PRODUCTIVITY CONVERGENCE

A vast new literature on the sources of economic growth has now accumulated. This book critically reviews the most significant works in this field and summarizes what is known today about the sources of economic growth. The first part discusses the most important theoretical models that have been used in modern growth theory as well as methodological issues in productivity measurement. The second part examines the long-term record on productivity among Organisation for Economic Co-operation and Development (OECD) countries, considers the sources of growth among them with particular attention to the role of education, investigates convergence at the industry level among them, and examines the productivity slowdown of the 1970s. The third part looks at the sources of growth among non-OECD countries. Each chapter emphasizes the factors that appear to be most important in explaining growth performance.

Edward N. Wolff is a professor of economics at New York University. He is also a research associate at the National Bureau of Economic Research. He served as managing editor of the *Review of Income and Wealth* from 1987 to 2004 and was a council member of the International Association for Research in Income and Wealth from 1987 to 2012. He is the author (or coauthor) of numerous books, including *Growth, Accumulation, and Unproductive Activity* (Cambridge University Press, 1987); *The Transformation of the American Pension System: Was It Beneficial for Workers?* (2011); and *Productivity Growth: Industries, Spillovers and Economic Performance* (with Thijs ten Raa, 2012). He received his Ph.D. from Yale University.

CAMBRIDGE SURVEYS OF ECONOMIC LITERATURE

Series Editor
Professor Frank Wolak, *Stanford University*

Series Advisor
Professor John Pencavel, *Stanford University*

The literature of economics is rapidly expanding, and within just a few years, many subjects have changed in recognition. Perceiving the state of knowledge in fast-developing subjects is difficult for students and time consuming for professional economists. This series of books is intended to help with this problem. Each book gives a clear structure to and balanced overview of the topic and is written at an intelligible level for the senior undergraduate. They will be useful for teaching as well as provide a mature, yet compact, presentation of the subject for economists wishing to update their knowledge outside their own specialties.

Productivity Convergence

Theory and Evidence

EDWARD N. WOLFF
New York University

CAMBRIDGE
UNIVERSITY PRESS

CAMBRIDGE
UNIVERSITY PRESS

32 Avenue of the Americas, New York, NY 10013-2473, USA

Cambridge University Press is part of the University of Cambridge.

It furthers the University's mission by disseminating knowledge in the pursuit of
education, learning, and research at the highest international levels of excellence.

www.cambridge.org
Information on this title: www.cambridge.org/9780521664417

© Cambridge University Press 2014

First published 2014

Printed in the United States of America

A catalog record for this publication is available from the British Library.

Library of Congress Cataloging in Publication data
Wolff, Edward N.
Productivity convergence : theory and evidence / Edward N. Wolff, New York University.
    pages   cm. – (Cambridge surveys of economic literature)
Includes bibliographical references and index.
ISBN 978-0-521-66284-0 (hardback) – ISBN 978-0-521-66441-7 (pbk.)
1. Production (Economic theory)   2. Endogenous growth (Economics)
3. Industrial productivity.   I. Title.
HB241.W65   2013
338'.0601–dc23   2013020608

ISBN 978-0-521-66284-0 Hardback
ISBN 978-0-521-66441-7 Paperback

Contents

Acknowledgments

Certain portions of the book were drawn from joint work with William Baumol, David Dollar, and Maury Gittleman. I would like to thank them each for their comments and help during the preparation of the manuscript. I would also like to acknowledge comments received from Moses Abramovitz, Bart van Ark, Magnus Blomström, Jan Fagerberg, Zvi Griliches, Alan Heston, Nazrul Islam, Robert Lipsey, Angus Maddison, Pierre Mohnen, Richard Nelson, Thijs ten Raa, Robert Summers, Bart Verspagen, and Michael Ward on various parts of the manuscript. The manuscript also benefited enormously from the comments of John Pencavel, who is currently the Advisor of the Cambridge Surveys of Economic Literature Series and was the Series Editor during the early stages of the manuscript, and of Frank Wolak, who is the current Series Editor, as well as Scott Parris, who was the Economics Editor at Cambridge University Press during the preparation of the manuscript.

Introduction

1.1 Scope of the Book

Over the past three decades there has accumulated a vast new literature on the sources of economic growth. Indeed, these studies have now formed the basis of what is referred to as the "new growth theory." The purpose of this book is to review critically the most significant works in this field and to summarize what is today known about the sources of economic growth. Where appropriate, I will add my own empirical analyses as well as update some of my previous work on the subject.

The book will first discuss methodological issues as well as the most important theoretical models that have been used in modern growth theory (Chapter 2). Chapter 3 summarizes some of the most important papers on methodological issues in the measurement of productivity. The next four parts will survey the empirical literature on the subject. This literature can be most conveniently divided into six groups. The first of these examines the long-term historical record of productivity growth among OECD countries (that is, the advanced industrial countries) (Chapter 4). The second considers the sources of growth among OECD countries over the postwar (that is, post–World War II) period (Chapter 5). The third of these focuses more closely on the role of education in the growth process among OECD countries (Chapter 6). The fourth looks at the pattern of growth and convergence at the industry level among OECD countries (Chapter 7). The next takes a slight digression to look into the source of the productivity slowdown of the 1970s in the United States (Chapter 8). The next part conducts an analysis similar to that of Chapter 5 of the sources of growth among newly industrialized countries (NICs), middle-income countries, and less developed countries or LDCs (Chapter 9). In each chapter, the emphasis will be to isolate those factors that appear to be most important in explaining their performance. The last chapter of the book, Chapter 10, will recap the findings of the previous chapters.

I generally take a "history of thought" approach, focusing on the earliest works on different topics. I also try to highlight the most important works on each topic. However, because of the now-voluminous literature on the subject of growth, I have inevitably left out other important articles and papers on this subject.

1.2 Factors Affecting Economic Growth

Before presenting a detailed summary of the book, it might be useful to list the factors that appear most germane in accounting for the pattern of economic growth on the basis of the recent literature on the subject. It should be noted at the outset that the explanatory variables considered here by no means represent an exhaustive list of relevant factors.

I divide these factors into two groups. The first of these is what I call "strong forces." These are variables that almost consistently show up with a positive and significant coefficient in growth regressions. Moreover, as a group, they explain the vast majority (often of the order of 80 to 90 percent) of the variation in economic or productivity growth in the sample of countries used. This group includes (1) the "catch-up" effect; (2) investment, including embodied technological change (or the "vintage" effect); (3) the level of educational attainment of the population or workforce (the "threshold" effect); (4) science and technology and, in particular, investment in research and development (R&D); and (5) the establishment of certain basic social institutions such as a stable state and the rule of law (what are also called "social capabilities").

The second group constitutes the "weak forces." These are variables that give mixed or statistically insignificant results in growth regressions or are ones in which the direction of causation is not clear. Individually and collectively, they explain only a small fraction of the variation in economic or productivity growth in the sample of countries used. In this group are, among others, (1) trade openness and foreign direct investment (FDI); (2) structural change (population growth); (3) and various sociopolitical variables such as the degree of democracy in a country, its level of income inequality, and the extent of government spending.

1.2.1 The Catch-Up Process

The first of the strong forces is the so-called catch-up effect. The catch-up hypothesis rests on the view that the historical course of technological progress operates through a mechanism that enables countries whose standard of productivity performance is reasonably close to that of the leader(s) to catch up. Through the constant transfer of new technology, leader countries and those most closely in their van learn the latest productive techniques from one another, but virtually by definition the follower countries have more to learn from the leaders than the leaders have to learn from them (the so-called advantages of backwardness). This mechanism has two implications: First, it means that those countries that lag somewhat behind the leaders can be expected systematically to move toward the level of achievement of the leaders. Second, the mechanism undermines itself automatically as follower countries gradually eliminate the difference between their own performance and that of the countries that were ahead of them – that is, the very fact of convergence means that the differential learning opportunities that are the source of these advantages of (slight) backwardness will exhaust themselves. On an analytical level, this hypothesis would imply faster productivity growth for the (initially) more backward economies relative to the more advanced ones, but the gap in productivity performance would gradually diminish over time as convergence was achieved.

1.2.2 Investment

The second of the strong forces is investment. It seems generally agreed that there are two prime ingredients in the growth of labor productivity: technological innovation and the accumulation of capital through saving (and the subsequent investment of those savings). Innovation and the international transfer of its products play a prime role in the converging productivity levels of a number of relatively successful industrialized economies. But even if technological innovation is the more important factor in the scenario (which is by no means certain), substantial capital accumulation very likely would have been required to put the inventions into practice and to effect their widespread employment. If, moreover, saving and investment play a primary role of their own, it becomes all the more important to explore the nature of that role. However, recognizing that unavoidable interactions may exist between the rates of innovation and investment, any attempt to separate the two may prove to be artificial, if not ultimately unworkable (see Abramovitz and David, 1973, for an extremely illuminating analysis of the data and the theoretical issues, as well as some references to other discussions by economic historians).

1.2.2.1 Vintage Effect

There are several ways in which capital formation and total factor productivity growth may have positive interactions or complementarities. First, it is likely that substantial capital accumulation is necessary to put new inventions into practice and to effect their widespread employment. This association is often referred to as the "embodiment effect," since it implies that at least some technological innovation is embodied in capital (see, for example, Kuznets, 1973; Abramovitz and David, 1973; or Solow, 1988). It is also consistent with the "vintage effect," which states that new capital is more productive than old capital per (constant) dollar of expenditure (see, for example, Nelson, 1964, or Hulten, 1992). If the capital stock data do not correct for vintage effects, then a positive correlation should be observed between the rate of technological gain and the change in the growth rate of capital.

A second avenue is that the introduction of new capital may lead to better organization, management, and the like. This may be true even if no new technology is incorporated in the capital equipment. A third is through learning by doing, which would also imply a positive relation between technological advance and the accumulation of capital stock (see Arrow, 1962). A fourth is that potential technological advance may stimulate capital formation, because the opportunity to modernize equipment promises a high rate of return to investment. Wolff (1991a, 1996a), for example, finds that the vintage effect is of particular importance in the early postwar period among OECD countries.

1.2.2.2 Public Infrastructure

One form of capital that has been singled out for being particularly productive is social infrastructure. This may take the form of networks of roads and other transportation systems, power generation, communications systems, and the like. Most of this type of infrastructure may be government financed or government owned. Work by Aschauer (1989a, 1989b) has shown that the rate of return to public infrastructure may be far in excess of that to private investment, though these estimates have been criticized by other economists.

1.2.2.3 Computers and Information Technology

Another form of capital that has also been singled out for special consideration is computers and the associated information technology. Particular interest is focused on the post-1980 period, which has seen a tremendous growth in the use of computers in production and which Freeman (1987) and others have termed a new "technoeconomic paradigm," based on computer-driven information technology. Fantastic increases in productivity have been found for both computers and software. Berndt and Griliches (1993) estimated a real price decline of microcomputers of 28 percent per year between 1982 and 1988. Gandal (1994) estimated a real price reduction in computer spreadsheets of 15 percent per year over the 1986–91 period. Many economists have felt that the growing use of IT throughout the sectors of the economy resulted in an acceleration of TFP growth during the 1990s and early 2000s.

1.2.3 Education

Another critical factor in economic growth is education, the third of the strong forces considered in the book. It will be seen that the statistical evidence is consistent with the hypothesis that the quantity of education provided by an economy to its inhabitants is one of the major influences determining whether per capita income in that society is growing rapidly enough to narrow the gap with per capita income in the more prosperous economies. This is important for policy because it suggests that a country can do a great deal to improve its performance in the convergence arena by increasing the resources it devotes to education. It is at the secondary school level, and to an even greater degree in higher education, that large differences persist. The book will consider the statistical evidence on the magnitude of the role that education plays in determining the growth rate of an economy.

One apparent paradox that will receive some attention is that while education levels are found to be highly significant in growth equations, the growth of education attainment is generally not found to be significant. This is a disturbing result for two reasons. First, it opens the question of causality – perhaps, rising educational levels are an outcome of the growth in per capita income rather than the reverse. Second, it raises profound policy issues about the one seemingly important mechanism for promoting economic growth.

1.2.4 Science and Technology

The role of science and technology is the fourth strong force considered in these works. There is a vast literature that supports the view that research and development (R&D) is positively associated with productivity growth. This has been demonstrated on the aggregate (national) level, the industry level, and the firm level (see, for example, Griliches, 1979; Mohnen, 1992; and Nadiri, 1993, for reviews of the literature). This work considers the role of two variables in particular – R&D expenditures as a percentage of GDP and scientists and engineers employed in R&D per capita – on productivity performance.

A related issue is whether there has been a slowdown in the process of invention and innovation. In a way, most of the major products that form the contemporary lifestyle were invented in the latter part of the nineteenth century or the first half of the twentieth century – electrification, the light bulb, the telephone, radios, televisions, phonographs, motion pictures, airplanes, automobiles, plastics, and so on. Since World War II, a comparable list might include computers, the jet engine, satellites, and bioengineering – an impressive list but, perhaps, not as significant as the earlier list. Some assessment will be made of this issue.

1.2.5 Social Institutions

The last of the strong forces considered in this work are basic social institutions. There is a large literature on how institutions affect economic development, beginning, perhaps, with North and Thomas (1973), who defined institutions as the formal and informal rules that govern human, social, economic, and political interactions. They argued that progress in the Western world occurred because of the development of basic economic institutions that fostered economic growth through establishing the rule of law and granting and protecting property rights of individuals. The establishment of a strong, stable government was another necessary ingredient to sustained economic growth.

1.2.6 Foreign Trade

The first of the weak forces is foreign trade. Another factor that may be directly relevant to the international transfer of technology is the extent of international trade and the pattern of trade. It is generally argued that trade is a mechanism for the transmission of information concerning new technologies and products. For example, imports of computers may revolutionize the production technology of importing industries. Also, the exposure to new products may induce local competitors to imitate. The argument on the export side is weaker. Competition in export markets may lead to the exposure to new foreign products; it may also lead to more rapid developments of new technology in industries competing in export markets. The evidence on this score generally supports a positive role played by international trade on economic growth, though it appears stronger on the import side than the export side.

1.2.6.1 Foreign Direct Investment

Related to trade is the role that foreign direct investment (FDI) may play in the process of economic growth, particularly that of LDCs. FDI constitutes the second of the weak forces considered in this work. Technology transfer through foreign direct investment can also result in indirect productivity gains for host developing countries through the realization of external economies. Generally these benefits are referred to as "spillovers," a characterization that indicates the importance of the way in which the influence is transmitted. There are several ways in which these spillovers may occur. Presumably the most important channel is via competition. Existing inefficient local firms may be forced by the competition of foreigners to make themselves more productive by investing in physical or human capital or importing new technology.

Another source of gain to the host economy is the training of labor and management provided by the multinationals, which may then become available to the economy in general. Since such resources are in short supply in developing countries, this type of spillover efficiency is expected to be more important there. A third potential source of spillover efficiency benefits is through the impact made by the foreign subsidiaries in the host economy on their local suppliers, by insisting that they meet standards of quality control, delivery dates, prices, and so forth.

1.2.7 Structural Change

Another major issue in understanding aggregate economic growth is to analyze how countries deal with differential productivity growth among the sectors of their economy and the inevitable dislocations it introduces – that is, sectoral shifts in employment. Do countries try to protect backward sectors, as Japan does for agriculture, or do they allow market forces to operate?

Structural change refers to shifts in the industrial composition of employment. This is another weak force in explaining economic growth. There are two principal mechanisms by which structural change may influence the rate of aggregate productivity growth. First, employment may shift from low productivity spheres to high productivity ones. The prime example is the shift out of agriculture, a sector in which marginal productivity is usually quite low, to manufacturing, a sector with a higher marginal productivity. Such a shift in employment, will, ceteris paribus, cause average productivity to rise. This type of structural shift is usually referred to as a "levels effect," since it arises from the difference in productivity levels between industries.

Second, employment may shift from a high productivity growth sector to one in which the rate of productivity growth is lower. Since the rate of overall productivity growth is the weighted sum of the rates of productivity growth of the individual sectors, where the employment shares are the weights, such a shift will cause aggregate productivity growth to decline. The prime example of this type of shift is from manufacturing to services. This type of structural shift is usually referred to as a "growth effect," since it arises from the difference in productivity growth rates between sectors. Both types of shift effects will be examined in the ensuing chapters.

The analysis of structural change will lead to a related set of issues, concerning productivity growth on the industry level. We will be particularly interested in the pace of technological advance in services, a sector that has been singled out for its "stagnancy." As will become evident, there is a dualistic structure to the service sector. There are some service industries, such as telecommunications, that have enjoyed and continue to enjoy rapid rates of technological progress. There are others, like government, community, and personal services, that seem to be permanently stagnant.

A related issue is "outsourcing," which refers to the process of replacing in-house services, such as legal, advertising, accounting, and related business services with services purchased from outside the firm (see, for example, Postner, 1990, for a discussion of this issue from an accounting point of view). This process has two effects of interest for us. First, it may speed up the shift of employment out of goods industries to services. Second, by sloughing off the more stagnant service activities, manufacturing should experience more rapid TFP growth (see, for example, Carter, 1970; Barker and Forssell, 1992; Siegel and Griliches, 1991; and ten Raa and Wolff, 1996).

1.2.8 Population Growth

This factor is often included in analyses of economic growth in order to control for any country whose population growth is so rapid as to swamp any gains from the advantages of backwardness. In these cases, any gains in productivity from the introduction of new technology may be offset by rapid population growth and, as a result, do not show up as increases in per capita income. An opposing argument, often made, is that rapid population growth may stimulate production by providing a rapidly expanding domestic market. Thus, population growth may act as a positive stimulant to the growth in per capita income. On net, population growth acts as an additional weak force in explaining countrywide productivity growth.

1.2.9 Sociopolitical Variables

A large set of sociopolitical variables have also been investigated by researchers to determine whether they exert any independent influence on the growth in per capita income. As a group, they also constitute a weak force in accounting for productivity convergence. The first of these is military expenditure as a percentage of GNP. The usual argument is that military spending diverts resources from investment and other productive uses and will therefore dampen economic growth. However, there is the opposing argument that while military spending diverts resources from productive investment, it might also stimulate the acquisition of advanced technology.

The second includes various indicators of the degree of democracy or civil rights in a country, such as the extent of voting rights. Another indicator is a variable that might reflect the presence or absence of official "violence" against citizens. A related factor is involvement in war or civil strife, which may also slow economic growth by diverting factors of production from productive to unproductive uses. Another factor is the use of central planning, which historically has often been cited as an inhibiting factor in economic growth.

Recent work has also emphasized the degree of economic inequality in a country. There are several theories as to why inequality might be good or bad for growth, and, perhaps not surprisingly, evidence is rather mixed as to whether inequality helps or hurts economic growth.

Another factor is the extent of government spending. I have already talked about public infrastructure, which many studies have found to have a positive effect on economic growth. However, generally speaking, government spending is viewed as a "bad," detracting potentially productive resources into unproductive pursuits. Many studies now include the size of the government as one important element in explaining aggregate growth.

Another key role played by governments is to regulate various industries in their economy. Indeed, many of the service industries in OECD countries are tightly regulated by the state, though rules have been loosened in recent years. Most economists have argued that this creates a serious restriction on their potential for future productivity advance. Fortunately, the United States has undergone deregulation in several key service industries, and this may provide some guidance as to the possible productivity enhancement benefits of deregulation. The first case is the U.S. telephone industry, which underwent a partial deregulation in 1984. Before that year, there was one telephone system, AT&T, for the whole United States. In the 1984 divestiture, long-distance service was opened to competition and effectively deregulated, while local telephone service continued to be supplied by regulated Regional Bell Operating Companies. Deregulation has also occurred in Japan.

Several studies have now examined the effects of deregulation in this industry on productivity growth (see, for example, Oniki, Oum, Stevenson, and Zhang, 1994; and Olley and Pakes, 1994). Berndt, Friedlaender, Chiang, and Vellturo (1993) made a study of the effects of deregulation on the U.S. rail industry. Lichtenberg and Kim (1989) looked indirectly at the effects of deregulation in the U.S. air transportation industry on productivity performance. Gordon (1992) also examined the effects of deregulation in both the U.S. airlines and trucking industry. Another aspect of regulation is provided by Gray and Shadbegian (1993, 1994), who looked at the effects of environmental regulation on plant level productivity performance in U.S. manufacturing over the period 1979 to 1985.

1.3 Why Is Productivity Growth Important?

1.3.1 Productivity Growth versus Economic Growth

Before proceeding to the actual literature review, it might be helpful to say a few words about why productivity growth matters at all. However, before even commencing this topic, it might be useful to distinguish between productivity growth and economic growth. Economic growth is typically defined as the growth of national output, GDP. Productivity growth, on the other hand, is usually defined as the rate of growth of output *per* unit of input. The latter is normally interpreted as an indicator of the rate of technological change in an economy. Thus, there are two ways of increasing economic growth. The first is by augmenting the factors available for production ("factor augmentation"), typically labor and capital. The second is by raising the rate of productivity growth. As we shall see in the literature review, there are numerous examples of researchers decomposing overall economic growth into these two components.

As developed in Chapter 2, we can formulate the relationship between output growth and productivity growth more formally as follows: Let ρ be the rate of total factor productivity (TFP) growth. TFP growth, ρ, is often defined as:

$$\rho_t = dY_t / dt - \alpha dL_t / dt - (1-\alpha) dK_t / dt \qquad (1.1)$$

where Y is output, dY_t/dt is the rate of output growth, L is the labor input, K is the capital input, α is the share of wages in national output, and t is a time subscript. TFP growth is used as a measure of technological advance in an economy. It then follows that:

$$dY_t / dt = \rho_t + \alpha dL_t / dt + (1-\alpha) dK_t / dt \qquad (1.2)$$

This equation makes it clear that overall output growth depends on the rate of TFP growth and the growth in the factors labor and capital. It is rather hard, at least through policy, to affect the growth rate of labor since this depends mainly on demographics – the birth rate, the death rate, increases in life expectancy, and the like. However, the rate of growth of capital is quite variable and depends mainly on the national investment rate and therefore the national savings rates. Here, policy interventions are more effective, and, as we shall see in the ensuing chapters, there is considerable variation in investment rates both across countries and over time.

As an alternative, many economists will analyze the rate of labor productivity growth, defined as the growth of output per unit of labor. In this case,

$$\pi_t = \rho_t + (1-\alpha) dk_t / dt \qquad (1.3)$$

where π is the rate of labor productivity growth and k is defined as the capital-labor ratio. In this formulation, the rate of labor productivity growth depends on the rate of technological change (TFP growth) and rate of growth of the capital-labor ratio.

1.3.2 Productivity Growth in the Long Run

Productivity growth is a vital subject that has to a large extent fallen into the hands of macroeconomists.[1] This is not to say that macroeconomist have

---

[1] Sections 1.3.2 through 1.3.6 are adapted from Baumol, Blackman, and Wolff (1989), chapters 1 and 2. See these chapters for sources.

not made important contributions to the subject but rather that there are regrettable features to this situation. In particular, macrotheory is to a large extent oriented to the short-run. However, productivity growth is essentially a long-run issue. In fact, it can probably be said without exaggeration that in the long-run nothing matters as much for economic welfare as the growth of productivity.

Until the Keynesian revolution in economic theory, most economists were pre-occupied with the long run. Classical economists framed the subject in terms of long-run tendencies, long-run equilibria, and the secular expansion or decline of entire nations over protracted periods of time. The advent of macrotheory changed this orientation. Issues of recession, depression, unemployment, and inflation are by their very nature short-run in scope. Because of the work of John Maynard Keynes, macroeconomics became almost exclusively concerned with short-run problems. In particular, macroeconomists tended to transform productivity growth into a short-run issue. For example, they study the effect of the business cycle on the rate of productivity growth, analyzing why growth characteristically slows down during a downturn and why it rises during an upturn. Similarly, they examine whether a stimulus to productivity growth is a way of dampening an inflationary spiral. In contrast, relatively little attention is paid to productivity growth in the long term.

It is only in the long term that productivity growth makes a large difference to the welfare of a country, and it is only in the long term that the rate of productivity growth is subject to fundamental change. Since the beginning of the nineteenth century labor productivity growth in the U.S. has averaged about 1½ percent per year. Yet, that was enough to produce an estimated twentyfold increase in total productivity and in living standards, a figure so large that it is hard to comprehend. In addition, a one percentage point lag in the rate of productivity growth for a single century was sufficient to transform the United Kingdom from the world's industrial leader into a second-rate economy that it is today. It was also enough to reduce real wages in the U.K. from about 1½ times that of other leading European economies to about two thirds of those countries today. These examples indicate why it is necessary to concern ourselves with America's productivity standing today and what it is likely to be a half century in the future.

1.3.3 Investment and Productivity Growth

There was considerable disagreement about the causes of what was regarded as a major U.S. productivity problem – the lag in U.S. productivity growth behind that of Japan during the 1970s and 1980s. One key factor was the disparity in savings behavior between the two countries. From the end of World War II until about 1990 or so, the savings rate in Japan was two to three times as large as that in the U.S. Between 1970 and 1980, for example, the net savings rate in the U.S. averaged about 8 percent of disposable income whereas it was over 25 percent in Japan. The average for OECD countries over this period was 16 percent. Likewise, net fixed investment as a share of GDP between 1971 and 1980 was 7 percent in the U.S., 12 to 13 percent in Germany and France, and 20 percent in Japan. Investment in manufacturing in the 1960s was 9 percent of output in the U.S., 16 percent in Germany, and 30 percent in Japan. These differences ranged from 15 to 20 percentage points.

The major point is that even such huge disparities in saving and investment rates make little difference in the relative productivity capacities of two countries if they go on for only a few years. On the other hand, if they persist for long time periods, *compounding* makes their influence enormous. As an illustration, consider two economies, J and U, and assume that in 1950 U starts off with 10 times as much capital per worker as J. Assume also that capital per worker expands at 10 percent per year in country U and 20 percent in J. Simple calculations indicate that by 1955 the relative positions of the two economics will hardly have changed, with capital per worker in J rising from 10 percent to 16 percent of U's level. However, after 25 years, in 1975, capital per worker in J will have attained 88 percent of U's level; and 10 years after that, in 1985, J will have more than *twice* the capital per worker as U. This example illustrates the "tyranny of compounding", which manifest itself only over long periods of time. It is clear that persistent compounded differences in savings and investment rates played a large, if not dominant role, in explaining Japan's productivity catch-up to the U.S. level over this period of time (see Chapter 5 for more discussion).

This example is not inconsistent with historical experience elsewhere. For example, the U.K. had a fairly low savings rate (about 9–10 percent per year) between 1760 and 1982, compared to the OECD average of 16 percent over the postwar period. Moreover, the U.K. had a very low investment rate in the period from 1790 to 1820, a phenomenon often ascribed to "crowding out" by government expenditures on the Napoleonic wars. As a result, most of the labor productivity gains of the early Industrial Revolution must be ascribable to the "wave of gadgets" – that is, the burst of innovation that characterized this period – rather than to capital deepening. These new inventions were impressive enough, including an improved steam engine, a chronometer for ships (which allowed sailors to calculate longitude, thereby speeding voyages and reducing the danger of shipwreck), and the various well-known improvements in textile manufacturing. Yet, despite these dramatic innovations per capita income in the United Kingdom improved by only 0.33 percent per year. It is noteworthy that this figure is about one tenth the growth rate of per capita income in less developed countries in the 1990s. This rather disappointing early increase in British labor productivity and per capita income, which happened despite the enormous outburst of innovation, is likely due to the low level of investment made by Britain over this time period.

This is not to say that innovation is unimportant. Indeed, innovation *does* count very much. In fact, it is hardly plausible that anything else played as important a role in the Industrial Revolution and the explosion in living standard in the two centuries that succeeded it. However, historically innovation seems to count less in the intermediate term than rates of investment.

1.3.4 American Productivity Growth in Historical Perspective

As we shall see in Chapter 5, the growth rate of American labor productivity from the end of World War II through the 1990s was considerably below that of Japan, France, Germany, Italy, and a slew of other industrialized countries. Today, it is substantially below that of China, India, Brazil, and a number of other "emerging" economies. This issue is a cause of concern both for the absolute prosperity of the U.S. economy and for its relative position. But in evaluating the danger that this signals, it is necessary to determine whether this phenomenon is merely transitory or reflects a long term change in the underlying relationships. There is probably no doubt that the U.S. is still among the leading economies in the world and that, on average, its populace still enjoys a very high standard of living. A short period when the productivity of other nations increases more rapidly than that of the U.S. is certainly not a reason for great concern. Only if the developments persist over the long run do they matter seriously.

The evidence presented in the ensuing chapters seems to suggest that there is no basis for believing that the long run productivity growth rate in the U.S. has fallen below its historical average or that it will in the near or distant future. Moreover, it is likely that the superior productivity performance of Europe and Japan in the 1960s, 1970s, and 1980s and that of China, India, and other emerging nations today is likely to be a temporary affair, representing a period of catch-up during which other nations are learning industrial techniques from the U.S. and other industrial leaders. Thus, the long-run data should not lend themselves to undue concern about the future of productivity growth in the U.S. Conversely, the historical record provides no guarantees that U.S. productivity growth will continue unabated into the future. Indeed, unless American productivity performance improves somewhat, it is possible that the U.S. will lose its economic leadership and its *relatively* high standard of living within a matter of a few decades. In fact, if the U.S. productivity level were to fall substantially below that of its leading industrial rivals, it may be the case that the U.S. would no longer have to fear the competition of cheap foreign labor since its comparative advantage may be heading in this direction.

1.3.5 Why Productivity Matters – and Why It Does Not

For real economic miracles one must look to the growth of productivity. An economic miracle it has in fact provided. Until at least the seventeenth century all of human history entailed an unending struggle against starvation. Except during periods of very favorable climate, famines every three to ten years were actually the normal state of affairs. Yet, even this marginal existence usually required some 90 percent of the employed workers to be involved in agricultural production. Even during periods of surprisingly fertile invention and practical application of these new ideas (there were several such periods before the Industrial Revolution), livings standards were not significantly improved because other activities produced so small a share of the economy's output. Today, in contrast (at least in the U.S. and most developed economies) the principal economic problem of agriculture is the disposal of its vast output, which threatens to leave unmanageable surpluses. Yet, instead of occupying the vast bulk of the labor force, agriculture today requires less than 3 percent of the work force of an industrialized country to produce this abundance. And this development, which clearly deserves the term "miracle," is clearly ascribable to two centuries of productivity growth whose magnitude is without historical precedent.

There is, in fact, nothing that matters as much *in the long term* for human welfare as productivity growth. On the other hand, productivity matter much less for short-run and transitory issues such as inflation, international competitiveness of individual industries in an economy, and the availability of jobs. Ultimately, productivity policy is not a useful instrument to deal with these problems. Rather, what productivity policy does contribute to effectively is real wages and the populace's general standard of living. When each worker produces more with a given outlay of effort, that person can generally expect to have more real income. But what is not generally known is just *how much* productivity growth has contributed to living standards. As we shall see, even when the facts are presented, the magnitude of the change is so immense as to defy comprehension.

Some of the immensity of the productivity achievement of the last 150 years is imparted by contrast with the preceding centuries. Though the data are not as reliable as more recent figures, it is likely that the standard of living in ancient Rome was likely to have been not lower and perhaps higher than in eighteenth century England (see Appendix Table 4.6 of Chapter 4, based on Angus Maddison's calculations). This was probably the case even for the lower classes – certainly for the free urban working class and perhaps even for Roman slaves. As for the upper classes, a Roman household was served by sophisticated technical devices for heating and bathing not found in an eighteenth century home of similar socio-economic position. Had an ancient Roman found himself in such an eighteenth century English house, it is likely that only a limited number of products would have surprised him. Few items other than window panes, clocks, the printed books and newspapers, and the musket represented technological breakthroughs achieved in the intervening 15 or 16 centuries.

It is true that by the middle of the eighteenth century and even during the Middle Ages there had been some technological changes in the workplace and elsewhere. Ship design, for example, had improved substantially. Lenses, the telescope, and microscope had been major innovations of the sixteenth century and had generated demand for specialized skills to produce them. Before these, the stirrup, the harness, and the heavy plow changed agriculture dramatically, and the water mill relieved humans of the tasks of grinding grain, polishing metal, sawing wood, hammering metal, processing wool, and the like. The eighteenth century also yielded the chronometer, which revolutionized water transport by allowing longitude to be calculated accurately. Yet, none of these inventions yielded rates of labor productivity growth even close to those of the nineteenth and twentieth centuries.

Nor is it the case that productivity growth reached a standstill for two millennia. It is likely that from the fall of Rome to about the Carolingian Renaissance of the eight century, productivity declined substantially and then started to increase in fits and starts until the eighteenth century. The early agricultural revolution brought by the heavy plow, the horse harness, and the three-field crop rotation system expanded food output for several centuries before the fourteenth century. There appears to have been at least two early "industrial revolutions" in Europe, one in the twelfth and the thirteenth centuries and the other from about 1550 to 1650. Yet, all the accompanying spurts in productivity could not have yielded a growth rate of more than a negligible magnitude. Maddison (1982) provides estimates of real GDP per capita in France and the U.K. in 1700 of the order of $600 of 1980 dollars. This is somewhat below the figure for India in 1980. If we somewhat arbitrarily take one quarter of the 1980 Indian GDP per capita as the minimum needed for sheer survival, real GDP per capita in the year 700 could not have been much lower than the equivalent of 200 1980 dollars. Direct arithmetic calculations then suggests that the average annual rate of productivity growth over the 1000 years since year 700 was not likely to have been much greater than 0.11 percent. In contrast, the average growth rate in labor productivity among the world's leading industrial economies from 1870 to 1979 was in excess of 2 percent per year, according to the Maddison (1982) figures (see Appendix Table 4.1 in Chapter 4.).

The Industrial Revolution is generally believed to have been underway in the last third of the eighteenth century. However, what is not usually recognized is how minor an affair it was in the context of the whole economy. At first the bulk of newly invented equipment was confined to textile production. Yet, an "industrialist" could undertake the new types of textile operations with a very small capital outlay, perhaps of the order of a few hundred pounds (about $100,000 1980 dollars). Williamson (1984) calculated that real per capita income grew at an annual rate of about 0.33 percent during the first half century of the Industrial Revolution in England. In contrast, the corresponding growth rate for less developed countries during the decade of the 1990s came to nearly 3 percent – almost ten times the British figure.

The Maddison (1982) data shows the remarkable contrast of developments from 1870 to 1979 with those of the earlier period (see Appendix Table 4.1). For these 16 industrialized countries, output per work hour grew by multiples ranging from about 5 for Australia to 26 in the case of Japan. For the U.S., the multiple was 12, which puts the U.S. in the middle of the pack, and even the U.K. managed a sevenfold increase. Thus, after not manifesting any substantial increase for at least *15 centuries*, in the course of *11 decades* the median increase in productivity among these 16 industrialized countries was a factor of 11! The productivity increase was sufficient to allow a rise in output per capita of more than 300 percent in the U.K., almost 1400 percent in Germany, over 1600 percent in Japan, and nearly 700 percent in France and the U.S.

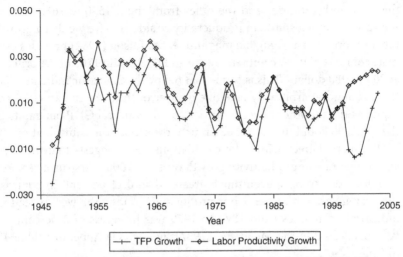

Figure 1.1 Annual rates of labor productivity and TFP growth, 1947–2003 (three-year running averages).

1.3.6 Limitations of Productivity as a Short Term Policy Instrument

While the primary purpose here is to clarify the importance of productivity growth, it is also useful to try to clear up some misconceptions attributing to productivity policy more than can reasonably be expected of it. Productivity has often been invoked as a suitable policy instrument for dealing with problems such as inflation, unemployment, and deficits in the balance of trade. The central shortcoming of these types of suggestions for the use of productivity policy to deal with short-run problems is that productivity growth is not readily amenable to attempts to change its magnitude, at least in the short-run. Besides, for each of these problems there are policy instruments already better suited to deal with them.

Productivity growth rates are surprisingly volatile. An examination of even three-year running averages of TFP and labor productivity growth in the U.S. over five and a half decades, from 1947 to 2003, as shown in Figure 1.1, reveals just how volatile these are.[2] This figure suggests that policy can not quickly change an economy's productivity growth at least in the short-run. The main reason is that an economy can hardly carry out overnight the introduction of profoundly new productivity techniques

---

[2] The figures are based on National Income and Product Account data. The source is Wolff (2009), chapter 11. See the data appendix of chapter 11 for sources and methods.

(much less the requisite research and development) or substantial expansion of plant and equipment in a short time period. Such measures can often require as much as a decade or more for their implementation. The short-run problem at hand may have well disappeared or at least to have changed its nature drastically before an economy can hope to bring substantial productivity changes to bear upon it.

It is true that, other things being equal, a jump in productivity can reduce the rise in price level that inflation may have otherwise brought. In an economy in which prices are increasing, a leap in annual productivity growth of, say, one percentage point, can slow the rate of inflation commensurately, about one percentage point. But such a spectacular rise in the productivity growth rate is no easy accomplishment, and we certainly know no policy programs that can be used to bring it about so quickly. The conclusion that follows is that one must continue to relay on monetary or fiscal policy for an effective way to deal with inflation. Productivity policy is simply not a major contender for that role.

1.3.7 Productivity, Unemployment, and "Deindustrialization"

There is another set of misunderstandings about productivity. Productivity issues are often mistakenly taken as a major source of long-run problems such as unemployment and balance of trade deficits. First, it is sometimes contended that rapid increases in labor productivity will destroy jobs, even in the long-run. Second, it is also sometimes argued that if an economy's productivity growth lags behind that of other countries, it will lose jobs to foreign workers, its industry will decline (that is, "deindustrialization"), and its balance of trade will be in deficit. However, the data do not support any of these conclusions.

If the specter of long-term unemployment were a reality, one would expect that the 12-fold rise in output per hour in the U.S. from 1870 to 1980 would have had devastating effect on the demand for labor over those years. Even with a 50 percent decline in working hours per year, output per capita in the U.S. over these eleven decades would have been about constant if employment had been cut to one-sixth of its initial size relative to population. However, this did not happen. Unemployment rates from 1874 to 1973 show that aside from the Great Depression there was no upsurge in unemployment and the trend, if anything, has been somewhat in the downward direction. This was the case despite the fact that the ratio of employment to the total population, according to the Maddison (1982) data, rose substantially in the U.S. Comparative data also show what a country like the U.K. which was a laggard in terms of productivity growth, was not subject to greater unemployment problems than the U.S. In fact the U.K. generally had lower unemployment rates than the U.S. over this 100-year period. In sum, neither rapid absolute productivity growth nor a slow relative rate of productivity growth need subject a country to a secular rise in unemployment rates.

The main reason is that in the long-run, comparative advantage and the equilibrating mechanisms of international exchange will create new jobs in other sectors of the economy to replace those lost as a result of the economy's relative or absolute productivity performance. Moreover, as Keynesians and monetarists agree, the "natural" rate of unemployment depends primarily on macroeconomic influences. Productivity growth itself automatically expands purchasing power and effective demand, thus in the long term off-setting the reduction in required labor time per unit of output that the rise in labor productivity automatically brings about.

Much of this argument is related to the view falsely held that a persistent lag in a country's productivity growth will place it an increasing competitive disadvantage in international trade, and that it will, as a result, be excluded increasingly from its export markets, with negative effects upon its export industries and its balance of trade. However, standard economic analysis suggest that this will generally happen – that, if nothing else, a falling exchange rate for the laggard country caused by low foreign demand for its products (and therefore its currency) will eventually bring its balance of trade into equilibrium, whatever the nation's productivity performance. In addition, since export markets depend on comparative rather than absolute advantage, a country whose lagging industry is no longer able to compete will find itself capable instead of exporting the products of agriculture or mining or some other industry in the economy.

Data compiled by Matthews, Feinstein, and Odling-Smee (1982) generally support this view. Over the period from 1855 to 1975, three countries with exceptional records of productivity growth – Japan, Germany, and Italy – all increased their share of world trade. Japan's share of world exports, in particular, went from essentially zero to 13 percent. The U.S.'s share, despite its mediocre productivity record, was still about 2 1/2 times as large in 1973 as in the 1880s. However, the U.K.'s share fell steadily from 43 percent to only 9 percent. On the surface, these findings seem to support the popular view.

However, there is more to the story. First, though it operates slowly, the equilibrating mechanism has apparently not failed in the long term. In the case of Britain, in fact, its net exports of goods and services actually moved in its favor from the 1870s through the 1970s. Moreover, the *volume* of British exports rose spectacularly despite its declining *share* of the world total. Between 1870 and 1979, total British exports increased by a factor of 10, and from 1855 to 1973, British exports of *goods* increased by a factor of 13.

Nor has the U.K. been forced to deindustrialize internally. According to Maddison's (1982) figures on the share of the labor force employed in industry (mining, construction, and manufacturing), the U.K. declined from first place among 16 in 1870 to fourth place in 1979. But the U.K.'s industry share was still 88 percent that of the leader in this respect (Germany). If this is deindustrialization, it is certainly very modest.

Here, too, there is a marked contrast between the relative and absolute performance of the U.K. In comparison to other countries, its export record is mediocre but in absolute terms it is quite spectacular. Yet, there is a significant relative sense in which lagging productivity does impede a nation's competitiveness in terms of the *share* of world exports. While the U.K.'s absolute productivity performance was indeed impressive, the problem was that productivity in other industrialized countries grew even faster.

At first glance, it then appears that there is no real penalty for the productivity laggard. In the long term such an economy will suffer little unemployment and little in the way of a balance of trade deficit. However, there is a cost and the cost is that the country must transform itself into a supplier of *cheap labor*. When a country lags behind others in terms of productivity growth, the prices of inputs such as fuel, raw materials and capital that are purchased by all nations will continue to be more or less the same for everyone. Only the price of inputs that do not readily move between countries can change their relative levels materially. This is particularly true of the price of labor – that is, wages. Suppose, however, that wages in the laggard country at first resist reduction. Then the exports of the productivity laggard will become more expensive in comparison with high productivity countries. The principle of supply and demand will then operate, and the quantities of the laggard's goods sold on foreign markets will fall.

The next step will be a decline in foreign demand for the laggard's currency. As always, declining demand for an item means that its relative price will fall. In particular, the exchange rate of this country must ultimately decline, and the decline must be sufficient to restore competitiveness to the country's exports. This process is enough to ensure that the country's exports will eventually become competitive, that its balance of trade will tend to zero, and that its labor force will not be beset by chronic unemployment.

However, there is a second layer to the story and that is a fall in the real wages of the laggard country. It is only necessary to recognize that a fall in a country's exchange rate is implicitly a disguised means to cut real wages. For example, a 50 percent cut of the exchange rate of the pound relative to the dollar means that a British worker must work twice as long as before to pay for a bottle of Coke produced in the U.S. In other words, the laggard's workers can only continue to compete by accepting a cut in their relative wage.

Another consequence of lessening real wages is that the laggard nations must find that is comparative advantage pattern has changed. In other words, it will no longer be able to specialize in the same industries as before. In particular, instead of being able to complete in technologically advanced industries with a high capital-labor ratio (in which an economy with high productivity and high wages does best), it will find itself better suited to specialize in industries that make heavy use of large amounts of cheap labor and relatively little capital. Here, the primary cost is the social cost of labor's transition from one industry to another.

Productivity growth also provides the resources that smooth out the political process. Education, environmental protections, widely available public health care, and similar programs are most easily financed out of the yields of productivity growth. This is particularly so because in an economy where productivity is growing, an increase in outlays on social programs can be paid for almost entirely out of the annual increment in national output that productivity contributes, thus entailing no offsetting reduction in private disposable incomes and expenditures. It is just for this reason that widespread public expenditures on universal education, the environment, and the like are a product of the modern era and why the world's poorer countries are still far behind in these areas.

That is why in the remainder of the book we look at the determinants of productivity growth, because of its importance for the improvement of living standards.

1.3.8 Productivity Growth and the 2012 Presidential Campaign

The 2012 presidential campaign between Mitt Romney and Barack Obama was one of the hardest fought in recent memory. Interestingly enough, productivity growth featured as a key campaign issue. There were several topics, in particular, which stood out during the campaign. The first of these was the relationship between tax rates and productivity growth.[3] In particular,

---

[3]   This issue is not directly addressed in this book.

the Republicans asserted that cutting tax rates for the wealthy was a way to stimulate investment and therefore spur productivity growth. However, this notion was put to rest by a Congressional Research Service Report for Congress, which was released on September 14, 2012, and entitled "Taxes and the Economy: An Economic Analysis of the Top Tax Rates Since 1945" by Thomas L. Hungerford.

As Hungerford notes, income tax rates have been at the center of recent policy debates. Some members of Congress have argued that raising tax rates, especially on higher income taxpayers, to increase tax revenues is part of the solution for long-term debt reduction. For example, one proposal would allow the 2001 and 2003 Bush tax cuts to expire for taxpayers with income over $250,000 ($200,000 for single taxpayers). Another proposal would implement the "Buffett rule" by raising the tax rate on millionaires.

Other recent budget and deficit reduction proposals would reduce tax rates. President Obama's 2010 Fiscal Commission recommended reducing the budget deficit and tax rates by broadening the tax base. The plan advocated by House Budget Committee Chairman Paul Ryan that is embodied in the House Budget Resolution (H.Con.Res. 112) also proposes to reduce income tax rates by broadening the tax base. Both plans would broaden the tax base by reducing or eliminating tax expenditures.

Advocates of lower tax rates argued that reduced rates would increase economic growth, raise saving and investment, and boost productivity. Proponents of higher tax rates argued that higher tax revenues are necessary for debt reduction, that tax rates on the rich are too low, and that higher tax rates on the rich would moderate increasing income inequality.

The Hungerford report attempted to ascertain whether or not there is an association between the tax rates of the highest income taxpayers and the rate of economic growth. Data was analyzed using econometric analysis on the association between the tax rates of the highest income taxpayers and measures of economic growth. Throughout the late 1940s and 1950s, the top marginal tax rate was typically above 90 percent; in 2012 it was 35 percent. Additionally, the top capital gains tax rate was 25 percent in the 1950s and 1960s, 35 percent in the 1970s, but only 15 percent in 2012. The real GDP growth rate averaged 4.2 percent and real GDP per capita increased annually by 2.4 percent in the 1950s. In the 2000s, the average real GDP growth rate was 1.7 percent and real per capita GDP increased annually by less than 1 percent.

As Hungerford concluded, there was no conclusive evidence to substantiate a clear relationship between the 65-year steady reduction in the top tax rates and economic growth. Analysis of such data indicated that the reduction in the top tax rates had little association with saving, investment, or productivity growth. However, the top tax rate reductions appear to be associated with the increasing concentration of income at the top of the income distribution. The share of income accruing to the top 0.1 percent of U.S. families increased from 4.2 percent in 1945 to 12.3 percent by 2007 before falling to 9.2 percent due to the 2007–2009 recession. The evidence does not indicate a relationship between tax policy with regard to the top tax rates and the size of the economic pie, but there appears to be a relationship between tax policy and how the economic pie is sliced.

1.3.8.1 Productivity Growth and Infrastructure Investment

A second issue that received some attention in the presidential campaign was the relationship between public infrastructure investment and productivity growth. I treat this topic in some detail in Section 4.7.1 of Chapter 4. At the basis of this interest is the belief that infrastructure investment is an important ingredient in economic growth. The argument is that there are spillovers (externalities) from public capital investment on that of the private capital stock. This is particularly true for the connection between transport infrastructure and transport related private activities. For example, good public roads should increase the efficiency of the trucking industry. In the case of the U.S., many believed that the low productivity growth of that country during the 1970s and 1980s could be attributed, at least in part, to inadequate infrastructure investment.

One of the earliest studies on the subject was an article by Aschauer (1989), who found on the basis of time-series data for the U.S. that public sector capital exerted a substantial effect on private sector productivity growth. However, later studies disputed this finding. In particular, Holtz-Eakin and Schwartz (1995), using an augmented neo-classical growth model, estimated that raising the rate of infrastructure investment would have had a negligible impact on productivity growth in the U.S. In sum, when the proper specifications are used and endogeneity is controlled for, later studies on this subject suggest that public infrastructure investment plays at best a minor role in explaining country level and, particularly, industry level productivity growth.

1.3.8.2 Productivity Growth and Inequality

A third issue raised in the campaign was the relationship between income inequality and productivity growth. Democrats were asserting that

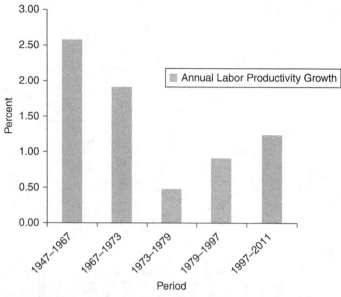

Figure 1.2 Average annual rates of overall labor productivity growth by period in the United States, 1947–2011.

inequality is bad for economic growth, while Republicans were arguing just the opposite – inequality is good for economic growth. Before looking at trends in inequality in the U.S., it is helpful to consider the historical picture of productivity growth in post-war United States.[4] I have divided the postwar period into five sub-periods as is standardly done. As shown in Figure 1.2, labor productivity growth was quite robust from 1947 to 1967, averaging 2.6 percent per year. It then fell to 1.9 percent per year over the 1967–73 period and fell even further to 0.5 percent per year over the 1973–79 period. This latter period is often referred to as the "productivity slowdown" period and is discussed at length in Chapter 8. Productivity picked up in the 1979–97 period, averaging 0.9 percent per annum and then even further over years 1997 to 2011, averaging 1.2 percent per year. However, it is clear that the very rapid productivity growth during the early postwar period has yet to be fully regained in the United States.

[4] Labor productivity is defined here as GDP in constant dollars per persons engaged in production (PEP). PEP is the broadest measure of labor input and equals the number of full-time equivalent employees plus the number of self-employed persons. The source is Bureau of Economic Analysis, National Income and Product Accounts, http://www.bea.gov/iTable/iTable.cfm?ReqID=9&step=1.

Figure 1.3 Gini coefficient for family income in the U.S., 1947–2011.

In contrast, as shown in Figure 1.3, inequality, as measured by the Gini coefficient,[5] was fairly low and steady from about 1947 to 1974 and then increased steeply thereafter. On the surface, at least, it appears that productivity growth was high in the U.S. when inequality was low and declining but it was low when inequality was high and rising. The Gini coefficient fell moderately from 1947 to 1974, by 0.021 Gini points, and then rose sharply through 2001, by 0.095 Gini points.

This subject is discussed in detail in Section 9.8.2 of Chapter 9. According to Barro (2000), theories on the relationship between inequality and growth emphasize four broad categories: credit-market imperfections, political

[5] The Gini coefficient is an index that ranges from zero (perfect equality) to one (maximum inequality). The formula for the Gini coefficient G is:

$$G = \sum_{i=1}^{n}\sum_{j=1}^{n} |Y_i - Y_j| / \left(2\,\bar{Y}\,n^2\right)$$

where Y_i is the income of individual i, n is the number of individuals, and, $\bar{Y}$ is mean income. The source for the data is the U.S. Census Bureau's Current Population Survey, http://www.census.gov/hhes/www/income/data/historical/families/.

economy, social unrest, and saving rates. In the case of the first view, with limited access to credit, the exploitation of investment opportunities will depend on the income of individuals. As a result, poor people may forego investments in education that offer relatively high rates of return. In this case, a reduction in inequality will allow poor people to increase their educational investment and thereby raise the rate of economic growth.

In the second view, political economy explanations typically revolve around voting models. If the mean income in a nation exceeds the median income, then majority voting will often lead to a redistribution of resources from rich to poor. More inequality will generally induce more redistribution through the political process. Typically, the transfer payments and associated taxes distort economic decisions. In such a case, more redistribution will lead to more distortions and will tend, in general, to reduce the level of investment. As a result, economic growth will decline. Greater inequality leads to a greater amount of redistribution and to lesser growth.

The third view focuses on the possibility that inequality may induce poor people to engage in crime, riots, and other socially disruptive activities. The participation of the poor in these socially disruptive activities wastes economic resources that could otherwise be devoted to productive activity. Moreover, defensive efforts taken by potential victims such as buying burglar alarm systems are a further loss of economic resources. In addition, the threat to property rights may reduce investment. Because of the threat of political unrest, more inequality will lead to lower productivity of an economy, and the rate of economic growth will be lower.

The fourth set of models focuses on the effects of inequality on the saving rate. There is ample empirical evidence that personal saving rates increase with income. If this relationship holds, then a redistribution of resources from the poor to the rich would lead to a higher aggregate saving rate in an economy. By this mechanism, a decline in inequality would actually lower overall investment and lower economic growth.

The empirical findings, not surprisingly, have also been ambiguous and, in any case, not very robust. Most of these studies use cross-country datasets and regress overall growth of GDP or of GDP per capita on control variables plus a measure of income inequality. Some studies use straight cross-country regressions, others use panel data estimates, and still others use instrumental variable techniques. The samples range from advanced countries only to ones that span all levels of development. The results are very mixed, with some finding a positive effect of inequality on productivity growth, others finding a negative effect, and most finding no statistically significant effect.

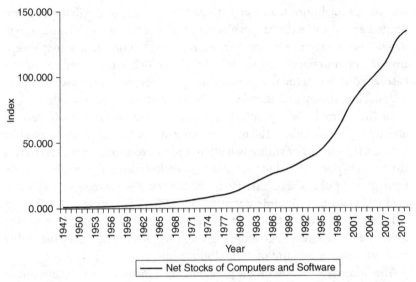

Figure 1.4 Net stocks of information processing equipment and software per worker in the United States, 1947–2011 [Index, 2005=100].

1.3.8.3 Productivity Growth and High Tech Investment

A fourth issue that received some attention in the recent election is the relationship between growth and high tech investment. Both sides seemed to concur that investment in information technology (IT) and the like is the key to future economic growth in the U.S.

As shown in Figure 1.4, there was a spectacular rise in IT investment from 1947 to 2011. The net stocks of information processing equipment and software (my measure of IT) per worker in the U.S. increased by a factor of 154 between 1947 and 2011 or at a growth rate of about 8 percent per year.[6] The gains were fairly steady over time. There was no noticeable acceleration (or deceleration) in the growth rate after 1973 compared to before 1973. As a result, at least on the surface, there is no noticeable correlation between IT investment and the overall rate of productivity growth over this time period in the U.S.

I briefly discus this issue in Section 10.4.6 of Chapter 10. Computer and other IT investment did not seem to play a notable role in explaining the pattern of productivity growth in advanced countries like the U.S. during

---

[6] The source for the data on IT investment is Bureau of Economic Analysis Fixed Assets data series, http://www.bea.gov/iTable/iTable.cfm?ReqID=10&step=1.

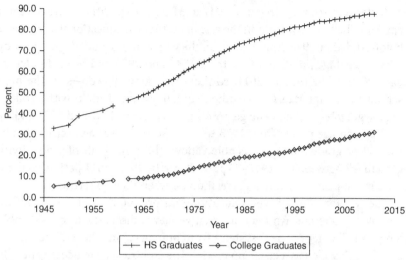

Figure 1.5 Percent of adults 25 years old or over with a high school and college degree, 1947–2011.

the 1980s and 1990s. However, some evidence has accumulated that it may have become more important during the first decade of the twenty-first century. For example, Van Ark, O'Mahony, and Timmer (2008), examining the growing productivity gap between Europe and the United States in the 1995–2006 period, concluded that slower emergence of IT in Europe compared to the U.S. was responsible for the growing divergence in productivity performance.

1.3.8.4 Productivity Growth and Education

The virtues of education as a source of productivity growth is another topic that was extolled by both sides of the political aisle during the 2012 presidential campaign. Here, too, there was basic agreement between the two candidates. On the surface, this appears to be little doubt that education is a key ingredient for economic growth.

As shown in Figure 1.5, there has been a steady rise in educational attainment in the U.S. over the postwar period.[7] The percent of adults (ages 25 and over) with a high school degree increased from 33 percent in 1947 to 88 percent in 2011, and the share of adults with a four-year college degree

---

[7] The source is U.S. Bureau of the Census, Current Population Survey, table P-16, available at http://www.census.gov/hhes/www/income/data/historical/people/.

or better rose from 5 percent in 1947 to 31 percent in 2011. There does not appear to be any slowdown in the rate of increase in educational attainment before and after 1973. The share of adults with a high school degree grew by 1.03 percentage points per year from 1947 and 1973 and by 0.74 percentage points from 1973 to 2011, so there was some slowdown in the high school graduation rate. On the other hand, the share of adults with a college degree grew by 0.28 percentage points per year from 1947 and 1973 and by 0.50 percentage points from 1973 to 2011, so there was an acceleration in the college graduation rate. As noted above, the annual rate of productivity growth fell between the 1947–73 period and the 1973–2011 period, so there does not appear to be much correlation between the two series.

The relationship between education and productivity growth is rather complex. There are two main alternative views, discussed in considerable length in Chapter 6. The first stems from human capital theory. The second could be classified as a catch-up model. The empirical evidence is generally positive on the second model but rather mixed on the first.

Human capital theory views schooling as an investment in skills and hence as a way of augmenting worker productivity This line of reasoning leads to growth accounting models which posit a linear relationship between the growth rate of labor productivity and the *change* in schooling levels. The early studies on this subject showed very powerful effects of changes in schooling on productivity growth. Griliches (1970), for example, estimated that the increased educational attainment of the U.S. labor force between 1940 and 1967 accounted for one-third of TFP growth. However, later studies such as Benhabib and Spiegel (1992) found no statistically significant effect of the growth in mean years of schooling on the growth in GDP per capita among a sample of countries at all levels of economic development. In contrast, Hanushek and Woessman (2010c) found that the growth of *cognitive skills* rather than educational attainment had a positive and significant effect on economic growth among a sample of developed (OECD) countries.

The second strand views the role of education in the context of a "catch-up" or "convergence" model. Explanations of productivity convergence among countries of the world rely on the so-called "advantages of backwardness", by which it is meant that catch-up can be explained, at least in part, by the diffusion of technical knowledge from the leading economies to the more backward ones (see Gerschenkron, 1952, for example). Competitive pressures in the international economy lead to the dissemination of superior productive techniques from one country to another. Through the continual transfer of knowledge, countries learn about the latest technology from each other, but virtually by definition the followers have more to learn from the leaders than the leaders have to learn from those further behind. One implication of this hypothesis that countries which lag behind the leaders can be expected to increase their productivity performance toward the level of the leading nations and, *ceteris paribus*, should experience higher *rates* of productivity growth.

However, being backward does not itself guarantee that a nation will catch up. Other factors must be present, such as strong investment, an educated work force, research and development, and the like. Indeed, Abramovitz (1986 and 1994) summarized this group of characteristics under the rubric of *social capability*. From this viewpoint, education is viewed as one index of the social capability of the labor force to borrow existing technology. In this context, education may be viewed as a *threshold effect* in that a certain level of education input might be considered a necessary condition for the absorption of advanced technology. Here, the literature is much more consistent on this effect. Baumol, Blackman and Wolff (1989, Chapter 9) were among the first to report a very strong effect of educational attainment on the growth in per capita income among a cross-section of countries covering all levels of development. Since that time, numerous other studies have confirmed the positive relationship between the rate of productivity growth and the *level* of educational attainment, at least when the sample is wide enough to include countries at all levels of development. However, among a sample of developed countries by themselves, the relationship is much weaker and, in many studies, not even statistically significant.

1.4 Plan of the Book

Chapter 2 considers the methodological underpinnings of the modern growth literature. It will also discuss the theoretical foundations of modern growth theory and critically compare the different models.

It begins with a discussion of production function theory, beginning with the standard Cobb-Douglas production function, and growth accounting. Growth accounting is a method first developed Denison (1967) which seeks to decompose the growth of output into different components like investment and education. The next section introduces research and development (R&D) into the production function. It shows how the standard Cobb-Douglas production function can be extended to include R&D investment. It also briefly discusses R&D spillovers both between industries in an economy and between countries.

The next section presents another view of the process of technological change which develops from the work of Schumpeter (1950) and evolutionary biology. The central idea is that new technology originates from a search process occurring in the neighborhood of existing technology. A related view can be found in the "technology gap" literature, which emphasizes innovativeness as the basis for technological change and growth.

The next three sections discuss the central models of modern growth theory. The first of these presents the classic Solow (1956) growth model. As will be seen, the basic model appears quite at odds with the empirical findings that different countries experience very different rates of productivity growth and that the rate of productivity growth in a given country will fluctuate over time. There are two principal ways in which growth theorists have modified the original Solow model to account for these discrepancies. First, they have viewed part of the discrepancy as a movement toward equilibrium rather than as a state of equilibrium. This leads to various forms of dynamics in approaching steady-state equilibrium. Second, they have modified the assumption of the same production function across countries (which underlies the Solow model) in two ways. First, the underlying production function at a given point of time may differ among countries, and changes in the production function over time might reflect the catch-up effect. Second, the production function can be modified to reflect human capital accumulation, and thus education is given a role in the growth model. One important example of the modified Solow growth model can be found in Mankiw, Roemer, and Weil (1992), which is also discussed in this section.

The following section sketches the Lucas (1988) growth model, which emphasizes the role of human capital in growth. Endogenous growth models are developed in the next section. In the Cobb-Douglas production function, technological change is viewed as being exogenous to the system of production. The Solow residual is used to estimate the rate of exogenous technical change. In endogenous growth theory, production itself creates the conditions of technical change. The works of Romer (1990) and Aghion and Howitt (1992) are highlighted here.

The last three sections also discuss basic methodology. The first of these introduces two different notions of convergence which have been used in the literature. The first, referred to as β-convergence, is defined as a narrowing of initial differences in income levels over some time horizon, with poorer countries growing faster than richer ones. The second concept used in the literature is referred to as σ-convergence and refers to the reduction over time in the cross-country variance of productivity. The differences between conditional and unconditional convergence is also highlighted. Econometric issues in model estimation are then reviewed in the following section, and the last one discusses data sources and methods used in this literature.

Chapter 2 presented an overview of modern growth theory and touched on some measurement and econometric issues. Chapter 3 provides technical details on both the measurement and estimation of productivity growth, particularly total factor productivity (TFP) growth. The chapter develops the theoretical foundation for much of the empirical literature dealing with issues of productivity measurement.

According to Diewert (1976), TFP is a production function-based concept. Although all researchers would agree that productivity growth has occurred if a firm is able to produce more output from the same vector of inputs, the quantitative estimate of the magnitude of TFP growth depends on how TFP is measured.

There are alternative methods to measure TFP – empirically-based index numbers, econometric methods, stochastic frontier methods, and data envelopment analysis (DEA). Another issue is that on the theoretical level TFP is typically measured in terms of physical output units even though, empirically, deflated dollar sales is used (see Bartelsman and Doms, 2000). In addition, since most of the empirical work reviewed in subsequent chapters is typically made with the use of aggregate industry-level or country-level data, it is necessary to derive these input and output aggregates from firm level data. Theoretical restrictions on firm level production functions necessary for an aggregate production function to exist need to be indicated as well. Consequently, there are a number of reasons why the growth in the country-level output aggregate is less than the growth in the country-level input aggregate that are not the result of productivity growth.

Section 3.2 starts with a rigorous definition of TFP using the neoclassical theory of production. It demonstrates that TFP depends on the assumed form of the production function – specifically the functional forms for both the input aggregator function and the output aggregator function. The theoretical treatment starts at the firm level because the existence of an aggregate economy-wide or industry-wide production function requires several additional assumptions. This framework is then used to introduce the distinction between Hicks-neutral technical change and factor-biased technical change. This is followed by a treatment of the theoretical framework for measuring productivity change using the minimum cost function. I also discuss the additional assumptions required by the dual (cost function) approach. This section develops the standard Laspeyres and Paasche price indices. the so-called "ideal" index, Diewart's superlative index, the Törnqvist-Theil "Divisia" index, and the translog function

Section 3.3 discusses econometric issues associated with the estimation of productivity growth. There are five common approaches to productivity measurement: (a) index numbers, (b) data envelopment analysis (DEA), (c) stochastic frontiers, (d) instrumental variables (GMM) and (e) semi-parametric estimation. This section reports the results of a paper by Van Biesebroeck (2007) of a simulation study to examine the sensitivity of productivity estimates and growth rates to the five approaches. Using simulated samples of firms, he analyzed the sensitivity of alternative methods to the randomness properties in the data generating process from introducing randomness via (a) factor price heterogeneity, (b) measurement error and (c) heterogeneity in the production technology.

Section 3.4 addresses the issue of the theoretical conditions necessary to measure productivity growth at the industry-level or country-level. Diewert and Nakamura (2007) provided a comprehensive discussion of this issue. Although it is always possible to construct index numbers and compute the difference between the growth in the output and input indices, only with certain assumptions on the true input and output aggregator functions does this resulting difference in growth rates equal the growth in TFP. Denny, Fuss, and Waverman (1981) discussed this issue when the assumption of constant returns to scale is dropped. The only assumption required is that the firm continuously minimizes costs over the time period of interest.

Section 3.5 addresses the major data availability and quality issues that must be dealt with in measuring TFP empirically. The first of these is how to measure the quantity of capital services used by the firm, industry, or economy. Even at the firm level, this is a complex task because capital is typically categorized as any expenditures on a long-lasting factor of production. This creates problems with aggregation over time and across different types of capital goods.

A second data aggregation issue is how to compute an aggregate input from similar inputs of different quality. This is particularly germane when firms hire different types of workers. The third input measurement issue discussed in this section is the distinction between a firm's capital stock and the services it receives from this capital stock. Berndt and Fuss (1986) discussed this problem and showed how the productivity residual can be adjusted in a consistent manner to accommodate forms of temporary equilibria, such as the variation in the utilization rates of quasi-fixed capital plant and equipment inputs.

Section 3.6 discusses another data issue related to the fact that the theory of productivity measurement is developed in terms of physical units of output, but dollar sales is often the only data that is available to the researcher. This is particularly true in industries with multi-product firms or differentiated products. Klette (1999) provides an econometric modeling framework that explicitly accounts for these factors in measuring productivity.

Section 3.7 also discusses problems associated with the use of deflated dollar sales instead of physical output as the output measure based on the work of Bartelsman and Doms (2000). Their work uses microdata like the Longitudinal Research Database (LRD), which has physical output measures for a small subset of products produced by a subset of establishments. An issue of particular interest is the relation between aggregate and micro-level (establishment) productivity growth. Aggregate productivity growth is a weighted average of establishment-level productivity growth, where the weights are related to the importance of the establishment in the industry. Typically, aggregate TFP growth is decomposed into components related to within-establishment TFP growth, reallocation, and the effects of exit and entry. The major finding is that aggregate TFP growth is significantly affected by compositional changes, such as shifts in output toward establishments with relatively high (or low) TFP.

Chapter 4 undertakes an examination of long-term trends among OECD (advanced industrial) countries. This is important for two reasons. First, it helps to put the postwar performance of OECD countries in historical perspective. Second, it also helps to isolate some of the salient factors that are responsible for productivity performance. As such, it provides good lessons for today's LDCs and middle-income countries, since their (current) level of productivity resembles in many ways the level of productivity of today's advanced countries 75 or 100 years ago.

Explanations of the productivity catch-up almost all involve so-called "advantages of backwardness", a term first coined by Gerschenkron (1952). The basic idea is that much of the catch-up can be explained by the diffusion of technical knowledge from the leading economies to the more backward ones (also, see Kuznets, 1973). Through the transfer of new technology, leading and following countries learn the latest productive techniques from one another, but virtually by definition the follower countries have more to learn from the leaders than the leaders have to learn from them (the "advantages of backwardness"). This mechanism has two implications: First, it means that those countries that lag somewhat behind the leaders can be expected systematically to move toward the productivity level of the leaders. Second, the mechanism undermines itself automatically as follower countries gradually eliminate the difference between their own performance and that of the countries that were ahead of them. However, backwardness *per se* does not itself guarantee that a nation will catch up. Other factors must be present, such as strong investment, an educated work force, a suitable product mix, and developed trading relations with advanced countries (Abramovitz' (1986) "social capabilities").

Chapter 4 begins with a review of the evidence on long term convergence in labor productivity and per capita income. Several of these studies, including Abramovitz (1986), Baumol (1986), and Baumol, Blackman, and Wolff (1989), made use of data provided in Maddison (1982) on output and employment for 16 OECD countries covering the period from 1870 to 1979. The next section summarizes the analogous evidence on long term convergence in total factor productivity (TFP). The following section surveys the various studies on convergence in the long term. There are very few long-term series on many of the explanatory variables of interest (such as education). As a result, the analysis focuses on three sets of factors: (1) the catch-up effect, (2) the role of capital formation, and (3) the vintage effect. The next section considers the evidence on convergence in per capita income in the very long term (two millennia), and the last section surveys the literature on this subject.

Chapter 5 reviews the extensive number of studies examining trends in economic growth among OECD countries since World War II (principally, since 1950). The availability of a large number of additional variables, such as education, R&D spending, international trade, government expenditures, and so on has made it much easier to analysis the role of these factors in explaining economic growth. Two noted papers, Barro (1991), and Mankiw, Romer and Weil (1992), considered a wide range of factors, including investment, education, trade, government spending, and political structure. Another factor that may be directly relevant to the international transfer of technology is the extent of international trade and the pattern of trade. Wolff (1991a) considered whether there are positive interactions between capital accumulation and technological advance. This association is often referred to as the "embodiment effect," since it implies that at least some technological innovation is embodied in capital.

The chapter begins with descriptive statistics on trends in output per worker over the post war period. The next section considers the most important determinants of growth among this group of countries and presents an econometric analysis of these factors on productivity growth. In addition, data for key variables such as education and R&D are also shown. The following section provides a survey of the literature on the convergence process among advanced countries. The next reviews the literature on the role of technology and R&D in particular on productivity growth among the advanced industrialized countries. The following section surveys the literature on the role of trade and foreign direct investment on growth among this group of countries. The last section provides a summary of the literature on other factors that have proved important in convergence among OECD countries.

Chapter 6 highlights the importance of education in the convergence process among OECD countries. There are three paradigms which appear to dominate current discussions of the role of education in economic growth. The first stems from human capital theory. Human capital theory views schooling as an investment in skills and hence as a way of augmenting worker productivity (see, for example, Schultz, 1960, and Becker, 1975). This approach leads to growth accounting models in which productivity growth is related to the *change* in educational attainment.

The second strand views the role of education in the context of a productivity "catch-up" or "convergence" model. In this context, education is viewed as one index of the social capability of the labor force to borrow existing technology. One of the prime reasons for the relatively weak growth performance of the less developed countries is their failure to absorb new technological information. One of the elements that can be expected to explain an economy's ability to absorb new technology is the education of its population. In this context, education may be viewed as a *threshold effect* in that a certain level of education input might be considered a necessary condition for the borrowing of advanced technology. On an econometric level, the correct specification would then relate the *rate* of productivity growth to the *level* of educational attainment.

The third approach, emanating from the work of Arrow (1962) and Nelson and Phelps (1966), emphasizes interactions between education and technological change. Arrow introduced the notion of *learning-by-doing*, which implies that experience in the application of a given technology or new technology in the production process leads to increased efficiencies over time. As a result, measured labor productivity in an industry should increase over time, at least until diminishing returns set in. One implication of this is that an educated labor force should "learn faster" than a less educated group and thus increase efficiency faster. In the Nelson-Phelps model, it is argued that a more educated workforce will make it easier for a firm to adopt and implement new technologies. Firms value workers with education because they are more able to evaluate and adapt innovations and to learn new functions and routines than less educated ones. Thus, by implication, countries with more educated labor forces should be more successful in implementing new technologies. The Arrow and Nelson-Phelps line of reasoning suggests that there may be interaction effects between the educational attainment of the labor force and measures of technological activity, such as the R&D intensity of a country.

This chapter investigates the validity of these three major approaches. The first part of the chapter provides descriptive statistics on educational enrollment and attainment for OECD countries. The next reports econometric results on the effects of educational enrollment and attainment levels and the growth in educational capital on per capita income growth. The following section investigates evidence on interactive effects between education and R&D, and the next discusses results from the Mankiw, Romer, and Weil (1992) model. The following provides a survey of literature on the relation between education and growth among advanced countries. The last section presents concluding remarks and discusses the implications of this work.

Chapter 7 investigates the convergence of productivity on the industry and sectoral level. If the theory behind productivity convergence is correct, then we should observe stronger convergence in productivity levels at the industry level than for the total economy, since the catch-up effect should operate most strongly at the industry level. Yet, the work of Dollar and Wolff (1988) and, later, Dollar and Wolff (1993), found just the opposite. They analyzed changes in productivity levels on the industry level for a sample of 9 OECD countries covering the period from 1960 to 1986. While they found strong evidence of convergence on the economy-wide level in GDP per worker, the capital-labor ratio, aggregate labor productivity and total factor productivity (TFP), convergence at the industry level was generally not as strong as that for the economy as a whole. In fact, aggregate convergence in productivity was to a large extent attributable to the modest productivity leads that different countries enjoyed in different industries. They argued that industry specialization was an important component in aggregate productivity convergence. Moreover, they did not find that structural change was an important factor in overall productivity convergence.

The first two sections of the chapter present statistics on sectoral trends in both labor productivity and TFP growth and in labor productivity and TFP levels for the period 1970–95 for about 12 OECD countries (those with the pertinent data). In addition, they look at changes in the composition of employment in these countries over time. The last part of the chapter surveys the available literature on this subject, including Dollar and Wolff (1988, 1993), and Bernard and Jones (1996a, 1996b, 2001), among others.

Chapter 8 takes a slight digression by looking into the causes of the dramatic slowdown in the rate of productivity growth that occurred first in the U.S. and later in Europe and other OECD countries in the early 1970s. This development spawned a large literature on the subject of productivity, particularly in the U.S. The watershed year was 1973. In this chapter, I review the literature on this subject, principally for the U.S. but with some attention paid to the more limited literature on the European slowdown.

The main candidates for the causes of the productivity slowdown, at least in the U.S., are the following five factors: (1) the slowdown in the rate of capital formation; (2) changes in the composition of the labor force; (3) energy price shocks; (4) declines in R&D spending and the productivity of R&D; and (5) structural change in the economy. It should be mentioned at the outset that these five factors are not necessarily mutually exclusive. For example, much of the discussion concerning the effect of the energy price rise on productivity growth involves its impact on capital formation.

The chapter begins with a consideration of some measurement issues involved in the definition of productivity since this is crucial for understanding some of the differences between the various studies. The next presents estimates of the magnitude of the productivity slowdown both for the economy as a whole and for individual industrial sectors in the United States. The following surveys much of the earlier literature on the subject, and the following section considers more recent literature on the productivity slowdown. The final section of the chapter evaluates the relative merits of the arguments on the causes of the productivity slowdown put forth in the literature on the subject.

Chapter 9 considers the postwar economic performance among all countries of the world, with particular attention paid to the less developed countries (LDCs). A sizable literature has also emerged on the growth performance of all countries of the world, with special attention to the newly industrialized countries (NICs), middle-income countries such as Mexico and Brazil, and low-income countries, such as sub-Saharan Africa and South Asia. Chapter 8 will survey this literature. Special attention will be paid to whether the lessons learned for the growth of the advanced industrialized countries also apply to other countries of the world.

This chapter first reports on the basic evidence on convergence for the postwar period. I then consider some of the factors that have been shown to influence the convergence process. The most important of these is investment, and the next section considers the evidence on capital formation and its role in the productivity catch-up process. Previous work on the subject has shown that the next most important factor in the catch-up process is education, and the following section reports on evidence on the magnitude of the role that education plays in determining the productivity catch-up rate of an economy.

A third important economic factor in the catch-up process is the extent of openness of an economy, which reflects the degree to which a country is involved in international trade. Work on this subject is considered next. In the following section, I look at the role of science and technology and, in particular R&D spending on the catch-up process among less developed countries. I then consider several other factors that appear to play a role in the next section. The first of these is population growth. A second is the extent of military expenditures. The third factor relates to political structure and the degree of democracy of a country's government, measured in various ways, such as the extent of voting rights within a country or the presence or absence of "official violence" against citizens. A fourth factor considered in this survey is the type of economy a nation has – free market versus centrally planned.

In the section following, I look into the role inequality plays in economic growth. Various theories have been proposed as to why income inequality may affect economic growth, which I will review in this section, as well as the available evidence. I then look into how institutions may impact economic growth. There is a large literature on how institutions affect economic development, beginning, perhaps, with North and Thomas (1973). The penultimate section considers a potpourri of additional factors. The first of these is financial development. Several researchers have found that a more developed financial system in a country is positively associated with a higher rate of economic growth. The second is the role of natural resources and climate. There are several avenues by which the abundance (or lack thereof) of natural resources may affect economic growth that have been discussed in the pertinent literature. The third is the role of foreign aid. There are two opposing views with regard to the effectiveness of foreign aid in promoting economic growth. The fourth is how the regulatory framework impacts on economic growth. In the final part, special attention is given to the economic fortunes of Sub-Saharan Africa, East Asia, and the former Communist Bloc countries.

Chapter 10 provides a recap of the major findings reported in the book, as well as a brief prognosis on the prospects for future growth around the world. It first reviews the basic results on convergence around the world and among OECD countries in particular both over the long term and over the postwar period. The next two sections summarize the evidence on the factors that have been found to play a role in the convergence process.

I divide the myriad of factors into two groups, "strong forces" and "weak forces." The former include the catch-up effect, capital formation, education, and R&D and technological spillovers. These factors explain the vast majority of the variation in the growth rates of GDP per capita or productivity. The second set of factors include international trade and FDI, the role of democracy and political institutions, social institutions, inequality, financial development, geography and resource availability, and structural change. These factors collectively might account for another five percent of the variation in the growth rates of GDP per capita or productivity.

The final section provides a summary of the "lessons" about growth that can be inferred from the works surveyed in the book. It starts out with a brief review of the major factors affecting growth and convergence. It then provides a short overview of the state of the world in terms of development and recent growth experiences. It then gives a brief assessment of the prospects for future growth among (today's) advanced industrialized countries and speculates on some of the lessons that are most relevant for today's middle income and less developed countries.

On a prefatory note, it should be mentioned that that because of the extensive number of works covered in the book, I have kept mathematical symbols consistent within each chapter but not necessarily across chapters. The only exception is Chapter 3 in which symbols are consistent only within *each section* of the chapter. The reason for this is that I have followed each author's presentation of theoretical material as closely as possible in order to allow the reader to consult their work for more details.

An Overview of Modern Growth Theory

2.1 Introduction

This chapter provides an overview of both the methodological and theoretical foundations for modern growth theory. This chapter lays the foundations for an understanding of the basic issues underlying the vast majority of empirical studies on convergence. A technical discussion of issues in productivity measurement is reserved for Chapter 3.

This chapter begins (in Section 2.2) with an introduction to production function theory and growth accounting. Section 2.3 introduces research and development (R&D) into the production function. It also briefly discusses R&D spillovers. There have been two main approaches to measuring R&D spillovers. One approach is to view R&D spillovers as the direct knowledge gains of customers from the R&D of the supplying industry. R&D spillovers are then typically measured on the basis of interindustry sales between producers and customers. An alternative approach is to measure R&D spillovers on the basis of the "technological closeness" between industries.

In Section 2.4, I present an alternative view of the process of technological change that develops from the work of Schumpeter (1950) and evolutionary biology. The central idea is that new technology originates from a search process occurring in the neighborhood of existing technology. A related view can be found in the "technology gap" literature, which emphasizes innovativeness as the basis for technological change and growth. Feedback effects also play a crucial role in maintaining technological advantage.

The next three sections develop the central models of modern growth theory. Section 2.5 presents the Solow (1956) and the Mankiw, Romer, and Weil (1992) growth models. Section 2.6 summarizes the Lucas (1988) growth model. Endogenous growth models are developed in Section 2.7.

In the Cobb-Douglas production function, technological change is viewed as originating outside the system of production. The Solow residual is treated as exogenous technical change. In endogenous growth theory, production itself creates the conditions of technical change. The work of Romer (1990) and Aghion and Howitt (1992) is highlighted here.

Section 2.8 discusses the two different notions of convergence that have been used in the literature. The first, referred to as β-convergence, is defined as a narrowing of initial differences in income levels over some time horizon, with poorer countries growing faster than richer ones. The second concept used in the literature is referred to as σ-convergence and relates to the reduction over time in the cross-country variance of productivity. Basic econometric issues in model estimation are reviewed in Section 2.9, and Section 2.10 then discusses data sources and methods used in this literature. A more technical discussion of these two sets of issues will be presented in Chapter 3. Section 2.11 presents a summary of the chapter.

2.2 Production Functions and Growth Accounting

One of the first attempts to derive a production function was made by Cobb and Douglas (1928). In this piece, they showed how a mathematical function could be used to describe the actual change of output when both labor and capital inputs changed. The function they derived, aptly known as the Cobb-Douglas production function today, is as follows:

$$Y = c\,L^{\alpha}K^{(1-\alpha)} \tag{2.1}$$

where Y denotes output, L is the labor input, K is the capital input, c is a constant, and α is the share of wages in total output. This function produces isoquants that have a negative slope and are convex to the origin. This function still serves as the foundation for most of the empirical work done on productivity growth.

Work on production functions was stimulated by Robert Solow's classic 1956 article developing a theory of economic growth. In the following year (1957) appeared another important paper on the measurement of technological change from an aggregate production function. This article has given rise to numerous applications and serves as the basis of our standard measures of technological change and total factor productivity (TFP) growth.

Solow's measure was derived from the Cobb-Douglas production function as follows: If we assume that the rate of technological change is constant over time, then we can rewrite equation (2.1) as:

$$Y_t = ce^{\rho t}L_t^{\alpha}K_t^{(1-\alpha)} \tag{2.2}$$

where t refers to time. By taking the time derivative of the logarithms of both sides of equation (2.2), we obtain:

$$dY_t / dt = \rho + \alpha \, dL_t / dt + (1-\alpha) \, dK_t / dt \tag{2.3}$$

Then the rate of (Hicks-neutral) TFP growth, ρ, is given by:

$$\rho_t = dY_t / dt - \alpha \, dL_t / dt - (1-\alpha) \, dK_t / dt \tag{2.4}$$

This is also referred to as the Divisia index of technological change and the Solow residual (see Chapter 3 for more discussion). The measure can be applied at the firm or industry level or to the total economy. Three key assumptions in the derivation of the index are perfect competition, no externalities, and constant returns to scale. The importance of this measure is that it allows one to separate out the efficiency of factor use from the quantities of factors used in accounting for output growth over time.

By the early 1960s, the literature branched in two directions. The first line followed up the production function approach and continually refined both the function used and the econometric techniques used to estimate the function. The simplest production function, the Cobb-Douglas, could be econometrically estimated from equation (2.3) as:

$$GDPGRT_t = \beta_0 + \beta_1 LABGRT_t + \beta_2 CAPGRT_t + \varepsilon_t \tag{2.5}$$

where $GDPGRT_t$ is the rate of output growth of the unit of observation (firm, industry, or total economy) over a given period; $LABGRT_t$ and $CAPGRT_t$ are the corresponding growth rates of labor and capital input; β_0, β_1, and β_2 are the coefficients to be estimated; and ε_t is a stochastic error term (usually assumed to be independently distributed). Under the three assumptions of perfect competition, no externalities, and constant returns to scale, a comparison of (2.1) and (2.2) reveals that β_1 should equal the wage share in that unit, β_2 the capital share (which, in turn, should equal 1 less the wage share), and β_0 is the rate of exogenous technical change.

This production function has the advantage of being simple but the disadvantage of imposing conditions on the data. As a result, many economists started to develop more complex and less restrictive production functions. One implicit assumption of the Cobb-Douglas production function, for example, is unitary elasticity of substitution between capital and labor. A more general class of production functions would maintain the assumption of constant elasticity of substitution (CES) between capital and labor but allow the data to estimate what the elasticity actually is (rather than imposing the condition that it equal unity).

Another restrictive assumption of the Cobb-Douglas function is constant returns to scale (which means that if we increase all inputs by a factor of x, then output must also increase by the same factor x). Here, again, there may be cases of diminishing or rising returns to scale. The CES production function allows the returns to scale to be directly estimated from the data. A very valuable review of the CES and other production functions is provided by Nadiri (1970).

The second branch is growth accounting. As originally developed by Denison (1962) and expanded in Denison (1974), this approach also devolves directly from equation (2.3), where actual factor shares, computed from national accounting data, are used to decompose output change into a set of sources of growth. One advantage of this approach is that the number of factors included in the analysis can be extended almost indefinitely. Moreover, factors such as labor can be built up from disaggregated data on employment by industry, occupation, gender, age, education, or the like. The analysis assumes that firms minimize cost and that factors are paid their marginal product. For example, to obtain a measure of labor input, the inputs of different kinds of labor are weighted by their actual market earnings.

This technique is very open with respect to the set of factors included in the analysis and the procedures used to calculate factor shares. A very interesting interchange on exactly this issue took place between Denison and Jorgenson and Griliches (1967), particularly with regard to the role of capital in U.S. output growth. Jorgenson, Gollop, and Fraumeni (1987) extended this approach to include quality-adjusted measures of both labor and capital inputs.

The residual in this analysis (the difference between output growth and the weighted sum of factor input growth, where factor shares are weights) is similar to the Solow residual in production function analysis and therefore a measure of the rate of technological change. However, as Denison noted in his work, the residual also picks up the contribution of factors not included in the analysis and might reflect the influences of omitted factors as well as technological change.

Growth accounting can be usefully extended to international comparisons of the sources of growth. Denison (1967) presented the first such analysis, where his primary interest was to explain why growth rates differed among advanced industrial countries. He was particularly concerned whether higher growth was due to the fact that certain inputs, like capital, grew faster in one country than another or was due to more rapid techno-logical change in one than another. Maddison (1987) also developed inter-national comparisons for six OECD countries.

2.3 R&D and Technological Spillovers

The 1950s saw a new institutional development in American corporations – the creation of separate units within the company responsible for research and development (R&D). This was partly a result of tax incentives given to U.S. business to invest in R&D. The National Science Foundation in the United States began collecting statistics on company R&D, and this pair of developments led economists to consider explicitly the role of this new fac-tor in economic growth.

The work on R&D is one of the forerunners of endogenous growth the-ory. Rather than viewing technical change as occurring exogenously, this approach views technological change as a consequence of choices made by firms. Firms make investment decisions about how much money to put toward R&D, and this is an important factor in influencing their subse-quent rate of productivity advance.

The standard production function approach is to consider a "stock" of R&D capital as an additional factor of production along with labor and cap-ital. Following Mansfield (1965, 1980) and Griliches (1979), we can rewrite equation (2.2) as:

$$Y_t = ce^{\eta t}L_t{}^{\alpha}K_t{}^{(1-\alpha)}R_t{}^{\beta} \qquad (2.6)$$

where R_t is the stock of R&D capital at time t and η is the rate of technolog-ical progress. Taking the time derivatives of the logarithm of both sides of equation (2.6) and using the definition of TFP growth from equation (2.,4), we obtain:

$$\rho_t = \eta + \beta[dR_t / dt] / R_t \qquad (2.7)$$

Since $\beta = (\partial Y_t / Y_t) / (\partial R_t / R_t)$ (where "∂" is the sign for the partial deriva-tive), then (2.7) can be rewritten as:

$$\rho_t = \eta + \zeta[dR_t / dt] / Y_t \qquad (2.8)$$

where $\zeta = \partial Y_t / \partial R_t$ and is usually interpreted as the "rate of return to R&D." Noting that dR_t is the change in R&D stock, which is approximately equal to R&D expenditures during the course of the year (assuming that the rate of obsolescence of R&D is small), then the corresponding estimating form becomes:

$$TFPGRT_t = a_0 + a_1 RDGDP_t + \varepsilon_t \qquad (2.9)$$

where $TFPGRT_t$ is the rate of TFP growth of a unit at time t, $RDGDP_t$ is the ratio of R&D expenditures to GDP (output) of the unit at time t, a_0 is a constant, and a_1 is the rate of return of R&D. This analysis assumes that the rate of return to R&D is equal across the units of observation in the sample (typically, firms or industries). Estimated rates of return to R&D typically fall in the range of 10 to 30 percent.

Griliches (1979) raised several important issues regarding the effects of R&D on productivity growth. One that has occupied many researchers involves the existence and magnitude of R&D or technological spillovers. By its very nature, R&D is knowledge production and knowledge has a way of "spilling over" from the producers of that knowledge to other firms. Another way of stating this issue is that the gains from R&D are not fully "appropriable" by the firm performing this activity, and some part of the gains may leak over to other firms in the industry and to firms in related industries.

There have been several approaches to measuring R&D spillovers. Terleckyj (1980) viewed R&D spillovers as the direct knowledge gains of customers from the R&D of the supplying industry. He measured R&D spillovers on the basis of interindustry sales between producers and customers and developed measures of the amount of R&D "embodied" in customer inputs (proportional to the interindustry sales and the R&D intensity of the supplying industry). Scherer (1983) distinguished two types of R&D expenditures: (1) process R&D, geared toward improving efficiency in production, and (2) product R&D, aimed at improving output quality. He used the latter as a measure of R&D spillovers, based on the amount of R&D expenditures devoted by one industry to products used by another.

An alternative approach is to measure the "technological closeness" between industries. If two industries use similar processes (even though their products are very different or they are not directly connected by interindustry flows), one industry may benefit from new discoveries by the other industry. Such an approach is found in Jaffe (1986), who relied on patent data to measure technological closeness between industries.

Estimates of the spillover effects of R&D are often quite high – in the range of 30 to 50 percent. The sum of the private gains from R&D and the spillover effects is often interpreted as the 'social rate of return to R&D.'

These estimates range as high as 50 to 80 percent and often serve as the basis of the argument that R&D should be subsidized by the government, since the social return exceeds the private return.

A related issue is raised by Cohen and Levinthal (1989), who argued that firms invest in R&D not only to generate their own product and process innovations but also to develop absorbative capacity, so that they are better able to use knowledge produced outside the firm boundaries. They emphasized that learning from others is a central part of the innovation process within the firm and serves as a motive for conducting its own R&D.

2.4 Evolutionary, Schumpeterian, and Technology Gap Models

An alternative view of the process of technological change devolves from the work of Schumpeter (1950) and evolutionary biology. The central idea is that new technology originates from a search process occurring in the neighborhood of existing technology. The search process has random components (much like genetic mutations) and results in a continuing modification of existing technology. Sometimes distinctly new technologies may evolve, replacing old technologies – a process Schumpeter called "creative destruction." However, though the fittest may be the only ones surviving in the long term, alternative technologies may coexist in both the short and medium term. This view was developed in a pair of articles, Nelson, Winter, and Schuette (1976) and Winter (1984), and in an influential book by Nelson and Winters (1982).

A related view can be found in the "technology gap" literature. This approach, first developed by Pavitt and Soete (1982), emphasized innovativeness as the basis for technological change and growth. Feedback effects also play a crucial role in maintaining technological advantage. Dosi, Pavitt, and Soete (1990), for example, argued that a dynamic relationship exists between "early innovative leads, economies of scale, learning by doing, oligopolistic exploitation of these advantages, and international competitiveness" (p. 34).

Fagerberg (1987) presented a relatively straightforward model in which output growth depends on the growth in knowledge, whether produced domestically or abroad, and efforts to make use of the available knowledge. The empirical implementation of the model used three independent variables: (i) GDP per capita of the countries in the sample, which served as a proxy for the availability of foreign-produced knowledge; (ii) patents, which served as an indicator of the extent of national innovative activity; and (iii) domestic investment, which reflected the degree to which a country attempted to exploit existing knowledge. All three variables were found to be statistically significant in explaining economic growth across a cross section of countries at different levels of development.

Verspagen (1991) developed a nonlinear model to incorporate the same set of factors. In addition, he included an educational variable as an indicator of the capacity of a country to absorb knowledge produced at home and abroad. Using a sample of more than one hundred countries, he found that the nonlinear model had greater predictive power than a simple linear form. His results also suggested that countries characterized by a large technological gap and low absorbative capacity (low educational levels) could wind up in a permanent low-growth trap.

Amable (1993) focused on the feedback effects among output growth, investment, and innovative activity. In his model, the ability to absorb foreign-produced knowledge (catch-up) depends on equipment investment and the level of education in the country. Investment depends on output growth (an accelerator model). Innovative activity depends on the level of education. Using data for fifty-nine countries covering the period 1960–85, he concluded that most countries will converge toward a productivity level considerably below that of the most advanced nations in the world.

History can play an important role. Arthur (1989) analyzed one peculiar phenomenon, referred to as the "lock-in" effect, whereby one technology may become the dominant one in an industry, even though it might not be the best. The classic example is the QWERTY keyboard, which became the standard for typewriters even though it is not the most efficient in terms of typing speed. An example from the 1980s was the DOS operating system, which became the standard for PCs during this period. The lock-in effect depends on the costs of learning the new technology and the cumulative spread of the technology.

Nelson and Wright (1992) applied some of these ideas in their historical analysis of the rise and fall of American technological leadership across a wide swath of industries. U.S. dominance of many key industries in the early part of the twentieth century, such as steel, automobiles, and electrical equipment, was in large part due to the emergence of mass production techniques and the size of the domestic American market. Its postwar leadership in high-tech industries such as aircraft, certain chemical products, electrical equipment, and computers was largely attributable to massive investments in research and development. The gradual erosion of American dominance, after 1960 or so, was a consequence of the development of world markets in most manufacturing lines and investment by other advanced countries in R&D.

2.5 The Solow and MRW Growth Models and Factor-Augmenting Technical Change

I start the formal treatment of growth models with the standard Solow (1956) growth model.[1] The Solow model assumes that the rates of saving, population growth, and technological change are exogenous. There are two inputs, capital and labor, which are paid their marginal product. A Cobb-Douglas production function is assumed, so that

$$Y(t) = K(t)^{\alpha} \left(A(t)L(t) \right)^{1-\alpha} \tag{2.10}$$

with $0 < \alpha < 1$ and A(t) the level of technology. Labor and technology are assumed to grow exogenously at rates n and g:

$$L(t) = L(0)e^{nt} \tag{2.11}$$

$$A(t) = A(0)e^{gt} \tag{2.12}$$

Therefore, the number of effective units of labor, A(t)L(t), grows at the rate $n + g$.

The Solow model also assumes that a constant fraction of output, q, is invested. If we let k be the amount of capital per effective unit of labor, k = K/AL, and y be the level of output per effective unit of labor, y = Y/AL, then

$$dk(t)/dt = qy(t) - (n+g+\delta)k(t) \tag{2.13}$$

$$= qk(t)^{\alpha} - (n+g+\delta)k(t)$$

where δ is the depreciation rate. Equation (2.13) implies that k converges to a steady-state value, k*, where

$$k^* = [q/(n+g+\delta)]^{1/(1-\alpha)} \tag{2.14}$$

As a result, the steady-state capital-labor ratio is positively related to the investment rate and negatively related to population growth.

By substituting (2.14) into (2.10) and taking logarithms of both sides, we obtain the steady-state level of GDP per worker as:

---

[1]   This treatment is based on Mankiw, Romer, and Weil (1992).

$$\ln\left[Y(t)/L(t)\right] = \ln A(0) + gt + [\alpha/(1-\alpha)]\ln(q) - \\ + [\alpha/(1-\alpha)]\ln(n+g+\delta)$$

(2.15)

If the capital share in income (α) is about one-third, then the elasticity of income per worker with respect to the investment rate q is approximately 0.5 and its elasticity with respect to $n+g+\delta$ is about -0.5. The model thus predicts that per capita income is higher in countries with higher investment rates and with lower values of $n+g+\delta$. This model thus provides directly testable predictions about the effects of these variables on output per worker across countries.

Mankiw, Romer, and Weil (1992) [MRW hereafter] augmented the basic Solow model by including human capital accumulation. MRW first modified the basic production function (2.10) as follows:

$$Y(t) = K(t)^{\alpha} H(t)^{\beta} \left(A(t)L(t)\right)^{1-\alpha-\beta}$$

(2.16)

where H is the stock of human capital. Let q_k be the fraction of output invested in physical capital and q_h be the fraction invested in human capital. The dynamics of the economy is then determined by:

$$dk(t)/dt = q_k y(t) - (n+g+\delta)\, k(t)$$

(2.17a)

$$dh(t)/dt = q_h y(t) - (n+g+\delta)\, h(t)$$

(2.17b)

where, as before, $y = Y/AL$ and $k = K/AL$, and now $h = h/AL$ are the quantities per effective unit of labor. MRW assumed that the same production function applies to consumption, physical capital, and human capital. In other words, one unit of consumption can be transformed costlessly into either one unit of human capital or one unit of physical capital. MRW also assumed that the same depreciation rate applies to both physical and human capital.[2]

MRW also assume that $\alpha + \beta < 1$. In other words, there are decreasing returns to all capital.[3] Equations (2.17a) and (2.17b) imply that the economy converges to a steady state given by:

$$k^* = [q_k^{1-\beta} q_h^{\beta} / (n+g-\delta)]^{1/(1-\alpha-\beta)}$$

(2.18a)

---

[2] Lucas (1988), in contrast, assumed that the production function for human capital differed from that of other goods.

[3] If $\alpha + \beta = 1$, then there would be constant returns to scale in the reproducible factors. In this case, there would be no steady-state solution for the model.

$$h^* = [q_k{}^\alpha q_h{}^{(1-\alpha)} / (n+g-\delta)]^{1/(1-\alpha-\beta)} \tag{2.18b}$$

Substituting (2.18a) and (2.18b) into (2.16) and taking logarithms yield a steady-state equation for output per worker similar to equation (2.15):

$$
\begin{aligned}
\ln\left[Y(t)/L(t)\right] = \ln A(0) + gt &- [(\alpha+\beta)/(1-\alpha-\beta)] \\
&\ln(n+g+\delta) + [\alpha/(1-\alpha-\beta)]\ln(s_k) \\
&+ [\beta/(1-\alpha-\beta)]\ln(s_h)
\end{aligned}
\tag{2.19}
$$

Equation (2.19) indicates how output per worker depends on population growth and the accumulation of physical and human capital. MRW estimated that the physical capital share of income was about a third, and that the share of human capital (β) was between one-third and one-half. If human capital is ignored in econometrically estimating the production function (as in the standard Solow model), then two types of biases will creep in. First, even if s_h is independent of the other regressors, the coefficient of $\ln(s_k)$ will be greater than $\alpha/(1-\alpha)$. For example, if both α and β are about one-third, then the coefficient of $\ln(s_k)$ would be about unity. Because higher investment leads to higher output, it also leads to a higher steady-state level of human capital even if the share of output devoted to human capital investment is unchanged. Hence, the presence of human capital increases the impact of physical capital accumulation on output. Second, the coefficient of $\ln(n+g+\delta)$ is larger in absolute value than the coefficient on $\ln(s_k)$. If, again, $\alpha = \beta = 1/3$, the coefficient on $\ln(n+g+\delta)$ would be -2. In this model, high population growth lowers output per worker because both physical and human capital must be spread more thinly over the workforce.

There is an alternative formulation for equation (2.19), as follows:

$$
\begin{aligned}
\ln\left[Y(t)/L(t)\right] = \ln A(0) + gt &- [\alpha/(1-\alpha)]\ln(n+g+\delta) \\
&+ [\alpha/(1-\alpha)]\ln(s_k) + [\beta/(1-\alpha)]\ln(h^*)
\end{aligned}
\tag{2.20}
$$

This is achieved by combining equation (2.19) with (2.18a) and (2.18b). The difference is that output per worker is now given as a function of the rate of investment in human capital, the rate of population growth, and the *level* of human capital. Equation (2.20) is almost identical to equation (2.15) except for the last term of equation (2.20). Here, it is now clear that omitting human capital from the standard Solow model estimation biases the coefficients of investment and population growth. Because investment and population growth influence h*, we should expect human capital to be positively correlated with the investment rate and negatively correlated with the growth rate of population. As a result, omitting the human capital term biases the coefficients on the investment rate and population growth.

A comparison of equations (2.19) and (2.20) suggests two alternative ways of estimating the influence of human capital on the level of output per worker. The first way is to include a term for the rate of human capital accumulation, $\ln(s_h)$, as a regressor. The second way is to include a term for the level of human capital, $\ln(h^*)$. These alternative regressions also predict different coefficients on the physical investment rate and population growth terms. A primary issue is whether the "levels" model produces better econometric results than the "growth" model. We shall return to this issue in Chapter 6 of this book.

Another modification of the basic Cobb-Douglas model of production is to drop the assumption of Hicks-neutral technical change and to assume, instead, that technological change is of the factor-augmenting form. I follow the treatment of Sato and Beckman (1970). The production function, as in the case of Cobb-Douglas, is assumed to be homogeneous of degree one and can be written as:

$$Y(t) = f\big(a(t)L(t),\ b(t)K(t)\big) \qquad (2.21)$$

where a(t) is an index of labor's productivity and b(t) is an index of capital's productivity. Sato and Beckman then define $\hat{L} \equiv aL$ as labor measured in efficiency units and $\hat{K} \equiv bK$ as capital measured in efficiency units. If it is assumed that a and b grow at constant rates:

$$a = e^{\alpha t} \quad \text{and} \quad b = e^{\beta t}$$

then the case when b = 1 is known as Harrod-neutral technical change and the case when b = a is Hick-neutral technical change. Factor-augmenting technical progress may thus be considered a combination of Harrod- and Hicks-neutral changes.

Sato and Beckman next showed that with a constant savings rate, s, and capital-augmenting technical progress, the labor-capital ratio measured in efficiency units decreases asymptotically to zero. Let:

$$\hat{x} = \hat{L} / \hat{K} = aL / bK$$

Then,

$$\overset{\circ}{\hat{x}}/\hat{x} = \overset{\circ}{a}/a - \overset{\circ}{b}/b + n - s(Y/K), \ 0 < s < 1, \qquad (2.22)$$

where it is assumed that labor increases at a constant rate n so that $L = L(0) e^{nt}$. Now write $a = a_0 e^{\alpha t}$ and $b = b_0 e^{\beta t}$, where $\alpha > 0$ and $\beta > 0$. Consider the case when

$$Y/K = f(aL/K, \ b) = bf(aL/bK, \ 1)$$

and then write $f(\hat{x}, 1) = \Phi(\hat{x})$. Because of the assumption of linear homogeneity,

$$Y/K = b\Phi(aL/bK) = b\Phi(\check{x})$$

where, as noted previously, $\hat{x}$ is the labor-capital ratio measured in efficiency units. Substituting in equation (2.22) yields

$$\overset{\circ}{\hat{x}}/\hat{x} = \alpha - \beta + n - sb\Phi(\hat{x}). \qquad (2.23)$$

Since b(t) is assumed to be increasing over time without limit, for large t the right-hand side turns negative, unless $\Phi(\hat{x})$ declines sufficiently. In either case, the result is that $\hat{x}$ approaches zero in the limit.

Sato and Beckmann then go on to show that the labor-capital ratio in physical terms, x, can approach a finite nonzero equilibrium only if the technical change is purely capital augmenting. This result does not apply in the case of a Cobb-Douglas production function.

2.6 The Lucas (1988) and Romer (1990) Growth Models

The third widely used model was developed by Lucas (1988). He actually presented three different models; the one of most interest is the one that relates human capital to growth. He defined human capital as the general skill level of a worker, so that a worker with human capital h(t) at time t is the productive equivalent of two workers with h(t)/2 each. One key point of the model concerns the manner in which an individual allocates his time over alternative activities in the current period, which affects his h(t) level in future periods. Introducing human capital into the model then involves defining how human capital affects current production and how current time allocation affects the accumulation of human capital.

In his model, he assumed that there were N workers in total, with skill levels h ranging from 0 to infinity. Let there be N(h) workers with skill level h, so that $N = \int H(h)dh$. Moreover, he supposed that a worker with skill level h devotes the fraction u(h) of his nonleisure time to current production and $1 - u(h)$ to human capital production. Then the effective labor force in production is given by $N^e = \int u(h)H(h)dh$. Moreover, if output is a function of total capital K and effective labor N^e, then total output $Y = F(K, N^e)$, the wage of a worker with skill level h is $w_h = F_N(K, N^e)h$, and the worker's total earnings are $W_h = F_N(K, N^e)hu(h)$.

Lucas argued that human capital has both an "internal effect" on individual earnings and an "external effect" on economywide productivity. Let the average level of human capital be given by:

$$h_a = \int_h N(h)dh / \int N(h)dh.$$

To simplify the analysis, Lucas assumed that all workers have skill level h and all choose time allocation u, so that the effective workforce is $N^e = uhN$ and the average skill level h_a is h. The technology of goods production is then given by:

$$N(t)c(t) + dK(t)/dt = AK(t)^\beta \left[u(t)h(t)N(t)\right]^{1-\beta} h_a(t)^\gamma \quad (2.24)$$

where c(t) is consumption at time t, the technology level A is assumed constant over time, β and γ are constants where $0 < \beta, \gamma < 1$, and the term $h_a(t)^\gamma$ is intended to capture the external effects of human capital. It should be noted that this model implicitly assumes increasing returns to scale.

Lucas also assumed that the growth of human capital is related to the current level of human capital and the amount of time devoted to acquiring more:

$$dh(t)/dt = h(t)G(1 - u(t)) \quad (2.25)$$

where the function G is increasing with $G(0) = 0$. Lucas also assumed that the function G is linear, so that

$$dh(t)/dt = h(t)\delta(1 - u(t)) \quad (2.26)$$

According to (2.25), if no effort is devoted to investing in human capital, then none accumulates. Alternatively, if all effort is devoted to human capital accumulation, then h(t) grows at a maximum rate of δ.

As in the standard Solow model, it is assumed that population grows at the rate n. Lucas then showed that on the balance growth equilibrium, the rate of growth of output is given by:

$$(dY/dt)/Y = [(1-\beta+\gamma)/(1-\beta)] \, (dh/dt)/h \qquad (2.27)$$

There are several interesting features of this equilibrium path. First, the rate of output growth is directly proportional to the rate of growth of human capital. Thus, an economy could maintain a high level of growth for the economy if it could maintain a high rate of growth of human capital. Second, this model is consistent with the permanent maintenance of per capita income differentials of any size (though not with differences in growth rates). Thus, the model is more consistent with the lack of convergence among countries of the world than is the standard Solow model (see Chapter 9 for more details).

Third, the model predicts multiple equilibria. Economies that are initially poor will remain poor in relative terms though their long-run growth rate will be the same as that of the initially (and permanently) richer countries. A world consisting of such economies would then exhibit uniform rates of growth across countries and would maintain a perfectly stable distribution of per capita income over time. As Lucas noted, this model fits the main features of the world economy: the very wide diversity in per capita output levels across countries, sustained growth in per capita output at all income levels, and the absence of any marked tendency for growth rates to differ systematically at different income levels (and certainly not inversely to initial per capita income).

2.7 Endogenous Growth Theory

In the Cobb-Douglas production function, technological change is viewed as originating outside the system of production. The Solow residual is treated as exogenous technical change. In endogenous growth theory, production itself creates the conditions of technical change. In other words, the determinants are endogenous to the economic system. We saw one example, in Section 2, where R&D is a producer of technical change and is determined within the economic system as an investment decision by firms depending on its rate of return. Earlier versions of the idea of endogenous growth can be found in Verdoorn (1949) and Kaldor (1956). In these two works, production itself sowed the seeds of continued growth in productivity, through a positive feedback effect between output growth and productivity growth. The general form of the argument is that increased output associated with an expanding market will lead to increased economies of scale, greater specialization of production, and new investment embodying the latest technology, which, in turn, allow price to decline and result in a further expansion of the market. Both arguments suggest a positive relation between the change in output growth and the rate of labor productivity advance.

The more recent literature cited in this section represents the "new growth theory" and formalizes these relations, as well as highlighting the potential importance of externalities and increasing returns to scale as part of the engine of economic growth. The articles of Romer (1986, 1990) and Lucas (1988) stress the importance of both physical capital and human capital as vehicles for the transmission of technological change. They both constructed models essentially of the form $Y = aK$, where a is a constant and K reflects both physical and human capital. There are no diminishing returns to capital, as in the Cobb-Douglas production function, because of externalities emanating from investment (the social returns to investment exceed the private gain). In the case of education, for example, a more educated labor force will make each individual worker more productive because of the opportunities of learning from his or her fellow workers.

An alternative route to obtaining an equation like $Y = aK$ is to assume that an increasing variety of intermediate inputs or increasing quality in machinery and equipment will offset the inherent tendencies to diminishing returns associated with new investment (see Romer, 1990, or Grossman and Helpman, 1991). In these models, K represents either the quality or variety of inputs, and a knowledge-producing sector (research and development, for example) is added as a second sector to the goods-producing industry. A monopolistic competitive market for goods is also assumed in order to allow the firms to recoup their investment in R&D.

Another approach derives from the idea of "learning by doing" developed by Arrow (1962). His argument is that a firm that first develops a product or introduces a new production technique may be able to descend the cost curve by acquiring the expertise that accrues through experience in making the product. This idea has led to a related group of models that emphasize the role of increasing internal returns to scale and learning by doing in the formation of industry specialization. The underlying theory was originally developed by Krugman (1979, 1980) in the context of international trade theory. This line of analysis suggests that it is the presence of economies of scale and/or high startup costs that allows different countries to achieve specialization in different products. The country that enters a new field or new product line first may be able to dominate that line by increasing production to the point at which its costs are so low that potential new competitors are unable to enter the field successfully (at least, without sufficient subsidies from their government). Even more important is the accumulation of specialized knowledge that is acquired only by being in the industry. This may include knowledge of the details of production steps, as well as specialized skills that are mainly acquired on the job, knowledge of marketing channels, and a knowledgeable sales force that is known to customers.

Which industries a country may specialize in may depend on history and a variety of influences, some of them perhaps fortuitous. Moreover, an important role can be played by the availability or unavailability of ancillary industries that can substantially facilitate a country's success in the production of some particular product or type of product. Geographical externalities may also play an important role, since once an industry is established in a country or place, there is greater likelihood of suppliers and customers also specializing there (see Krugman, 1991).

The Romer (1990) model is one of the earliest examples of an endogenous growth model.[4] Romer based his model on three premises. The first is that technological change lies at the heart of economic growth. The second premise is that technological change arises in large part because of intentional actions that firms take in response to market incentives. This assumption makes this model one of endogenous rather than exogenous technological change. The third premise is that research knowledge is inherently different from other economic goods and services. Once the cost of creating new knowledge has been incurred, the same knowledge can be used over and over again at no additional cost. Developing such research knowledge is equivalent to incurring a fixed capital cost. This property is taken to be the defining characteristic of technology.

In the particular specification of his model, a firm incurs fixed R&D costs when it creates a new good or service. The firm then recovers these costs by selling the new product for a price in excess of its constant cost of production. Since there is free entry into the R&D activity, a firm earns zero profits in equilibrium in terms of present value. The fact that R&D entails fixed

---

[4] Actually, as noted previously, the Lucas (1988) model is partially an endogenous growth model because human capital is produced internally to the model and diverts resources from other outputs.

costs implies that firms doing R&D gain from increases in the size of the market. In equilibrium, increases in the size of the market have effects not only on the level of output but also on the rate of growth of output. Larger markets induce more R&D and therefore faster growth.

The production function used by Romer has four inputs – capital, labor, human capital H, and an index of the level of technology, where H is a measure of the cumulative effect of formal education and on-the-job training. The economy has three sectors. The first, the R&D sector, uses human capital and the existing stock of knowledge to produce new knowledge. The second, the intermediate goods sector, uses the knowledge produced in the first sector together with other produced inputs. The third sector, the final goods sector, uses labor, human capital, and the set of producer durables produced by the second sector to create final output. This output can be either consumed or saved as new capital. Romer also assumed that the population, the labor supply, and the total stock of human capital are all constant over time. The production function for final output Y is a modified Cobb-Douglas form given by:

$$Y\left(H_Y, L, x\right) = H_Y^{\alpha} L^{\beta} \sum x_i^{1-\alpha-\beta} \tag{2.28}$$

where H_Y is the portion of human capital devoted to final output, L is the labor input, x_i is produced input number i, and α and β are fixed parameters of the production function. The production function for the technology level A is given by:

$$dA / dt = \delta A H_A \tag{2.29}$$

where δ is a productivity constant and H_A is the total human capital employed in research and development. Romer then showed that in balanced growth equilibrium,

$$Y\left(H_A, L, x\right) = \left(H_Y A\right)^{\alpha} \left(LA\right)^{\beta} \left(K\right)^{1-\alpha-\beta} \left(\eta\right)^{1-\alpha-\beta} \tag{2.30}$$

where η is another technology constant. Finally, the equilibrium growth rate g of output is given by:

$$g = \delta H - \{\alpha / [(1-\alpha-\beta)(\alpha+\beta)]\}r \tag{2.31}$$

where r is the equilibrium interest rate. Perhaps, the main result of interest here is that the growth rate of output depends directly on the *level* of human capital in an economy. This has important implications for growth regressions (see Chapter 6).

The second model considered here was developed by Aghion and Howitt (1992). Like the Romer model, this one also considered the role of the research sector in generating growth endogenously. They concluded that both the average growth rate and the variance of the growth rate are increasing functions of the size of innovations, the size of the skilled labor force, and the productivity of R&D as measured by the rate at which innovations arrive.

Their model took into account the factor of obsolescence, in which new and better products render previous ones obsolete (so-called creative destruction). They argued that the amount invested in R&D depends on two effects. The first is creative destruction, whereby the payoff from research in this period is the prospect of monopoly rents in the next period. This payoff will last only until the next innovation occurs, at which time the rents from the previous innovation are rendered obsolete. The second effect is a general equilibrium effect on the wages of skilled labor. The expectation of more research next period will correspond to an expectation of higher demand for skilled labor in R&D next period, which results in a higher expected real wage for skilled labor. Higher wages next period will reduce the monopoly rents gained from the innovation and thus discourage research this period by reducing the rents next period.

The formal model is developed as follows: First, the technology of the consumption good y is given by:

$$Y = AF(x)$$

where Y is output, x is intermediate input, and A is a parameter indicating the productivity of the intermediate input. Second, the intermediate good is produced using skill labor H alone according to the linear technology:

$$x = H.$$

Third, the introduction of a new intermediate good increases the productivity parameter A by a factor γ so that

$$A_t = A_0 \gamma^t$$

where A_0 is the initial value.

In balanced growth equilibrium, output growth g is given by

$$g = \lambda \varphi(n^*) \ln \gamma$$

where λ is a parameter that refers to the length of interval during which the research is conducted and $\phi(n^*)$ is the total flow of skilled labor used in research during the interval or research. Thus, the rate of output growth depends positively on the rate of innovation, the size of innovations, and the size of the skilled labor endowment.

2.8 Definitions of Convergence

Two different notions of convergence have been used in the literature. The first, referred to as β-convergence, is defined as a narrowing of initial differences in income levels over some time horizon, with poorer countries growing faster than richer ones. Many cross-section analyses have used this concept when focusing on the transition to equilibrium growth paths. The second concept used in the literature is called σ-convergence and refers to the reduction over time in the cross-country variance of productivity. One concept does not necessarily imply the other. These interpretations of convergence are associated with predicted productivity paths from a neoclassical growth model with different initial endowments of capital stock. β-convergence implies that countries with low initial capital stocks and hence low initial income levels accumulate capital faster than average, while countries with higher than average initial capital stocks grow more slowly. σ-convergence, in contrast, predicts that the cross-country dispersion in productivity will decline during the transition to a steady-state equilibrium. Once countries attain their steady-state levels of capital, no further reduction in the cross-country dispersion of productivity is expected, and expected growth rates after this point become identical.

β-convergence also implies a negative correlation between the initial income level and the subsequent growth rate. This is often tested by running what is known as the "growth-initial level" regression. The coefficient of the initial income variable in these regressions (say, β) is predicted to be negative (and significant). Convergence is thus assessed by the sign and significance level of the coefficient β.

However, a negative β coefficient does not necessarily imply a reduction in the cross-country dispersion of per capita income. As a result, some have argued that it is more appropriate to look directly at the dispersion of per capita income levels across countries. This gave rise to the concept of σ-convergence, where σ is the notation for the standard deviation of the cross-sectional distribution of per capita income levels. β-convergence is a necessary though not sufficient condition for σ-convergence (see Bernard and Durlauf, 1996, for further discussion of these issues).

Another distinction is often drawn between *unconditional* and *conditional* convergence. These two concepts usually refer exclusively to β-convergence. Unconditional convergence implies that the coefficient β in a growth-initial level regression should be negative even if no other variable is included on the right-hand side of the equation. In contrast, conditional convergence requires that appropriate variables be included on the right-hand side of the growth-initial level regression equation in order to control for the effects of other factors on growth. Typical variables include investment, education, and trade openness. After controlling for these other factors, a negative and significant coefficient on β would be evidence of conditional convergence in productivity levels.

The concept of *club convergence* (or "group convergence") is related to the concept of conditional convergence. In the case of unconditional convergence it is implicitly assumed that there is only one equilibrium level to which all economies converge. However, in the case of conditional convergence, equilibrium levels differ by country and each particular country approaches its own unique equilibrium. The notion of club convergence is based on models that yield multiple equilibria. The actual equilibrium that a particular economy approaches depends on its initial conditions as well as other factors (such as educational level). A group of countries may approach a similar (or identical) equilibrium if they share similar initial conditions and a similar set of other factors. This process is referred to as club (or group) convergence.

2.9 Econometric Issues

As Temple (1999) noted, the early cross-sectional Ordinary Least Squares (OLS) regressions (including my own early work) were subject to different types of econometric problems. The first is specification error. The researcher typically does not know the "true" model that determines the rate of growth of productivity or per capita income. As a result, she is forced to select explanatory variables that appear to be the most reasonable determinants of growth (often on the basis of what data are available). Levine and Renelt (1992) in an important article discussed this problem. As they noted, many variables were found to be significant in these growth regressions, but many of these were found to be "fragile" in the sense that their statistical significance evaporated when a different group of explanatory variables were selected. As a result, presenting the results of a single model may be misleading. However, even the finding that a variable's coefficient is robust to changes in the model specification is not sufficient for valid inference about its statistical significance since the specification may be subject to other types of econometric problems (see later discussion).

One particular form of specification bias is the omitted variable bias. This occurs when an explanatory variable that is likely to have an important effect on the dependent variable is omitted from the equation (perhaps because of a lack of appropriate data). In this case, there are well-established ways to assess the degree of omitted variable bias. In the simple bivariate case, the omission of a significant variable positively correlated with the included right-side variable will bias upward the coefficient estimate on the included variable (and conversely if the two are negatively correlated).

The second type of econometric problem is measurement error. In most data sets such as the widely applied Penn World Tables (discussed later) that are used in cross-section growth regressions, the variables are likely to suffer from measurement error. However, few studies in this literature attempt to assess the sensitivity of the regression results to measurement error. Normally, measurement error will bias the coefficient estimates toward zero. However, this is not always the case, and when there are several variables in the regression with severe measurement error, then biases may be either upward or downward. Multivariate reverse regressions is one technique that can be used in the case of measurement error, as well as classical method-of-moments estimators. Another approach is to use instrumental variables, though one common problem with this approach is a shortage of suitable instruments.

A third problem is so-called unobserved heterogeneity in the parameter estimates. This problem is especially acute in cross-country growth regressions involving countries at all levels of development. In particular, countries varying widely in terms of their political, social, and institutional framework are unlikely to occupy a common space. For example, in a regression of the investment rate on income growth, the coefficient on the investment rate is likely to be much lower in politically unstable countries (and ones suffering through wars) than in stable and peaceful countries. A standard approach to this problem is to include time and country-industry fixed effects in a cross-sectional regression in order to account for unobserved heterogeneity across countries (and also industries if the unit of observation is the industry). Panel data estimation (see later discussion) may also alleviate some of the problems associated with heterogeneity.

A fourth problem and perhaps the one most frequently discussed in the growth literature is the possible endogeneity of some of the explanatory variables. This problem is also referred to as simultaneity bias, since both the dependent and independent variables are determined simultaneously (or, alternatively, codetermined). There are various techniques that have been used to overcome this problem. First, some researchers often use the initial value of the independent variable in a growth regression – for example, regressing the growth in per capita income from 1950 to 1990 on the 1950 secondary school enrollment rate. However, this solution is not foolproof, since some omitted variable such as the degree of democracy in a country may affect both per capita income growth and the initial level of schooling.

Many of the earlier papers on this subject (including my own) used the investment rate as an explanatory variable. However, it is possible that causality could go from income growth to investment (for example, growth probably raises the saving rate). One way around this problem is to use instrumental variables (IV). IV estimates typically produce a smaller coefficient on the investment rate than OLS. However, one major problem with the IV technique is that there is usually a paucity of possible instruments. The reason is that there are many variables that could be used to explain income growth so that it is difficult to find ones that not only are highly correlated with the endogenous variables but can also be reasonably excluded from the regression. Another possibility is to use lagged values of the endogenous variables as instruments, but their exogeneity is not always clearly determined.

An alternative solution is to use panel data estimation (that is, a pooled cross-section, time-series sample) instead of cross-section analysis. This approach has several advantages. First, it allows the researcher to control for omitted variables that are persistent over time. For example, standard cross-section productivity growth regressions usually produce a biased coefficient on the initial level of productivity because of the variations of technical efficiency across countries that are likely to be correlated with the explanatory variables. In contrast, a panel data estimation will control for unobserved heterogeneity in the initial efficiency level. Another advantage is that several lagged values of the explanatory variables can be used as instruments, thereby reducing measurement error and endogeneity biases. GMM (generalized method of means) estimation can also be used with panel data. However, the sample properties of GMM estimation are not as yet well understood. Moreover, the power of the estimation can also be increased by using first difference estimation (as well as differences in differences) in a fixed effect model. Such fixed effect estimation assumes that the variables remain fairly constant over long periods or that they affect income growth only after a long lag. First difference techniques are likely to increase the problem of measurement error if these errors are not persistent over time. An alternative to the first difference approach is to introduce regional dummy variables into the growth equation since much of the variation in productivity levels occurs within regions rather than between them.[5]

2.10 Data Sources and Methods

It is useful to introduce this section with a review of basic number indices. The two most commonly used are the Laspeyres, L, and the Paasche, P, indices, given by:

$$L = \sum_{i=1}^{n} p_{it+1} q_{it} \Big/ \sum_{i=1}^{n} p_{it} q_{it}$$

$$P = \sum_{i=1}^{n} p_{it+1} q_{it+1} \Big/ \sum p_{it} q_{it+1}$$

where p refers to the price, q refers to the quantity, and t refers to time. The Laspeyres index uses base year quantity weights, while the Paasche index uses second year quantity weights. They can be interpreted as indices based on fixed baskets from year t and t + 1, respectively. A third index, the Fisher index, F, is the geometric mean of the two sets of weights:

$$F = [L \cdot P]^{1/2}$$

The Laspeyres and the Paasche indices can also be expressed in terms of expenditure weights. For example,

$$L = \sum_{i=1}^{n} \left(p_{it+1} / p_{it} \right) \cdot w_{it}$$

where $w_{it} = p_{it} q_{it} / \sum_i p_{it} q_{it}$ is the expenditure share of the i-th product in total expenditure. Here the price index is expressed as an expenditure share weighted average of price relatives for different products. We shall have much more to say on index numbers in Chapter 3.

When comparing per capita income levels across countries in the world, the usual method is to value each country's final products at domestic prices

---

[5] See Chapter 3 as well as Temple (1999) and Islam (2003) for further discussion of econometric issues in this literature.

and then convert these figures into a common monetary unit using the pertinent exchange rates. However, market exchange rates do not often reflect the fact that a given number of U.S. dollars will buy different amounts of goods and services in different countries. In other words, there are often large and persistent differences between market exchange rates and so-called purchasing power parity or PPP exchange rates. Most researchers in this field prefer to use PPPs so that incomes are converted into a special currency index that is calculated so that one unit will purchase the same bundle of goods and services in each country.

The development of a complete table of national accounts based on PPPs with figures that are comparable across both space and time requires price data for a wide range of goods in each country. The United Nations International Comparison Program (ICP), begun in the late 1960s, was the first systematic attempt to construct such estimates for about ninety countries. These estimates were then combined with national accounts tables in these countries to produce the Penn World Tables (PWT).[6] This is the principal research tool used by those engaged in empirical growth research. Most of the countries provided their own data to the project, and these are referred to as "benchmark" countries. However, other countries did not participate in the ICP project and the PWT estimates are based on extrapolations. It is likely that the quality of data for these countries is rather low.

According to Maddison (2005), the early international comparisons were initiated by the OECD (see Gilbert and Kravis, 1954). These early estimates were based on binary comparisons of differences in price levels between pairs of countries. The three options that were used were (1) a Paasche PPP, with own country quantity weights; (ii) a Laspeyre PPP, with quantity weights from the numeraire country – in this case, the United States; and (iii) a geometric (Fisher) average of the first two measures. The corresponding measures of real expenditures were (i) Laspeyres comparisons of GDP levels based on the prices (or unit values) of the numeraire country; (ii) a Paasche level comparison based on own country prices (or unit values); and (iii) a Fisher geometric average of the two measures. On the basis of this method, it was possible to make binary comparison between, say, Germany and the United States and France and the United States and these could be linked to make a Germany-France comparison. However, such a comparison would not be transitive in the sense that the results would be different from one based on a direct Germany-France

---

[6] See Summers and Heston (1984, 1988, 1991) for details.

comparison. This was not a great drawback for the OECD countries since the intercountry deviations in performance levels were not too wide. However, the PWT project encompassed a much wider range of countries and therefore performance levels.

The PWT project therefore adopted the Geary (1958)-Khamis (1970) or GK method, which multilateralized the results of international comparisons. The set of "international prices" (reflecting relative product values) and country PPPs so derived are estimated simultaneously from a system of linear equations. The resulting set of prices has the properties of base-country invariance, matrix consistency, and transitivity.

The GK method is an average price method that can be used to compute real final expenditures by product type. It entails valuing a matrix of quantities using a vector of international prices. The vector is obtained by averaging national prices across countries after they have been converted to a common currency with PPPs and weighted by quantities. The PPPs are obtained by averaging within countries the ratios of national and international prices weighted by expenditure. The international prices and the PPPs are defined by a system of interrelated linear equations that require solving simultaneously:

(i) $\quad P_i = [\sum_{j=1}^{M}(p_{ij}q_{ij})/ PPP_j]/\sum_{j=1}^{M}q_{ij}$

(ii) $\quad PPP_j = \sum_{i=1}^{N}p_{ij}q_{ij}/\sum_{i=1}^{N}P_iq_{ij}$

where P_i refers to the international average price of product i for the N products in the system, q_{ij} is the output of good i in country j in the M countries in the system, and p_{ij} is the price of good i in country j.

The GK method produces PPPs that are transitive and real final expenditures that are additive. One important disadvantage of this method is that a change in the composition of the group can change significantly the international prices as well as the relationships between countries.

The Maddison data (see Maddison, 2005, for example) are also based on the GK methodology. As will be seen, the Maddison data have been used extensively for long-term country comparisons (see Chapter 4 in particular). Other sources of international data are the International Monetary Fund, whose GDP figures are based on market exchange rates, and the World Bank, whose GDP figures are based on PPPs. The most recent World Bank figures (as of 2010) used different national prices than the PWT. In particular, their figures show a substantially lower relative level of GDP per capita in China than the PWT. This has been a source of much controversy recently.

2.11 Summary

Chapter 2 discussed the methodological underpinnings of the modern growth literature. It also considered the theoretical foundations of modern growth theory and touched on some measurement and econometric issues.

The chapter began with a discussion of production function theory, beginning with the standard Cobb-Douglas production function, and growth accounting. Growth accounting is a method that attempts to decompose the growth of output into different components such as investment and education. The next section introduced R&D into the production function. It indicated how the standard Cobb-Douglas production function can be modified to include R&D investment and discussed R&D spillovers both between industries in an economy and between countries.

Section 2.4 introduced another view of the process of technological change, which is based on the work of Schumpeter (1950) and evolutionary biology. The central idea is that new technology originates from a search process occurring in the neighborhood of existing technology. A related view can be found in the "technology gap" literature, which emphasizes innovativeness as the basis for technological change and growth.

The next three sections discuss the central models of modern growth theory. The first of these (Section 2.5) presented the classic Solow (1956) growth model. The basic model is quite at odds with the empirical findings that different countries experience very different rates of productivity growth and that the rate of productivity growth in a given country fluctuates over time.

There are three principal ways in which growth theorists have modified the original Solow model to account for these discrepancies. First, they have viewed part of the discrepancy as a movement toward equilibrium rather than as a state of equilibrium. This leads to various forms of dynamics in approaching steady-state equilibrium. Second, they have modified the assumption of the same production function across countries (which underlies the Solow model) in two ways. First, the underlying production function at a given point of time may differ among countries, and changes in the production function over time might reflect the catch-up effect. Second, the production function can be modified to reflect human capital accumulation, and thus education is given a role in the growth model. One important example of the modified Solow growth model can be found in

Mankiw, Roemer, and Weil (1992), which is also discussed in this section. Third, the assumption of Hicks-neutral technical change can be dropped and factor-augmenting technical change can be assumed instead.

Section 2.6 outlined the Lucas (1988) growth model, which emphasizes the role of human capital in growth. Endogenous growth models are developed in the next section. In the Cobb-Douglas production function, technological change is viewed as being exogenous to the system of production. The Solow residual is used to estimate the rate of exogenous technical change. In endogenous growth theory, production itself creates the conditions of technical change. The works of Romer (1990) and Aghion and Howitt (1992) were discussed here.

The last three sections discussed basic methodological issues. The first of these, Section 2.8, presented two different notions of convergence that have been used in the literature. The first, referred to as β-convergence, is defined as a narrowing of initial differences in income levels over some time horizon, with poorer countries growing faster than richer ones. The second concept used in the literature is σ-convergence, which refers to the reduction over time in the cross-country variance of productivity. The differences between conditional and unconditional convergence are also highlighted. Some basic econometric issues in model estimation were then reviewed in Section 2.9, while Section 2.10 provided an overview of some of the most common data sources and methods used in this literature.

3

The Measurement and Estimation of Productivity Growth

3.1 Introduction

In the last chapter I presented an overview of modern growth theory and touched on some measurement and econometric issues. It is now helpful to provide technical details on both the measurement and the estimation of productivity growth, particularly total factor productivity (TFP) growth. In this chapter, I present the theoretical foundation for much of the empirical literature dealing with issues of productivity measurement.

As Erwin Diewert emphasized in a number of papers, TFP is a production function–based concept (see, for example, Diewert, 1976). Although all researchers would agree that productivity growth has occurred if a firm is able to produce more output from the same vector of inputs, the quantitative estimate of the magnitude of TFP growth depends on how each researcher chooses to measure it. There are several different ways to measure TFP – empirically based index numbers, econometric methods, stochastic frontier methods, and data envelopment analysis (DEA). It is important to address this issue, as well as many other important theoretical issues associated with defining and measuring productivity change. For instance, an uncritical reader might get the mistaken impression that there is such a thing as an industry-level or country-level production function and that it has the Cobb-Douglas functional form, because almost all empirical work in this literature uses this functional form.

A number of important data issues need to be discussed in some detail for the reader to be able to judge the quality of the empirical evidence presented. For example, the economic theory of TFP measurement is typically derived in terms of physical output units even though, empirically, deflated dollar sales is used in place of physical output. This issue is discussed in, for example, Bartelsman and Doms (2000). Most of the analysis discussed in subsequent chapters is also carried out using aggregate industry-level or country-level data. As a result, we need to provide a discussion of how industry-level and country-level input and output aggregates are computed. Moreover, the theoretical restrictions on firm level production functions necessary for an aggregate production function to exist need to be spelled out as well. Consequently, there are a number of reasons why the growth in the country-level output aggregate is less than the growth in the country-level input aggregate that are not the result of productivity growth. Some discussion of these data-to-theory issues and how important they are likely to be quantitatively is necessary for the reader to understand how to interpret many of the empirical results discussed in later chapters.

As a result, this chapter tries to provide enough theoretical background on productivity measurement and the data challenges researchers face in measuring productivity growth to give readers the necessary foundation to evaluate the subsequent discussion of the strengths and weaknesses of the empirical evidence discussed in the remaining chapters of the book. These later chapters will focus on explaining the important results from the literature and why they are important, as well as pointing out any shortcomings.

Section 3.2 presents a systematic treatment of the theory of productivity growth. Section 3.3 discusses econometric issues associated with the estimation of productivity growth. Section 3.4 addresses the question of the theoretical conditions necessary to measure productivity growth at the industry level or country level. Section 3.5 treats the major data availability and quality issues that must be dealt with in measuring TFP empirically. Section 3.6 discusses another data issue related to the fact that the theory of productivity measurement is developed in terms of physical units of output, but dollar sales is often the only information that is available to the researcher. Section 3.7 also discusses problems associated with the use of deflated dollar sales instead of physical output as the output measure based on the work of Bartelsman and Doms (2000). A summary and concluding remarks are provided in Section 3.8.

3.2 Theory of Productivity Growth

I begin with a systematic treatment of the theory of productivity. This should provide the necessary theoretical foundation for the remaining chapters of the book. Later discussion will identify the major data-to-theory challenges that must be confronted in measuring productivity empirically.

This section begins with a rigorous definition of TFP using the neoclassical theory of production. It demonstrates that TFP depends on the assumed form of the production transformation function, specifically the functional forms for both the input aggregator function and the output aggregator function. This theoretical discussion begins at the firm level because the existence of an aggregate economywide or industrywide production transformation function requires many additional assumptions that may or may not hold empirically. This framework is then used to introduce the distinction between Hicks-neutral technical change and factor-biased technical change. This is then followed by a discussion of the theoretical framework for measuring productivity change using the minimum cost function. In this regard, I also explain the additional assumptions required by the dual (cost function) approach relative to the primal production function–based approach to productivity measurement. For example, measuring productivity in terms of the production function only requires the firm to produce in a technically efficient manner, whereas productivity measurement from the dual approach requires both technically efficient and allocatively efficient production.

As a preface, it should be noted that I have presented the main results from the studies surveyed here and have, as a result, skipped over some important steps in the mathematical derivations. Because of this, I have presented the article summaries using the *original* mathematical symbols of the authors. Such an approach will enable the reader to refer to the individual articles for more details on the mathematical derivations. As a result, it should be noted that while the symbols used are consistent within each subsection, they may not be consistent between subsections of the paper.

3.2.1 Diewert's Superlative Index

As noted in Section 3.1 Diewert (1976) argued that TFP is a production function–based concept. Although all researchers would agree that productivity growth has occurred if a firm is able to produce more output from the same vector of inputs, the quantitative estimate of the magnitude of TFP growth depends on how each researcher chooses to measure it.

Diewert (1976) notes that one of the most troublesome problems facing economic researchers who construct a data series is the question of which functional form for an index number should be used. Diewert considers this question and relates functional forms for and index number to the underlying production or utility function (or aggregator function, to use a neutral terminology). He rationalizes certain functional forms for index numbers with functional forms for the underlying aggregator function. An aggregator functional form is said to be "flexible" if it can provide a second-order approximation to an arbitrary twice-differentiable linearly homogeneous function. An index number functional form is said to be "superlative" if it is exact (that is, consistent with) for a "flexible" aggregator functional form. The paper shows that a certain family of index number formulae is exact for the "flexible" quadratic mean of order r aggregator function, $(\Sigma_i \Sigma_j a_{ij} x_i^{r/2} x_j^{r/2})^{1/r}$. For r equal to 2, the resulting quantity index is Fisher's so-called ideal index. Diewert also utilizes the Malmquist quantity index in order to rationalize the Tornqvist-Theil quantity index in the nonhomothetic case.

Diewert begins the formal presentation by defining a quantity index between periods 0 and 1, $Q(p^0, p^1; x^0, x^1)$, as a function of the prices in periods 0 and 1, $p^0 > 0_N$ and $p^1 > 0_N$, where 0_N is an N-dimensional vector of zeroes, and the corresponding quantity vectors, $x^0 > 0_N$ and $x^1 > 0_N$, while the price index between periods 0 and 1, $P(p^0, p^1, x^0, x^1)$, is a function of the same price and quantity vectors. On the basis of either a price index or a quantity index, the expenditure function can be defined implicitly by the following equation:

$$P\left(p^0, p^1, x^0, x^1\right) Q\left(p^0, p^1, x^0, x^1\right) = p^1 \cdot x^1 / p^0 \cdot x^0 \qquad (3.1)$$

In other words, the product of the price index times the quantity index should yield the expenditure ratio between the two periods, where the inner product of two vectors is given by p·x or $p^T x$.

The Laspeyres (La) and Paasche (Pa) price indices are given as:

$$P_{La}\left(p^0, p^1, x^0, x^1\right) = p^1 \cdot x^0 / p^0 \cdot x^0$$

$$P_{Pa}\left(p^0, p^1, x^0, x^1\right) = p^1 \cdot x^1 / p^0 \cdot x^1$$

The so-called ideal (Id) index is the geometric mean of the Paasche and Laspeyres indices:

$$P_{Id}\left(p^0, p^1, x^0, x^1\right) = [(p^1 \cdot x^1 p^0 \cdot x^1)/(p^1 \cdot x^0 p^0 \cdot x^0)]^{1/2} \qquad (3.2)$$

The Laspeyres, Paasche, and ideal quantity indices are defined in a similar manner except that quantities and prices are interchanged in the preceding formulae. In particular, the ideal quantity index is defined as:

$$Q_{Id}\left(p^0, p^1, x^0, x^1\right) = [(p^1 \cdot x^1 p^0 \cdot x^1)/(p^1 \cdot x^0 p^0 \cdot x^0)]^{1/2} \qquad (3.3)$$

It should be noted that $P_{Id}Q_{Id} = p^1 \cdot x^1 / p^0 \cdot x^0$. In other words, the ideal price and quantity indexes satisfy the "adding up" property (3.1). It follows that the ideal quantity index may be used to compute the quantity aggregates $f(x^r)$. It can then be shown that

$$f(x^r)/f(x^0) = Q_{Id}(p^0, p^r, x^0, x^r), r = 1, 2, \ldots, R \qquad (3.4)$$

Thus given the base period normalization $f(x^0) = 1$, the ideal quantity index may be used to calculate the aggregate $f(x^r) = (x^{rT} A x^r)^{1/2}$ for $r = 1, 2, \ldots, R$. It is of note that it is not necessary to estimate the unknown coefficients in the A matrix. This is the major advantage of this method for determining the aggregates $f(x^r)$, and it is particularly important when N (the number of goods to be aggregated) is large compared to R (the number of observations in addition to the base period observation p^0, x^0).

If a quantity index $Q(p^0, p^r, x^0, x^r)$ and a functional form for the aggregator function f satisfy equation (3.4) then we say that Q is "exact" for f. It appears that out of all the exact index numbers, only the ideal index corresponds to a functional form for f that is capable of providing a second-order approximation to an arbitrary twice-differentiable linear homogeneous function. Diewert calls such a quantity index Q "superlative" if it is exact for a function f that can provide a second-order approximation to a linear homogeneous function.

3.2.2 The Törnqvist-Theil "Divisia" Index and the Translog Function

Diewert begins with a homogeneous translog aggregator function from Christensen, Jorgenson, and Lau (1971) defined by:

$$\ln f(x) = \alpha_0 + \sum_{n=1}^{N} \alpha_n \ln x_n + 1/2 \sum_{j=1}^{N} \sum_{k=1}^{N} \gamma_{jk} \ln x_j \ln x_k$$

where $\sum \alpha_n = 1$, $\gamma_{jk} = \gamma_{kj}$, and $\sum \gamma_{jk} = 0$ for $j = 1, 2, \ldots, N$.

Christensen, Jorgenson, and Lau show that the homogeneous translog function can provide a second-order approximation to an arbitrary twice–continuously differentiable linear homogeneous function. Using the parameters that occur in the translog functional form, define the following function:

$$f^*(z) = \alpha_0 + \sum_{j=1}^{N} \alpha_i z_i + 1/2 \sum_{i=1}^{N} \sum_{j=1}^{N} \gamma_{jk} z_i z_j \qquad (3.5)$$

Since the function f^* is quadratic, it is possible to use the quadratic approximation to obtain:

$$f^*(z^1) - f^*(z^0) = \tfrac{1}{2}[\bar{V}f^*(z^1) + \bar{V}f^*(z^0)] \cdot (z^1 - z^0) \tag{3.6}$$

The f^* function can now be related to the to the translog function f as follows:

$$\partial f^*(z^r)/\partial z_j = \partial \ln f(x^r)/\partial \ln x_j = \left[\partial f(x^r)/\partial x_j\right]\left[x^r_j/f(x^r)\right] \tag{3.7}$$

$$f^*(z^r) = \ln f(x^r)$$

$$z^r_j = \ln x^r_j, r = 0,1 \text{ and } j = 1,2,\ldots,N$$

If (3.7) is substituted into (3.6), then:

$$\ln f(x^1) - \ln f(x^0) = \tfrac{1}{2}[\hat{x}^1 \bar{V}f(x^1)/f(x^1) + \hat{x}^0 \bar{V}f(x^0)/f(x^0)] \cdot [\ln x^1 - \ln x^0] \tag{3.8}$$

where $\ln x^1 \equiv [\ln x^1_1, \ln x^1_2, \ldots, \ln x^1_N]$, $\ln x^0 \equiv [\ln x^0_1, \ln x^0_2, \ldots, \ln x^0_N]$, and $\hat{x}^1$ is the vector x^1 diagonalized into a matrix, and likewise for $\hat{x}^0$.

Let it be assumed that $x^r \gg 0_N$ is a solution to the aggregator maximization problem $\text{Max}_x f(x)$: $p^r \cdot x = p^r \cdot x^r$, $x \geq 0_N\}$, where $p^r \gg 0_N$ for $r = 0, 1$ and f is the homogeneous translog function. The first-order conditions for the two maximization problems (after elimination of the Lagrange multipliers) yield the relations $p^r / p^r \cdot x^r = \bar{V} f(x^r)/x^r \cdot \bar{V} f(x^r)$ for $r = 0, 1$. Since f is linear homogeneous, $x^r \cdot \bar{V} f(x^r)$ can be replaced by $f(x^r)$ in the preceding, and substitution of these last two relations into (3.8) yields:

$$\ln\left[f(x^1)/f(x^0)\right] = \tfrac{1}{2}[(\hat{x}^1 p^1/p^{1T} x^1) + (\hat{x}^0 p^0/p^{0T} x^0)]\left[\ln x^1 - \ln x^0\right]$$

$$= \sum_{n=1}^{N} \tfrac{1}{2}\left[s^1_n + s^0_n\right] \ln\left[x^1_n / x^0_n\right]$$

or, alternatively,

$$f(x^1)/f(x^0) = \prod_{n=1}^{N}\left[x^1_n / x^0_n\right]^{\tfrac{1}{2}\left[s^1_n + s^0_n\right]} \equiv Q_0\left(p^0, p^1, x^0, x^1\right) \tag{3.9}$$

where $s^r_n \equiv p^r_n x^r_n / p^r \cdot x^r$, the nth share of cost in period r. This quantity index is exact for a homogeneous translog aggregator function, and in view of the second-order approximation property of the homogeneous translog function, the right-hand side of equation (3.9) is a superlative quantity index. It is also the case that the homogeneous translog function is the only differentiable linear homogeneous function that is exact for the Törnqvist-Theil quantity index.

The preceding argument can be repeated (with some changes in notation) if the unit cost function for the aggregator function is the translog unit cost function defined by:

$$\ln c(p) = \alpha^*_0 + \sum_{n=1}^{N} \alpha^*_n \ln p_n + \frac{1}{2} \sum_{j=1}^{N} \sum_{k=1}^{N} \gamma^*_{jk} \ln p_j \ln p_k$$

where $\sum \alpha^*_n = 1$, $\gamma^*_{jk} = \gamma^*_{kj}$, and $\sum \gamma^*_{jk} = 0$ for $j = 1, 2, \ldots, N$.

Now under the assumption of cost-minimizing behavior in periods 0 and 1, one can derive:

$$\ln c(p^1) - \ln c(p^0) = \sum_{n=1}^{N} \frac{1}{2} \left[s^1_n + s^0_n \right] \ln \left[p^1_n / p^0_n \right]$$

or, alternatively,

$$c(p^1)/c(p^0) = \prod_{n=1}^{N} \left[p^1_n / p^0_n \right]^{\frac{1}{2}\left[s^1_n + s^0_n \right]} \tag{3.10}$$

where $s^r_n \equiv p^r_n x^r_n / p^r \cdot x^r$, the nth share of cost in period r; $p^r \gg 0_N$ for $r = 0$, 1; $x^r \geq 0_N$ for $r = 0$, 1; and $c(p)$ is the translog unit cost function. This price index is exact for a translog unit cost function, and this is the only differentiable unit cost function that is exact for this price index.

Next, denote the right-hand side of (3.10) as the price index function P_0 (p^0, p^1, x^0, x^1) and denote the right-hand side of (3.9) as the quantity index Q_0 (p^0, p^1, x^0, x^1). It can then be shown that $P_0 (p^0, p^1, x^0, x^1) Q_0 (p^0, p^1, x^0, x^1)$ does not, in general, equal $p^1 \cdot x^1 / p^0 \cdot x^0$. In other words, the price index P_0 and the quantity index Q_0 do not satisfy the weak factor reversal test (3.1). This is perfectly reasonable, since the quantity index Q_0 is consistent with a homogeneous translog (direct) aggregator function, while the price index P_0 is consistent with an aggregator function that is dual to the translog unit cost function, and the two aggregator functions do not in general coincide – that is, they correspond to different (aggregation) technologies. Thus, given Q_0, the corresponding price index, which satisfies (3.1), is defined by $\tilde{P}_0(p^0, p^1, x^0, x^1) \equiv p^1 \cdot x^1 / p^0 \cdot x^0 \, [Q_0 \, (p^0, p^1, x^0, x^1)]$.

The quantity index Q_0 and the corresponding (implicit) price index P_0 were used by Christensen and Jorgenson (1969, 1970) in order to measure U.S. real input and output. On the other hand, given P_0, the corresponding (implicit) quantity index, which satisfies (3.1), is defined by $\tilde{Q}_0(p^0, p^1, x^0, x^1)$ $\equiv p^1 \cdot x^1 / p^0 \cdot x^0 [P_0 (p^0, p^1, x^0, x^1)]$. The price-quantity index pair $(\tilde{P}_0, \tilde{Q}_0)$ might be preferred to (P_0, Q_0), because as we disaggregate more and more, we can expect the individual consumer or producer to utilize positive amounts of fewer and fewer goods (that is, as N grows, components of the vectors x^0 and x^1 will tend to become zero), but the prices that the producer or consumer faces are generally positive irrespective of the degree of disaggregation. Since the logarithm of zero is not finite, Q_0 tends to be indeterminate as the degree of disaggregation increases, but P_0 will still be well defined (provided that all prices are positive).

Theil (1968) provided a somewhat different interpretation of the indices P_0 and Q_0, one that does not require the aggregator function to be linear homogeneous. Let the aggregate u be defined by u = f(x), where f is a not necessarily a homogeneous aggregator function that satisfies certain regularity conditions for a production function. For $p >> 0_N$ define the total cost function by $C(u;p) = \min_x \{p \cdot x: f(x) \geq u; x >> 0_N\}$ and the indirect utility function by $g(p/ Y) = \max_x \{f(x): p \cdot x \leq Y, x \leq 0_N\}$. The true cost of living price index evaluated at "utility" level u is defined as $P(p^0, p^1; U) \equiv C(u; p^1) / C(u; p^0)$ and the Theil index of quantity (or 'real income') evaluated at prices p is defined as $Q_T (p; u^0, u^1) = C(u^1 ; p)/C(u^0; p)$. The Theil results are that (i) P_0 $(p^0, p^1; x^0, x^1)$ is a second-order approximation to $P(p^0, p^1; g(v^*))$, where the nth component of v^* is $v_n^* \equiv (p^0_n p^1_n / p^0 \cdot x^0 p^1 \cdot x^1)^{\frac{1}{2}}$, for n = 1,2, ..., N, and (ii) $Q_0(p^0, p^1, x^0, x^1)$ is a second-order approximation to $\tilde{Q}_T(p^*; g(p^0/ p^0 \cdot x^0), g(p^1 / p^1 \cdot x^1))$, where the nth component of p^* is $p^*_n \equiv (p^0_n p^1_n)^{\frac{1}{2}}$.

It can be shown that the index number P_0 is exact for any general (non-homothetic) functional forms for the cost function $C(u; p)$. In contrast to the case of a linear homogeneous aggregator function where the cost function takes the simple form $C(u; p) = c(p)u$, the index number P_0 $(p^0, p^1; x^0, x^1)$ is exact for functional forms for $C(u; p)$ other than the translog. In fact, the same price index P_0 is exact for more than one functional form (and reference utility level) for the true cost of living.

It is also possible to provide a justification for the quantity index Q_0 in the context of an aggregator function f that is not necessarily linearly homogeneous. In order to provide this justification, it is necessary to define the quantity index that was proposed by Malmquist (1953). On the basis of an aggregator function f and an aggregate u = f(*x*), define f's distance function as $D[u; x] \equiv \max_k \{k; f(x/k) \geq u\}$. In the language of utility theory, the distance function indicates the proportion it is necessary to deflate (or inflate) the given consumption vector x in order to obtain a point on the utility surface indexed by u. It can be shown that if f satisfies certain regularity conditions, then f is completely characterized by D. In particular, $D[u; x]$ is linear homogeneous nondecreasing and concave in the vector of variables x and nonincreasing in u.

Define the Malmquist quantity index as $Q_M(x^0, x^1; u) \equiv D[u; x^1] / D[u; x^0]$. Note that the index depends on x^0 (the base period quantities), x^1 (the current period quantities), and the base indifference surface (which is indexed by u) onto which the points x^0 and x^1 are deflated. As was the case with the price index P_0, the quantity index Q_0 is equal to Malquist quantity indexes that are defined by nontranslog distance functions. However, there is a rather strong justification for the use of P_0 or Q_0, since the translog functional form provides a second-order approximation to a general cost or distance function (which in turn are dual to a general nonhomothetic aggregator function).

3.3 Econometric Estimation of Productivity Growth

I next look at issues associated with the estimation of productivity growth. There are four common approaches to productivity measurement described previously. Here I discuss the strengths and weaknesses of each approach. It should be noted that in general each methodology estimates a different magnitude. However, there are certain conditions necessary for each approach to estimate the same magnitude. It should be pointed out that although the quantitative magnitudes obtained from each approach to measuring productivity are, in general, different, often the qualitative conclusions about the patterns of productivity growth over time are similar across the methodologies. This part of the chapter will also describe the circumstances when the patterns of measured productivity are likely to be invariant to the approach employed.

Van Biesebroeck (2007) performs a simulation study to examine the sensitivity of productivity estimates and growth rates to the four approaches to measuring described earlier. He finds that many qualitative features of the time path of TFP are invariant to the measurement methods employed. Van Biesebroeck (2006) assesses the extent to which conclusions about three important productivity debates in the economic development literature are sensitive to the productivity estimation method employed.

As Van Biesebroeck (2007) notes, researchers interested in estimating productivity can choose from different methodologies, each with its strengths and weaknesses. He compares the robustness of five widely used techniques, two nonparametric and three parametric: (a) index numbers, (b) data envelopment analysis (DEA), (c) stochastic frontiers, (d) instrumental variables (GMM), and (e) semiparametric estimation. Using simulated samples of firms, he analyzes the sensitivity of alternative methods to the randomness properties in the data generating process. Three experiments are used: introducing randomness via (a) factor price heterogeneity, (b) measurement error, and (c) heterogeneity in the production technology. He finds that when measurement error is small, the index number method is excellent for estimating productivity growth and ranks among the best for estimating productivity levels. The DEA method is particularly applicable with heterogeneous technology and nonconstant returns to scale. On the other hand, when measurement errors are nonnegligible, parametric methods are preferable. In rank order, the preferred techniques are stochastic frontiers, GMM, and then semiparametric estimation methods.

There is typically a large amount of heterogeneity even among firms in a single industry. Despite this high degree of heterogeneity, most studies that estimate productivity or production functions rely on relatively simple models that ignore most of the relevant heterogeneity. For instance, nonparametric models tend to be deterministic, and parametric methods tend to assume a homogeneous production technology with the same degree of input substitutability for all firms.

Van Biesebroeck (2007) employs a Monte Carlo method to investigate the sensitivity of these five estimation methods for productivity to different sources of heterogeneity among firms. The first two methods, index numbers and DEA, are very flexible in the specification of technology but do not allow for unobservables. The three parametric methods differ in the way they deal with the problem of simultaneity of inputs and unobserved productivity and these are evaluated as well. Stochastic frontiers make explicit distributional assumptions on the unobserved productivity; the GMM system estimator (GMM-SYS) relies on instrumental variables; and the semiparametric estimator inverts the investment function nonparametrically to obtain an observable expression for productivity.

In the actual empirical analysis, Van Biesebroeck simulates samples of hypothetical firms by introducing heterogeneity in the three different ways noted previously. The first is factor price heterogeneity, which in the model can also be interpreted as high frequency productivity. The second is measurement error. The third is differences in production technology. Estimated productivity levels and growth rates are then compared with the true values of these two variables.

As Van Biesebroeck argues, the objective of productivity measurement is fundamentally to identify output differences that cannot be explained by input differences. To perform this task, one needs to observe inputs and outputs accurately and control for the input substitution allowed by the production technology. Methodologies differ by the choice of statistical techniques and economic assumptions they use to control for input substitution and for unobservable differences. The three different experiments considered in the chapter map into different situations that researchers often encounter. For example, depending on the source of the data and the type of observations the sample covers, a researcher will have different priors on the importance of measurement error or heterogeneity in technology. The relative performance of the different methods should be informative in choosing the most appropriate estimator for the situation.

When measurement error is small, the index number method produces consistently accurate productivity growth estimates. In the case when firms are likely to employ different technologies, productivity level estimates are among the most robust as well. DEA is the preferred estimator for productivity levels if technology is likely to vary across firms and scale economies are not constant. Examples would include situations where one has to pool firms from very different industries, at different stages in their life cycle or operating in countries with different levels of development.

Because of the well-known simultaneity problem between inputs and unobserved productivity, estimating a production function by least squares (OLS) is generally not advisable. Its disadvantages are less acute for productivity growth than for productivity levels. When there is good reason to believe that productivity differences are constant over time, that output is measured accurately, and that firms share the same technology, stochastic frontier estimation produces accurate productivity level estimates. When there is considerable measurement error or some heterogeneity in technology, the GMM-SYS estimator provides the most robust estimates of productivity level and growth among the parametric methods. When firms are subject to idiosyncratic productivity shocks that are not entirely transitory, the semiparametric proxy estimator will provide reliable estimates.

3.3.1 The Specification of the Production Function

In the absence of price setting power at the firm level, information on deflated sales or value added and input levels is very often used in conjunction with a production function to calculate a firm's productivity. However, it should be noted that when firms have market power, but information on prices is not available, as is the usual situation, a model of product demand is required to isolate quantity changes from price changes.

One firm is considered more productive than another if it can produce the same output with fewer inputs or if it produces more output from the same inputs. Similarly, a firm is said to have experienced positive productivity growth if outputs increase more than inputs or inputs decrease more than outputs. To compare two production plans in which one uses more of a first input and the other more of a second input, it is necessary to specify a transformation function that links inputs to output. Input substitution possibilities are determined by the technology and each productivity measure is defined only with respect to that specific production technology.

Van Biesebroeck begins with a simple production function of the form:

$$Q_{it} = A_{it} F_{(it)} (X_{it})$$ (3.11)

where A_{it} is the unobservable productivity term, which, in general, differs across firms and across time. The deterministic part of the model – the technology – is represented by the production function $F(\cdot)$, which takes a vector of inputs X_{it} as arguments. The analysis here is limited in a number of ways. First, only the single output case is considered, because most studies use value added or sales as the output measure. Second, all productivity differences are Hicks-neutral, as the most widely used Cobb-Douglas production function cannot identify factor bias in technological change (see Chapter 2). Third, the productivity measure used is output-based – that is, it measures how much extra output a firm produces relative to another firm, conditional on its (extra) input use

It is next possible to rearrange the production function as follows:

$$\ln (A_{it} / A_{j\tau})_k = \ln (Q_{it} / Q_{j\tau}) - \ln [F_k (X_{it}) / F_k (X_{j\tau})]$$ (3.12)

This formulation underscores the point that productivity is intrinsically a relative concept. If the technology is allowed to vary across observations one has to be explicit as to which technology underlies the comparison. As a result, a k subscript is introduced. The calculation of the last term in (3.12) – the ratio of input aggregators – distinguishes the different methods used by researchers. It is here that different studies make different assumptions. Van Biesebroeck distinguishes three approaches:

First, index numbers assume that firms make input choices optimally, with some restrictions on the nature of the technology differences. An exact Taylor expansion of the production function can be calculated using the information on the slope of the F(.) function contained in the factor price ratios.

If the first-order conditions for input choices hold, the factor price ratio will equal the slope of the input isoquant at the optimum, which determines local input substitution possibilities. Suppose production occurs at two production points of a firm, P_0 and P_1, at time 0 and time 1. With information contained in the relative factor price ratio for either production plan, one can control for input differences without having to estimate the shape of the (local) isoquant. Instead, it is possible to use the average labor share in costs for both production plans to control for the input substitution possibilities. As will be seen later, this productivity measure corresponds to the geometric mean of the measures using either production technology.

Second, nonparametric frontiers, such as DEA, construct for each observation a linear combination of all other observations (normalized by output) for explicit comparison. Weights are chosen to maximize productivity for the unit considered. The same "technology" is used in the numerator and denominator of the input aggregator ratio in (3.12), but for each unit, a separate comparison is performed – that is, technology is still firm-specific.

The second approach is entirely nonparametric. It constructs a piecewise linear isoquant to maximize the productivity estimate for P_0, without allowing any other observation to lie below the isoquant. The relevant section of the isoquant implicitly defines relative weights for labor and capital. Weights are chosen to minimize the distance from P_0 to the isoquant. For each observation, different weights are calculated using linear programming techniques. The productivity of P_0 relative to the frontier indicates how much its inputs can be reduced for the plan to equal a linear combination of the two comparison plans.

Third, parametric methods explicitly assume a functional form for the technology, the F(.) function, to be estimated econometrically. Random errors can be introduced straightforwardly in the model, multiplying the right-hand side of (3.11). If we compare two production points of a firm, P_0 and P_1, at time 0 and time 1, then the parametric method allows one to decompose the movement between the two points into a shift along the technology frontier in period 0, exploiting the input substitution that the technology allows, and a shift in the technology frontier between the two periods.

The parametric approach to measure the shift relies on the functional form assumptions made about the technology to be used (that is, on the input trade-off) to estimate the exact shape of the unit isoquant. Most studies use a simple functional form and virtually all applications restrict parameters to be equal across firms. One reason for the restrictiveness in the deterministic portion of the model is that unobserved productivity differences make input choices endogenous. Estimating flexible functional forms is likely to exacerbate this simultaneity problem. It also explains the popularity of nonparametric approaches that are able to calculate productivity without estimating the exact input trade-off.

3.3.2 The Estimation Procedures

3.3.2.1 Index Numbers (IN)

Index numbers, as discussed previously, provide a theoretically motivated aggregation method for inputs and outputs, without needing to specify the exact shape of the production technology. For example, Solow (1957) used the following formula for total factor productivity (TFP) growth in his original growth accounting exercise:

$$\ln\left(A^{IN}_{it} / A^{IN}_{it-1}\right) = \ln\left(Q_{it} / Q_{it-1}\right) - \left[\left(s^{L}_{it} + s^{L}_{it-1}\right)/2\right] \ln\left(L_{it} / L_{it-1}\right) \\ - \left[1 - \left(s^{L}_{it} + s^{L}_{it-1}\right)/2\right] \ln\left(K_{it} / K_{it-1}\right) \tag{3.13}$$

where the left-hand side is the estimated rate of TFP growth, the superscript IN stands for the index number approach, and s^{L} is labor's share of national output. All variables on the right-hand side of (3.13) are observable: output, inputs, and the fraction of the wage bill in output (s^{L}).

While Solow rationalized the TFP formula as a discrete approximation to the continuous Divisia index, Caves, Christensen, and Diewert (1982a) show that the so-called Törnqvist index has a much more general application. It exactly equals the geometric mean of the two Malmquist productivity indices – using either production plan's technology – if the technology is characterized by a translog (output) distance function. Some heterogeneity in production technology across observations is allowed; only the coefficients on the second-order terms have to be equal for the two units compared. The relative weights on the input factor ratios (labor versus capital shares in output) make use of the information on the slope of the input trade-off contained in the factor prices.

For multilateral productivity level comparisons, Caves, Christensen, and Diewert (1982b) propose an index in which each firm is compared to a hypothetical firm, with average log output, average log labor input, average log capital input, and average labor share. The productivity level of firm i at time t is

$$\ln A^{IN}_{it} - \overline{\ln A^{IN}}_t = \left(\ln Q_{it} - \overline{\ln Q_t} \right) - \left[\left(s^L_{it} + s^L_t \right) / 2 \right] \left(\ln L_{it} - \overline{\ln L_t} \right)$$
$$- \left[1 - \left(s^L_{it} + s^L_t \right) / 2 \right] \left(\ln K_{it} - \overline{\ln K_t} \right) \tag{3.14}$$

This yields bilateral comparisons that are transitive and still allows for technology that is firm-specific.

For the index number technique theory to be applicable, several assumptions need to be satisfied. The most important ones are perfect competition in output and input markets, optimizing behavior by firms, and the absence of measurement error. While it is not strictly necessary to assume constant returns to scale, outside information on scale economies would be needed to control for them in the productivity estimates. To absorb the scale effect, an additional factor has to be added to (subtracted from) equation (3.14) for each input if returns to scale are decreasing (increasing). Estimating scale economies parametrically or obtaining information on the cost of capital would be sufficient, but here the common practice of assuming the constant returns to scale case will be used.

The main advantages of the index number approach are the straightforward computations (with no econometric estimation needed), the ability to handle multiple outputs and multiple inputs, and the flexible and heterogeneous production technology such an approach permits. Technical change can be factor-biased, and the only separability assumption needed is that between outputs and inputs. The main disadvantage of the index number approach are the assumptions it is necessary to make on firm behavior and market structure. It is also not possible to deal with measurement errors or outliers, except for some ad hoc data trimming.

3.3.2.2 Data Envelope Analysis (DEA)

Data envelopment analysis (DEA) is a nonparametric frontier estimation procedure. No particular production function is assumed. Instead, efficiency is defined as the ratio of a linear combination of outputs over a linear combination of inputs. Weights on inputs (u_l, u_k) and output (v_q) are chosen directly to maximize efficiency (productivity) for the unit under consideration, indicated by Θ. Observations that are not dominated are referred to as "100 percent efficient." Domination occurs when another firm, or a linear combination of other firms, produces more of all outputs with the same input aggregate, using the same weights to aggregate inputs.

A linear programming problem is solved separately for each observation. For unit (firm-year) 1, in the single-output case, the problem amounts to:

$$\max_{v_q, u_1, u_k} \Theta_1 \left[v_q Q_1 + v^* \right] / \left[u_1 L_1 + u_k K_1 \right] \tag{3.15}$$

$$\text{subject to } \left[v_q Q_1 + v^* \right] / \left[u_1 L_1 + u_k K_1 \right] \leq 1 \qquad i = 1 \dots N$$

$$v_q, u_1 + u_k > 0, \ u_1, u_k \geq 0$$

$$v^* \geq 0 \left(v^* = 0 \text{ for constant returns to scale} \right)$$

In addition to sign restrictions on the weights, the only constraints are that the efficiency of all firms i cannot exceed 100 percent when the same weights are applied to them. For the problem to be well defined, a normalization is needed; doubling all input and output weights in (3.15) would leave productivity estimates unchanged. The usual choice is to make $u_1 L_1 + u_k K_1$ equal to unity. The variable v^* is included as a complementary slack variable to allow for the case of variable returns to scale. Under constant returns to scale ($v^* = 0$), the production frontier is a ray through the origin in output-aggregate input space; under variable returns to scale, it is a piecewise linear envelope of all production plans.

The efficiency measure Θ_i can be interpreted as the productivity difference between unit i and the most productive unit: $\Theta_i = A_i / A_{max}$. Estimates of productivity levels and growth rates comparable to the ones obtained with other methodologies can be defined as:

$$\ln A^{DEA}{}_{it} - \overline{\ln A}{}^{DEA}{}_t = \ln \Theta_{it} - \left(1/N_t \right) \sum_{j=1}^{N_t} \ln \Theta_{jt} \tag{3.16a}$$

$$\ln A^{DEA}{}_{it} - \ln A^{DEA}{}_{it-1} = \ln_{it} \Theta - \ln \Theta_{it-1} \tag{3.16b}$$

The Θ coefficients are estimated on the full sample that includes all firm-years as separate observations. The transformations do not change the ranking of firms, only the absolute productivity levels and growth rates.

The main advantage of DEA is that a specification of functional form or behavioral assumptions are not required. The underlying technology is left entirely unspecified and allowed to vary across firms. The linear aggregation is natural in an activities analysis framework. Each firm is considered a separate process that can be combined with others to replicate the production plan of the unit under investigation. On the other hand, the flexibility in weighting has drawbacks: Each firm with the highest ratio for any output-input combination is considered 100 percent efficient. Under variable returns to scale, each firm with the lowest input or highest output level in absolute terms is also fully efficient. The most widely used implementations do not include a stochastic element, thus making estimates sensitive to outliers. Because each observation is compared to all others, measurement error for a single firm can affect all productivity estimates.

3.3.2.3 Parametric Estimation Using Ordinary Least Squares (OLS)

The parametric methods make much stronger assumptions on the production structure of firms. First, they assume the same input trade-off (substitutability) and returns to scale for all firms. The functional form assumption on the production function concentrates all heterogeneity in the productivity term, but the explicitly stochastic framework is likely to make estimates less susceptible to measurement error. The most common production function in the literature is the Cobb-Douglas production function (see Chapter 2). These are presented in logarithm form as follows:

$$q_{it} = \alpha_0 + \alpha_l l_{it} + \alpha_k k_{it} + \omega_{it} + \varepsilon_{it} \qquad (3.17)$$

where lowercase letters represent logarithms; ω_{it} represents a productivity difference known to the firm, but unobservable to the econometrician; and ε_{it} captures other sources of i.i.d. (independently and identically distributed) error.

Consistent estimation of the input parameters faces a particular endogeneity problem. Firms choose inputs knowing their own level of productivity, and an OLS regression of output on the various inputs in the production function will produce inconsistent estimates of the production function coefficients. However, it is helpful to use OLS estimates as a benchmark and then to implement three estimators that explicitly address the endogeneity problem.

The stochastic frontier method in Section 3.3.2.4 makes explicit distributional assumptions on the unobserved productivity term; the GMM-SYS estimator discussed in Section 3.3.2.5 relies on instrumental variables; and the semiparametric estimator discussed in Section 3.3.2.6 inverts the investment function nonparametrically to obtain an expression for productivity.

Because the input aggregator is the same for all periods and firms, the calculation of productivity levels and productivity growth rates is straightforward:

$$\ln A^{OLS}_{it} - \overline{\ln A}^{OLS}_t = (q_{it} - \overline{q}_t) - \hat{\alpha}_l^{OLS} (l_{it} - \overline{l}_t) - \hat{\alpha}_k^{OLS} (k_{it} - \overline{k}_t) \qquad (3.18a)$$

$$\ln A^{OLS}_{it} - A^{OLS}_{it-1} = \left(q_{it} - q_{it-1}\right) - \hat{\alpha}_1^{OLS}\left(l_{it} - l_{it-1}\right) - \hat{\alpha}_k^{OLS}\left(k_{it} - k_{it-1}\right) \quad (3.18b)$$

To obtain a "clean" estimate of ω_{it} it is necessary to subtract an estimate for the difference in error terms from the right-hand sides in (3.18a) and in (3.18b). However, generally this is not possible and is ignored.

3.3.2.4 Parametric Estimation Using Stochastic Frontiers (SF)

The stochastic frontier literature uses assumptions on the distribution of the unobserved productivity component to separate it from the random error term. Estimation is usually with a maximum likelihood estimator. In the production function (3.17), the term ω_{it} is weakly negative and is interpreted as the inefficiency of firm i at time t relative to the best-practice production frontier. An alternative interpretation is that in the firm-specific production function ω_{it} lies below the most productive observation in the sample.

Initially developed to measure productivity in a cross section of firms, the model is generalizable for panel data in a number of ways. One way is to model the inefficiency term as:

$$\omega_{it} = -e^{\eta(t-T)}\omega_i \text{ with } \omega_i \text{ drawn from } N+(\gamma, \sigma^2) \quad (3.19)$$

where N+ is the half-normal distribution of positive values only. The relative productivity of each firm (ω_i) is a time-invariant draw from the truncated normal distribution indicated earlier. Inefficiency increases (decreases) deterministically over time if Z is positive (negative) at the same rate for all firms. If firms are observed only once, it is necessary to make strong assumptions in order to separate the productivity component from the random error. However, panel data contain more information on each firm and allow identification under weaker assumptions. Equations (3.18a) and (3.18b) can then be used to calculate the expected value of log-productivity.

An advantage of the stochastic frontiers method is that the deterministic part of the production function can be generalized easily to allow for more complicated specifications, such as incorporating factor bias in technological change or flexible functional forms. This particular model trades off flexibility in the characterization of productivity with estimation precision. The assumption that the relative position of firms never changes, in equation (3.19), only requires the estimation of three coefficients, but it will be less appropriate for panel data with longer samples. However, one drawback is that identification results solely from distributional assumptions, which are especially restrictive in this model.

3.3.2.5 Parametric Estimation: Instrumental Variables (GMM)

In this approach, the productivity term is modeled as a firm fixed effect (ω_{it}) with an additive autoregressive component ($\omega_{it} = \omega_{it-1} + \eta_{it}$). An additional term ε_{it} captures measurement error and transitory productivity shocks. Quasi-differencing the production function gives the estimating equation in its dynamic representation:

$$q_{it} = \rho q_{it} + \alpha_1(l_{it} - \rho l_{it-1}) + \alpha_k(k_{it} - \rho k_{it-1}) + \omega'_i + (\eta_{it} + \varepsilon_{it} - \rho \varepsilon_{it-1}) \quad (3.20)$$

There is still a need for moment conditions to provide instruments, because the inputs will be correlated with the composite error ε_{it} through η_{it}, the annual productivity innovation, and the transitory productivity shocks ε_{it} and ε_{it-1}. Estimating equation (3.20) in first-differenced form takes care of the firm fixed effects. Three and more periods' lagged inputs and output will be uncorrelated with $\Delta\varepsilon_{it}$ under standard exogeneity assumptions on the initial conditions. Three lags are necessary as the first-differenced equation will contain errors as far back as ε_{it-2}. This error directly affects twice-lagged output and firms will have based their input choices two periods ago on this shock. Additional lags can be used to increase precision.

Blundell and Bond (1998) illustrate theoretically and with a practical application that these instruments can be weak. If one is willing to make the additional assumption that input changes are uncorrelated with the firm fixed effects and that the same holds for the initial output change, twice-lagged first differences of the variables are valid instruments for the production function in levels. As before, the presence of the lagged error ε_{it-1} in equation (3.20) requires an additional lag on the instruments. However, in this case, including more distant lags does not provide additional information. The production function is estimated as a system combining the first-differenced and level equations, each with the appropriate set of instruments. Productivity is here too calculated using equations (3.18a) and (3.18b).

The GMM system estimator is flexible in generating instruments, and one can test the overidentification restrictions if many instruments are used for the first-differenced equation. This estimator allows for an autoregressive component to productivity, in addition to a fixed component and an idiosyncratic component. Relative to the simple fixed effects estimator, it also uses the information contained in the levels, which may help with measurement error. The major disadvantage is that at least four periods are required in the panel if transitory productivity shocks are included. If instruments are weak, the method risks underestimating the input elasticities, just like the fixed effects estimator.

3.3.2.6 Semiparametric Estimation (OP)

The last method considered in the Van Biesebroeck (2007) work was introduced by Olley and Pakes (1996) to estimate the productivity effects of restructuring in the U.S. telecommunications equipment industry. They make two important assumptions. First, productivity – a state variable in the firm's dynamic problem – is assumed to follow a Markov process unaffected by the firm's control variables. Second, investment, which acts as one of the control variables of the firm, becomes part of the capital stock with a one-period lag.

In a first step, coefficients on the variable inputs in the production function and the joint effect of all state variables on output are estimated. Under relatively mild conditions, investment is shown to be a monotonically increasing function of productivity. Inverting the investment equation nonparametrically provides an observable expression for productivity. This expression is used to substitute the unobserved productivity term (ω_{it}) from the production function. This thereby allows identification of the variable input elasticities. If market structure or factor prices change over time, the inversion can even be performed separately by year.

In the second step, the coefficients of the observable state variables are identified, exploiting the orthogonality of the quasi-fixed capital stock and the current innovation in productivity. A nonparametric term is included in the production function to absorb the impact of productivity, to the extent it was known to the firm when it chose investment in the last period. The second term is included in equation (3.22) and uses the results of the first stage.

The estimating equations for the two steps are given by:

$$q_{it} = \alpha_0 + \alpha_1 l_{it} + \phi_t \left(l_{it}, k_{it} \right) + \varepsilon^1_{it} \tag{3.21}$$

$$q_{it} - \hat{\alpha}_1 l_{it} = \alpha_k k_{it} + \psi(\hat{\varphi}_{it-1} - \alpha_k k_{it-1}) + \varepsilon^2_{it} \tag{3.22}$$

The functions φ_t and ψ are approximated nonparametrically by a fourth-order polynomial or a kernel density. Productivity is calculated from (3.18a) and (3.18b).

A major advantage of this approach is the flexible characterization of productivity. The only assumption needed is that it evolves according to a Markov process. A potential weakness is the use of nonparametric approximations. The functions that are inverted are complicated mappings from states to actions, since they have to hold for all firms regardless of their size or competitive position. The prevalence of zero investment observations in many data sets also weakens the mapping.

3.3.3 Monte Carlo Estimation Results

Van Biesebroeck compared the different methods using simulated data, constructed from a representative firm model. The model used is the simplest possible that still allows for input substitution in the production function and optimal input choices over time. The firm chooses labor input and investment over time to maximize the net present value of profits, subject to a production function, an exogenously evolving productivity level, the initial capital stock, and a capital accumulation equation. The firm observes all variables at time t, including its own productivity level.

The sample simulation begins by drawing values for the initial values of capital and productivity for all firms, the industry wage rate, and firm-specific productivity shocks. Van Biesebroeck shows results for all experiments that are the averages over 50 simulated samples, each consisting of 200 firms that are observed over ten years. Using the simulated data, he estimates the production function parameters, productivity levels, and growth rates on the basis of each methodology. The productivity estimates for each of the six methods are compared with the true values of the data generating process. For the productivity level, he reports the Spearman rank correlation between estimates and true productivity, and for productivity growth he shows the simple correlation statistic. Correlations are calculated by year and then averaged over the ten-year sample period.

For each of the three experiments, a different source of heterogeneity is introduced. The first is heterogeneity of factor prices. It is assumed that productivity is the sum of two processes: a firm fixed effect and decaying productivity shocks following an AR(1) process, with $\rho = 0.3$. Selected results are shown in Panel A of Table 3.1. All six estimation methods produce high correlations between true and estimated productivity levels. Generally, the correlations are even higher between true and estimated productivity growth rates. The parametric methods in this case produce particularly accurate estimates of productivity levels and growth rates, with correlation of 0.97 and 0.99, respectively. The parametric estimators for productivity levels

Table 3.1. *Van Biesebroeck (2007) Simulation Results Based on Monte Carlo Experiments*

Estimation Technique	Correlation with True Productivity	
	Level	Growth
A. Wage Heterogeneity[a]		
IN	0.969	0.942
DEA	0.771	0.568
OLS	0.792	0.963
SF	0.969	0.975
GMM	0.975	0.996
OP	0.973	0.990
B. Measurement Error in Output		
IN	0.307	0.131
DEA	0.090	0.086
OLS	0.027	0.079
SF	0.024	0.077
GMM	0.212	0.077
OP	−0.011	0.078
C. Measurement Error in Inputs		
IN	0.390	0.159
DEA	0.446	0.170
OLS	0.417	0.177
SF	0.725	0.252
GMM	0.776	0.455
OP	0.734	0.252
D. Hetereogeneity in Production Technology[b]		
IN	0.918	0.995
DEA	0.822	0.632
OLS	0.236	0.734
SF	0.213	0.737
GMM	0.490	0.884
OP	0.352	0.764

Notes: See the text for a description of each of the estimators

[a] It is assumed that productivity is the sum of an AR(1) process and a fixed effect

[b] It is assumed that constant returns to scale are imposed on the production function

perform much better than OLS in this regard, though differences for productivity growth are much smaller. The index number estimators (IN) are almost as reliable as the parametric estimators. The DEA estimates for both productivity levels and growth are the least reliable of all six techniques.

The second is measurement error, and the third is heterogeneity in production parameters. These two problems are likely to be important when the analysis is performed on large census data sets in developed countries on narrowly defined industries. In developing countries, where data are likely to be more noisy, these problems may apply to agricultural applications or even to manufacturing firms where output and inputs are more straightforward to measure.

These results will be especially relevant if we expect wage (or relative price) heterogeneity to be important. One case is when labor markets are geographically or functionally segregated or when firms face radically different costs of capital, particularly when smaller firms have limited access to formal credit markets. If optimization errors are expected to be particularly important, these results will once again apply. Examples of this would be data sets with many new firms or with inexperienced owners, or firms facing rapid technological change or other changes in their environment. High frequency productivity shocks, occurring after one input is fixed but before investment for next period's capital takes place, constitute a third situation when these two types of problems may arise.

Van Biesebroeck adds measurement error to both inputs and outputs. He does by using mean-zero, independent, and standard normally distributed error draws, which are added to the logarithmic values of labor, capital, output, investment, and the wage bill. Panel B of Table 3.1 shows the results when only output is measured with measurement error. Here, it is clear that none of the six estimation methods produces estimates of productivity levels or productivity growth that are close to the true measures. The best method with regard to productivity levels and growth rates is the index method, IN, though even here the maximum correlation is only 0.31. The other methods produce much lower correlations. The results for the case when measurement error is in the inputs are better (Panel C). In this case, the best estimation methods are SF, GMM, and OP, which result in correlations of more than 0.7 in the case of productivity levels and more than 0.25 in the case of productivity growth rates.

The results in Panels B and C of Table 3.1 apply when measurement errors are important, begging the question of how is one to know this. In some cases variables will fail obvious consistency checks – for example, the wage bill might exceed value added for a substantial number of firms, output levels might display large spikes that are not matched by corresponding input increases and disappear after a single year, and so on. Another situation in which these results are relevant occurs when input measures are relatively crude. For example, they might lump together workers of varying quality, do not adjust for intensity of input use such as capacity utilization or the presence of temporary workers, or ignore cross-firm differences in the number of hours that are worked. Similarly, the output measure may combine different products and the composition may change over time or between firms. If such data imperfections are exogenous or at least uncorrelated with productivity, the effect will be similar to measurement error. When variables are constructed from firm surveys that use recall information in the absence of accounting data, as is often the case in developing countries, measurement errors are an important issue.

Panel D shows the case of heterogeneity in production technology when constant returns to scale is imposed on the production function. In this case, normally distributed errors were added to the input elasticity parameters in the production function. These errors are assumed to differ by firm, but to be constant over time. In this case, the parametric approaches are very unreliable, as is evident from the low correlations for productivity levels. In contrast, the IN and DEA estimators are quite reliable and deal very well with the technological heterogeneity.

Because of the marked differences between estimators in these experiments, it would be particularly useful to know when the results in Panel D are applicable. One situation would be if one's data set pools firms from different industries or from different countries and the sample size is not large enough to split the sample into subsamples. If observations are aggregate entities, such as industries, or are mostly larger firms in developed economies, the results under the constant returns to scale assumption are likely to be most appropriate. If the sample contains firms from developing economies, firms from a new industry, or many new entrants, the variable returns results are likely to be more relevant.

Even if all firms are in a single industry, there might be good reason to suspect that they do not all use the same production technology. For example, a plant producing steel has the choice to operate as an integrated mill using the basic oxygen furnace to melt iron ore or operate as a minimill using electric furnaces to process scrap metal. Automobile plants can use highly automated mass manufacturing methods to maximize scale economies or alternatively rely on lean, more flexible manufacturing techniques. Larger textile firms in developing countries that produce for the export market are often much more automated than domestically oriented, smaller companies. In each case, one might be hesitant to split the sample a priori, but when diverse firms are pooled, heterogeneity in technology is likely to be an important problem.

In summary, van Biesebroeck introduced three sources of variation in the data generating process for his simulated samples of firms: factor price heterogeneity (which alternatively can be interpreted as optimization error or productivity shocks occurring after inputs are chosen), measurement error, and differences in production technology. Each of the six econometric methods showed both strengths and weaknesses. Different simulations tend to favor different estimators.

The index numbers method (IN) produces consistently accurate productivity growth estimates, unless the data are subject to considerable measurement error. When the units of analysis such as firms or industries are likely to use different technologies, productivity level estimates are among the most robust as well. The data envelopment method (DEA) is the preferred estimator for productivity levels if technology is likely to vary across firms and scale economies are not constant, though it is never the ideal method for estimating productivity growth. DEA is particularly suitable when it is necessary to pool firms from very different industries, at different stages in their life cycle, or operating in countries with different levels of development.

Given the well-known problem of simultaneity among inputs and unobserved productivity, Ordinary least squares (OLS) is generally not advisable. A simple fixed effects estimator will perform better in most situations. Its disadvantage is less acute for productivity growth than for productivity levels. The stochastic frontiers (SF) method works well when there is good reason to believe that productivity differences are constant over time, that output is measured accurately, and that observations share the same technology. In these cases, this method produces accurate productivity level estimates.

The GMM method provides the most robust productivity level and growth estimates of the parametric methods when there is measurement error or heterogeneous production technology. In the absence of these forms of heterogeneity, it provides the most reliable results overall if at least part of the productivity difference is constant over time. When firms are subject to idiosyncratic productivity shocks that are not entirely transitory, the semiparametric estimator (OP) will make use of the firm's knowledge about these shocks. In addition, if output is measured with error, an alternative estimator, which purges random noise from the productivity estimates, provides accurate results, especially for productivity levels.[1]

3.4 Industry-Level and Country-Level Productivity Growth

This part of the chapter turns to the question of the theoretical conditions necessary to measure productivity growth at the industry or country level. Diewert and Nakamura (2007) provides a comprehensive discussion of this issue. This discussion helps provide the necessary theoretical foundation to understand the different conceptual meanings of TFP growth at the industry or country level. Although it is always possible to construct index numbers and compute the difference between the growth in the output aggregate index and that in the input aggregate index, as Diewert has shown in a number of papers, most notably in Diewert (1976), only under certain assumptions on the true input and output aggregator functions that constitute the true production transformation function does this resulting difference in growth rates equal the growth in TFP.

I will also try to clarify the frequently misunderstood point in empirical productivity analysis that measured productivity change often contains other factors besides actual productivity change. Particularly for index-number-based approaches, it is always possible to compute the index of productivity growth, but what this index actually measures is often very difficult to determine. Caves, Christensen, and Diewert (1982a), as discussed in Section 3.3.2.1 and Denny, Fuss, and Waverman (1981) discuss this issue in some detail.

3.4.1 The Relaxation of the Assumption of Constant Returns to Scale

As I noted previously, it is always possible to compute the index of productivity growth with index-number-based approaches, but what this index actually measures is often very difficult to determine. Denny, Fuss, and Waverman (1981) discuss this issue when the assumption of constant returns to scale is dropped. In particular, they relate the Divisia TFP measure to shifts in the cost function without assuming constant returns to scale.

While the general index number approach does not require cost minimizing behavior on the part of firms, the Denny, Fuss, and Waverman approach

---

[1] Also, see Van Biesebroeck (2006) for further discussion of these estimators in the context of data on manufacturing firms for two developing countries, Colombia and Zambia.

does require the assumption that the firm continuously minimizes costs over the period of interest: $0 \leq t \leq 1$. The firm's unit cost function can be written here as $c(y,w,t)$, where $y(t) \equiv [y_1(t), \ldots, y_M(t)]$ denotes the vector of outputs and $w(t) \equiv [w_1(t), \ldots, w_N(t)]$ denotes the vector of input prices. (The t variable in $c(y,w,t)$ is viewed as representing the fact that the cost function is continuously changing as a result of technical progress.) Under the assumption of cost minimizing behavior, we obtain:

$$C(t) \equiv \sum_n w_n(t) x_n(t) = c[y(t), w(t), t] \qquad (3.23)$$

The continuous time technical progress measure is defined as minus the (percentage) rate of increase in cost at time t:

$$TP(t) \equiv -\{\partial c[y(t), w(t), t]/\partial t\}/c[y(t), w(t), t] \qquad (3.24)$$

According to Shephard's lemma,

$$x_n(t) = \partial c[y(t), w(t), t]/\partial w_n, \quad n = 1, 2, \ldots, N. \qquad (3.25)$$

With algebraic manipulation, Denny, Fuss, and Waverman then obtain:

$$C'(t)/C(t) = \sum_m \varepsilon_m(t)[y'_m(t)/y_m(t)] + \sum_n S^c_n(t)[w'_n(t)/w_n(t)] - TP(t) \qquad (3.26)$$

where

$$\varepsilon_m(t) \equiv \{\partial c[y(t), w(t), t]/\partial y_m\}/\{c[y(t), w(t), t]/y_m(m(t))\}$$

is the elasticity of cost with respect to the mth output volume and

$$S^c_n(t) \equiv [w_n(t) x_n(t)]/C(t)$$

is the nth input cost share.

Denny, Fuss, and Waverman then define the rate of change of the continuous time output aggregate, $Q(t)$, as:

$$Q'(t)/Q(t) \equiv \sum_m \varepsilon_m(t) \left[y'_m(t)/y_m(t)\right]/\sum_i \varepsilon_i(t) \qquad (3.27)$$

The Divisia expression for the output growth rate weights the individual output growth rates, $y'_m(t)/y_m(t)$, by the revenue shares, $s^R_m(t)$. Alternatively, $y'_m(t)/y_m(t)$ is weighted by the mth cost elasticity share, $\varepsilon_m(t)/\sum_i \varepsilon_i(t)$. The authors show that $\sum_i \varepsilon_i(t)$ is the percentage increase in cost due to a 1 percent increase in scale for each output. They then define the reciprocal of this sum to be a measure of (local) returns to scale:

$$RS(t) \equiv [\Sigma_i \, \varepsilon_i(t)]^{-1} \qquad (3.28)$$

They then show that

$$TP(t) = [RS(t)]^{-1}[Q'(t)/Q(t)] - [X'(t)/X(t)] \qquad (3.29)$$

and derive the following expression:

$$TFPG(t) = TP(t) + \{Q'(t)/Q(t)\}\{1 - [RS(t)]^{-1}\} \\ + \{[Y'(t)/Y(t)]\} - [Q'(t)/Q(t)]\} \qquad (3.30)$$

This equation indicates that the Divisia productivity index equals the technical progress measure TP(t) plus the marginal cost weighted output growth index, $Q'(t)/Q(t)$, times a term that depends on the returns to scale term, $\{1 - [RS(t)]-1\}$, and that will be positive if and only if the local returns to scale measure $RS(t)$ is greater than 1, plus the difference between the Divisia output growth index, $Y'(t)/Y(t)$, and the marginal cost weighted output growth index, $Q'(t)/Q(t)$.

Denny, Fuss, and Waverman (1981, p. 197) interpret the term $Y'(t)/Y(t) - Q'(t)/Q(t)$ as the effect on TFP growth of nonmarginal cost pricing of a nonproportional variety. If marginal costs are proportional to output prices, then the term $Y'(t)/Y(t) - Q'(t)/Q(t)$ vanishes from equation (3.30), and this approach provides a continuous time counterpart to the economic approaches to productivity measurement developed in previous sections.

3.5 How Do We Move from Data to Theory?

This section of Chapter 3 treats the major data availability/quality issues that must be dealt with in measuring TFP empirically. The first is how to measure the quantity of capital services used by the firm, industry, or economy. Even at the firm level, this is an extremely complex task because capital is typically categorized as any expenditures on a long-lasting factor of production. This creates problems with aggregation over time and across different types of capital goods, in addition to the even more difficult problem of how to distinguish the amount of capital services that flow from a given piece of capital stock each period.

For example, on the issue of aggregation over time, expenditures on different vintages of machinery are aggregated into a single capital stock figure for machinery, and from this stock of machinery the firm receives capital services. These expenditures are made in nominal dollars, and particularly during times of nominal price inflation, how these nominal expenditures are converted into real magnitudes can dramatically impact the measured size of the firm's or industry's capital stock. Particularly in the developing world, historical information on capital expenditures for a firm, industry, or economy is not available, so the researcher must make other assumptions to estimate the capital stock.

A second data aggregation issue is how to compute an aggregate input from similar inputs of different quality. For example, firms hire many different types of workers, yet productivity analysts typically assume a single labor input. A discussion of how different qualities of an input such as labor are aggregated to create the single input called labor used to compute aggregate TFP is necessary to judge the results of cross-country studies of productivity growth. A fixed quantity of labor input measured in number of workers or hours of work in the United States is of dramatically different quality than the same number of workers or hours of work in a developing country. The dual approach to productivity measurement can prevent some of the challenges associated with measuring the firm's capital stock or different qualities of inputs, but as mentioned, this approach requires additional assumptions beyond the production function–based approach to measure productivity growth.

The final input measurement issue is particularly important in capital intensive industries, where there is a distinction between a firm's capital stock and the services it receives from this capital stock. As Berndt and Fuss (1986) demonstrate, how this distinction is modeled can dramatically impact the sign and magnitude of measured productivity growth in economically meaningful ways. These issues are also discussed later.

Another data issue that will be discussed is the fact that the theory of productivity measurement is developed in terms of physical units of output, but dollar sales is often the only data available to the researcher. This is particularly true in industries with multiproduct firms or differentiated products, which characterize the vast majority of firm-level sales in virtually all countries. Consequently, productivity measurement is confounded with how the competitiveness of the industry changes over time, because one way for a firm's sales to increase is for the firm to cut its prices. Klette (1999) discusses these issues and provides an econometric modeling framework that explicitly accounts for these factors in measuring productivity.

This section also treats the major data quality/measurement issues associated with input prices, including a discussion of how to construct the price of capital services, a nontrivial measurement task. Measuring the price of labor and other aggregate inputs has similar challenges to the process of measuring the quantity of labor. The problem with measuring input prices is particularly acute in the developing country context, where firms typically do not keep standardized accounts.

It is hoped that this discussion of both the theoretical foundation for productivity measurement and the data challenges associated with doing this empirically will provide the reader with the ability to judge the quality of the evidence presented in subsequent chapters.

3.5.1 Measurement of Capital Services

As noted earlier, an important measurement issue, particularly in capital intensive industries, is the distinction between a firm's capital stock and the services it provides from its capital stock. Berndt and Fuss (1986) demonstrate how this distinction can be modeled and how it can affect the sign and magnitude of measured productivity growth in economically meaningful ways.

Berndt and Fuss note that one of the greatest puzzles addressed by preceding productivity research is the substantial decline in measured productivity growth during the 1970s (the so-called productivity slowdown).[2] They find that a substantial portion of the measured decline is due to the fact that traditional methods of productivity measurement assume that producers are in long-run equilibrium when in fact they may be in short-run or temporary equilibrium. They utilize the Marshallian framework of a short-run production or cost function with certain inputs quasi-fixed to provide a theoretical basis for accounting for temporary equilibrium. Within this theoretical framework it is the value of services from stocks of quasi-fixed inputs that should be altered rather than the *quantity*. The empirical application to U.S. manufacturing data over the period from 1958 to 1981 shows that, depending on the measurement procedure, one can attribute somewhere between 18 percent and 65 percent of the traditionally measured decline in TFP growth between 1965–73 and 1973–81 to the effects of temporary equilibrium.

The authors note that a temporary equilibrium may occur when unexpected demand shocks lead to under- or overutilization of capacity, or

---

[2] See Chapter 8 for more discussion of the productivity slowdown in the United States.

when sudden changes in factor prices, such as the energy price shocks of 1973 and 1979, result in short-run relative factor usage that is inappropriate for the long run. It has long been recognized that the existence of temporary equilibrium, especially that associated with the business cycle, can bias measured productivity growth away from its long-run path.

Their paper provides a set of theoretical underpinnings to clarify how the productivity residual can be adjusted in a consistent manner to accommodate forms of temporary equilibria, such as the variation in the utilization rates of quasi-fixed capital plant and equipment inputs. A nice feature of their approach is that it can be implemented on the basis of either nonparametric procedures (with some simple revisions to traditional growth accounting practices) or parameters estimated using econometric techniques.

They first show that the traditional method for TFP measurement is appropriate only if the firm's output is always produced at the long-run equilibrium point – that is, at the point of tangency between the short-run unit or average total cost (SRUC) curve and the long-run unit cost (LRUC) curve. They then demonstrate the consequences of temporary rather than long-run equilibrium and, in particular, that in temporary equilibrium the contributions of quasi-fixed (fixed in the short run, but variable in the long run) inputs should be valued at their shadow prices, not at their market transaction prices. Within this theoretical framework, adjustment of the productivity residual for temporary equilibrium effects such as variations in capacity utilization is made by altering the value and not the quantity of capital (when capital is the only factor assumed to be quasi-fixed). They then extend the temporary equilibrium framework to the dual approach to the measurement of TFP growth. They also consider a common example of temporary equilibrium, the existence of excess capacity (hence, capacity underutilization).

3.5.1.1 Standard Productivity Measurement

The economic theory underlying traditional productivity measurement is closely related to the theory of cost and production. Let there be a constant returns to scale production function with traditional neoclassical curvature properties relating the maximum possible output Y obtainable during period t from the flows of services of n inputs, $X_1, X_2, ..., X_n$, and the state of technology, represented by time t:

$$Y(t) = F\left[X_1(t), X_2(t), ..., X_n(t); t\right] \qquad (3.31)$$

Over time t, it is assumed that the state of technology improves from dis-embodied technical change. A logarithmic differential of (3.31) can be written as

$$d \ln Y(t)/dt = \Sigma_i [\partial \ln Y(t)/\partial \ln X_i(t)] \cdot d \ln X_i(t)/dt + \partial \ln Y(t)/\partial t$$

$$(3.32)$$

Denoting the output elasticities $\partial \ln Y(t)/\partial \ln X_i(t)$ by W_i, setting $\partial \ln Y(t)/\partial t$ to $\mathring{A}(t)/A(t)$, and interpreting logarithmic derivatives as rates of growth, one can rewrite (3.32) as

$$\mathring{Y}/Y = \Sigma_i W_i \mathring{X}_i /X + \mathring{A}/A \qquad (3.33)$$

or

$$\mathring{A}/A = \mathring{Y}/Y - \Sigma_i W_i \mathring{X}_i /X \qquad (3.34)$$

The *actual* (as opposed to measured) multifactor productivity growth rate $\mathring{A}/A$ is given by (3.34). Under the assumption of constant returns to scale $\Sigma_i W_i = 1$ and the last term in (3.34) can be interpreted as the elasticity-weighted aggregate input. If output elasticities and all service flows were observable, (3.34) would always provide the correct measure of TFP growth irrespective of temporary equilibrium issues. These latter issues arise from the different possible ways of measuring W_i, and the flow of services from quasi-fixed inputs, and hence $\mathring{A}/A$.

The conventional method of measuring $\mathring{A}/A$ is based on the assumption that the observed inputs and outputs are generated by firms in competitive long-run equilibrium. With prices of output and inputs fixed, the firm chooses input levels so as to maximize profits. The first-order condition for profit maximization is then

$$\partial Y(t)/\partial X_i(t) = P_i(t)/P(t) \qquad (3.35)$$

where $P(t)$ is the output price and $P_i(t)$ is the market price of the ith input. One can substitute (3.35) into (3.34) to obtain the empirical approximation to $\mathring{A}/A$:

$$\mathring{A}/A = \mathring{Y}/Y - \Sigma_i S_i \mathring{X}_i /X \qquad (3.36)$$

where

$$S_i = P_i(t)X_i(t)/P(t)Y(t) \tag{3.37}$$

is the long-run competitive equilibrium approximation to W_i. Alternatively,

$$\overset{o}{A}/A = \overset{o}{Y}/Y - \overset{o}{X}/X \tag{3.38}$$

where aggregate input growth $\overset{o}{X}/X$ is the revenue or cost share-weighted aggregate of the individual input growth rates:

$$\overset{o}{X}/X = \sum_i S_i \overset{o}{X}_i/X \tag{3.39}$$

Under competitive conditions and long-run constant returns to scale, $P(t)$ is the long-run equilibrium price, profits are zero and revenue equals costs, implying that S_i is also the cost share and $\sum_i S_i = 1$. Hence the denominator of (3.37) can be rewritten as $\sum_i P_i(t)X_i(t)$, where $P_i(t)$ are ex ante prices, including the imputed service prices of quasi-fixed inputs that are purchased as stocks, such as capital equipment and structures. Also, under the assumption of competitive long-run equilibrium, all quasi-fixed inputs are optimally utilized in the sense that the total cost of production per unit of output is minimized. This long-run optimal utilization is what Berndt and Fuss call "full" economic utilization. When economic utilization is full, flows from quasi-fixed inputs can be assumed to be proportional to the stocks – that is, the available services from quasi-fixed inputs are fully utilized. This leads to the replacement of unobserved service flows in (3.36) by observed stocks. The rate of TFP growth is then computed from (3.36), which can be calculated from observed price and quantity data.

The measure of TFP growth obtained from (3.36) is not appropriate if firms are not in long-run cost-minimizing equilibrium. It can be assumed that a firm is not in long-run equilibrium whenever the firm's input-output bundle does not correspond to a point on its long-run unit cost function. For example, if the temporary equilibrium were due entirely to underutilization of capacity (caused, for example, by a demand shock), then a perfectly competitive firm would not be in long-run equilibrium if its output were not produced at the minimum point on the firm's SRUC curve. This serves as the relevant condition for a perfectly competitive industry. If the firm was not in a perfectly competitive industry, it would not be in long-run equilibrium whenever it produced output at a level other than that corresponding to the tangency point of a SRUC and the LRUC curve.

3.5.1.2 A Generalized Approach to Productivity Measurement

In the traditional long-run equilibrium treatment, it is assumed that all inputs are variable and that for each input, marginal product equals P_j/P. This assumption can now be relaxed. Partition the set of n inputs into two exhaustive and mutually exclusive subsets, one subset of J variable inputs, v = $[v_1, v_2, . ., v_j]$, and another subset of M quasi-fixed inputs, f = $[f_1, f_2, ..., f_M]$. The quasi-fixed inputs are fixed in the short run and can be varied over time but only by incurring increasing marginal costs of adjustment. Using this partition of inputs, the short-run production function is given as:

$$Y(t) = F[v_1(t), v_2(t), ..., v_j(t); f_1(t), f_2(t), ..., f_M(t); t]$$
$$= F[v(t); f(t); t] \tag{3.40}$$

In (3.40), Y(t) is the maximum amount of output obtainable during period t on the basis of given flows of variable inputs v(t), stocks of quasi-fixed inputs f(t), and the state of technology. It should be noted that in (3.40) it is no longer assumed that there is a flow-stock identification problem since the quasi-fixed inputs are specified as stocks. The logarithmic differential of (3.40) can now be written as:

$$d \ln Y(t)/dt = \sum_{j=1}^{J} [\partial \ln Y(t)/\partial \ln v_j(t)] \cdot d \ln v_j(t)/dt$$
$$+ \sum_{m=1}^{M} [\partial \ln Y(t)/\partial \ln f_m(t)] \cdot d \ln f_m(t)/dt + \partial \ln Y(t)/\partial t$$

$$\tag{3.41}$$

Let $\partial \ln Y(t)/\partial t \equiv \overset{\circ}{A}/A$ and $W_m \equiv \partial \ln Y(t)/\partial \ln f_m(t)$. Then, from (3.41),

$$\overset{\circ}{A}/A = \overset{\circ}{Y}/Y - [\sum_{j=1}^{J} W_j \overset{\circ}{v_j}/v_j + \sum_{m=1}^{M} \overset{\circ}{f_m}/f_m] \tag{3.42}$$

Now suppose a firm is not in long-run competitive equilibrium but instead is in a short-run competitive or temporary equilibrium. A firm maximizing short-run variable profits, given f(t), will choose input levels so that:

$$\partial Y(t)/\partial v_j(t) = P_j(t)/P(t) \tag{3.43}$$

As a result,

$$W_j(t) \equiv \partial \ln Y(t) / \partial \ln v_j(t) = [\partial Y(t) / \partial v_j(t)] \cdot [v_j(t) / Y(t)]$$

$$W_j(t) = [P_j(t) \cdot v_j(t)] / [P(t) \cdot Y(t)] \equiv S_j(t), j = 1, \ldots, J \qquad (3.44)$$

which has the same form as (3.37). However, (3.44) differs from (3.37) in two ways. First, (3.44) holds only for variable inputs, not the quasi-fixed factors. Second, P(t) is no longer the long-run equilibrium output price but rather the short-run equilibrium price.

Since by definition the f_m are quasi-fixed in the short-run, it follows that for the short-run (one-period) profit-maximizing firm, marginal product values of f_m are not necessarily equal to transactions prices $P_m(t)$, where P_m is now the market user cost or one-period market rental price of the mth input stock. As a result, output elasticities will, in general, differ from value shares. Define the ex post realized shadow user cost of the mth quasi-fixed input as Z_m:

$$Z_m(t) \equiv P(t) \cdot [\partial Y(t) / \partial f_m(t)] \qquad (3.45)$$

As a result,

$$P(t) \cdot Y(t) = \sum_j P_j(t) \cdot v_j(t) + \sum_m Z_m(t) \cdot f_m(t)$$

Define the ex ante expected shadow user cost as:

$$Z^*_m(t) \equiv P^*(t) \cdot [\partial Y(t) / \partial f_m(t)] \qquad (3.46)$$

where $P^*(t)$ is the expected output price. As a result, the income-expenditure identity becomes:

$$P^*(t) \cdot Y^*(t) = \sum_j P^*_j(t) \cdot v^*_j(t) + \sum_m Z^*_m(t) \cdot f_m(t)$$

where the asterisk indicates expected values and $f_m(t) = f^*_m(t)$.

It should be noted that this is a temporary equilibrium process (relative to the long-run equilibrium) and that nonrealized expectations are possible. Also implicit here is the assumption that at the beginning of the period, the firm forms expectations about future input and output prices. Its optimal response in adjusting quasi-fixed factors is based on these expectations. As a result, the expected value of the marginal product $[Z^*_m(t)]$ is the relevant shadow rental price, corresponding with observed levels of the quasi-fixed inputs. However, ex post, after actual input and output prices are known, the firm chooses the levels of its variable factors and output, conditional on the prior choice of the quasi-fixed factors. This implies that the actual value shares [$S_j(t)$ in (3.44)] are the correct weights for the variable factors.

$Z^*_m(t)$ represents the additional expected variable profits during period t that are obtained by adding one more unit of f_m for one period. Differences between the transactions rental prices $P_m(t)$ and expected shadow rental prices $Z^*_m(t)$ may be due to factors like the presence of increasing marginal costs of adjustment for the quasi-fixed inputs. When $Z^*_m > P_m$, the firm expects a relative shortage of f_m and has incentives to invest in additional units; conversely, when $Z^*_m < P_m$, the firm expects to find itself with a relative surplus of f_m and has incentives to disinvest; finally, when $Z_m = P_m$, the short- and long-run levels of f_m coincide, and there is no incentive to change the level of f_m.

The output elasticity of the mth quasi-fixed input can be expressed in terms of the expected shadow prices $Z_m(t)$ as follows:

$$W^*_m(t) \equiv \partial \ln Y(t)/\partial \ln f_m(t) = [\partial Y(t)/\partial f_m(t)] \cdot [f_m(t)/Y^*(t)]$$

$$W^*_m(t) = [Z^*_m(t) \cdot f_m(t)]/[P^*(t) \cdot Y^*(t)], \quad m = 1,...,M \qquad (3.47)$$

On the basis of (3.40), (3.43), and (3.46), an alternative measure of TFP growth, $\mathring{A}_2/A_2$, which is consistent with short-run or temporary equilibrium, can be derived as follows:

$$\mathring{A}_2/A_2 = \mathring{Y}/Y - [\sum_{j=1}^{J} S_j \mathring{v}_j/v_j + \sum_{m=1}^{M} W^*_m \mathring{f}_m/f_m] \qquad (3.48)$$

By definition, the ex post elasticities S_j plus W_m sum to unity, where

$$W_m(t) \equiv [Z_m(t) \cdot f_m(t)]/[P(t) \cdot Y(t)] \qquad (3.49)$$

However, even though $Y = F(v; f; t)$ is homogeneous of degree one in v and f, the output elasticities S_j plus $w^*_m(t)$ do not necessarily sum to 1.

Equation (3.48) can be rewritten as

$$\mathring{A}_2/A_2 = \mathring{Y}/Y - \mathring{X}^*/X^* \qquad (3.50)$$

where

$$\mathring{X}^*/X^* = [\sum_{j=1}^{J} S_j \mathring{v}_j/v_j + \sum_{m=1}^{M} W^*_m \mathring{f}_m/f_m] \qquad (3.51)$$

When Z^*_m decreases from $Z^*_m = P_m$ to $Z^*_m < P^*_m$ for all m (a relative sur-plus of stocks of f_m exist), f_m is valued less highly and therefore aggregate input growth $\overset{\circ}{X}{}^*/X^*$ is less than $\overset{\circ}{X}/X$, implying by (3.40) and (3.50) that $\overset{\circ}{A}_2/A_2 > \overset{\circ}{A}_1/A_1$. If, for example, the firm is only in temporary equilibrium because capacity has become underutilized between periods t − 1 and t, $\overset{\circ}{A}_2/A_2$ is the correct measure of $\overset{\circ}{A}/A$, and the traditional measure $\overset{\circ}{A}_1/A_1$ understates true TFP growth (since $Z^*_m < P_m$). It should be noted that the utilization of f_m, when $Z^*_m \neq P_m$ is accounted for in (3.50) by the adjustment stock values f_m, not their quantities of service flows. It should also be noted that when $P_m = Z^*_m$ for all m, $\overset{\circ}{X}/X = \overset{\circ}{X}{}^*/X^*$ and the traditional and the alternative measures of TFP growth are equal.

3.5.1.3 The Dual Approach to TFP measurement

The dual approach to traditional TFP measurement under the assumption of competitive long-run equilibrium derives from the unit cost function dual to the production function (3.31):

$$c(t) = G\left[P_1(t), P_2(t), ..., P_n(t); t\right] \tag{3.52}$$

where c(t) denotes the minimum possible unit cost of producing output at time t with input prices given. Constant returns to scale implies that c(t) is independent of Y(t). As before, the state of technology (reductions in unit cost) is assumed to increase over time t as a result of disembodied technical progress. A logarithmic differential of (3.52) can be written as:

$$d\ln c(t)/dt = = \Sigma_i [\partial \ln c(t)/\partial \ln P_i(t)] \cdot d\ln P_i(t)/dt + \partial \ln c(t)/\partial t \tag{3.53}$$

On the basis of Shephard's lemma, with output quantity and input prices fixed, the cost-minimizing firm's demand for the ith input is given by:

$$X_i(t) \cdot \partial c(t)/\partial P_i(t), \quad i = 1, 2, ..., n \tag{3.54}$$

Since

$$\partial \ln c(t)/\partial \ln P_i(t) = \left[\partial c(t)/\partial P_i(t)\right] \cdot \left[P_i(t)/c(t)\right], \tag{3.55}$$

it is possible to substitute (3.53) into (3.54) to obtain cost shares $S_i(t)$. Equation (3.53) can then be rewritten as:

$$\overset{\circ}{B}_1/B_1 = \overset{\circ}{c}/c - \Sigma_i S_i(t) \cdot \overset{\circ}{P_i}(t)/P_i(t) \tag{3.56}$$

where $\overset{o}{B}_1/B_1$ is the measured rate of cost reduction due to technical progress. By rearranging terms and rewriting, the authors obtain:

$$\overset{o}{B}_1/B_1 = \overset{o}{c}/c - \overset{o}{P}_X/P_X = \overset{o}{P}/P - \overset{o}{P}_X/P_X \qquad (3.57)$$

where $\overset{o}{P}_X/P_X$ is the rate of growth of the price of aggregate input X,

$$\overset{o}{P}_X/P_X \equiv \Sigma_i S_i \cdot \overset{o}{P}_i / P_i \qquad (3.58)$$

Equation (3.57) indicates that the calculated cost reduction due to technical change is equal to the difference in growth rates between unit cost (price) and the price of aggregate input. Hence, equation (3.57) is the dual of (3.38). Moreover, it can be shown that in the case of constant returns to scale, the primal and dual rates are negatives of one another:

$$\overset{o}{A}_1/A_1 = -\overset{o}{B}_1/B_1 \qquad (3.59)$$

Hence, in the case of long-run competitive equilibrium conditions, either $\overset{o}{A}_1/A_1$ or $\overset{o}{P}_1/B_1$ can be used to measure TFP growth.

In analogous fashion, a dual measure of TFP growth under conditions of temporary equilibrium can also be derived. Define the short-run unit variable cost function as:

$$c^v = \left[1/Y(t)\right] \cdot H\left[P_1(t), \dots P_j(t); f_1(t), \dots, f_M(t); t\right] \qquad (3.60)$$

The short-run unit shadow cost function can then be defined as:

$$c^*(t) = [1/Y(t)] \cdot [c^v \cdot Y(t) + \sum_{m=1}^{M} Z^*_m(t) \cdot /f_m(t)] \qquad (3.61)$$

It should be noted that $c^*(t)$ is the unit cost that would prevail in the long run if the firm faced factor prices $[P_j(t), Z^*_m(t)]$ and produced output $Y(t)$. Hence $c^*(t) = P^*(t)$, since F is linear homogeneous. As a result, if the firm is a short-run profit maximizer, $c^*(t)$ is just the short-run expected marginal cost curve, with $P^*(t)$ exogenous.

Berndt and Fuss next show that by totally differentiating (3.61) with respect to time and using Shephard's lemma they obtain:

$$\overset{o}{B}_2/B_2 = \overset{o}{c^*}/c^* - [\sum_{j=1}^{J} S_j \cdot (\overset{o}{P}_j/P_j) + \sum_{m=1}^{M} W^*_m \cdot (\overset{o}{Z}^*_m/Z^*_m)] \qquad (3.62)$$

Equation (3.62) is the dual to equation (3.48). They are related in exactly the same way as the traditional dual equations (3.36) and (3.56). It should be noted that in (3.62) shadow prices replace market prices for the quasi-fixed factors.

If the term in the bracket of equation (3.62) is defined as $\overset{\circ}{P}{}^*_X / P^*_X$, then the dual measure may be expressed as:

$$\overset{\circ}{B}_2 / B_2 = \overset{\circ}{c}{}^*/c^* - \overset{\circ}{P}{}^*_X / P^*_X = \overset{\circ}{P}{}^*/ P^* - \overset{\circ}{P}{}^*_X /P^*_X \tag{3.63}$$

The dual measure of TFP growth under temporary equilibrium is once again the difference between the growth rates in output price and aggregate input price, analogous to (3.57). The primal and dual TFP measures $\overset{\circ}{A}_2 / A_2$, and $\overset{\circ}{B}_2 / B_2$ are related in the same way as $\overset{\circ}{A}_1 / A_1$, and $\overset{\circ}{B}_1 / B_1$: $B_2 / B_2 = - \overset{\circ}{A}_2 / A_2$.

As Berndt and Fuss note, one of the most common examples of temporary equilibrium is the existence of excess capacity because of a reduction in demand for output or the like. In this case, by assuming that the firm was in long-run equilibrium, the researcher would be attributing to improvements in the state of technology increases in output per unit labor due partly to increases in the rate of capacity utilization. The use of the temporary equilibrium measures $\overset{\circ}{A}_2 / A_2$ and $\overset{\circ}{B}_2 / B_2$ would correct for these short-run effects.

3.6 Physical Units versus Dollar Amounts

Another issue raised in the beginning of Section 3.5 is that the theory of productivity measurement is developed in terms of physical units of output, but most researchers only have dollar sales data available to them to measure output. This problem occurs particularly in the case of industries with multiproduct firms or differentiated products. Consequently, productivity measurement is confounded with how the competitiveness of the industry changes over time, because one way for a firm's sales to increase is for the firm to cut its prices.

Klette (1999) provides a good treatment of these issues and provides an econometric modeling framework that explicitly accounts for these factors in measuring productivity. In particular, he develops an econometric framework that permits *simultaneous* estimation of price-cost margins, scale economies, and productivity from a panel of establishment data. The model contains only a few parameters to be estimated, but it is nevertheless consistent with a flexible (translog) underlying technology, quasi-fixed capital, and the presence of persistent differences in productivity between establishments.

The theoretical model begins with a consideration of the nature and consequences of imperfect competition and scale economies. It shows how the usual approach to estimate market power can be extended to account for scale economies, and for the quasi-fixity of capital. When estimating price cost margins, it is necessary to adjust for scale economies, because the estimate of scale economies will tend to be closely linked to the estimate of the ratio of price to marginal costs. For example, with price and average costs as the observable point of departure, overestimating scale economies will lead to underestimated marginal costs, which in turn provides an overestimated price-marginal cost ratio.

Most studies in this area are based on industry-level data. However, microdata are essential for a simultaneous study of price-cost margins and scale economies, since scale economies at the industry level are affected by externalities, entry, and exit. These are phenomena that have little to do with the scale economies relevant for the firms' price setting decisions. The use of plant- or firm-level panel data has the additional benefit that the model is implemented at the level for which it is developed. This eliminates problems of aggregation and permits the researcher to control for permanent productivity differences between plants (that is, "fixed effects"). Permanent productivity differences between plants are common to most data sets on establishments and firms, and their presence raises questions about the interpretation of results from aggregate data that are based on the idea of a representative firm.

The model that Klette develops is as follows. It is assumed that firms within an industry are constrained by a production function $Q_{it} = A_{it} F_t (X_{it})$, where Q_{it} and X_{it} represent output and a vector of inputs for firm i in year t. A_{it} is a firm-specific productivity factor, while $F_t(\cdot)$ is the portion of the production function that is common to all firms. The time subscript on the F function indicates that the function can change freely between years. In other words, the model does not impose constraints on the form of technical progress that is common across the firms within the industry, and the model is consequently consistent with, for example, factor-augmenting technical progress (see Chapter 2).

On the basis of a version of the generalized mean value theorem, the production function can be rewritten in terms of logarithmic deviations from a point of reference. This point of reference can be thought of as the representative firm's level of output and inputs for each year. Rewriting the production function in terms of logarithmic deviations from the representative firm, we obtain:

$$\hat{q}_{it} = \hat{a}_{it} + \sum \bar{\alpha}^j_{it} \hat{x}^j_{it} \qquad (3.64)$$

where a lowercase letter with a hat ($\wedge$) is the logarithmic deviation from the point of reference of the corresponding uppercase variable. For example, $\hat{q}_{it} \equiv \ln(Q_{it}) - \ln(Q_t)$, where Q_t is the level of output for the representative firm in year t. In the empirical application, this reference point was chosen as the median value of output within the industry in each year. A similar (industry-year) median value is used as a reference point for each of the inputs, and $X_t = \{X^1_t, X^2_t, ..., X^m_t\}$ is the reference vector for the inputs. The set of the m inputs is denoted by M. $\bar{\alpha}^j_{it}$ is the output elasticity for factor j evaluated at an internal point $\bar{X}^j_{it}$ between X^j_{it} and the reference point X_{it}. A bar over a variable such as $\bar{\alpha}^j_{it}$ indicates that it is evaluated at the internal point. By changing the estimated reference point from year to year, the model allows for unrestricted technical change.

Klette goes on to argue that according to basic producer theory, the profit-maximizing behavior of firms requires that marginal cost should equal marginal revenue product. It is assumed that the firm has some market power in the output markets, while it acts as a price taker in the input markets when determining its factor inputs. This assumption is perfectly consistent with a bargaining situation where the firm and the union bargain over the wage rate, while the firm unilaterally determines the number of hours employed. The first-order conditions with these behavioral assumptions are as follows:

$$A_{it} \partial F_t (X_{it}) / \partial X_{it} = W^j_{it} / [(1 - 1/\varepsilon_{it}) P_{it}] \qquad (3.65)$$

where W^j_{it} is the factor price for input j, while the denominator on the right-hand side is marginal revenue. In particular, P_{it} is the output price and ε_{it} is the (conjectured) price elasticity of demand. According to the theory of imperfect competition, the factor $(1 - 1/\varepsilon_{it})^{-1}$ represents the ratio of price to marginal cost. He denotes the ratio between price and marginal costs by μ_{it} and uses the first order conditions in equation (3.65) to obtain:

$$\bar{\alpha}^j_{it} = \mu_{it} (\bar{W}^j_{it} \bar{X}^j_{it}) / (\bar{P}_{it} \bar{Q}_{it}) = \mu_{it} \bar{s}^j_{it} \qquad (3.66)$$

where $\bar{s}^j_{it}$ is the cost share of input j relative to total revenue.

Various rigidities make it unlikely that equation (3.66) holds for capital – that is, the imputation of the marginal product of capital from observed prices on new equipment, tax rules, interest, and depreciation rates. However, this problem can be handled in the following way. The elasticity of scale in production is defined by

$$\bar{\eta}^j_{it} = \sum \bar{\alpha}^j_{it} \tag{3.67}$$

It follow from equation (3.66):

$$\bar{\alpha}^K_{it} = \bar{\eta}_{it} - \mu_{it} \sum_{j \neq K} \bar{s}^j_{it} \tag{3.68}$$

The output elasticity of capital as constructed in equation (3.68) will vary across firms and over time. If, for the moment, the randomness in $\bar{\eta}_{it}$ and μ_{it} is neglected, then equation (3.68) implies that the capital elasticity will be high, ceteris paribus, when the labor elasticity is low, and vice versa. This is quite sensible since a low labor elasticity tends to reflect a shortage of capital – that is, a situation with a high capital elasticity.

If equation (3.66) is used for the noncapital inputs and equation (3.68) for the capital input, then equation (3.64) can be rewritten as:

$$\hat{q}_{it} = \hat{a}_{it} + \mu_{it} \sum_{j \neq K} \bar{s}^j_{it} (\hat{x}^j_{it} - \hat{x}^K_{it}) + \eta_{it} \hat{x}^K_{it} \tag{3.69}$$

On the basis of this relationship and the addition of stochastic assumptions, an econometric model can be estimated.

In sum, the model developed previously imposes only mild regularity conditions on the production technology in order to derive equation (3.69). This model is consistent with nonconstant returns to scale and the presence of market power since price can exceed marginal cost. The model also allows for the possibility that capital is not fully adjusted to its equilibrium value but is considered, instead, a (quasi-) fixed factor of production, while the firm solves its short-run profit maximizing problem. The two terms η_{it} and μ_{it} can be interpreted as scale elasticity and the ratio of price to marginal costs.

This framework can be used to analyze interfirm differences in productivity and technical change. In fact, the productivity measure a_{it} in equation (3.69) is just an extension of "the multilateral TFP index" developed by Caves, Christensen, and Diewert (1982b) for multilateral comparisons of productivity (see earlier discussion). The productivity index of Caves *et al.* is also based on the concept of the representative firm as a benchmark for comparing productivity differences across a number of firms. However, this multilateral TFP index assumes constant returns to scale and competitive output markets, while Klette's measure does not require these assumptions.

3.6.1 The Fixed Effects Model

In order to implement equation (3.68) in an econometric framework, additional assumptions need to be made. One common assumption is the presence of fixed effects. Productivity differences between firms tend to be highly persistent over time. These productivity differences are important determinants of growth. The term $\hat{a}_{it}$, which represents the firm's productivity *relative* to the reference firm, can be represented by an error component structure, as follows:

$$\hat{a}_{it} = a_i + u_{it} \tag{3.70}$$

where a_i is treated as a fixed (correlated) effect, while u_{it} is a random error term. Treating a_i as a fixed effect means that we allow the cross-sectional differences in productivity between establishments to be freely correlated with all the variables in the estimating equation – in particular, with output and all factor inputs. It should be noted that technical change common among plants within an industry can be neglected since all variables are measured *relative* to the reference firm in each year separately, and there is consequently no need to introduce year-dummies in equation (3.70).

There can be several explanations for the presence of fixed effects as captured in a_i. Establishments might differ in the effectiveness of the management, labor quality, vintage of the capital, and so forth. Such productivity differences will typically be positively correlated with size, since more productive establishments will tend to gain larger market shares. To eliminate the fixed effects, the model is estimated in terms of first differences.

The scale coefficients developed in Klette's model are long-run scale elasticities, because they incorporate changes in both variable factors such as materials, energy and working hours, and capital. The econometric model, however, focuses on *changes* in the level of operation in the longitudinal dimension and disregards the cross-sectional information about efficiency differences in small versus large plants. Some people have argued that cross-sectional comparisons of establishments are more relevant in understanding long-run scale economies. However, the comparison in efficiency between small and large plants raises the question of causality: Are large plants more efficient because they are large (which would support the claims about scale economies), or have they grown larger than other plants because they are more efficient (because of better technology or better management or the like)? This question raises doubt about whether cross-sectional differences in efficiency can be interpreted as evidence of scale economies.

The actual estimating equation can be derived by combining equation (3.70) with equation (3.69) and then taking first differences to eliminate the fixed effect term (a_i):

$$\Delta \hat{q}_{it} = \mu \Delta \hat{x}^V_{it} + \eta \Delta \hat{x}^K_{it} + \Delta v_{it} \tag{3.71}$$

where the variable $\hat{x}^V_{it} = \sum_{j \neq K} \bar{s}^j_{it} (\hat{x}^j_{it} - \hat{x}^K_{it})$, $\Delta \hat{q}_{it} = \hat{q}_{it} - \hat{q}_{i,t-1}$, and $\Delta v_{it} = v_{it} - v_{i,t-1}$. The latter term is given by:

$$v_{it} = u_{it} + (\mu_{it} - \mu)\hat{x}^V_{it} + (\eta_{it} - \eta)\,\hat{x}^K_{it} \tag{3.72}$$

The last two terms in equation (3.72) indicate that the error term, v_{it}, captures differences in the mark-up and scale parameters across firms, because the μ- and η- parameters in the estimating equation (3.71) are restricted to be common across firms. The first term on the right-hand side of equation (3.72) represents transitory and idiosyncratic differences in productivity.

Equation (3.71) cannot be consistently estimated by OLS for two reasons. First, even allowing for fixed effects by estimating the model in first differences does not solve the problem of correlation between the productivity differences, u_{it}, and the differences in the firms' choices of factor inputs. To the extent that a firm experiences *changes* in productivity over time relative to the average firm, a productivity shock might be correlated with changes in factor inputs to the extent that the shock is anticipated before the factor demands are determined. If productivity improvements stimulate growth, this will tend to create a positive correlation between the right-hand side variables and the error term in equation (3.71), thereby creating an upward bias in the OLS estimates. Second, errors in variables due to, for example, reporting errors will create another endogeneity problem, which typically biases the OLS estimates downward. The preferred estimator according to Klette is GMM (see earlier discussion).

3.7 Physical Output versus Deflated Dollar Sales

As noted in the Introduction to this chapter the economic theory of TFP measurement is typically derived in terms of physical output units. However, empirically, deflated dollar sales is usually used in place of physical output. This issue is discussed in detail in Bartelsman and Doms (2000).

As they note, the main choice that researchers make is whether to analyze labor productivity or TFP. After that, they must choose whether the output concept is in physical terms, in deflated gross production, or in (double) deflated value added. Among methods of calculating TFP, choices can be made among index number approaches, econometric estimation of cost or production functions, or nonparametric methods, such as data envelopment analysis (see the discussion in Section 3.3). If one is interested only in productivity measures per se, it is best not to take a dogmatic stance on methodology but rather to explore the sensitivity of productivity measures to variations in methodology. In assessing the effect of certain factors on productivity, one must take care that the chosen empirical framework allows proper identification of the relationship.

TFP can be thought of in a manner analogous to labor productivity, namely, as a ratio of output to input. A simple measure of the level of labor productivity is given by:

$$LP_{it} = y_{it}/L_{it}$$

where LP shows the output, y, for firm i, period t, per unit of labor input, L. Numerous complications arise concerning measurement of outputs and inputs or aggregation of inputs across types, across agents, and over time. For example, labor input may be measured in employees, in hours worked, or in quality-adjusted hours worked.

Although TFP is an analogous concept, in a general multioutput multi-input setting, the level of productivity cannot be measured in any meaningful units. Instead, productivity changes of a firm over time or productivity movements relative to other firms need to be measured in terms of index numbers. The equation

$$\pi_{it}/\pi_{it-1} = \left(y_{it}/x_{it}\right)/\left(y_{it-1}/x_{it-1}\right)$$

shows, for firm i, productivity (π) change between period t and period t − 1, where y is an index of output quantity and x is an index of aggregate inputs.

Likewise, the equation

$$\pi_i/\pi_j = \left(y_i/x_i\right)/\left(y_j/x_j\right)$$

shows productivity of firm i relative to that of firm j, at a given time.

The choice between TFP or labor productivity is fundamental since increases in labor productivity can result from increases in the capital-labor ratio without changes in underlying technology. TFP provides more information about changes in technology than does labor productivity and is usually the preferred concept despite problems arising from the measurement of capital service flows. However, for certain purposes, labor productivity may be the preferred appropriate concept. In particular, for welfare comparisons, value added per capita can be more informative than TFP. Moreover, at a more disaggregated level, the use of labor productivity allows a comparison of unit labor costs of production across establishments. When establishments are known to have the same capital, labor productivity is sufficient. Heterogeneity in labor productivity has been found to be accompanied by similar heterogeneity in TFP in most empirical applications where both measures are used.

The choice of output measure is often determined by available data. When possible, physical output with unchanging quality is the best measure. Microdata, like the Longitudinal Research Database (LRD), have physical output measures for a small subset of products produced by a subset of establishments. However, these data are not corrected for quality changes over time; nor are they necessarily comparable across establishments. In general, researchers rely on deflating nominal variables at the sectoral level (with all establishments in an industry using the same deflators). Most studies using the LRD use production and materials deflators at the four-digit SIC level. The use of deflated production to measure productivity has one drawback, which is the same whether applied at the microlevel or at the sectoral or aggregate level: Any quality improvement in output that is not reflected in the deflator will result in a downward bias in productivity.

The lack of availability of microlevel prices introduces other problems. For example, the application of quality-adjusted industry deflators to microlevel data would be acceptable under perfect competition because the price per unit of quality-adjusted output would be the same among firms. However, the persistent dispersion of productivity or costs across firms calls into question the empirical relevance of perfect competition. Under monopolistically competitive markets with differentiated products, prices may differ across firms or establishments. In this case, the assumption of constant prices implies that an establishment with higher-than-average prices will mistakenly be assigned higher productivity. Disentangling price and quantity movements, even if microlevel market prices are available, requires knowledge of the demand side for the differentiated goods.

Another choice facing researchers is the use of gross production or value added as the output concept. Value added may be more useful for making welfare statements at an aggregate level but less useful for understanding the sources of productivity growth. Shifts in the use of intermediate inputs relative to capital and labor over time may create biases in productivity measured with the use of value-added output.

Measures of TFP can be calculated using a wide variety of methods, and the comparative advantage of each measure depends on the particular question that is being addressed and the available data. A general decomposition of an index of TFP change allows the computation of the contributions from technological change, changes in technical and allocative efficiency, effects of nonmarginal cost pricing, and effects of nonconstant returns to scale. With k inputs and m outputs, the k-vector of input prices and quantities and the m-vector of output prices and quantities at time 0 and 1 can be used to compute TFP change:

$$\pi^1 / \pi^0 = \left\{ \left[\left(p^1 y^1 \right) / \left(p^0 y^0 \right) \right] \, / \, P\left(y^1, y^0, p^1, p^0 \right) \right\}$$
$$/ \left\{ \left[\left(w^1 x^1 \right) / \left(w^0 x^0 \right) \right] \, / \, W\left(x^1, x^0, w^1, w^0 \right) \right\}$$

This equation states that the change in TFP equals the deflated change in revenues divided by the deflated change in costs, where the functions P and W represent a price index for output and input deflation, respectively.

The Solow residual is a special case of this ratio and measures technological change if certain "standard" assumptions hold (see Chapter 2 also). These assumptions are (i) that factors of production are utilized in a technically efficient manner and are paid their marginal products, and (ii) that outputs are produced under constant returns to scale and priced at marginal cost. The equation

$$\hat{\pi}_t = \hat{y}_t - \sum_k \hat{x}_{k,t} s_{k,t}$$

indicates the growth rate of the Solow residual measure of TFP, where a caret ($\wedge$) denotes the first difference in logarithms, and s is the average of current and lagged factor shares. Factor shares are computed as revenue shares, where the share of capital is usually computed as 1 minus the shares of the other factors.

Deviations from marginal cost pricing and constant returns will sever the link between the preceding Solow residual and the "true" rate of technological change. One adjustment, for example, uses cost shares as weights (requiring data on the user cost of capital and the assumption of a constant elasticity of demand for output) and explicitly estimates the degree of returns to scale. Other departures between the TFP change index and technological change occur if factor inputs do not receive payments equal to their marginal products or if factors are not utilized fully. Then, allocative and technical inefficiency changes may result in deviations between the Solow residual movements and actual technological change. A large empirical literature exists that deals with these departures from the basic assumptions and decomposes residuals into efficiency changes and technological change.

A widely used method for computing a productivity index for sectoral data is through estimation of a cost function and factor demand equations. The advantage of using this approach for the measurement of productivity is that the estimated parameters are not biased because of simultaneity of productivity and factor demand. However, the advantages of this method over directly estimating production functions are questionable in the case of microdata because identification of the factor demand equations requires variation in factor prices, which are not available at the microlevel. Instead, prices vary over time only at the sectoral level.

No data set is ideal for every question because of issues related to frequency, coverage, sampling, unit of analysis, time series properties, and missing variables, among others. Longitudinal microdata like LRD are no different. For instance, studies that examine the relationships between R&D and productivity may be appropriately conducted at the firm level, but not at the establishment level. For the LRD, although all the manufacturing establishments of a firm are known in census years, much of the research to date has neglected other parts of the firm, such as headquarters, sales offices, R&D labs, and the other parts that lie outside manufacturing. Another shortcoming of longitudinal microdata is that they tend to focus mainly on manufacturing, a sector whose share of GDP and employment has been decreasing.

Other problems with longitudinal microdata arise from productivity measurement. The difficulties that affect aggregate measures of either TFP or labor productivity, in particular, getting accurate measures of inputs and outputs, may actually prove worse at the microlevel. In a standard capital, labor, energy, materials (KLEM) model of production, the measurement of each factor has its own problems. Capital stocks or service flows are notoriously difficult to measure at the microlevel because of composition effects and the time series of investments required. In the case of the labor input, the LRD classifies employees only as production or nonproduction workers rather than providing more detailed information on occupations, education, or experience. Output measurement is also difficult, with most data being deflated by four-digit industry deflators. Therefore, differentiating between productivity differences and differences in markups is difficult, if not impossible.

It should also be noted that the quality of data collected at the establishment level is largely unknown. Although input and output measures may be noisy at the microlevel, aggregate measures may be more precise if the noise is random. A question therefore arises of how much of the dispersion in productivity at the microlevel is noise and how much is real.

Another issue concerns the relation between aggregate and average productivity growth. One interest in examining microproductivity growth is to gain a better understanding of the sources of aggregate productivity growth. Aggregate productivity growth is a weighted average of establishment-level productivity growth, where the weights are related to the importance of the establishment in the industry:

$$\Delta \Pi_t = \sum_i s_{it} \Delta \pi_{it}$$

where Δ denotes first difference, π_i is the logarithm of productivity for unit i, and s is the share of firm i (or establishment i) in the total. Different economists have used various methods for computing the contributions of compositional shifts of output and within-establishment productivity growth to aggregate productivity over the industry, but the results are quite similar. Aggregate TFP growth in the periods studied is significantly affected by compositional changes, such as shifts in output toward establishments with relatively high (or low) TFP.

Typically, aggregate TFP growth is decomposed into components related to within-establishment TFP growth, reallocation, and the effects of exit and entry. One such decomposition is as follows:

$$\Delta \Pi_t = \sum_{i \varepsilon C} s_{i,t-1} \Delta \pi_{it} + \sum_{i \varepsilon C} s_{i,t-1} \Delta \pi_{it}$$
$$+ \sum_{i \varepsilon C} s_{i,t-1} (\pi_{it} - \Pi_{t-1}) \Delta s_{it} + \sum_{i \varepsilon C} \Delta \pi_{it} \Delta s_{it}$$
$$+ \sum_{i \varepsilon N} s_{it} (\pi_{it} - \Pi_{t-1}) - \sum_{i \varepsilon X} s_{i,t-1} (\pi_{it} - \Pi_{t-1})$$

In this particular decomposition, aggregate productivity growth between two periods is divided into five parts. The first three add up to the contribution of continuing plants (set C), and the last two, of entry (set N) and exit (set X), respectively. The labor shares, s, are computed over all establishments in the relevant period.

The five components distinguish (1) a within-plant effect – within-plant growth weighted by initial output shares; (2) a between-plant effect – changing output shares weighted by the deviation of initial plant logarithm TFP and initial logarithm industry TFP; (3) a covariance term – a sum of plant TFP growth times plant share change; (4) an entry effect – a year-end share-weighted sum of the difference between (log) TFP of entering plants and initial (log) industry TFP; and (5) an exit effect – an initial-share-weighted sum of the difference between initial (log) TFP of exiting plants and initial (log) industry TFP.

The between-plant and the entry and exit terms use the deviation between plant productivity and the industry average in the initial period. A continuously operating firm with an increasing share makes a positive contribution to aggregate productivity only if it initially has higher productivity than the industry average. Entering (exiting) plants contribute only if they have lower (higher) productivity than the initial average. This treatment of births and deaths ensures that the contribution to the aggregate does not arise because the entering plants are larger than exiting plants, but because there are productivity differences.

Bartelsman and Doms (2000) provide a very useful summary of the research findings from the use of longitudinal microdata to date. The first general finding of note is that productivity levels are quite dispersed, that productivity differences between plants may be very persistent, that entry and exit of plants with different productivity levels are an important source of productivity growth, and that plants' long-run employment changes and productivity changes are not correlated. The existence of productivity heterogeneity, even among producers of comparable products with comparable equipment, forces productivity researchers to rethink conventional wisdom in this field. In particular, these results cast some doubt on the validity of an "aggregate" production function that is based on a representative firm. Industry output is not produced with industry inputs in such an orderly fashion. Factor output elasticity, which is considered a structural property of a production function, does not represent a property of "industry technology." If, for example, labor input in an industry were to double, the resulting change in industry output would depend not only on the production technology at each plant but also on the allocation of inputs and output among plants within the industry before and after the change. The properties associated with an aggregate production function, such as factor substitution and scale elasticities, do not represent marginal responses of the industry or of a plant. Instead, the elasticities capture both some average over time and across plants of microlevel production technology and the effects of past changes in composition within the industry.

An important implication of the problems associated with elasticities estimated with aggregate data is that the elasticities may be time varying and nonlinear and that they do not reflect structural characteristics of the production technology in any case. As a result, a researcher cannot rely on aggregate elasticities in order to compute the marginal response to changes in relevant variables. Rather, the researcher must understand the microlevel technology and the mechanism of compositional response to changes in the variable to calculate marginal responses.

3.8 Summary and Concluding Remarks

Chapter 2 presented an overview of modern growth theory and touched on some measurement and econometric issues. This chapter provided technical details on both the measurement and estimation of productivity growth, particularly TFP growth, and developed the theoretical foundation for much of the empirical literature dealing with issues of productivity measurement.

According to Diewert (1976), TFP is a production function–based concept. Although all researchers would agree that productivity growth has occurred if a firm is able to produce more output from the same vector of inputs, the quantitative estimate of the magnitude of TFP growth depends on how TFP is measured. There are alternative methods to measure TFP – empirically based index numbers, econometric methods, stochastic frontier methods, and data envelopment analysis (DEA). Another issue is that the economic theory of TFP measurement is typically derived in terms of physical output units even though, empirically, deflated dollar sales is used in place of physical output (see Bartelsman and Doms, 2000). Also, since the analysis discussed in subsequent chapters is typically made with the use of aggregate industry-level or country-level data, it is necessary to indicate how industry-level and country-level input and output aggregates are computed. Theoretical restrictions on firm level production functions necessary for an aggregate production function to exist need to be indicated as well. As a result, there are several reasons why the growth in the country-level output aggregate is less than the growth in the country-level input aggregate that are not the result of productivity growth.

Section 3.2 began with a rigorous definition of TFP using the neoclassical theory of production. It demonstrates that TFP depends on the assumed form of the production transformation function, specifically the functional forms for both the input aggregator function and the output aggregator function.

This theoretical discussion began at the firm level because the existence of an aggregate economywide or industrywide production transformation function requires many additional assumptions. This framework was then used to introduce the distinction between Hicks-neutral technical change and factor-biased technical change. This was followed by a treatment of the theoretical framework for measuring productivity change using the minimum cost function. I also discussed the additional assumptions required by the dual (cost function) approach relative to the primal production function–based approach to productivity measurement. For example, measuring productivity in terms of the production function only requires the firm to produce in a technically efficient manner, whereas productivity measurement from the dual approach requires both technically efficient and allocatively efficient production.

In this section, I developed first the standard Laspeyres and Paasche price indices. This was followed by a treatment of the so-called ideal index, which is the geometric mean of the Paasche and Laspeyres indices, Diewart's superlative index, the Törnqvist-Theil Divisia index, and the translog function

Section 3.3 discussed econometric issues associated with the estimation of productivity growth. There are five common approaches to productivity measurement: (a) index numbers, (b) data envelopment analysis (DEA), (c) stochastic frontiers, (d) instrumental variables (GMM), and (e) semiparametric estimation. This section reports the results of a paper by Van Biesebroeck (2007) of a simulation study to examine the sensitivity of productivity estimates and growth rates to the five approaches. Using simulated samples of firms, he analyzed the sensitivity of alternative methods to the randomness properties in the data generating process from introducing randomness via (a) factor price heterogeneity, (b) measurement error, and (c) heterogeneity in the production technology. He found that when measurement error is small, the index number method is excellent for estimating productivity growth and ranks among the best for estimating productivity levels. The DEA method is particularly applicable with heterogeneous technology and nonconstant returns to scale. On the other hand, when measurement errors are nonnegligible, parametric methods are preferable. In rank order, the preferred techniques are stochastic frontiers, GMM, and then semiparametric estimation methods.

Section 3.4 addressed the question of the theoretical conditions necessary to measure productivity growth at the industry level or country level. Diewert and Nakamura (2007) provided a comprehensive discussion of this issue. Although it is always possible to construct index numbers and compute the difference between the growth in the output and input indices, only with certain assumptions on the true input and output aggregator functions does this resulting difference in growth rates equal the growth in TFP. Denny, Fuss, and Waverman (1981) discussed this issue when the assumption of constant returns to scale is dropped. In particular, they related the Divisia TFP measure to shifts in the cost function without assuming constant returns to scale. The only assumption required was that the firm continuously minimizes costs over the period of interest.

Section 3.5 addressed the major data availability and quality issues that must be dealt with in measuring TFP empirically. The first of these is how to measure the quantity of capital services used by the firm, industry, or economy. Even at the firm level, this is a complex task because capital is typically categorized as any expenditures on a long-lasting factor of production. This creates problems with aggregation over time and across different types of capital goods, in addition to the even more difficult problem of how to distinguish the amount of capital services that flow from a given piece of capital stock each period.

A second data aggregation issue was how to compute an aggregate input from similar inputs of different quality. This is particularly germane when firms hire different types of workers. The third input measurement issue discussed in this section is particularly important in capital intensive industries, where there is a distinction between a firm's capital stock and the services it receives from this capital stock. Berndt and Fuss (1986) discussed this problem. Their paper provided a set of theoretical underpinnings to clarify how the productivity residual can be adjusted in a consistent manner to accommodate forms of temporary equilibria, such as the variation in the utilization rates of quasi-fixed capital plant and equipment inputs.

Section 3.6 discussed another data issue related to the fact that the theory of productivity measurement is developed in terms of physical units of output, but dollar sales is often the only data available to the researcher. This is particularly true in industries with multiproduct firms or differentiated products. Consequently, productivity measurement is confounded with how the competitiveness of the industry changes over time, because one way for a firm's sales to increase is for the firm to cut its prices. Klette (1999) discussed these issues and provides an econometric modeling framework that explicitly accounts for these factors in measuring productivity. In particular, he developed an econometric framework that permits *simultaneous* estimation of price-cost margins, scale economies, and productivity from a panel of establishment data. The model contains only a few parameters to be estimated, but it is nevertheless consistent with a flexible (translog) underlying technology, quasi-fixed capital, and the presence of persistent differences in productivity between establishments.

Section 3.7 also discussed problems associated with the use of deflated dollar sales instead of physical output as the output measure based on the work of Bartelsman and Doms (2000). Their work used microdata like the Longitudinal Research Database (LRD), which has physical output measures for a small subset of products produced by a subset of establishments. An issue of particular interest is the relation between aggregate and microlevel (establishment) productivity growth. Aggregate productivity growth is a weighted average of establishment-level productivity growth, where the weights are related to the importance of the establishment in the industry. Different economists have used various methods for computing the contributions of compositional shifts of output and within-establishment productivity growth to aggregate productivity over the industry, but the results are quite similar. Typically, aggregate TFP growth is decomposed into components related to within-establishment TFP growth, reallocation, and the effects of exit and entry. The major finding is that aggregate TFP growth is significantly affected by compositional changes, such as shifts in output toward establishments with relatively high (or low) TFP.

4

Long-Term Record among the Advanced
Industrial Countries

4.1 Introduction

Explanations of the productivity catch-up almost all involve so-called advantages of backwardness, a term first coined by Gerschenkron (1952). The basic idea is that much of the catch-up can be explained by the diffusion of technical knowledge from the leading economies to the more backward ones (also, see Kuznets, 1973). Through the constant transfer of new technology, leader countries and those most closely in their van learn the latest productive techniques from one another, but virtually by definition the follower countries have more to learn from the leaders than the leaders have to learn from them (hence the advantages of backwardness).

This mechanism has two implications: First, it means that those countries that lag somewhat behind the leaders can be expected systematically to move toward the level of achievement of the leaders. Second, the mechanism undermines itself automatically as follower countries gradually eliminate the difference between their own performance and that of the countries that were ahead of them – that is, the very fact of convergence means that the differential learning opportunities that are the source of these advantages of (slight) backwardness will exhaust themselves. On an analytical level, this hypothesis would imply faster productivity growth for the (initially) more backward economies relative to the more advanced ones, but the gap in productivity performance would gradually diminish over time as convergence was achieved.

However, being backward does not itself guarantee that a nation will catch up. Other factors must be present, such as strong investment, an educated workforce, a suitable product mix, and developed trading relations with advanced countries (Abramovitz's (1986) "social capabilities"). Indeed, when the catch-up hypothesis is tested across all countries of the world, the finding is generally that there is no or very little correlation between the rate of productivity growth and the initial productivity level. However, when other variables such as investment or education are included in the model to allow for "conditional convergence" (that is, that poorer countries experience faster productivity growth than richer ones given other characteristics such as the investment rate and the stock of human capital), the catch-up term has been found to be highly significant in a wide range of specifications.

The next section (section 4.2) reviews the evidence on long-term convergence in labor productivity and per capita income. Several of these studies, including Abramovitz (1986), Baumol (1986), and Baumol, Blackman, and Wolff (1989), made use of data provided in Angus Maddison's 1982 book *Phases of Capitalist Development*, on output and employment for sixteen OECD countries covering the period from 1870 to 1979. Section 4.3 reviews the analogous evidence on long-term convergence in total factor productivity (TFP). Section 4.4 surveys related studies on convergence in the long term. Section 4.5 presents statistical evidence on convergence in per capita income in the very long term (two millennia). Section 4.6 reviews the related literature on the subject. A summary and concluding remarks are presented in Section 4.7.

4.2 Convergence in Labor Productivity and Per Capita Income

Maddison (1982, pp. 96–9) provided the first evidence of catch-up. Interestingly enough, his work was based on long-term data, covering the period from 1870 to 1979, for what are today the advanced industrial countries. Results from the 1982 book are shown in Figure 4.1 (also see Appendix Table 4.1.) The labor productivity measure used here is GDP in 1970 U.S. dollars per hour worked, standardized so that U.S. labor productivity in 1950 was 100. A trend line is included in Figure 4.1, which is sharply negative (and also statistically significant at the 1 percent level).

Several indices of convergence were computed. The first is the ratio of the difference between the maximum and minimum labor productivity (the "range") in a given year to the (unweighted) average labor productivity for that year among all sixteen countries. The second is the coefficient of variation, defined as the ratio of the standard deviation to the mean. The coefficient is computed for labor productivity levels in each year. The third is the ratio of the unweighted average labor productivity of all countries except the leading country to the productivity level of the leader. The fourth is the same ratio, except that the labor productivity level of the United States is

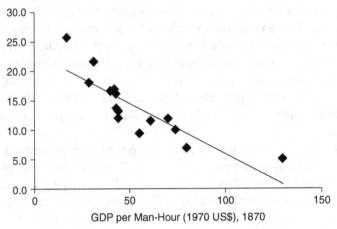

Figure 4.1. Ratio of 1979 GDP per man-hour to 1870 GDP per man-hour for 16 OECD countries (*Source*: Maddison, 1982).

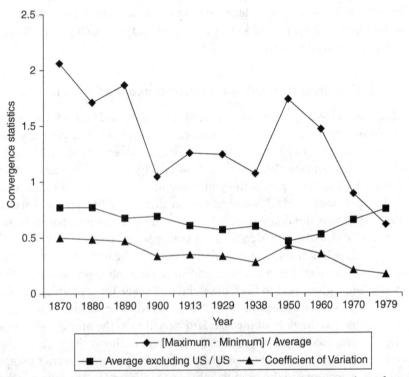

Figure 4.2. Labor productivity convergence, 1870–1979 (GDP per man-hour for 16 OECD countries).

used instead of that of the leader. The trends in several of these indices are also illustrated in Figure 4.2.

There are a number of interesting patterns that emerge. First, convergence in labor productivity levels means that the spread or dispersion among countries should narrow over time. The first two indices show that this was the case. The ratio of the range to the mean productivity level declined by 70 percent from 1870 to 1979, and the coefficient of variation declined by two-thirds. On the basis of the coefficient of variation as the measure of convergence, we find a more or less steady pattern of productivity convergence among these sixteen countries. Between 1870 and 1938, the coefficient of variation fell almost by half. However, as a result of the destruction of capital stock in many European countries and in Japan during World War II, the coefficient of variation in 1950 climbed back to a level just below its 1890 level. There followed a remarkable degree of convergence from 1950 to 1979, with the coefficient of variation falling by three-fifths.

Second, if convergence is occurring, then the average labor productivity level of follower countries should be closing in on that of the leader. This is also verified by the data, since this ratio increased from 0.38 in 1870 to 0.75 in 1979. Likewise, the ratio of the highest productivity level to the lowest also registered a very sharp drop. Its value plummeted from 7.7 in 1870 to 1.9 in 1979.

Third, it is of interest to note that, perhaps somewhat surprisingly, neither the United States nor the United Kingdom was the early leader in labor productivity but rather Australia. The United States ranked only fifth. Among the major economies, the United Kingdom was the most productive. Indeed, according to the Maddison data, Australia was far out ahead of the other countries in this dimension during the late 1800s. By 1900, the United States had surpassed the United Kingdom, and by 1929 it went ahead of Australia and became the country with the highest level of labor productivity.

Fourth, the final statistic, the ratio of average labor productivity of all countries except the United States to that of the United States, in fact does not show convergence. The ratio was, in fact, slightly higher in 1870 than in 1979. The reason is that U.S. labor productivity increased very rapidly from 1870 to 1929 – much faster than the average of the other countries. It was not until the 1930s that other countries began to catch up to the United States.

Fifth, another way of demonstrating convergence is to examine the correlation between initial labor productivity levels and labor productivity growth rates. According to the convergence hypothesis, countries that were further behind initially should exhibit higher growth rates as they narrow the gap with the leader. Productivity growth statistics for the 1870–1979 period are shown in the last two columns of Appendix Table 4.1, the first in terms of annual average growth rates and the second in terms of total growth over the period. Some of the growth multiples are quite impressive – a 12-fold increase in productivity for the United States, a 22-fold growth for Sweden, and a 26-fold increase for Japan. Moreover, a quick inspection by eye suggests that there is a strong inverse correlation between productivity growth and initial relative productivity levels in 1870. Australia, with the highest level of productivity in 1870, had the lowest increase of productivity over the period – a factor of 5. In contrast, Japan, which began at the bottom of the pack in 1870, had by far the greatest increase in productivity – a factor of 26. Indeed, the overall correlation coefficient between 1870 productivity levels and the annual rate of productivity growth from 1870 to 1979 is –0.93.

Baumol (1986) was among the first to document this convergence in labor productivity levels over the last century or so. The results are almost as strong for the postwar period alone. In this case, the correlation coefficient between initial labor productivity levels in 1950 and the rate of labor productivity growth over the 1950–79 period is –0.89.

Three studies questioned the Baumol results. The first of these, by Abramovitz (1986), investigated subperiods using the same Maddison data. He found that the pattern of convergence was far from uniform over time, and, indeed, for some periods, there was actually divergence in productivity levels. He also found that labor productivity convergence was considerably slower between 1870 and 1938 than between 1950 and 1979. Moreover, between 1938 and 1950, productivity levels actually diverged, though this was partly attributable to the differential effects of World War II on the various economies of the world (note in particular the absolute declines in productivity levels in Germany and Japan).

The postwar period was notable for the strong catch-up exhibited by the followers. Indeed, the correlation coefficient between 1950 productivity levels and productivity growth rates over the 1950–79 period was 0.89 for this 29-year period, compared to 0.93 for the 109-year period. However, even in the postwar period, there is evidence from Abramovitz that productivity convergence slowed during the 1970s. Abramovitz also found that there were significant changes in leadership and the rank order of countries over time (for example, Australia was the early leader in productivity but ranked only ninth of sixteen in 1979). This result is at variance with a simple convergence hypothesis.

The second study was by Dowrick and Nguyen (1989). They added a key variable to the analysis, which was the rate of capital formation. With the addition of this variable, they disputed Abramovitz's result that the rate of productivity convergence varied over time and, in particular, found considerable parameter stability in their catch-up model between the pre- and post-1973 periods when controlling for factor intensity growth.

The third and sharpest criticism was that of de Long (1988). His basic argument was that Baumol's results suffered from what might be called "sample selection bias." In particular, the countries chosen for the Maddison sample included only those countries that had proved successful – that is, the OECD countries. Thus, regressing annual productivity growth on initial productivity level would tend to ensure the finding of a strong negative correlation between the two. If the sample of countries included the full range of countries in the world, including those that proved to be successful in the postwar period as well as those that did not succeed, then the correlation between initial productivity and productivity growth would be much weaker. In fact, using data from a wider sample of countries, de Long demonstrated exactly that. Indeed, he selected twenty-two of the richest countries in 1870, including Ireland, Chile, Portugal, and Spain. Since many of these countries turned out to be economic failures in the late postwar period, the correlation between initial productivity and productivity growth for this group of countries turned out to be slightly negative or, in some cases, positive, depending on the assumption regarding measurement error.[1]

Baumol and Wolff (1988) provided a rebuttal and showed that the De Long criticisms were not as cutting as they first appeared. Baumol first admitted that admirable though the Maddison data are, they do not permit us to overcome the bulk of the major problems besetting any attempt to test the convergence hypothesis more or less definitively. In particular, without adding data on countries other than those in Maddison's sample, we cannot reject the conjecture that the convergence result is simply an artifact of ex post selection of a sample of industrial (i.e., relatively successful) economies.

Baumol and Wolff first used Bairoch's (1976) estimates of GNP per capita for nineteen European countries, essentially by decade, for the period 1830 to 1913. Arranging the countries in descending order of GNP per

---

[1] De Long also included a rather interesting analysis of measurement error in convergence analysis, since it is likely that these early statistics on GDP have a great deal of uncertainty about them. Moreover, the measurement error is likely to bias the regression coefficient of productivity growth on initial productivity level downward – that is, tend to make it more negative.

capita in 1830, they constructed a sample of countries consisting of the top eight economies (that is, the set of eight countries at the top of the list). Then they successively constructed samples of the top nine, the top ten, and so on, until they got to the top fourteen (beyond that number of countries too many data points were missing to permit an illuminating calculation). For each sample size they calculated a time series of the coefficients of variation (i.e., the standard deviation divided by the mean) for each year for which estimates were provided. This ex ante classification was also replaced by an intermediate period (1870) ranking of countries, with the analogous sets of countries and similar time series calculated under this classification.

The results showed a straightforward pattern. For the period 1830 to 1900, under the 1830 ranking, the coefficient of variation for every group of countries grew fairly steadily. That is, there was general growth in *divergence* in GDP per capita. After 1900, a pattern of convergence seemed to make its appearance for the set of countries ranging in number of members from eight to fourteen. However, if the remaining countries in Bairoch's table were added to the 1900–13 calculations, divergence continued.

Predictably, when the calculations were based on the intermediate year, 1870, rather than the initial period (1830) ranking, convergence in the top group (eight countries) appeared to begin far earlier, perhaps as early as 1860, and certainly by 1880. Use of the Gini coefficient instead of the coefficient of variation also showed earlier convergence (since about 1880) for a group as large as the top ten countries on an 1870 ranking.

These calculations then suggested that much of the nineteenth century was a period of divergence in standards of living of the leading European economies. Then, some time toward the end of the century, this process began to erode and was replaced by convergence among the initially (or later) more affluent of the countries. This is precisely what one should have expected. Before the Industrial Revolution the countries of Europe were relatively homogeneous in their general poverty. Then Great Britain pulled ahead of the others, inaugurating a growth in heterogeneity that was intensified as a small set of European leaders, including Belgium, Switzerland, the Netherlands, France, and Germany, also jumped ahead of the others. Only toward the end of the century was the leaders' example able to spread, so that convergence could extend to a group of any considerable size.

Because Bairoch's figures stopped in 1913, and his sample of countries was still far too small, they were insufficient to permit any conclusive exante test of the reality and prevalence of convergence. However, for the period 1950–80 Summers and Heston (1984) provided consistent data on GDP per capita for seventy-two countries (data for additional countries were provided for a somewhat briefer period). The figures for different countries were rendered comparable by using purchasing power parity (PPP) exchange rates rather than currency (market) exchange rates. They were expressed in 1975 "international dollar" units, and the statistics were referred to as RGDP (real per capita GDP). These figures permitted a comparison of the performance of the LDCs, the Soviet countries, and other groupings with that of the leading industrial countries. But more importantly, it permitted the selection of an ex ante (or an intermediate period) sample of countries.

Baumol and Wolff used those figures to test the hypothesis of their earlier study that among wealthier countries homogenization had occurred, but not among poorer countries. They tested this by calculating whether initially poorer countries subsequently grew faster than initially richer ones, as convergence required. To reduce scatter and obtain a coherent pattern they calculated moving averages for sets of ten countries at a time. That is, the first set was made up of the ten countries ranked lowest in terms of 1950 GDP per capita. The second set added the eleventh lowest and removed the lowest, et cetera. For each such group they graphed its average 1950 RGDP on the horizontal axis, and the growth rate of its RGDP between 1950 and 1980 on the vertical axis. The resulting graph constituted an automatic ex ante stratification, since poorer countries at that date clearly must lie to the left of the graph, while initially wealthier countries lie to its right. Their hypothesis, consequently, entailed the conjecture that the moving average graph would be roughly positively sloping toward the left, and distinctly negatively sloping toward the right, meaning that per capita incomes among LDCs, selected ex ante, had diverged, while the opposite had been true among initially "industrialized" countries.

This was, indeed, something like what the figure showed. For nations with initial per capita real GDPs below about seven hundred dollars, the curve's slope was highly erratic and could, perhaps, be interpreted to be positive in slope overall. Beginning possibly with a $700 dollar annual figure, and certainly above $1,300, the slope was clearly negative. Correspondingly, of the seventy-two countries in the sample, something between twenty-nine and fifty-two fell in the group represented in the downward sloping portion of the curve, while between twenty and forty-three fell in the more or less positively sloping segment. What all of this suggested was that somewhere near the median in their sample of countries "the advantages of backwardness" did indeed begin to overbalance the counteracting forces, sociological, educational, and other.

In a more formal regression analysis, both a nonlinear relationship and a piecewise-linear relation composed of two line segments were fitted to the RGDP data. The quadratic regression yielded the equation:

$$\ln \text{RATIO} = 0.586 + 0.00038 \; \text{RGDP50} - (9.9/10^7) \; \text{RGDP50}^2, R^2 = 0.07, N = 72$$
$$\quad\quad [4.2] \quad\quad [2.1] \quad\quad\quad\quad\quad\quad [2.2]$$

where RATIO = 1980 RGDP divided by 1950 RGDP, RGDP50 = 1950 per capita GDP, and t-ratios are shown in brackets beneath the corresponding coefficient. The maximum of the equation occurred at a 1950 RGDP value of about $1,900. Both variables were significant at the 5 percent level, with the predicted signs. The results again showed divergence among the 1950 lower income countries and convergence among the higher income ones.

A piecewise linear regression was designed to attain its maximum near that of the nonlinear one, putting seventeen of the seventy-two countries into the ex ante upper income category. The resulting regression equation was:

$$\ln \text{RATIO} = 0.658 + 0.00019 \; \text{RGDP50} - 0.00044 \; \text{D1900}, R^2 = 0.07, \; N = 72$$
$$\quad\quad [5.8] \quad\quad\quad [1.9] \quad\quad\quad\quad [2.2]$$

where D1900 = RGDP50 if RGDP50 ≥ $1,900 and 0 if RGDP50 < $1,900. The first variable was significant at the 10 percent level and the second at the 5 percent level, and both had the predicted signs, thus confirming the results of the quadratic equation. Finally, two separate regressions were run, one for the upper income sample and the other for the lower income group. For the upper income group,

$$\text{RATIO} = 3.3 - 0.00038 \; \text{RGDP50}, \; R^2 = 0.30, N = 17$$
$$\quad\quad [7.7] \; [12.5]$$

and for the lower income group

$$\text{RATIO} = 2.1 + 0.0005 \; \text{RGDP50}, R^2 = 0.03, N = 55.$$
$$\quad\quad [5.5] \quad [1.3]$$

The results provided strong support for convergence among the countries in the upper income group but much weaker support for divergence among the lower income group.

The preceding tests could be criticized because they compared only 1950 and 1980, with no attention to intermediate year figures. It could be argued that 1950 was characterized by atypical diversity in RGDP as a result of the great differences in damage done to various economies by World War II, notably to those of Germany, France, the United Kingdom, and Japan. Recovery of the most heavily damaged countries would naturally contribute abnormal convergence and would thereby bias the results of their calculation in the direction of their hypothesis.

To prevent such problems, they calculated for different ex ante country samples the time path of the coefficient of variation *for each year* in the period 1950–81. The Summers and Heston countries were again ranked on a 1950 basis (it was also done on a 1960 basis with no noteworthy changes in results, though not all of the tests were replicated for the 1960 base). The time series of coefficient of variation was calculated for the top ten countries as well as the top twelve, fourteen, sixteen, eighteen, twenty-two, twenty-four, twenty-six, twenty-eight, thirty, thirty-five, forty, forty-five, fifty, fifty-five, and sixty countries.

There was a sharp break in the pattern of behavior between the samples that included fewer than sixteen countries and those that included sixteen or more. The curve for the sample of the top fourteen countries was typical for the smaller country sets, containing the countries with the highest RDGP values in 1950. The coefficient of variation fell quite steadily and sharply throughout the period, except at its very beginning and very end. Noteworthy was the fairly steady rise since 1975, a rise whose overall magnitude remained fairly modest – at least so far.

For larger samples of countries divergence, as measured by coefficient of variation, began much earlier and continued far longer. The curve for the sample of the top twenty-six countries was not atypical. This curve showed a fairly steady rise in divergence ever since 1961. The coefficient of variation in 1981 was still about midway between its 1950 high and its 1961 low, so that about half of the initial increase in homogenization had been lost.

These then were the facts so far as they were ascertained from the available data back then. They indicated that for perhaps the top fifteen countries convergence had been marked and unambiguous, though there had been something of a retreat in the late 1970s. For all countries together, excluding the LDCs, there had also been some overall convergence. Yet, larger samples did not display convergence, in part because of the heterogeneous performance of the LDCs and the failure of South American countries to live up to their growth promise.

4.3 Convergence in Total Factor Productivity

4.3.1 Descriptive Statistics

Several papers have considered the convergence in TFP or multifactor productivity (MFP). The two are a purer measure of technology than labor productivity since both measures adjust for the amount of capital employed per worker. Indeed, as will be shown later, TFP can be shown to be a weighted sum of labor productivity and the capital-labor ratio.

Wolff (1991a) was one of the first papers to look at the convergence of TFP over the long term. This was followed up by a related paper (Wolff, 1996a), which considered in more detail the so-called vintage effect. I begin with results from Wolff (1991a).

The TFP level for country h is defined as the ratio of total output (Y^h) to a weighted average of labor input (L^h) and capital input (K^h). The formula is easier to grasp in logarithmic form, as follows:

$$\ln TFP^h = \ln Y^h - \alpha^h \ln L^h - (1 - \alpha^h) \ln K^h \qquad (4.1)$$

where the labor input is measured by hours of work, the capital stock is measured by gross nonresidential fixed plant and equipment, and α_h is the wage share in country h. The TFP formula used in this paper is the Divisia index (see Sections 3.2.2 and 3.4.1 of Chapter 3 for further discussion of the Divisia index). The empirical implementation of the TFP measure is the Törnqvist-Divisia index based on average period shares (see Section 3.2.2).

The basic data on output, employment, and capital stock are from Maddison (1982). The capital stock data in this Maddison work are basically drawn from national sources. The only standardization is to convert the capital stock figures of different nations into 1970 U.S. relative prices.[2] The sample is the so-called Group of Seven – Canada, France, Germany, Italy, Japan, the United Kingdom, and the United States. Factor shares are based on the average ratio of employee compensation to national income for the United Kingdom and the United States for the 1880–1979 period, because these are the only data available for the full period.[3]

---

[2] Problems of comparability of measures across countries are extensively discussed in Maddison (1982), Abramovitz (1986), and Wolff (1991a).

[3] Data on wage shares are computed from the following sources: (1) Data for 1950–87 are from the United Nations' *Yearbook of National Accounts Statistics*, selected years. (2) Data for 1937–50 are from the International Labour Organization's *Yearbook of Labor Statistics*, various years. (3) For the United Kingdom, data for 1870–1938 are from Deane and Cole (1964), p. 247. (4) For the United States, data for 1870–1938 are from Johnson (1954).

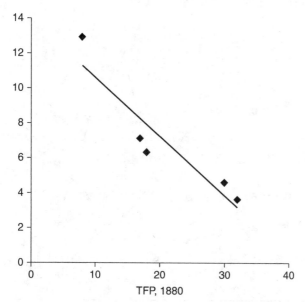

Figure 4.3. Ratio of TFP, 1880 to 1979, for Germany, Italy, Japan, United Kingdom, and United States (*Source*: Wolff, 1991).

The main results are shown in Figure 4.3 (also see Appendix Table 4.2 for computations of TFP levels for selected years in the period from 1870 to 1979).[4] Once again, a trend line is included that is sharply negative (and statistically significant at the 1 percent level). Results are quite similar to those for labor productivity. The United Kingdom was the early leader in total factor productivity (as it was for labor productivity when Australia is excluded). The United States caught up to the United Kingdom by 1890 and led thereafter. Japan was last throughout the period, though its TFP relative to the United States increased from a fourth in 1880 to three-fourths in 1979.

According to three indices, the ratio of the range to the unweighted average TFP level, the coefficient of variation, and the average TFP level of the other countries relative to the United States, there was only moderate convergence between 1880 and 1929 and particularly between 1880 and 1913 (see Figure 4.4). This is similar to labor productivity movements among the five countries. The Depression years did produce some convergence in TFP levels, followed by a sharp increase in dispersion between 1938 and 1950.

---

4   It should be noted that the sample of countries diminishes as one goes further back in time because of data availability.

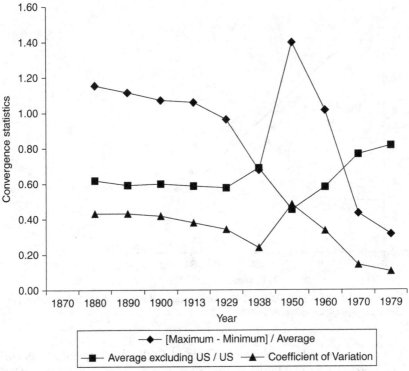

Figure 4.4. TFP convergence, 1880–1979, for Germany, Italy, Japan, the United Kingdom, and the United States.

As with labor productivity, this was partly a consequence of the deleterious effect of World War II on German and Japanese productivity, which declined in absolute terms, but mainly due to a tremendous increase in U.S. productivity. Another indicator of catch-up is a negative correlation of TFP growth rates with initial TFP levels. These coefficients show the same pattern: –0.20 for 1880–1913, –0.33 for 1880–1929, –0.64 for 1880–1938, and --0.83 for 1880–1979. Over the postwar period, the coefficient of variation fell by more than two-thirds, the ratio of the range to average TFP declined by about three-fourths, and average TFP relative to the United States rose from 0.54 to 0.85. Moreover, the correlation of TFP growth rates with initial TFP levels (in 1950) was –0.96 (see Wolff, 1991a, for more details).[5]

---

[5] For the postwar period, data availability is much greater and TFP was also computed using country-specific factor shares. Results did not materially differ from those reported here and are not shown.

These long-term results have been criticized on two other grounds as well. The first, and most telling, critique concerns the so-called sample selection bias. Since the sample consists of OECD countries, it is by nature limited to countries whose economies have been successful in recent years. What if the sample included countries that were strong in the late 1800s but have since faded away, such as Argentina and Uruguay? Results of de Long (1988) show very little evidence of productivity convergence over the last century when the sample is no longer restricted to OECD countries but includes such other countries as well. The second involves issues of statistical bias. In particular, the fact that the early data in many of these series were constructed by "backward extrapolation" of more recent data and the fact that early data are characterized by more measurement error than later data may each induce false correlations. In particular, they can be shown to bias upward in absolute value the correlation coefficient (that is, overstate the inverse correlation) between initial productivity levels and productivity growth rates (see Baumol, 1986, and De Long, 1988, for more discussion of these statistical problems).

Figure 4.5 (and Appendix Table 4.3) shows related statistics on rates of growth for the period 1880 to 1979, based on data from Maddison (1982). Cross-country average labor productivity growth for these seven countries remained fairly stable between 1870 and 1938, at about 2 percent per year; fell precipitously during World War II, to about 1 percent per year; climbed to 4 percent in the 1950s and then to 5 percent in the 1960s; and fell off to about 3.5 percent in the 1970s.

TFP growth, ρ, is then defined on the basis of the standard Divisia index as:

$$\rho^h_t = d \ln Y^h_t / dt - \alpha^h d \ln L^h_t / dt - (1 - \alpha^h) d \ln K^h_t / dt \qquad (4.2)$$

The Törnqvist approximation based on average period shares is employed. It also follows directly that

$$\pi^h_t = \rho^h_t + (1 - \alpha^h) d \ln k^h_t / dt \qquad (4.3)$$

where $LP \equiv Y/L$, the level of labor productivity, and π is the rate of labor productivity growth; and $k \equiv K/L$, the ratio of the capital stock to labor. From this formula, it should be clear that TFP growth is equal to labor productivity growth minus factor accumulation. As such, it is *not* a pure measure of technological change since it reflects the contribution of various factors to this measure of TFP growth (such as education).

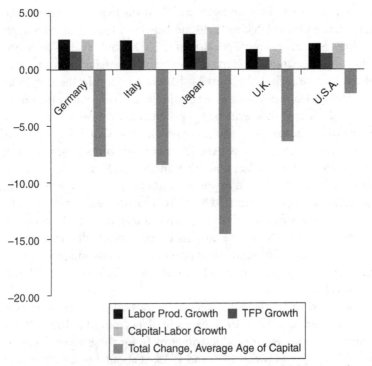

Figure 4.5. Annual labor productivity, TFP, and capital-labor growth, 1880–1979 (*Source*: Maddison, 1982).

Average TFP growth remained rather steady at about 1 percent per year from 1880 to 1938 (Panel B of Appendix Table 4.3). World War II, not unexpectedly, caused severe damage to the three Axis powers – Germany, Italy, and Japan – and, for Japan and Germany, TFP growth was actually negative between 1938 and 1950. However, the Allied powers did well. Both Canada and the United States enjoyed their highest TFP growth ever (4.5 and 3.6 percent per year, respectively), while the United Kingdom averaged 1.6 percent per year, its second highest level. The 1950s and 1960s were the boom years, with TFP growth averaging around 3 percent per year. The 1970s showed a substantial fall-off in TFP growth among OECD countries. Perhaps most dramatic was Japan, whose annual rate of TFP growth fell from 5.6 percent in the 1960s to 1.6 percent in the 1970s. However, overall the pattern over time was quite similar to that for labor productivity growth.

Between 1880 and 1938, the international average annual growth in capital intensity tended to remain relatively stable, at about 2 percent per year (Panel C of Appendix Table 4.3). During the war and war recovery years,

1938–50, it fell to about 1 percent, and then increased to 2.7 percent during the 1950s. The 1960–70 period thus represents an unusual departure from the long-term historical trend, with an average annual rate of *5.6 percent*. The average rate then declined to 4.9 percent in 1970–9.

Results on average age are shown in Figure 4.5 (and Panel D of Appendix Table 4.3).[6] The average age for the five countries declined from twenty-three years in 1880 to twenty-one years in 1913, rose steadily to twenty-eight years in 1950, then rapidly declined to fifteen years in 1979. Perhaps the most telling result is the extreme *rejuvenation* of the capital stock during the 1950s and 1960s, during which the average age fell by 6.1 and 5.6 years, respectively. Germany during the 1950s and Japan during the 1960s experienced extremely sharp drops in the age of their capital stock. In contrast, the average age of capital remained virtually unchanged during the 1970s. Changes were also relatively modest in the periods before 1938.

The United States had by far the newest capital stock from 1880 to 1913 (a third younger than the other four countries in 1900), a consequence of its high rate of capital growth. U.S. capital stock aged relative to the other countries from 1900 onward, and by 1979, it was 13 percent older than the other countries. From 1929 onward, Japan had the youngest capital stock; in 1979, its average age was two-thirds of its nearest rival, Germany, and 0.58 that of the United States. In contrast, the United Kingdom had the oldest capital stock, a position it maintained for one hundred years. In fact, in 1900, the UK capital stock was 70 percent older than that of the United States.

Figure 4.6 (and Appendix Table 4.4), from Wolff (1996a), shows a similar set of results based on the Maddison (1991, 1993a) data. In this case, capital stock estimates are standardized across countries by using the same service lives (a thirty-nine-year life for nonresidential structures and a fourteen-year life for machinery and equipment), as well as the same (U.S.) prices, and figures are provided separately for both plant and machinery and equipment. Moreover, estimates of average age are taken from Maddison (1993b) for selected years. The data are also now updated through 1989, and the periods 1973–9 and 1979–89 are highlighted. The new country sample includes the Netherlands but excludes Canada and Italy.

---

[6] Estimates of the average age of the capital stock were derived from capital stock data for 1870, 1880, 1890, 1900, 1913, 1929, 1938, 1950, 1960, 1970, and 1979. It was assumed that the service life was 50 years and that the average age of the capital stock was 25 years in 1870. Estimates were not provided for Canada or France, because the capital stock series are not long enough.

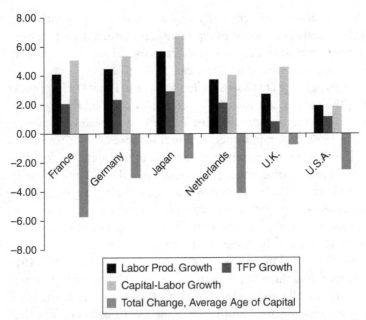

Figure 4.6. Annual labor productivity, TFP, and capital-labor growth, 1950–1989 (*Source*: Maddison 1991, 1993a).

Results are similar to Appendix Table 3.2. According to the new data, average annual labor productivity growth fell off sharply from a peak of 5.0 percent in 1960–73 to 2.8 percent per year in 1973–9 and then more moderately to 2.1 percent per year in 1979–89, close to its historical average. The slowdown in productivity growth between 1960–73 and 1973–9 occurred for all six countries, and that between 1973–9 and 1979–89 for four of the six countries. Annual productivity growth in the United States in particular picked up between the two last periods, from 0.8 to 1.4 percent.

Annual TFP growth averaged 2.9 percent in 1950–60 among the six countries, declined to 2.5 percent in 1960–73, and then fell off precipitously to 0.9 percent in 1973–9 and 0.8 percent in 1979–89. Here too TFP growth fell in all countries between 1960–73 and 1973–9, with Japan's fall-off the most dramatic, from 4.0 to 0.1 percent per year, and in four of the six between 1973–9 and 1979–89. The two exceptions are Japan and the United States, both of which experienced a rapid increase in TFP growth in the 1980s.

The growth in capital intensity (the ratio of gross capital to hours worked), averaged among the six countries, surged from 3.3 percent per year in the 1950s to 6.3 percent per year in 1960–73, then declined to 4.9 percent per year in 1973–9, and further to 3.4 percent per year during the 1980s. The slowdown occurred for all countries except France between 1960–73 and 1973–9 and for all countries between the latter period and the 1980s. Japan, in particular, saw its annual percentage rate of capital-labor growth decline from 11.7 in 1960–73 to 7.5 in 1973–9, and then to 5.0 in 1979–89.

The average age of the capital stock among the six countries (Panels D and E of Appendix Table 4.4) declined from 15.4 years in 1950 to 13.1 years in 1960 and further to 10.2 years in 1973. This "youthening" effect occurred for every country and was particularly notable in Germany during the 1950s and in France, Japan, and the Netherlands between 1960 and 1973. After 1973, the trend reversed, with the average age first increasing to 10.6 years in 1979 and then to 12.5 years in 1989. The aging effect happened in every country except France between 1973 and 1979 and in each of the countries between 1979 and 1989.

4.3.2 Analysis of Long-Term Trends

A regression analysis was employed to analyze the long-term data. The results are described in the Appendix and shown in Appendix Table 4.5. Using the results of these regressions, we can now understand some of the factors behind the slowdown in labor productivity growth in the 1970s and 1980s. A decomposition, based on the regression results of Appendix Table 4.5, is shown in Table 4.1. For example, on the basis of the Maddison (1982) data, for the 1880–1990 period, of the 1.5 percent per year average growth in labor productivity, 0.3 percentage point could be attributed to the catch-up effect (RELTFP), 0.6 percentage point to the growth in the capital-labor ratio, 0.02 percentage point to the vintage effect (the decline in the average age of the capital stock), and 0.5 percentage point to general technological advance (with 0.04 point unexplained).

Between 1880 and 1938, average annual labor productivity growth increased from 1.5 to 2.1 percentage points, mainly because of an increasing catch-up effect (as U.S. technology advanced relative to other OECD countries) and rising growth in the capital-labor ratio. Between 1929–39 and 1950–60, labor productivity growth doubled, to 4.2 percent per year. Of this *increase*, 42 percent $((1.51-0.62)/(4.22-2.07))$ could be attributed to the increasing catch-up effect from the rising technological advantage of the United States, as the TFP of other OECD countries slipped to 39 percent below the U.S. level; 15 percent to increased capital-labor growth; and *50 percent* to the increasing vintage effect, as the average age of capital stock declined at an annual rate of *0.6 year* over this period.

Table 4.1. *Contribution by Component to Average Labor Productivity Growth by Period on the Basis of the Long-Term Maddison Data*

A. Maddison (1982) Data: 5–Country Summary Statistics[a]

	1880–1890	1890–1900	1900–1913	1913–1929	1929–1938	1938–1950	1950–1960	1960–1970	1970–1979
1. Average Value of Explanatory Variables									
RELTFP	−0.07	−0.09	−0.08	−0.1	−0.16	−0.09	−0.39	−0.34	−0.26
KLGRT (% pts)	1.44	2.06	2.23	2.28	1.93	1.04	2.68	6.34	5.34
AGEKCHG	−0.02	−0.09	−0.11	0.14	0.19	0.24	−0.61	−0.56	−0.05
2. Percentage Point Contribution of Each Variable to Average Labor Productivity Growth[b]									
Constant	0.52	0.52	0.52	0.52	0.52	0.52	0.52	0.52	0.52
RELTFP	0.27	0.37	0.32	0.39	0.62	0.35	1.51	1.32	1.03
KLGRT	0.62	0.88	0.95	0.98	0.83	0.45	1.15	2.71	2.28
AGEKCHG	0.02	0.13	0.15	−0.2	−0.26	−0.33	0.85	0.77	0.07
Sum	1.43	1.9	1.95	1.7	1.71	0.99	4.03	5.33	3.91
Unexplained	0.04	−0.16	−0.24	0.42	0.36	−0.36	0.19	0.27	−0.28
LPGRT	1.47	1.74	1.71	2.12	2.07	0.63	4.22	5.61	3.63

B. Maddison (1991, 1993) Data: 6–Country Statistics

	1950–1960	1960–1973	1973–1979	1979–1989
1. Average Value of Explanatory Variables				
RELTFP	-0.32	-0.30	-0.27	-0.20
KLGRT (% pts)	3.34	6.35	4.87	3.41
AGEKCHG	-0.22	-0.23	0.07	0.23
2. Percentage Point Contribution of Each Variable to Average Labor Productivity Growth[b]				
Constant	1.10	1.10	1.10	1.10
RELTFP	1.03	0.96	0.85	0.65
KLGRT	1.31	2.49	1.91	1.34
AGEKCHG	0.68	0.69	-0.21	-0.70
Sum	4.12	5.23	3.65	2.39
Unexplained	0.12	-0.18	-0.82	-0.25
LPGRT	4.24	5.05	2.83	2.14

Notes: Key:
RELTFP: percentage difference of country's TFP from U.S. TFP at the beginning of the period
KLGRT: country's annual rate of capital-labor growth
AGEKCHG: annualized change in the average age of country's capital stock over the period
[a] Coefficients from Regression 1 in Appendix Table 4.5
[b] Defined as coefficient value multiplied by the average value of the variable by period
[c] Coefficients from regression 2 in Appendix Table 4.5

During the 1960s, labor productivity growth increased to 5.6 percent per year, exclusively as a result of rising capital-labor growth (as it reached its highest point over the century), and despite a slight diminution of both the catch-up effect and the vintage effect. More than a third (35 percent) of the fall-off in productivity growth during the 1970–9 period, to 3.6 percent per year, was attributable to the reduction in the vintage effect, as the average age of capital remained almost constant over the 1970s; 15 percent was attributable to the continued diminution of the catch-up effect, as the average TFP of other countries approached 26 percent of the U.S. level; and 22 percent to a slowdown in capital-labor growth.

The results from the newer Maddison (1991) data for the postwar period are shown in Panel B. As with the Maddison (1982) data, the contribution of the catch-up effect diminished over time, from 1.03 percentage points in 1950–60 to 0.65 percentage point in 1979–89, as other countries' TFP converged on the U.S. level. Also, as with the Maddison (1982) data, the contribution of capital-labor growth increased from the 1950–60 to the 1960–73 period and then declined in 1973–9 and then again in the 1979–89 period.

The vintage effect was quite strong and positive in the 1950–60 and 1960–73 periods, averaging about *two-thirds* of a percentage point, but then fell to –0.21 during the 1973–9 period and even further to –0.70 in the 1979–89 period, reflecting the aging of the capital stock in OECD countries.

Comparing the 1960–73 and 1973–9 periods, we can understand some of the reasons for the fall-off in labor productivity growth between these two periods of 2.6 percentage points. The slowdown in total capital-labor growth accounted for *26* percent of the decline in labor productivity growth, resulting about equally from reduced investment in structures and machinery and equipment; the aging of the capital stock accounted for *41* percent; the diminution of the catch-up only 5 percent; and 29 percent was due to the unexplained portion. Most of the further fall-off in labor productivity growth between the 1973–9 and 1979–89 periods was attributable to the slowdown in capital-labor growth and the continued aging of the capital stock.

4.4 Related Studies on Convergence in the Long Term

Crafts (1998) delved into the issue of how Britain came to be the leading industrialized country in the last few decades of the eighteenth century and the first few of the nineteenth century. To understand the British Industrial Revolution and the subsequent American overtaking of Britain, he examined data on technological and structural change in the two economies. He reported that Britain's trend rate of real GDP growth grew steadily rather than spectacularly over several decades from about 1780 and reached a peak in the mid-nineteenth century at about 2.5 percent per year. While output growth in some specialized sectors such as cotton textiles, which had seen dramatic technological change, was indeed extremely high, these sectors constituted only a small part of the aggregate economy, and a large part of traditional economic activity grew very slowly. Between 1780 and 1870, according to the Maddison data (see Appendix Table 4.6), per capita income in the United Kingdom almost doubled to $3,300, which was about 20 percent ahead of the Netherlands, 70 percent ahead of both France and Germany, and about a third higher than the United States. Between 1780 and 1870 the share of the British labor force employed in agriculture fell by half, to 23 percent, a level not reached in the United States until about 1920 or in Germany until 1950. While employment in manufacturing accounted for about one-third of the British labor force in 1870, the corresponding figure in the United States was only about one-sixth. On the other hand, by 1870 labor productivity in manufacturing was actually twice as great in the United States as in the United Kingdom.

Britain's investment rate (the ratio of investment to GDP) was also relatively low during the period from 1780 to 1913, averaging around 8 percent, and TFP growth was also relatively modest over this period, running around 1 percent per year. Craft offered a number of reasons for Britain's low rate of TFP growth. First, technological change in the United Kingdom was very uneven over this period, and productivity growth in many activities, particularly the service sectors, which constituted more than 40 percent of employment, was negligible. Second, even the most important inventions of the period such as the steam engine had a very modest impact on the sector in which they were initially used and even a smaller impact on the total economy. Third, overall productivity growth remained low during the early nineteenth century because this was long before the era of Fordism, and scale effects in British industrial productivity were not an important source of productivity growth at this time. Fourth, as a pioneer in new technology, the United Kingdom could not take advantage of catching up in total factor productivity as a source of growth, unlike the follower countries.

The American overtaking of Britain was completed by 1929 when the gap in GDP per person widened to 31 percent. In contrast, in 1870, U.S. GDP per capita was only 75 percent of the British level, despite the fact that labor productivity in American manufacturing was twice the British level in that year. The main factor for the emergence of the United States as the overall productivity leader by 1929 was the redistribution of the American labor force out of agriculture and toward manufacturing. With the widespread adoption of Fordist practices, productivity in American manufacturing really took off after this point. During the 1920s TFP growth in U.S. manufacturing averaged 5.3 percent per year, much higher than in Britain. By 1929, labor productivity in American manufacturing was 2.5 times the level in Britain (also see Broadberry, 1994a and 1994b).

Wright (1990) examined the factor content of trade in order to explain how the United States became the preeminent manufacturing nation at the turn of the twentieth century. He found that the most distinctive characteristic of U.S. manufacturing exports was their intensity in nonreproducible natural resources (such as iron ore) rather than American technological leadership in the broad sense of the term. Moreover, this relative intensity increased over time between 1880 and 1920. Furthermore, he found that this relative intensity mainly reflected greater exploitation of the United States' geological endowment rather than a greater geological endowment of these resources. Wright found that American innovation during the late nineteenth century and early twentieth century was largely driven by the specific resource environment that characterized the United States during this period.

Another view on the American "takeover" was voiced by Ehrlich (2008), who argued that human capital acquisition was the main reason why the United States overtook the United Kingdom and other European countries in the early part of the twentieth century in both aggregate and per capita GDP. In particular, he conjectured that the ascendancy of the United States as an economic superpower was due in large measure to its relatively faster rate of human capital formation. He reported evidence that the United States led other advanced countries in schooling attainment per adult population by the middle of the twentieth century, particularly at the secondary and tertiary levels. He attributed the ascendancy of the United States in terms of educational attainment to such historical factors as the Morrill Acts of 1862 and 1890, which enabled state governments to create so-called land grant universities; the high school movement of 1910 to 1940, which increased secondary school enrollment enormously; and the GI Bill (technically, the Servicemen's Readjustment Act) of 1944, which mandated the federal government to subsidize tuition and educational fess for veterans returning from World War II.

Nelson (1991) presented an interesting argument for why the American lead in terms of GDP per worker and per capita eroded over the latter half of the twentieth century, particularly after 1960 or so. He argued that the American lead after World War II stemmed from two factors – its dominance in mass production industries and in high-tech industries. The American ascendancy in mass production, in turn, stemmed from two main features. First, by the late nineteenth century, the United States had become the world's largest common market. Second, large-scale production tended to be capital intensive. High American wages and a relative scarcity of skilled labor encouraged such capital intensive production. The American dominance in high-tech industries resulted from massive investments in R&D made after World War II. By the early 1960s, R&D as a fraction of GDP was about twice as high in the United States as in European countries. However, after 1960 or so, the U.S. lead in mass production started to evaporate because of the opening of world trade in manufactured goods. It then became sensible for European and Japanese firms to rebuild their production capacity along U.S. lines. Likewise, the U.S. domination of high-tech fields also started to erode as European and Japanese companies started to mimic the United States by making very large investments in R&D (see Chapter 5 of the book for more details).

Maddison (2008) provided an insightful analysis of why the West grew faster than the rest of the world before 1820. He argued that the greater dynamism of Western Europe than Asia in particular was due to five major changes. First, in the eleventh and twelfth centuries, two important trading centers emerged in Flanders and northern Italy. These new centers provided for autonomous property rights and fostered entrepreneurship and eliminated feudal restrictions on the purchase and sale of property. Accounting developed and this helped make contracts enforceable. New financial and banking institutions emerged, providing for credit access and insurance and helping facilitate the development of risk assessment and large-scale business organizations throughout Western Europe.

The second development included the introduction of printed books in the fifteenth century, the Renaissance, the evolution of Galilean and Newtonian science, the beginnings of systematic experimentation (with Francis Bacon), and the spread of university education. Together, these forces led to a rapid advance in secular knowledge, which was a prerequisite for later technological advances.

The third was the influence of the Christian Church and marital arrangements. The Christian Church made sure that marriage was monogamous and banned concubines, divorce, and even the remarriage of widows. Inheritance was strictly limited to close family relations, and primogeniture was widely adopted, helping to break down tribal loyalties and promoting individualism. This development contrasted sharply with the extended family systems of India and China.

A fourth feature was the development of nation-states in close proximity to each other in Western Europe. This, in turn, helped to create substantial trading relations and relatively easy intellectual interchanges among the nations. Competition and innovation were thereby stimulated, as well as a sharing of technological developments, and economic gains were spread out throughout most of Western Europe.

Fifth, advances in maritime technology and the introduction of new navigation techniques revolutionized the Europeans' knowledge of world geography. The discovery of the Americas, in particular, led to the development of mercantile capitalism and colonialism around the world. The Americas were repopulated by Europeans and slaves, and substantial profits became available from trade with the New World.

4.5 Convergence in the Very Long Term

For reasons of comparability with Figure 4.1 (and Appendix Table 4.1), we return to data on the "Maddison 16." Moreover, we use Maddison's data in order to retain consistency with the earlier data. Figure 4.7 shows summary statistics and Appendix Table 4.6 shows time trends in GDP per capita from the year 1 to 2006 AD. Maddison switched from labor productivity to GDP per capita because of the difficulty of obtaining data on employment for these early years.[7] The differential between per capita income and average labor productivity reflects differences in the ratio of employment to population – that is, the employment rate. Countries with relatively large numbers of children, nonworking spouses, and old people will have, ceteris paribus, lower employment rates.

The story that emerges here is not as straightforward as for the period from 1870 to 1979. It is first of note that the leading "country" in the year 1 was Italy – that is, the Roman Empire located in now what is called "Italy." Its GDP per capita was about twice that of any of the other countries in the group. However, between the year 1 and 1000, with the breakup of the Roman Empire and the emergence of the medieval period, there were a sharp decline in Rome's per capita income and a dramatic convergence in GDP per capita among countries. The coefficient of variation fell from 0.23 in the year 1 to 0.04 in the year 1000. By the year 1500, there was again a strong divergence in per capita incomes led once again by Italy (particularly Venice). Other Western European countries including Belgium and France advanced as well, while North America and Australia remained far behind. The coefficient of variation rose to 0.29. Further divergence was in evidence from 1500 to 1700 with the emergence of mercantile capitalism in places like the Netherlands

---

[7] Sources and methods for the data series are documented in Maddison (1995, 2001, 2003, 2005, and 2007).

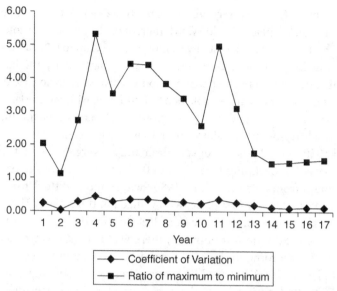

Figure 4.7. GDP per capita convergence, year 1 to 2006 (*Source*: Maddison, 2008).

and the beginnings of the Industrial Revolution in the United Kingdom. Over these years, the Netherlands took leadership in per capita income. The United Kingdom was a distant second, though it was followed closely by Italy, Belgium, and Denmark. The coefficient of variation advanced to 0.45.

With industrialization spreading to other countries in Western Europe and to the United States, there was a marked convergence in per capita income from 1700 to 1820. The Netherlands remained in first place but was now closely followed by the United Kingdom. Many other Western European countries including Austria, Belgium, Denmark, and Sweden were also experiencing a growth spurt. The coefficient of variation fell to 0.31 from 0.45.

With continuing industrialization in selected countries, the pattern reversed again from 1820 to 1870. Australia now took leadership in per capita income followed closely by the United Kingdom. Belgium pulled into third place and the United States into fourth. Austria, Switzerland, Germany, and Italy also showed large gains. The coefficient of variation increased from 0.31 to 0.35. With industrialization continuing, the years 1870 to 1890 marked another period of divergence, with the coefficient of variation rising to 0.37. Australia remained in first place, still followed by the United Kingdom, Belgium, and the United States.

The period from 1890 to 1938 was one of convergence, with strong catch-up by countries out of the original core of industrialized countries. The coefficient of variation fell sharply from 0.37 to 0.24. Switzerland took over first place and the United Kingdom second. The United States was third, while Australia faded to fourth place. World War II interrupted this process of convergence, and by 1950 the coefficient of variation was back up to 0.36, about the same level as in 1890. Both Germany and Japan, particularly the latter, showed large declines in real per capita income between 1938 and 1950. The United States was now firmly established in first place, with Switzerland close behind. The United Kingdom also lost ground. The ratio of maximum to minimum reached close to 5.0, almost back to where it was in 1700.

The period 1950 to 1980 was one of very dramatic convergence, with the coefficient of variation declining from 0.36 to 0.12 and the ratio of maximum to minimum from 4.98 to 1.45. By 1980 Switzerland and the United States were in a virtual tie for first place, with Canada in third place. There was virtually no additional convergence from 1980 to 2006. Indeed, according to the ratio of maximum to minimum, there was a slight divergence, from 1.45 to 1.57. According to the Maddison data, the United States was firmly in first place in 2006, followed by Norway in second. Looking over the whole 1870 to 2006 period, we find a very strong negative correlation, –0.94, between the growth in per capita income by country and its initial (1870) level of per capita income. This compares with a correlation coefficient of –0.93 between the growth in average labor productivity by country between 1870 and 1979 and the country's 1870 level of productivity for the same sixteen countries (see Appendix Table 4.1).

As is apparent, over the very long term (and even the more recent long term) there was no clear pattern of convergence even among this select sample of countries. Indeed, the very long term was as much marked by divergence in per capita income levels as in convergence of per capita income. Divergence characterized the periods 1000–1700, 1820–90, and 1938–50; convergence occurred during the 1700–1820, 1890–1938, and 1950–80 periods; and no clear trend occurred during the 1980–2006 period.

4.6 Related Studies on Convergence in the Very Long Term

Fogel (1999) pushed the clock back to 9000 BC and recorded mankind's early developments of technology in relation to population growth. The year 9000 BC is widely regarded as the approximate beginning of the first agricultural revolution. In 6000 BC was the beginning of pottery, and at around 4500 BC the invention of the plow occurred, greatly enhancing productivity in agriculture. The first irrigation works arose shortly after (maybe around 4200 BC), and the first cities appeared to emerge around 4000 BC. The beginnings of metallurgy are usually dated around 3200 BC, and writing first appeared around 3000 BC. Mathematics first started 1000 years later (around 2000

BC). Despite these technological developments, population grew slowly. The real breakthrough occurred not until 1700 AD or so with the second agricultural revolution. This was much more dramatic than the first (in 9000 BC) and was associated with a tremendous increase in population.

Galor and Weil (2000) considered the long transition process from thousands of years of Malthusian stagnation through the demographic transition to modern growth as documented by Fogel (1999). They developed a unified growth model that attempted to capture the transition among three regimes that have historically characterized economic development. The first is the Malthusian regime, which is characterized by slow technological progress and population growth high enough to prevent any sustained increase in income per capita. The second is what they called the post-Malthusian period, in which technological progress increases relative to the first period and population continues to increase but not enough to absorb the full increase of output growth. The third (and final) one is the modern growth regime. This is entered when a demographic transition that reverses the positive association between income growth and population growth occurs. The modern regime is characterized by sustained income growth and lowered population growth.

During the Malthusian regime that characterized almost all of human history until the last few centuries, both technological progress and population growth were extremely slow, particularly by modern standards. Moreover, in contrast to the modern period, there was a positive relationship between population growth and income per capita. During the post-Malthusian regime, the positive association between population growth and income per capita continued, but output grew enough so that per capita income rose during this period. Finally, in the modern growth regime, the relationship between per capita income and population growth reversed and became negative. Today, for example, the highest rates of population growth are found in the poorest countries, and many advanced nations have population growth rates close to zero.

The model itself is rather complex and a full treatment is beyond the scope of this book. However, the central features are as follows: First, while most models of the demographic transition focus on the effect of a high income *level* in inducing parents to switch to giving birth to fewer but "higher-quality" children, the Galor-Weil model puts the emphasis on *technological progress*. In particular, in their model, the reduction in the birth rate is seen as a response to technological change. Technological change raises the rate of return to education and thus provides an incentive to parents to trade off quality for quantity of children.

This argument was first developed by Schultz (1964). Looking at the agriculture sector in historical terms, he argued that when technology in the sector is constant over long periods, farmers will learn to use their resources efficiently. Children likewise will acquire knowledge about farming directly from their parents and formal schooling will add little of economic value. However, when technology is changing over time, knowledge gained from the parents will have less value. New technology will create a demand for the ability to evaluate and analyze new possibilities about production techniques, and this, in turn, will raise the return to schooling. One piece of evidence for this is from Foster and Rosenzweig (1996), who found that the so-called green revolution in India raised the return to education and led to an increase in school enrollment rates. Likewise, the large increase in schooling levels in Europe over the nineteenth century was likely a response to the new technology that was being developed on the continent. Galor and Weil maintain that new technology is most likely to be skill biased in the short run.

Second, Galor and Weil argue that high levels of human capital are, in turn, more likely to advance the technological frontier or increase the rate at which advanced technologies are adopted. Thus, higher levels of education will lead to a higher rate of technological progress. Third, with the level of education held constant, the speed of technological change is assumed to be a positive function of the overall size of the population. Higher population will generate a larger supply, larger demand, and more rapid rate of diffusion of new technology. This part of the model is crucial to explain the takeoff from the Malthusian regime into the post-Malthusian regime.

Fourth, it is assumed that the economy is characterized by the existence of a fixed factor or production, land, and a subsistence level of consumption, below which individuals cannot survive. If technological change allows output per worker to exceed this subsistence level, then population will rise, the land-to-labor ratio will fall, and, without further technological change, wages will be back to the subsistence level of consumption. Without technological change, income per capita is self-equilibrating and remains in the "Malthusian trap." However, sustained technological change can overcome the offsetting effect of population growth and may lead to sustained income growth.

The Malthusian "steady state" can remain stable over very long periods but it can then vanish endogenously in the long run. During the Malthusian period, output per capita remains stationary. Technology progresses very slowly and is reflected in proportional increases in both output and population. Shocks to the ratio of land to labor lead to temporary changes in the real wage and fertility, but these in turn drive per capita income back to its stationary equilibrium level. Because of slow technological change, the return to education is low and parents have little incentive to substitute child quality for the number of children.

In the long run, however, the Malthusian trap vanishes because of the impact of population size on the rate of technological change. When population size reaches a certain threshold, the resulting rate of technological progress is sufficiently high to induce parents to provide their children with some education. At this point, a "virtuous cycle" develops in which higher human capital raises the rate of technological progress, which, in turn, increases the value of human capital.

Increased technological progress at first has two effects on population growth. First, the improved technology eases households' budget constraint and allows families to spend more money on raising children. Second, it induces a reallocation of these added resources toward human capital acquisition. During the post-Malthusian period, the first effect dominates and, as a result, population growth rises. However, eventually, the greater rate of technological change that results from the increase in the level of human capital triggers a demographic transition: Wages and the return to human capital continue to rise, the shift away from child quantity to child quality becomes even more significant, and the rate of population growth finally declines. In the modern growth regime, technology and output per capita continue to increase rapidly while the rate of population growth remains moderate.[8]

Some evidence on these three regimes was provided in Goodfriend and McDermott (1995, p. 117) on the basis of data from Maddison (1982), as follows:

Average Annual Growth Rates

Period	Population	Per Capita GDP
500–1500	0.1	0.0
1500–1700	0.2	0.1
1700–1820	0.4	0.2
1820–1980	0.9	1.6

The period from year 500 to 1500 corresponds to the Malthusian period, when population growth was very low and productivity growth as measured by per capita income was essentially zero. The next period, from 1500 to 1700, corresponds to the post-Malthusian era. Population growth doubled to 0.2 percent per year and per capita GDP finally began to grow, though only at a minuscule 0.1 percent per year. The years from 1700 to 1820 mark the beginning of the modern growth era. Annual population growth picked up to 0.4 percent and annual per capita GDP growth to 0.2 percent. Finally, from 1820 to 1980, we enter the period of the modern growth era proper, with population growing at 0.9 percent per year and GDP per capita at 1.6 percent per year.

[8]   Related models on very long term economic growth were also developed by Kremer (1993) and Goodfriend and McDermott (1995).

4.7 Summary and Concluding Remarks

Chapter 4 examined long-term trends in productivity among (today's) advanced industrial countries. This is important for two reasons. First, it helps to put the postwar performance of OECD countries in historical perspective. Second, it also helps to isolate some of the salient factors that are responsible for productivity performance.

Explanations of the productivity catch-up almost all involve the "advantages of backwardness," a term first coined by Gerschenkron (1952). The basic idea is that much of the catch-up can be explained by the diffusion of technical knowledge from the leading economies to the more backward ones. Through the transfer of new technology, leading and following countries learn the latest productive techniques from one another, but virtually by definition the follower countries have more to learn from the leaders than the leaders have to learn from them (the advantages of backwardness). This mechanism has two implications: First, it means that those countries that lag somewhat behind the leaders can be expected systematically to move toward the productivity level of the leaders. Second, the mechanism undermines itself automatically as follower countries gradually eliminate the difference between their own performance and that of the countries that were ahead of them.

Section 4.2 of this chapter began with a review of the evidence on long-term convergence in labor productivity and per capita income. Several of these studies, including Abramovitz (1986), Baumol (1986), and Baumol, Blackman, and Wolff (1989), made use of data provided in Maddison (1982) on output and employment for sixteen OECD countries covering the period from 1870 to 1979.

Strong evidence of convergence in labor productivity levels was found among this group of countries. On the basis of the coefficient of variation, we found a more or less steady pattern of productivity convergence among these sixteen countries. Between 1870 and 1938, the coefficient of variation fell almost by half. However, as a result of the destruction of capital stock in many European countries and in Japan during World War II, the coefficient of variation in 1950 climbed back to a level just below its 1890 level. There followed a remarkable degree of convergence from 1950 to 1979, with the coefficient of variation falling by three-fifths. Moreover, the overall correlation coefficient between 1870 productivity levels and the annual rate of productivity growth from 1870 to 1979 is –0.93.

Section 4.3 of this chapter presented the analogous evidence on long-term convergence in total factor productivity (TFP) based on Wolff (1991a). The sample consists of Germany, Italy, Japan, the United

Kingdom, and the United States. Factor shares are based on the average ratio of employee compensation to national income for the United Kingdom and the United States for the 1880–1979 period. According to the coefficient of variation, there was only moderate convergence in TFP between 1880 and 1929. This is similar to labor productivity movements among the five countries. The Depression years did cause some convergence in TFP levels, followed by a sharp increase in dispersion between 1938 and 1950. However, over the postwar period, the coefficient of variation fell by more than two-thirds.

There are very few long-term series on many of the explanatory variables of interest (such as education). As a result, the analysis focuses on three sets of factors: (1) the catch-up effect, (2) the role of capital formation, and (3) the vintage effect. A regression analysis was employed to analyze the long-term data in Wolff (1991a). A decomposition, based on these regression results, indicated that for the 1880–1990 period, of the 1.5 percent per year average growth in labor productivity, 0.3 percentage point could be attributed to the catch-up effect, 0.6 percentage point to the growth in the capital-labor ratio, 0.02 percentage point to the vintage effect (the decline in the average age of the capital stock), and 0.5 percentage point to general technological advance (with 0.04 point unexplained).

Section 4.5 considered the evidence on convergence in per capita income in the very long term (two millennia) on the basis of sixteen OECD countries (the "Maddison 16"). Maddison (2008) showed time trends in GDP per capita from the year 1 to 2006 AD (Figure 4.7). The story that emerges here is not as straightforward as for the period from 1870 to 1979. It is first of note that the leading "country" in the year 1 was Italy – that is, the Roman Empire. However, between the year 1 and 1000, with the breakup of the Roman Empire and the emergence of the medieval period, there were a sharp decline in Rome's per capita income and a dramatic convergence in GDP per capita among countries. By the year 1500, there was again a strong divergence in per capita incomes led once again by Italy (particularly Venice). Further divergence was in evidence from 1500 to 1700 with the emergence of mercantile capitalism in places such as the Netherlands and the beginnings of the Industrial Revolution in the United Kingdom. With industrialization spreading to other countries in Western Europe and to the United States, there was a marked convergence in per capita income from 1700 to 1820. With continuing industrialization in selected countries, the pattern reversed again from 1820 to 1870, with rising dispersion in per capita income. The story after that is similar to the one for labor productivity described previously. As is apparent, over the very long term (and even the more recent long term) there was no clear pattern of convergence even among this select sample of countries.

Several studies discussed in Section 4.6 considered the very long-term, going back as far as 9000 BC. Galor and Weil (2000), for example, considered the long transition process from thousands of years of Malthusian stagnation through the demographic transition to modern growth. They developed a unified growth model that attempted to capture the transition among three regimes that have historically characterized economic development. The first is the Malthusian regime, which is characterized by slow technological progress and high enough population growth to prevent any sustained increase in income per capita. The second is what they called the post-Malthusian period, in which technological progress increases relative to the first period and population continues to increase but not enough to absorb the full increase of output growth. The third (and final) one is the modern growth regime. This is entered when a demographic transition occurs to reverse the positive association between income growth and population growth. The modern regime is characterized by sustained income growth and lowered population growth.

I think that additional work on growth over the very long terms might be a fruitful research objective. Though several models of this process have now been developed, empirical evidence in support of them has been rather scanty to date. This is particularly so for the so-called demographic transition and the factors behind this process.

APPENDIX TO CHAPTER 4
REGRESSION ANALYSIS OF LONG-TERM LABOR
PRODUCTIVITY TRENDS

As developed in Wolff (1996a), we first distinguish between capital stock measured in natural units (constant prices), K, and capital stock measured in "efficiency units," K^*. Suppose that this year's capital investment is s percent more productive than last year's, and the parameter s is constant over time. Then, K^* measured in today's efficiency units is approximately given by:

$$K^* = Ke^{-s\bar{A}} \qquad (A.4.1)$$

where $\bar{A}$ is the average age of the capital stock (see Nelson, 1964, for more details).[9] Assuming a Cobb-Douglas aggregate production function, with capital measured in efficiency units, we then obtain for country h:

$$\mathrm{Ln}\, Y^h_t = \zeta^h + \alpha^h \mathrm{Ln}\, L^h_t + (1 - \alpha^h)\, \mathrm{Ln}\, K^h_t - (1 - \alpha^h)\, s^h \bar{A}^h_t \qquad (A.4.2)$$

From (A.4.1) and (A.4.2) and with the added assumption that s is equal across countries, it follows that

$$\pi^h_t = \rho^h_t + (1 - \alpha^h)\, d\, \mathrm{Ln}\, k^h_t\, /\, dt - (1 - \alpha^h) s \Lambda_{ht} \qquad (A.4.3)$$

where $\Lambda_{ht} \equiv d\, \bar{A}_{ht}\, /\, dt$, the rate of change in the age of the capital stock in country h.

From (A.3.3), the basic estimating form is:

$$LPRGRT^h_t = b_0 + b_1 RELTFP^h_t + b_2 KLGRT^h_t + b_3 AGEKCHG^h_t + \varepsilon^h_t$$
$$(A.4.4)$$

where $LPRGRT^h_t$ is country h's annual rate of labor productivity growth, $RELTFP^h_t$ is country h's (Translog) TFP relative to the United States at the start of each period, $KLGRT^h_t$ is country h's rate of capital-labor growth, $AGEKCHG^h_t$ is the (annual) change in the average age of country h's capital stock, and ε^h_t is a stochastic error term. The RELTFP term is included as a crude index of technology gap with respect to the United States and hence of the catch-up potential. Where appropriate, the total capital stock is also divided into structures (S) and machinery and equipment (ME).

---

[9]　This formulation is actually only an approximation to the average age of the capital stock. See Gittleman, ten Raa, and Wolff (2006) for more details.

157

Column 1 of Appendix Table 4.5 shows the results based on the Maddison (1982) data. The catch-up effect (the initial relative TFP level) is significant at the 1 percent level in explaining labor productivity growth and its coefficient has the expected negative sign. The coefficient value of RELTFP is –0.04. Thus a 50 percent difference between a country's initial TFP and that of the United States is associated with about a 2 percentage point per year (half of –0.04) growth in labor productivity. Capital-labor growth is also significant at the 1 percent level and has the expected positive sign. A 1 percentage point increase in capital-labor growth is associated with a 0.4 percentage point increase in labor productivity growth. The constant term is 0.005, suggesting an average growth of TFP of about one-half a percentage point per year.

The change in the average age of the capital stock has the expected negative sign and the variable is significant at 5 percent. The effect is surprisingly large: a one year reduction in the average age of capital is associated with about a *1* percentage point increase in labor productivity growth.

Results based on the Maddison (1991, 1993a) data are shown in column 2 of Appendix Table 4.5. The catch-up effect, as before, has the expected negative sign and is significant at the 1 percent level, though the coefficient value is slightly smaller in absolute terms. Capital growth has the expected positive sign and remains significant at the 1 percent level, though, again, the coefficient value is slightly smaller. The vintage effect is now significant at the 1 percent level and is considerably stronger in the new sample.

The constant term from the 1991 and 1993 Maddison data is 0.011, compared to 0.005 from the 1982 Maddison data. This suggests a "natural" rate of technological advance of 1.1 percent per year, rather than 0.5 percent per year. The difference, however, may simply reflect the fact that the observations from the Maddison (1991, 1993a) data are more heavily weighted toward the postwar period. The goodness of fit, as measured by the adjusted-R^2 statistic and the standard error of the regression, is higher on the basis of the Maddison (1991, 1993a) data. This, again, may reflect the fact the observations are primarily from the postwar period.

Appendix Table 4.1. Labor Productivity (LP) in 16 Advanced Countries, 1870–1979 (GDP in 1970 U.S. Relative Prices ($) per Man-Hour)

Country	1870	1880	1890	1900	1913	1929	1938	1950	1960	1970	1979	Annual Growth Rate [%]	Ratio of 1979/1870
Australia	130	156	162	149	170	216	234	305	402	502	648	1.47	5.0
Austria	43	50	61	74	90	101	103	125	221	399	589	2.40	13.7
Belgium	74	89	102	112	126	168	184	211	289	471	731	2.10	9.9
Canada	61	76	86	102	145	176	175	333	454	596	703	2.24	11.5
Denmark	44	51	62	75	100	151	157	182	245	400	527	2.28	12.0
Finland	29		37		71	97	115	148	220	416	526	2.66	18.1
France	42	53	58	71	90	131	169	185	287	492	711	2.60	16.9
Germany (West)	43	50	62	79	95	119	147	140	272	462	693	2.55	16.1
Italy	44	45	47	53	72	98	128	137	210	410	583	2.37	13.3
Japan	17		24		37	64	87	59	103	279	439	2.98	25.8
Netherlands	74		97	107	123	182	180	227	317	519	748	2.12	10.1
Norway	40	46	56	63	82	128	162	203	304	478	665	2.58	16.6
Sweden	31	37	45	59	83	122	155	234	330	533	671	2.82	21.6
Switzerland	55		74		101	168	184	221	298	431	512	2.05	9.3
United Kingdom	80	94	106	120	135	170	184	240	299	427	548	1.77	6.9
United States	70	88	106	129	167	245	262	425	541	696	828	2.27	11.8
Summary Statistics													
Mean	54.8	69.6	74.1	91.8	105.4	146.0	164.1	210.9	299.5	469.4	632.6		
Standard Deviation	26.9	33.6	34.4	30.0	36.3	47.5	44.6	88.6	102.3	93.5	104.8		

(continued)

159

Appendix Table 4.1. (*continued*)

Country	1870	1880	1890	1900	1913	1929	1938	1950	1960	1970	1979	Annual Growth Rate [%]	Ratio of 1979/1870
(Max. – Min.)/ Average	2.06	1.71	1.86	1.05	1.26	1.24	1.07	1.74	1.46	0.89	0.61		
Coeff. of Variation	0.49	0.48	0.46	0.33	0.34	0.33	0.27	0.42	0.34	0.20	0.17		
Arithmetic Average of 15 Countries													
(Excluding USA)	0.77	0.77	0.68	0.69	0.61	0.57	0.60	0.46	0.52	0.65	0.75		
Ratio of Maximum to Minimum	7.65	4.22	6.75	2.81	4.59	3.83	3.01	7.20	5.25	2.49	1.89		
Correlation of Productivity Growth Rate with 1870 LP							-0.93						

Source: Maddison (1982), table C10, p. 212. Labor productivity is computed as the ratio of GDP in 1970 U.S. relative prices to hours worked. Missing values are estimated by geometric interpolation.

Appendix Table 4.2. *Total Factor Productivity (TFP) for the Group of Seven, Selected Years, 1880–1979 (Index Numbers, U.S., 1950 = 100)*

Country	Year							Annual	
	1880	1890	1913	1929	1938	1950	1979	Percentage Growth 1880–1979	TFP Ratio 1979/1880
Canada				50	49	86	123		
France						54	131		
Germany	18	22	31	38	46	43	112	1.86	6.3
Italy	17	18	26	34	42	45	121	1.98	7.1
Japan	8	9	14	24	32	21	101	2.58	12.9
UK	32	36	44	53	57	72	115	1.29	3.6
USA	30	36	49	65	65	100	138	1.53	4.6
5 Country Statistics									
(Max. – Min.)/ Average	1.16	1.11	1.06	0.96	0.68	1.40	0.31		
Coefficient of Variation	0.43	0.43	0.38	0.34	0.24	0.48	0.10		
Avg. (excl. US)/ U.S. Level	0.62	0.59	0.59	0.57	0.69	0.45	0.81		
7 Country Statistics									
(Max. – Min.)/ Average						0.79	0.27		
Coefficient of Variation						0.42	0.09		
Avg. (excl. U.S.)/ U.S. Level						0.54	0.85		

Source: Wolff (1991), table 1. TFP levels are computed according to equation (4.1) and standardized so that U.S. TFP equals unity in 1950. Output is measured by GDP, labor by hours worked, and capital by gross nonresidential fixed plant and equipment (net for Germany). Factor shares are based on the average ratio of employee compensation to national income for the UK and the U.S. over the 1870–1979 period.

Appendix Table 4.3. *Basic Statistics on Labor Productivity, TFP, and Capital-Labor Growth, and Average Age of Capital Stock, Drawn from Maddison (1982), 1880–1979*

	1880–1890	1890–1900	1900–1913	1913–1929	1929–1938	1938–1950	1950–1960	1960–1970	1970–1979
A. Average Annual Rate of Labor Productivity Growth (%)									
Canada	1.24	1.71	2.71	1.21	-0.06	5.36	3.10	2.72	1.83
France	0.90	2.02	1.82	2.35	2.83	0.75	4.39	5.39	4.09
Germany	2.15	2.42	1.42	1.41	2.35	-0.41	6.64	5.30	4.51
Italy	0.43	1.20	2.36	1.93	2.97	0.57	4.27	6.69	3.91
Japan	1.72	1.88	1.88	3.42	3.41	-3.24	5.57	9.96	5.04
UK	1.20	1.24	0.91	1.44	0.88	2.21	2.20	3.56	2.77
USA	1.86	1.96	1.99	2.40	0.75	4.03	2.41	2.52	1.93
Arithmetic Average									
5-Country Sample[a]	1.47	1.74	1.71	2.12	2.07	0.63	4.22	5.61	3.63
7-Country Sample	1.36	1.78	1.87	2.02	1.87	1.33	4.08	5.16	3.44
B. Average Annual Rate of TFP Growth (%)									
Canada					-0.45	4.49	1.48	1.74	0.88
France							3.34	3.40	2.06
Germany	1.27	1.53	0.67	1.02	2.26	-0.78	5.07	2.58	1.91
Italy	0.58	0.60	1.29	0.86	1.19	0.26	3.16	3.93	1.66
Japan	1.38	1.14	0.75	1.72	2.45	-3.67	4.72	5.61	1.58
UK	1.11	0.86	0.42	0.85	0.79	1.62	1.41	1.65	1.16
USA	1.30	0.43	0.93	1.54	-0.23	3.64	1.33	1.49	1.10
Arithmetic Average (%)									
5-Country Sample[a]	0.89	0.91	0.81	1.20	1.29	0.21	3.14	3.05	1.48
7-Country Sample							2.93	2.92	1.48

C. Average Annual Rate of Growth of Gross Capital to Hours (%)

Canada					0.95	2.17	4.01	2.44	2.37
France							2.62	4.95	5.04
Germany	2.20	2.21	1.87	0.95	0.22	0.92	3.90	6.74	6.44
Italy	2.51	1.48	2.65	2.64	4.41	0.75	2.76	6.85	5.60
Japan	0.85	1.85	2.81	4.23	2.38	1.08	2.11	10.82	8.58
UK	0.23	0.94	1.21	1.47	0.23	1.47	1.96	4.75	4.01
USA	1.40	3.81	2.62	2.12	2.42	0.98	2.68	2.54	2.05
Arithmetic Average (%)									
5-Country Sample[a]	1.44	2.06	2.23	2.28	1.93	1.04	2.68	6.34	5.34
7-Country Sample							2.86	5.58	4.87

D. Average Age of Capital Stock at the Beginning of the Period (in years)[b]

Germany	23.0	21.9	20.4	20.0	27.3	28.7	30.9	19.4	15.3	
Italy	24.3	22.9	24.2	21.9	22.8	21.5	25.9	21.2	15.8	
Japan	24.6	25.9	24.3	20.5	16.9	18.4	23.4	19.6	10.0	
UK	25.6	27.1	27.0	25.7	28.5	30.1	31.4	24.8	19.2	
USA	19.5	18.4	15.8	16.5	20.3	25.5	26.7	22.7	17.3	
Arithmetic Average (in years)										
5-Country Sample[a]	23.4	23.2	22.3	20.9	23.2	24.8	27.7	21.5	16.0	15.5

Notes: Output is measured by GDP, labor by hours worked, and capital by gross nonresidential fixed plant and equipment (net for Germany).

Factor shares are based on the average ratio of employee compensation to national income for the UK and the U.S. over the 1880–1979 period

TFP levels are computed according to equation (4.1) and standardized so that TFP in the U.S. is equal to unity in 1950. See the text for data sources and methods

[a] Germany, Italy, Japan, UK, and U.S.

[b] Average age is estimated from capital stock data for 1870, 1880, 1890, 1900, 1913, 1929, 1938, 1950, 1960, 1970, and 1979. It is assumed that the service life is 50 years and that the average age of the capital stock was 25 years in 1870

Appendix Table 4.4. *Basic Statistics on Labor Productivity, TFP, and Capital-Labor Growth, and Average Age of Capital Stock, Drawn from Maddison (1991, 1993b), 1890–1989*

	1890–1913	1913–1929	1929–1938	1938–1950	1950–1960	1960–1973	1973–1979	1979–1989
A. Average Annual Rate of Labor Productivity Growth (%)								
France	1.74	2.35	2.82	0.64	4.46	5.15	3.73	2.66
Germany	1.85	1.37	2.36	-0.39	6.65	5.09	3.62	2.03
Japan	1.74	3.38	2.34	-0.67	5.54	8.70	3.14	3.21
Netherlands	1.13	2.84	-0.12	0.32	4.08	5.12	3.40	1.73
UK	1.04	1.44	0.92	2.22	2.27	3.82	2.34	1.86
USA	2.20	2.40	1.42	3.14	2.44	2.42	0.76	1.35
Arithmetic Average	1.62	2.30	1.62	0.88	4.24	5.05	2.83	2.14
B. Average Annual Rate of TFP Growth (%)								
France					2.93	2.72	1.11	0.95
Germany					4.82	2.09	1.60	0.60
Japan	0.84	1.49	1.42	-1.65	4.92	4.01	0.11	1.21
Netherlands					2.64	3.01	1.76	0.57
UK	0.52	0.54	0.43	1.63	0.50	1.47	0.64	0.52
USA	0.73	1.49	0.19	3.14	1.56	1.65	0.00	0.75
Arithmetic Average					2.89	2.49	0.87	0.77

C. Average Annual Rate of Growth of Gross Capital to Hours (%)

France				2.22	3.80	6.03	6.49	4.24
Germany					4.53	7.46	5.02	3.55
Japan		4.71	2.27	2.43	1.53	11.65	7.54	4.97
Netherlands					3.58	5.23	4.05	2.90
UK	1.29	2.24	1.22	1.49	4.41	5.83	4.22	3.32
USA	3.65	2.26	3.06	0.01	2.18	1.91	1.89	1.50
Arithmetic Average					3.34	6.35	4.87	3.41

D. Average Age of Capital Stock at the Beginning of the Period (in years)

France					17.3	14.8	9.8	9.7	11.6
Germany				17.6	16.3	12.4	10.4	11.0	13.3
Japan			11.7	11.2	12.1	11.1	7.7	8.6	10.4
Netherlands					18.0	15.1	11.3	11.5	13.9
UK	15.9	15.1	13.9	13.2	12.6	10.9	9.7	10.2	11.8
USA	14.2	13.7	15.1	17.3	16.1	14.6	12.4	12.8	13.6
Arithmetic Average					15.4	13.1	10.2	10.6	12.5

Note: Output is measured by GDP (1985 US$), labor by hours worked, and capital by gross nonresidential fixed plant (structures) and machinery and equipment. Factor shares are based on the average ratio of employee compensation to national income for the UK and the U.S. over the 1890–1987 period. TFP levels are computed according to equation (4.1) and standardized so that TFP in the U.S. is equal to unity in 1950

Appendix Table 4.5. *Regression of Annual Labor Productivity Growth (LPGRT) on Relative TFP Level, Capital-Labor Growth, and the Change in the Average Age of Capital*

Independent Variables	Maddison (1982) Data[a] (1)	Maddison (1991, 1993) Data[b] (2)
Constant	0.005	0.011**
	(1.80)	(3.20)
RELTFP	-0.039**	-0.032**
	(2.94)	(2.98)
KLGRT	0.428**	0.392**
	(4.21)	(3.76)
AGEKCHG	-0.0138*	-0.0304**
	(2.05)	(3.98)
R^2	0.72	0.81
Adjusted R^2	0.70	0.78
Standard Error	0.012	0.009
Sample Size	45	34
Degrees of Freedom	41	28

Notes: t-ratios are shown in parentheses below the coefficient estimate. Key:

RELTFP: percentage difference of country's TFP from U.S. TFP at the beginning of the period;

KLGRT: country's annual rate of capital-labor growth;

AGEKCHG: annualized change in the average age of country's capital stock over the period

[a] Observations are for Germany, Italy, Japan, the UK, and the U.S. for nine periods: 1880–90, 1890–1900, 1900–13, 1913–29, 1929–38, 1938–50, 1950–60, 1960–70, and 1970–79

[b] Observations are for the UK and the U.S. for eight periods: 1890–1913, 1913–29, 1929–38, 1938–50, 1950–60, 1960–73, 1973–9, and 1979–89; Japan, for 1929–38, 1938–50, 1950–60, 1960–73, 1973–9, and 1979–89; and France, Germany, and the Netherlands for 1950–60, 1960–73, 1973–9, and 1979–89

* significant at the 5 percent level

** significant at the 1 percent level

Appendix Table 4.6. GDP per Capita in 16 Advanced Countries, Year 1 to 2006 (1990 International Geary-Khamis Dollars)

Country	1	1000	1500	1700	1820	1870	1890	1913
Australia	400	400	400	400	518	3,273	4,458	5,157
Austria	425	425	707	993	1,218	1,863	2,443	3,465
Belgium	450	425	875	1,144	1,319	2,692	3,428	4,220
Canada	400	400	400	430	904	1,695	2,378	4,447
Denmark	400	400	738	1,039	1,274	2,003	2,523	3,912
Finland	400	400	453	638	781	1,140	1,381	2,111
France	473	425	727	910	1,135	1,876	2,376	3,485
Germany	408	410	688	910	1,077	1,839	2,428	3,648
Italy	809	450	1,100	1,100	1,117	1,499	1,667	2,564
Japan	400	425	500	570	669	737	1,012	1,387
Netherlands	425	425	761	2,130	1,838	2,757	3,323	4,049
Norway	400	400	610	722	801	1,360	1,709	2,447
Sweden	400	400	695	977	1,198	1,662	2,086	3,096
Switzerland	425	410	632	890	1,090	2,102	3,182	4,266
United Kingdom	400	400	714	1,250	1,706	3,190	4,009	4,921
United States	400	400	400	527	1,257	2,445	3,392	5,301
Summary Statistics								
Coefficient of Variation	0.23	0.04	0.29	0.45	0.31	0.35	0.37	0.31
Ratio of Maximum to Minimum	2.02	1.13	2.75	5.33	3.55	4.44	4.41	3.82

Appendix Table 4.6. (continued)

Country	1929	1938	1950	1960	1970	1980	1990	2000	2006	Annual Growth Rate, 1870–2006 [%]
Australia	5,263	5,886	7,412	8,791	12,024	14,412	17,106	21,605	24,614	1.48
Austria	3,699	3,559	3,706	6,519	9,747	13,759	16,895	20,691	22,742	1.84
Belgium	5,054	4,832	5,462	6,952	10,611	14,467	17,197	20,656	22,729	1.57
Canada	5,065	4,546	7,291	8,753	12,050	16,176	18,872	22,360	24,618	1.97
Denmark	5,075	5,762	6,943	8,812	12,686	15,227	18,452	22,975	24,898	1.85
Finland	2,717	3,589	4,253	6,230	9,577	12,949	16,866	19,770	23,241	2.22
France	4,710	4,466	5,271	7,546	11,664	15,106	18,093	21,025	23,691	1.86
Germany	4,051	4,994	3,881	7,705	10,839	14,114	15,929	18,944	19,993	1.75
Italy	3,093	3,316	3,502	5,916	9,719	13,149	16,313	18,774	19,802	1.90
Japan	2,026	2,449	1,921	3,986	9,714	13,428	18,789	20,742	22,471	2.51
Netherlands	5,689	5,250	5,996	8,287	11,967	14,705	17,262	22,161	23,388	1.57
Norway	3,387	4,262	5,430	7,204	10,027	15,076	18,466	25,102	27,867	2.22
Sweden	3,869	4,725	6,739	8,688	12,716	14,937	17,609	20,710	24,204	1.97
Switzerland	6,332	6,390	9,064	12,457	16,904	18,779	21,487	22,475	23,862	1.79
United Kingdom	5,503	6,266	6,939	8,645	10,767	12,931	16,430	20,353	23,013	1.45
United States	6,899	6,126	9,561	11,328	15,030	18,577	23,201	28,449	31,049	1.87
Summary Statistics										
Coefficient of Variation	0.30	0.24	0.36	0.25	0.18	0.12	0.11	0.11	0.11	
Ratio of Maximum to Minimum	3.41	2.61	4.98	3.12	1.77	1.45	1.46	1.52	1.57	

Source: Angus Maddison, Statistics on World Population, GDP and Per Capita GDP, 1–2006 AD (September 2008) available at: www.ggdc.net/maddison/horizontal_file_09–2008.

5

Postwar Record on Productivity Performance on the Aggregate Level among the Advanced Industrial Countries

5.1 Introduction

The term "aggregate convergence" refers to the gradual diminution of differences in productivity levels for the overall economy of countries over time. Explanations of the productivity catch-up almost all involve the so-called advantages of backwardness or Gerschenkron effect, by which it is meant that much of the catch-up can be explained by the diffusion of technical knowledge from the leading economies to the more backward ones (see Gerschenkron, 1952, and Kuznets, 1973, for example). From this view, technological progress operates through a mechanism that enables countries whose level of productivity is behind (but not too far behind) that of the leading country(ies) to catch up. Through the constant transfer of knowledge, countries learn about the latest technology from one another, but virtually by definition the followers have more to learn from the leaders than the leaders have to learn from the laggards. On the other hand, those countries that are so far behind the leaders that it is impractical for them to profit substantially from the leaders' knowledge will generally not be able to participate in the convergence process at all, and many such economies will find themselves falling even further behind.

Two noted papers looked at the process of conditional convergence – Barro (1991), and Mankiw, Romer, and Weil (1992). Like Baumol, Blackman, and Wolff (1989), the authors considered a wide range of factors, including investment, education, trade, government spending, and political structure. They found that the investment rate (the ratio of investment to GDP) had a positive and significant effect on the rate of growth of GDP per capita among countries at all levels of development. Another critical factor was education. The two studies showed that the quantity of education provided by an economy to its inhabitants (as measured by school enrollment rates) was another major influence determining the rate of growth of per capita income among a wide range of countries.

Other factors that may be directly relevant to the international transfer of technology are the extent of international trade and the pattern of trade. It is generally argued that trade is a mechanism for the transmission of information concerning new technologies and products. For example, imports of computers may revolutionize the production technology of importing industries. Also, the exposure to new products may induce local competitors to imitate. Competition in export markets may lead to the exposure to new foreign products; it may also lead to more rapid developments of new technology in industries competing in export markets. The results showed that the shares of both imports and exports in GDP were generally statistically significant as determinants of GDP per capita growth, though the import effect was somewhat stronger than the export effect.

Wolff (1991a) considered whether there are positive interactions between capital accumulation and technological advance. It is likely that substantial capital accumulation is necessary to put new inventions into practice and to effect their widespread employment. This association is often referred to as the "embodiment effect," since it implies that at least some technological innovation is embodied in capital. It is also consistent with the "vintage effect," which states that new capital is more productive than old capital per (constant) dollar of expenditure. If the capital stock data do not correct for vintage effects, then a positive correlation should be observed between the rate of technological gain and the change in the growth rate of capital. This study found strong evidence of the existence of this effect among the G-7 countries (Canada, France, Germany, Italy, Japan, the United Kingdom, and the United States) over the period 1880–1979.

A somewhat different but related issue was raised by Dollar and Wolff (1988) and, later, Dollar and Wolff (1993), who analyzed changes in productivity levels on the industry level for a sample of thirteen OECD countries covering the period from 1960 to 1986. They found strong evidence of convergence on the economywide level in GDP per worker, capital-labor ratio, aggregate labor productivity and total factor productivity (TFP), and average real wages. They also examined the same variables for nine manufacturing sectors and found that, except for real wages, convergence at the industry level was generally not as strong as that for the economy as a whole. In fact, aggregate convergence in labor productivity was to some extent attributable to the modest labor productivity leads that different countries enjoyed in different industries. The results were similar for TFP and capital intensity.

In this chapter, I review the studies that have focused on convergence among the industrialized (OECD) countries of the world. I focus here almost exclusively on the postwar period (that is, after World War II) and on the "club" or rich countries. In contrast, in Chapter 4, I investigated productivity convergence over a longer period (indeed, stretching back to the year 1) and for a larger group of nations. Moreover, in this chapter, I look into some of the mechanisms accounting for productivity convergence in this group of counties. This feature provides the rationale for concentrating on the postwar period, since data for the pertinent explanatory variables are generally available only for the period after the Second World War.

In Section 5.2, I present descriptive statistics on trends in output per worker over the postwar period. Section 5.3 reports on trends among the most important determinants of growth among this group of countries and presents an econometric analysis of factors affecting productivity growth. Section 5.4 surveys other literature on the convergence process among advanced countries. Section 5.5 reviews some of the pertinent literature on the role of technology and R&D in particular on productivity growth among the industrialized countries. Section 5.6 surveys the literature on the role of trade and a related factor, foreign direct investment, in the convergence process for this group. Section 5.7 considers a potpourri of other factors that have been considered in the pertinent literature. Concluding remarks are provided in Section 5.8.

5.2 Descriptive Statistics on TFP and Labor Productivity Growth

Two data sets are used here to examine the postwar record of OECD countries during the catch-up phase. The first is the OECD International Sectoral Database (ISDB). This source provides statistics on GDP, which is measured in 1985 prices and expressed in U.S. dollars; gross capital stock, which is also measured in 1985 prices and expressed in U.S. dollars; total employment; and employee compensation. Moreover, data on each of these variables are also provided on the sectoral and industry levels – a total of thirty-one sectors and industries. The ISDB data cover fourteen industrialized countries (ICs) – Australia, Belgium, Canada, Denmark, Finland, France, Germany (West), Italy, Japan, Netherlands, Norway, Sweden, the United Kingdom, and the United States. The period covered is from 1960 to 1992. The second is the Penn World Tables, Version 6.1 This source provides statistics on real GDP, denominated in 1985 international dollars per worker.

Descriptive statistics on labor productivity growth are presented in Figures 5.1a and 5.1b (also see Appendix Table 4.1 for more details). I have divided the years 1950–92 into four subperiods – 1950–60, 1960–73, 1973–9, and 1979–92. I have highlighted the two largest Industrialized Countries (ICs), the United States, and Japan. Arithmetic averages for the other ICs are shown as a separate entry, as well as all ICs. In the case of the Penn World Tables data, a separate entry is provided for the non-IC OECD countries (Greece, Portugal, Spain, and Turkey), and arithmetic averages for all OECD countries are also presented.

Among the ICs, labor productivity growth averaged 3.6 percent per year in both the 1950–60 and 1960–73 periods, fell off considerably to 1.2 percent per year during the slowdown period of 1973–9, and then rebounded slightly to 1.5 percent per year between 1979 and 1992. The trends were even more dramatic for the United States and Japan. In the case of the United States, annual labor productivity growth fell from 2.2 percent in 1960–73 to 0.1 percent in 1973–9 and then recovered to 1.4 percent during the 1979–92 period. For Japan, the drop-off was even sharper, from 7.7 percent per year in 1960–73 to 2.4 percent per year in 1973–9, and the recovery was stronger, 3.4 percent per year in 1979–92.

Comparisons are provided with computations of the same variable based on the ISDB data. Because of the difference in sources and methods and country samples between the two databases, the time patterns were rather different. Average labor productivity growth among the ICs computed from the two sources was almost equal for the 1960–73 period. However, it was almost 50 percent higher using the ISDB data for the 1973–9 period and slightly higher for the 1979–92 period. The ISDB data, like the Penn World Tables, showed a sharp drop in labor productivity growth between the 1960–73 and 1973–9 periods, but the former did not indicate any recovery in the post-1979 data, while the Penn data showed a modest rebound.

Figure 5.1c shows a similar set of statistics for TFP growth (see equation 3.3.3 for the formula used to estimated TFP growth and Chapter 3 for more discussion of the measurement of TFP). The U.S. results were pointed. They showed a very precipitous falloff in the rate of TFP growth between the 1960–73 period, 1.2 percent per year, and the 1973–9 period, to *negative* 0.3 percent per year. This was followed by a recovery to 0.5 percent per year in 1979–92. For Japan, the calculations show a major recovery in the 1979–92 period, from a TFP growth of 0.0 percent per year in 1973–9 to 1.0 percent per year in the following period.

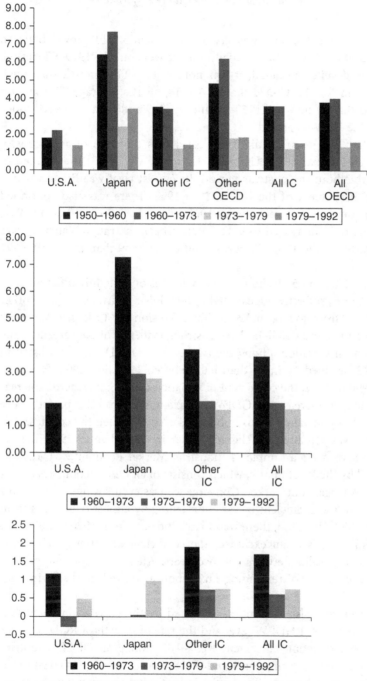

Figure 5.1 (a) Average annual percentage rate of aggregate labor productivity growth (*Source*: Penn World Tables); (b) average annual percentage rate of aggregate labor productivity growth; (c) average annual percentage rate of TFP growth (*Source*: ISDB).

Among other ICs, there was also a sharp falloff of TFP growth between 1960–73 and 1973–9, but virtually no recovery in the 1979–92 period. However, despite the falloff, it was notable that TFP growth was much higher than for the United States. Among all ICs, average TFP growth declined sharply between 1960–73 and 1973–9 and then recovered modestly in the 1979–92 period.

The last line of Appendix Table 5.1 shows the ratio of average TFP among all ICs except the United States to the U.S. level. The U.S. led in TFP throughout the postwar period. Its closest rival was France, which reached 97 percent of the U.S. TFP in 1992. There was also continued catch-up on the U.S. level between 1960, when the ratio was 0.64, to 1992, when the ratio increased to 0.82. Interestingly, the rate of catch-up was much faster in the 1960–73 period and the 1973–9 than in the 1979–92 period.

Figures 5.2a and 5.2b shows country figures on a slightly different concept of labor productivity, real GDP (2000 dollar equivalents) per worker (RGDPW), from the Penn World Table Version 6.1 (also see Appendix Table 5.2 for more details). There is strong evidence of convergence. The coefficient of variation among the twenty-four OECD countries listed in Table 4.2 declined by more than half between 1950 and 1990. However, from 1990 to 2002, the coefficient of variation actually increased. The reason is the huge increase in RGDPW in Luxembourg over this period, more than doubling in value. If Luxembourg is excluded, then the coefficient of variation was actually only slightly higher in 2002 than in 1990. Results are also shown for a sample of Industrial Market Economies (IMEs), as classified by the World Bank, which consists of all OECD countries except Greece, Portugal, and Turkey. Convergence was even stronger among this group, with the coefficient of variation falling by almost two-thirds from 1950 to 1990. Here, too, there was a large increase from 1990 to 2002. But if Luxembourg is again excluded, the coefficient of variation remained unchanged in value between the two years. After 1980, the rate of convergence in RGDPW (excluding Luxembourg) slowed markedly in both samples.

Catch-up was also evident, as indicated by the correlation coefficient between the 1950 RGDPW level and the rate of growth of RGDPW after 1950. The correlation coefficient was –0.85 among all OECD countries (–0.90 excluding Luxembourg) and –0.88 among the IMEs (–0.94 again excluding Luxembourg). The results indicate that the countries with the lowest productivity levels in 1950 generally experienced the fastest increase in labor productivity.

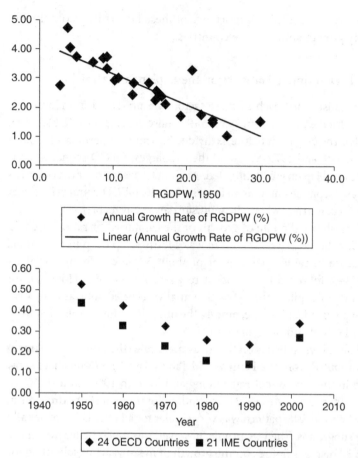

Figure 5.2 (a) Annual growth rate of RGDPW in 24 OECD countries, 1950–2002; (b) coefficient of variation of RGDPW by year (*Source*: Penn World Tables).

5.3 Regression Analysis of Factors Affecting Postwar Productivity Performance

Five sets of factors that may influence the rate of productivity growth among the industrialized nations of the world are considered here: (i) the investment rate and the growth in capital intensity, (ii) the increase in schooling levels in the workforce, (iii) the amount of resources devoted to research and development, (iv) the extent and pattern of foreign trade, and (v) the structure of employment and the rate of structural change in the economy. Section 5.3 first presents descriptive statistics on each of these factors; second, reports on the regression results; and third, presents a decomposition analysis to assess the relative importance of these factors in accounting for productivity growth among these countries.

5.3.1 Descriptive Statistics on the Explanatory Variables

Descriptive statistics for each of these factors are presented in Figures 5.3a through 5.3h for the period from 1950 to 1992 (also see Appendix Table 5.3 for more details). The period, as before, is divided into four subperiods – 1950–60, 1960–73, 1973–9, and 1979–92 – and the two largest OECD economies, the United States and Japan, are highlighted. Arithmetic averages for the other ICs are shown as a separate entry, as well as the non-IC OECD countries, all ICs, and all OECD countries (where the requisite data are available).

Figure 5.3a shows the rate of growth of the capital-labor ratio, based on the ISDB. For the United States, there was a fairly steep drop in the annual rate of increase in capital per worker of about 50 percent between 1960–73 and 1973–9, followed by a modest recovery in 1979–92. However, for Japan, the rate of capital-labor growth actually declined substantially over the latter two periods. Likewise, among the other ICs, the rate also fell from 1960–73 to 1973–9 and once again to 1979–92.

Figure 5.3b shows statistics on the investment rate (the ratio of investment to GDP) computed from the Penn World Tables data. The results here show an increase in the investment rate among all ICs from 1950–60 to 1960–73 and another increase to the 1973–9 period, followed by a slight drop-off in the 1979–92 period. The pattern was very similar for all OECD countries and each of the subgroups. The U.S. profile, however, was much flatter over time.

Figure 5.3c displays figures on the growth of mean years of schooling for the total adult population in OECD countries for the period from 1960 to 1992 from Barro and Lee (1996). It is interesting to note first that the rate of growth was quite high among ICs and OECD generally – on the order of 1.0 to 1.5 percent per year. Average years of schooling among ICs grew from 6.9 years in 1960 to 9.5 years in 1992. However, it is somewhat paradoxical that the pattern of growth of mean years of schooling was exactly the opposite that of labor productivity growth. Among all ICs, for example, the annual growth of mean schooling increased from 1960–73 to 1973–9 and then fell in 1979–92. A similar pattern is evident for all OECD countries, the United States (the falloff in 1979–92 was particularly marked), Japan, other ICs, and other OECD countries.

Figure 5.3d shows figures on average R&D intensity – the ratio of R&D expenditures to GNP (or GDP) from the *UNESCO Statistical Yearbooks*, 1963–90. The R&D expenditures include both private and governmental

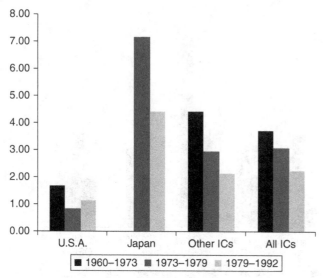

Figure 5.3a Average annual percentage growth rate, gross capital stock to total employment (*Source*: OECD International Sectoral Database).

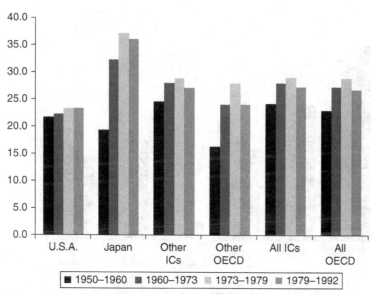

Figure 5.3b Average investment rate (%) over period (*Source*: Penn World Tables).

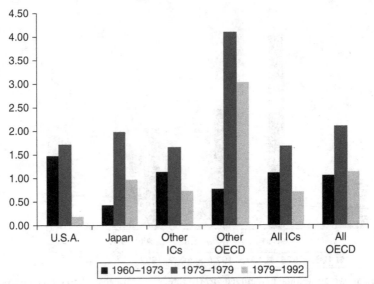

Figure 5.3c Average annual percentage growth rate, mean years of schooling (*Source*: Barro and Lee, 1996).

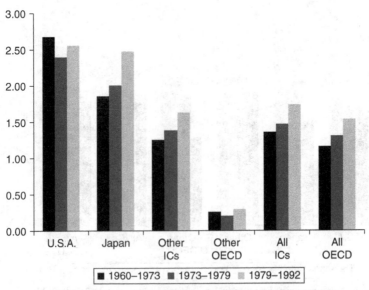

Figure 5.3d Expenditures on R&D as a percentage of GNP or GDP (*Source*: *UNESCO Statistical Yearbooks*).

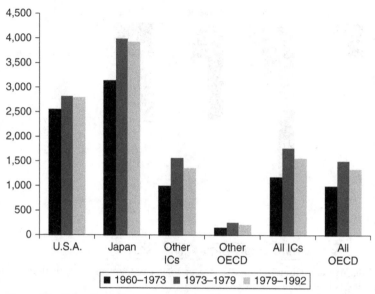

Figure 5.3e Scientists and engineers engaged in R&D per million of population (*Source*: *UNESCO Statistical Yearbooks*).

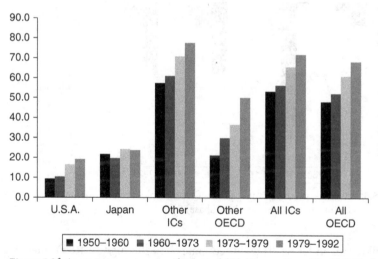

Figure 5.3f Average openness over the period (%) (*Source*: Penn World Tables).

sources. The main finding here is that R&D intensity was increasing rather steadily between the 1960s and 1990. For this factor also, there was no fall-off during the slowdown period of 1973–9 but rather an increase (except for a moderate decline for the United States). It is also interesting to note

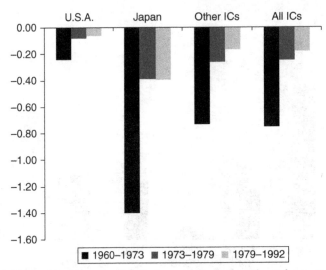

Figure 5.3g Average annual change, share of total employment in agriculture (%) (Source: OECD International Sectoral Database).

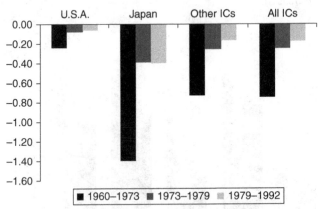

Figure 5.3h Average annual change, share of total employment in manufacturing (%) (*Source*: OECD International Sectoral Database).

the differences in levels. The United States had the highest R&D intensity throughout the postwar period, but during the 1979–92 period Japan was a very close second. The average of the other ICs in 1979–92 was lower and that of other OECD countries much lower.

Another measure of R&D activity is the number of scientists and engineers engaged in R&D per capita, also from the *UNESCO Statistical Yearbooks*. This measure shows a slightly different pattern than R&D expenditures for two reasons. First, R&D performed in different industries differs in their degree of capital intensity. As a result, countries with different mixes of industries may have different numbers of scientists and engineers employed in R&D per dollar of R&D expenditure. Second, the relative salaries of R&D personnel may vary across countries. This also may account for differences in scientific personnel employed per dollar of R&D expenditure.

According to this measure, Japan was the most R&D intensive country over the period from 1960 to 1992, with the United States in second place. This measure shows a fairly substantial increase in the degree of R&D activity between the 1960–73 and 1973–9 periods, followed by a moderate drop in the 1979–92 period. This is exactly opposite to the time pattern in productivity growth. Interestingly, the falloff in scientists and engineers engaged in R&D per capita between 1973–9 and 1979–92 was minuscule in both Japan and the United States.

Figure 5.3f show the degree of trade openness, the ratio of the sum of exports and imports to GDP, based on the Penn World Tables (Panels F through J of Appendix Table 5.3 show different indices of trade intensity). This index had a very similar time pattern to R&D expenditures, rising steadily over time. This is another factor that showed no falloff during the slowdown period of 1973–9. It is also interesting to note the difference in levels – both the United States and Japan were much lower than the average of the other ICs.

Panels G and H of Appendix Table 5.3 show the ratio of exports and imports, respectively, to GNP, calculated from figures in the World Bank's *World Tables 1994*. Here, too, a steady rise in these two measures was evident between the 1960–73 and 1973–9 periods and again between the 1973–9 and 1979–92 periods. However, as with the ratio of the sum of exports and imports to GDP, the rate of increase of trade openness slowed down in the 1979–92 period. Panels I and J show the ratio of merchandise exports and merchandise imports, respectively, to GNP, also calculated from figures in the World Bank's *World Tables 1994*. Here, again, the pattern was very similar. Both measures of trade intensity increased between the 1970–73 and 1973–9 periods and again between the latter and the 1979–92 period. Moreover, there was a slowdown in the rate of growth in trade openness between the 1973–9 and 1979–92 periods.

Figures 5.3g and 5.3h show statistics on structural change among the ICs, as measured by the average annual change of the share of total employment in agriculture and manufacturing, respectively. The average employment share in agriculture among the ICs declined sharply from 20 percent in 1960 to 5 percent in 1992. However, the greatest rapidity of change occurred in the 1960–73 period. For Japan, the rate of decline in the agricultural share was especially high during the 1960–73 period, but it should be noted that in 1960 agriculture accounted for 34 percent of Japanese employment (compared to 7 percent in the United States).

The average share of total employment in manufacturing in the ICs declined from 27 percent in 1960 to 19 percent in 1992. Its rate of change accelerated between the first and second periods and then declined slightly during the third. The acceleration was particularly marked for the United States. However, Japan was somewhat of an anomaly, because the share of employment in manufacturing actually increased substantially over the 1960–73 period, fell sharply during the 1973–9 period, but was virtually unchanged over the 1979–92 years.

In Panel M of Appendix Table 5.3, I aggregated four of the service industries – (i) trade, restaurants, and hotels; (ii) finance, insurance, and real estate; (iii) community, social, and personal services; and (iv) government services – to form what I call the "stagnant" service sector. The term "stagnant" indicates that these sectors have historically experienced very little productivity growth over time. In particular, I have excluded transportation and communications from this grouping, since its productivity has historically behaved more like that of a "progressive" manufacturing industry than like that of most other service industries.[1]

The average share of employment in the stagnant service industries in the ICs grew dramatically over the postwar period, from 36 percent in 1960 to 59 percent in 1992. In the case of the United States, the share of employment in services reached 69 percent in 1992. The rate of increase in the stagnant service share increased between the 1960–73 and 1973–9 periods, and then slowed down in 1979–92. The rate of increase of the share of employment in services in the United States was much lower than in other ICs in the first two periods, but this was due to the fact that the share had already reached 53 percent in 1960, much higher than that in the other ICs.

5.3.2 Regression Analysis

The basic estimating form is:

$$\text{TFPGRT}^h_t = b_0 + b_1 \text{ RELTFP}^h_t + b_2 \text{ KLGRT}^h_t + b_3 \text{ AGEKCHG}^h_t + \varepsilon_{ht} \tag{5.1}$$

where TFPGRT^h_h is country h's annual rate of TFP growth, RELTFP^h_t is country h's (Translog) TFP relative to the United States at the start of each

---

[1] See Baumol, Blackman, and Wolff (1989), chapter 6, for more discussion of these concepts.

period, KLGRT^h_t is country h's rate of capital-labor growth, AGEKCHG^h_t is the (annual) change in the average age of country h's capital stock, and ε is a stochastic error term.[2] The RELTFP term is included as a crude index of technology gap with respect to the United States and hence of the catch-up potential.

Columns 1 and 2 of Table 5.1 show the results based on data from the ISDB. The regression is run on three periods: 1960–73, 1974–9, and 1979–92. The sample of countries is restricted to the fourteen countries in the ISDB database. The first column shows the results for the catch-up variable (RELTFP), and the change in the annual rate of growth of the capital stock between the beginning and end of the period, DEL(KGRT), which is used as a proxy for the vintage effect (see Wolff, 1991a, for more details). The coefficient of RELTFP has the expected negative sign and is significant at the 5 percent level. The coefficient of DEL(KGRT) has the expected positive sign (an acceleration in capital growth is equivalent to a reduction in the average age of the capital stock) and is significant at the 1 percent level.

In the second column, I add in the other variables of interest – the annual growth in mean years of schooling (EDUCGRTH), R&D intensity (RDGNP), ratio of imports to GNP (IMPGNP), and average annual change of the share of employment in agriculture and services – DEL(AGRSHR) and DEL(SERSHR), respectively. It is first of interest to examine the coefficients of the previously included variables. The coefficient of RELTFP becomes smaller (in absolute value) and statistically insignificant. The coefficient of DEL(KGRT) also falls and also becomes insignificant.

Growth in mean years of schooling has the expected positive coefficient. However, the coefficient is relatively small – an increase of 1 percentage point in schooling growth is associated with a 0.17 percentage point increase in TFP growth – and statistically insignificant. R&D intensity has the expected positive coefficient, 0.31. This is somewhat higher than a previous estimate of Wolff and Nadiri (1993) of about 11 percent among exclusively manufacturing sectors and 20 percent among all sectors in the United States. However, this estimate falls in the range of previous estimates of the direct rate of return to R&D, which ranges from about 3 percent (Griliches and Lichtenberg, 1984a) to 76 percent (Griliches and Lichtenberg, 1984b). (Also see Mohnen (1992) or Nadiri (1993) for a summary of previous results.) However, the variable is not statistically significant. I also substituted the

---

[2]   See the Appendix to Chapter 4 for the derivation of this regression equation. Also, see Chapter 3 for a discussion of some of the econometric issues associated with estimating growth equations.

Table 5.1. *Regression of Annual TFP Growth (TFPGRT) on the Change in Capital Growth, R&D Intensity, Schooling Growth, Trade Openness, and Structural Shifts*

Independent	ISDB Data[a]		Maddison (1991, 1993)[b]
Variables	(1)	(2)	(3)
Constant	0.0264**	−0.0053	−0.0052
	(4.16)	(0.84)	(0.88)
RELTFP	−0.0201*	−0.0152	−0.0278**
	(2.43)	(1.44)	(3.28)
DEL(KGRT)	0.221**	0.109	
	(4.49)	(1.62)	
AGEKCHG			−0.044**
			(3.83)
EDUCGRTH		0.172	0.331
		(1.05)	(1.52)
RDGNP		0.312	0.228
		(1.32)	(1.66)
IMP/GNP		0.0232*	
		(2.12)	
OPEN			0.014
			(1.33)
DEL(AGRSHR)		−1.002**	−0.643
		(2.85)	(0.35)
DEL(SRVSHR)		−0.527	−0.109
		(0.96)	(0.83)
R^2	0.53	0.78	0.84
Adjusted-R^2	0.5	0.73	0.75
Standard Error	0.0064	0.0048	0.013
Sample Size	42	42	22
Degrees of Freedom	39	33	14

Notes: t-ratios are shown in parentheses below the coefficient estimate
Key:
RELTFP: percentage difference of country's TFP from U.S. TFP at the beginning of the period *Source*: OECD International Sectoral Database, or Maddison (1991), as indicated.
DEL(KGRT): change in average annual rate of growth of capital stock between end and beginning of period. Source: OECD International Sectoral Database
AGEKCHG: annualized change in the average age of country's capital stock over the period. *Source*: Maddison (1993)
EDUCGRTH: average annual growth in mean years of schooling. Source: Barro and Lee (1996)
RDGNP: the ratio of R&D expenditures to GNP. Source: UNESCO Statistical Yearbooks, 1963–1990

Table 5.1. (*continued*)

IMP/GNP the ratio of imports to GNP, all in nominal terms. Source: World Bank, World Tables, 1994

OPEN: the ratio of exports plus imports to GDP, all in nominal terms. Source: Penn World Tables, Version 6.2

DEL(AGRSHR): average annual change of the share of employment in agriculture. *Source*: OECD International Sectoral Database

DEL(SRVSHR): average annual change of the share of employment in services. *Source*: OECD International Sectoral Database

[a] Observations are for Australia, Belgium, Canada, Denmark, Finland, France, Germany (West), Italy, Japan, Netherlands, Norway, Sweden, the United Kingdom, and the United States, for three periods: 1960–73, 1973–9, and 1979–92

[b] Observations are for France, Germany, Japan, the Netherlands, the UK and the U.S. for four periods: 1950–60, 1960–73, 1973–9, and 1979–89

* significant at the 5 percent level

** significant at the 1 percent level

number of scientists and engineers engaged in R&D per capita, but this variable is also insignificant.

Import intensity has the expected positive sign and is significant at the 5 percent level. A 1 percentage point increase in import openness is associated with an increase of TFP growth of 0.023 percentage point – a relatively small effect. Four other measures of trade openness were also tried – (i) the ratio of exports to GNP, (ii) the ratio of exports plus imports to GNP, (iii) the ratio of merchandise imports to GNP, and (iv) the ratio of merchandise exports to GNP. The best fit was provided by the ratio of imports to GNP, though all of the other indices, with the exception of the ratio of merchandise exports to GNP, proved to be statistically significant. In addition, I substituted the annual change in the various ratios of trade to GNP for the actual trade ratios. None of the changes in trade intensity variables proved to be statistically significant.

The change in the share of employment in agriculture has the expected negative sign and is significant at the 1 percent level. The coefficient is also quite large – a 1 percentage point decline in the agricultural share is associated with a 1.0 percentage point increase in TFP growth. The change in the share of employment in services also has the expected negative sign but is insignificant. The coefficient is also quite large – a 1 percentage point decline in the services share is associated with a 0.5 percentage point increase in TFP growth. This form also provides a good fit, with a R^2 of 0.76 and an adjusted-R^2 of 0.72.

The third column of Table 5.1 shows the results of a similar specification estimated with the Maddison (1991, 1993a) sample. The vintage variable is AGEKCHG, the change in the average age of the capital stock. The periods are 1950–60, 1960–73, 1973–9, and 1979–89. RELTFP and AGEKCHG are both significant at the 1 percent level and with the expected signs. The growth in the mean years of schooling has a moderate effect, 0.33, though the coefficient is insignificant. A 1 percentage point growth in mean years of schooling leads to a 0.3 percentage point increase in TFP growth. The coefficient of R&D intensity is 0.23, smaller than in the regressions on the ISDB data, but is again not significant. Trade openness, measured by the ratio of exports plus imports to GNP (the only trade variable available for the 1950–60 period), has a positive but insignificant coefficient. The effect remains quite small, at 0.014.

The coefficient of the change in the share of employment in agriculture is negative but insignificant in this regression. Its effect is still relatively large: a 1 percentage point decline in the agricultural share is associated with a 0.64 percentage point increase in the aggregate rate of TFP growth. The change in the share of employment in services has the expected negative coefficient, but it is also insignificant. The effect is relatively small – a 1 percentage point increase is associated with a 0.10 percentage point decline in the aggregate rate of TFP growth. The goodness of fit, as measured by the adjusted-R^2 statistic, is quite high in this regression – 0.75.

5.3.3 Decomposition of Postwar Trends in Productivity

A decomposition based on the regression results of Table 5.1 is shown in Table 5.2. The first panel shows the results based on the ISDB data, and the second panel the results from the Maddison data. The results are roughly similar. In the ISDB results, the contribution of the catch-up effect was 0.46 percentage point to aggregate TFP growth in the 1960–73 period, but this diminished somewhat over time to 0.30 percentage point in 1979–93. The vintage effect, as reflected in the acceleration of the growth in the capital stock, changed from a positive 0.34 percentage point contribution in 1960–73 to negative 0.1 in both 1973–9 and 1979–93. This reflected the aging of the capital stock among OECD countries after 1973.

The contribution of the growth in mean years of schooling was quite small but rose from 0.19 percentage point in 1960–73 to 0.25 percentage point in 1973–9, before declining to 0.11 percentage point in 1979–93. The ratio of imports to GNP had a strong and increasing effect on TFP growth, rising from 0.54 percentage point in 1960–73 to 0.68 percentage point in 1979–93.

This was accounted for by the increasing openness of OECD economies over the postwar period. R&D intensity also made a sizable and increasing contribution to TFP growth, from 0.48 percentage point in 1960–73 to 0.59 percentage point in 1979–93, reflecting rising R&D intensity over the period.

The shift of employment out of agriculture contributed a very sizable 0.75 percentage point to aggregate TFP growth in the 1960–73 period. As the movement out of agriculture slowed, so did its positive contribution to aggregate TFP growth, falling to 0.25 percentage point in 1973–9 and 0.18 percentage point in 1979–93. The rate of shift of employment into the service industries increased between the 1960–73 and 1973–9 periods but then slowed in the 1979–93 period. As a result, its drag on aggregate TFP growth first increased, from –0.33 percentage point in 1960–73 to –0.44 percentage point in 1973–9, and then fell to –0.33 percentage point in the most recent period.

Comparing the results for the 1960–73 and 1973–9 periods can give us some indication of the sources of the slowdown in TFP growth in the latter period. The diminution of the catch-up had a small effect, only 0.1 percentage point. The aging of the capital stock, as reflected in the change in the growth of the capital stock, accounted for 0.5 percentage point. The slowing of the shift of employment out of agriculture explained another 0.5 percentage point. The increasing drag on productivity from the shift of employment into services was responsible for another 0.1 percentage point. These factors were offset by an increasing contribution of educational growth, rising trade openness, and rising R&D activity. Together, they helped increase TFP growth by 0.2 percentage point. However, there was a large unexplained residual in this decomposition.

The results from the Maddison data for the postwar period are shown in Panel B. As before, the contribution of the catch-up effect lessened over time, from 0.89 percentage point in 1950–60 to 0.57 percentage point in 1979–89, as productivity in other countries converged on the United States. The vintage effect remained quite strong and positive in the 1950–60 and 1960–73 periods, averaging almost *a full* percentage point, but then declined to –0.30 during the 1973–9 period and even further to –1.0 in the 1979–89 period, as the capital stock in OECD countries aged.

The contribution of the growth in mean years of schooling was modest but increased from 0.19 percentage point in 1950–60 to 0.36 percentage point in 1979–89. The degree of trade openness had a surprisingly strong effect on TFP growth, ranging from a half to three-quarters of a percentage point. Its contribution also increased over the postwar period. The

Table 5.2. *Contribution by Component to Average TFP Growth by Period on the Basis of the ISDB and Maddison Data*

Variable	1950–60	1960–73	1973–9	1979–89/93
A. ISDB Data: 14–Country Statistics[a]				
1. Average Values of Explanatory Variables				
RELTFP		−0.30	−0.24	−0.20
DEL(KGRT) [% points]		3.11	−1.28	−1.05
EDUCGRTH [% points]		1.12	1.44	0.66
RDGNP [% points]		1.55	1.61	1.90
IMPGNP [% points]		23.1	28.2	29.4
DEL(AGRSHR) [% points]		−0.75	−0.25	−0.18
DEL(SERSHR) [% points]		0.63	0.83	0.62
2. Percentage Point Contribution of Each Variable to Average TFP Growth[b]				
Constant		−0.55	−0.55	−0.55
RELTFP		0.46	0.37	0.30
DEL(KGRT)		0.34	−0.14	−0.11
EDUCGRTH		0.19	0.25	0.11
RDGNP		0.48	0.50	0.59
IMPGNP		0.54	0.65	0.68
DEL(AGRSHR)		0.75	0.25	0.18
DEL(SERSHR)		−0.33	−0.44	−0.33
Unexplained		0.42	−0.28	−0.13
TFPGRT		2.30	0.62	0.75
B. Maddison (1991, 1993) Data: 6–Country Statistics[c]				
1. Average Values of Explanatory Variables				
RELTFP	−0.32	−0.3	−0.27	−0.2
AGEKCHG	−0.22	−0.23	0.07	0.23
EDUCGRTH [% pts]	0.57	0.74	0.76	1.07
OPEN [% pts]	37.1	37.7	46.6	50.9
RDGNP [% pts]	0.97	1.93	2.08	2.34
DEL(AGRSHR) [% pts]	−0.6	−0.51	−0.22	−0.16
DEL(SERSHR) [% pts]	0.2	0.69	0.73	0.2
2. Percentage Point Contribution of Each Variable to Average TFP Growth[b]				
Constant	−0.52	−0.52	−0.52	−0.52
RELTFP	0.89	0.83	0.74	0.57
AGEKCHG	0.98	0.99	−0.30	−1.00
EDUCGRTH	0.19	0.24	0.25	0.36
OPEN	0.53	0.54	0.66	0.72
RDGNP	0.22	0.44	0.47	0.53
DEL(AGRSHR)	0.39	0.33	0.14	0.11
DEL(SERSHR)	−0.02	−0.08	−0.08	−0.02
Unexplained	0.22	−0.36	−0.59	0.01
TFPGRT	2.89	2.49	0.87	0.77

Table 5.2. (*continued*)

Notes: Key:
RELTFP: percentage difference of country's TFP from U.S. TFP at the beginning of the period
DEL(KGRT): change in average annual rate of growth of capital stock between end and beginning of period
AGEKCHG: annualized change in the average age of country's capital stock over the period
EDUCGRTH: average annual growth in mean years of schooling
RDGNP: the ratio of R&D expenditures to GNP (or GDP)
IMP/GNP the ratio of imports to GNP, all in nominal terms
OPEN: the ratio of exports plus imports to GDP, all in nominal terms
DEL(AGRSHR): average annual change of the share of employment in agriculture
DEL(SRVSHR): average annual change of the share of employment in services
[a] Coefficients from Regression 2 in Table 5.1. The sample includes 14 countries – Australia, Belgium, Canada, Denmark, Finland, France, Germany (West), Italy, Japan, Netherlands, Norway, Sweden, the United Kingdom, and the United States – over three periods – 1960–73, 1973–9, and 1979–93
[b] Defined as coefficient value multiplied by the average value of the variable by period
[c] Coefficients from Regression 3 in Table 5.1. The sample includes 6 countries – France, Germany (West), Japan, Netherlands, the United Kingdom, and the United States – over four periods – 1950–60, 1960–73, 1973–9, and 1979–89

contribution of R&D intensity also increased over the postwar period, from 0.22 percentage point in 1950–60 to 0.53 percentage point in 1979–89, as average R&D intensity rose over the period.

The shift of employment out of agriculture contributed 0.39 percentage points to aggregate TFP growth in the 1950–60 period. However, the share of employment in agriculture fell less rapidly after 1960 than during the early postwar period, and its contribution to TFP growth correspondingly declined, to 0.33 percentage point in 1960–73, 0.14 percentage point in 1973–9, and 0.11 percentage point in 1979–89. The shift of employment into the service industries, though substantial during the 1960–73 and 1973–9 periods, had a very small negative effect on overall TFP growth over the entire postwar period.

We can again analyze some of the factors responsible for the TFP slowdown between the 1960–73 and 1973–9 periods. The aging of the capital stock was again the primary culprit, accounting for a decline of 1.3 percentage points in TFP growth. The diminution of the catch-up again had a small effect, only 0.1 percentage point. The lessening of the gains from the shift of employment out of agriculture explained another 0.2 percentage point of the aggregate TFP slowdown. However, these factors were offset by slightly increasing contributions to TFP growth from rising trade openness and rising R&D activity. Most of the further reduction in TFP growth between the 1973–9 and 1979–89 periods was attributable to the continued aging of the capital stock and the further decrease in the catch-up effect. Offsetting these factors were increased contributions from the growth in mean years of schooling, increasing trade openness, and further increases in R&D activity.

5.4 Other Literature on the Convergence Process among Advanced Countries

A large number of studies have investigated factors behind growth among industrialized countries alone in the postwar period. I summarize a few of them here. Alam (1992) also used data from Maddison (1982, 1989) to investigate the determinants of productivity growth for a sample of sixteen OECD countries. Three periods of analysis were pooled: 1950–69, 1960–73, and 1973–86. Explanatory variables include the initial GDP per capita (the catch-up effect), the gross investment rate, the share of manufacturing in total output, the size of the population at the start of the period, the trade intensity measured as the ratio of the sum of exports and imports to GDP, and the percentage of the population enrolled in higher education. The initial level of GDP per capita was highly significant, at the 1 percent level, and had the predicted negative sign. The investment rate was likewise significant at the 1 percent level and had the predicted positive sign. The trade intensity variable had the predicted positive sign and was significant at the 5 percent level in two specifications, at the 10 percent level in a third, and not significant in a fourth. The share of manufacturing output in GDP had a positive coefficient and was marginally significant, at the 10 percent level. The education variable, however, was not significant.

Skoczylas and Tissot (2005) looked at more recent data on OECD TFP levels for twenty OECD countries. Their work covered the period from 1966 to 2004. Their main finding was that the United States was pulling ahead of the other OECD countries in terms of output per person and output per hour worked. This trend was particularly notable after 1996. From 1996 to 2004, output per hour grew at an annual rate of 2.8 percent in the United States but only at 1.7 percent in the other OECD countries. They also noted that not only did the United States have the highest TFP growth rate among the OECD countries in the period from 1996 to 2004, but it had also been rising the fastest among these countries. Indeed, productivity growth decelerated among in many of the other OECD countries. They also found that the U.S. performance in the 1996 to 2004 period reflected a higher rate of technological progress rather than stronger capital accumulation.

In contrast, the rate of capital formation remained quite high in the other OECD countries in the most recent period.

Gust and Marquez (2004) also looked into the growing gap in productivity growth between the United States and other industrialized countries during the 1990s. They used panel data from 1992 to 1999 for thirteen OECD countries. They found that both the production and the adoption of information technology (IT) played an important role in the divergence of productivity growth between the United States and European countries. They used two variables to measure the extent of IT. The first was IT production as a share of GDP. The second was the ratio of expenditures on IT to GDP. They found that both these variables were positive and significant (at the 5 percent level) in explaining cross-country differences in labor productivity growth over time.

They then tried to explain cross-country differences in IT spending on the basis of regulation. They used three variables to measure the extent of regulation in a country. The first was an index of employment protection legislation. The second was an index of overall administrative regulatory burdens. The third was an index of regulatory burdens on start-up companies. They found that the extent of regulation in a country played an important (and negative) role in accounting for differences in IT spending, especially regulations restricting labor market practices.

Pyyhtiä (2007) also examined the growing gap between European countries and the United States. He used data from the OECD STAN database covering twelve European Union (EU) countries and the United States over the period 1987 to 2003. He also included R&D data taken from the OECD ANBERD data bank and the Eurostat Data base. Using panel data estimation methods, he estimated both Cobb-Douglas and CES production functions. He found that in many ICT-producing and -using countries such as Denmark, Finland, Ireland, Sweden, and the United States the rate of technical progress accelerated during the decade of the 1990s. His main finding was that the acceleration in the rate of technological progress was associated with increased R&D investment. He concluded that R&D expenditures explained a substantial part of the divergent growth performance between the United States and Europe in general and among European countries as well, particularly between the ICT-intensive and the non-ICT-intensive economies.

Van Ark, O'Mahony, and Timmer (2008) also examined the growing productivity gap between Europe and the United States. They first of all reported that the average annual rate of labor productivity growth (measured as GDP per work hour) in the United States accelerated from the

1973–95 period to the 1995–2006 period. In contrast, among the fifteen European Union countries, annual labor productivity growth declined from the first period to the second. The authors found that the slower emergence of IT in Europe compared to the United States was responsible for the growing divergence in productivity performance. The paper also emphasized the key role played by market services in accounting for the widening of the productivity gap. In particular, while productivity growth stagnated or fell in European market services, it increased on the American scene. This difference was attributable to the greater investment made by American service providers in IT.

In summary, it appears that while other IC and OECD countries were converging on the U.S. level in terms of both labor productivity and TFP from about 1960 through the early 1990s, the United States has since pulled out ahead of these other countries. The increasing gap between the United States and these other countries over the last twenty years or so appears due to the higher rate of technological progress in the United States relative to these other countries, and this, in turn, appears due to greater investment in ICT by the United States.

5.5 The Role of Science and Technology

There is, of course, a voluminous literature that has demonstrated that R&D makes an important contribution to growth at the firm, industry, and national levels.[3] There is also recent empirical literature that has examined this issue in a cross-country context among OECD countries. Coe and Helpman (1995) found a positive and statistically significant effect of (domestic) R&D stock on TFP growth among twenty-two OECD countries over the period 1971–90. They also included an estimate of foreign (imported) R&D capital stock and found this variable to have a positive and significant effect on TFP growth, particularly among the smaller OECD countries. However, it should be stressed that the authors did not include a catch-up term in their regression. A related study, from Working Party No. 1 of the OECD Economic Policy Committee (1993), reported a positive but insignificant effect of the growth in R&D capital stock on labor productivity growth for a sample of nineteen OECD countries over four subperiods between 1960 and 1985 (table 19 of the report). This analysis did include a catch-up term.

---

[3] See, for example, the literature reviews of Griliches (1979) and Mohnen (1992).

Fagerberg (1988) reported a significant and positive effect of the average annual growth in civilian R&D on GDP growth for twenty-two countries over the 1973–88 period, with a catch-up term included. Verspagen (1994) used a cross-country sample consisting of twenty-one OECD countries, South Korea, and Yugoslavia and covered the period 1970–85. He found that with a catch-up term (the initial labor productivity gap) in the specification, the growth in total R&D stock was a positive and significant determinant of GDP growth. Also, distinguishing between business and nonbusiness R&D, he reported that only the former had a statistically significant effect on output growth (the coefficient of nonbusiness R&D was actually negative).[4]

Several studies examined the relation of R&D investment to productivity growth on the industry or sectoral level among OECD countries. Three such studies are of note. Fecher and Perelman (1989) used data for nine manufacturing industries and eleven OECD countries for the period 1971 to 1986 and found that R&D intensity (the ratio of R&D expenditures to GDP) was a positive and significant determinant of TFP growth in a pooled cross-section regression specification. The estimated rate of return to R&D was 15 percent. Dosi, Pavitt, and Soete (1990) looked at the relation between labor productivity *levels* and the cumulative number of patents registered by each country in the United States (an index of technological innovativeness) for thirty-nine industrial sectors. They found that their patent index had a positive and significant coefficient for most but not all industrial sectors.[5]

Griffith, Redding, and van Reenen (2004) also analyzed the relation between R&D and TFP growth on the industry level for a sample of twelve OECD countries. Nine manufacturing industries were used in the analysis. The data covered the period from 1974 to 1990. The data source was the

---

[4] A negative coefficient on government-financed R&D was often reported in single-country studies (see, for example, Wolff and Nadiri, 1993). In the case of the United States, this result was often attributed to the high defense component of government R&D. In defense-related work, R&D expenditures usually show up in improved weaponry, which is not reflected in standard productivity measures. In other countries, the negative coefficient may reflect the fact that private industry will finance profitable R&D opportunities out of their own funds, leaving the government to subsidize outlets that may be socially desirable but privately unprofitable.

[5] Surprisingly, I could not find any studies containing regressions of productivity growth on R&D by individual industries pooled across countries. Verspagen (1993), for example, analyzed this relation in time series regressions for individual OECD countries. Interestingly, he found that the effects of R&D on productivity growth varied by type of industry – most important and significant in high-tech industries and least important and insignificant in low-tech ones.

OECD ISDB and ANBERD data sets, supplemented with education data from the UNIDO database. Their major contribution to the literature was to consider the absorptive capacity of each industry in each country on the basis of the industry's distance from the productivity frontier. They argued that the further a country lies behind the technological frontier, the greater the potential gain from R&D to increase TFP growth through technology transfer from more advanced countries. The distance from the frontier was measured by the gap in TFP between the leader in the industry and the industry in that country. They found the interaction term between R&D intensity and the technology gap was positive and statistically significant (though at only the 10 percent level). They concluded that the return to R&D was much larger than that estimated on the basis of standard cross-industry or cross-country regressions.

In sum, R&D almost consistently shows up as making a positive and statistically significant contribution to productivity growth among OECD countries. This result generally shows up on both the aggregate level and the industry level as well. These results and many others reinforce the notion that R&D acts a *strong* force in explaining productivity growth.

5.6 The Role of International Trade and Foreign Direct Investment (FDI)

The role of international trade and FDI on productivity convergence, as discussed in Chapter 1, is connected with the transfer of new technological knowledge. The argument is, first of all, that imports often embody the latest technology. Indeed, if would make little sense for a country to import products that are already produced by it. The acquisition of imports thus enables a country to acquire new knowledge of production techniques, and this, in turn, may enable the country to improve its own production processes. Moreover, these "spillovers" of knowledge may be greater if the imports themselves embody a high content of R&D. Likewise, FDI may produce similar transfers of knowledge from the host country to the receiving country. The export "story" is somewhat different. Here the argument is that firms in a country engaged in export competition will have a strong incentive to acquire the latest production technology in order to compete with the local producers and exporters from other countries of similar products.

Helliwell and Chung (1991) used OECD national accounts data for nineteen industrialized countries over the 1960–85 period. They first reported strong evidence of international convergence in the rates of growth of labor efficiency for this sample of countries over the years 1960 to 1985. They then included in their model both a catch-up term and a measure of openness, which was the log difference of current and lagged values of five-year moving averages of the sum of exports and imports divided by GNP. They found for this sample evidence that convergence was faster for countries whose degree of openness to international trade was increasing over time, with the coefficients of their trade openness variable typically significant at the 5 percent level.

Ben-David (1993) used a sample of EU countries over the 1950–85 period. He found a very strong relation between the degree of trade liberalization and the convergence in per capita income among this sample of countries. The latter occurred almost in step with the reductions in import tariffs and quotas. Rassekh (1992) used a sample of OECD countries for the 1950–85 period and a measure of trade openness defined as the ratio of the sum of exports and imports to GDP in each country. He found a positive relation between per capita GDP growth and the growth of this index of trade openness.

Many of the earlier studies of the effect of trade on growth have been criticized for relating the size of trade to the growth in income per capita (or per worker). This approach suffers from both problems of endogeneity and an omitted variable bias. The former refers to the issue of causality. In particular, it was not clear from the earlier studies whether increased trade caused income convergence or whether the increasing similarity of countries in regard to per capita income was responsible for increasing trade among these countries.

One way around the endogeneity problem is to look at changes in (exogenous) trade policy. Ben-David (1993) chose a small number of advanced countries that decided formally to liberalize trade. He was then able to examine the degree of disparity among these countries before, during, and after the implementation of the trade reform. He found that for each of these countries no evidence of income convergence was apparent during the decades prior to the reduction of trade barriers. However, as these nations began to liberalize trade, the income gaps started to decline, and they remained below the preliberalization levels in the years after the trade reform began. He argued that insofar as the trade reforms could be viewed as exogenous events, his finding provided support for the hypothesis that movements toward freer trade led to convergence rather than the converse.

Another way around the endogeneity problem is to look at first differences – that is, the relation between the change in import or export intensity and income growth. Ben-David and Kimhi (2004) examined the impact of changes in trade between countries on changes in the rate of reduction in the size of the income gap between these countries. They used export and import data as the criteria for measuring bilateral trade between major trade partners. Their country sample consisted of twenty industrial market economies and five middle income countries (including Argentina, Chile, Uruguay, and South Africa). Their data covered the years from 1960 to 1985. This resulted in 127 pairs of countries on the basis of export data and 134 pairs from import data. Their major finding was that an increase in trade between trade partners was positively related to an increase in the rate of convergence in per capita income between the two countries. The effect was particularly strong for increased exports by a poorer country to a richer trading partner.

Bernard and Jensen (2004) analyzed a related issue in the case of the United States. They were interested in the effects of increased exporting on increasing industry level productivity growth in U.S. manufacturing. They noted first that contemporaneous levels of exports and productivity are positively correlated across manufacturing industries, but tests on industry data indicate that causality runs from productivity to exporting, not the reverse. They used data from the Annual Survey of Manufactures (ASM) compiled together in the Longitudinal Research Database (LRD) of the U.S. Bureau of the Census. The period covered 1983 to 1992.

They found, first of all, evidence that exporting plants had higher productivity levels than nonexporters but, second of all, no evidence that exporting increases the rate of plant labor productivity growth. Third, they found that exporting plants grew faster than nonexporters within the same industry in terms of both output and employment. Exporting was therefore associated with a reallocation of employment from less efficient to more efficient plants within an industry. This reallocation (or shift effect) was associated with increased productivity growth *at the industry level*. Overall, the reallocation effect was quite large and accounted for more than 40 percent of the TFP growth at the industry level (also see Section 3.7 of Chapter 3 for an extended discussion of the reallocation effect).

As Keller (2004) noted, technology has three major characteristics in terms of its effect on productivity growth. First, technology is nonrival in the sense that the marginal costs for an additional firm (or individual) to use the technology are negligible. This means that technological knowledge can serve users beyond those who are currently using the technology without raising the costs to the current set of users. In contrast, physical capital is a "rival" input in that it can be used by only one firm at a time.

Second, the returns to investments in new technology are partly private and partly public. This means that the individual or firm who develops the new technology receives a benefit (such as a patent or a license) but that part of the new knowledge "spills over" to other users. That is to say, new technology benefits both the original inventor (the private return) and potential users external to the inventor by adding to their knowledge base as well (the public return). Third, technological change is the outcome of activities by private agents who devote resources to the invention of new products and processes. This means that individuals who invest in new technologies expect to receive a monetary return on their investment. It is hoped that the private return to the investment is strong enough to provide an incentive to innovate.

Both international trade and foreign direct investment (FDI) can be viewed in these terms as conveyors of new technological knowledge. Coe and Helpman (1995) were among the first to provide evidence on the importance of trade as a vehicle for the international diffusion of technology. They argued that if there is evidence (as seems to be the case) that innovation or R&D performed in one industry leads to technological gains in using industries, then is it possible that R&D performed in one country leads to technological gains in countries that import products from the first country? Coe and Helpman gathered data for twenty-two OECD countries covering the period from 1971 to 1990. They constructed measures of (domestic) R&D stock by country and estimated import flows between countries. Their major contribution was to construct a measure of "foreign R&D capital," which they defined as the import-share weighted average of the domestic R&D capital stocks of trade partners. Using bilateral import shares to weight foreign R&D expenditures, they calculated the variable S^f_i, which represented the foreign R&D stock of country i, as:

$$S^f_i = \sum_j m_{ik} RD_k$$

where m_{ik} is the quantity of imports from country k as a share of total imports into country i and RD_k is the stock of R&D in country k. Thus, the more R&D intensive the imports are from other countries, the higher is a country's stock of foreign R&D capital.

They then regressed a country's annual TFP growth on both its domestic and its foreign R&D capital. They found like most studies that domestic R&D was a significant determinant of a country's TFP growth. However, their most important finding was that foreign capital was also a significant determinant of TFP growth within a country. They calculated a domestic

R&D elasticity of 23 percent for the G-7 countries and about 8 percent for the fifteen smaller OECD countries. However, their estimated elasticities for foreign R&D (i.e., R&D embodied in imports into these countries) were 6 percent for the G-7 countries and 12 percent for the other OECD countries. They concluded that imported R&D was a more important factor in explaining domestic productivity growth in the smaller OECD countries, and the converse was true for the larger OECD economies. They also found that the more open a country was, the higher the return to foreign R&D.

They then looked at two additional issues. First, they wanted to determine whether a country's productivity growth was greater to the extent that it imported goods and services from countries with a high (domestic) R&D intensity relative to imports from countries with low R&D expenditures. Second, after controlling for the composition of its imports, they were interested in whether a country's productivity growth would be higher the higher its overall import share. They found support for both predictions. In particular, they found that international R&D spillovers were related to both the composition of a country's imports as well as its overall import intensity.

This paper stimulated a lot of additional work on the importance of foreign spillovers from trade and R&D. Park (1995), using aggregate data for ten OECD countries (including the G-7 countries), had similar results. He estimated that foreign R&D accounted for about two-thirds of the total effect of R&D on domestic productivity. He estimated a domestic R&D elasticity of 7 percent and a foreign R&D elasticity of 17 percent.

However, Verspagen (1997) challenged the findings of Coe and Helpman. Verspagen constructed a technology flow matrix based on European patent data that indicated not only in which sector the patent originated but also in which sectors the patent was used. This approach allowed the researcher to identify explicitly the pattern of intersectoral spillovers of knowledge. In contrast, Coe and Helpman based their spillover calculations on intersectoral trade (import) flows. Another difference was that Verspagen related TFP growth on the *sectoral* level to both direct and indirect R&D capital stocks.

Using a panel data set of twenty-two sectors, fourteen OECD countries, and nineteen years (1974–92, though there were missing data for some countries, sectors, and years), Verspagen was able to distinguish between R&D effects across sectors (the so-called between effect) and R&D effects over time (the so-called within effect). He found that foreign R&D spillovers were significant only in the "within" estimation (that is, the time series effect). Foreign spillovers were positive in the "between" estimation (that is, between sectors) but not statistically significant. It thus appeared that the Coe and Helpman results overstated the contribution of foreign R&D to domestic productivity growth.

Eaton and Kortum (1999) used a broader approach to calculating the relative importance of domestic and foreign R&D in domestic productivity growth. In their model, they included not only the direct effects on productivity growth but also a contribution from the transitional adjustment path to long-run equilibrium. They estimated that the portion of productivity growth attributable to domestic as opposed to imported R&D was about 13 percent in Germany, France, and the United Kingdom; around 35 percent for Japan; and up to 60 percent in the United States. Keller (2002) used a more general form of the R&D productivity function by allowing for multiple channels by which the diffusion of R&D can interact with domestic TFP growth. Using this method, he estimated that over the period from 1983 to 1995, the contribution of technology diffusion from France, Germany, Japan, the United Kingdom, and the United States to nine other OECD countries amounted to about 90 percent of the total R&D effect on TFP growth.

Eaton and Kortum (1996), on the other hand, controlled for both distance and other effects. They found that once these other influences are controlled for, bilateral imports were not significant as a predictor of bilateral patenting activity, which they used as an indicator of international technology diffusion. Moreover, Keller (1998) replicated the set of regressions used by Coe and Helpman (1995) with what he termed "counterfactual import shares." These were simulated import shares based on alternative assumptions rather than actual import shares that were used to create the imported R&D variable in the regression equations. Keller argued that for there to be strong evidence for trade induced international R&D spillovers, one should expect a strong positive effect from foreign R&D when actual bilateral import shares were used but a weaker and likely insignificant effect when the made-up "import" shares were used. Keller found high and significant coefficients when counterfactual import shares were used instead of actual import shares. The magnitude of the coefficients and the level of significance were similar in the two sets of regressions. On the basis of these results, he disputed the claim of Coe and Helpman that the import composition of a country was an important factor in explaining the country's productivity growth.

Xu and Wang (1999) showed that the import composition effect remained strong when trade in capital goods was used instead of trade in goods produced in total manufacturing. Xu and Wang obtained a R^2 statistic of 0.771

when the weights used in the construction of the imported R&D variable were based on imports of capital goods. In comparison, Keller obtained an R^2 statistic of 0.749 on the basis of his counterfactual import weights, and Coe and Helpman (1995) obtained a R^2 statistic of 0.709 in their original regressions.

Sjöholm (1996) took a different approach by analyzing citations in patent applications of Swedish firms to patents owned by inventors in other countries. Patent citations have been used in a number of studies now as an indicator for knowledge flows either between firms or between countries (see, for example, Jaffe, Trajtenberg, and Henderson, 1993). Sjöholm controlled for a number of other variables and found a positive and significant relation between Swedish patent citations and bilateral imports. He concluded that imports contributed to international knowledge spillovers.

Acharta and Keller (2008) looked at two channels by which imports affect productivity. The first is that import competition may lead to market share reallocation among domestic firms with different levels of production. This they called the "selection effect." The second is that imports can also improve the productivity of domestic firms through learning externalities or spillovers. They used a sample of seventeen industrialized countries covering the period 1973 to 2002. They reported two principal findings. First, increased imports lowered the productivity of domestic industries through selection. Second, if imports embodied advanced foreign technologies (as measured by their R&D intensity), increased imports could also generate technological learning through spillovers that on net raised the productivity of domestic industries.

Madsen (2007) took an even longer perspective on the relationship between trade and productivity growth. His data covered the period from 1870 to 2004. Using data for sixteen OECD countries from Maddison (1982) and augmenting them with data on bilateral trade flows and patents for each of the countries, he constructed a measure of knowledge imports from foreign countries. Using a cointegration method, he estimated that as much as 93 percent of the TFP growth of the average OECD country could be attributed to the international transmission of knowledge through the channel of imports.

An alternative vehicle for the transmission of technical know-how is through FDI. This involves the transfer of knowledge from one country to another and could be an important mechanism for the international technology diffusion (see Blomström and Kokko, 1998, for a survey of the various mechanisms involved in FDI spillovers).

Braconier and Sjöholm (1998) used a sample of nine industries for six large OECD countries covering the period from 1979 to 1991 to analyze the role of both R&D embodied in imports and R&D embodied in FDI. They found evidence of R&D spillovers, but these spillovers occurred within industry, and they were confined to industries that were relatively R&D intensive. They found very little evidence of spillovers between industries. Moreover, they did not find any effect on productivity growth from R&D embodied in intermediate imports.

Lichtenberg and van Pottelsberghe de la Potterie (2001) analyzed the importance of FDI as a source of international technology diffusion in thirteen OECD countries over the period from 1971 to 1990. They started out with the same twenty-two countries as Coe and Helpman (1995) but had to eliminate nine of these for lack of suitable data. They used the same R&D weighting approach as Coe and Helpman (1995) used for imports. However, it should be noted that reliable data on bilateral FDI were available to a much smaller extent than corresponding data for trade. Therefore, their data on FDI stocks were derived from balance-of-payments accounts. Other measures of multinational activity, such as subsidiary output, sales, or employment, are related also to FDI flows, and FDI data derived from balance-of-payment data only were likely to have a considerable amount of error.

Interestingly, Lichtenberg and van Pottelsberghe de la Potterie (2001) found that a country's *outward* FDI gave access to foreign technology. However, surprisingly, they did not find significant effects on country productivity from *inward* FDI. In other words, the country providing the investment was the one that benefited from FDI, not the one receiving the investment. Baldwin, Braconier, and Forslid (2005) reported some positive inward FDI spillover effects on the industry level, but overall, the results were decidedly mixed. Their study used the same technique to compute FDI flows as did Lichtenberg and van Pottelsberghe de la Potterie (2001) and might be subject to the same type of measurement error.

Xu (2000) used data on U.S. multinational enterprise (MNE) activity provided by the U.S. Bureau of Economic Analysis in order to analyze the relation between U.S. outward FDI and productivity growth in the host country. His analysis covered total manufacturing between 1966 and 1994 for forty countries, of which about half consisted of developed economies and the other half of less developed countries. Xu generally found a positive and significant relation between the host country's rate of productivity growth and the ratio of subsidiary value added to host country GDP. However, this association was decidedly stronger and more robust in the more developed countries than in the less developed ones.

Blitzer, Geishecker, and Görg (2007) used the OECD STAN database combined with input-output tables for OECD countries to examine the importance of FDI on the industry level. The data covered nine manufacturing industries in seventeen OECD countries, as well as ten Central and Eastern European (CEEC) transition economies over the period 1989 to 2003. Their main contribution was to look at both forward and backward linkages of the effects of FDI on output growth. Forward linkages refer to the relation between an output producer and its customer, while backward linkages refer to the relation between a producer and its suppliers. Their main finding was that there were strong backward linkages between multinationals and domestic firms for both groups of countries, and this effect was much higher for CEEC than OECD countries. This implies that FDI increases the productivity growth of industries that supply the multinational firms.

Several studies used microdata on the relation between firm (or plant) level productivity growth and FDI. Girma and Wakelin (2001) used microdata from the UK Census of Production to analyze the effects of inward FDI on productivity in the United Kingdom. They focused on the electronics industry between 1980 and 1992. Girma and Wakelin analyzed whether plant productivity growth was related to the ratio of foreign-owned plants to all plants in a given four-digit industry. They also looked at which countries provided the foreign investment and considered FDI in particular geographic regions within the United Kingdom and FDI in a particular (two-digit) industry. Their first test was for the presence of intraindustry FDI spillovers. In this regard, they found a positive effect from Japanese and other (excluding the United States and Japan) foreign FDI on industry productivity growth within the United Kingdom but not from U.S. FDI. The second examination looked for the presence of FDI spillovers based on geographic proximity. They found no evidence that within-region spillovers were stronger than those across regions. The third test was for the presence of FDI spillovers on the basis of technological proximity (that is, within the same industry). The authors did find statistical support for this.

Haskel, Pereira, and Slaughter (2002) used the same database as Girma and Wakelin (2001) but included both more years and plants from all of manufacturing in the sample. They first confirmed the findings of Girma and Wakelin that technological proximity had a positive effect on FDI spillovers, whereas geographic proximity within the United Kingdom did not. However, in contrast to Girma and Wakelin, they found positive spillovers from U.S. and French FDI on UK productivity but negative spillovers from Japanese FDI.

Kinoshita (2001) reported firm-level evidence on the effects of inward FDI in the Czech Republic between 1995 and 1998. The data were from the Czech Statistical Office though little documentation was provided. Unlike the two other studies reported previously, Kinoshita had information on R&D expenditures of the domestic firms, which might be an important omitted variable in the other two studies. After controlling for R&D spending, Kinoshita found no evidence of positive spillovers from inward FDI into the Czech Republic. However, he did find that if the FDI variable was interacted with the firm's own R&D expenditure, the coefficient on the interaction effect was positive and significant. One interpretation of this result is that the effects of international technology diffusion via FDI depend on a relatively high "absorptive capacity" of the firm as measured by the firm's own R&D expenditure.

Globermann, Kokko, and Sjöholm (2000) analyzed 220 patent applications by Swedish MNEs and non-MNEs for 1986. Patent citations were contained in these applications, and the authors were able to relate the patent citations to both inward FDI from the cited countries as well as outward FDI to the cited countries. On the basis of a conditional logit estimation framework, the three authors estimated a positive and significant association between outward FDI and patent citations. This was the case for both MNEs and non-MNEs. However, they failed to find a significant relation between patent citations and inward FDI.

In sum, the studies discussed earlier (and a host of others on these topics) were generally supportive that international trade, particularly imports, is positively related to a country's rate of productivity growth. However, several studies reported no statistical significant effect of the trade variables on country productivity growth. Moreover, the econometric results are generally much weaker at the industry (or sectoral) level. Econometric results are also sensitive to the econometric specification, particularly the exclusion or inclusion of a catch-up term, and to the sample of countries used and the time chosen. There is also the issue of causality, particularly in the case of exports – that is, do greater exports lead to higher productivity growth or the reverse? The results on the effect of R&D embodied in imports on country or industry productivity growth are mixed, particularly on the industry level. The same is true for the effects of FDI on the aggregate and industry levels. Overall, I would conclude that trade and FDI qualify as weak forces in productivity convergence.

5.7 Other Explanatory Factors

5.7.1 Infrastructure

Another factor that has steadily gained attention in recent years is the quantity and quality of infrastructure and its effects on economic growth. At the basis of this interest is the belief that infrastructure capital is an important ingredient in economic growth. The argument is that there are spillovers (externalities) from investment in public capital stock on that of the private capital stock. This is particularly true for the transport infrastructure and the transport related activities. For example, good public roads should increase the efficiency of the trucking industry. In the case of the United States, many believed that the low productivity growth of that country in the 1970s through the early 1990s could be attributed in part to the inadequate accumulation of infrastructure capital.

One of the earliest and most influential studies on the subject was an article by Aschauer (1989a). Using time series data for the United States, he included public sector capital in an aggregate production function for the U.S. economy and found that it exerted a very large effect on private sector productivity growth. Munnell (1990) and Eberts (1990) also reported qualitatively similar though smaller effects. Morrison and Schwartz (1996), using state-level cost functions, found that public infrastructure was a cost-saving input for manufacturing industries. Holtz-Eakin and Schwartz (1995) developed an augmented neoclassical growth model to simulate the effects of public capital accumulation on aggregate economic growth. They found little support for claims of a dramatic productivity boost from increased infrastructure outlays. In a specification designed to provide an upper bound for the influence of infrastructure, they estimated that raising the rate of infrastructure investment would have had a negligible impact on annual productivity growth in the United States between 1971 and 1986.

In sum, when the proper specifications are used and endogeneity is controlled for, the later studies cited here (as well as numerous other more recent studies) suggest that investment in public infrastructure plays at best a minor role in explaining country level and, particularly, industry level productivity growth.

5.7.2 Economic Geography

Physical distances between trading partners may affect both transport costs and the speed of knowledge transfers (through shipping time). One study that analyzed this factor is Boulhol, de Serres, and Molnar (2008), who examined how much of the disparities in productivity growth among OECD countries could be explained by economic geography factors. In particular, they focused on two aspects of economic geography: (1) the proximity of individual countries to areas of dense economic activity and (2) differences in endowments of natural resources. Selected indicators of distance to markets, transportation costs, and dependence on natural resources were added as explanatory variables in an augmented Solow model. Their econometric analysis was based on a panel data set comprising twenty-one countries and thirty-five years of observations (1970–2004). They found that three measures of distance to markets had a statistically significant effect on GDP per capita: the sum of bilateral distances, market potential, and the weighted sum of market access and supplier access. They estimated that the reduced access to markets relative to the OECD average contributed negatively to GDP per capita by as much as 10 percent in Australia and New Zealand. Conversely, a favorable impact of around 6 to 7 percent of GDP was found in the case of Belgium and the Netherlands.

5.7.3 Regulation

Many of the service industries in the industrialized countries have been until recently tightly regulated by the state. Many economists have argued that this has created a serious restriction on their potential for future productivity advance. There are two rationales. First, regulation may restrict competition and thus lead to a misallocation of resources within industry (and possibly between industries). Second, regulation may reduce the incentives for innovation, particularly if cost-plus pricing (that is, a fixed markup on costs) is used by the regulator. However, in many countries deregulation has occurred recently in several key service industries. Single country studies generally find enhancement benefits of deregulation.

The U.S. telephone industry underwent a partial deregulation in 1984. Before that year, there was one telephone system, AT&T, for the whole United States. In the 1984 divestiture, long-distance service was opened to competition and effectively deregulated, while local telephone service continued to be supplied by regulated Regional Bell Operating Companies.

My own calculations show that TFP growth increased after 1984 in the U.S. telecommunications industry as a whole. TFP growth averaged 3.0 percent per year between 1960 and 1984 and 3.7 percent per year from 1984 to 1993. On the surface, it appeared that deregulation helped to increase TFP growth in this industry. However, in a regression analysis of TFP growth on a constant and a dummy variable for the post-1984 period, the coefficient of the dummy variable was positive but not statistically significant (the t-value was 0.92). (The same result held with a time trend variable added.) Moreover, the telephone industry was characterized by two major technological innovations after 1984 – the introduction of digital switches and the replacement of copper cable by fiber optic cable. So even if the dummy variable for the post-1984 period was significant, it would still not be possible to ascribe the effect entirely to deregulation.

There are several other pertinent studies that also provide evidence on this question. A study of the Japanese telecommunications industry by Oniki, Oum, Stevenson, and Zhang (1994) did find a major gain in productivity growth after deregulation. In the early 1980s, the Japanese government opened the way for privatization of the Nippon Telegraph and Telephone Company and opened the market to competition. They reported that over the 1954–87 period TFP in the Japanese telecommunication industry grew by 3.4 percent per year. However, it increased much faster, 5.1 percent per year, in the postderegulation period, 1982–7. After controlling for scale, technology, and capacity utilization effects, they concluded that liberalization was the major source of TFP improvement in the industry.

Olley and Pakes (1994) analyzed the effects of the AT&T divestiture in the United States on productivity performance in the telecommunications equipment industry. Before 1984, all telephone equipment was manufactured by Western Electric, a subsidiary of AT&T. With divestiture, the equipment market was opened to competition. The authors found significant productivity gains in this industry after 1984. Between 1978 and 1987, TFP growth average 3.4 percent per year, but during the 1984–7 period, it averaged 4.1 percent per year. However, they pointed out that TFP growth was *negative* between 1981 and 1983 (–8.7 percent per year), and this appeared to be due to a massive reorganization of the industry in anticipation of divestiture.

Berndt, Friedlaender, Chiang, and Vellturo (1993) made a study of the effects of deregulation on the U.S. rail industry. The railroad freight industry was deregulated in 1979 by (1) easing rate setting restrictions, (2) simplifying merger procedures, and (3) allowing unprofitable routes to be abandoned. The period of analysis covered in the study was 1974 to 1986, which allowed a comparison between prederegulation and postderegulation cost performance of the rail freight industry. The authors controlled for other factors – particularly, the effect of mergers per se on railroad cost performance. They found that deregulation by itself reduced costs in the rail industry by 0.6 percentage point per year. This effect was statistically significant and persisted over time. By inference, this result implied that deregulation increased TFP growth in the rail industry by 0.6 percentage point per year.

Lichtenberg and Kim (1989) looked indirectly at the effects of deregulation in the U.S. air transportation industry on productivity performance. The airline industry in the United States was deregulated in the late 1970s, and this induced a wave of mergers and consolidations. The authors analyzed productivity performance over the 1970–84 period to isolate the effects of mergers on productivity performance in the industry. They found that TFP growth was increased by about 0.7 percentage point per year as a result of the merger activity. The primary reason was an increase in capacity utilization in the industry (the load factor).

Gordon (1992) created some doubt about the beneficial effects of deregulation in both the U.S. airlines and trucking industries. Gordon also found an acceleration in TFP growth in the railroad industry in the postderegulation 1978–87 period in comparison to the pre-1987 period, of about 1.7 percentage points per year. However, for the trucking industry, TFP growth in the postderegulation period of 1978–87 was estimated to be about 2 percentage points lower than in the 1969–78 period and for the airline industry, 1 percentage point lower. This latter result contrasted with the findings of Lichtenberg and Kim (1989).

Another aspect of regulation was provided by Gray and Shadbegian (1993), who looked at the effects of environmental regulation on plant level productivity performance in U.S. manufacturing over the period 1979 to 1985. They found very strong negative effects of environmental compliance on productivity growth – a 0.9 percentage point per year reduction in the paper industry, a 0.5 percentage point per year decrease in oil products, and 1.3 percentage point decline in the steel industry. Later work by the same two authors, Gray and Shadbegian (1994), seemed to suggest that these earlier estimates overstated the negative effects of pollution abatement expenditures on productivity. However, even in the later paper, the effects remained negative and statistically significant.

Several papers have investigated the importance of regulation as a factor in productivity convergence among OECD countries. I have already mentioned the work of Gust and Marquez (2004), who used three variables to measure the extent of regulation in a country. The first was an index of employment protection legislation. The second was an index of overall administrative regulatory burdens. The third was an index of regulatory burdens on start-up companies. They found that the extent of regulation in a country had a negative effect on IT spending.

Barone and Cingano (2008) used data from the OECD Stan database for seventeen OECD countries combined with corresponding OECD input-output tables over the period from 1996 to 2002. Their analysis was based on fifteen manufacturing industries. The main focus of the paper was the effect of regulation in service industries on the productivity performance of manufacturing industries that used these services. Cross-country measures of service sector regulation were obtained from the OECD Product Market Regulation (PMR) database. These measures attempted to quantify the degree to which the regulatory settings in a given service industry created barriers to entrepreneurship and restricted competition in domestic markets in cases where competition could be otherwise viable. They focused on three types of regulations. The first were entry barriers, which restricted entry into a service industry. The second were vertical integration restrictions, in which competitive activities such as electricity generation are separated from natural monopolies such as the national distribution network. The third was conduct regulation, which included restrictions on pricing and fees, advertising, and other forms of business activity. They found that countries with lower levels of regulation of their service industries exhibited faster rates of productivity growth among manufacturing industries using these services. This negative effect was particularly strong in the case of professional services and energy provision.

Buchele and Christiansen (1999) reached the opposite conclusion with regard to the effects of worker rights (including collective bargaining rights, employment protection, and income security) on productivity growth in a sample of fifteen advanced economies over the period from 1979 to 1994. They argued in favor of the cooperative model of labor relations, in which it is posited that increased worker participation in decisions and the firm organization can significantly raise worker effort. They used five measures of worker rights within a country: (1) collective bargaining coverage, (2) notification plus severance pay in months, (3) importance of regulatory obstacles to dismissal, (4) the unemployment insurance replacement rate, and (5) the degree of social protection as measured by public spending on health and income security as a share of GDP. They found that an index combining measures of worker rights and labor-management cooperation had a positive effect on the overall rate of growth of labor productivity.

In sum, deregulation may reduce productivity growth for two main reasons: (i) stifling competition and leading to a misallocation of resources and (ii) providing little incentive for innovation. The results of the studies cited previously (and elsewhere) are generally supportive that deregulation spurs productivity growth, though several studies found little (positive) effect. As a result, I would classify deregulation as a weak force in promoting productivity convergence.

5.7.4 Technology and Specialization

A related argument is that specialization itself might matter for overall growth performance. The argument harkens back to Adam Smith's *Wealth of Nations* (1776) that the division of labor might lead to increasing returns and therefore higher productivity gains. His classic example was the pin factory, where he argued that as the tasks performed by workers became more specialized, output per worker would rise. The argument has been extended in the recent literature to industry specialization. The argument today is that countries that specialize its production in particular industries will, ceteris paribus, have higher productivity growth than those that do not.

Several studies have provided some verification for this argument. Dalum, Laursen, and Verspagen (1999) constructed a measure of industry specialization using a measure called "revealed comparative advantage" (RCA) for eleven manufacturing industries, as follows:

$$RCA^h_j = [X^h_j / X_j] / [X^h / X]$$

where X is exports, the superscript h refers to country h, the subscript i indicates a product group (or sector), X_j is the total exports of product j, X^h is the total exports of country h, and X is the world total of exports. RCA^h_j thus measures country h's share of total exports of product j relative to h's share of total exports. RCA thus shows in what products (or industries) a country is particularly strong in terms of exports.

Dalum, Laursen, and Verspagen then used data for twenty OECD countries and the eleven manufacturing sectors and three periods: 1965–73, 1973–9, and 1979–88. They regressed industry output growth by country and period on the industry's RCA measure, as well as a number of control variables (such as the ratio of the sector's productivity in that country to the maximum sectoral value in order to pick up the "catch-up" effect). They generally found positive coefficients on RCA, a result that indicated that industries in which a country specialized did grow faster than other industries in the country. In other words, specialization did matter for growth.

Archibugi and Pianta (1992) investigated the relation between a country's size and level of development and its degree of industry specialization. They used data on patents filed in the United States, Germany, and the European

Patent Office in order to determine in which industries different countries specialize their research activity. They constructed a measure they called "technological revealed comparative advantage" or TRCA. This measure is similar to the RCA measure discussed earlier and measures the share of patents by country h in the class j to the overall share of country h in total patents. Examining data for eighteen OECD countries over the 1979–88 period, they found a clear inverse relation between a country's technological size (as measured by their cumulative R&D expenditures) and degree of technological specialization. In other words, while small and medium size countries are in a way forced to specialize in narrow niches, large countries can spread their technological activity across a wide variety of industries.

In a follow-up article, Archibugi and Pianta (1994) developed a measure of "technological distance" between pairs of countries on the basis of their pattern of patenting. Using data for the eighteen OECD countries over the years 1971 to 1990, they found that while these countries converged in terms of GDP per capita, their degree of technological specialization actually widened over these years. In other words, aggregate productivity advanced through greater industry specialization in new technology.

5.8 Concluding Comments

Empirical results on aggregate, countrywide productivity levels provide strong evidence of productivity convergence among the group of advanced industrialized nations over the period from about 1950 through the early to mid-1990s. For example, the ratio of the average TFP level of all countries except the United States to the U.S. level rose from 0.64 in 1950 to 0.82 in 1992 on the basis of the ISDB data. Moreover, the correlation coefficient between initial labor productivity level in 1950 and the rate of labor productivity growth from 1950 to 2002 was −0.85 among all twenty-four OECD countries on the basis of the Penn World Tables (PWT). Moreover, regressions of annual TFP growth on the relative TFP level reported in Table 5.1 negative coefficients that were statistically significant at the 5 percent level in the case of the ISDB data and the 1 percent level in the case of the Maddison data.

However, since about the mid-1990s or so, the United States has pulled further ahead of most of the other OECD countries in terms of productivity level. Several researchers, notably van Ark, O'Mahony, and Timmer (2008), attribute this to relatively greater investment in ICT on the part of the United States than other OECD countries.

This chapter also examined some of the factors responsible for the convergence of productivity levels among the group of OECD countries. Several "strong" forces played a major role. These include R&D investment, which most studies on the subject found to be highly significant (though in the regressions reported in Table 5.1 the R&D variable was not statistically significant). A second factor is the vintage effect, which in my own work reported earlier has consistently been shown to play a strong and statistically significant role. A third factor, education, will be discussed in detail in the next chapter.

Weaker forces were also at play. These include, first, structural change – notably the movement of employment out of low productivity agriculture and into other sectors. However, the importance of this factor has dissipated over time as the size of the agricultural sector has shrunk in almost all OECD countries. A second is geographical distance from the European trading base, which may explain a small part of the relatively poorer productivity growth of outlying countries like Australia and New Zealand. A third is technological specialization, which appears to have a positive though relatively small impact on aggregate productivity growth. A fourth, investment in public infrastructure, also appears to have a positive though relatively small effect on productivity growth (and an effect that was vastly overstated in the earlier literature on the subject).

The last of these examined in the chapter, international trade, the degree of openness, and FDI, has produced mixed results in the literature on this subject. The general argument in support of the import of this group of factors is that imports, exports, FDI, and R&D embodied in imports all constitute mechanisms for indirect knowledge transfer and associated knowledge spillovers. The general argument is compelling. However, the empirical work as noted previously on each of these factors has produced mixed results (including my own regression analysis reported in Table 5.1).

A further examination of the group of factors might prove to be a fruitful avenue for future research. Indeed, given the volume of research on this subject, it is surprising that no consensus has been reached in the literature. One would think that the degree of knowledge transfer mediated through imports and FDI would depend on the level of technological sophistication of the receiving country relative to the exporting country. Moreover, one might also think that the degree of knowledge transfer would be *industry-specific*, since technological sophistication would vary across industries within a particular country. I believe that further progress on this subject can come about only through an examination of trade patterns using industry level data of both the receiving country and the exporting country.

Appendix Table 5.1. *Average Annual Rates of Labor Productivity and Total Factor Productivity (TFP) Growth, 1950–1992*

Country Sample	1950–60	1960–73	1973–79	1979–92	1992
I. Penn World Tables Data[a]					
A. Average Annual Rate of Aggregate Labor Productivity Growth (%)					
USA	1.81	2.20	0.09	1.35	
Japan	6.40	7.68	2.41	3.41	
Other IC Countries[b]	3.53	3.40	1.21	1.43	
Other OECD Countries[b]	4.85	6.20	1.79	1.85	
All IC Countries[b]	3.59	3.56	1.21	1.53	
All OECD Countries[b]	3.80	4.00	1.31	1.58	
II. ISDB Data[c]					
A. Average Annual Rate of Aggregate Labor Productivity Growth (%)					
USA		1.84	0.05	0.93	
Japan		7.28	2.94	2.75	
Other IC Countries[b]		3.85	1.93	1.61	
All IC Countries[b]		3.6	1.87	1.65	
B. Average Annual Rate of Aggregate TFP Growth (%)					
USA		1.16	−0.29	0.47	
Japan		–	0.04	0.96	
Other IC Countries[b]		1.9	0.74	0.76	
All IC Countries[b]		1.71	0.62	0.75	
Ratio of average TFP level of all countries except the U.S. to the U.S. Level at the Beginning of the Period					
		0.64	0.74	0.78	0.82

Notes: [a] Defined as real GDP in 1985 international dollars per worker. Sources: 1950–90 – Penn World Tables, Version 6.1. OECD countries include Australia, Austria, Belgium, Canada, Denmark, Finland, France, Germany (West), Greece, Iceland, Ireland, Italy, Japan, Luxembourg, Netherlands, New Zealand, Norway, Portugal, Spain, Sweden, Switzerland, Turkey, the United Kingdom, and the United States. ICs (industrialized countries) include all OECD countries except Greece, Portugal, Spain, and Turkey

[b] Arithmetic average

[c] Labor productivity is defined as the ratio of GDP measured in 1985 prices and expressed in U.S. dollars to total employment. TFP is based on GDP in 1985 prices, total employment, and gross capital stock

Sources: OECD International Sectoral Database, diskettes, updated with data from OECD, National Accounts. ICs include Australia, Belgium, Canada, Denmark, Finland, France, Germany (West), Italy, Japan, Netherlands, Norway, Sweden, the United Kingdom, and the United States. The data for all countries cover the period 1960–92.

Appendix Table 5.2. *Real GDP per Worker (RGDPW) in OECD Countries,
1950-2002 (Figures are in 1,000s, 2,000 Dollar Equivalents)*

Country	1950	1960	1970	1980	1990	2002	Annual Growth Rate (percentage) 1950–2002
Australia	23.5	28.2	36.8	39.9	44.3	53.1	1.57
Austria	8.6	15.6	26.3	34.3	39.0	59.3	3.71
Belgium	15.9	20.9	32.4	40.5	46.3	61.1	2.58
Canada	23.5	28.5	36.4	41.9	50.3	51.2	1.49
Denmark	15.8	21.6	29.2	31.4	36.5	51.1	2.26
Finland	10.2	17.0	24.8	31.9	40.0	47.1	2.94
France	12.9	19.7	31.6	39.2	44.4	56.6	2.85
Germany, West	10.7	20.3	31.1	39.9	43.1	51.4	3.02
Greece	5.0	7.6	15.9	22.7	25.9	34.4	3.72
Iceland	12.7	18.4	22.8	32.9	36.5	44.9	2.43
Ireland	9.2	12.3	19.3	26.9	35.2	63.8	3.72
Italy	9.2	16.2	28.4	39.2	45.0	51.9	3.33
Japan	3.8	7.3	16.8	23.8	33.0	44.4	4.73
Luxembourg	20.8	27.5	37.1	41.7	55.4	115.9	3.31
Netherlands	16.7	25.0	37.1	42.7	45.6	57.1	2.37
New Zealand	25.4	31.1	35.2	36.0	37.1	43.4	1.03
Norway	14.9	20.9	28.4	37.0	42.7	65.4	2.84
Portugal	4.2	7.2	12.3	16.5	24.3	34.5	4.03
Spain	7.3	12.0	24.3	31.3	38.6	46.0	3.54
Sweden	19.3	25.4	33.9	36.4	41.5	47.5	1.73
Switzerland	21.9	29.4	39.8	43.1	47.9	54.6	1.76
Turkey	2.8	4.7	7.0	9.8	12.6	11.5	2.74
United Kingdom	17.1	21.6	27.2	31.0	39.2	50.9	2.10
United States	30.0	35.7	44.6	46.3	53.8	66.8	1.54
Summary Statistics: All 24 OECD Countries							
Mean	14.2	19.8	28.3	34.0	39.9	52.7	
Std. Deviation	7.5	8.3	9.2	8.9	9.5	17.8	
Coeff. of Var.	0.52	0.42	0.33	0.26	0.24	0.34	
Correlation with 1950 RGDPW							−0.85
Summary Statistics: 21 Industrial Market Economies (All Countries except Greece, Portugal, and Turkey)							
Mean	15.7	21.7	30.6	36.5	42.6	56.4	
Std. Deviation	6.8	7.0	7.0	5.8	6.0	15.3	
Coeff. of Var.	0.43	0.32	0.23	0.16	0.14	0.27	
Correlation with 1950 RGDPW							−0.88

Note: own computations from the Penn World Table Version 6.2

Appendix Table 5.3. *Growth in Capital Intensity, Investment Rate, Mean Years of Schooling, R&D Intensity, Openness, and Sectoral Composition, 1950–1992*

Country	1950–60	1960–73	1973–9	1979–92	1992
A. Average Annual Growth Rate, Gross Capital Stock to Total Employment (%)[a]					
USA		1.69	0.84	1.15	
Japan		--	7.17	4.43	
Other ICs		4.41	2.94	2.15	
All ICs		3.73	3.09	2.25	
B. Average Investment Rate over the Period (%)[b]					
USA	21.7	22.3	23.4	23.4	
Japan	19.4	32.3	37.2	36.1	
Other ICs	24.6	28.0	28.9	27.0	
Other OECD	16.3	24.0	28.0	24.1	
All ICs	24.2	27.9	29.0	27.3	
All OECD	22.9	27.3	28.8	26.7	
C. Average Annual Rate of Growth, Mean Years of Schooling (%)[c]					
USA		1.48	1.72	0.19	
Japan		0.42	1.98	0.96	
Other ICs		1.12	1.66	0.73	
Other OECD		0.76	4.10	3.03	
All ICs		1.10	1.68	0.71	
All OECD		1.04	2.10	1.12	
D. Average Level of Schooling, Beginning of the Period					
All ICs		6.92	7.89	8.71	9.47
All OECD		6.22	7.11	7.92	8.84
D. Expenditures on R&D as Percentage of GNP (or GDP)[d]					
USA		2.68	2.40	2.56	
Japan		1.86	2.00	2.47	
Other ICs		1.25	1.39	1.63	
Other OECD		0.25	0.20	0.29	
All ICs		1.36	1.47	1.73	
All OECD		1.16	1.31	1.54	
E. Scientists and Engineers Engaged in R&D per Million of Population[e]					
USA		2,560	2,833	2,800	
Japan		3,145	4,001	3,927	
Other ICs		1,000	1,576	1,368	
Other OECD		170	264	231	
All ICs		1,195	1,770	1,578	
All OECD		1,016	1,508	1,344	

Country	1950–60	1960–73	1973–9	1979–92	1992
F. Average Openness over the Period (%)[f]					
USA	9.2	10.3	16.7	19.1	
Japan	21.7	19.6	24.1	23.7	
Other ICs	57.5	61.0	70.9	77.4	
Other OECD	21.3	30.1	36.8	50.1	
All ICs	53.3	56.4	65.9	71.8	
All OECD	48.0	52.0	61.0	68.2	
G. Average Ratio of Exports to GNP over the Period (%)[g]					
USA		5.4	8.0	8.4	
Japan		10.1	12.3	12.4	
Other ICs		30.1	34.0	36.0	
Other OECD		12.5	14.7	20.1	
All ICs		27.7	31.5	33.3	
All OECD		25.1	28.6	31.0	
H. Average Ratio of Imports to GNP over the Period (%)[h]					
USA		4.9	8.4	9.7	
Japan		9.4	11.9	11.1	
Other ICs		29.8	34.2	35.5	
Other OECD		16.8	21.9	26.5	
All ICs		27.4	31.7	32.9	
All OECD		25.6	30.0	31.8	
I. Average Ratio of Merchandise Exports to GNP over the Period (%)[i]					
USA		4.4	6.4	6.5	
Japan		9.4	10.7	10.9	
Other ICs		20.2	22.7	24.4	
Other OECD		8.6	9.3	13.1	
All ICs		18.6	21.0	22.6	
All OECD		16.7	18.8	20.8	
J. Average Ratio of Merchandise Imports to GNP over the Period (%)[j]					
USA		4.5	7.0	8.1	
Japan		7.1	9.4	8.6	
Other ICs		22.2	25.7	26.5	
Other OECD		15.1	18.1	22.3	
All ICs		20.3	23.8	24.5	
All OECD		19.4	22.7	24.1	
K. Average Annual Change, Share of Total Employment in Agriculture (%)[k]					
USA		−0.24	−0.08	−0.06	
Japan		−1.40	−0.39	−0.40	
Other ICs		−0.73	−0.26	−0.17	
All ICs		−0.75	−0.25	−0.18	
Share of Total Employment in Agriculture, Beginning of Period					
All ICs		19.7	9.0	7.5	5.1

(*continued*)

Country	1950–60	1960–73	1973–9	1979–92	1992
L. Average Annual Change, Share of Total Employment in Manufacturing[k]					
USA		–0.12	–0.33	–0.47	
Japan		0.46	–0.56	0.00	
Other ICs		–0.06	–0.44	–0.39	
All ICs		–0.01	–0.44	–0.37	
Share of Total Employment in Manufacturing, Beginning of Period					
All ICs		27.1	26.5	23.9	19.2
M. Average Annual Change, Share of Total Employment in Stagnant Services (%)[l]					
USA		0.40	0.41	0.65	
Japan		0.52	0.77	0.44	
Other ICs		0.58	0.87	0.63	
All ICs		0.63	0.83	0.62	
Share of Total Employment in Stagnant Services, Beginning of Period					
All ICs		36.0	46.0	50.8	58.7

Notes: Main sources are (i) OECD International Sectoral Database (ISDB) diskettes, updated with data from OECD, National Accounts. ICs include Australia, Belgium, Canada, Denmark, Finland, France, Germany (West), Italy, Japan, Netherlands, Norway, Sweden, the United Kingdom, and the United States. The data for all countries cover the period 1960–92

(ii) Penn World Tables, Version 6.2. OECD countries include Australia, Austria, Belgium, Canada, Denmark, Finland, France, Germany (West), Greece, Iceland, Ireland Italy, Japan, Luxembourg, Netherlands, New Zealand, Norway, Portugal, Spain, Sweden, Switzerland, Turkey, the United Kingdom, and the United States. ICs (industrialized countries) include all OECD countries except Greece, Portugal, Spain, and Turkey.

Figures for Other ICs, All ICs, Other OECD, and All OECD are based on arithmetic averages

[a] Gross capital stock is measured in 1985 prices, expressed in U.S. dollars. *Source:* OECD International Sectoral Database, diskettes

[b] Defined as the ratio of real gross domestic investment to GDP, both in current international dollars. Source: Penn World Tables, Version 6.2

[c] Source: Barro and Lee (1996), appendix tables

[d] R&D expenditures include both private and governmental sources. Source: UNESCO Statistical Yearbooks, 1963–1992

[e] *Source:* UNESCO Statistical Yearbooks, 1963–1992

[f] Defined as the ratio of exports plus imports to GDP, all in nominal terms. Source: Penn World Tables, Version 6.2

[g] Defined as the ratio of exports of goods and nonfinancial services (national accounts measure) to GNP, both in local currency and current prices. *Source:* World Bank, World Tables, 1994, diskettes

[h] Defined as the ratio of imports of goods and nonfinancial services (national accounts measure) to GNP, both in local currency and current prices. *Source:* World Bank, World Tables, 1994, diskettes

[i] Defined as the ratio of merchandise exports, fob (balance of payments measure) to GNP, both converted to U.S. dollars. *Source:* World Bank, World Tables, 1994, diskettes

[j] Defined as the ratio of merchandise imports, fob (balance of payments measure) to GNP, both converted to U.S. dollars. *Source:* World Bank, World Tables, 1994, diskettes

[k] *Source:* OECD International Sectoral Database, diskettes

[l] "Stagnant" services are defined to include (i) trade, restaurants, and hotels; finance, insurance, and real estate; (iii) community, social, and personal services; and (iv) government services. *Source:* OECD International Sectoral Database, diskettes

Further Details on the Role of Eduction and Technology in the Productivity Performance among the Advanced Industrial Countries

6.1 The Role of Education

There are three paradigms that appear to dominate current discussions of the role of education in economic growth. The first has stemmed from human capital theory. The second could be classified as a catch-up model. And the third important approach has stressed the interactions between education and technological innovation and change.

6.1.1 The Human Capital Approach

Human capital theory views schooling as an investment in skills and hence as a way of augmenting worker productivity (see, for example, Schultz 1960, 1961, and 1971; and Becker, 1975).[1] This line of reasoning leads to growth accounting models in which productivity or output growth is derived as a function of the change in educational attainment.

The early studies on this subject showed very powerful effects of educational change on economic growth. Griliches (1970) estimated that the increased educational attainment of the U.S. labor force accounted for one-third of the Solow residual, the portion of the growth of output that could not be attributed to the growth in (unadjusted) labor hours or capital stock, between 1940 and 1967. Denison (1979b) estimated that about one-fifth of the growth in U.S. national income per person employed between 1948 and 1973 could be attributed to increases in educational levels of the labor force.[2] Jorgenson and Fraumeni (1993) calculated that improvements in labor quality accounted for one-fourth of U.S. economic growth

---

[1] Adam Smith (1776) was, perhaps, the first to put forward this view.
[2] Edward Denison's 1962 book appears to be the first work to provide detailed estimates of the contribution of education to economic growth.

between 1948 and 1986. Maddison (1987), in a growth accounting study of six OECD countries covering the years 1913 to 1984, generally found that increases in educational attainment explained a significant proportion of productivity growth, though the contributions varied by country and subperiod.

Yet, some anomalies appeared in this line of inquiry. Denison (1983) in his analysis of the productivity slowdown in the United States between 1973 and 1981 reported that the growth in national income per person employed (NIPPE) fell by 0.2 percentage point whereas increases in educational attainment contributed a *positive* 0.6 percentage point to the growth in NIPPE. In other words, whereas educational attainment was increasing, labor productivity growth was falling. Maddison (1982) reported similar results for other OECD countries for the 1970–9 period. Benhabib and Spiegel (1992), using the Kyriacou series on educational attainment (see Chapter 9), found no statistically significant effect of the growth in mean years of schooling on the growth in GDP per capita among a sample of countries at all levels of economic development, when a "catch-up" term was included.

6.1.2 Catch-Up Models

The second strand views the role of education in the context of a productivity "catch-up" or "convergence" model. Previous explanations of the productivity convergence process almost all involve the advantages of backwardness, by which it is meant that much of the catch-up can be explained by the diffusion of technical knowledge from the leading economies to the more backward ones (see Gerschenkron, 1952, and Kuznets, 1973, for example). Competitive pressures in the international economy ensure rapid dissemination of superior productive techniques from one country to another. Through the constant transfer of knowledge, countries learn about the latest technology from each other, but virtually by definition the followers have more to learn from the leaders than the leaders have to learn from the laggards. One direct implication of this view is that countries that lag behind the leaders can be expected to increase their productivity performance toward the level of the leading nations and, ceteris paribus, should experience higher *rates* of productivity growth.

However, being backward does not itself guarantee that a nation will catch up. Other factors must be present, such as strong investment, an educated and well-trained workforce, research and development activity, developed trading relations with advanced countries, a receptive political structure, low population growth, and the like. Indeed, Abramovitz (1986 and 1994) summarized this group of characteristics under the rubric of *social capability*.[3]

In this context, education is viewed as one index of the social capability of the labor force to borrow existing technology. One of the prime reasons for the relatively weak growth performance of the less developed countries is their failure to keep up with, absorb, and utilize new technological and product information, and to benefit from the international dissemination of technology. One of the elements that can be expected to explain an economy's ability to absorb information and new technology is the education of its populace. In this context, education may be viewed as a *threshold effect* in that a certain level of education input might be considered a necessary condition for the borrowing of advanced technology. Moreover, varying levels of schooling might be required to implement technologies of varying sophistication. On an econometric level, the correct specification would then relate the *rate* of productivity growth to the *level* of educational attainment.

Baumol, Blackman and Wolff (1989, chapter 9) were among the first to report an extremely strong effect of educational level on the growth in per capita income among a cross section of countries covering all levels of development (the chapter was originally written and circulated in 1986). For the educational variable, they used the (gross) enrollment rate, defined as the ratio of the number of persons enrolled in school to the population of the corresponding age group. Enrollment rates were constructed for primary school, secondary school, and higher education. They also used various country samples and periods – 66 countries for 1950–81, 112 countries for 1960–81, and 105 countries for 1965–84. The first two data sets were based on the Summers-Heston sample described in Summers and Heston (1984) and the last was calculated from the World Bank's *World Development Report, 1986*.

Since that time, many other studies have reported similar results on educational enrollment rates using both more recent data, particularly the 1960–85 Summers-Heston sample described in Summers and Heston (1988), and data from Penn World Table Mark V (see Summers and Heston, 1991) covering the period 1960–88, and a more varied assortment of country samples (see, for example, Barro, 1991; and Mankiw, Romer, and Weil,

---

[3]   This process was also referred to as conditional convergence by Mankiw, Romer, and Weil (1992). See Chapter 2 for more discussion.

1992). In these two, as well as in most others, the *secondary school enrollment rate* was used as the measure of educational input.

However, several cracks appeared to have formed in this strand of research (see Wolff and Gittleman, 1993, for details). First, the introduction of a number of "auxiliary" variables – most notably, investment – mitigated the importance of education in the growth process. Second, whereas primary and secondary school enrollment rates both remained statistically significant as a factor in explaining economic growth, the *university enrollment rate* often appeared statistically insignificant.

Third, the use of enrollment rates in productivity growth regressions was aptly criticized because they are not indices of the educational attainment of the current labor force but of the future labor force.[4] Moreover, high enrollment rates may be a consequence of high productivity growth – that is, the causation may go the other way. As a result, several studies have used educational attainment at a particular point in time instead of educational enrollment rates in cross-country regressions in which growth in GDP per capita is the dependent variable. However, measures of the direct *educational attainment of the labor force* (or of the adult population) often produced weaker results than the use of enrollment rates (see Wolff and Gittleman, 1993, for details).

6.1.3 Interactions with Technical Change

A third strand emanates from the work of Arrow (1962) and Nelson and Phelps (1966). Arrow introduced the notion of *learning by doing*, which implies that experience in the application of a given technology or new technology in the production process leads to increased efficiencies over time. As a result, measured labor productivity in an industry should increase over time, at least until diminishing returns set in. One implication of this is that an educated labor force should "learn faster" than a less educated group and thus increase efficiency faster.

In the Nelson-Phelps model, it is argued that having a more educated workforce may make it easier for a firm to adopt and implement new technologies. Firms value workers with education because they are more able to evaluate and adapt innovations and to learn new functions and routines than less educated ones. Thus, by implication, countries with more

---

[4] Mankiw, Romer, and Weil (1992) tried to avoid this problem in their regression analysis by using the ratio of secondary school enrollment to the working-age population, a variable that they interpreted as a proxy for the human capital investment rate.

educated labor forces should be more successful in implementing new technologies.[5]

The Arrow and Nelson-Phelps line of reasoning suggests that there may be interaction effects between the educational level of the workforce and measures of technological activity, such as the R&D intensity of a country. Several studies provided some corroboration of this effect. Welch (1970) analyzed the returns to education in U.S. farming in 1959 and concluded that a portion of the returns to schooling resulted from the greater ability of more educated workers to adapt to new production technologies. Bartel and Lichtenberg (1987), using industry-level data for sixty-one U.S. manufacturing industries over the 1960–80 period, found that the relative demand for educated workers was greater in sectors with newer vintages of capital. They inferred from this that highly educated workers have a comparative advantage with regard to the implementation of new technologies.

A related finding was reported by Mincer and Higuchi (1988), using U.S. and Japanese employment data, that returns to education were higher in sectors undergoing more rapid technical change. Another was from Gill (1989), who calculated on the basis of U.S. Current Population Survey data for 1969–84 that returns to education for highly schooled employees were greater in industries with higher rates of technological change. Howell and Wolff (1992) and Wolff (1996b), using industry level data for forty-three industries covering the period 1970–85, found that the growth of cognitive skill levels (as defined by the *Dictionary of Occupational Titles*) of employees was positively related to indices of industry technological change, including computer intensity, capital vintage, and R&D activity.

6.1.4 Methodological Issues

There are several methodological problems in the types of cross-country growth regressions cited in the preceding literature (see Levine and Renelt, 1992). First, there may be problems of comparability with cross-country measures of many of the independent variables used in this type of analysis, particularly between countries at very different levels of development. Behrman and Rosenzweig (1994), for example, stressed the difficulties in comparing educational measures across countries, particularly in regard to the quality of schooling. Second, a related problem is that the availability of educational attainment data is much more limited than that of enrollment

---

[5]   These ideas were revived and reformulated in the "new growth theory" of Lucas (1988) and Romer (1990).

data. This may bias the sample of countries and the regression results. Also, imputations of missing educational data can also be misleading (again, see, Behrman and Rosenzweig, 1994). Third, there may be specification problems in the equations that relate education and other variables to productivity or output growth. Levine and Renelt (1992) reported that econometric results for certain exogenous variables were very sensitive to the form in which they were entered into the regression equation.

6.1.5 Objective

The objective of this chapter is to examine the three alternative models of the relation of education to economic growth described through an empirical analysis. I will also try to account, at least in part, for any discrepancies in results and, perhaps, to shed some new light on the role of education in economic growth.

In this study, I will confine the analysis to OECD countries. This has two methodological advantages. First, it will provide a relatively consistent sample of countries to be used in testing a wide range of models (though, in some cases, missing observations will force the exclusion of one or more of these countries). Second, it will mitigate, to some extent, problems of comparability of educational data. However, it should be stressed even at this point that educational systems do differ even among OECD countries. For example, as Maddison (1991) noted, scores on standardized tests of cognitive achievement were usually much lower in the United States than in other industrialized countries at the same grade level. Moreover, some countries, such as Germany, have an extensive system of apprentice training integrated with part-time education, which is not reflected in the figures for formal schooling.[6] Thus, comparisons of standard measures of formal schooling even in this select sample of countries must be interpreted cautiously. We shall return to this point again in the conclusion of the chapter.

The remainder of this chapter is organized as follows: The following section (Section 6.2) provides descriptive statistics on productivity levels and on educational enrollment and attainment for OECD countries. Section 6.3 reports econometric results on the effects of educational enrollment and attainment levels on per capita income growth. Section 6.4 analyzes the role of the growth in educational capital in productivity and output growth. Section 6.5 investigates evidence on interactive effects between education

---

[6] The OECD has recently changed this in their published education figures and now counts German apprentices as enrolled in full-time postsecondary education.

and R&D. Section 6.6 discusses results from the model developed by Mankiw, Romer, and Weil (1992). Section 6.7 surveys other literature on the relation between education and growth among advanced countries. Section 6.8 presents concluding remarks and discusses the implications of this work.

6.2 Comparative Statistics among OECD Countries

Figures 6.1 through 6.3 (and Appendix Tables 6.1 to 6.3) show measures of educational levels among OECD countries (these results update the work of Wolff, 2000). Figures 6.1a and 6.1b show gross enrollment rates, defined as the ratio of the number of persons enrolled in school to the population of the corresponding age group by educational level (also see Appendix Table 6.1).[7] There was almost 100 percent enrollment at the primary school level and almost no variation among countries in this group. In contrast, the average secondary school enrollment rate increased rather steadily over time from 60 percent in 1965 to 116 percent in 2002 among all OECD countries and from 63 to 120 percent among the Industrial Market Economies (IMEs). The standard deviation remained relatively stable between 1965 and 1991 and then jumped in 2002. The increase between 1991 and 2002 reflected the surge in secondary school enrollment in Australia, Denmark, Finland, Sweden, and the United Kingdom. Because of the rising mean, the coefficient of variation fell from 0.27 in 1965 to 0.16 in 1991 among all OECD nations and from 0.20 in 1965 to 0.11 in 1991 among IMEs. However, because of the surge in secondary school enrollment in the five countries, the coefficient of variation climbed back to 0.20 in 2002 among all OECD countries and to 0.19 in 2002 among IMEs.

The largest dispersion is found on the higher education level. In 1965, on average, only 13 percent of college-age adults were enrolled in tertiary school, with the United States the highest at 40 percent and Turkey the lowest at 4 percent (Spain was the lowest at 6 percent among IMEs). However, by 1991, the average enrollment rate had tripled to 39 percent, and then almost doubled again to 63 percent in 2002, with Finland now leading at 88 percent and Turkey the lowest at 28 percent (Austria and Switzerland were the lowest at 49 percent among IMEs).[8] The standard deviation actually rose over time for both country samples between 1965 and 1991 (particularly, 1983 to

---

[7] These ratios can exceed 100 percent. For example, secondary schools can enroll students who are older than the "normal" secondary school range.

[8] The Canadian figure seems unrealistically high for 1991, but that is what is reported in the UNESCO data source.

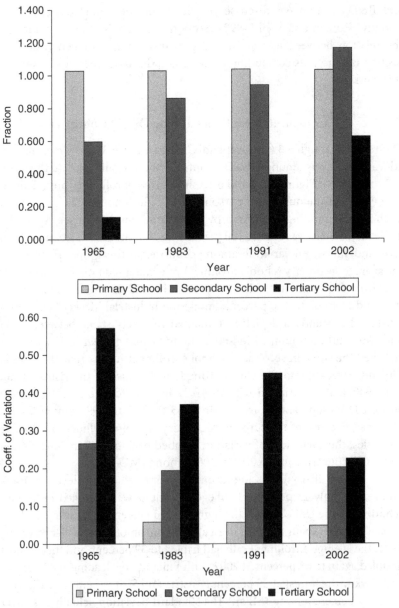

Figure 6.1 (a) Average gross enrollment rates in 23 OECD countries by educational level, 1965–2002; (b) coefficient of variation of gross enrollment rates in 23 OECD countries by educational level, 1965–2002 (*Source: UNESCO Statistical Yearbooks*).

1991), and then declined between 1991 and 2002. The coefficient of variation fell from 0.57 in 1965 to 0.37 in 1983, then increased to 0.45, and then declined again to 0.22 among all OECD countries, for a net decline over the full 1965 to 2002 period. A similar pattern is evident for the IMEs.[9]

Educational attainment rates, defined as the proportion of the population twenty-five and older who have attained the indicated level of schooling or greater, are shown in Figures 6.2a and 6.2b for years 1960, 1970, 1979, and 1996 (also see Appendix Table 6.2). A word should be said about the reliability of the data. Unlike the enrollment rate data of the preceding table, which appear to be relatively consistent over time, there are several anomalies in the attainment rate data. At the primary school level, there appear to be substantial declines in attainment rates for Greece and Ireland between 1960 and 1970; for Australia, Italy, the Netherlands, and the United Kingdom between 1970 and 1979; and for Switzerland over the entire 1960–79 period. Moreover, Australia's attainment rate at the secondary school level seems to have fallen from 70 to 51 percent and at the higher education level from 22 to 13 percent between 1970 and 1979 though both picked up a bit by 1996, whereas Norway's secondary school rate appears to increase from 30 to 91 percent from 1970 to 1979 though it then fell back to 82 percent by 1996. In Canada, the attainment rate at the tertiary level appears to have fallen from 37 percent in 1979 to only 17 percent in 1996, despite the huge increase in the enrollment rate at this level, and in New Zealand from 27 to 11 percent over the same period.

Insofar as enrollment rates rose in all these countries between 1965 and 1983, it is hard to believe that attainment rates could have fallen. One possible explanation is the immigration of people with low schooling levels to these countries (Australia, perhaps) or the emigration of highly educated individuals (Britain, perhaps). The more likely explanation is errors in the data. These figures are derived from *UNESCO Yearbooks* and are based on country responses to questionnaires. There may have been changes in country reporting methods over time and/or compilation errors on the part of UNESCO. In any case, I am not in a position to improve on these results.

Despite these reservations, the overall pattern of results is quite sensible. Attainment rates are, not surprisingly, lower than the corresponding enrollment rates, since enrollment rates have been increasing over time (that is, attainment rates for the adult population in a given year reflect the

---

[9] If we exclude Canada, the standard deviation still rose for both country samples between 1965 and 1991, though the coefficient of variation fell between 1983 and 1991 for all OECD countries and rose slightly among the IMEs.

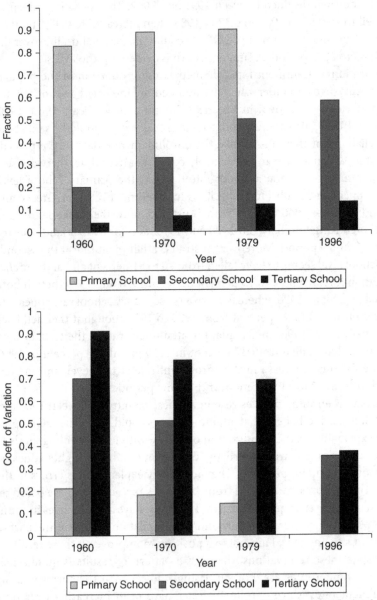

Figure 6.2 (a) Mean educational attainment rates in 24 OECD countries by level, 1960–1996; (b) coefficient of variation of educational attainment rates in 24 OECD countries by level, 1960–1996 (*Source: UNESCO Statistical Yearbooks*).

enrollment rates when the adults were children). However, changes over time and differences between countries in attainment rates present a similar picture to those based on enrollment rates. Between 1960 and 1996 (1979 in the case of primary schooling), average attainment rates among the adult population rose at all three educational levels. Secondary school attainment rates almost tripled and higher education attainment rates more than tripled. The coefficient of variation in attainment rates fell at all three educational levels, particularly at the higher education level, though the standard deviation increased at both the secondary and tertiary levels.

Figures 6.3a and 6.3b show data on mean schooling of the total population aged twenty-five and above, derived from Barro and Lee (2000) (also see Appendix Table 6.3). They began with benchmark data from UNESCO sources on attainment rates by educational level and then updated (or backdated) the attainment figures on the basis of school enrollment rates by level in preceding and succeeding years. Their data show a reasonable amount of internal consistency over time.

Average schooling levels rose continuously from 1960 to 1999. In 1999, the United States had the highest mean schooling level at 12.3 years. Norway was second at 11.9, and New Zealand third at 11.5. At the bottom of the list were Turkey, at 4.8 years, Portugal, at 4.9 years, and Italy, at 7.0 years. The standard deviation of schooling levels remained fairly constant over time, while the coefficient of variation in schooling levels showed a decline between 1960 and 1999, from 0.33 to 0.21. This result was due to rising mean schooling levels.

In summary, two important trends are evident with regard to education. First, there was a significant increase in average schooling levels in OECD countries since 1960, particularly at the secondary and tertiary levels (primary school levels were already high at the beginning of the post–World War II period). Second, the dispersion in educational levels among the various OECD countries declined substantially over the postwar period, particularly at the secondary level, though it appears to have risen for enrollment rates at the secondary and higher education levels during the 1990s.

Figures 6.4a and 6.4b show statistics on one important indicator of the technology intensity of production, the ratio of research and development (R&D) expenditure to GNP (also see Appendix Table 6.4).[10] The ranges are considerable. In the 1969–72 period, R&D expenditure as a percentage of GNP ranged from lows of 0.20 in Greece and 0.25 in Spain to a high of

---

[10] Both public and private sources of funding are included in the tabulations. In later years, GDP is used as the denominator.

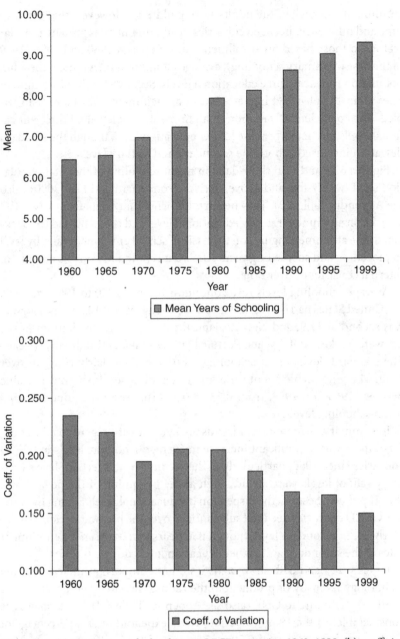

Figure 6.3 (a) Mean years of schooling in OECD countries, 1960–1999; (b) coefficient of variation of schooling in OECD countries, 1960–1999 (*Source*: Barro and Lee, 2000).

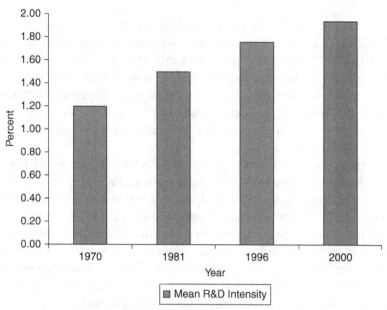

Figure 6.4a Mean R&D intensity among OECD countries, 1970–2000 (*Source*: OECD Analytical Business Enterprise Research and Development database [ANBERD]).

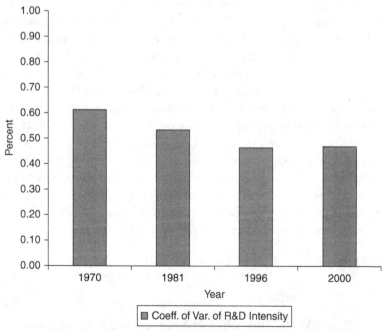

Figure 6.4b Coefficient of variation of R&D intensity among OECD countries, 1970–2000 (*Source*: ANBERD database).

2.70 in the United States and from a low of 0.20 in Greece to a high of 2.80 in Sweden in 1982–5. In 1996, the range went from 0.45 in Turkey to 3.59 in Sweden, and in 1999–2001 from 0.64 in Turkey to 4.21 in Sweden. In 1999–2001, the United States ranked fourth, behind Sweden, Finland, and Japan. Two trends are apparent. First, the average R&D intensity increased between 1970 and 2001; and, second, the coefficient of variation declined. The trends were stronger among the industrial market economies than among all OECD countries.

On the surface, at least, there appears to be a direct relation between schooling levels and labor productivity levels, as reported in Appendix Table 6.2. First, the convergence in educational levels among OECD countries appears to correspond to the convergence in labor productivity levels over the post–World War II period. Second, the increase in schooling levels seems to correspond to the growth in labor productivity over this period. Moreover, as productivity and educational levels were growing and converging among OECD countries, so was their R&D intensity of production. We now turn to regression analysis to analyze these relations more systematically.

6.3 Catch-Up Models

For heuristic reasons, I begin the econometric analysis with the catch-up model. As noted in Section 6.1.2, this approach implies that education should be interpreted as a threshold effect and leads to an econometric specification in which the rate of productivity growth is a function of the *level* of schooling. Of course, one is still left with the difficulty of deciding which year to use for the educational variable. When productivity growth is measured over a short period, the model would suggest using educational attainment as of the beginning of the period. However, when productivity growth is measured over a long period, educational levels will likely be rising and initial education may not be relevant for characterizing the ability of the workforce to adopt new technology toward the end of the period. In this case, one might use the average educational level over the period. Of course, as a matter of practicality, one is limited in choice by the available data.

The basic model specification is as follows:

$$\ln\left(\text{RGDPW}_1 / \text{RGDPW}_0\right) / \left(t_1 - t_0\right) = b_0 + b_1 \text{RGDPW}_{0'} + b_2 \text{INVRATE} \\ + b_3 \text{RDGNP} + b_4 \text{EDUC} + \varepsilon$$

$$(6.1)$$

where $\ln(\text{RGDPW}_1/\text{RGDPW}_0)/(t_1 - t_0)$ is the annual rate of growth in real GDP per worker from time 0 to time 1; $\text{RGDPW}_{0'}$ is RGDPW near the beginning of the period; INVRATE is the average investment rate, defined as the ratio of investment to GDP, both in 1985 dollar equivalents, averaged over the period of analysis; RDGNP is the average ratio of R&D expenditures to GNP, averaged over the period; EDUC is a measure of educational input; and ε is a stochastic error term.[11] Also, the coefficient b_3 is usually interpreted as the rate of return to R&D. Mankiw, Romer, and Weil (1992) provide theoretical justification for this approach, deriving this specification from an augmented Solow model (see Chapter 2 for a discussion).

The convergence hypothesis predicts that the coefficient b_1 will be negative (that is, countries further behind near the beginning of the period will show more rapid increases in GDP per worker). The coefficients of the investment rate (b_2), R&D intensity (b_3), and education (b_4) should be positive. Results are shown in Table 6.1 for all OECD countries over the 1950–2000 period and for selected educational measures.

The RGDPW level of the country relative to the U.S. level is by far the most powerful explanatory variable in accounting for differences in labor productivity growth among OECD countries. By itself, the catch-up variable explains 74 percent of the variation in RGDPW growth over the 1950–2000 period. The coefficient of INVRATE is positive and significant at the 1 or 5 percent level except in three cases where it is significant at the 10 percent level. The average investment rate, together with the catch-up variable, explains 80 percent of the variation in RGDPW growth. R&D intensity is significant in most cases (and typically at the 10 percent level).

The educational enrollment rates have positive coefficients in all three cases but are not significant. The coefficients of attainment rates are insignificant for secondary and university attainment but significant for primary school attainment levels (at the 5 percent level). The results for primary education are unexpected, because this is the level of schooling that would appear to have least relevance to the types of sophisticated technology in use among OECD countries in the post–World War II period. Also there is little variation in this measure among OECD countries, except for Greece,

[11] In order partially to allay the criticisms of Friedman (1992), I use the value of RGDPW near the beginning of the period rather than $RGDPW_0$ in the regression analysis. See his comment for more details. I also use labor productivity growth, as opposed to the growth in GDP per capita, as has been used in most previous studies, including my own, or GDP per adult, as used in Mankiw, Romer, and Weil (1992). As a result, the results reported here will differ somewhat from those of previous studies. Also see Chapter 3 for a discussion of econometric issues regarding the estimation of productivity growth equations.

Table 6.1. *Regressions of the Annual Growth in Real GDP per Worker (RGDPW) on Initial RGDPW, the Investment Rate, R&D, and Educational Enrollment and Attainment Levels, All OECD Countries, 1950–2000*

Relative $RGDPW_{55}$	INVRATE	Ratio of R&D to GNP (GDP)	Education Variable	R^2	Adjusted R^2	Standard Error	Sample Size	Education Variable
-0.017** (7.99)				0.74	0.73	0.0056	24	
-0.016** (8.35)	0.063* (2.38)			0.80	0.78	0.0051	24	
-0.018** (8.20)	0.064* (2.51)	0.314# (1.80)		0.83	0.80	0.0050	24	
-0.018** (8.12)	0.074** (2.93)	0.366* (2.16)	0.031 (1.66)	0.85	0.82	0.0048	23	PRIM–ENRL65–02
-0.019** (6.81)	0.059# (2.01)	0.308 (1.72)	0.004 (0.38)	0.83	0.79	0.0051	23	SCND–ENRL65–02
-0.021** (7.92)	0.073** (2.93)	0.274 (1.51)	0.033 (1.72)	0.86	0.82	0.0048	22	UNIV–ENRL65–02
-0.022** (8.92)	0.039 (1.60)	0.264 (1.59)	0.029* (2.54)	0.88	0.85	0.0044	22	PRIM–ATTN60–79
-0.017** (5.67)	0.061* (2.31)	0.421# (2.03)	-0.008 (0.66)	0.84	0.80	0.0051	22	SCND–ATTN60–96
-0.018** (5.35)	0.059# (2.10)	0.364# (1.93)	-0.016 (0.49)	0.84	0.80	0.0051	23	UNIV–ATTN60–96
-0.015** (4.60)	0.072* (2.85)	0.344# (2.02)	-0.001 (1.48)	0.85	0.81	0.0048	23	MEAN–EDUC60–99

Notes: The absolute values of t-ratios are shown in parentheses below the coefficient estimate.

Key:

Dependent variable: ln(RGDPW00/RGDPW50)/50

RGDPWt: GDP per worker in year t, measured in 1985 international prices (in units of $10,000).

Source: Penn World Table Mark 5.6

Relative RGDPW55: RGDPW level of the country relative to the RGDPW level of the U.S. in 1955.

Source: Penn World Table Mark 5.6

INVRATE: Ratio of investment to GDP (both in 1985 dollar equivalents) averaged over the regression period. *Source:* Penn World Table Mark 5.6

RDGNP: Expenditure for R&D as a percentage of GNP (GDP).

Source: UNESCO Statistical Yearbook, 1963–2001

PRIM-ENRLt: Total enrollment of students of all ages in primary school in year t as a proportion of the total population of the pertinent age group.

PRIM-ENRLt-t': Average primary school enrollment rate in t and t'

SCND-ENRLt: Total enrollment of students of all ages in secondary school in year t as a proportion of the total population of the pertinent age group.

SCND-ENRLt-t': Average secondary school enrollment rate in t and t'

UNIV-ENRLt: Total enrollment of students of all ages in higher education in year t as a proportion of the total population of the pertinent age group.

UNIV-ENRLt-t': Average tertiary school enrollment rate in t and t'

PRIM-ATTNt: Proportion of the population age 25 and over who have attended primary school or higher in year t

SCND-ATTNt: Proportion of the population age 25 and over who have attended secondary school or higher in year t

UNIV-ATTNt: Proportion of the population age 25 and over who have attended an institution of higher education in year t

MEAN-EDUCt: Mean years of schooling of the of the total population aged 25 and over in year t, from Barro and Lee (2000). BL-EDUCt-t': Average years of schooling from t to t'

significant at the 10 percent level, 2-tail test

* significant at the 5 percent level, 2-tail test

** significant at the 1 percent level, 2-tail test

Portugal, and Turkey (the three nonindustrial market economies). However, even when these three countries are excluded from the sample, the coefficient remains significant at the 5 percent level. I shall comment more on this result in Section 6.7. The last line shows results for mean educational levels. Its coefficient is insignificant and, indeed, has a negative value.[12]

It is possible that the use of cross-sectional regressions, where variables are averaged over time, might cause relatively low variability of the education variables and thus result in low significance levels. In Table 6.2, I use pooled cross-section, time series data for the twenty-four OECD countries and periods 1960–80 and 1980–2000. As a result of data limitations, the only education variables that could be used are the enrollment rates. The regression results are similar to those in the cross-section analysis of Table 6.1. The coefficients of the enrollment rates remain insignificant. In fact, for the secondary and tertiary levels, the coefficients are negative. The catch-up term is less significant than before (because of the shorter time), as are the R^2 and adjusted-R^2 statistics, but the investment rate variable is stronger. There is little change in the coefficients of the R&D variables.

6.4 Human Capital Models

I next turn to the human capital model, which posits a positive relation between the rate of productivity growth and the rate of change of schooling levels. For this, I use the same specification as (1), except that I substitute the change in educational level for the educational level itself. The model becomes:

$$\ln\left(RGDPW_1 / RGDPW_0\right)/\left(t_1 - t_0\right) = b_0 + b_1 RGDPW_{0'} + b_2 INVRATE + b_3 RDGNP + b_4 \Delta\left(EDUC\right) + \varepsilon$$

$$(6.2)$$

where $\Delta(EDUC)$ is the change in level of schooling. Results are shown in Table 6.3 for the 1960–2000 period. I have used this shorter period (instead of 1950–2000), since data on schooling levels are not available for the 1950s for the full set of OECD countries.

---

[12] When RDGNP is omitted from the equation, both the coefficients and significance levels of the educational variables remain substantially unchanged. Various combinations of the educational variables were also included in different regression specifications, with no material difference in results.

Table 6.2. *Pooled Cross-Section, Time Series Regressions of the Annual Growth in Real GDP per Worker (RGDPW) on Initial RGDPW, the Investment Rate, R&D, and Educational Enrollment Levels, All OECD Countries, 1960–1980 and 1980–2000*

Relative RDGPW$_{55}$	INVRATE	Ratio of R&D to GNP (GDP)	Education Variable	R^2	Adjusted R^2	Standard Error	Sample Size	Education Variable
-0.032**	0.145**	0.691#		0.45	0.41	0.0145	46	
(4.77)	(3.01)	(1.72)						
-0.032**	0.149**	0.723#	0.021	0.46	0.41	0.0146	46	PRIM–ENRL
(4.69)	(3.06)	(1.78)	(0.80)					
-0.021**	0.157**	0.591	-0.013	0.56	0.52	0.0132	46	SCND–ENRL
(2.80)	(3.58)	(1.62)	(1.54)					
-0.024**	0.103#	0.818#	-0.031	0.51	0.46	0.0142	44	UNIV–ENRL
(2.96)	(2.01)	(1.96)	(1.53)					

Notes: The sample consists of pooled cross section, time series data for periods 1960–80 and 1980–2000. The absolute values of t-ratios are shown in parentheses below the coefficient estimate. See Table 6.1 for definitions of the variables

\# significant at the 10 percent level, 2-tail test

* significant at the 5 percent level, 2-tail test

** significant at the 1 percent level, 2-tail test

Table 6.3. *Regressions of the Growth in GDP per Worker (RGDPW) on Initial RGDPW, the Investment Rate, R&D Intensity, and the Change in Educational Levels, 1960–2000*

Relative $RGDPW_{65}$	INVRATE	Ratio of R&D to GNP (GDP)	Education Variable	R^2	Adjusted R^2	Standard Error	Sample Size	Education Variable
-0.018**	0.055*	0.369*	0.325	0.85	0.82	0.0048	23	$\Delta SCND\text{-}ENRL_{02\text{-}65}$
(8.49)	(2.21)	(2.17)	(1.65)					
-0.022**	0.058*	0.467*	0.489#	0.86	0.83	0.0047	22	$\Delta UNIV\text{-}ENRL_{02\text{-}65}$
(8.10)	(2.36)	(2.57)	(1.87)					
-0.017**	0.050	0.187	0.127	0.80	0.74	0.0052	21	$\Delta SCND\text{-}ATTN_{96\text{-}60}$
(5.82)	(1.65)	(0.74)	(0.53)					
-0.015**	0.052#	0.131	0.877	0.81	0.76	0.0050	21	$\Delta UNIV\text{-}ATTN_{96\text{-}60}$
(4.98)	(1.93)	(0.55)	(1.27)					
-0.019**	0.061*	0.324#	0.019	0.83	0.79	0.0051	23	$\Delta MEAN\text{-}EDUC_{99\text{-}60}$
(7.90)	(2.29)	(1.82)	(0.58)					

Notes: The dependent variable is $\ln(RGDPW0_0/RGDPW_{60})/40$. The absolute values of t-ratios are shown in parentheses below the coefficient estimate. See Table 6.1 for definitions of the variables. In addition, Δ indicates the annual change in the variable over the period

significant at the 10 percent level, 2-tail test

* significant at the 5 percent level, 2-tail test

** significant at the 1 percent level, 2-tail test

The results are again disappointing. The coefficient of the change in schooling is positive in all five cases but statistically significant in only one: the change in university enrollment rates at the 10 percent level. One possibility, at least for the educational attainment rate, is that the anomalies in the basic data are undermining the regression results (the enrollment rate data seem sensible, as do the mean schooling levels). I eliminated all observations that seemed to be unreasonable and reran the regressions. The results were virtually unchanged.

Another possibility is that there are both a threshold effect as well as a positive influence of the growth in human capital on labor productivity growth. The same five equations were reestimated with initial level of schooling also included (results not shown). In all five cases, the change in schooling was insignificant (including the case of the university enrollment rate).

6.5 Interactions with Technical Change

There is now a voluminous literature supporting the argument that the rate of productivity growth of a country is strongly related to the R&D intensity of its production (see, for example, Griliches, 1979, a review of the literature). Moreover, the Arrow and Nelson-Phelps models suggest that there may be interaction effects between the educational level of the workforce and the R&D intensity of a country. I introduce the interaction effect into the model as follows:

$$
\ln\left(RGDPW_1 / RGDPW_0\right)/\left(t_1 - t_0\right)
$$
$$
= b_0 + b_1 RGDPW_{0'} + b_2 INVRATE + b_3 EDUC
$$
$$
+ b_4 RDGNP + b_5 RD * EDUC + \varepsilon \tag{6.3}
$$

An interaction term is included between EDUC and R&D, because, according to the Arrow and Nelson-Phelps models, a more educated labor force should be more successful in implementing the fruits of the R&D activity. For example, it is frequently argued that the Japanese economy is successful in adapting new technology to direct production because of the high level of education of its workforce. In this sense, of two countries with the same R&D intensity but different education levels, the one with the more educated labor force should adopt new technology more quickly and effectively, and this should show up in higher measured productivity growth.[13] This formulation is admittedly crude

---

[13] This assumes, of course, that the output of new inventions is directly proportional to R&D activity.

Table 6.4. *Regressions of the Annual Growth of Real GDP per Worker (RGDPW) on Initial RGDPW, the Investment Rate, R&D Intensity, Schooling, and the Interaction between Schooling and R&D, 1960–2000*

Relative $RGDPW_{65}$	INVRATE	Education Variable	R&D	EDUC*R&D	R^2	Adj. R^2	Stand. Error	Sample Size	Education Variable
-0.021** (5.92)	0.100** (3.19)		0.57* (2.42)		0.71	0.67	0.006	23	
-0.023** (5.02)	0.092** (2.69)	0.007 (0.61)	0.58* (2.41)		0.72	0.66	0.006	23	$SCND-ENRL_{65-02}$
-0.021** (3.61)	0.098* (2.61)	-0.002 (0.09)	0.02 (0.02)	0.008 (0.44)	0.72	0.64	0.006	23	$SCND-ENRL_{65-02}$
-0.026** (5.53)	0.116** (3.51)	0.035 (1.43)	0.55 (2.18)		0.74	0.68	0.006	22	$UNIV-ENRL_{65-02}$
-0.027** (4.30)	0.111** (3.03)	0.056 (0.82)	0.74 (1.15)	-0.009 (0.33)	0.75	0.67	0.006	22	$UNIV-ENRL_{65-02}$
-0.018** (3.83)	0.103** (3.05)	-0.012 (1.02)	0.67* (2.51)		0.73	0.66	0.007	21	$SCND-ATTN_{1970}$
-0.015** (2.97)	0.135** (3.71)	-0.047# (2.08)	-0.09 (0.19)	0.022 (1.58)	0.77	0.70	0.006	21	$SCND-ATTN_{1970}$
-0.019** (3.86)	0.097* (2.77)	-0.032 (0.91)	0.59* (2.24)		0.73	0.66	0.006	21	$UNIV-ATTN_{1970}$
-0.015** (3.30)	0.129** (3.68)	-0.169** (2.36)	-0.02 (0.05)	0.081 (1.43)	0.79	0.72	0.006	21	$UNIV-ATTN_{1970}$
-0.019** (3.45)	0.100** (3.15)	-0.001 (0.57)	0.55* (2.29)		0.72	0.66	0.006	23	$MEAN-EDUC_{1970}$
-0.018** (3.01)	0.108** (2.87)	-0.001 (0.67)	0.20 (0.22)	0.001 (0.43)	0.72	0.64	0.006	23	$MEAN-EDUC_{1970}$

Notes: The absolute values of t-ratios are shown in parentheses below the coefficient estimate

A constant term is included in the equation but its coefficient is not shown. The dependent variable is $\ln(RGDPW_{00}/RGDPW_{60})/40$

Significant at the 10% level

* Significant at the 5% level

** Significant at the 1% level

and specification problems might arise if, for example, the variability in the education variable is low enough to cancel out the variability in the R&D variable. In this case, the interaction term might also show low explanatory power.

Results for all OECD countries over the 1960–2000 period are shown in Table 6.4 (note that these results differ somewhat from those of Table 6.1, whose regressions cover the 1950–2000 period). In specifications without an interaction effect, RDGNP is positive and significant at the 5 percent level in all cases. Moreover, the coefficients are generally in the range of 0.50 to 0.60, suggesting extraordinarily high returns to R&D investment.[14] However, the interaction term is insignificant in all cases, casting some doubt, at least, on this interpretation of the Arrow and Nelson-Phelps models. Another striking result is that the coefficient of every educational variable is statistically insignificant in this set of regressions.

Another interpretation of the two models is that having an educated labor force might make the adoption and/or adaptation of foreign technology easier and thus expedite the international transfer of technology. This argument suggests that there might exist an interaction effect between the educational level of the workforce and the technology gap, as reflected in the initial productivity level of the country relative to the United States. However, using a variety of measures of educational level, I found no case in which this interaction variable proved significant.

6.6 The MRW Model

I next model the effects of education on economic growth using the model developed by Mankiw, Romer, and Weil, or MRW (1992) (also see Chapter 2 for a discussion of the MRW model). The same three types of models can be derived from this framework: (i) the catch-up model, (ii) the human capital model, and (iii) interactions with technical change.

6.6.1 Catch-Up Effect

I first derive a formal model of the catch-up effect from MRW (1992). Their model is derived from an augmented Solow (1956, 1957) growth model,

---

[14] These returns are much higher than found in most of the literature. The difference in results is apparently due to the inclusion of a catch-up term here. When it is dropped, the return to R&D falls to the more normal 10 to 20 percent range.

where output is determined as a Cobb-Douglas production function of physical capital, human capital, and efficiency units of labor:

$$Y(t) = K(t)^{\alpha} H(t)^{\beta} (A(t)L(t))^{1-\alpha-\beta}$$

(6.4)

where K is the stock of physical capital, H is the stock of human capital, L is the stock of labor, A is the level of technology, and α and β are parameters roughly corresponding to the elasticity of output with respect to labor and capital, respectively. It is assumed that labor grows at a fixed rate n, A grows at the constant rate g, and K depreciates at the constant rate δ. The choice of specification implies constant returns to all factors and therefore diminishing returns to physical or human capital taken separately. Two alternative productivity growth equations can be derived from (6.4). First,

$$\ln(y(t)) - \ln(y(0)) = (1 - e^{-\lambda t})[(\alpha/(1-\alpha-\beta))\ln(s_k) \\ + (\beta/(1-\alpha-\beta))\ln(s_h) \\ -((\alpha+\beta)/(1-\alpha-\beta))\ln(n+g+\delta) - \ln(y(0))]$$

(6.5)

where s_k is the fraction of output invested in physical capital and s_h is the fraction invested in human capital; or

$$\ln(y(t)) - \ln(y(0)) = (1 - e^{-\lambda t})[(\alpha/(1-\alpha))\ln(s_k) \\ + (\beta/(1-\alpha))\ln(H) \\ -(\alpha/(1-\alpha))\ln(n+g+\delta) - \ln(y(0))]$$

(6.6)

where H is the *level* of human capital. Equation (6.6) is consistent with a threshold model of education.

In order to implement this model in a cross-country sample, five assumptions must be made: (1) technology is the *same* across all countries; (2) g is fixed over time and constant across countries; (3) n is fixed over time and exogenous; (4) the savings rate s_k is fixed over time and exogenous; and (5) the human capital investment rate s_h is fixed over time and exogenous. MRW also imposed the reasonable assumptions that g is .02 and δ is 0.03 and estimated equation (6.5) over the 1960–85 period, using (an estimate of) the average percentage of the working age population in secondary school over the period as an index for s_h. Interestingly, for a sample of twenty-two OECD countries over this period, they found that while the coefficient of s_h was positive, it was not statistically significant. MRW do not attempt to estimate equation (6.6).

Following Lichtenberg (1992), I modify equation (6.6) by introducing a term for R&D investment (with corresponding changes in the coefficients). The basic model specification is as follows:

$$\ln\left(\text{RGDPW}_1 / \text{RGDPW}_0\right) / \left(t_1 - t_0\right) = b_0 + b_1 \ln\left(\text{RGDPW}_{0'}\right) +$$
$$b_2 \ln\left(\text{INVRATE}\right) + b_3 \ln\left(\text{RDGNP}\right) + b_4 \ln\left(\text{EDUC}\right) + \quad (6.7)$$
$$b_5 \ln(\text{LABGRT} + g + \delta) + \varepsilon$$

where LABGRT is the rate of growth of the labor force (estimated here as employment growth).

The convergence hypothesis, as well as the MRW model, predicts that the coefficient b_1 will be negative (that is, countries further behind near the beginning of the period will show more rapid increases in GDP per worker). The coefficients of the investment rate (b_2), R&D intensity (b_3), and education (b_4) should be positive, while the coefficient of $(n+g+\delta)$ should be negative. I follow MRW but setting $g+\delta$ equal to 0.05. Results are shown in Table 6.5 for all OECD countries over the 1950–2000 period and for selected educational measures.

The logarithm of RGDPW of the country relative to the U.S. level is by far the most powerful explanatory variable in accounting for differences in labor productivity growth among OECD countries. By itself, the catch-up variable explains 80 percent of the variation in RGDPW growth over the 1950–2000 period. The coefficient of the logarithm of INVRATE is positive and significant at the 1 or 5 percent level except in two cases, where it is significant at the 10 percent level. The average investment rate, together with the catch-up variable, explains 85 percent of the variation in RGDPW growth. The coefficient of the logarithm of R&D intensity is positive in all cases but statistically significant in only a few cases (and typically at the 10 percent level). The coefficient of the logarithm of (LABGRT+$g+\delta$) is negative in all cases, as predicted, and significant at the 1 or 5 percent level in all cases except one.

The logarithms of the educational enrollment rates have positive coefficients in all three cases. The coefficients of both the primary and secondary school enrollment rates are significant at the 10 percent level, while that of the university enrollment rate is highly significant, at the 1 percent level. The coefficients of the logarithm of the attainment rates are insignificant for secondary and university attainment but highly significant (at the 1 percent level) for the primary school attainment level. The results for primary education are, as before, unexpected, because this is the level of schooling that would appear to have least relevance to the types of sophisticated technology in use among

Table 6.5. *MRW Regressions of the Annual Growth in Real GDP per Worker (RGDPW) on Initial RGDPW, the Investment Rate, R&D, and Educational Enrollment and Attainment Levels and Changes, 1950–2000*

Relative RGDPW$_{55}$	Log of INVRATE	Log of RDGNP	Log of LABGRTA	Log of Education	R^2	Adj. R^2	Std. Error	Sample Size	Education Variable
-0.015** (9.37)					0.80	0.79	0.0049	24	
-0.015** (10.96)	0.016* (2.72)				0.85	0.84	0.0043	24	
-0.017** (9.78)	0.014* (2.34)	0.224# (1.80)			0.86	0.84	0.0043	23	
-0.016** (10.67)	0.016** (3.18)	0.184# (1.80)	-0.024** (3.20)		0.91	0.89	0.0035	23	
-0.016** (10.86)	0.019** (3.75)	0.229* (2.16)	-0.026** (3.64)	0.032# (1.83)	0.93	0.91	0.0033	23	PRIM–ENRL$_{65\text{-}02}$
-0.018** (9.97)	0.010# (1.82)	0.191 (1.51)	-0.018* (2.24)	0.008# (1.76)	0.93	0.91	0.0033	23	SCND–ENRL$_{65\text{-}02}$
-0.019** (12.74)	0.012* (2.72)	0.132 (1.51)	-0.024** (3.90)	0.009** (3.60)	0.95	0.94	0.0028	22	UNIV–ENRL$_{65\text{-}02}$
-0.018** (12.13)	0.010# (2.04)	0.174 (1.52)	-0.014# (1.98)	0.017** (3.13)	0.95	0.93	0.0029	22	PRIM–ATTN$_{60\text{-}96}$
-0.016** (8.27)	0.016* (2.85)	0.159 (1.33)	-0.023* (2.85)	0.001 (0.36)	0.91	0.89	0.0037	22	SCND–ATTN$_{60\text{-}96}$
-0.017** (8.21)	0.016** (3.01)	0.153# (1.93)	-0.030* (2.85)	0.002 (0.93)	0.92	0.89	0.0036	22	UNIV–ATTN$_{60\text{-}96}$
-0.016** (7.20)	0.016* (2.75)	0.179 (1.41)	-0.024** (3.04)	0.001 (0.15)	0.91	0.89	0.0036	23	MEAN–EDUC$_{60\text{-}99}$

242

									Dependent variable
−0.017** (7.78)	0.016* (2.55)	0.002 (1.26)	−0.022* (2.34)	0.294 (1.60)	0.88	0.84	0.0042	23	ΔSCND–ENRL$_{02-65}$
−0.019** (8.36)	0.014* (2.35)	0.002 (1.31)	−0.036** (3.80)	0.517* (2.43)	0.90	0.86	0.0039	22	ΔUNIV–ENRL$_{02-65}$
−0.017** (6.55)	0.017* (2.27)	0.001 (0.71)	−0.032* (2.57)	0.097 (0.67)	0.85	0.80	0.0047	22	ΔSCND–ATTN$_{02-60}$
−0.018** (7.15)	0.018* (2.59)	0.001 (0.78)	−0.048** (3.06)	0.688 (1.66)	0.87	0.83	0.0044	22	ΔUNIV–ATTN$_{02-60}$
−0.017** (7.20)	0.016* (2.34)	0.001 (0.82)	−0.029** (3.16)	0.029 (0.46)	0.86	0.82	0.0044	23	ΔMEAN–EDUC$_{99-60}$

Notes: The absolute values of t-ratios are shown in parentheses below the coefficient estimate

See footnotes to Table 6.1 for sources and methods. A constant term is also included in the regression. Key:

Dependent variable: $\ln(\text{RGDPW}_{00}/\text{RGDPW}_{50})/50$

LABGRTA: rate of growth of the labor force plus the rate of technological change (assumed to be 0.02 per year) plus the depreciation rate of physical capital (assumed to be 0.03 per year). *Source*: Penn World Table Mark 5.6

\# Significant at the 10% level

* Significant at the 5% level

** Significant at the 1% level

OECD countries in the post–World War II period. The coefficient on average education for the adult population is positive but insignificant.[15]

As noted previously, the assumptions in implementing this model are very strong, and we would expect that coefficient estimates of variables that change over time in conjunction with labor productivity growth are biased upward. This would be the case for INVRATE and RDGNP as well as the enrollment rates. The coefficient of the university enrollment rate, in particular, is likely to be heavily biased upward if university enrollment responds positively to increases in per capita income. The coefficients of the educational attainment rates are also likely to be biased upward, though less severely than the coefficients of the enrollment rates, since the attainment rates measure the educational levels of the existing labor force and reflect enrollment rates with a lag. The average level of schooling of the labor force will rise slowly over time as more highly educated students enter the labor force and less educated older workers exit the labor force.

6.6.2 Human Capital Model

I next turn to the human capital model, which posits a positive relation between the rate of productivity growth and the rate of change of schooling levels. The standard human capital earnings function is given by (see Mincer, 1974):

$$\text{Ln } w = a_0 + a_1 S$$

where w is the wage, S is the worker's level of schooling, and a_0 and a_1 are constants. It follows that

$$(d\text{Ln } w) / dt = a_1 (dS / dt) \tag{6.8}$$

In the case of a standard aggregate Cobb-Douglas production function of the form

$$Y(t) = A(t)K(t)^{\alpha}L(t)^{1-\alpha}$$

---

[15] When the log of RDGNP is omitted from the equation, both the coefficients and significance levels of the educational variables remain substantially unchanged. Various combinations of the educational variables were also included in different regression specifications, with no material difference in results. Regressions were also run on subperiods 1950–73 and 1973–90, with no notable change in results. As before, I also used pooled cross-section, time series data for the 24 OECD countries and periods 1960–73 and 1973–90 for enrollment rates. The regression results are similar to those in the cross-section analysis of Table 6.5.

labor productivity is given by:

$$Y / L = (K / L)^{\alpha}.$$

The wage w is given by:

$$w = \partial Y / \partial L = (1 - \alpha) AK^{\alpha} / L^{\alpha} = (1 - \alpha)(Y / L) . \qquad (6.9)$$

In this case, the wage is directly proportional to overall labor productivity. Combining (6.8) and (6.9), we obtain:

$$[dLn(Y / L)] / dt = (a_1 / (1 - \alpha))(dS / dt)$$

In other words, the rate of labor productivity growth should be proportional to the *change in the level of schooling* over the period.

Equation (6.7) is correspondingly modified by substituting the change in educational level for the educational level itself to obtain the new model:

$$\begin{aligned}
\ln\left(RGDPW_1 / RGDPW_0\right) / \left(t_1 - t_0\right) = b_0 &+ b_1 \ln\left(RGDPW_{0'}\right) \\
&+ b_2 \ln\left(INVRATE\right) + b_3 \ln\left(RDGNP\right) \\
&+ b_4 \Delta\left(EDUC\right) + b_5 \ln\left(LABGRT\right. \\
&+ g + \delta) + \varepsilon
\end{aligned}$$

$$(6.10)$$

where $\Delta(EDUC)$ is the change in level of schooling. Results are shown in Table 6.5 for the 1960–2000 period. I have used this shorter period (instead of 1950–2000), since data on schooling levels are not available for the 1950s for the full set of OECD countries.

The coefficient of the log of initial RGDPW is again negative and significant at the 1 percent level, that of the logarithm of the investment rate positive and significant at the 5 percent level, and that of the logarithm of $(LABGRT+g+\delta)$ is negative and significant at the 1 or 5 percent level. The coefficient of R&D intensity is positive but not significant.

The coefficient of the change in schooling is positive in all five cases but statistically significant in only one: the change in university enrollment rates, at the 5 percent level. Here, as earlier, we might expect this coefficient to be biased upward because university enrollment rates will depend on increases in per capita income. One possibility for the failure to find significant coefficients on the educational attainment rate is that the anomalies in the basic data are undermining the regression results (the enrollment rate data seem sensible, as do the mean schooling levels). I eliminated all observations that seemed to be unreasonable and reran the regressions. The results are virtually unchanged.

Another possibility is that there are both a threshold effect as well as a positive influence of the growth in human capital on labor productivity growth. The same five equations were reestimated with initial level of schooling also included (results not shown). In all five cases, the change in schooling is insignificant (including the case of the university enrollment rate).

6.6.3 Interactions with Technical Change

As in equation (6.3), I introduce the interaction effect as follows:

$$
\ln\left(RGDPW_1 / RGDPW_0\right)/\left(t_1 - t_0\right) = b_0 + b_1\ln\left(RGDPW_{0'}\right) + b_2\ln\left(INVRATE\right)
$$
$$
+ b_3\ln\left(RDGNP\right) + b_4\left(EDUC * RDGNP\right)
$$
$$
+ b_5\ln\left(LABGRT + g + \delta\right) + \varepsilon
$$

$$(6.11)$$

The rationale for the interaction effect is that a more educated labor force should be more successful in implementing the fruits of the R&D activity. Results are shown in Table 6.6 for the 1960–2000 period. The coefficient of the interaction term is positive in all cases. The results for the enrollment rates seem to make sense since the coefficient of the interaction term is not significant for primary enrollment but is positive and significant at the 5 percent level for the secondary school enrollment rate and at the 1 percent level for the university enrollment rate. One would expect the interaction term to be stronger at higher levels of schooling. However, the results make little sense for the attainment rates since the coefficient is significant at the 1 percent level for primary school attainment but not significant at higher levels of education. The coefficient is also not significant for mean years of schooling.

An alternative interpretation of the Nelson-Phelps model is the existence of an interaction effect between the educational level of the workforce and the investment rate of a country. The rationale is similar (as I argued in the Introduction): a more educated workforce might acquire the new skills needed to implement the new equipment faster and more effectively than a less educated one. According to this interpretation, the appropriate model is:

$$
\ln\left(RGDPW_1 / RGDPW_0\right)/\left(t_1 - t_0\right) = b_0 + b_1\ln\left(RGDPW_{0'}\right)
$$
$$
+ b_2\ln\left(INVRATE\right) + b_3\ln\left(RDGNP\right)
$$
$$
+ b_4\left(EDUC * INVRATE\right)
$$
$$
+ b_5\ln\left(LABGRT + g + \delta\right) + \varepsilon
$$

$$(6.12)$$

The results for this interaction effect, shown in Table 6.7, are very similar to those in Table 6.6. The coefficient of this term is positive in each case. As

Table 6.6. *MRW Regressions of the Annual Growth of Real GDP per Worker (RGDPW) on Initial RGDPW, the Investment Rate, R&D Intensity, Schooling, and the Interaction between Schooling and R&D, 1960–2000*

Relative RGDPW$_{55}$	Log of INVRATE	Log of RDGNP	Log of LABGRTA	Education x R&D	R^2	Adj. R^2	Std. Error	Sample Size	Education Variable
-0.016** (7.25)	0.020** (3.07)	-0.031 (1.42)	-0.030** (3.35)	0.033 (1.48)	0.88	0.84	0.0042	23	PRIM–ENRL$_{65-02}$
-0.020** (7.38)	0.010 (1.40)	-0.010 (1.71)	-0.022* (2.43)	0.012# (1.99)	0.89	0.85	0.0040	23	SCND–ENRL$_{65-02}$
-0.022** (10.42)	0.013* (2.64)	-0.011** (3.45)	-0.032** (4.47)	0.012** (4.25)	0.93	0.91	0.0031	22	UNIV–ENRL$_{65-02}$
-0.021** (9.00)	0.010# (1.80)	-0.020** (2.99)	-0.019* (2.14)	0.022** (3.26)	0.91	0.89	0.0036	22	PRIM–ATTN$_{60-96}$
-0.018** (6.58)	0.017* (2.43)	-0.003 (0.69)	-0.031** (3.00)	0.004 (1.09)	0.87	0.83	0.0044	22	SCND–ATTN$_{60-96}$
-0.019** (6.61)	0.017* (2.61)	-0.003 (0.76)	-0.039** (3.08)	0.004 (1.31)	0.87	0.83	0.0044	22	UNIV–ATTN$_{60-96}$
-0.017* (5.20)	0.017* (2.38)	0.000 (0.04)	-0.028** (2.99)	0.001 (0.24)	0.86	0.82	0.0044	23	MEAN–EDUC$_{60-99}$

Notes: The dependent variable is $\ln(RGDPW0_0/RGDPW_{60})/40$. The absolute values of t-ratios are shown in parentheses below the coefficient estimate. A constant term is also included in the equation. See Table 6.1 for definitions of the variables

\# Significant at the 10% level

* Significant at the 5% level

** Significant at the 1% level

Table 6.7. *MRW Regressions of the Annual Growth of Real GDP per Worker (RGDPW) on Initial RGDPW, the Investment Rate, R&D Intensity, Schooling, and the Interaction between Schooling and the Investment Rate, 1960–2000*

Relative RGDPW$_{55}$	Log of INVRATE	Log of RDGNP	Log of LABGRTA	Education x INVRATE	R^2	Adj. R^2	Std. Error	Sample Size	Education Variable
-0.016**	-0.013	0.002	-0.030**	0.033	0.88	0.84	0.0042	23	PRIM–ENRL$_{65-02}$
(7.25)	(0.60)	(1.02)	(3.35)	(1.48)					
-0.020**	-0.002	0.002	-0.022*	0.012#	0.89	0.85	0.0040	23	SCND–ENRL$_{65-02}$
(7.38)	(0.15)	(0.94)	(2.43)	(1.99)					
-0.022**	0.001	0.001	-0.032**	0.012**	0.93	0.91	0.0031	22	UNIV–ENRL$_{65-02}$
(10.42)	(0.22)	(0.70)	(4.47)	(4.25)					
-0.021**	-0.012	0.001	-0.019*	0.022**	0.91	0.89	0.0036	22	PRIM–ATTN$_{60-96}$
(9.00)	(1.13)	(1.01)	(2.14)	3.26					
-0.018**	0.013#	0.000	-0.031**	0.004	0.87	0.83	0.0044	22	SCND–ATTN$_{60-96}$
(6.58)	(1.86)	(0.24)	(3.00)	(1.09)					
-0.019**	0.014*	0.001	-0.039**	0.004	0.87	0.83	0.0044	22	UNIV–ATTN$_{60-96}$
(6.61)	(1.94)	(0.45)	(3.08)	(1.31)					
-0.017**	0.016#	0.001	-0.028**	0.001	0.86	0.82	0.0044	23	MEAN–EDUC$_{60-99}$
(5.20)	(1.79)	(0.65)	(2.99)	(0.24)					

Notes: The dependent variable is $\ln(RGDPW_{90}/RGDPW_{60})/30$. The absolute values of t-ratios are shown in parentheses below the coefficient estimate. A constant term is also included in the equation. See Table 6.1 for definitions of the variables.

Significant at the 10% level
* Significant at the 5% level
** Significant at the 1% level

before, it is not significant for primary school enrollment rate, significant at the 5 percent level for the secondary school enrollment rate, and significant at the 1 percent level for the university enrollment rate. It is also significant at the 1 percent level for the primary school attainment rate, but it is not significant for attainment rates for higher levels of schooling or for mean schooling.

6.7 Other Literature on the Relation of Schooling and Growth

Frantzen (2000) used educational data from Barro and Lee (1993) to analyze the relations among human capital, R&D spending, and TFP growth for twenty-one Industrialized Market Economies in the OECD. His period spanned 1961 to 1991. His particular interest was to investigate the complementarity between R&D and human capital investments. Using average data over the period for each of the variables of interest, he first estimated equations that related TFP growth over this period to domestic and foreign R&D intensity. Foreign R&D intensity was estimated as a bilateral import-share weighted average of the domestic R&D capital stocks of the country's twenty trading partners, expressed in dollars at PPP exchange rates. He then expanded the specification to include either the rate of growth or the level of human capital. A cointegration analysis was then performed on the equations in level terms, where the log of TFP was related to the logs of the stocks of domestic and foreign capital and the log of human capital. The cointegration equations were estimated on a panel of pooled annual time series for the same countries over the period from 1965 to 1991.

In the first set of regressions, he found that the coefficients of the R&D intensity variables and the catch-up term were both positive and statistically significant at the 5 percent level. The estimated rate of return to domestic R&D was very high, indicating substantial social returns, and was of the same order of magnitude as reported by Gittleman and Wolff (1995). The coefficient of foreign R&D was also positive and significant at the 5 or 1 percent level and larger in magnitude than the coefficient on domestic R&D.

When the *growth* in human capital was added to the basic estimating equation, Frantzen found that its coefficient was positive but not statistically significant. However, he found that the addition of the initial level of human capital (as of 1960) and an interaction term between the initial human capital level and the initial level of TFP (in 1960) were both highly significant, at the 1 percent level. The coefficient of the former was positive, as expected, and that of the latter was negative, as predicted. The addition of this interaction term derived from the Nelson and Phelps (1966) model, in which it was argued that the introduction of new technology or more advanced foreign technology depends on the skill level of the labor force. A more educated (domestic) labor force will make the adoption of new technology more effective and therefore speed productivity growth. The cointegration regression results were consistent with the single equation estimates, and, if anything, the coefficient estimates were even stronger.

Fuente and Doménech (2006) found stronger results of the effect of education on growth for OECD countries by attempting to improve on the data quality of some of the initial education data sets. Fuente and Doménech worked with the Barro and Lee (1996) data on years of schooling and educational attainment. They argued that the counterintuitive results of human capital on growth might be due, at least in part, to deficiencies in the underlying data on human capital. However, another possibility was connected with basic trends in human capital and productivity growth. As productivity growth rates declined among OECD countries after 1980 while both enrollment rates and schooling levels rose sharply, a negative sign on the human capital variable was, perhaps, not really surprising when the cross-section variation of the data was eliminated. But this result might also reflect the omission of some other factors that might account for the slowdown in productivity growth.

Most of the paper was concerned with corrections to the basic Barro and Lee data using UNESCO data and other sources. Using their corrected data, they did obtain stronger results of education on productivity growth than those reported in Sections 6.3 to 6.6. In their first set of specifications, they regressed the level of the logarithm of output per employed worker on the logarithm of the stock of physical capital and the logarithm of the average number of years of schooling of the adult population (their measure of human capital). Using their corrected data on schooling, they obtained a positive and very significant (at the 1 percent level) coefficient on the logarithm of human capital. Their results were stronger when including fixed country and period effects. However, the results were weaker when the rate of TFP growth was used as the dependent variable and this was regressed on the rate of change of physical and human capital. In this case, the coefficient of the rate of change of human capital was positive but significant at only the 10 percent level when no country dummies or catch-up term was included. The coefficient did become significant at the 1 percent level when country dummies, period dummies, and a catch-up term were included. In their "preferred specification," which was a constant returns to scale production function in first differences with a technological catch-up term and fixed period and country effects, they again found that the coefficient of the rate of change of human capital was positive and significant at the 1 percent level.

Apergis (2007) examined data from a panel of European Union (EU) manufacturing industries over the period from 1980 to 2000. He used both the Barro and Lee (2000) and the de la Fuente and Doménech (2006) data on mean years of schooling. He related the growth in industry-level TFP within a country to the growth in the country's level of human capital. Using a GMM estimator, he found a positive and significant (at the 1 percent level) coefficient on the growth in human capital on the basis of both data sets on schooling levels. He also added a human capital "threshold effect" (that is, countries with mean years of schooling above a critical level) interacted with industry R&D intensity and found a positive and significant coefficient on this variable as well.

Wasmer (2003) provided another interesting interpretation of why the standard educational data such as years of schooling might not provide reliable comparisons across countries. Wasmer argued that American workers tend to invest in general human capital especially since they face little employment protection and low unemployment benefits, while the European model (generous benefits and higher duration of jobs) favors specific human capital investments. This conjecture provided, among other things, a rationale for differences in labor mobility and reallocation costs. The main argument was based on a fundamental property of human capital investments: They are not independent of the aggregate state of labor markets, and, in particular, frictions and slackness of the labor market raise the returns to specific human capital investments relative to general human capital investments. As a result, mobility costs are typically higher in Europe. Jobs do last longer in Europe than in the United States, but when they are destroyed, the welfare loss for workers is higher. A simple comparison of years of schooling would not be sufficient to capture differences in human capital because of the difference in the relative amounts of specific and general human capital embodied in formal schooling between European countries and North American ones.

A related argument is that of Krueger and Kumar (2003). They noted that European economic growth, compared to that of the United States, was relatively weak since the 1980s. They argued that the European focus on specialized, vocational education might have been effective during the 1960s and 1970s in promoting growth but resulted in a growth gap relative to the United States during the subsequent information age, when new technologies emerged at a more rapid pace. They attempted to assess the quantitative importance of education policy in comparison to labor market rigidity and product market regulation – other policy differences more commonly suggested to be responsible for United States–Europe differences. Using a decomposition analysis based on a calibration exercise, they found that differences in education policy between Europe and the United States accounted for more than 50 percent of the United States–Europe disparity in overall growth over a twenty-year period.

Middendorf (2005) considered another dimension to education, which is the quality of schooling. His measure of quality was based on the results of the Programme for International Student Assessment (PISA) conducted in 2000. PISA is an internationally standardized assessment that is administered to fifteen-year-olds in school. PISA assesses the extent to which students near the end of compulsory education have acquired some of the knowledge and skills that are essential for full participation in society. In all cycles, the domains of reading and mathematical and scientific literacy are covered not merely in terms of mastery of the school curriculum, but in terms of important knowledge and skills needed in adult life. Concentrating on the twenty-nine OECD member countries that participated in PISA 2000 (except Luxembourg), Mittendorf used panel data estimation techniques over the period from 1965 to 2000. Estimation results revealed a positive and significant impact (mainly at the 10 percent level) of the level of human capital, as measured by average years of schooling and the secondary school attainment rate. However, when possible endogeneity was taken into account in an instrumental variables approach, these conclusions on the impact of the level of human capital on economic growth were demonstrated to be rather fragile. Moreover, the *change* in average years of schooling was found to be negatively related to economic growth, though its coefficient was statistically insignificant.

In a series of recent papers, Hanushek and Woessman (2009a, 2009b, 2010a, 2010b, and 2010c) examined the effects of the change in the average level of *cognitive skills* rather than that of educational attainment per se on countrywide productivity growth. They used various samples in their empirical analysis, including countries at all levels of development, Latin American nations, and OECD countries alone. Though the first two samples are more relevant for Chapter 9, which considers countries at all levels of development, the OECD sample is relevant for the current chapter. Since it makes more sense to review the full set of Hanushek and Woessman papers together, I will comment on all five papers here rather than splitting the commentary between this chapter and Chapter 9.

Their central argument is that educational attainment per se is a poor indicator of the output of the schooling process. A better indicator is the achievement level on standardized tests, which serves as a measure of the cognitive skills gained in the educational process. Most of their work relies on PISA test score results, mentioned earlier in relation to the Middendorf (2005) study, though these test results are augmented with a variety of different sources, depending on the country. In the work of Hanushek and Woessman, as well as Middendorf (2005), these test score results are considered an indicator of schooling quality.

Hanushek and Woessman (2009a) is the first of their papers to provide evidence of a robust association between cognitive skills and economic growth. Their sample was fifty countries covering nations at all levels of development. Their paper also showed that this association reflects a causal effect of cognitive skills on growth and supported the economic benefits of effective school policy. They developed a new common metric that allowed tracking student achievement across countries, over time, and along the within-country distribution. This measure combined results from PISA with a variety of other sources. Extensive sensitivity analyses of cross-country growth regressions generated remarkably stable results across specifications, periods, and country samples. In addressing causality, they found significant growth effects of cognitive skills when instrumented by institutional features of school systems. Moreover, countries that improved their cognitive skills over time experienced relative increases in their growth paths.

Hanushek and Woessman (2009b) considered economic development in Latin America. As they noted, this has trailed that of most other world regions over the past forty years or so despite the region's relatively high initial development and school attainment levels. They resolved this apparent puzzle by considering the actual learning as expressed in tests of cognitive skills, on which Latin American countries consistently perform at the bottom. In growth models estimated across world regions, these low levels of cognitive skills can account for the poor growth performance of Latin America. Given the limitations of worldwide tests in discriminating performance at low levels, they also introduced measures from two regional tests designed to measure performance for all Latin American countries with internationally comparable income data. Their growth analysis using these data confirmed the significant effects of cognitive skills on variations in growth within the region. By splicing the new regional tests into the worldwide tests, they also confirmed this effect in extended worldwide regressions, although it appears somewhat smaller in the regional Latin American data than in the worldwide data.

Hanushek and Woessman (2010a) noted that critics of international student comparisons argue that results on national average scores may be influenced by differences in the extent to which countries adequately sample their entire student populations. In this research note, they showed that larger exclusion and nonresponse rates are related to better country average scores on international tests, as are larger enrollment rates for the relevant age group. However, even accounting for sample selectivity does not alter existing research findings that tested academic achievement can account for a majority of international differences in economic growth and that institutional features of school systems have important effects on international differences in student achievement.[16]

Hanushek and Woessman (2010c) noted first that existing growth research provides little explanation for the very large differences in long-run growth performance across OECD countries. In this paper, they showed that cognitive skills can account for economic growth differences within the OECD, whereas a range of economic institutions and quantitative measures of tertiary education cannot. Under the growth model estimates and plausible projection parameters, they found that school improvements falling within currently observed performance levels yielded very large gains. They also conducted extensive sensitivity analyses, which indicated that while differences between model frameworks and alternative parameter choices made a difference, the economic impact of improved educational outcomes remained enormous.

6.8 Concluding Remarks

The descriptive statistics presented in this chapter suggest a positive association between years of formal education and labor productivity levels among OECD countries over the post–World War II years. First, the increase in educational attainment seems to correspond to the growth in labor productivity over this period. Second, the convergence in labor productivity levels among these nations appears to correspond to their convergence in schooling levels.

However, my econometric results reported here using standard growth equations and showing a positive and significant effect of formal education on productivity growth among OECD countries are spotty at best. It is an understatement to say that the relationship between education and growth is not very robust, at least among OECD countries.

---

[16] Also, see Hanushek and Woessman (2010b) for an extended review of the international literature covering educational achievement differences across countries and their relation to economic growth and labor market outcomes.

Three types of models were considered in this chapter. The first is the threshold model of education, in which a certain level of educational attainment of the workforce is viewed as a necessary condition for the adoption of advanced technology. With regard to this model, none of the measures of mean years of schooling proves to be significant, and, indeed, in many instances, their coefficient is negative. Educational enrollment rates are generally found to be insignificant as determinants of productivity growth with the sole exception of the primary school enrollment rate in 1965 at the 10 percent level. Likewise, educational attainment rates are generally insignificant, with the sole exception of the primary school attainment rate.

There is also little support found for the second model, the human capital approach. The growth in levels of formal schooling appears to have no bearing on the growth in labor productivity. This is true despite the surface evidence that mean years of schooling in OECD countries continued to grow over the post–World War II period, as did productivity levels, and schooling levels converged among these countries in conjunction with productivity levels. One exception is the change in university enrollment rates between 1965 and 2000, whose coefficient is significant at the 10 percent level.

These results also appear to be inconsistent with growth accounting models, which have attributed a substantial portion of the growth in productivity to increases in schooling levels. There are three potential reasons for the difference in results. The first is that growth accounting exercises typically exclude a catch-up effect. Evidence from the Penn World Table Mark 5.6 data does suggest that with the absence of a catch-up effect, the growth in mean schooling does contribute significantly to the growth in productivity.

The second stems from methodological differences in the two techniques. Growth accounting simply *assigns* to schooling (or measures of labor quality) a (positive) role in productivity growth based on the share of labor in total income. In contrast, regression analysis lets the data *tell us* whether a variable such as education is a significant factor in productivity growth. The third is that growth accounting is typically performed with data for a single country, whereas the regression results reported here are based on a cross-country sample. Insofar as there are problems in comparability of educational data across countries, individual country studies that use a consistent definition of education over time within a particular country may produce more reliable results than cross-country comparison data (though see later discussion for more analysis of the comparability problem).

However, three studies reported on here did find a positive effect of the change in schooling on productivity growth. Fuente and Doménech (2006) found stronger results of the effect of education on growth for OECD countries by attempting to improve on the data quality of some of the initial education data sets. When the rate of TFP growth was used as the dependent variable and this was regressed on the rate of change of physical and human capital, the coefficient of the rate of change of human capital was positive and significant at the 1 percent level when country dummies, period dummies, and a catch-up term were included. Apergis (2007), using data from a panel of EU manufacturing industries over the period from 1980 to 2000 and a GMM estimator, also found a positive and significant (at the 1 percent level) coefficient on the growth in human capital. However, it should be stressed that the results applied only to manufacturing, not the whole economy. Hanushek and Woessman (2010c) found that the growth of cognitive skills rather than educational attainment was a positive and significant determinant of countrywide economic growth among OECD countries.

The third model is based on the argument that a more educated labor force might facilitate the adoption of new technology. However, the regression evidence provides no corroboration that there is any kind of interaction effect between the degree of technological activity, as measured by R&D intensity, and the educational level of the workforce. On the other hand, R&D intensity by itself does play a powerful role in explaining differences in productivity growth among OECD countries. However, as reported in the previous section, Frantzen (2000) found in his growth regression that the coefficient of an interaction term between the initial human capital level and the initial level of TFP (in 1960) was highly significant, at the 1 percent level, and with the predicted positive sign.

The MRW econometric results showing a positive and significant effect of formal education on productivity growth among OECD countries are mixed. The same three models were considered in this chapter. The first is the threshold model of education, in which a certain level of educational attainment of the workforce is viewed as a necessary condition for the adoption of advanced technology. With regard to this model, the coefficients of all the educational variables are found to be positive. Moreover, all three enrollment rate variables are statistically significant, as well as the primary school attainment rate and the mean years of schooling of the labor force. The coefficients of the secondary school and university attainment rates are not significant; nor is that of the mean years of schooling.

There is strong reason to believe that the coefficients of the enrollment rate variables, particularly the higher education enrollment rate, are biased upward. Moreover, we would expect the attainment rate variables to prove more significant, since they better reflect the schooling level of the workforce. On the surface, it may also appear somewhat anomalous that of the three attainment measures, the best fit is provided by the primary school attainment rate, since this is the level that would appear to be least relevant to implementing the advanced technology of the OECD countries. However, primary schooling is the level at which the basic literacy and numerical skills required for almost all types of work are acquired. This result is consistent with Wolff and Gittleman (1993), which showed that primary schooling was the most powerful educational variable in explaining growth in per capita income among countries at all levels of development. It may still be the case that this level is most relevant to OECD countries as well.

There is once again little support found for the human capital model in the MRW variant. The one exception is the change in university enrollment rates, whose coefficient is significant at the 5 percent level. However, as suggested previously, there is strong reason to suspect that this coefficient is biased upward.

The third model, derived from Nelson and Phelps (1966), is based on the argument that a more educated labor force might facilitate the adoption of new technology. This suggests interaction effects between R&D intensity or the investment rate and the educational level of the workforce. The econometric results are similar to those for the threshold model (which are not surprising since the two models are algebraically close). The coefficients of the interaction effects are all positive. They are significant at the 10 percent level for the secondary school enrollment rate and at the 1 percent level for the university enrollment rate, the primary school attainment rate, and the mean years of schooling of the labor force but not significant for the other educational variables.

In sum, the MRW econometric analysis provides mixed support for the threshold and interaction models but very little support to the human capital model. What may explain the generally poor results for measures of formal education in accounting for productivity growth in advanced countries? There are five possible reasons. The first is the poor quality of the education data. Though I have used three different sources for these figures, they all generally derive from UNESCO sources, which, in turn, are based on compilations of country responses to questionnaires. I have already noted some anomalies in the raw data for some of these educational indices – particularly, the figures on educational attainment rates and mean years of schooling of the labor force. However, it should be noted that when corrections were applied to these data – primarily, through averaging techniques – the econometric results remained largely unchanged. Moreover, as long as there is no systematic correlation between errors in measurement of schooling and productivity growth rates, the measurement errors should be captured in the stochastic error term of the regression and not bias the coefficient estimators.

Another point is that even if there is a systematic bias in measures of education by country, as long as these biases remain relatively constant over time, they should not affect the results of the production function equations. In particular, assume that schooling is mismeasured and that the true educational attainment of country h at time t, E^h_t, is given by:

$$E^h_t = v^h_t S^h_t$$

where S^h_t is measured schooling of country h at time t and v^h_t is the correction factor. Then, in a Cobb-Douglas production function, with quality-adjusted labor input,

$$d\left(\ln Y^h_t\right) = c + \alpha d\left(\ln L^h_t\right) + \beta d\left(\ln E^h_t\right) + \gamma d\left(\ln K^h_t\right)$$

where Y is output, L is (unadjusted) labor input, K is capital input, and α, β, γ, and c are constant terms. Substituting for E^h_t, we obtain:

$$d\left(\ln Y^h_t\right) = c + \alpha d\left(\ln L^h_t\right) + \beta d\left(\ln S^h_t\right) + \beta d(\ln v^h_t) + \gamma d\left(\ln K^h_t\right)$$

It is now clear that as long as v^h is constant over time (though it may differ across countries), the measurement error will be captured in the constant term

$$d\left(\ln Y^h_t\right) = c' + \alpha d\left(\ln L^h_t\right) + \beta d\left(\ln S^h_t\right) + \gamma d\left(\ln K^h_t\right)$$

Such systematic measurement errors in education should not bias the results of regressions, such as equation (6.2), where labor productivity growth is regressed on the rate of growth of or change in educational attainment. However, if v^h_t varies over time, then biased coefficient estimates will result.[17]

A second and more likely reason may be problems of comparability in formal education measures across countries. As discussed in OECD (1998), there are substantial differences in schooling systems among OECD countries, and years of schooling may be a particularly unreliable indicator of

[17] Also, see Krueger and Lindahl (2001) and Chapter 9 of this book for a related discussion of measurement error in educational variables and its implications for cross-country growth regressions.

achievement and knowledge gain (as measured by test scores). Moreover, the failure of measures of formal schooling to include time spent in apprenticeship programs will also create systematic biases across countries, particularly for a country like Germany.

How do such problems affect the regression results? Here, one might suspect systematic errors in measurement across countries, so that regressions of labor productivity growth on educational *levels* would produce biased coefficient estimates. However, one might also suspect that this type of measurement error would be relatively fixed over time within country, so that the coefficient estimators of production function regressions, such as equation (6.1), would not be unduly biased.

A third possibility is specification errors. Levine and Renelt (1992) showed the sensitivity of cross-country regression results to changes in specification. However, I have used a large number of alternative specifications in this work. With only a few exceptions, the coefficient estimators of the educational variables have been largely unaffected by adding or deleting variables.

A fourth possibility is that the causal relation between productivity and schooling may be the reverse of what I have assumed – namely, that schooling levels respond to per capita income levels instead of productivity growth to educational levels. In many ways, the acquisition of schooling responds to social forces. This may be particularly true in an "elitist"-type schooling system such as France has developed. Insofar as schooling is a luxury good, rising per capita income would lead to greater availability of schooling opportunity and hence rising schooling levels, particularly at the university level. This hypothesis might account for the positive and significant coefficient on the change in university enrollment rates in the cross-country productivity growth regression (Tables 6.3 and 6.5). It might also reconcile the apparent inconsistency between rising educational levels in OECD countries and the weak relation observed between productivity gains and the rise in schooling levels.

The fifth possibility is that formal education per se may not have much relevance to productivity growth among advanced industrial countries. Rather, it may be the case that only some forms of schooling (and training) are related to growth. Two types have already been highlighted in the results. The first of these is the attainment rate of primary education in the labor force. Primary schooling is the level at which the basic literacy and numerical skills required for almost all types of work are acquired (also see Wolff and Gittleman, 1993).

It is rather surprising that secondary education as a whole appears so weak as an explanatory factor of productivity growth. However, there is also strong suggestion that alternative institutional arrangements like worker-based or employer-based training, apprenticeship programs, and technical education may bear a stronger relation to productivity growth than average years of secondary schooling (see OECD, 1998). The lack of cross-country statistics on these programs prevents a systematic econometric analysis of their influence.

It is also surprising that with the explosive growth of university education in OECD countries in recent years, its relation to economic growth is so tenuous. There are two possible explanations. The first is that higher education may perform more of a screening function (see Arrow, 1973, or Spence, 1973) than a training function. According to this explanation, the skills acquired in university education are not relevant to the workplace but serve employers mainly as a signal of potential productive ability. As enrollment rates rise, screening or educational credentials may gain in importance, and a higher proportion of university graduates may become overeducated relative to the actual skills required in the workplace.

A second possibility is that university education may encourage more rent-seeking activities than directly productive ones. For example, a study by Murphy, Schleifer, and Vishny (1991) reported that per capita GDP growth is *negatively* related to the number of lawyers per capita of a country. Here, too, with rising enrollment rates, the rent-seeking bias in higher education may have been increasing in recent years.

A third and related explanation might be the increasing absorption of university graduates by "cost disease" sectors characterized by low productivity growth, such as health services, teaching, law, and business services (see Baumol, Blackman, and Wolff, 1989). These are essentially labor activities and, as such, are not subject to the types of automation and mechanization that occur in manufacturing and other goods-producing industries. These sectors are also plagued by difficulties in measuring output, and, therefore, the low productivity growth figures that are found for them may also reflect output measurement problems, particularly in regard to quality change. If this is so, there might, indeed, be a positive relation between productivity growth and university education, but inadequate output measures prevent us from observing it.

A sixth possibility, suggested by Griliches (1996), is that much, if not most of the growth in human capital since 1970 or so was absorbed in the public sectors of many of these countries. This was definitely true of Israel, where more than 80 percent of highly educated labor is employed in the public sector, in services, and in other "unmeasurable" (as far as output is concerned) sectors. This does not necessarily imply that such workers are unproductive in these sectors; indeed, they may instead contribute to the efficient functioning of the economy. However, their contribution to measured productivity such as real output per worker is not reflected in such data because the national income and product accounts provide no good measures of the real output of these sectors.

My own surmise on the basis of my own work and a review of existing studies is that the threshold model is unlikely to yield much explanatory power at least among OECD countries alone, though, as we shall see in Chapter 9, differences in educational levels constitute an important factor in explaining cross-country differences in economic growth among countries at all levels of development. Interaction models of educational attainment and technological innovation and change yield very spotty results, which are quite sensitive to model specification and country sample. Perhaps the use of an interaction term between cognitive skills and technological change may yield more consistent results. Otherwise, this avenue is likely to be a research dead end.

Models of output or productivity growth on the *change* in educational attainment have generally yielded very poor results, and further work along this line is also likely to prove to be a dead end. However, the use of the change in cognitive skills instead of the change in schooling as shown, at least in the work of Hanushek and Woessman, appears to be a promising avenue of research in growth models. The use of cognitive skill test scores instead of educational attainment is one way of avoiding the problem, noted earlier, of the variation of school quality among countries. Of course, one is still left with the task of explaining why school quality varies so much among OECD countries at least, conditional on educational expenditures.

APPENDIX TO CHAPTER 6

Appendix Table 6.1. *Gross Enrollment Rates in OECD Countries by Educational Level, 1965–2002*

Country	Primary School				Secondary School				Higher Education			
	1965	1983	1991	2002	1965	1983	1991	2002	1965	1983	1991	2002
Australia	0.99	1.05	1.07	1.04	0.62	0.92	0.82	1.54	0.16	0.26	0.39	0.74
Austria	1.06	0.99	1.07	1.03	0.52	0.74	1.04	1.00	0.09	0.25	0.35	0.49
Belgium	1.09	0.97	0.99	1.05	0.75	1.08	1.02	1.61	0.15	0.28	0.38	0.61
Canada	1.05	1.03	1.07	1.01	0.56	1.01	1.04	1.05	0.26	0.42	0.99	0.58
Denmark	0.98	1.01	0.96	1.04	0.83	1.05	1.08	1.29	0.14	0.29	0.36	0.67
Finland	0.92	1.02	0.99	1.02	0.76	1.03	1.21	1.28	0.11	0.31	0.51	0.88
France	1.34	1.08	1.07	1.04	0.56	0.89	1.01	1.09	0.18	0.28	0.43	0.56
Germany[a]	1.06	1.00	1.07	0.99	0.63	0.74	0.99	1.00	0.09	0.30	0.36	0.51
Greece	1.10	1.05	0.97	1.01	0.49	0.82	0.98	0.97	0.10	0.17	0.25	0.74
Iceland	0.97	1.01	1.01	1.00	0.80	0.88	0.99	1.14			0.29	0.63
Ireland	1.08	0.97	1.03	1.06	0.51	0.93	1.01	1.07	0.12	0.22	0.34	0.52
Italy	1.12	1.03	0.94	1.01	0.47	0.75	0.76	0.99	0.11	0.26	0.32	0.57
Japan	1.00	1.00	1.02	1.00	0.82	0.94	0.97	1.02	0.13	0.30	0.31	0.51
Netherlands	1.04	0.96	1.02	1.08	0.61	1.01	0.97	1.22	0.17	0.31	0.38	0.58
New Zealand	1.06	1.02	1.04	1.02	0.75	0.87	0.84	1.18	0.15	0.28	0.45	0.74
Norway	0.97	0.98	1.00	1.01	0.64	0.96	1.03	1.15	0.11	0.28	0.45	0.81
Portugal	0.84	1.22	1.22	1.15	0.42	0.47	0.68	1.13	0.05	0.11	0.23	0.56
Spain	1.15	1.11	1.09	1.08	0.38	0.90	1.08	1.17	0.06	0.24	0.36	0.62
Sweden	0.95	0.98	1.00	1.11	0.62	0.85	0.91	1.39	0.13	0.39	0.34	0.83
Switzerland	0.87	1.02	1.03	1.08	0.50	0.85	0.91	0.98	0.08	0.23	0.29	0.49
Turkey	1.01	1.12	1.10	0.91	0.16	0.38	0.51	0.79	0.04	0.07	0.15	0.28
United Kingdom	0.92	1.01	1.04	1.00	0.66	0.85	0.86	1.79	0.12	0.20	0.28	0.64
United States	1.06	1.00	1.04	0.98	0.63	0.85	0.90	0.94	0.40	0.56	0.76	0.83

Summary Statistics: All 23 OECD Countries

Mean	1.03	1.03	1.04	1.03	0.60	0.86	0.94	1.16	0.13	0.27	0.39	0.63
Std. Deviation	0.10	0.06	0.06	0.05	0.16	0.17	0.15	0.23	0.08	0.10	0.18	0.14
Coeff. of Var.	0.10	0.06	0.06	0.05	0.27	0.19	0.16	0.20	0.57	0.37	0.45	0.22
Number	23	23	23	23	23	23	23	23	22	22	23	23

Summary Statistics: 21 Industrial Market Economies (All Countries except Greece, Portugal, and Turkey)

Mean	1.03	1.01	1.03	1.03	0.63	0.91	0.97	1.20	0.15	0.30	0.42	0.64
Std. Deviation	0.10	0.04	0.04	0.04	0.12	0.10	0.10	0.23	0.08	0.08	0.17	0.12
Coeff. of Var.	0.10	0.04	0.04	0.03	0.20	0.11	0.11	0.19	0.52	0.28	0.41	0.19
Number	20	20	20	20	20	20	20	20	19	19	20	20

Notes: The gross enrollment rate is defined as the ratio of total enrollment of students of all ages in primary school, secondary school, and higher education to the population of the age group for that schooling level. The age groups vary somewhat among countries, depending on the normal age coverage of that country for a given schooling level. The enrollment rates may therefore exceed 100 percent. Sources: World Bank, World Development Report 1988, 1994; World Bank, World Tables, 1991; UNESCO Statistical Yearbooks, 1970 and 1996; and UNESCO Institute for Statistics, www.uis.unesco.org (downloaded June 7, 2005)

[a] West Germany in 1965, 1983, and 1991

Appendix Table 6.2. *Educational Attainment Rates in OECD Countries by Level, Selected Years, 1960–1996*

Country	Primary School			Secondary School				Higher Education			
	1960	1970	1979	1960	1970	1979	1996	1960	1970	1979	1996
Australia		0.99	0.87		0.70	0.51	0.57		0.22	0.13	0.15
Austria			0.87	0.07	0.35	0.43	0.71	0.02	0.03	0.03	0.06
Belgium			0.99	0.31	0.37	0.57	0.54	0.04	0.03	0.08	0.11
Canada	0.98	0.99	0.98	0.30	0.32	0.74	0.76	0.08	0.10	0.37	0.17
Denmark	0.78	0.82	1.00	0.27	0.41	0.58	0.66	0.04	0.08	0.11	0.15
Finland			0.92	0.10	0.30	0.39	0.67	0.04	0.06	0.11	0.12
France			0.98	0.10	0.15	0.52	0.60	0.02	0.03	0.14	0.10
Germany, West		1.00	0.99		0.35	0.42	0.82		0.04	0.09	0.13
Greece	0.84	0.80	0.89	0.11	0.14	0.27	0.44	0.02	0.04	0.08	0.12
Iceland											
Ireland	0.87	0.85	0.92	0.19	0.36	0.46	0.50	0.04	0.05	0.07	0.11
Italy	0.87	0.92	0.83	0.15	0.20	0.31	0.38	0.02	0.03	0.04	0.08
Japan	0.96	0.99	1.00	0.34	0.39	0.52		0.02	0.06	0.13	
Luxembourg							0.29				0.11
Netherlands		0.99	0.93	0.12	0.49	0.57	0.63	0.01	0.07	0.15	0.23
New Zealand	0.95	0.99	0.99	0.26	0.40	0.56	0.60	0.05	0.12	0.27	0.11
Norway		0.99	0.98	0.16	0.30	0.91	0.82	0.02	0.07	0.11	0.16
Portugal	0.55	0.56	0.82	0.05	0.08	0.37	0.20	0.01	0.02	0.05	0.08
Spain	0.76	0.87	0.91	0.05	0.10	0.18	0.30	0.01	0.04	0.06	0.13
Sweden			0.86		0.43	0.58	0.74		0.08	0.15	0.13
Switzerland	1.00	0.95	0.62	0.31	0.09	0.36	0.80	0.09		0.10	0.10
Turkey	0.41	0.44	0.47	0.05	0.09	0.12	0.17	0.01	0.02	0.03	0.06
United Kingdom		0.97	0.88		0.37	0.54	0.76	0.05	0.09	0.12	0.13
United States	0.98	1.00	1.00	0.60	0.72	0.98	0.86	0.17	0.21	0.30	0.26

Summary Statistics: All 24 OECD Countries

Mean	0.83	0.89	0.9	0.2	0.33	0.5	0.58	0.04	0.07	0.12	0.13
Std. Deviation	0.18	0.16	0.13	0.14	0.17	0.2	0.2	0.04	0.05	0.09	0.05
Coeff. of Var.	0.21	0.18	0.14	0.7	0.51	0.41	0.35	0.91	0.78	0.69	0.37
Number	12	17	22	18	21	22	22	19	21	22	22

Summary Statistics: 21 Industrial Market Economies (All countries except Greece, Portugal, and Turkey)

Mean	0.81	0.95	0.92	0.21	0.37	0.53	0.63	0.05	0.08	0.13	0.13
Std. Deviation	0.28	0.06	0.09	0.14	0.15	0.19	0.17	0.04	0.05	0.09	0.05
Coeff. of Var.	0.35	0.06	0.1	0.69	0.41	0.35	0.26	0.84	0.71	0.65	0.34
Number	9	14	19	15	18	19	19	16	18	19	19

Note: The educational attainment rate is defined as the proportion of the population 25 and over who have attained the indicated level of schooling or greater. The original data sources are UNESCO, Statistics of Educational Attainment and Literacy, 1945–1974; UNESCO Statistical Yearbook 1990; and OECD, Education at a Glance: OECD Indicators, 1998. See Wolff and Gittleman (1993) for details on sources and methods

Appendix Table 6.3. *Average Years of Schooling of the Total Population Aged 25 and Older in OECD Countries, Selected Years, 1960–1999*

Country	1960	1965	1970	1975	1980	1985	1990	1995	1999
Australia	9.43	9.30	10.09	9.81	10.02	10.06	10.12	10.31	10.57
Austria	6.71	6.91	7.01	6.83	8.43	8.26	8.22	8.44	8.80
Belgium	7.46	7.67	8.40	7.88	7.85	8.16	8.43	8.55	8.73
Canada	8.37	8.07	8.80	9.54	10.23	10.40	10.50	11.18	11.43
Denmark	8.95	8.86	8.78	8.95	9.16	9.42	10.13	9.86	10.09
Finland	5.37	5.78	6.50	7.23	8.33	7.96	9.48	9.82	10.14
France	5.78	5.86	5.86	6.08	6.77	7.31	7.56	7.94	8.38
Germany, West	8.28	8.25	8.27	7.73	8.41	8.98	9.06	9.57	9.75
Greece	4.64	4.95	5.19	5.67	6.56	6.95	7.66	8.05	8.52
Iceland	5.63	5.89	6.22	6.65	7.11	7.55	7.96	8.35	8.75
Ireland	6.46	6.45	6.52	6.70	7.61	7.87	8.50	8.79	9.02
Italy	4.56	4.77	5.22	5.28	5.32	5.76	6.16	6.60	7.00
Japan	6.87	7.22	6.89	7.36	8.23	8.51	9.22	9.44	9.72
Netherlands	5.27	5.58	7.59	7.75	7.99	8.32	8.61	8.96	9.24
New Zealand	9.56	9.42	9.36	11.00	11.43	11.43	11.18	11.31	11.52
Norway	6.11	6.18	7.36	7.71	8.28	8.40	10.85	11.82	11.86
Portugal	1.94	2.24	2.44	2.79	3.27	3.57	4.33	4.54	4.91
Spain	3.64	3.75	4.69	4.49	5.15	5.32	6.09	6.62	7.25
Sweden	7.65	7.66	7.47	8.44	9.47	9.22	9.57	11.24	11.36
Switzerland	7.30	7.32	8.28	8.28	10.07	9.90	9.92	10.18	10.39
Turkey	2.00	2.05	2.16	2.26	2.80	3.38	3.95	4.57	4.80
United Kingdom	7.67	7.17	7.66	8.01	8.17	8.44	8.74	9.03	9.35
United States	8.67	9.25	9.79	10.01	11.91	11.71	12.00	12.18	12.25

Summary Statistics: All 24 OECD Countries

Mean	6.45	6.55	6.98	7.24	7.94	8.12	8.62	9.01	9.30
Std. Deviation	2.14	2.05	2.07	2.15	2.27	2.12	2.03	2.05	1.96
Coeff. of Var.	0.33	0.31	0.30	0.30	0.29	0.26	0.23	0.23	0.21
Number	23	23	23	23	23	23	23	23	23

Summary Statistics: 21 Industrial Market Economies (All Countries except Greece, Portugal, and Turkey)

Mean	6.99	7.07	7.54	7.79	8.50	8.65	9.12	9.51	9.78
Std. Deviation	1.64	1.55	1.47	1.60	1.74	1.61	1.53	1.57	1.45
Coeff. of Var.	0.23	0.22	0.19	0.21	0.20	0.19	0.17	0.16	0.15
Number	20	20	20	20	20	20	20	20	20

Note: The methodology is as follows: benchmark estimates on attainment rates by six educational levels were first obtained from UNESCO Statistical Yearbooks, various years. Attainment rates for other years were estimated on the basis of school enrollment rates by level in preceding and succeeding years. The labor force was then "aged" backward and forward in time and school attainment estimated using the enrollment rates

Source: Barro and Lee (2000), appendix.

Appendix Table 6.4. *Research and Development (R&D) Intensity of Production in OECD Countries, 1960–2001*

Country	Expenditures for R&D as a Percentage of GDP (or GNP)			
	1969–72	1982–85	1996	1999–2001
Australia	1.40	1.30	1.68	1.53
Austria	0.60	1.30	1.52	1.87
Belgium	1.20	1.70	1.59	1.98
Canada	1.25	1.43	1.64	1.89
Denmark	1.00	1.25	2.01	2.15
Finland	0.85	1.47	2.58	3.32
France	1.87	2.30	2.32	2.20
Germany, West	2.05	2.60	2.29	2.47
Greece	0.20	0.20	0.48	0.68
Iceland	0.40	0.80	1.51	2.70
Ireland	0.75	0.85	1.39	1.18
Italy	1.03	1.17	1.03	1.06
Japan	1.83	2.63	2.83	3.00
Netherlands	2.20	2.03	2.09	2.00
New Zealand	0.50	0.90	0.97	1.03
Norway	1.18	1.40	1.71	1.67
Portugal	0.35	0.40	0.58	0.80
Spain	0.25	0.50	0.87	0.95
Sweden	1.45	2.80	3.59	4.21
Switzerland	2.05	2.20	2.74	2.64
Turkey	0.30	0.40	0.45	0.64
United Kingdom	2.15	2.20	1.94	1.89
United States	2.70	2.65	2.62	2.71
Summary Statistics: All 24 OECD Countries				
Mean	1.20	1.50	1.76	1.94
Std. Deviation	0.73	0.80	0.82	0.91
Coeff. of Var.	0.61	0.53	0.46	0.47
Number	23	23	23	23
Summary Statistics: 21 Industrial Market Economies (All except Greece, Portugal, and Turkey)				
Mean	1.34	1.67	1.95	2.12
Std. Deviation	0.69	0.70	0.70	0.83
Coeff. of Var.	0.51	0.42	0.36	0.39
Number	20	20	20	20

Note: The original data sources are UNESCO Statistical Yearbook, 1963–1990, 1999; the OECD ANBERD database, 1998 version; and UNESCO Institute for Statistics, Statistic Tables, at www. uis.unesco.org (downloaded on Feb. 8, 2005). Period averages are shown for 1969–72 and 1982–85. See Gittleman and Wolff (1994) for details on sources and methods for the 1960–89 data

Productivity Performance on the Industry Level among the Advanced Industrial Countries

7.1 Sectoral Level Performance and Comparative Advantage

Chapter 5 established that the aggregate productivity levels of advanced economies converged on the leader, the United States, from about 1950 through 1980. The question remained, however, What was the source of this aggregate convergence? In Section 7.2 we examine the extent to which labor productivity at the industry level converged among OECD economies. We also examine the role of changes in employment mix. In Section 7.3 we consider the role of technological gains and capital formation in labor productivity growth. Section 7.4 surveys the more recent literature on this subject, including Bernard and Jones (1996a, 1996b), among others. Concluding remarks are provided in Section 7.5.

Some industries produce more value added per worker than others, owing to the use of large amounts of capital or skilled labor or of advanced technology. It is possible for countries to have the same labor productivity at the industry level but nevertheless to have different levels of aggregate productivity because one economy's employment mix is shifted toward the high value– added sectors. One of the leading models of international trade, the Heckscher-Ohlin model, predicts that this will be the case among fairly similar countries, such as those in the OECD. Thus aggregate convergence can result from labor productivity converging at the industry level and/or from employment mixes becoming more similar.

If the theory behind productivity convergence is correct, then we should observe stronger convergence in productivity levels at the industry level than for the total economy, since the catch-up effect should operate most strongly at the industry level. Yet, the work of Dollar and Wolff (1988) and, later, Dollar and Wolff (1993) found just the opposite. They analyzed changes in productivity levels on the industry level for a sample of nine

OECD countries covering the period from 1960 to 1986. While they found strong evidence of convergence on the economywide level in GDP per worker, the capital-labor ratio, aggregate labor productivity, and total factor productivity (TFP), convergence at the industry level was generally not as strong as that for the economy as a whole. In fact, aggregate convergence in productivity was to a large extent attributable to the modest productivity leads that different countries enjoyed in different industries. They argued that industry specialization was an important component in aggregate productivity convergence. Moreover, they did not find that structural change was an important factor in overall productivity convergence.

7.2 Labor Productivity Convergence by Industry

In this section I report on work by Dollar and Wolff (1993, chapter 3), which examined trends in labor productivity in twenty-eight manufacturing industries of thirteen industrial countries over the period 1963 to 1986.[1] The main empirical finding of Dollar and Wolff (DW hereafter) was that among these industrial countries there was in fact convergence of labor productivity levels in virtually every manufacturing industry during the postwar period. Furthermore, throughout this period there was more intercountry variation in productivity at the industry level than at the level of all manufacturing. Productivity convergence was stronger for all manufacturing than within individual industries; this was especially true for heavy industries (like chemicals and steel) and for high technology industries (like transport equipment and machinery). In 1986 the productivity leader in these industries had an advantage ranging from 25 percent to 150 percent over the average of the other countries. It may seem paradoxical that there was stronger convergence at an aggregate level, but this result can be explained by the fact that in 1986 different countries led in different industries.

The second major finding was that variation in the employment mix among industrial countries apparently did not play an important role in

[1] See Chapter 3 for an extended methodological discussion of measurement issues associated with industry-level productivity levels and growth. From a methodological point of view, this chapter should precede Chapter 4 on aggregate productivity convergence. However, from a historical perspective on the literature and a logical perspective on the substantive results, it makes more sense to have this chapter follow the ones on aggregate convergence. First, the earliest work in this field dealt with productivity convergence on the aggregate level. Second, the main finding of the chapter – namely, that aggregate convergence occurs because of convergence on the industry level and not because of shifts in the composition of output – makes sense only after I discuss aggregate convergence.

explaining cross-country differences in aggregate productivity in all manufacturing; nor were changes in employment mixes an important source of convergence. Convergence in value added per work hour in all manufacturing among these countries resulted from convergence of productivity levels within individual industries.

7.2.1 Trade Theory and Labor Productivity

The traditional Heckscher-Ohlin (HO) model of international trade provides a useful framework for analyzing differences in labor productivity among a group of countries that engage in trade.[2] In the simple version of the model there are two factors of production (labor and capital) and two goods, one of which is capital intensive compared to the other. Trade will take place between countries if they have different aggregate capital-labor ratios. In particular, the relatively capital abundant country will export the capital intensive good. In the process, it is possible that for each industry the capital-labor ratio will be the same in the two economies, with the result that at the industry level labor productivity (and wages) will be identical as well. Such an equilibrium is characterized by factor price equalization.

What is interesting about this model from the point of view of productivity research is that it points out the possibility that two countries with different aggregate factor endowments can have the same factor intensities and levels of productivity in each industry. In particular, if factor-price equalization holds among a group of countries, then for each individual industry labor productivity should be identical across such countries.[3] The key to the factor-price equalization result is that countries will be using the same techniques of production (that is, capital-labor ratios) at the industry level.

In this model there will still be differences in *aggregate productivity*. Aggregate output in any country h will be the sum of factor earnings:

$$Y^h = rK^h + wL^h, \tag{7.1}$$

where Y^h is aggregate value added (GDP), K^h and L^h are aggregate quantities of capital and labor, and r and w are the relevant factor prices (which are the same across countries). Aggregate labor productivity is then

---

[2] The basic model was developed by Hecksher (1919) and Ohlin (1933). It was formalized in a series of papers by Samuelson, notably Samuelson (1953).

[3] Leamer (1984) discussed the conditions under which factor-price equalization holds and demonstrated that certain implications of factor-price equalization were borne out empirically for a large group of countries in 1958 and 1975.

$$Y^h / L^h = r\left(K^h / L^h\right) + w. \tag{7.2}$$

Across countries, aggregate labor productivity will vary (linearly) with the capital-labor ratio.

At the industry level, on the other hand, labor productivity will not vary across countries. This is possible because countries will have different distributions of output and employment across industries. In particular, a capital abundant country will have more of its labor force in the capital-intensive industry. That industry will have relatively more value added per unit of labor input than the labor-intensive sector. Differences in aggregate endowments of nonlabor factors such as capital hence will be reflected in different distributions of employment across industries, not in different techniques of production at the microlevel. This model implies that differences in aggregate productivity can then only result from differences in industry mixes.

While the exposition of the HO model with factor-price equalization is easiest in a 2 by 2 model, these basic results can hold with many factors and industries.[4] Formally, let v^h be an nx1 vector of fixed factor supplies for country h. With factor-price equalization there will be an nx1 factor-price vector, w, that is the same for all countries. GDP or aggregate value added for country h can then be expressed as the sum of factor earnings:

$$Y^h = w'v^h. \tag{7.3}$$

Let the first factor in the vector v^h be the aggregate labor supply, L^h. Then aggregate labor productivity can be expressed as

$$Y^h / L^h = w_L + \Sigma_{i=2}\left(w_i v_i^{\ h} / L^h\right). \tag{7.4}$$

where w_L is the wage. In the more general model, one country will have greater aggregate productivity than another if the value of its nonlabor factors (per work hour) is greater. Aggregate labor productivity is also, by definition, a weighted average of labor productivity in individual industries,

---

[4] Exposition is also easiest if the number of factors equals the number of goods. However, this highly unrealistic assumption is not necessary to generate the basic results. In particular, the number of goods can be greater than the number of factors, and still there can be an equilibrium with factor-price equalization. With more goods than factors, the pattern of trade *in goods* is not uniquely defined; nevertheless, it remains true that countries tend to be implicit exporters of their relatively abundant factors through their trade in goods. For details, see Chang (1979) and Vanek (1968).

$$Y^h / L^h = \Sigma_i \left(a_i^h y_i^h / L_i^h \right), \tag{7.5}$$

where the weights are employment shares ($a_i^h = L_i^h/L^h$).

The HO model with factor-price equalization predicts that value added per work hour at the industry level is identical across countries, so that high labor productivity at the aggregate level must result from having an employment mix shifted toward high productivity industries. Industries with high value added per work hour are those that employ much human capital, physical capital, or other nonlabor resources per work hour. It should also be noted that, even with factor-price equalization, exact equality across countries in industry labor productivity would only be observed at a very disaggregated level. Improper aggregation would necessarily introduce some cross-country variation in industry labor productivity. In this case the implication of factor-price equalization can be stated in the following form: The cross-country variation in labor productivity at the industry level should be significantly less than variation at the aggregate level, though not necessarily zero.

7.2.2 Convergence in All Manufacturing

DW's examination of the convergence of labor productivity at the industry level covered thirteen industrial countries––the so-called G-7 (Canada, France, Germany, Italy, Japan, the United Kingdom, and the United States) plus six smaller economies (Australia, Austria, Denmark, Finland, Norway, and Sweden). Data availability dictated the countries selected.

To investigate labor productivity at the industry level they used data from the *United Nations Yearbook of Industrial Statistics*, which reports manufacturing output and employment disaggregated into twenty-eight industries. Their output measure was value added, which was reported in current prices, denominated in domestic currency.[5] They used the GNP deflator of each country to convert values of different years into 1983 prices, and then

---

[5] Using value added rather than gross output introduces biases if materials prices change significantly and countries differ in their dependence on materials. This concern is more relevant for studies of aggregate labor productivity, since intercountry variation in the use of materials at the industry level is likely to be small. DW made productivity calculations using U.S. input-output data for 1958 and 1977 in order to compare the value added measure with the gross output one. Using an 85-industry breakdown, they calculated both the annual rate of growth of value added (in 1972 dollars) per worker and that of gross output (in 1972 dollars) per worker over the period. The correlation coefficient between the two series was 0.80. Thus, value added per worker at the industry level appeared to be a good proxy for gross output per worker.

applied PPP exchange rates calculated by the OECD to convert all values into 1983 dollars.[6]

The ideal labor input measure would be hours worked; unfortunately, this was not available at the industry level. So DW used number of employees in the industry, adjusted by the average number of hours worked in the country and year in question.[7] Their primary measure of labor productivity then was value added per work hour, denominated in 1983 dollars. If hours worked in the whole economy were not good proxies for hours worked in individual manufacturing industries, then this procedure would introduce some bias (of unknown direction). Hence they also used value added per worker as an alternative measure of labor productivity to ensure that the results were not heavily dependent on any such bias.

For all manufacturing, the United States maintained a labor productivity lead over the other twelve countries throughout the period under consideration. This can be seen in Appendix Table 7.1, which presents cross-country indices of value added per work hour in all manufacturing for 1963, 1970, 1982, and 1986. The U.S. productivity lead, however, diminished over time. The unweighted average productivity in the other twelve countries was 47 percent of U.S. productivity in 1963; there was a strong trend toward convergence between 1963 and 1970 (see Figure 7.1). By the latter year, the average of the other countries had risen to 58 percent of U.S. productivity. This convergence of productivity levels can also be seen in the coefficient of variation: This measure of cross-country dispersion declined from 0.36 in 1963 to 0.24 in 1970.[8]

The trend toward convergence is much less clear in the period after 1970. There appears to have been some additional convergence during the 1970s, and by 1982 the average productivity in the manufacturing sector of the other industrial countries was 66 percent of the U.S. level. Between 1982 and 1986 U.S. productivity grew relative to that of the other countries. In 1986, the average productivity of the twelve industrial countries compared to the United States was 60 percent, about the same as in 1970. The lack of any strong secular trend between 1970 and 1986 is also reflected in the

---

[6] See Ward (1985) for an explanation of how these PPP exchange rates were calculated. If data were available, it would be preferable to deflate the output measures with industry-specific deflators, then convert to a common currency with PPP exchange rates for tradable goods. Unfortunately, neither industry-level deflators nor PPP exchange rates for tradables were available.

[7] The hours data were from Maddison (1982).

[8] The convergence is slightly weaker if value added per worker rather than value added per work hour is used, though the difference is not large.

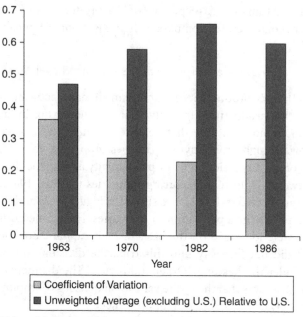

Figure 7.1 Value added per work hour in manufacturing in 12 industrial countries relative to the United States, 1963 to 1986.

coefficient of variation, which was virtually the same in 1970 (.24), 1982 (.23), and 1986 (.24).

It is interesting that different countries follow different patterns of convergence. Japan gained steadily on the United States throughout the period examined, though it must be remembered that it had by far the lowest productivity among industrial countries at the beginning of the period. Many of the countries followed the general pattern of gaining on the United States between 1963 and 1970, and then showing little further progress subsequently. Germany, Australia, and France were all examples of this pattern. Canada was somewhat of an anomaly. It started out with the productivity level closest to the United States in 1963 but showed little progress between 1963 and 1982. In the 1980s, however, Canada gained strongly on the United States, reaching 93 percent of the U.S. productivity level in 1986. The figures for Italy and the United Kingdom show implausibly large productivity increases between 1970 and 1982, followed by implausibly large decreases between 1982 and 1986. Those anomalies may reflect the manner in which the 1982 recession affected their productivity statistics. Note also that productivity convergence on the United States was strongest for the large economies: The average for Japan, Germany, France, Italy, the United

Kingdom, and Canada was 65 percent of U.S. productivity by 1986. For the six smaller economies, the comparable figure was only 55 percent.

7.2.3 Convergence at the Industry Level

In theory, the U.S. productivity advantage in all manufacturing could result from superior productivity in individual manufacturing industries and/or from an employment mix that, relative to other industrial countries, is shifted toward high productivity industries. Appendix Table 7.2 provides measures of the dispersion in labor productivity among the thirteen countries for twenty-eight manufacturing industries in 1963, 1982, and 1986. Statistics for selected industries are shown in Figures 7.2a and 7.2b.

Industries were grouped into four categories. Heavy, medium, and light industries were identified on the basis of their capital-labor ratio. Several industries did not fit easily into this tripartite division and were placed together under the heading "Other Industries." The distinctive feature of these industries was that they were very small in terms of employment and/or were closely connected to primary products.

A number of interesting results emerge from the results. In 1963 the United States was the productivity leader in virtually every industry, with the only exceptions occurring in small industries like coal products. This was reflected in the average of productivity in the twelve countries relative to the United States. At the industry level the U.S. productivity lead was related to the capital intensity of the industry, with the U.S. advantage noticeably greater in heavy industries than in light industries.

On the basis of the coefficients of variation, which measure the dispersion in industry labor productivity across the thirteen countries, in 1963 there was considerably more dispersion in heavy industries (.50) than in all manufacturing (.36). There was less dispersion in medium industries (.40), but still more than in all manufacturing. Light industries (.33) evidenced less variation than the whole manufacturing sector.

Between 1963 and 1986 the coefficient of variation declined for virtually every industry, indicating that among these countries labor productivity was converging at the industry level. The average of productivity in the twelve countries, relative to the United States, also rose in all but three industries (food products, tobacco products, and coal products). The convergence was strongest in the light industries: The other countries had on average achieved 66 percent of U.S. productivity, whereas the comparable figure for all manufacturing was 60 percent. In heavy and medium industries, as well, the other countries made substantial gains relative to the United States. Nevertheless, it

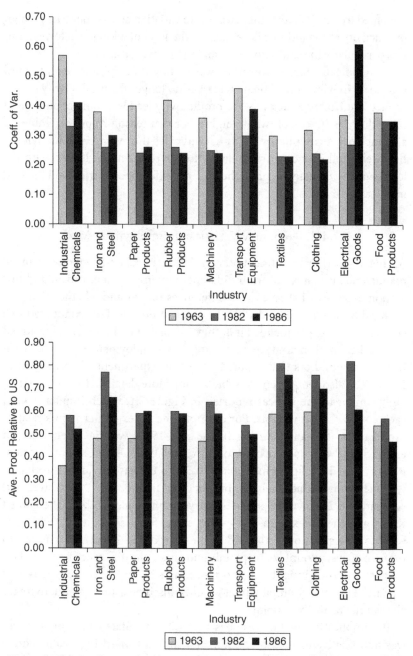

Figure 7.2 (a) Coefficient of variation in value added per work hour across 13 industrial countries for selected manufacturing industries, 1963, 1982, and 1986; (b) average value added per work hour in 12 industrial countries relative to the United States for selected manufacturing industries, 1963, 1982, and 1986.

remained true in 1986 that there was more variation across countries in labor productivity at the industry level than at the level of all manufacturing. This was particularly the case with heavy and medium industries.

An important change from 1963 was that by 1986 there were quite a few industries in which the United States was no longer the productivity leader. In fact, the United States was the productivity leader in only about half of the industries (fifteen of twenty-eight). For that reason Appendix Table 7.2 also includes a column for 1986 that indicates the average productivity of the twelve follower countries relative to the productivity leader, with the lead country indicated in parentheses. Five different countries held the lead in at least one industry.

7.2.4 Intercountry Variation in Employment Mix

As noted previously, intercountry variation in labor productivity in all manufacturing can result from differences in employment mixes, and this section explores what role these differences played and whether that role changed between 1963 and 1982. In order to do this, DW conducted two counterfactual experiments. First, they calculated an index of value added per worker in all manufacturing using U.S. employment shares for each country. The indices that resulted from this experiment are presented in Figure 7.3 (also see Appendix Table 7.3 for more details). They were strikingly similar to the indices reported in Figure 7.1, which implicitly used each country's own weights. For example, the index of Germany's relative productivity in manufacturing in the mid-1960s was 54 when German employment weights were used for the calculation. Using U.S. employment weights raised the figure marginally to 58. In the case of Japan the change was even more minor: relative productivity in 1963 of 27 (U.S. weights) compared to 26 (own weights). The largest difference was with the United Kingdom: The index with own weights was 52 and rose to 57 with U.S. weights. The situation at the end of the period, 1986, was very similar. In the case of every country except Italy and Japan, the difference between U.S. weights and own weights was no more than 2 points. For both Italy and Japan, the use of U.S. employment weights raised measured productivity for all manufacturing by 3 points.

The implication of this result is that U.S. manufacturing employment was not, relative to the other countries, shifted toward high value added industries, either at the beginning of this period or at the end. Differences in employment mixes could explain virtually none of the cross-country differences in labor productivity at the level of all manufacturing. Thus the

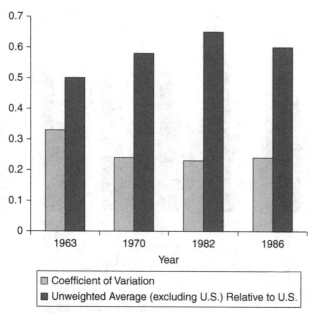

Figure 7.3 Value added per work hour in manufacturing in 12 industrial countries relative to the United States, calculated with U.S. employment shares of that year, 1963 to 1986.

United States had higher aggregate productivity in 1963 not because its output and employment mix were substantially different from those of other industrial countries, but rather because it had higher labor productivity in every two-digit manufacturing industry.

The second counterfactual experiment involved calculating an index of value added per worker in all manufacturing holding each country's employment weights constant through time. For this DW used 1982 employment weights; the results are presented in Figure 7.4 for the United States, Germany, and Japan (see Appendix Table 7.4 for all thirteen countries), along with indices calculated with actual employment weights (changing over time). Again, there is strikingly little difference between the constant weights and actual weights indices. In the case of Germany, for example, applying that country's 1982 weights to its mid-1960s productivity levels raised the index of productivity for all manufacturing to only a small degree (from 59 to 63). This indicated that between the mid-1960s and the mid-1980s there was a minor adjustment in the German employment mix, in the direction of higher value added industries. In the case of Japan, the use of 1982 weights on 1963 productivity levels resulted in no change in the

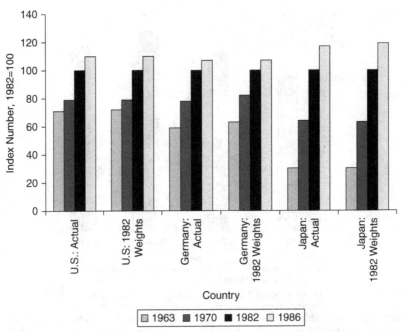

Figure 7.4 Value added per work hour in manufacturing in 3 countries, using actual and 1982 weights, 1963 to 1986.

index of manufacturing productivity. The only exception to this rule was Austria, where the use of 1982 weights results in a large increase in the productivity index for all manufacturing. Except for that one anomaly, all of the countries evidenced only minor changes in the index as a result of using contemporary employment weights.

This result implied that in twelve of these thirteen economies changes in employment mixes did not play an important role in productivity growth and hence in the convergence of labor productivity at the level of all manufacturing. It should be emphasized that this result does not mean that employment mixes did not change over time; they almost certainly had. What the results here established was that the changes cannot be characterized as a shift from low value added (presumably labor intensive) to higher value added (capital and/or technology intensive) industries.

7.2.5 Interpretation of the Results

DW concluded that in 1963 the U.S. lead in labor productivity for all manufacturing was rooted in superior productivity at the industry level. Between

1963 and 1986 labor productivity of the industrial countries covered by this study converged on the U.S. level in virtually every industry, though the degree of convergence differed markedly across industries. This convergence of productivity at the industry level was the proximate source of the convergence in aggregate productivity that has been noted in the many studies covered in Chapter 5 of this book. Changes in the distribution of employment across industries played virtually no role in the aggregate convergence.

One of the interesting implications of this last result is that the key to aggregate productivity growth was not a shifting of the nation's employment and output into a few special sectors. Countries such as Japan grew well not because they captured a small number of high value added industries but rather because their productivity growth was high in all sectors. What employment shifts did occur cannot be characterized as a shift from low to high value added activities. In addition to growing well in all industries, successful economies also had a few industries in which their productivity growth was especially high. These high growth sectors, however, appeared to be different in each country, a finding that explained the greater cross-country dispersion of productivity in individual industries than that of the aggregate.

In interpreting these results, the question that naturally arises is how we can account for the observed intercountry variation in industry labor productivity. Discovering the source of the productivity differentials should also lead to an explanation of why those differentials have diminished over time. Two hypotheses, not mutually exclusive, suggest themselves: first, that industry level capital-labor ratios converged among the countries in this sample; second, that technology levels converged among the countries.

DW argued that in 1963 the United States had a much greater aggregate capital-labor ratio than other industrial countries, and probably more human capital per worker as well, though the latter was hard to prove. The HO model predicts that in this situation the U.S. output mix will be shifted toward industries that use physical and human capital intensively, and there is evidence that this was the case.[9] The factor-price equalization theorem demonstrates that it is possible that the shift in the output mix is of such magnitude that at the industry level the use of capital and other factors per worker is identical across countries, equalizing labor productivity at

---

[9] Baldwin (1971), for instance, found that in the 1960s the United States was exporting from high productivity industries and importing goods produced in low productivity industries.

the industry level. This was clearly not the case among industrial countries in 1963. The United States had a large productivity lead in virtually every industry, and in the heavy industries the U.S. lead was considerably greater than in all manufacturing.

On the basis of the results reported previously, it seems likely that in each industry the United States was employing more capital per worker than other countries in 1963. Between 1963 and 1982 the aggregate capital-labor ratios of industrial countries converged on the U.S. level (see Section 7.3). The countries with low capital-labor ratios in 1963 accumulated capital extremely rapidly; this was especially true for Japan, and the importance of capital accumulation as a source of Japanese labor productivity growth has been well documented.[10] This apparently resulted in the convergence of capital-labor ratios at the industry level, a hypothesis that will be examined in Section 7.3.

This interpretation is consistent with empirical studies of changing U.S. comparative advantage. Bowen (1983, p. 409), for instance, found that the U.S. position as a capital abundant country declined relative to other developed countries, and that "as capital accumulation proceeded in developed countries they were increasingly able to compete with the United States in capital-intensive sectors." DW argued that this development should be understood in the context of the HO model without factor-price equalization.

Convergence of industry labor productivity can be reconciled with the HO model, if the productivity convergence is driven by convergence of factor endowments. The fact that different countries hold productivity leads in different industries in 1986, on the other hand, is not easily reconciled with HO theory. Such a result is more compatible with technology based trade theories and is the expected outcome if the technological advance of industrial nations is concentrated in different industries.

Hence another plausible hypothesis that needs to be considered is that these findings concerning industry labor productivity are primarily the result of variation in technology, both across countries and over time. It is possible that there were important technology differences among industrial countries in 1963, and that in general these differences diminished over time, partly as a result of international diffusion of technology. A general convergence of technology levels is not inconsistent with individual countries developing modest technology leads in different industries, which would account for the fact that in 1986 productivity differentials were somewhat larger at the industry level than at the level of all manufacturing.

---

[10] See, for example, Norsworthy and Malmquist (1983).

7.3 TFP Convergence by Industry

Several works have demonstrated that OECD countries have become more similar in terms of aggregate characteristics. This growing similarity is evident in the marked convergence of overall labor productivity among industrialized countries in the postwar period, as well as in the convergence of aggregate total factor productivity (TFP) and capital-labor ratios.[11] Section 7.2 began the investigation of how this productivity convergence was manifested in particular industries. DW addressed two issues in particular: the extent to which shifts in employment from low value added to high value added activities within manufacturing contributed to aggregate labor productivity convergence and the extent to which there had been labor productivity convergence in individual industries.

DW left open the question of the source of the intercountry variation in industry labor productivity, as well as the explanation for the changes in these differentials over time. This section takes up these issues by considering two, not mutually exclusive hypotheses: first, that there were differences in degree of technological sophistication, though these narrowed among the countries; and, second, that industry level capital-labor ratios differed but converged among industrialized countries.

The evidence reported by DW (1993, chapter 4) pointed to the convergence of TFP levels both in the aggregate and within industry between 1963 and 1985. However, this process of technological catch-up was much faster in the period before 1972 than after. Moreover, the degree of convergence varied considerably among industries and was particularly strong in the heavy industries, which had much greater dispersion in TFP levels in the early 1960s. As a result, by 1985 the cross-country disparity in TFP levels was very similar among industries.

The evidence also indicated convergence in capital-labor ratios both in the aggregate and by industry, though this process was also much stronger before

---

[11] On convergence of aggregate labor productivity see Chapters 4 and 5 of this book; Baumol (1986); Mathews, Feinstein, and Odling-Smee (1982); Abramovitz (1986); and Maddison (1987). Wolff (1991) found convergence in aggregate total factor productivity (TFP), defined as the ratio of output to a weighted sum of labor and capital inputs, during the postwar period among the G-7 countries. Dowrick and Nguyen (1989) similarly demonstrated significant catch-up in TFP levels among 24 OECD countries over the 1950–85 period. In addition, Wolff (1991a) found that aggregate capital-labor ratios became more similar among the G-7 countries: The coefficient of variation in the aggregate capital-labor (gross capital to hours) ratio fell from 0.52 in 1950 to 0.23 in 1979. Bowen (1983) also found that the U.S. position as a capital abundant country declined relative to that of other industrialized countries.

1972 than after. By 1985 the variation in capital intensity among countries was much greater in heavy industries than medium or light, helping to explain its greater dispersion in labor productivity levels. Differences in aggregate capital intensity were explained almost totally by differences in capital intensity at the industry level (more capital abundant countries had higher industry capital-labor ratios). Moreover, the convergence of aggregate capital-labor ratios was attributable almost entirely to the convergence of capital intensity within industries, rather than to changes in employment mix.

There also appeared to be two distinct phases. During the 1963–72 period TFP, capital intensity, and labor productivity all converged rapidly, though most of the catch-up in labor productivity was attributable to the catch-up in TFP. Furthermore, industries and countries that were particularly far behind the leader, the United States, demonstrated the greatest degree of TFP catch-up, a finding consistent with Gerschenkron's notion that backward countries can benefit from borrowing advanced technology pioneered by the leader. In the 1963–72 period it was also the case that convergence of industry TFP was correlated with convergence of capital-labor ratios. This result could mean that some advanced technology was embodied in machinery so that rapid capital accumulation occasioned fast TFP growth. Alternatively, it could be that rapid TFP growth brought about by acquiring disembodied technology made an industry especially profitable and attractive for investment. It is quite plausible that causality ran in both directions, with high investment spurring TFP growth, which in turn attracted more investment. After 1972, convergence slowed in both TFP and labor productivity, and labor productivity catch-up to the United States was achieved primarily through increasing capital intensity. Indeed, several countries surpassed the United States in terms of the capital intensity of production.

It was also found that the variation in TFP, capital intensity, and labor productivity was greater at the industry level than in aggregate manufacturing. These results indicated that the countries specialized in different industries, particularly since the mid-1970s. Countries invested heavily in new technology in different industries; that explained the emergence of countries other than the United States as productivity leaders in some industries. Changes in international comparative advantage thus could be attributed to a combination of worldwide shifts in technology leadership and investment strategies.

7.3.1 Total Factor Productivity Comparisons

Because of the nature of the available data, the total factor productivity of industry i (TFP_i) index is measured as the ratio of a sector's value added (Y_i)

to a weighted average of employment (L_i) and gross capital stock (K_i), or in logarithmic form:

$$\ln \text{TFP}_i = \ln Y_i - \alpha_i \ln L_i - (1 - \alpha_i) \ln K_i \qquad (7.6)$$

where α_i is the wage share in industry i. Two different wage shares are used for each industry: (1) individual country averages of the ratio of wages to value added over the full period in each industry and (2) the mean over all the countries of the individual country wage shares for each industry, which they called the "international average wage share." The TFP index was normalized so that the U.S. TFP index in 1963 equaled 1.0 in each industry. The proper choice between the wage share figures is debatable; hence results for the two choices were reported.[12]

Two different databases were used. The first, called the "Dollar-Wolff" database, was assembled from a variety of sources and included information on employment, value added, wages, and gross capital stock (see Dollar and Wolff, 1993, for details on sources and methods). The data were available for nine countries: Belgium, Canada, France, Federal Republic of Germany (Germany, for short), Italy, Japan, the Netherlands, the United Kingdom, and the United States. Because of differences in data classification schemes from the various sources, the data were aggregated to twelve industries: ferrous & nonferrous metals; nonmetallic minerals and products; chemicals; (finished) metal products, excluding machinery & transportation; machinery; electrical goods; transport equipment; food, beverages, and tobacco; textiles, clothing, footwear and leather; paper and printing; rubber and plastic products; and other industries.

As before, data on output, employment, and labor compensation were taken from the United Nations' *Yearbook of Industrial Statistics* for various years. The output measure was value added, which is reported in current prices, denominated in domestic currency. The GNP deflator of each country was used to convert output values of different years into 1983 prices, and then the PPP index calculated by OECD was used to convert all output values into 1983 U.S. dollars. The labor input measure was employment. The capital stock data for the EC countries were from Eurostat worksheets, for Canada from Statistics Canada worksheets and Statistics Canada (1987), for Japan from the Japan Economic Planning Agency (1988), and for the United States from Musgrave (1986a, 1986b). Only gross capital stock data were available for the nine countries.

---

[12] See Chapter 3 for a more extended discussion of methodological issues associated with the estimation of TFP on the industry level.

The second data source was the OECD International Sectoral Databank (the ISDB). This contained data for fourteen countries, which include the nine listed plus Australia, Denmark, Finland, Norway, and Sweden, and nine manufacturing industries: (1) food, beverages, and tobacco; (2) textiles; (3) wood and wood products; (4) paper, printing, and publishing; (5) chemicals; (6) nonmetal mineral products; (7) basic metal products; (8) machinery and equipment; and (9) other manufactured products. The data consist of GDP, already calculated in 1980 U.S. dollar equivalents, and total employment, number of employees, compensation of employees, and gross capital stock, already measured in 1980 U.S. dollars.

Appendix Table 7.5 shows TFP levels for the whole manufacturing sector relative to the United States for selected years over the period 1963–85 (selected statistics are shown in Figure 7.5 on the basis of the Dollar-Wolff database). Though the United States maintained its lead in TFP for the manufacturing sector as a whole, there was strong evidence that other countries were catching up. Using the Dollar-Wolff data set and own country factor shares, they reported that the unweighted average of TFP levels of other countries increased from 61 percent of the U.S. level in 1963 to 76 percent in 1983. In fact, every country except Canada gained relative to the United States over the period, with the largest relative gains made by the United Kingdom and Belgium. The coefficient of variation declined from 0.24 in 1963 to 0.14 in 1983. The ratio of maximum to minimum TFP levels fell from 2.16 in 1963 to 1.52 over the same period.

Because of data availability, the sample of countries in the preceding calculation changed over the period. Therefore, the same set of summary statistics is shown for two constant sample sets of countries (Panels B and C of Appendix Table 7.5). The pattern was similar, as were the summary statistics.[13]

Another point of interest is that the dispersion in labor productivity was larger than that of TFP in the early 1960s but its rate of convergence was greater than that of TFP. For the same sample of nine countries in the Dollar-Wolff data set, the coefficient of variation of labor productivity fell from 0.37 in 1963 to 0.15 in 1982, the unweighted average of labor productivity levels relative to the United States increased from 0.52 to 0.73, and the ratio

---

[13] The same set of results was also computed for TFP measures based on international average factor shares (results not shown). The summary statistics were almost identical. Most of the convergence occurred by the early 1970s. In 1972, the coefficient of variation in TFP levels was 0.15. The unweighted average of TFP levels of other countries relative to the United States was 0.73, and the ratio of maximum to minimum TFP was 1.63.

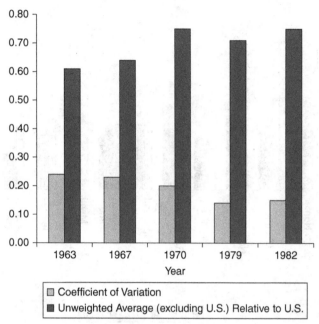

Figure 7.5 TFP levels in total manufacturing in all industrial countries with available data, 1963 to 1982.

of maximum to minimum labor productivity declined from 2.9 to 1.7. By 1982, the dispersion in labor productivity levels was almost identical to that of TFP.[14]

The same pattern is seen for individual industries, as shown in Figures 7.6a and 7.6b (also see Appendix Table 7.6 for more details). On the basis of the Dollar-Wolff database, convergence, as indicated by the decline in the coefficient of variation, occurred in every industry between 1967 and 1979. Moreover, the average TFP level of other countries relative to the United States increased in nine of the twelve industries in this classification scheme. However, the average dispersion of TFP in manufacturing industries (the unweighted average of the coefficient of variation) was still substantially greater than the degree of dispersion in the total manufacturing sector (0.34 versus 0.23 in 1967 and 0.26 versus 0.15 in 1985).

[14] The results were almost identical for the two seven-country samples shown in Panels B and C of Appendix Table 7.5. Moreover, results from the OECD database indicated that the coefficient of variation of labor productivity levels declined from 0.19 in 1970 to 0.15 in 1985 and the average labor productivity relative to the United States increased from 0.68 to 0.73. The 1985 figures for labor productivity were almost identical to those for TFP.

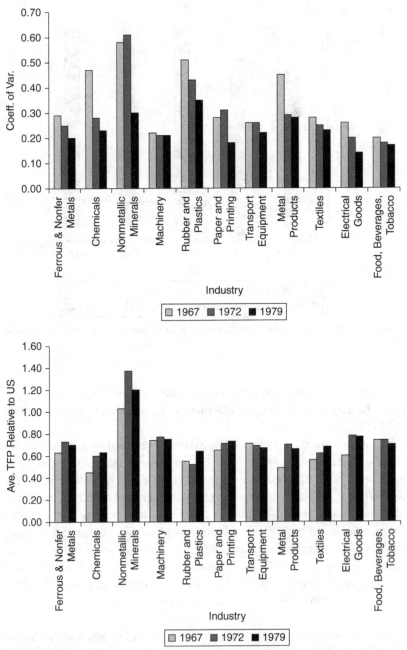

Figure 7.6 (a) Coefficient of variation of TFP levels by manufacturing industry; (b) average TFP relative to United States by manufacturing industry (*Source*: Dollar-Wolff Data Set, 1967, 1972, and 1979).

The industries were divided into three groups again – heavy, medium, and light – on the basis of the unweighted average of the capital-labor ratios among the relevant group of countries.[15] Convergence was strongest among heavy industries, in which the (unweighted) average coefficient of variation of industries within this group fell by almost half over the 1967–79 period according to the Dollar-Wolff data and by 20 percent between 1970 and 1985 according to the ISDB data. The average TFP level of the other countries exceeded that of the United States by 1979 according to the first data set and reached 87 percent of the U.S. level by 1985 according to the second.

Among medium and light industries, the average coefficient of variation fell by about a third between 1967 and 1979 by the first data set, and the average productivity of the other countries pulled to about 70 percent of the U.S. level. According to the ISDB data, dispersion remained unchanged among both medium and light industries between 1970 and 1985. By 1985, the dispersion of TFP levels within the three groups of industries was almost equal, whereas it was considerably higher among heavy industries in 1967. This finding was an interesting contrast to the results in Section 7.2 earlier, where it was found that convergence in labor productivity was strongest among light industries and weakest in heavy industries, and, by 1982, there was considerably more dispersion among heavy industries than among medium or light ones.

The leading country in terms of TFP level is also indicated for each industry in Appendix Table 7.6. In the Dollar-Wolff data set, the United States led in ten of the twelve industries in 1967 and ten in 1979. According to the ISDB data, the United States led in four of the nine OECD industries in 1970 and five in 1985. In Section 7.2, it was found that the United States led in virtually all of the twenty-eight manufacturing industries in our sample in 1963 in terms of labor productivity but in only ten of the twenty-eight in 1982. Seven countries, besides the United States, held the lead in at least one industry in 1982. Part of the reason for the difference in results was that the sample of countries used in this study was different and the industry classifications were more aggregated than in Section 7.2. However, the major explanation, as we shall see, was that other countries not only caught up to but surpassed the United States in terms of capital intensity.

Productivity movements are sensitive to business cycle fluctuations (see, for example, Chapter 3 and Chapter 8 for a discussion). There is a sizable literature on the proper techniques to use to adjust output and input measures

---

[15] The food, beverages, and tobacco industry did not fit easily into this three-way division because of several anomalies and, as a result, was tabulated separately.

for business cycle changes. Because of data availability, capacity utilization indices are used here to adjust the TFP measures. The new measure is:

$$\ln TFP_i = \ln Y_i - \alpha_i \ln - L_i - (1 - \alpha_i) \ln(uK_i) \qquad (7.6')$$

where u was the capacity utilization rate. Unfortunately, there were no data on capacity utilization by individual industry for each of the countries, so that the utilization index for the whole manufacturing sector was used to compute the adjusted TFP index. Data on utilization rates were from OECD (1980) and Coe and Holtham (1983). Results for the coefficient of variation of TFPU are almost identical to (unadjusted) TFP (see Appendix Table 7.6).

7.3.2 Capital Intensity at the Aggregate and Industry Levels

As noted, several studies documented a convergence in aggregate, economywide capital-labor ratios among industrialized countries over the postwar period. DW next looked at the extent to which the convergence in aggregate capital-labor ratios was translated into a convergence in capital-labor ratios in individual industries. Because the summary statistics were very sensitive to the sample of countries chosen, results are shown only for constant sample sets of countries (see Figures 7.7a and 7.7b and Appendix Table 7.7 for more details). The choice of countries was based on data availability. For each industry, the set of countries that had employment and capital stock data for the maximum number of years was chosen.

There was strong evidence of convergence in capital intensity among the group of nine countries in the Dollar-Wolff database. The coefficient of variation fell from 0.36 to 0.20, while the ratio of maximum to minimum capital-labor ratio fell from 3.4 to 1.8. For the whole manufacturing sector, the (unweighted) average capital-labor ratio among countries other than the United States increased from three-fourths of the U.S. level in 1965 to almost perfect equality by 1983. Catch-up in capital intensity was much stronger than in TFP (in 1985 the average TFP of other countries was only 72 percent that of the United States). Every country gained on the U.S. in terms of capital intensity over the 1963–83 period, and countries with lower initial capital endowments gained more (the correlation coefficient between the 1965 capital-labor ratio and the annual rate of growth of the capital-labor ratio over the 1965–83 period was –0.85 among the nine countries). The aggregate capital-labor ratio of Japan, in particular, increased from 40 percent of the U.S. level in 1965 to

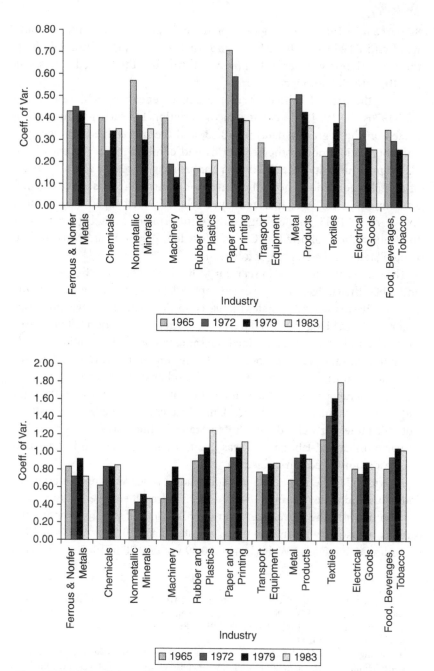

Figure 7.7 (a) Coefficient of variation of capital-labor ratios by manufacturing industry; (b) average capital-labor ratio relative to United States by manufacturing industry (*Source*: Dollar-Wolff Data Set, 1965–1983).

83 percent in 1983.[16] Aggregate capital stock data indicated that Canada was first in 1963 and the U.S. second. In 1983 Canada still ranked first, the Netherlands was second, Italy was third, and the United States was fourth, with Belgium a close fifth.

As in the case of TFP, most of the convergence was achieved by the mid-1970s. In 1974, the coefficient of variation for total manufacturing (based on the aggregate data) was 0.23, and the unweighted average capital-labor ratio among other countries had climbed to 91 percent of the U.S. capital intensity. The ISDB data confirmed this result. The dispersion of capital-labor ratios among the fourteen countries in this sample reached a minimum in 1975 and then remained relatively unchanged over the next ten years. In 1985, the leading country in terms of capital intensity was the Netherlands, followed by Canada, Sweden, Belgium, and Norway. The United States ranked eighth of fourteen.

The same pattern was also seen for individual industries. Between 1965 and 1983, the (unweighted) average capital-labor ratio in the eight countries relative to the United States increased in eleven of the twelve industries according to the Dollar-Wolff data; the coefficient of variation fell in nine of the twelve industries and remained the same in one; and the ratio of maximum to minimum capital-labor ratio fell in nine of the twelve and in two remained almost unchanged. By 1983 the other countries were, on average, considerably ahead of the United States in capital intensity in the light industries, at virtual parity with the United States in the medium industries, but still rather far behind the United States in the heavy industries. The disparity in capital-labor ratios was greatest among heavy industries and smallest among medium industries.[17]

As with TFP, the dispersion of capital-labor ratios was more marked in individual industries than in the aggregate. This result emerged from a comparison between the unweighted average coefficient of variation among the various industries with that of the aggregate data: 0.30 versus 0.20 in 1983 according to the Dollar-Wolff data and 0.39 versus 0.20 in 1985 on the basis

---

[16] The importance of capital accumulation as a source of Japanese productivity growth was well documented. See, for example, Jorgenson and Nishimizu (1978), Norsworthy and Malmquist (1983, 1985), Kendrick (1984), Bronfenbrenner (1985), and Jorgenson, Kuroda, and Nishimizu (1987).

[17] According to the OECD data, by 1985, other countries had far surpassed the United States in capital intensity in the light industries, were ahead of the United States in the medium industries, and had reached equality with the United States in the heavy industries. However, as with the first set of results, the dispersion in capital-labor ratios was greatest among heavy industries and smallest among medium industries.

of the ISDB data. This finding was somewhat surprising. In a comparison between a developed and developing country, one generally finds capital-labor ratios more similar in industries than in the aggregate. Dollar (1991), for instance, found that for South Korea and West Germany, differences in capital-labor ratios were modest at the industry level, though Germany had a far higher aggregate ratio. The reason for this was that, compared to South Korea's, Germany's employment mix was shifted toward capital inten-sive industries. This pattern is predicted by the Heckscher-Ohlin model of international trade. Given the capital abundance of the United States in the early postwar period, a similar relationship was expected between the United States at that time and the other OECD countries: greater dispersion of cap-ital-labor ratios in the aggregate than within industries. However, such was not the case.

Another interesting issue is the extent to which convergence in the overall capital-labor ratio among countries resulted from the convergence of industry employment mix. This issue can be addressed formally, as follows. Define:

s^h_i: country h's employment in industry i as a proportion of country h's total employment;

κ^h_i: ratio of country h's capital-labor ratio to U.S. capital-labor ratio in industry i;

where the industry capital-labor ratios in each country are standardized by expressing them as ratios to the U.S. levels. Then,

$$\kappa^h = \sum_i s^h_i \kappa^h_i \qquad (7.7)$$

where κ^h is country h's capital-labor ratio in all manufacturing. From (7.7) it follows that

$$\Delta\kappa^h = \sum_i s^h_i (\Delta\kappa^h_i) + \sum_i (\Delta s^h_i)\kappa^h_i \qquad (7.8)$$

where a "Δ" indicates change over time (for example, $\Delta\kappa^h_i \equiv \kappa^h_t - \kappa^h_{t-1}$). From Table 7.1, it is apparent that almost all the change in aggregate country cap-ital-labor ratios over the 1972–85 period could be attributed to the change in industry capital-labor ratios rather than to changes in employment mixes among industries. This was the case for each country, with the exception of Canada, and for each of the periods considered – 1972–9 and 1979–85.

Finally, it should be noted that in the 1980s, the dispersion of capital-labor ratios in all manufacturing, as measured by the coefficient of varia-tion, was greater than that of TFP levels. This was also true for each of the three industry groups and for the great majority of individual industries.

Table 7.1. *Decomposition of Country Capital-Labor Ratios into Industry-Level Employment and Capital-Labor Effects*

Country	1972–9			1979–85			1972–85		
	$\Delta\kappa^h$	$\Delta\kappa^h_i$	Δs^h_i	$\Delta\kappa^h$	$\Delta\kappa^h_i$	Δs^h_i	$\Delta\kappa^h$	$\Delta\kappa^h_i$	Δs^h_i
Belgium	22.5	25.3	-2.9	5.4	5.4	0.0	28.1	30.7	-2.6
Canada	26.8	-1.2	28.0	1.9	2.7	-0.8	28.6	1.5	27.1
Denmark	18.7	19.9	-1.2	-17.8	-17.8	0.0	0.8	2.1	-1.3
France	15.1	16.2	-1.2	5.3	5.1	0.3	20.5	21.3	-0.8
Germany	4.6	6.6	-2.1	-7.8	-6.0	-1.8	-3.3	0.6	-4.0
Italy	-2.2	-1.8	-0.4	-2.5	-2.1	-0.4	-4.4	-3.9	-0.4
Japan	22.8	24.5	-1.6	1.8	2.7	-0.9	23.9	27.2	-3.3
Netherlands	18.1	24.0	-5.9	-12.3	-9.5	-2.9	7.0	14.6	-7.6
Norway	19.7	19.3	0.4	8.2	8.8	-0.6	28.3	28.1	0.2
Sweden	19.4	19.1	0.3	-7.4	-6.8	-0.5	12.9	12.3	0.6
UK	3.7	5.4	-1.7	7.4	6.6	0.7	10.9	12.0	-1.1
Average	15.4	14.3	1.1	-1.6	-1.0	-0.6	13.9	13.3	0.6

Note: This decomposition is based on equation (7.8). The U.S. is excluded from this panel, because its capital-labor ratio is used as the base value
Source: Dollar and Wolff (1993).

This suggests that technology transfer was relatively easy among industrialized countries and, as a result, the state of technology was becoming very similar among these nations, but that national investment rates, as well as investment rates in particular industries, still displayed relatively great differences among countries.

7.3.3 Decomposition of Labor Productivity Growth

As was seen in Section 7.2, the convergence of aggregate labor productivity among industrial countries resulted from convergence of labor productivity within industries. Here we investigate the sources of this labor productivity convergence within individual industries. As shown previously, between the early 1960s and the mid-1980s, both TFP and capital-labor ratios converged toward the U.S. level, though most of this occurred by the early 1970s. The next issue addressed is the extent to which the convergence in labor productivity within industries was attributable to the convergence in TFP and to what extent it was a result of the catch-up in capital deepening.

A standard growth accounting framework is used. Formally, assume that for each industry i and country h there is a Cobb-Douglas value added production function:

$$\mathrm{Ln} Y^h_i = \xi^h_i + \alpha_i \mathrm{Ln} L^h_i + (1-\alpha_i)\,\mathrm{Ln} K^h_i \qquad (7.9)$$

The parameter ξ^h_i is country-specific and indicates country h's technology level in industry i. The output elasticity of labor in industry i, α_i, is assumed to be the same among countries. If factors are paid their marginal products, then the output elasticity is equal to labor's distributive share. DW took the cross-country (unweighted) average of labor's share in industry i as the estimate of α_i.[18]

The Divisia index is used to measure TFP growth, as follows:[19]

$$\rho = \mathrm{d\ln} Y^h_i\,/\,dt\, - \alpha_i \mathrm{d\ln} L^h_i\,/\,dt\, - (1-\alpha_i)\,\mathrm{d\ln} K^h_i\,/\,dt \qquad (7.10)$$

Consistent with this measure of TFP growth is a second method of calculating TFP level, often referred to as the Translog Index of TFP:

$$\mathrm{Ln\ TFP}^h_i = \mathrm{Ln\ } Y^h_i - \alpha_i \mathrm{Ln\ } L^h_i - (1-\alpha_i)\,\mathrm{Ln\ } K^h_i \qquad (7.11)$$

Comparison of equation (7.11) with equation (7.9) reveals that this measure of TFP is implicitly based on a Cobb-Douglas form for the production function.

It is now possible formally to decompose the convergence of labor productivity growth into a component attributable to technology convergence and a part attributable to convergence in capital-labor ratios. Let the United States be the benchmark country and define:

λ^h_i: ratio of country h's labor productivity to U.S. labor productivity in industry i;

τ^h_i: ratio of country h's technology level to U.S. technology level in industry i;

and, as before,

κ^h_i: ratio of country h's capital-labor ratio to U.S. capital-labor ratio in industry i.

Equations (7.9) and (7.11) then imply that

$$\mathrm{Ln} \lambda^h_i = \mathrm{Ln} \tau^h_i + (1-\alpha_i)\mathrm{Ln} \kappa^h_i \qquad (7.12)$$

Differentiating this with respect to time yields

$$\mathrm{dLn} \lambda^h_i\,/\,dt = \mathrm{Ln\ } \tau^h_i\,/\,dt + (1-\alpha_i)\mathrm{Ln\ }''^h_i\,/\,dt \qquad (7.13)$$

[18] See Chapter 2 for more discussion of the Cobb-Douglas model.
[19] See Chapter 3 for additional details on the Divisia index and the Translog index.

Hence, the convergence of country h's labor productivity in industry i on the U.S. level can be decomposed into the convergence of technology and the convergence of capital-labor ratios.

Results for equation (7.13) are shown in Table 7.2 for the Translog Index of TFP. During the period 1963–72, most of the catch-up in labor productivity was attributed to the catch-up in technological capabilities. Though there was some variability among countries, the unweighted cross-country average indicates that about two-thirds of labor productivity convergence was attributable to technology transfer and the remaining third to increasing capital intensity. Japan's results were interesting. They indicated that a little more than half of their labor productivity convergence resulted from increasing capital intensity. There are also differences among individual industries. However, for the aggregate heavy, medium, and light industries, the preponderance of the catch-up was achieved from convergence in technology.

In contrast, between 1970 and 1985, labor productivity catch-up toward the United States was achieved primarily through increasing capital intensity (three-fourths on the basis of the unweighted cross-country average). Though there are both country and industry differences, this result held for eight of the thirteen countries and seven of the nine industries. Japan was, again, an exception, since about two-thirds of its labor productivity convergence to the United States was achieved through technology catch-up. The heavy industries, particularly basic (ferrous and nonferrous) metals and chemicals, were another exception, for which about four-fifths of the labor productivity convergence was attributable to technology transfer.

This analysis still begs the question of whether there is any connection between technology catch-up and the rate of capital accumulation in a country. DW next turned to a regression framework to test two hypotheses concerning technology convergence. The first, which can be labeled the "catch-up hypothesis," states simply that industries and countries that lagged furthest behind the United States in technological sophistication in the 1960s had the most opportunities to imitate and purchase advanced technology and hence should exhibit the fastest rate of technology convergence. Taking each industry in each country as an observation, this hypothesis implies that the rate of growth of τ^h_i between the mid-1960s and the mid-1980s was inversely correlated with the level of τ^h_i at the beginning of the period. This approach provides a large number of observations to test this hypothesis.

Table 7.2. *The Decomposition of Labor Productivity Convergence into a Technology- and Capital-Intensity Component, 1970–1985 (Annual Rates of Growth in Percentages)*

	1963–72			1970–85		
	LPROD	TFP	K/L	LPROD	TFP	K/L
A. Total Manufacturing by Country						
Australia				−0.03	−0.23	0.20
Belgium				2.41	1.62	0.78
Canada	0.61	0.50	0.11	−0.53	−0.55	0.02
Denmark				0.09	−0.01	0.10
Finland				0.42	0.36	0.06
France	0.51	−0.30	0.81	0.55	0.12	0.42
Germany	2.23	1.38	0.85	0.00	−0.15	0.15
Italy	0.29	1.87	−1.58	0.17	0.24	−0.06
Japan	6.82	3.20	3.62	2.74	1.77	0.97
Netherlands				1.70	0.99	0.71
Norway				−0.85	−1.32	0.46
Sweden				−0.53	−0.78	0.25
United Kingdom	2.11	1.49	0.61	−0.05	−0.61	0.55
B. Unweighted Industry Average across Countries						
All Manuf.	2.09	1.36	0.74	0.47	0.11	0.35
Heavy Industry	2.90	2.43	0.47	1.93	1.62	0.31
Basic Metals	3.42	3.87	−0.46	2.78	2.95	−0.17
Chemicals	4.32	2.72	1.60	2.22	1.86	0.36
Minerals	4.71	1.77	2.94	0.53	−0.17	0.71
Medium Industry	0.64	0.82	−0.18	0.07	−0.27	0.34
Machinery	0.86	−0.53	1.39	0.08	−0.15	0.23
Rubber, Plastics	0.70	1.09	−0.39			
Paper, Printing	1.62	0.81	0.82	0.88	0.32	0.56
Transport Equipment	1.87	2.37	−0.49			
Food, Beverages	1.70	0.27	1.43	−0.49	−0.80	0.31
Light Industry	1.71	1.43	0.28	−0.40	−0.79	0.39
Metal Products	3.48	2.38	1.10			
Textiles	1.34	0.28	1.06	−0.01	−0.57	0.56
Electrical Goods	2.06	3.65	−1.59			
Wood Products				−0.29	−0.69	0.40
Other Industry	0.28	−1.26	1.53	−2.00	−2.52	0.52

Notes: The decomposition is based on equation (7.13). The Translog index of TFP growth is used. Calculations for 1963–82 are based on the Dollar-Wolff database and those for 1970–85 are based on the ISDB. International average wage shares are used.
Source: Dollar and Wolff (1993).

A second hypothesis is the "vintage hypothesis," which states that a dollar's worth of new capital is more productive than a (constant) dollar's worth of old capital. (This might also be called the "embodiment effect," since it implies that at least some technological innovation is embodied in capital.) If the capital stock data do not correct for vintage effects, then this hypothesis suggests that the rate of growth of τ^h_i will be positively correlated with the rate of growth of κ^h_i. Again, each industry in each country can be treated as an observation to test this hypothesis.

Both hypotheses can be tested using the following regression specification:

$$RELLPGR^h_{it} = b_0 + b_1 RELTFP^h_{it} + b_2 RELKLGR^h_{it} + \sum c_h CNTYDUM^h_i + \sum d_i INDDUM^h_i + \varepsilon^h_{it}$$

where $RELLPGR^h_{it}$ is the labor productivity growth of industry i in country h at time t relative to the United States; $RELTFP^h_{it}$ is country h's (Translog) TFP relative to the United States at the start of each period t in industry i; $RELKLGR^h_{it}$ is the rate of growth of the capital-labor ratio of industry i in country h at time t relative to the United States; $CNTYDUMM_h$ is a dummy variable for each country h (except the United States); $INDDUM_i$ is an industry dummy variable (excluding other industry); and ε is a stochastic error term. Country and industry dummy variables were included to control for country-specific effects, such as the degree of trade openness, culture, and government policy, and industry-specific effects, such as market structure and diffusion patterns for new technology. Both two-year and three-year averages were used for the growth variables to reduce random noise. The regression was performed on both the Dollar-Wolff database and the ISDB. For the former, DW introduced an additional dummy variable, D6372, defined as unity on or before 1972 and zero thereafter, which interacts with $RELKLGR^h_{it}$ to control for period effects. The United States was excluded from this regression equation, since the value of the dependent variable was always unity.

The results, shown in Table 7.3, confirmed the catch-up hypothesis, showing a highly significant inverse relation between the rate of TFP convergence by industry and country and its initial TFP level, relative to the United States. The results on the vintage hypothesis were interesting. The term RELKLGR had a negative and significant coefficient for the regressions performed on the ISDB data over the period 1970–85; the term also had a negative coefficient in the Dollar-Wolff database, but the interactive term, RELKLGR*D6372 was positive and highly significant. These results

Table 7.3. *Regression of Relative Productivity Growth on Relative Productivity Level and Growth in Relative Capital Intensity*

Dependent Variable	Independent Variables				R^2	Adjusted R^2	Std. Error of Reg.	Sample Size
	Constant	RELTFP	RELKLGR	RELKLGR* D6372				
A. ISDB, 1970–85								
1. Two-Year Averages								
RELLPGR	0.0097	−0.057**	−0.227**		0.18	0.15	0.055	643
	(0.4)	(4.6)	(5.7)					
2. Three-Year Averages								
RELLPGR	0.0006	−0.042**	−0.194**		0.25	0.21	0.039	457
	(1.0)	(4.0)	(4.9)					
B. Dollar-Wolff Database, 1963–83								
1. Two-Year Averages								
RELLPGR	0.054**	−0.048**	−0.673**	0.490**	0.21	0.18	0.065	694
	(4.2)	(5.8)	(9.9)	(6.3)				
2. Three-Year Averages								
RELLPGR	0.066**	−0.061**	−0.646**	0.455**	0.30	0.26	0.047	460
	(5.6)	(7.8)	(8.4)	(6.1)				

Notes: t-ratios are shown in parentheses below the coefficient estimate. Country and industry dummy variables are included in the specification but results are not shown. The observations are based on two- or three-year averages, as indicated

Key:

RELLPGR: annual rate of growth of country i's labor productivity relative to the U.S. labor productivity growth in industry i

RELTFP: ratio of country i's technology level to U.S. technology level in industry i at the beginning of the period

RELKLGR: annual rate of change of ratio of country i's capital-labor ratio to U.S.' capital-labor ratio in industry i

D6273: dummy variable, defined as unity on or before 1972 and zero thereafter

* Significant at the 5 percent level

** significant at the 1 percent level

Source: Dollar and Wolff (1993).

suggested that the embodiment effect was likely important during the 1963–72 period, when productivity convergence was very strong among OECD countries, but inoperative between the mid-1970s and the mid-1980s. Indeed, the negative sign of the coefficient suggested that adjustment costs associated with the introduction of new capital equipment may actually have inhibited productivity growth once an industry reached the technological frontier.[20]

7.4 Other Literature on Sectoral Productivity Growth

Bernard and Jones (1996a, 1996b) and Bernard and Jones (2001) in a reply to Sørenson (2001) followed up the work of Dollar and Wolff (1993) by investigating TFP convergence by major sector of the economy. Whereas Dollar and Wolff focused on manufacturing industries, Bernard and Jones looked at six major divisions of the economy: (i) agriculture, (ii) mining, (iii) manufacturing, (iv) utilities, (v) construction, and (vi) services. They used data on industry-level value added, capital stocks, and employment to construct TFP estimates for fourteen OECD countries over the period 1970 to 1987. The data source was the OECD Intersectoral Database or ISDB (see Meyer-zu-Schlochtern, 1988, for a description of the data set).

Bernard and Jones (1996a) reported that there was substantial heterogeneity in productivity movements across sectors. They also found differential results regarding convergence in TFP levels within sectors. Whereas aggregate TFP was converging among the fourteen countries over the 1970 to 1987 period, this convergence was driven primarily by the nonmanufacturing sectors of the economy, particularly services and utilities. Within manufacturing, they found no evidence for convergence over this period as a whole and, in actuality, divergence during the 1980s.

Bernard and Jones (1996b) reported that among the fourteen OECD countries, the gap in overall TFP for total industry between the most productive country (the United States) and the least productive country declined consistently from 120 percent in 1970 to 85 percent in 1987. The standard deviation of the logarithm of TFP for total industry, a measure of overall dispersion, fell from 0.175 in 1970 to 0.135 in 1987. A regression of the change in log TFP for total industry on a constant term and initial TFP

---

[20] It is, perhaps, not coincidental that the post-1970 period is also associated with the rapid introduction of computerization among manufacturing industries. Many commentators have suggested that there were sizable adjustment costs associated with this new technology. See, for example, David (1991).

(in 1970) yielded a highly significant (t-ratio of 4.03) coefficient of -0.0226, and the R^2 was 0.54.

However, regression results differed by sector. For agriculture, services, and utilities, there was strong evidence of TFP convergence across countries. For agriculture, the coefficient on initial TFP was -0.039, the t-ratio was 3.45, and the R^2 was 0.46. For services, the coefficient on initial TFP was -0.012, the t-ratio was 3.69, and the R^2 was 0.56; and for utilities, the coefficient on initial TFP was -0.025, the t-ratio was 3.49, and the R^2 was 0.46. In contrast, for manufacturing, the coefficient on initial TFP was -0.015, the t-ratio was 1.11, and the R^2 was 0.02; and for mining, the coefficient on initial TFP was -0.027, the t-ratio was 1.35, and the R^2 was 0.07. The construction industry was marginal. The coefficient on initial TFP was -0.028, the t-ratio was 1.90, and the R^2 was 0.17.

Moreover, the standard deviation of the logarithm of TFP showed a fairly steady decline for agriculture, services, and utilities over the period from 1970 to 1987. In contrast, for manufacturing, the same statistic fell from 0.22 to 0.18 during the 1970s. However, after 1982, it rose sharply and reached 0.23 in 1987. Thus, over the entire period, the evidence indicated divergence in TFP levels within manufacturing.[21] The mining sector also showed an increase in the standard deviation of the logarithm of TFP between 1970 and 1987, while the construction sector showed no clear trend.

Gouyette and Perelman (1997) also used the OECD ISDB to look at convergence. Using data on output, labor, and capital, they compared the performance of manufacturing and services over the 1970–87 period for thirteen OECD countries. Their main results showed, like those of Bernard and Jones, very limited convergence of TFP levels over this period, but, in spite of low overall growth rates, productivity levels did converge in services. Using a Divisia index to measure TFP, they reported for the services sector that the ratio of minimum to maximum TFP levels increased from 52.5 percent in 1970 to 63.9 percent in 1987; the average TFP level also increased from 70.0 to 81.4 percent of the U.S. level; and the coefficient of variation of TFP levels fell from 0.20 to 0.14. Moreover, the correlation between the initial TFP level (in 1970) and the rate of annual TFP growth over the 1970–87 period was -0.67. In contrast, for manufacturing, the ratio of minimum to maximum TFP levels declined from 54.8 percent in 1970 to 49.2 percent in 1987; the average TFP level relative to the United States fell from 72.0 to 67.4 percent;

[21] Sørenson (2001) took issue with the conclusion of TFP divergence for manufacturing. He showed that the result was sensitive to the choice of base year for the PPPs used to convert each country's manufacturing output to a common currency.

and the coefficient of variation of TFP levels actually increased from 0.21 to 0.25. Moreover, the correlation between the initial TFP level and the rate of TFP growth over the period was only –0.23.

Boussemart *et. al.* (2006) updated some of the earlier results of Bernard and Jones and Gouyette and Perelman to the period from 1970 to 1996 on the basis of the ISDB. They used data for nine sectors: agriculture, mining, utilities, construction, trade, transportation and communications, finance and insurance, nongovernmental services, and governmental services. They also used data for five manufacturing industries. They estimated a standard catch-up model, using a Generalized Method of Moments (GMM) regression estimating method. Of the fourteen sectors and industries, they found negative and significant catching-up coefficients (on the initial level of TFP) in all industries except textiles and government services. Estimated annual speeds of catching up ranged from 1.4 to 9.5 percent. These new results differed from those of Bernard and Jones in that they confirmed catching up in manufacturing (with the sole exception of textiles). These authors attributed the difference in results to the fact that they computed TFP indices using a nonparametric technique and to the fact that the United States was not considered the technology leader in each sector (see Chapter 3 for a discussion of alternative methods to compute TFP at the industry level).

A related issue is what portion of overall (aggregate) productivity growth can be ascribed to shifts of employment among the various sectors of the economy. Sectors of the economy differ in terms of both productivity levels and rates of productivity growth. If employment shifts out of low productivity sectors to high productivity sectors, this will, ceteris paribus, increase the level of aggregate productivity. Likewise, if employment shifts out of low productivity *growth* sectors to high productivity growth ones, this will, ceteris paribus, increase the overall rate of aggregate productivity growth. Bernard and Jones (1996a) decomposed aggregate TFP growth for the total industry sector into two components. The first was a weighted sum of the TFP growth rates of the individual sectors in the economy. The second was the share effect, which shows the contribution of changing sectoral composition on aggregate TFP growth, where the share changes are weighted by average relative TFP for the sector over the period. Their main result was that within sector growth accounted for fully 96 percent of the overall TFP growth among these countries over the period from 1970 to 1987. Correspondingly, shifts in the share of output among the six sectors contributed only 4 percent of total TFP growth.

7.5 Concluding Comments

As I noted in the introduction to Chapter 7, some industries produce more value added per worker than others because of the use of large amounts of capital or skilled labor or of advanced technology. It is possible for countries to have the same labor productivity at the industry level but nevertheless to have different levels of aggregate productivity because one economy's employment mix is shifted toward the high value added sectors. One of the leading models of international trade, the Heckscher-Ohlin model, predicts that this will be the case among countries at fairly similar levels of development, such as those in the OECD. Thus aggregate convergence can result from labor productivity converging at the industry level and/or from employment mixes becoming more similar.

If the theory behind productivity convergence is correct, then we should observe stronger convergence in productivity levels at the industry level than for the total economy, since the catch-up effect should operate most strongly at the industry level. Yet, the work of Dollar and Wolff (1988) and, later, Dollar and Wolff (1993) found just the opposite. They analyzed changes in productivity levels on the industry level for a sample of nine OECD countries covering the period from 1960 to 1986. While they found strong evidence of convergence on the economywide level in GDP per worker, the capital-labor ratio, aggregate labor productivity, and total factor productivity (TFP), convergence at the industry level was generally not as strong as that for the economy as a whole. In fact, aggregate productivity convergence was to a large extent attributable to the modest productivity leads that different countries enjoyed in different industries. They argued that industry specialization was an important component in aggregate productivity convergence. Moreover, they did not find that structural change was an important factor in overall labor productivity and TFP convergence.

In particular, Dollar and Wolff (1993) found between 1963 and 1986 the coefficient of variation declined for virtually every industry, indicating that among these countries labor productivity was converging at the industry level. The average of productivity in the twelve countries, relative to the United States, also rose in all but three industries. Nevertheless, it remained true in 1986 that there was more variation across countries in labor productivity at the industry level than at the level of all manufacturing. This was particularly the case with heavy and medium industries. Moreover, an important change from 1963 was that by 1986 there were quite a few industries in which the United States was no longer the productivity leader.

In fact, the United States was the productivity leader in only about half of the industries (fifteen of twenty-eight). Five different countries held the lead in at least one industry.

Bernard and Jones (1996a, 1996b) and Bernard and Jones (2001) in a reply to Sørenson (2001) followed up the work of Dollar and Wolff (1993) by investigating TFP convergence by major sector of the economy. Bernard and Jones (1996a) reported that there was substantial heterogeneity in productivity movements across sectors. They also found differential results regarding convergence in TFP levels within sectors. Whereas aggregate TFP was converging among the fourteen countries over the 1970 to 1987 period, this convergence was driven primarily by the nonmanufacturing sectors of the economy, particularly services and utilities. Within manufacturing, they found no evidence for convergence over this time as a whole and, in actuality, divergence during the 1980s. Gouyette and Perelman (1997) also reported very limited convergence of TFP levels over this period, but, in spite of low overall growth rates, productivity levels did converge in services.

In sum, the work reported here, at least, largely discredits the HO model as an explanatory mechanism in accounting for aggregate and industry level productivity convergence.

Appendix Table 7.1. *Value Added per Work Hour in Manufacturing in 12 Industrial Countries Relative to the U.S., 1963 to 1986 (Index Numbers, U.S. = 100)*

Country	1963	1970	1982	1986
United States	100	100	100	100
Canada	77	80	76	93
Germany	54	68	68	66
Japan	26	49	61	65
United Kingdom	52	60	88	54
Sweden	52	68	78	62
Denmark	41	54	59	58
Australia	47	53	56	56
France	53	64	67	56
Italy	45	50	88	55
Finland	34	48	51	51
Austria	37	47	49	51
Norway	46	58	49	51
Coefficient of Variation	0.36	0.24	0.23	0.24
Unweighted				
Average (excluding U.S.)	47	58	66	60

Note: Calculated from aggregate data for all manufacturing
Source: Dollar and Wolff (1993).

Appendix Table 7.2. *Measures of Productivity Convergence in 28 Manufacturing Industries of 13 Industrial Countries, 1963 to 1986*

Industry	Coefficient of Variation			Average Productivity in 12 Countries Relative to U.S.			Average Productivity in 12 Countries Relative to Leader
	1963	1982	1986	1963	1982	1986	1986
A. Heavy Industries	0.50	0.34	0.34	0.42	0.62	0.53	0.60
Industrial Chemicals	0.57	0.33	0.41	0.36	0.58	0.52	0.51 (Canada)
Other Chemicals	0.49	0.43	0.44	0.37	0.45	0.44	0.44 (US)
Iron and Steel	0.38	0.26	0.30	0.48	0.77	0.66	0.61 (Canada)
Nonferrous Metals	0.56	0.32	0.30	0.46	0.69	0.82	0.58 (Canada)
B. Medium Industries	0.40	0.26	0.25	0.48	0.67	0.60	0.60 (Canada)
Paper Products	0.40	0.24	0.26	0.48	0.59	0.60	0.60 (US)
Printing	0.38	0.31	0.21	0.49	0.72	0.66	0.66 (US)
Rubber Products	0.42	0.26	0.24	0.45	0.60	0.59	0.59 (US)
Plastic Products	0.35	0.23	0.18	0.51	0.72	0.70	0.70 (US)
Pottery	0.46	0.28	0.32	0.54	0.75	0.66	0.55 (Canada)
Glass Products	0.38	0.26	0.28	0.43	0.69	0.65	0.65 (US)
Nonmetal Products, n.e.c	0.36	0.23	0.21	0.53	0.80	0.74	0.63 (Canada)
Metal Products, n.e.c.	0.39	0.25	0.22	0.46	0.69	0.66	0.63 (Canada)
Machinery	0.36	0.25	0.24	0.47	0.64	0.59	0.59 (US)
Transport Equipment	0.46	0.30	0.39	0.42	0.54	0.50	0.50 (US)
C. Light Industries	0.33	0.25	0.20	0.59	0.79	0.66	0.66 (US)
Textiles	0.30	0.23	0.23	0.59	0.81	0.76	0.62 (Canada)
Clothing	0.32	0.24	0.22	0.60	0.76	0.70	0.70 (US)
Leather Products	0.26	0.30	0.22	0.63	0.79	0.79	0.62 (France)

Footwear	0.33	0.22	0.17	0.63	0.79	0.76	0.75 (Canada)
Wood Products	0.34	0.25	0.22	0.72	0.90	0.76	0.58 (Canada)
Furniture	0.37	0.27	0.14	0.50	0.82	0.78	0.78 (US)
Electrical Goods	0.37	0.27	0.61	0.50	0.82	0.61	0.61 (US)
D. Other Industries							
Food Products	0.38	0.35	0.35	0.54	0.57	0.47	0.47 (US)
Beverages	0.41	0.27	0.27	0.56	0.73	0.61	0.61 (US)
Tobacco Products	1.06	1.00	1.03	0.94	0.84	0.63	0.19 (Austria)
Petroleum Refining	0.65	0.63	0.76	0.82	0.79	1.04	0.33 (France)
Coal Products	0.86	0.35	0.97	1.01	0.77	1.00	0.17 (Germany)
Professional Goods	0.42	0.33	0.30	0.43	0.51	0.48	0.48 (US)
Manufactures, n.e.c.	0.40	0.26	0.20	0.46	0.69	0.66	0.66 (US)
E. All Manufacturing	0.36	0.23	0.24	0.47	0.66	0.60	0.60 (US)

Source: Dollar and Wolff (1993).

Appendix Table 7.3. *Value Added per Work Hour in Manufacturing in 12 Industrial Countries Relative to the U.S., 1963 to 1986 (Calculated with U.S. Employment Shares of That Year) (Index Numbers, U.S. = 100)*

Country	1963	1970	1982	1986
United States	100	100	100	100
Canada	78	80	75	91
Germany	58	64	64	65
Japan	27	52	64	68
United Kingdom	57	60	88	53
Sweden	52	69	75	62
Denmark	42	52	56	56
Australia	46	53	55	56
France	53	64	66	56
Italy	48	49	84	58
Finland	35	48	50	49
Austria	59	47	50	51
Norway	47	60	51	50
Coefficient of Variation Unweighted	0.33	0.24	0.23	0.24
Average (excluding U.S.)	50	58	65	60

Source: Dollar and Wolff (1993).

Appendix Table 7.4. *Value Added per Work Hour in Manufacturing in 13 Industrial Countries (Index Numbers, 1982 = 100)*

Country	1963	1970	1982	1986
United States				
Actual	71	79	100	110
1982 Weights	72	79	100	110
Canada				
Actual	72	83	100	135
1982 Weights	74	84	100	134
Germany				
Actual	59	78	100	107
1982 Weights	63	82	100	107
Japan				
Actual	30	64	100	117
1982 Weights	30	63	100	119
United Kingdom				
Actual	46	54	100	68
1982 Weights	46	55	100	68
Sweden				
Actual	49	70	100	87
1982 Weights	50	73	100	88
Denmark				
Actual	50	72	100	108
1982 Weights	52	73	100	109
Australia				
Actual	60	74	100	110
1982 Weights	59	77	100	109
France				
Actual	56	77	100	92
1982 Weights	55	76	100	93
Italy				
Actual	39	45	100	69
1982 Weights	40	45	100	70
Finland				
Actual	48	76	100	110
1982 Weights	50	77	100	110
Austria				
Actual	53	75	100	114
1982 Weights	85	75	100	114
Norway				
Actual	65	94	100	114
1982 Weights	68	98	100	114

Source: Dollar and Wolff (1993).

Productivity Performance on the Industry Level

Appendix Table 7.5. *TFP Levels in Total Manufacturing Relative to the U.S.,*
1963–1985 (Index Number, with U.S. = 100)

Country	Dollar-Wolff Data					ISDB		
	1963	1967	1970	1979	1982	1970	1979	1985
Australia						81	79	76
Belgium	46	47	61	63	66	63	78	81
Canada	68	65	69	72	NA	81	77	71
Denmark						56	62	59
Finland						61	59	61
France	69	71	84	72	80	79	84	75
Germany	NA	74	90	78	87	84	87	81
Italy	NA	47	52	60	63	83	85	82
Japan	NA	74	92	77	88	75	79	86
Netherlands	67	69	85	78	69	66	69	68
Norway						77	67	63
Sweden						74	66	65
United Kingdom	56	NA	65	70	73	66	63	65
United States	100	100	100	100	100	100	100	100
A. Summary Statistics Based on Available Data Only								
Coeff. of Variation	0.24	0.23	0.20	0.14	0.15	0.15	0.15	0.15
Maximum/Minimum	2.16	2.14	1.92	1.66	1.58	1.78	1.68	1.70
Unweighted Average (excluding U.S.)	0.61	0.64	0.75	0.71	0.75	0.73	0.74	0.72
Coeff of Var (TFPU)	0.24	0.21	0.19	0.13	0.15			

B. Summary Statistics Based on 7-Country Sample: Belgium, Canada,
  France, Germany,
Japan, Netherlands, and U.S.

Coeff of Variation	NA	0.20	0.15	0.14	NA	--	--	--
Unweighted Average (excluding U.S.)	NA	0.67	0.80	0.73	NA	--	--	--
Coeff of Var (TFPU)	NA	0.19	0.16	0.12	NA			

C. Summary Statistics Based on Seven-Country Sample: Belgium, France, Germany,
  Italy, Japan, Netherlands, and U.S.

Coeff of Variation	NA	0.25	0.20	0.16	0.16	--	--	--
Unweighted Average (excluding U.S.)	NA	0.63	0.77	0.71	0.76	--	--	--
Coeff of Var (TFPU)	NA	0.22	0.20	0.15	NA			

Note: Results are based on country-specific factor shares
Source: Dollar and Wolff (1993).

Appendix Table 7.6. *Indices of TFP Convergence by Manufacturing Industry,*
1967–1985

I. Dollar-Wolff Data Set	Coefficient of Variation			Average TFP Relative to U.S.[a]					
	1967	1972	1979	1967		1972		1979	
Heavy Industries[b]	0.45	0.38	0.24	0.70	(GER)	0.90	(GER)	0.84	(GER)
Ferrous & Nonferrous Metals	0.29	0.25	0.20	0.63	(USA)	0.73	(GER)	0.70	(USA)
Chemicals	0.47	0.28	0.23	0.45	(USA)	0.60	(USA)	0.63	(USA)
Nonmetallic Minerals	0.58	0.61	0.30	1.03	(FRA)	1.37	(NET)	1.20	(NET)
Medium Industries[b]	0.32	0.30	0.24	0.66	(USA)	0.67	(USA)	0.70	(USA)
Machinery	0.22	0.21	0.21	0.74	(USA)	0.77	(USA)	0.75	(CAN)
Rubber and Plastics	0.51	0.43	0.35	0.55	(USA)	0.52	(USA)	0.64	(USA)
Paper and Printing	0.28	0.31	0.18	0.65	(USA)	0.71	(JPN)	0.73	(USA)
Transport Equipment	0.26	0.26	0.22	0.71	(USA)	0.69	(USA)	0.67	(USA)
Light Industries[b]	0.33	0.28	0.23	0.60	(USA)	0.68	(USA)	0.69	(USA)
Metal Products	0.45	0.29	0.28	0.49	(USA)	0.70	(USA)	0.66	(USA)
Other Industries	0.32	0.38	0.28	0.73	(NET)	0.60	(USA)	0.64	(USA)
Textiles	0.28	0.25	0.23	0.56	(USA)	0.62	(USA)	0.68	(USA)
Electrical Goods	0.26	0.20	0.14	0.60	(USA)	0.78	(FRA)	0.77	(USA)
Food,Beverages, Tobacco	0.20	0.18	0.17	0.74	(USA)	0.74	(USA)	0.70	(USA)
All Manufacturing[b]	0.34	0.30	0.27	0.66	(USA)	0.74	(USA)	0.73	(USA)

II. ISDB	1970	1979	1985	1970		1979		1985	
Heavy Industries[b]	0.30	0.27	0.24	0.71	(USA)	0.77	(JPN)	0.87	(JPN)
Basic Metals	0.42	0.37	0.27	0.73	(NET)	0.83	(JPN)	1.05	(JPN)
Chemicals	0.31	0.26	0.20	0.69	(GER)	0.76	(GER)	0.93	(GER)
Nonmetallic Minerals	0.18	0.18	0.24	0.70	(USA)	0.71	(USA)	0.64	(USA)
Medium Industries[b]	0.22	0.22	0.23	0.73	(USA)	0.73	(USA)	0.71	(USA)
Machinery & Equipment	0.24	0.21	0.20	0.65	(USA)	0.67	(USA)	0.63	(USA)
Paper,Printing,Publ.	0.17	0.21	0.24	0.71	(USA)	0.72	(USA)	0.74	(ITA)
Food, Beverages,Tob.	0.25	0.24	0.25	0.83	(UK)	0.81	(JPN)	0.75	(ITA)
Light Industries[b]	0.20	0.23	0.22	0.88	(CAN)	0.78	(ITA)	0.72	(USA)
Textiles	0.20	0.21	0.20	0.88	(ITA)	0.77	(ITA)	0.71	(USA)
Wood & Wood Products	0.20	0.25	0.24	0.87	(CAN)	0.78	(ITA)	0.73	(ITA)
Other Industries	0.38	0.28	0.47	0.65	(CAN)	0.63	(USA)	0.42	(USA)
All Manufacturing[b]	0.26	0.24	0.26	0.75	(USA)	0.74	(USA)	0.73	(USA)

Notes: Calculations are based on country-specific wage shares

[a] The country leader in each year is shown in parentheses

[b] Unweighted average of industries within group

Source: Dollar and Wolff (1993).

Appendix Table 7.7. *Measures of Convergence in Capital-Labor Ratios by Industry, 1965–1985*

	Average Capital-Labor Ratio Relative to U.S.				Coefficient of Variation of Capital-Labor Ratios			
I. Dollar-Wolff Data Set	1965	1972	1979	1983	1965	1972	1979	1983
Heavy Industries[a]	0.59	0.66	0.76	0.68	0.47	0.37	0.36	0.36
Ferrous & Nonferrous Metals	0.83	0.72	0.92	0.72	0.43	0.45	0.43	0.37
Chemicals	0.62	0.83	0.83	0.85	0.40	0.25	0.34	0.35
Nonmetallic Minerals	0.34	0.43	0.52	0.47	0.57	0.41	0.30	0.35
Medium Industries[a]	0.74	0.83	0.95	0.99	0.39	0.28	0.22	0.25
Machinery	0.47	0.67	0.83	0.70	0.40	0.19	0.13	0.20
Rubber and Plastics	0.90	0.97	1.05	1.25	0.17	0.13	0.15	0.21
Paper and Printing	0.83	0.94	1.05	1.12	0.71	0.59	0.40	0.39
Transport Equipment	0.78	0.75	0.87	0.88	0.29	0.21	0.18	0.18
Light Industries[a]	0.85	1.07	1.21	1.26	0.35	0.44	0.31	0.33
Metal Products	0.69	0.94	0.98	0.93	0.49	0.51	0.43	0.37
Other Industries	1.08	1.44	1.40	1.60	0.29	0.50	0.29	0.29
Textiles	1.15	1.42	1.62	1.80	0.23	0.27	0.38	0.47
Electrical Goods	0.82	0.76	0.89	0.84	0.31	0.36	0.27	0.26
Food,Beverages, Tobacco	0.82	0.95	1.05	1.03	0.35	0.30	0.26	0.24
All Manufacturing[c]	0.75	0.88	1.00	1.00	0.39	0.36	0.29	0.30
II. ISDB		1970	1979	1985		1970	1979	1985
Heavy Industries[a]		0.88	1.04	1.02		0.50	0.45	0.46
Basic Metals		0.60	0.68	0.56		0.49	0.42	0.42
Chemicals		0.86	1.02	0.97		0.21	0.27	0.28
Nonmetallic Minerals		1.19	1.42	1.54		0.82	0.67	0.69
Medium Industries[a]		1.10	1.26	1.26		0.36	0.31	0.29
Machinery & Equipment		1.05	1.25	1.13		0.33	0.26	0.21
Paper,Printing,Publ.		1.19	1.37	1.56		0.53	0.45	0.46
Food, Beverages,Tob.		1.06	1.17	1.10		0.24	0.22	0.22
Light Industries[a]		1.44	1.64	1.79		0.29	0.32	0.31
Textiles		1.37	1.73	1.72		0.25	0.35	0.26
Wood & Wood Products		1.52	1.55	1.86		0.35	0.30	0.38
Other Industries		1.12	1.23	1.24		0.56	0.50	0.59
All Manufacturing[c]		1.11	1.27	1.30		0.41	0.38	0.39

Note: Unweighted average of industries within group
Source: Dollar and Wolff (1993).

8

The Productivity Slowdown

8.1 The Earlier Literature on the Productivity Slowdown

The slowdown in the rate of productivity growth that occurred from about 1965 to 1979 in the United States spawned a considerable literature and was also a major focus of policy debate. Because of its enormous implications for the improvement of per capita well-being, a whole host of possible causes were diagnosed and a corresponding menu of remedies proposed. It should be noted at the outset there were wide differences of opinion both on the identity of the relevant factors and on their likely quantitative importance.

A few words should be said at this point about some of the causes of the productivity slowdown of the 1965–79 period. The main candidates, in the case of the United States, have included the following five factors: (1) slowdown in the rate of capital formation, (2) changes in the composition of the labor force, (3) energy price shocks, (4) declines in R&D spending (and/or the productivity of R&D), and (5) changes in the composition of output (mainly, the shift to services).

The next part of this chapter (Section 8.2) considers some measurement issues involved in the definition of productivity since this is germane to understanding some of the differences between the various studies. Section 8.3 presents estimates of the magnitude of the productivity slowdown both for the economy as a whole and for individual industrial sectors. Section 8.4 surveys much of the earlier literature on the subject. Section 8.5 considers more recent literature. Section 8.6 evaluates the relative merits of the arguments on the causes of the productivity slowdown put forth in the early literature on the subject and presents an evaluation of the later literature in light of the earlier research.

8.2 Measurement Issues in Defining Productivity

Generally speaking, productivity is defined as the ratio of some measure of output to some measure of input. Disagreements arise as to what to include in the numerator of the ratio and what to include in the denominator. This is true for the measures of both overall and sectoral productivity.

For aggregate productivity, the numerator is some measure of the total output of the economy such as gross domestic product, GDP (or GNP in the earlier literature), or net national product, NNP. However, there was extensive discussion about the desirability of excluding certain components of traditional net output indices such as police services and including certain nonmarket activities such as homemaker services in the NNP (see, for example, Rees, 1979). There was also disagreement about how to define the output of the government sector, which is valued on the basis of its inputs in the national accounts.[1] Of particular relevance to the debate over the productivity slowdown in the earlier literature was the desirability of including such items as worker safety, environmental improvements, and other indicators of externalities as part of the output measure.

Another issue is whether to use GDP, as Kendrick (1980a) and Thurow (1979) did, or NNP, as Denison (1979a) did. The difference between the two is the depreciation of fixed capital. Many observers, particularly growth theorists, believe it is more proper to exclude depreciation because this is an intermediate cost that, like the consumption of raw materials and semifinished goods, is excluded from the measure of final output. However, others, particularly those looking at the issue from the standpoint of production theory, prefer the GNP measure because for them depreciation is part of the measure of the services of the primary factor, capital.

Two measures are commonly used for the denominator. The first is total labor input, and the resulting ratio is referred to as labor productivity. The second is a weighted sum of factor inputs including labor and capital stock and sometimes land and other natural resources, and the ratio is referred to as total factor productivity, TFP, or multifactor productivity, MFP. Labor productivity is usually considered the better measure of welfare because it bears a rough correspondence to per capita income. TFP is considered the better measure of an economy's efficiency and its rate of technical change because it measures the ratio of output to the sum of basic inputs. Moreover, whereas the labor productivity measure can, in essence, be used

---

[1] In education, for example, the labor input of teachers and other personnel, rather than the number of graduates or the improvement in test scores, are used to measure its output.

with any model or theoretical framework, the use of TFP entails some fairly restrictive assumptions. The reason is that the denominator is construed as a weighted average of the various inputs, where the weights are generally value shares (that is, the shares received by the factors in total income). For this to be analytically legitimate, the production function that characterizes each sector of the economy must fall within a certain class (in particular, those with constant elasticities of substitution), and labor and capital must receive in payment the value of their marginal product. In addition, it must be assumed that the economy is operating efficiently – that is, on the production-possibility frontier (see Hulten, 1978).[2]

There are also issues about the appropriate way to define the inputs used in the two kinds of measures. In the case of labor, the simplest measure is the total number of hours worked per year or the number of full-time equivalent workers. These are referred to as unweighted measures of labor input. In contrast, some researchers used weighted measures of labor input. The case for a weighted figure is that more skilled labor represents a larger number of input units per time worked and thus makes for a better measure of factor input in a production function. There was, however, disagreement about whether to use schooling, training, or some combined measure of human capital or relative wages as the appropriate weight.[3]

Three principal issues arise in the measurement of the other principal input, the capital stock. First, what is the appropriate measure of net capital stock? Gross investment in a given year can be measured adequately in standard national accounts. However, in any given year, part of the existing capital stock wears out physically, and part of it becomes obsolete technologically or economically. The net increase in capital stock is equal to gross investment less this depreciation. The difficulties concern the measure of *true* economic depreciation, which is necessary to estimate the net capital stock. Second, how should the capital stock of the business sector and its components be measured? The gross investment figure in the national accounts lumps together business investment in various sectors. Alignment of investment in plant and equipment with the sector making the investment is often a major measurement task. Third, what is the utilization rate of the capital stock? This issue is particularly important in the use of TFP

---

[2] Also, see Chapter 3 for a more extended discussion of issues in productivity measurement.

[3] The justification for the use of relative wages is that in a competitive labor market, wage differences reflect differences in marginal productivity. However, there is considerable reason to believe that discrimination, unions, and other factors make the assumption of perfectively competitive labor markets questionable.

because TFP is designed to measure the ratio of output to a weighted sum of actual labor services and capital services. The latter, in turn, depend on the amount of existing capital actually utilized in production. Failure to measure the utilization rate properly will bias the TFP measure (also see the presentation of the work of Berndt and Fuss, 1986, in Section 3.5 of Chapter 3).

Additional complications beset productivity measurement by sector. Almost all researchers used value added originating by sector divided by employment as the measure of sectoral productivity. Two problems affect the use of the sectoral value added measure: First, it is sometimes difficult to interpret what is meant by "value added in constant prices," a concept that is essential to the analysis of productivity change over time. The physical gross output of a sector, such as wheat, has a price whose movement over time can, in principle, be ascertained. But the components of value added, such as wages, profits, rent, net interest, and depreciation – all change at different rates over time. Therefore, researchers normally use a technique called double deflation, in which the prices of gross output and the material inputs are deflated by their respective price changes. The difference between the two is used as the measure of value added in constant prices. Second, the actual output produced by a sector and its value added may move in different directions over time. The agricultural sector provides the clearest example. A bumper crop causes the price of the output to fall, perhaps yielding lower profits and a reduction in value added, depending on the elasticity of demand in response to prices. For these two reasons, consequently, value added may not be the optimal measure of sectoral output. In summary, it is probably fair to say that different concepts of productivity are useful for different purposes and different ways of measuring productivity are advantageous for some uses but not for all.

8.3 Magnitude of the Productivity Slowdown

There was almost universal agreement among researchers that the rate of productivity growth in the United States began to decline from its postwar average rate in the mid- to late 1960s. Moreover, most researchers believed that there were two distinct phases in the decline, one lasting from about 1965 to 1973 and the other from about 1973 to 1978. Even though different definitions of productivity were used, the results were quite uniform (see Table 8.1). For the 1948–65(1966) period, the estimated annual rate of productivity growth ranged from 3.3 to 3.5 percent; for the 1965(1966)–72(1973) period, the range was 2.1 to 2.3 percent; and for the 1972(1973)–7(1978)

Table 8.1. *Selected Estimates of the Change in the Aggregate Rate of Productivity Growth over the Postwar Period (Percentage Points)*

Source	Productivity Concept	Period	Annual Rate of Productivity Growth
Denison (1979a)	National income per person employed	1948–73	2.43
	in nonresidential business	1973–76	-0.54
Kendrick (1980a)	Real product per unit of labor	1948–66	3.50
	in the business economy	1966–73	2.10
		1973–78	1.10
Kendrick (1980a)	TFP in the business economy	1948–66	2.70
		1966–73	1.60
		1973–78	0.80
Norsworthy, Harper, and Kunze (1979)	GDP per hour of labor input	1948–65	3.32
		1965–73	2.32
		1973–78	1.20
Thurow (1979)	GDP per labor hour in the private sector	1948–65	3.30
		1965–72	2.30
		1972–77	1.20

period, the range was 1.1 to 1.2 percent. Kendrick (1980a), Norsworthy, Harper, and Kunze (1979), and Thurow (1979) all found that there was about a 1 percentage point drop in the labor productivity growth rate between the first two periods and another decline of about 1 percentage point between the second and third periods. Denison (1979a) compared the rate of labor productivity growth in the 1947–73 and 1973–6 periods and found an even more precipitous drop of 3 percentage points.

Kendrick (1980a) presented a separate set of estimates for the rate of TFP growth. These were uniformly lower than his estimates of labor productivity growth because the effect of a rising capital-labor ratio on labor productivity is factored out. Even so, Kendrick found a 1 percentage point drop in the rate of TFP growth between the first and second periods and the second and third periods.

Table 8.2 presents estimates of the decline in the rate of productivity growth in particular industries. In contrast with the aggregate estimates, there was much greater variation in actual point estimates for particular sectors, although the assessments of the *direction* of change were fairly

Table 8.2. *Selected Estimates of the Change in Overall Annual Sectoral Productivity Growth Rates (Percentage Points)*

Source / Productivity Concept	Denison (1979a) GNP/Hours Worked[a]	Thurow (1979) Value added per Employee hour[b]	Kendrick (1980a) TFP[c]	Nadiri (1980) Value added per worker[d]	Norsworthy, Harper and Kunze (1979) GDP per Employee hour[e]
Periods	1948–73 / 1973–76	1948–65 / 1972–77	1948–73 / 1973–76	1948–74 / 1974–78	1948–65 / 1973–78
Overall	-2.97	-2.1	-1.8	-0.93	-2.1
Sectors:					
Agriculture, forestry, and fisheries	-3.4	-3.6	-2.2	-1.17	-2.6
Mining	-10.2	-9.4	-7.0	-6.79	-8.2
Construction	-0.7	-4.2	0.9	-1.06	-4.7
Nondurable manufacturing	-1.3	-0.7	-2.2	-0.94	-1.0
Durable manufacturing	-1.5	-1.5	-0.6	-1.07	-1.6
Transportation	-2.9	-1.0	0.1	-2.45	-2.4
Communications and utilities			-6.7		
Communications	3.2	1.1		2.52	1.6
Utilities	-4.0	-5.3		-2.66	-6.1
Wholesale and retail trade			-2.4	-1.86	
Wholesale trade	-4.6	-3.3			-2.9
Retail trade	-1.3	-1.6			-1.6
Finance, insurance & real estate		-0.6	0.3	1.59	0.4
Finance and insurance	---				
Real estate	---				
Services	-1.2	-1.0	--	-1.37	-1.0
Government	--	--	--	-0.33	--

Notes: [a] The overall productivity figure is national income per person employed in nonresidential business

[b] The overall figure is GNP per employee hour in the private sector

[c] The overall figure is for the business economy

[d] The overall figure is for the total economy; for the business economy, the overall figure is -0.78

[e] The overall figure is for the private business economy

uniform.[4] All seven researchers found that the rate of productivity growth of the mining sector declined and that this was the sector that experienced the largest decline. There was also general agreement that productivity growth declined in both durable and nondurable manufacturing, in construction (Kendrick found an increase), in agriculture, and in transportation, utilities, wholesale and retail trade, and general services. There were mixed reports for finance, insurance, and real estate, with four researchers reporting increases and two finding declines; and for the government sector, with two reporting modest declines and one a modest increase. By all accounts, the productivity growth slowdown before and after 1970 infected almost all sectors. However, the actual magnitude of the decline varied considerably among sectors, from a high in mining to a low in government services and to an actual increase in communications.

8.4 Causes of the Slowdown

A full explanation of the productivity slowdown would have to account not only for the aggregate slowdown but also for individual sectors as well. Moreover, it would have to account for the two-phase nature of the slowdown on the aggregate level and for the individual variation on the individual industry level as well. Most of the researchers were not able to provide a full explanation. Indeed, most of the research focused on explaining the slowdown in aggregate productivity growth.

Most of the aggregate analysis relied on growth accounting, in which the economy is treated as a single aggregate production function, with total output related to a set of input factors. Each factor is assigned a weight in the determination of total output, usually based on its factor share (that is, the proportion of total income received by the factor), and the total growth of output could then be related to the growth of these inputs over time. It is then possible to estimate the contribution of each factor to output growth, with the remaining part (or residual) attributed to technological change.[5]

Seven causes have been suggested as reasons for the productivity slowdown. The first three relate to inputs: the rate of capital formation, the composition of the labor force, and energy prices. The fourth relates to the residual in the production function: research and development (R&D) and the rate of technological progress. The fifth concerns the shares of the

---

[4] The differences in the estimates reflect the actual periods chosen, the productivity concept used, and the data sources.

[5] See Chapter 3 for more details on growth accounting methodology.

economy's different products: the composition of output. The remaining two are government regulation and the business cycle. It should be mentioned at the outset that these seven causes are not really mutually exclusive. For example, much of the discussion concerning the effect of the energy price rise on productivity growth involves its impact on capital formation. This division is made more for heuristic purposes than for analytical reasons.

8.4.1 Rate of Capital Formation

Many believed that the decline in capital formation was a major culprit in the overall productivity slowdown. On the surface, the evidence seemed to belie this belief because the ratio of gross private domestic investment to gross domestic product actually *rose* from 12.3 percent in 1948–65 to 13.5 percent in 1965–73 and then fell to 12.8 percent in 1973–8, a figure that was still above the level prior to the slowdown.[6] However, this was not the whole story; employment also increased more rapidly during the slowdown periods. The same source indicated that total hours of labor input increased at annual rates of 0.38 percent in 1948–65, 1.44 percent in 1965–73, and 1.42 percent in 1973–8. From the viewpoint of labor productivity, the important issue is what happened to the *capital-labor ratio* during this period because labor productivity increases as the capital-labor ratio rises. Despite the seeming simplicity of the issue involved, there are wide disparities in the results obtained in different studies depending on which definition and which data source were used.

Eckstein (1980) maintained that the stagnation in the capital-labor ratio was perhaps the largest element in the productivity slowdown. Kendrick (1980a), using a growth accounting framework, found that of the 2.4 percentage point decline in the rate of growth of real product per unit of labor between the 1948–66 and 1973–8 periods, 0.5 was accounted for by the deceleration in the substitution of capital for labor. Kopcke (1980), using an aggregate Cobb-Douglas production function, ascribed half of the productivity slowdown between 1950–65 and 1964–78 in the nonfarm, nonresidential economy to slower growth in plant and equipment.[7] In the case of manufacturing, he attributed the entire drop to slower growth in investment. Nadiri (1980), using a three-input Cobb-Douglas production function and sectoral data, estimated that the change in the capital-labor ratio accounted for 38 percent of the productivity slowdown between 1948–74

---

[6] See Norsworthy, Harper, and Kunze (1979), p. 390.
[7] See Chapter 2 for a description of the Cobb-Douglas production function.

and 1974–8 for the economy as a whole and 33 percent in the private economy. Tatom (1979) estimated that the slowdown in capital formation accounted for 0.7 percentage point of a 1.8 percentage point decline in the productivity growth rate between 1950–72 and 1972–9. Moreover, Clark (1979) estimated that 0.26 point of the 0.75 point decline in the 1965–73 trend rate in productivity growth resulted from the slow growth in the capital-labor ratio.

Another view of the effect of capital formation on the productivity slowdown was offered by Norsworthy and Harper (1979), who examined the effect of the rate of capital formation on labor productivity growth after 1965 in the nonfarm business sector. They found that the rate of capital formation had little to do with the slowdown during the 1965–73 period but played a significant role during 1973–7. Divisia aggregates of capital stock were used in conjunction with a Translog production function.[8]

A problem affecting the capital stock measures used in many studies is their misalignment with the output and labor input measures. The equipment and structures of nonprofit institutions are normally included but, for consistency, should be left out; the stock of tenant-owned housing is normally excluded but should be included. The misalignment is found to have significant effects on conclusions about the comparative rate of growth of capital stock and the capital-labor ratio. Norsworthy and Harper found that when this problem was corrected, there was about a 20 percent increase in the figure for the rate of growth of net stocks of equipment and structures in the nonfarm business sector in the 1965–73 period. They concluded on the basis of an examination of both corrected and uncorrected rates that there was no slowdown in the growth in the capital-labor ratio during the 1965–73 period regardless of the aggregation method. However, they did find a slowdown in the capital-labor ratio growth rate of 1 percentage point per year after 1973. Moreover, they concluded that the effect of capital accumulation on labor productivity growth was actually *greater* in 1965–73 than in earlier periods. In the 1973–7 period, on the other hand, they estimated that the contribution of capital stock growth to productivity growth fell by half. Of the 0.87 percentage point decline in productivity growth

---

[8] A Divisia aggregate is an index formed by weighting each component (in this case, of capital stock) according to its current value share. A Translog production function is a fairly complex representation of the technology of an industry. It relates the output of the sector to the various inputs used in production. See, for example, Gollop and Jorgenson (1980), pp. 25–8, for a discussion of the translog production function and Chapter 3 for more discussion.

between 1965–73 and 1973–7, the slowdown in capital formation explained 0.43 percentage point, or about half.

In a follow-up study, Norsworthy, Harper, and Kunze (1979) looked at productivity growth over the 1965–73 and 1973–8 periods for the entire business sector (including the farm sector). Using regression analysis, they concluded that capital formation was the main contributor to the productivity growth slowdown in the private business sector over the 1965–73 period. During the 1973–8 period, capital effects accounted for 0.79 percentage point of the 1.12 percentage point decline in productivity growth.

Denison (1979a) presented the opposing view that capital formation was not a major contributory factor in the productivity slowdown. His estimates showed that there was a very small decline in the rate of growth of the capital-labor ratio in the nonresidential business economy between the 1948–73 and 1973–6 spans and that this factor explained only a tiny portion (about one percent) of the slowdown in productivity growth. Denison (1980) extended his analysis through 1978. He found that for the nonresidential business economy, the growth rate of fixed capital to hours worked was only slightly lower in 1965–78 than in 1950–65 (0.1 percent for gross stocks and 0.5 percent for net stocks of capital). In manufacturing, in fact, the growth rate of gross stocks per hour worked *rose* 0.61 points in the second period, and the rate for net stocks *rose* 1.12 points. Denison's findings probably differ from those of the other studies because he excluded the residential sector and because he used NNP instead of GNP, which resulted in a lower estimate of capital's contribution to output. Finally, Wolff (1985), using sectoral capital stock data provided to the author by the Bureau of Labor Statistics, also found a very small retardation in the annual rate of increase in the overall capital-labor ratio from 2.49 percent in 1947–67 to 2.41 percent in 1967–76. However, because the unemployment rate was high in 1976 and low in 1967, the peak-to-peak decline might have been somewhat greater.

Besides holding back the rate of increase of the capital-labor ratio, a slowdown in capital formation will have secondary effects on the rate of growth of labor productivity (see Griliches, 1980). Because new technology is normally embodied in new capital stock, a decline in capital formation will slow the rate of introduction of new technology and therefore the rate of technical change. In this way, Kendrick (1980a) used the average age of capital goods as an indicator of the rate of diffusion of new technology. He found that between 1948 and 1966, the average age declined by three years, contributing 0.25 percentage point to the overall productivity growth rate. Between 1966 and 1973 the decline in average age slowed to one year; and between 1973 and 1978 there was no decline in the average age of capital stock. Clark (1979), using a Cobb-Douglas aggregate production function and assuming that new capital stock is 1 percent more productive than last year's capital stock, found a somewhat smaller vintage effect than Kendrick did. He estimated that of the 0.66 point decline in the labor productivity growth rate between 1948–65 and 1965–73, the vintage effect explained 0.09 point; of the 1.17 point decline between 1965–73 and 1973–8, the vintage effect accounted for 0.10 point.

One additional argument that was offered in connection with capital formation is that much of the new capital investment since the mid-1960s was made in order to comply with safety regulations and pollution rules and therefore did not add to productivity. Rama (1980) estimated that if one subtracted this unproductive portion from the total capital stock, the capital-labor ratio *actually fell* from an index of \$258 in 1967 to \$220 in 1973. Denison (1979a) estimated that the amount of capital installed to comply with pollution and safety regulations grew from 0 percent of net stocks in 1967 to 2.6 percent in 1975. Such compliance explained 0.30 point of the 3.07 point decline in the productivity growth rate from 1948–73 to 1973–6.

8.4.2 Composition of the Labor Force

Another candidate cause of the productivity slowdown is the changing composition of the labor force, particularly the increase after 1966 in the relative number of young workers and women. Eckstein (1980) and Perloff and Wachter (1980) argued that the productivity of these groups was generally lower than that of the labor force as a whole because they had fewer skills and less experience; therefore, a shift in labor force composition toward these groups would lower overall productivity. Perry (1977) estimated the labor-force participation rates of various demographic groups. For persons of both sexes aged sixteen to twenty-four and women aged twenty-five to forty-four, a statistically significant speedup in participation rates was found after 1966. For teenagers and women aged twenty-five to forty-four, this acceleration was 3 to 4 percent a year. Men aged twenty-five to sixty-four and women forty-five years of age and older showed a statistically significant slowing in participation rates. Perry also argued that these changes in labor force participation by women are the result of fairly permanent sociological changes, such as the deferral of marriage or child-bearing, rather than short-run influences, such as inflation and declining real earnings.

Kendrick (1980a), using a growth accounting framework, estimated that the changing proportion of women and youths in the labor force reduced annual productivity growth by 0.1 percentage point in 1948–66, 0.4 point in 1966–73, and 0.2 point in 1973–8. Filer (1980), using a correlation analysis from a regression model, estimated that a significant part of the productivity slowdown was caused by the accelerated influx of women into the labor force since 1966. Norsworthy, Harper, and Kunze (1979) estimated that the changing age composition of the workforce played some role in the productivity slowdown between 1948–65 and 1965–73 but not between 1965–73 and 1973–8, whereas they found that the changing sex composition was a factor in the second slowdown but not in the first. Denison (1979a) attributed only 0.08 point of the 2.97 percentage point productivity slowdown to the change in age-sex composition between the 1948–73 and 1973–6 periods. Clark (1979) estimated that the shifts in age and sex explained almost one-third of the 1965–73 slowdown.

A counteracting influence during this period was the increase in the education and training of the workforce. Kendrick (1980b) estimated that it accounted for 0.7 point in the overall productivity growth rate between 1973 and 1978, compared with 0.6 point between 1948 and 1966. Norsworthy, Harper, and Kunze (1979) also found that the contribution of this factor increased steadily, from 0.46 point in 1948–65 to 0.95 point in 1965–73 and 1.05 points in 1973–8, although these figures were not corrected for interactive effects with the change in the occupational mix. Denison's (1979a) figures indicated a rise in the contribution of this factor from 0.52 point in 1948–73 to 0.88 point in 1973–6, but because 1976 was a year of high unemployment, the average education of the labor force was probably overstated.

8.4.3 Energy Prices

Another event that many observers believed was connected with the productivity slowdown was the dramatic rise in energy prices that began in the early 1970s. A study by Rasche and Tatom (1977a) estimated that 4 to 5 percentage points of the decrease in national income in 1974 was due to the quadrupling of oil prices by the Organization of Petroleum Exporting Countries (OPEC). They concluded that this loss of national income was permanent, as was the associated reduction in potential GNP. The Council of Economic Advisers (1977) also cited evidence supporting the view that the drop in productivity of labor and capital resources since 1973–4 was permanent and was caused by the higher costs of energy resources. Rasche and Tatom (1977a, 1977b) estimated a Cobb-Douglas production function using annual data for the period from 1949 to 1975. The results indicated that capacity in the manufacturing sector fell 5 percent in 1974 as a result of the 45.3 percent increase in the nominal price of energy over the 1973–4 span. There was also evidence that these results were representative for the entire private business sector.

Hudson and Jorgenson (1978) also examined the effect of the 1973–4 oil price increase using a dynamic general equilibrium model of the U.S. economy to simulate two economic growth paths over the 1972–6 period. The first simulation used actual values for the exogenous variables, including world oil prices. This gave an estimate of the actual development of the economy over that period. A second simulation kept energy prices constant at their 1972 level for the entire period. A comparison of the two simulations indicated that the increase in the price of energy over that period reduced real GNP in 1976 by 3.2 percent. This was attributed to the behavior of producers who tried to substitute other inputs for energy in the production process. This tended to decrease productivity because the substitution was imperfect and the substitute inputs must be taken away from other uses. The decline in energy use was found to redirect the patterns of net input away from energy. The greatest relative reductions in energy use were estimated to have occurred in services and manufacturing.

At the same time, higher energy prices led to increased use of labor per unit of output as producers substituted labor for energy. The largest increases in the demand for labor occurred in services and manufacturing; significant increases were also found in agriculture and construction. However, because real GNP fell by 3.2 percent between 1972 and 1976, the demand for labor also fell by 3.2 percent. The net effect of the increase in the price of energy was found to be a decrease in labor demand of only 0.6 percent. As a result, there was a decrease in the average output per worker. The economic restructuring represented by the differences in the two simulations involves a 2.57 percent decline in the growth rate of average labor productivity over four years, or 0.6 percent a year. Hudson and Jorgenson noted that these are once-and-for-all effects; Denison (1979a) disputed this analysis. He argued that the value of energy used in the nonresidential business sector was less than 4 percent of the total value of the factor inputs in the entire economy. Hudson and Jorgenson (1978) estimated that the use of energy per unit of factor input was reduced 7.7 percent between 1973 and 1976. According to Denison, "The usual procedure would then yield a reduction in output per unit of labor, capital, and land of only 0.3 percentage points (7.7 x 0.04)"; this was about one-seventh of the Hudson-Jorgenson estimate of 2.57 percentage points. Denison thus estimated that the 1973–4 energy price increase reduced the productivity growth rate by 0.1 percentage point a year, not 0.6 percentage point a year. However, it should be noted that Denison's analysis implicitly assumed a Cobb-Douglas production function for the economy, an assumption that might not be entirely supportable.

Norsworthy, Harper, and Kunze (1979) used a dynamic model of the manufacturing sector to simulate the effect of energy price movements on productivity. In their analysis, the energy price effect on the productivity slowdown was subsumed in its effect on capital formation. The results showed a strong complementarity between labor and capital over both the short and the long term. The simulation assumed that the price of energy increased at the same rate as the implicit price deflator for manufacturing (rather than the 22.3 percent that actually occurred). On this basis, the model suggested that the capital-labor ratio would have risen at an annual rate of 2.3 percent instead of the actual 1.7 percent, implying that the annual growth rate of labor productivity would have increased 0.18 point if the change in the relative price of energy had not occurred.

Finally, Berndt (1980) argued that the direct effect of the energy price increase on the productivity slowdown in U.S. manufacturing during the 1973–7 period was not significant. He identified two reasons for the small direct effect: First, energy costs were a very small proportion of total costs, and therefore energy price variations did not weigh heavily in productivity calculations. Second, observed variations in energy-output ratios were very small between 1973 and 1977, despite the substantial energy price increases. Berndt granted that energy price increases could have had an indirect effect on labor productivity through price induced substitutions of labor for energy, which would have led to reductions in the ratios of capital to labor and of energy to labor. This required energy-capital complementarity and energy-labor substitutability. But he pointed out that the evidence on this was not strong. There was only a very slight slowdown in the rate of growth of the capital-labor ratio, from 2.88 percent in 1965–73 to 2.52 percent in 1973–7, and in the rate of growth of the energy-labor ratio, from 2.79 percent in the first period to 2.54 percent in the second period.

8.4.4 Research and Development

The decline in R&D expenditures since 1965 was cited by several authors as a contributor to the slowdown over the 1965–78 period. The ratio of R&D expenditures to GNP peaked in 1964 at 2.97 percent and then fell to 2.27 percent over the 1976–7 period (Denison, 1979a). The decline was ascribable primarily to the drop in federal expenditures on defense and space programs. Expenditures financed by other sources actually increased from 0.99 percent of GNP in 1963–4 to 1.15 percent in 1969–70. There was a decline in private R&D to GNP ratio to 1.07 percent in 1972–3, but it recovered to 1.12 percent in the 1974–7 period.

Research and development affects productivity through advances that reduce the unit cost of final outputs already available or through the introduction of new products. However, not all R&D expenditures contribute to productivity growth. Much is spent on defense and space exploration, health, environment, and goods and services, and the quality improvements brought about by such spending are not captured in the national income accounts. Because much of the relative decrease in R&D outlays occurred in these areas, the slowdown in productivity-augmenting research and development may be considerably smaller than these figures indicated.

Griliches (1980) estimated that there was a decline in R&D capital spending of approximately 3 to 6 percentage points during the period of the slowdown. Assuming an elasticity of aggregate output with respect to R&D capital of 0.06 point, Griliches estimated that the reduction in the R&D capital growth rate contributed only 0.14 percentage point to the productivity decline in manufacturing during the recent slowdown. Denison (1979a) estimated that the slowdown in R&D expenditures contributed only about 0.1 point to the decline in overall productivity growth rate. Thurow (1980) also argued that the retardation in R&D spending could not have contributed much to the productivity slowdown because whereas this lessened expenditure did not really begin until the early 1970s, the slowdown began in the mid-1960s, and there must be a substantial time lag between R&D expenditures and measured productivity growth.

On the other side of the ledger, Kendrick (1980a) claimed to find that 13 percent of the decline in TFP growth (0.25 of an overall decline of 1.9 percentage points) could be attributed to the decline in R&D. However, as Denison pointed out, Kendrick did not adjust his R&D series for that portion financed by the federal government for space and defense work. Moreover, Nadiri (1980), using a Cobb-Douglas production function with three inputs (labor, capital, and R&D stock), estimated that 17 percent of the productivity decline in the economy as a whole and 27 percent in the private sector could be attributed to diminished R&D investment. Nadiri's estimates might, however, have been biased upward because he omitted such variables as the average age of capital and total number of labor hours. The total number of labor hours, in particular, reflects the short-run productivity movements during the business cycle (see Section 8.4.7).

In a later work, Nadiri and Shankerman (1981) specified cost and demand functions for total durables and nondurables manufacturing. Cost, price, and income elasticities were estimated and used to examine the slowing of TFP growth over the 1958–65, 1965–73, and 1973–8 periods. Nadiri and Shankerman used an average variable cost function that is shifted by disembodied technological change and the change in the R&D stock, as well as an output demand function and a pricing rule that equates output price to average variable costs and quasi-rents accruing to capital. They found that the decline in the growth of R&D stock contributed only 5 to 10 percent of the slowdown in TFP growth for total manufacturing between the first two periods, with a similar figure applying to nondurables over the last two periods. For total manufacturing and durables, the R&D slowdown accounted for about one-fourth of the TFP growth slowdown between the last two periods.

In seeking to determine whether there was a slowdown in the rate of technical changes, most studies measured this variable by treating it as a residual in the analysis. Fraumeni and Jorgenson (1981) reported that after 1966, the rate of technical change measured in this way almost disappeared as a source of economic growth. Indeed, they calculated a *negative* rate of technical change for the 1973–6 period. However, it is hard to evaluate these findings because there was no independent measure of technical change. Indeed, since R&D investment continued during these years, their results would seem to imply that R&D activity yielded no innovative techniques.

8.4.5 Composition of Output

The relation between the composition of output and the productivity slowdown is also a topic on which there was some disagreement. It should be noted that this treatment of the productivity problem was distinct from the others discussed so far in that it dealt with a new set of issues, namely, how the composition of the product changed over time. However, this treatment was not entirely separable from the others; a change in the composition of output had direct implications concerning the growth of inputs, particularly the capital stock, and the composition of the labor force. Thus, effects on productivity growth estimated from the change in output composition might have been partly picked up in other analyses from changes in input or labor force composition. These results were not therefore strictly additive with other results.

The difference in findings concerning the effect of output composition on productivity growth was ascribable to differences in research methods.

Two basically different procedures were employed in this context. The first calculated the aggregate productivity level as a weighted average of the productivity *levels* of the individual sectors. A shift in employment or output between sectors would therefore change the level of overall productivity, assuming that the values of all other variables remained unchanged. It was then possible to isolate the effect of shifts in the composition of output or employment on the change in overall productivity. This decomposition technique was used by Nordhaus (1972); Kutscher, Mark, and Norsworthy (1977); Denison (1973, 1979a); and Thurow (1979). However, as shown in Baumol and Wolff (1984), this technique is methodologically flawed because the results are dependent on the choice of base year for the industry productivity series.

The second approach calculated the overall rate of productivity growth as a weighted average of individual sectoral rates of productivity growth. The theory underlying this approach was provided by Baumol (1967) in his model of unbalanced growth and was later extended by Grossman and Fuchs (1973) and Baumol, Blackman, and Wolff (1989). Using this technique, one can break down the change in overall productivity growth into two effects: the first ascribable to changes in sectoral rates of productivity growth and the second to the composition of output or employment. This technique was used by Wolff (1985).

In the earliest of these studies, Nordhaus (1972) estimated productivity levels for twelve sectors and then projected what the overall rate of productivity growth would have been if the sectoral productivity levels had remained constant over the period while the employment weights shifted as they did over that time. He found that of the 1.17 percentage point decline in aggregate productivity growth that occurred between 1948–65 and 1965–71 (from 3.20 to 2.03), 0.09 point was attributable to the change in the composition of output.

Kutscher, Mark, and Norsworthy (1977), using Bureau of Labor Statistics sectoral gross output and employment data, estimated that between 1947 and 1966, the shift in the labor force out of agriculture contributed 0.4 point a year to the overall productivity growth rate, whereas from 1966 to 1973, it contributed only 0.1 point annually. Moreover, the shift of employment toward services decreased the overall productivity growth rate by only 0.1 percentage point a year, and this effect was fairly steady over the entire 1947–73 period. Taken together, the shift in hours of work was responsible for 0.3 to 0.4 point of the 1.5 point decline in overall productivity (from 3.2 to 1.7 points) between 1947–66 and 1967–73.

Denison (1973) found that the shift to services had very little bearing on the productivity slowdown. Although the share of total employment in service industries rose from 54 percent in 1948 to 64 percent in 1969, service employment as a share of total employment in the nonfarm, nonresidential business sector remained almost constant. Moreover, service output as a percentage of total nonfarm, nonresidential business output also remained constant. As a result, Denison estimated that the change in composition between commodities and services had less than a 0.05 percentage point impact on the annual productivity growth rate.

Norsworthy, Harper, and Kunze (1979) used a sixty-two-sector breakdown of employment by industry. They estimated that despite the 1.00 percentage point decline in annual labor productivity growth between 1948–65 and 1965–73, the interindustry effect from employment shifts actually boosted productivity growth by 0.05 point. Between 1965–73 and 1973–8, the interindustry effect accounted for 0.27 of the 1.12 point decline in the productivity growth rate. However, these results may be understated because the farm-to-nonfarm shift was actually captured by the change in occupational composition, which they included as a separate effect.

In contrast, Thurow (1979) found somewhat stronger compositional effects on productivity growth. Using a twelve-sector breakdown and defining sectoral productivity as value added per worker, Thurow also found that between 1948–65 and 1965–72, changes in the industrial composition of employment had no effect on productivity. However, Thurow estimated that from 1965–72 to 1972–7, 45 to 50 percent of the observed decline in productivity growth was ascribable to the shifts in the mix of output toward low productivity sectors. However, this effect may result in part because the shift occurred to sectors with lower capital-to-labor ratios. Finally, Wolff (1985) used U.S. input-output data for 1947, 1967, and 1976 and separated the overall rate of productivity change into two effects: (1) that produced by changes in the sectoral composition of final output and (2) that stemming from changes in individual sectoral rates of technical change. He estimated that changes in the sectoral composition of final output, mainly because of its constancy, accounted for 20 to 25 percent of the decline in the overall productivity growth rate.

8.4.6 Government Regulation

Increased government regulation during the 1965–78 period was also cited as a contributing cause to the decline in productivity growth. Denison

(1979a) argued that there was a diversion of inputs in the process of complying with government regulations. Government regulations also imposed extra paperwork, which used resources. The federal government estimated that in 1976 this cost was between 2.4 and 3.1 percent of the GDP of the business sector. When state and local government regulations were included the cost jumped to approximately 3.0 to 4.6 percent. Regulation and taxes also divert executive attention. The profitability of business is affected by the way in which it responds to rapid changes in government regulations that discriminate among different types of income and business costs. Denison concluded that this was a psychological deterrent to performance. On balance, he thought the effect of such regulations on productivity growth accounted for perhaps 13 percent of the decline.

Government regulation also extends the maturation and fruition period of new investment projects, and this delay too retards productivity growth. In addition, regulation may lead to a misallocation of resources to those items in whose favor it is biased. The largest misallocation effect results from the induced uncertainty about the future. Future benefits of a project become more difficult to assess if there is uncertainty about future regulations. In this way, growing government regulation may serve to reduce growth. Kendrick's results suggested that 16 percent of the weakening in productivity growth between the 1948–66 and 1973–8 periods was attributable to increased government regulations and related policies. Fellner (1979) also concluded that 1 percentage point of the worsening in productivity growth was difficult to explain without including the effects of federal government policy changes.

Denison (1979b) estimated the effect of pollution controls on measured output per unit of input. He concluded that by 1975 the change in environmental controls introduced since 1967 diverted nearly 1 percent of labor, capital, and land used in the nonresidential business sector from production of measured output to pollution abatement, which does *not* result in measured output. By 1978 this had risen to 1.2 percent. He concluded that output per unit of input in 1978 was 98.8 percent as large as it would have been if environmental regulations had stayed as they were in 1967.

Crandall (1980) suggested that there are two ways in which government regulation may reduce productivity growth. First, government regulation restricts competition and protects regulated firms from new technology and new competitors. Second, health, safety, and environmental regulations divert large quantities of resources to the control of various hazards, thereby reducing normally measured output-to-input ratios. Between 1969 and 1972, for example, the Occupational Safety and Health Administration, the Environmental Protection Agency, the National Highway Traffic Safety Administration, the Consumer Product Safety Commission, and the National Environmental Policy Act all came into existence. However, the only hard evidence that Crandall presented was for the mining sector, where the annual rate of productivity growth declined from 4.2 percent in 1948–65 to 2.0 percent in 1965–73 and to -4.0 percent in 1973–8.

8.4.7 Cyclical Factors

Another view attributed much of the productivity problem to the business cycle and thus considered the problem temporary. Productivity growth is known to decrease during the tail end of an economic expansion and during recessions. But during periods of economic recovery, productivity growth usually increases.

An economic recovery begins with the resurgence of sales and decreases in inventory accumulation. Output is initially increased by more intensive use of the existing labor force and capital stock. This increases average weekly working hours and leads to a sharp increase in output per labor hour. As output increases, so do employment and productivity. In later stages, the increase in labor input continues to grow at a rapid rate for one or two quarters after output growth slows, thus decreasing the growth of output per labor hour.

Cyclical productivity movements are explained by the hoarding of labor by firms. During recessions, firms are reluctant to lay off workers because they want to avoid rehiring costs when the expansion occurs. For this reason, hours of employment per worker also display a cyclical pattern. As a result, hours worked vary more than employment. An alternative explanation of the observed cyclical behavior of productivity is that the use of capital relative to labor is procyclical. Firms use relatively more capital intensive methods as the economy expands and reduce capital usage relative to labor during economic contractions.

Gordon (1979) examined the short-run behavior of aggregate productivity from 1954 to 1977. Specifically he investigated the short-run increasing returns to labor and the tendency for productivity growth to decline during the last stages of the business expansion. Cyclical fluctuations in labor productivity were described in his model as a partial adjustment of the ratio of actual labor hours to potential hours (that is, the full employment level of labor hours) in response to the fluctuation in the ratio of actual to potential GDP. He included a dummy variable in the regression to capture the effect of overhiring in the last two quarters of the business expansion. His estimates showed that the dummy variable was highly significant. Of the total end-of-expansion effect of 1.8 percentage points, employment accounted for 1.26 points and hours per employee for 0.54 point. This implied that the end-of-expansion effect primarily involved the retention of too many workers relative to output. Gordon had two explanations for this phenomenon: First, labor and capital are interdependent factors of production. When capital investment is relatively high, additional employees are required for installation and training. This implies that experienced labor must work overtime to train new employees. When investment is low, installations of this type are decreased. Second, firms may maintain slack in their labor force when the quit rate is high to guard against being caught shorthanded.

Kendrick (1980a) noted that there was full employment in 1948 and 1966 and that, as a result, the ratio of actual to potential GNP in 1973 was 1.5 percent below that of 1966 and 2.7 percent lower in 1978 than in 1966. This subtracted 0.1 point from the annual growth rates in 1966–73 and 0.3 point in 1973–8. A related phenomenon is that the deceleration in the growth of total real GNP means a lessening of the contribution of economies of scale to productivity growth. Kendrick estimated that this factor explained 0.2 point of the decline in TFP growth between 1948–66 and 1973–8.

A basic difficulty with the cyclical explanations of the productivity slowdown was the evidence that this decline lasted for fifteen years and did not seem to be affected by changing business conditions. All in all, it is not easy to believe that the business cycle was one of the prime culprits.

8.5 More Recent Literature on the Productivity Slowdown

Later work on the subject of the productivity slowdown of the 1970s had the benefit of hindsight. It also had the benefit of new information on the productivity recovery after 1979 and new econometric techniques. Despite these factors, work on the productivity slowdown tailed off after 1980 or so as productivity growth recovered. Still, a few economists returned to this issue.

One important hypothesis warranting examination was that R&D was making less of a contribution to technical progress than previously. The results of Griliches (1980) and others led some to speculate that technological opportunities were being exhausted, reducing the contribution of

R&D to growth.[9] More recent work by Griliches and others since drew the opposite conclusion.[10] As Nadiri (1993) observed, however, a survey of the literature left one with the impression that the contribution of R&D to growth may have diminished in the early 1970s and then strengthened in the late 1970s and 1980s. For example, Lichtenberg and Siegel (1991), who analyzed the period 1973–85 in the United States, found that while R&D was significant in boosting TFP growth throughout the period, its impact strengthened in the latter half of the period.[11]

Another strand of the technical change literature took note of the fact that the ratio of patents to real R&D investment and its ratio to scientists and engineers employed in R&D (S&E) declined in the United States and other developed economies. The patent/S&E ratio in 1990 was at 55 percent of its level in 1969–70 in the United States, 44 percent in the United Kingdom, 42 percent in Germany, and 40 percent in France (Evenson, 1993). Whether this implied diminishing returns to R&D is a matter of some dispute. Evenson (1993) argued that there was some evidence that invention potential was being exhausted. Griliches (1989), on the other hand, favored an explanation focusing on a declining tendency to patent.

Wolff (1996a) used the Maddison data to analyze the productivity slowdown in seven OECD countries. He argued that the vintage effect explained a large part of the productivity slowdown. He first noted that the productivity slowdown of the 1970s characterized all seven countries. For example, the annual rate of TFP growth in Japan fell from 5.6 percent in the 1960s to 1.6 percent in the 1970s. He also found that whereas the average age of the capital stock fell sharply during the 1950s and 1960s, there was virtually no change during the 1970s.

On average, the falloff in labor productivity growth between the 1960–73 and 1973–9 periods amounted to 2.6 percentage points. On the basis of regression analysis, he estimated that the slowdown in total capital-labor growth accounted for 26 percent of the decline in labor productivity growth; the aging of the capital stock accounted for 41 percent; the diminution of the catch-up effect only 5 percent; and 29 percent was due to the unexplained portion. He concluded that the vintage effect explained a large

[9]   For a more detailed discussion, see Baily and Chakrabarti (1988).
[10] See, for example, Griliches and Lichtenberg (1984a), Griliches (1986), and Lichtenberg and Siegel (1991).
[11] It should be kept in mind that as Scherer (1983) argued, continued strong returns to R&D investment do not necessarily mean that technological opportunities are not diminishing, since firms can cut back on R&D expenditures if they do not deem them to be profitable.

part of the productivity slowdown in these countries (see Section 5.3 of this book for more details).

Bishop (1989) raised the provocative question of whether the productivity slowdown could be attributed in part to the decline in test scores among American students. A decline in general intellectual achievement (or GIA, as he termed it) would translate into a decline in labor quality. He first reported on the basis of an "intelligence test" administered as part of the Panel Survey of Income Dynamics a 1.25 grade level decline in test score achievement between 1967 and 1980. This test score decline coincided with the period of the productivity slowdown. He estimated that if test scores had continued to grow after 1967 at the same rate as prevailed from about 1945 to 1967 labor quality would have been 2.9 percent higher in 1980 than in actuality and 1980 GNP would have been 0.91 percent higher. He surmised that the test score decline explained 9.3 percent of the productivity slowdown between 1973 and 1980.

Another interesting argument was presented by Greenwood and Jovanovic (2001). They first noted three important facts about the postwar growth experience of the United States. First, since the early 1970s there was a slump in the advance of productivity. Second, the price of new equipment fell steadily over the postwar period. Third, in the early 1970s there began a huge upsurge in investment in computers and computer-related equipment. They developed a vintage capital model to explain these facts. They concluded that productivity growth slowed in the 1970s because the implementation of information technologies was both costly and slow (also, see David, 1991). They also showed that technological advance in the capital goods sector led to a decline in equipment prices, which in turn spurred the adoption of new information technology. Their results, while intriguing, are based on theoretical models. However, the authors did not supply any empirical corroboration.

A related paper by Samaniego (2006) also linked the productivity slowdown of the 1970s to the information technology (IT) revolution. However, the emphasis of his model is on the role of organizational capital. In particular, he argued that IT appeared to require plant level reorganization for its full implementation. His paper did not provide any empirical evidence directly, but his calibration of the model did support his contention that the "organizational" shock of introducing new IT could have depressed productivity growth.

Nordhaus (2004) revisited the productivity slowdown of the 1970s on the basis of new industry level data on output and employment provided by the U.S. Bureau of Economic Analysis. His major finding was that the productivity slowdown of the 1970s was primarily centered in those sectors that were most energy intensive, were hardest hit by the energy shocks of the 1970s, and therefore had large output declines. These included oil and gas extraction; motor vehicles and equipment; electric, gas, and sanitary services; and agriculture. Nordhaus concluded that industries with the largest slowdown in productivity were the ones hardest hit by the energy price surge of the 1970s.

8.6 An Evaluation of Past Research

It is rather difficult to form a consensus of the various factors cited by the studies discussed in this chapter as possible causes of the productivity slowdown. Results differed among researchers because of differences in data sources, periods, concepts, sector of the economy studied, research methods, measurement error in the raw data, and underlying assumptions and models used (for example, the specification of the production function). The range of estimates of the earlier studies is summarized in Table 8.3. Here I offer an evaluation of the evidence presented in the various studies. The key element, as I see it, is whether the factor was special to the slowdown period or whether it was part of a long-term secular trend. The benefit of hindsight is also useful here.

8.6.1 Capital formation

Except for Denison, most observers seemed to agree that the slowdown in the growth of the capital-labor ratio was an important cause of the productivity slowdown. In addition, there seemed to be a marked difference in its importance between the first slowdown period (1965–73) and the second (from 1973 onward). The evidence seemed to suggest, although not with unanimity, that this factor was not very important in explaining the first slowdown. However, the slowing in the growth of capital employed per worker did seem to explain between one-third and two-thirds of the second slowdown. It should be emphasized, though, that the underlying cause was not a decline in the gross-investment-to-GNP ratio but, rather, the rapid growth in the labor force after 1965. This speedup in labor force growth, a result of the "Baby Boom" generation's coming of working age, was special to the slowdown period, particularly in light of subsequent history. As a result, the sharp decline in the growth of the capital-labor ratio was unique to the slowdown period. Subsequent history shows that capital-labor growth picked up after 1980 or so.

Table 8.3. *Estimates of the Importance of Selected Factors in the Productivity Slowdown*

Factors and Source	Periods	Percentage of Slowdown
A. Capital Formation		
1) Capital-labor ratio growth		
Denison (1979a)	1948–73, 1973–76	4
Kendrick (1980a)	1948–66, 1973–78	21
Clark (1979)	1948–65, 1965–73	35
Nadiri (1980)	1948–74, 1974–78	38
Tatom (1979)	1950–72, 1972–79	39
Norsworthy and Harper (1979)	1948–65, 1965–73	--
	1965–73, 1973–77	49
Norsworthy, Harper,	1948–65, 1965–73	--
and Kunze (1979)	1965–73, 1973–78	71
2) Vintage effect		
Kendrick (1980a)	1948–66, 1973–78	10
Clark (1979)	1948–65, 1965–73	14
	1965–73, 1973–78	9
3) Pollution and regulation		
Denison (1979a)	1948–73, 1973–76	13
Kendrick (1980a)	1948–66, 1973–78	16
4) Energy price effect		
Denison (1979a)	1948–73, 1973–76	3
Norsworthy, Harper,	1965–73, 1973–78	16
and Kunze (1979)		
Hudson and Jorgenson (1978)	1948–72, 1972–76	20
B. Research and development		
Denison (1979a)	1948–73, 1973–76	3
Griliches (1980)	1965–73, 1973–77	10
Kendrick (1980a)	1948–66, 1973–78	13
Nadiri (1980)	1948–74, 1974–78	17
C. Output Composition		
Denison (1979a)	1948–73, 1973–76	13
Kutcher, Mark, and	1947–66, 1966–73	23
Norsworthy (1979)		
Norsworthy, Harper,	1948–65, 1965–73	--
and Kunze (1979)	1965–73, 1973–78	24
Thurow (1979)	1948–65, 1965–72	--
	1965–72, 1972–77	45–50
Wolff (1985)	1947–67, 1967–76	20–25
Nordhaus (1972)	1948–55, 1965–71	79
D. Government Regulation		
Denison (1979a)	1948–73, 1973–76	13
Kendrick (1980a)	1948–66, 1973–78	16

Moreover, when other effects associated with capital formation are included, its importance became even greater. The vintage effect stemming from a slowdown in capital formation might explain another 10 percent of the decline in both the first and second periods. Wolff (1996a) reported an even larger effect. The fact that a part of the new capital equipment went to meet new pollution and safety standards instead of increasing output directly meant the growth of the *effective* capital stock was overvalued by the investment data. This diversion of capital stock to meet new government regulations might have explained at least 10 percent of the slowdown in the second period.

And the rapid increase in energy prices after 1972 might have slowed the rate of new capital formation. Moreover, because higher energy prices made part of the existing capital stock uneconomical and therefore obsolete, the rate of growth of the net capital stock may have been even further depressed. This factor might explain another 10 percent of the productivity slowdown of the second period. Nordhaus (2004) also found that the biggest declines in productivity growth during the 1970s were localized in energy intensive sectors. Altogether, capital formation effects might well account for more than half of the productivity slowdown in the second period and perhaps a quarter in the first period.

8.6.2 Composition of the Labor Force

Changes in the labor force involved two counteracting tendencies during the slowdown period: (1) the increased rate of labor force participation of women and the relative rise in the number of young workers and (2) the increased educational level of new entrants into the labor force. On this, there was a strong consensus that the net contribution to the productivity slowdown was very small (and as a result, these estimates are not shown in Table 8.3). Bishop (1989), however, felt that the decline in test scores and the consequent deterioration of the quality of the U.S. labor force might have accounted for about 10 percent of the productivity slowdown. Moreover, the change in labor force composition has been an ongoing phenomenon and does not correlate with the subsequent increase in productivity growth after 1980.

8.6.3 R&D and Technical Change

The consensus seemed to be that the rate of disembodied technical change declined after 1965 (although perhaps not as much as Fraumeni and

Jorgenson, 1981, maintained). But because the ratio of privately financed research and development to GNP did not decline (and, in any event, was largely confined to manufacturing), research and development was probably not a major contributory factor to the productivity slowdown. There seemed to be general agreement that about 10 percent of the productivity slowdown of the second period was caused by a decline in R&D investment. However, as Nadiri (1993) concluded, a survey of the literature seemed to suggest that the contribution of R&D to growth may have diminished in the early 1970s and then rebounded in the late 1970s and 1980s. On net, and in retrospect, the relatively modest decline in R&D intensity during the slowdown period could not have been a major force in accounting for the productivity slowdown of the 1970s.

8.6.4 Composition of Output

Most observers seemed to concur that output shifts were responsible for part of the productivity slowdown, but their estimates differed quite widely. For the first period, the estimates varied from zero to three-fourths; for the second period, they varied from zero to one-fourth. These disparities largely reflected methodological differences. Estimates of the composition effect based on differences in productivity *levels* (for example, Nordhaus, 1972, and Thurow, 1979), as noted previously, were shown to be methodologically flawed. The proper procedure is to use differences in sectoral productivity growth *rates*. In any event, the shift to services is a secular process that has been steadily and gradually going on over the last seventy years and could not have explained the sharp slowdown in productivity growth in the 1970s.

8.6.5 Other Factors

Of the remaining possible causes (government regulation and cyclical factors), only increased government regulation might have played any significant role in the productivity problem, perhaps as much as 15 percent in the second period. On the surface, it is hard to believe that the increased stringency of safety, health, and environmental regulations did *not* divert some resources away from *measured output*. However, in this context in particular, measurement issues played an especially vital role, and if the benefits generated by those regulations had been reflected in the measures of utilized output, the reported productivity slowdown would have been smaller. This factor might have had some (albeit small) weight in the overall productivity slowdown of the period since many of these regulations took effect in the late 1960s and early 1970s.

In conclusion, the consensus view may have accounted for nearly all of the productivity slowdown in the second period and perhaps one-third of the decline in the first period. Of course, this chapter has not attempted to discuss all the proposed causes of the productivity slowdown. One major omission is contributing institutional factors, particularly those related to the structure of employer-employee relations. Unfortunately, there are almost no estimates of the quantitative importance of this factor. A second major omission is industry specific factors, such as the effect of the depletion of natural resources on the productivity performance of the mining sector. Here, too, estimates of the economywide effect are lacking. A third, mentioned by Greenwood and Jovanovic (2001) and Samaniego (2006), is that the beginnings of the IT revolution in the early 1970s may have slowed productivity growth as a result of adjustment costs associated with its introduction. Many researchers (e.g., Jorgenson Stiroh, 1999 and 2000) attribute a substantial part of the increase in U.S. productivity growth since 1995 or so to the finally realized benefits of the IT revaluation.

9

Postwar Economic Performance among
Countries of the World

9.1 Introduction

The term "aggregate convergence" refers to the gradual diminution of differences in productivity levels for the overall economy of countries over time. Previous explanations of the productivity catch-up almost all involve the advantages of backwardness or Gerschenkron effect, by which it is meant that much of the catch-up can be explained by the diffusion of technical knowledge from the leading economies to the more backward ones (see Gerschenkron, 1952, and Kuznets, 1973, for example). From this view, technological progress operates through a mechanism that enables countries whose level of productivity is behind (but not too far behind) that of the leading country(ies) to catch up. Through the constant transfer of knowledge, countries learn about the latest technology from each another, but virtually by definition the followers have more to learn from the leaders than the leaders have to learn from the laggards. On the other hand, those countries that are so far behind the leaders that it is impractical for them to profit substantially from the leaders' knowledge will generally not be able to participate in the convergence process at all, and many such economies will find themselves falling even further behind.

The most important influence underlying this process is the transfer of technology that occurs constantly among many of the world's economies. There is strong evidence that advanced industrial countries continuously acquire technical ideas from each other. Competitive pressures in the international economy ensure rapid dissemination of superior productive techniques from one country to another. However, in the process of reciprocal exchange of ideas, clearly it is the more backward countries that have more to learn from the leaders than the reverse. That is the heart of the explanation of a convergence process.

This mechanism has two implications: First, it means that countries that lag (somewhat) behind the leaders can be expected to increase their productivity performance toward the level of the leading nations. In other words, there should be an *inverse* relation between a country's initial productivity level and its rate of productivity growth. Second, the mechanism tends to undermine itself as the gap in productivity between follower countries and leading countries is gradually eliminated. As a result, the rate of catch-up should slow as the productivity gap is closed.

It should be stressed at this point that being backward does not itself guarantee that a nation will catch up. Other factors must be present, such as strong investment, an educated and well-trained workforce, research and development activity, a developed information sector, a suitable product mix, developed trading relations with advanced countries, foreign investment by multinational corporations, a receptive political structure, low population growth, and the like.

In this chapter, I report on the existing evidence relating to the convergence hypothesis for overall economic performance among countries at all levels of development, and then on some of the factors that affect the convergence process. The scope of this chapter differs from that of Chapters 4 and 5 in that the latter focused on the experience of the advanced industrial (that is, OECD) countries. This chapter instead considers not only this group of countries but middle income and low income ones as well. As such, because the data coverage includes developing countries and formerly planned economies, there will be many more issues of measurement error and greater data-to-theory challenges (see Chapter 3 for a discussion of these measurement issues).

In the next section (Section 9.2), I look at the basic evidence on convergence for the postwar period. These studies consider the success of countries at all levels of development. I then consider some of the factors that have been shown to influence the convergence process. I start with the so-called strong forces and then consider the weak forces. The most important of these is investment. There are two primary ingredients in the growth of labor productivity: technological innovation and the accumulation of capital through saving (and the subsequent investment of those savings). Most studies find that innovation and the international transfer of its products have played the major role in the converging productivity levels of a number of relatively successful industrialized economies. But many studies also find that substantial capital accumulation is also required to put the inventions into practice and to effect their widespread employment. In Section 9.3, I consider the evidence on capital formation and its role in the productivity catch-up process.

Previous work on the subject has shown that the next most important factor in the catch-up process is education (Section 9.4). The statistical evidence supports the hypothesis that the level of education provided by an economy to its inhabitants is one of the major influences determining whether per capita income in a country is growing rapidly enough to narrow the gap with per capita income in the more advanced economies. The major effects appear to result from schooling at the secondary school level, and to a lesser degree in primary education. I will report on evidence on the magnitude of the role that education plays in determining the productivity catch-up rate of an economy.

A third important economic factor in the catch-up process is the extent of openness of an economy, which reflects the degree to which a country is involved in international trade (Section 9.5). Results of previous studies strongly support the argument that openness is a primary ingredient in economic growth. Countries with more open economies have been found to have higher rates of productivity catch-up than those that close their borders to trade. Interestingly, import openness is a stronger factor than the degree of export orientation of an economy. This result is consistent with the advantages of backwardness argument, since imports from advanced countries provide a more direct source of information on new technologies than the exports sent abroad by a country.

In Section 9.6, I consider the role of science and technology and, in particular, research and development (R&D) spending on the catch-up process among less developed countries. There is a very extensive literature that has demonstrated that R&D makes an important contribution to growth at the firm, industry, and national levels. There are also several cross-country studies of the effect of R&D on growth, but these are mainly confined to developed economies. Here, I find little evidence that R&D aids development among less developed countries of the world.

I also consider several other factors that appear to play a role in Section 9.7. The first of these is population growth. This factor is included in order to control for any country whose population growth is so rapid as to overwhelm any gains from the advantages of backwardness. In these cases, any gains in productivity from the introduction of new technology may be offset by rapid population growth and, as a result, do not show up as increases in per capita income.

A second is the extent of military expenditures. There is some dispute about the import of this factor. Some have argued that military expenditures may drain resources from productive investment and thus inhibit the process of technological catch-up. In contrast, others have argued that the production or import of advanced military equipment may be a source of new technology. I summarize the statistical findings with regard to this factor.

The third factor relates to political structure and the degree of democracy of a country's government, measured in various ways, such as the extent of voting rights within a country or the presence or absence of "official violence" against citizens. Are democratic governments more conducive to economic growth? Some have argued that they are for several reasons. First, they may be more consonant with the freedom to invest and to make entrepreneurial decisions. Second, they may provide greater legal security to the owners of the enterprises within a country and reduce the fears of expropriation, thus increasing the incentive to invest. Third, such forms of government may create greater political stability, thus mitigating against capital flight out of the country. On the other hand, some have suggested that authoritarian regimes, particularly in the third world, may provide for greater political stability and legal security of ownership. These alternative views have also been subjected to empirical testing.

The next factor considered in this survey is the type of economy a nation has – free market versus centrally planned. Here, again, there has been considerable debate about the relative advantages and disadvantages of centrally planned economies. Some have argued that such a state apparatus introduced too much inflexibility into economic structure and might thus act as an impediment to economic growth. However, others have suggested that central planning increased the amount of capital available for expansion and improved its allocation over free market forms of economies. The role of this factor has also been investigated in the literature on economic growth.

In Section 9.8, I look into the role inequality plays in economic growth. Various theories have been proposed as to why income inequality may affect economic growth; I will review them in this section. For example, a political economy theory argues that a greater degree of inequality will generally induce more redistribution through the political process, and the transfer payments and associated taxes may distort economic decisions. This will lower growth.

Section 9.9 looks into how institutions may impact economic growth. There is a large literature on how institutions affect economic development, beginning, perhaps, with North and Thomas (1973). They argued that progress in the Western world occurred because of the development of economic institutions that fostered economic growth through granting and protecting property rights of individuals.

Section 9.10 considers a potpourri of additional factors. The first of these is financial development. Several researchers have found that a more developed financial system in a country is positively associated with a higher rate of economic growth. The second is the role of natural resources and climate. There are several avenues by which the abundance (or lack thereof) of natural resources may affect economic growth that have been discussed in the pertinent literature. For example, natural resource dependence is usually believed to "crowd out" other types of capital and thereby slow economic growth (the so-called natural resource curse). The third is the role of foreign aid. There are two opposing views with regard to the effectiveness of foreign aid in promoting economic growth. The fourth is how the regulatory framework impacts on economic growth. In Section 9.11, special attention is given to the economic fortunes of Sub-Saharan Africa, East Asia, and the former Communist bloc countries. Concluding remarks are provided in the final section, Section 9.12.

9.2 Postwar Convergence

I begin with some descriptive statistics from the Penn World Tables database (see Heston, Summers, and Aten, 2006, for a description of the variables). I use here their variable RGDPL, real GDP per capita in 2000 constant prices (using the Laspeyre price index). Their data currently extend from 1950 to 2004, but the period of greatest data availability is from 1970 to 2003. I generally follow the country groups as reported in Hulten and Isaksson (2007). Data for all countries with RGDP figures in 1970 and 2003 are included.[1]

As shown in Figure 9.1, there is no evidence of general convergence in per capita income among this set of countries between 1970 and 2003 (also see Appendix Table 9.1 for more details). The coefficient of variation of RGDPL was virtually the same in 2003 as in 1970 (actually, slightly higher). The correlation between the growth rate of RGDPL and initial RGDPL was slightly positive instead of negative. The average annual growth rate of RGDPL among the advanced industrialized countries was 2.13 percent over the period. This compares with a figure of 1.46 percent for the upper middle income countries, 2.18 percent for the lower middle income countries, and 1.63 percent for the low income countries.

---

[1] The only exceptions are Qatar, Kuwait, and Brunei, which are extreme outliers in 1970. Their per capita income in 1970 was more than three times that of the next highest country (Switzerland).

Table 9.1. *Regressions of Growth in Real GDP per Capita (RGDP) on Initial RGDP for Various Sample Sizes, 1950–1991 and 1960–1991*

Dependent Variable	Constant	Initial RGDP	R^2	Adjusted– R^2	Std. Err. Of Reg.	Sample Size
A. 1950–91 Period						
ln(RATIO)	1.350** (8.50)	−1.299** (2.85)	0.209	0.181	0.316	Top 30
ln(RATIO)	1.128** (8.08)	−0.732 (1.54)	0.059	0.034	0.404	Top 50
ln(RATIO)	0.822** (9.06)	−0.172 (0.45)	0.003	−0.013	0.438	All (63)
B. 1960–91 Period						
ln(RATIO)	0.799** (10.10)	−0.410** (6.28)	0.686	0.669	0.281	Top 20
ln(RATIO)	0.779** (11.50)	−0.410** (5.29)	0.424	0.409	0.353	Top 40
ln(RATIO)	0.773** (13.60)	−0.406** (5.13)	0.312	0.300	0.376	Top 60
ln(RATIO)	0.635** (11.00)	−0.322** (3.48)	0.133	0.122	0.454	Top 80
ln(RATIO)	0.524** (10.40)	−0.246* (2.59)	0.058	0.049	0.478	All (111)

Notes: t-ratios are shown in parentheses below the coefficient estimate
Key:
RATIO = $RGDP_1 / RGDP_0$
$RGDP_t$: GDP per capita in year t, measured in units of $10,000s (1980 international prices)
* significant at the 5 percent level, 2-tail test
** significant at the 1 percent level, 2-tail test
Source: Penn World Tables, Mark 5.

There were two major success stories. The first were the so-called Original Asian Tigers. These five countries registered an average annual growth rate of RGDPL of 4.66 percent. Taiwan and South Korea had growth rates of 5.86 and 5.77 percent, respectively. The "New Asian Tigers" also showed impressive gains. Their average annual growth rate of RGDPL was 4.45 percent over the period. China registered a figure of 6.96 percent (even higher after 1980).We will say more about the "East Asian Miracle" in Section 9.11 later.

Among the seventy-one low income countries, some did fairly well, including Cuba, Romania, Egypt, Pakistan, and Botswana. However, many

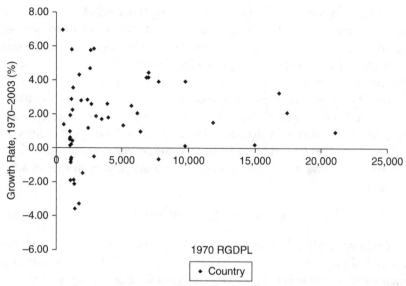

Figure 9.1 Real GDP per capita (RGDPL), 1970, selected countries, and average annual growth rate, 1970–2003.

did very poorly – in fact, showed up with a negative growth rate of RGDPL. In fact, of the seventy-one countries in this group, twenty had a negative growth rate in RGDPL. Many of these countries were in Sub-Saharan Africa (however, some Sub-Saharan African countries did well). We will say more about Sub-Saharan Africa in Section 9.11.

Because of both sample selection problems and measurement problems in early data, many studies have focused on the convergence issue for the postwar period only. Wolff (1994) used the Summers-Heston data set, which provided data on per capita GDP for 63 countries over the period 1950–91 and for 111 countries for the 1960–91 period (the source is the Penn World Tables Mark V; see Summers and Heston, 1988, for a description of the data). The figures for different countries were made comparable by converting the GDP data in each of the countries in terms of relative purchasing power parity (PPP) rather than currency exchange rates. They were expressed in units that Summers and Heston called "1980 international dollars," and the statistics were referred to as real per capita GDP (RGDP). These figures permitted a comparison of the performance of countries at different levels of development, including industrialized, middle income, centrally planned, and less developed ones.

I first show some of the early results from Wolff (1994) based on the Summers-Heston sample.[2] Most of the tests that will be described here are based on the 1960–91 sample, since this contained a larger sample of countries, though all of them were repeated for the 1950–91 sample, with rather similar results, except where noted otherwise. There were three measures of real GDP per capita in the early Summers-Heston data: the first, RGDP, based on PPP indices; the second, based on PPP with a term of trade adjustment; and the third, based on a chained price index of PPP indices. Results were quite similar among the three measures and are reported for only the first.

Table 9.1 shows regression results for the basic convergence estimating equation:

$$\ln \text{RATIO} = b_0 + b_1 \text{RGDP}_0 + \varepsilon \qquad (9.1)$$

where ln is the natural logarithm, RATIO = the ratio of RGDP at the end of the end of the period to that at the beginning, ln RATIO is the percentage increase in RGDP over the period, RGDP_0 is RGDP at the beginning of the period, and ε is a stochastic error term. The convergence hypothesis predicts that the coefficient b_1 will be negative (that is, countries further behind at the beginning will show more rapid increases in GDP per capita).

The analysis was conducted on different sample sizes. For the 1950–91 period, it began with the top thirty countries, as ranked by RGDP in 1950, and then expanded the sample to the top fifty and then the full sample of countries. The coefficient was negative in each case, but statistically significant (and at the 1 percent level) for only the sample consisting of the top thirty countries. For the 1960–91 sample, it began with the top twenty countries, as ranked by 1960 RGDP, and then the sample was expanded by successively adding the next twenty countries. The coefficient b_1 was negative for all samples, statistically significant at the 1 percent level for all samples except the full sample, where the coefficient was significant at the 5 percent level.

Thus, it is clear that convergence was a powerful force operating through all levels of development, though the force was stronger in the period after 1960 than before. Moreover, convergence was a much stronger force among the industrialized and middle income countries than among the less developed ones. This is apparent by examining the coefficient estimate of b_1 and its t-ratio, and the R^2 and adjusted-R^2 statistics, all of which declined as the sample was expanded to lower income countries, and the standard error of the regression, which increased as the sample size was enlarged. Among the

[2] The paper was originally presented at ESCAP/UNCTC Symposium on Transnational Technology toward the Year 2000 in the ESCAP Region in April 1990, in Bangkok.

top twenty countries, the R^2 statistic was 0.69 (69 percent of the variation in RGDP growth rates was explained solely by the country's initial RGDP level), whereas among the full sample, the R^2 was only 0.05 (5 percent of the differences explained).

Other studies have reached similar conclusions on the basis of this data source. Baumol and Wolff (1988) used the coefficient of variation in RGDP as their measure of convergence. They found that this index declined among the top third or so over the 1950–81 period, though its trend was weaker than among OECD countries alone. However, once all countries were included in the sample, the coefficient of variation failed to show a downward trend. Baumol and Wolff also found that productivity convergence slowed during the 1970s, as did Abramovitz (1986). However, this result was disputed by Dowrick and Nguyen (1989), who found for a sample of twenty-four OECD countries that, once differences in the rate of investment were controlled for, there was no evidence of a convergence "slowdown" in the 1970s.

Soete and Verspagen (1993) used data for 114 countries from the Penn World Tables Mark 5 over the periods 1950 to 1973 and 1973 to 1988. They used cluster analysis and identified four distinct groups of countries: (1) the "leading elite," consisting of the advanced industrialized countries of the time; (ii) the "strongly catching up countries," consisting of Israel, Korea, and Singapore; (iii) the "catching up" countries; and (iv) the "falling behind" countries, consisting of 26 less developed countries. They also found significant break points in time trends. First, they found that the period from 1950 to about 1973 appeared as a historically unique period of convergence among OECD countries. This convergence pattern came to an end in the OECD countries by the early 1970s. Second, among the Asian "tigers," the convergence pattern was of more recent origin, since the early 1970s. Third, for other Asian countries, South American countries, African countries, and other less developed countries, convergence in terms of GDP per capita or technological innovation did not really take off.

Castellacci and Archibugi (2008) and Castellacci (2008) argued that three distinct "convergence clubs" or "technology clubs" could be identified in the data on cross-country per capita income. They argued that cross-country differences in the ability to innovate and to imitate foreign technologies determined the existence of clustering, polarization, and convergence clubs. The studies investigated the characteristics of different technology clubs and the growth trajectories that they followed over time using cluster analysis and factor analysis. Their technology variables included patenting activity, the degree of Internet penetration, tertiary science and engineering enrollment, literacy rate, and mean years of schooling. The period of coverage was 1990 to 2000. The results identified three distinct technology clubs and showed that these were characterized by very different technological characteristics and growth behavior. These clubs corresponded to the advanced industrialized nations, the intermediate group, and a large group of less developed countries. The first two groups were found to be much more technologically dynamic than the less developed countries. The intermediate follower group in fact moved closer to the technological frontier over the 1990s while the marginalized third group experienced an enlargement of its gap in terms of per capita income and innovative capabilities.

Castellacci (2008) also found that different factors influenced development in the three groups. In the advanced group, the most important growth variables were the investment share of GDP, the degree of innovative activity (both patents and scientific articles), computers per capita, the percentage of the population at the tertiary educational level, and the catch-up variable. In the follower group, the most important variables were physical capital accumulation, the export share of GDP, patenting activity, traditional infrastructure, and secondary education. In the marginalized group, development was negatively related to the openness of the economy and positively related to structural change variables (industry and service shares of GDP), and traditional infrastructure. He argued that these three "clubs" that differed in terms of initial conditions tended to converge to different steady states (see the discussion of the Lucas model in Chapter 2).

Neumayer (2003) pointed out another issue related to the convergence in per capita income across countries. Using data from the World Bank and several other sources over the 1960 to 1999 period, he examined a wide range of fundamental aspects of living standards. These included life expectancy, infant survival, educational enrollment rates, literacy, and telephone and television availability. His country sample varied from 74 to 164 countries, depending on the variable used. He included several measures of convergence including changes in the coefficient of variation and regression analysis. His surprising finding was that despite the lack of convergence in income per capita among a wide range of countries, he found strong evidence of convergence in these other indicators of living standards. In contrast, Hobijn and Franses (2001), using a somewhat difference set of living standard indicators, including daily caloric and daily protein intake, infant mortality, and life expectancy at birth, found no evidence of convergence at least for these variables over the period 1965 to 1990.

Comin, Hobijn, and Rovito (2006) considered a related issue. They examined differences in the intensity with which ten major technologies were used in 185 countries across the world by calculating how many years ago these technologies were used in the United States at the same intensity as they were used in these countries. They focused on the period from 1950 to 2000. They referred to these time lags as technology usage lags and compared them with lags in real GDP per capita. Their list of technologies included (i) electricity production, (ii) Internet and PC usage, (iii) telephones and cell phones, (iv) airplane usage, and (v) tractors. They reported three main findings. First, technology usage lags were very large and of the same order as lags in real GDP per capita. Second, technology usage lags were highly correlated (on the order of 80 to 90 percent) with lags in per capita income. Third, technology usage lags were highly correlated across technologies. They concluded that technology usage disparities might account for a large part of cross-country TFP differentials.

Acemoglu and Zilibotti (2001) made a different type of argument to explain productivity differences across countries. They noted that many technologies used by the less developed countries (LDCs) were developed in the OECD economies and were designed to make optimal use of the skills of workers in these richer countries. However, differences in the supply of skills created a mismatch between the requirements of these technologies and the skills available among workers in LDCs. This mismatch, in turn, led to low productivity in the less developed countries. Therefore, even in the case when all countries have equal access to new technologies, this technology-skill mismatch could lead to sizable differences in TFP and output per worker between developed and less developed countries. They used data from the United Nations General Industrial Statistics to estimate TFP levels in twenty-seven three-digit manufacturing industries in twenty-two countries in 1990. The country sample included both advanced and less developed economies. Their results provided evidence that the mismatch between advanced technology and the low skill levels of the workforce in LDCs accounted for a large fraction of the difference in output per worker among these countries.

The greater difficulty of the less developed countries in achieving convergence is probably explained in good part by the likelihood that in very poor countries, low investment rates, lack of education, impeding social arrangements, and other such influences tend to swamp the advantages of backwardness – the fact that less developed countries have more to learn from the leaders than the leaders have to learn from them. Only in a country with a sufficient head start do these forces of convergence outweigh those promoting stagnancy.

9.3 The Role of Investment

The first factor considered is investment, one of the strong forces noted in Chapter 1. Previous work documented a remarkably close correspondence between output per worker (or GDP per capita) and capital stock per worker (or per capita). Maddison (1982, p. 52) and Baumol, Blackman, and Wolff (1989, chapter 8) both reported extremely high correlations between GDP per worker and capital (gross fixed nonresidential capital stock) per worker both over time within country and across countries by year among the Group of Seven over the 1870–1979 period. Lipsey and Kravis (1987, pp. 58–9) also computed very high correlation coefficients between per capita real non-residential capital stock and real per capita income among fifty countries in 1970 and thirty-four countries in 1975 (0.95 in the latter case).

Though the association between capital and output of an economy is very close, the direction of causation may run two ways. On the one hand, a nation with a large amount of capital can be expected to produce a relatively high output level. On the other, a nation with a large output can be expected to have a correspondingly high investment rate. Statistical tests tend to show that both effects are present, but their relative strengths are difficult to ascertain (see Abramovitz, 1979, for further discussion of these points).

Though Wolff (1994) did not have strong evidence on the issue here, he investigated the effects of investment on the rate of growth of RGDP. For the analysis, he again relied on the Summers-Heston data. The explanatory variable was INVRATE, the average investment rate, defined as the ratio of investment to GDP, both in 1980 international dollars, averaged over the period of analysis (1960–91). The estimating equation then becomes:

$$\ln\left(RGDP_{91} / RGDP_{60}\right) = b_0 + b_1 RGDP_0 + b_2 INVRATE + \varepsilon \quad (9.2)$$

Results, shown in Table 9.2, indicate strong support for the role of investment in explaining productivity convergence. The coefficient of INVRATE was positive and significant at the 1 percent level. Moreover, with the inclusion of INVRATE in the equation, the catch-up variable, $RGDP_{60}$, became significant at the 1 percent level for the full sample of countries.[3] Initial RGDP and the average investment rate explained 44 percent of the variation of country RGDP growth rates over the 1960–91 period.

---

[3]   It should be noted that the INVRATE variable was not available for centrally planned economies, so these countries were excluded in the analysis.

Table 9.2. *Regressions of Growth in RGDP on Initial Relative RGDP, the Investment Rate, Education, Population Growth, and Trade, 1960–1991*

Constant	$RGDP_{60}$	INVRATE	Education PRIM	Education SCND	POPGRT	Trade Variable	R^2	Adj. R^2	Std. Error	Sample Size	Trade Variable
0.52** (10.40)	-0.25* (2.59)						0.06	0.05	0.48	111	
-0.18 (1.91)	-0.30** (3.95)	0.039** (8.10)					0.44	0.42	0.38	102[a]	
-0.41** (3.15)	-0.40** (4.99)		1.14** (7.61)				0.39	0.38	0.39	111	
0.15* (2.27)	-0.49** (5.87)			1.17** (7.64)			0.39	0.38	0.38	111	
-0.48** (3.94)	-0.37** (4.93)	0.028** (4.99)	0.62** (3.56)				0.50	0.49	0.36	102[a]	
-0.14 (1.56)	-0.40** (4.81)	0.027** (4.09)		0.58** (2.61)			0.47	0.46	0.37	102[a]	
-0.44* (2.38)	-0.36** (4.53)	0.027** (4.55)	0.62** (3.50)		-1.00 (0.25)		0.50	0.48	0.36	102[a]	
-0.35 (1.90)	-0.48** (4.61)	0.026** (3.98)		0.81** (2.84)	6.90 (1.29)		0.48	0.46	0.37	102[a]	
-0.39** (3.09)	-0.39** (5.57)	0.020** (3.41)	0.53** (3.08)			0.54* (2.37)	0.50	0.48	0.33	90	EXPGDP
-0.42** (3.56)	-0.38** (5.48)	0.020** (3.43)	0.59** (3.57)			0.56** (2.70)	0.52	0.50	0.33	94	EXPMGDP
-0.49** (4.11)	-0.36** (5.28)	0.020** (3.61)	0.61** (3.78)			0.65** (3.49)	0.54	0.52	0.33	94	IMPMGDP

(continued)

Table 9.2. *(continued)*

Constant	RGDP$_{60}$	INVRATE	Education		POPGRT	Trade Variable	R^2	Adj. R^2	Std. Error	Sample Size	Trade Variable
			PRIM	SCND							EXIMGDP
-0.46**	-0.37**	0.019**	0.60**			0.66**	0.54	0.52	0.33	94	EXIMGDP
(3.89)	(5.45)	(3.45)	(3.69)			(3.25)					

Notes: t-ratios are shown in parentheses below the coefficient estimate

Key:

Dependent variable: ln(RGDP91/RGDP60)

RGDP$_{60}$: RGDP per capita in 1960, measured in units of $10,000s (1980 international prices). *Data source*: Penn World Tables, Mark 5, diskettes

RGDP$_{91}$: RGDP per capita in 1991, measured in units of $10,000s (1980 international prices). *Data source*: Penn World Tables, Mark 5, diskettes

INVRATE: ratio of investment to RGDP, both in 1980 international dollars, averaged over the 1960–91 period. Data source: Penn World Tables, Mark 5

PRIM: Proportion of age group enrolled in primary school, averaged between 1965 and 1983. *Data source*: World Bank, World Development Report 1986, Table 29

SCND: Proportion of age group enrolled in secondary school, averaged between 1965 and 1983. *Data source*: World Bank, World Development Report 1986, Table 29

EXPGDP: exports of goods and non-factor services as a proportion of GDP in 1984. *Data source*: World Bank, World

EXPMGDP: merchandise exports as a proportion of GDP in 1984. *Data source*: World Bank, World Development Report 1986, Table 10

IMPMGDP: merchandise imports as a proportion of GDP in 1984. *Data source*: World Bank, World Development Report 1986, Table 11

EXIMGDP: the average of merchandise exports and merchandise imports as a proportion of GDP in 1984. Data source: World Bank, World Development Report 1986, Tables 10 and 11

POPGRT: Average annual rate of population growth over the 1960–91 period. Data source: Penn World Tables, Mark 5

[a] Excludes centrally planned economies

* significant at the 5 percent level, 2-tail test

** significant at the 1 percent level, 2-tail test

Many other studies have reported similar econometric findings of a positive effect of the investment rate on either output or per capita output growth, when a catch-up term (such as initial per capita income) was included in the regression specification. These include Kormendi and Meguire (1985), who used a sample of forty-seven countries drawn from the *International Financial Statistics* of the International Monetary Fund for the period 1950–77; Hess (1989) for a sample of sixty-six LDCs over the 1970–85 period; Rassekh (1992) on the basis of a sample of OECD countries over the 1950–85 period; Barro (1991) for the Summers-Heston sample (excluding the oil exporters) over the 1960–85 period; and Dowrick and Nguyen (1989) for both a sample of twenty-four OECD countries over the 1950–81 period and the full Summers and Heston sample over this period. Interestingly, both Dowrick and Nguyen (1989) and Wolff (1994) found that as the Summers and Heston sample was enlarged from the top third of countries to the full sample, the R^2 statistic declined somewhat but the t-ratio of the investment rate variable did not generally decline.

Several studies have attempted to separate out the effects of investment and technical change on the growth in labor productivity. The objective is to determine the relative contributions of capital accumulation and technological progress to the increase in labor productivity over time. The standard model begins with an aggregate Cobb-Douglas production function of the form:

$$Y_t = A_t L_t^{\alpha} K_t^{(1-\alpha)} \qquad (9.3a)$$

where Y_t is total output (usually measured by GDP) at time t, L_t is employment at time t, K_t is total capital stock at time t, A_t is the level of technology at time t, and α is the average wage share over the period.[4] Two different wage shares are typically used: (1) individual country averages of the ratio of wages to GDP over the full period of analysis and (2) the mean over all the countries of the individual country wage shares, which will be called "the international average." TFP here is defined as:

$$TFP_t = Y_t / [L_t^{\alpha} K_t^{(1-\alpha)}]$$

or

$$Ln\, TFP_t = LnY_t - \alpha Ln\, L_t - (1-\alpha)\, Ln\, K_t \qquad (9.3b)$$

---

[4] See Chapter 2 for more discussion of the Cobb-Douglas model.

TFP growth, ρ, is then defined as:

$$\rho = d(\ln Y_t)/dt - \alpha d(\ln L_t)/dt - (1-\alpha) d(\ln K_t)/dt \qquad (9.3c)$$

In the case of the Cobb-Douglas production function,

$$d(\ln a_t)/dt = \rho_t$$

It also follows directly that

$$\pi_t = \rho_t + (1-\alpha) d(\ln k_t)/dt \qquad (9.3d)$$

where π is the rate of labor productivity growth, $k \equiv K/L$, the ratio of the capital stock to labor, and $d(\ln k_t)/dt$ is the rate of growth of the capital-labor ratio. From this formula, it should be clear that labor productivity growth is equal to TFP growth plus the rate of growth of the capital-labor ratio multiplied by the capital share.

Hulten and Isaksson (2007) examined the relative importance of capital accumulation and technological progress as factors explaining differences in output per worker among a sample of 112 countries over the period from 1970 to 2000. Their data source was the Penn World Tables Version 6.1. To check the robustness of their findings, they used several different models of the growth process and different assumptions about the underlying data. Although different models of growth produced different estimates of the relative contributions of capital formation and TFP to output per worker, they found that differences in technical efficiency as measured by relative levels of TFP were the dominant factor accounting for the difference in levels of labor productivity across countries.

The opposite conclusion was reached by Kumar and Russell (2002), whose decomposition differed from that of Hulten and Isaksson (2007). They decomposed labor productivity growth into three components: (1) technological change as measured by shifts in the world production frontier, (2) technological catch-up as measured by movements toward or away from the frontier, and (3) capital accumulation. They used a sample of fifty-seven countries over the period from 1965 to 1990 from the Penn World Tables Version 5.6. They estimated that both labor productivity growth and labor productivity convergence were driven primarily by capital accumulation, not TFP.

In sum, despite the somewhat disparate results on the decomposition of labor productivity growth, the vast bulk of evidence indicates that investment plays a major and significant role in productivity convergence among all nations of the world.

9.4 Education and Productivity Convergence

I suggested in the Introduction that one of the prime reasons, besides low investment rates, for the relatively weak catch-up performance of the less developed countries over the postwar period was the failure of the lagging countries to keep up with, absorb, and utilize new technological and product information, and to benefit from the international dissemination of technology. Countries only slightly behind the leaders, in contrast, have been extremely successful in doing so. Indeed, for these countries, having more to learn from the leaders than the leaders can learn from them has constituted a major element in what has been referred to as the "advantages of backwardness." But here, as elsewhere, there can be too much of a (not so) good thing. A bit of backwardness may contribute to growth, but beyond some point it seems clearly to become pure handicap.

One of the elements that can be expected to explain an economy's ability to absorb information and new technology is the education of its populace, the second of the strong forces. The LDCs are well behind the industrialized countries, particularly at the secondary and higher levels, in terms of share of the population receiving education. As with investment, Wolff (1994) tested statistically for the role of education in the growth process by adding another new variable, the share of a country's relevant age group receiving formal education, to the initial level of RGDP for the country in question. The resulting equation becomes:

$$\ln\left(RGDP_{91} \,/\, RGDP_{60}\right) = b_0 + b_1 RGDP_0 + b_2 EDUC + \varepsilon \qquad (9.4)$$

For the education variable, EDUC, Wolff (1994) used two alternative statistics, one indicating the proportion of the relevant age group receiving formal primary education (PRIM), and the other being the corresponding figure for secondary education (SCND).

The results, shown in Table 9.2, were almost as strong as those for investment. The coefficients of the two education variables were positive and significant at the 1 percent level. Both primary school and secondary school education appeared to have about the same effect. Moreover, with the inclusion of the education variable, the coefficient of $RGDP_{60}$ was negative and significant at the 1 percent level. Thus, in effect, countries with similar educational levels were shown quite consistently to be converging among themselves, in terms of RGDP, though not catching up with countries whose educational levels were higher.

Equation 9.5 shows the results when both the investment rate variable and the education variable are combined in a single regression equation:

$$\ln\left(RGDP_{91} / RGDP_{60}\right) = b_0 + b_1 RGDP_0 + b_2 INVRATE + b_3 EDUC + \varepsilon \quad (9.5)$$

In the combined regression, both investment and education were positive and significant at the 1 percent level. In the regression with PRIM, 50 percent of the variation among country growth rates was explained; with SCND, 47 percent of the variation was explained. Primary school enrollment appeared to be a slightly stronger determinant of growth than secondary school enrollment, once differences in investment rates were controlled for. This was probably due to the fact that investment behavior was positively correlated with the presence of a trained labor force, for which secondary school education was a necessity. In other words, the presence of a trained labor force likely acted as a stimulus to investment. However, the differences in statistical results between primary school and secondary school enrollment rates were not great.

Baumol, Blackman, and Wolff (1989, chapter 9) also reported similar (and more detailed) results for the 1960–81 period, as did Barro (1991) for the Summers-Heston sample (excluding the oil exporters) over the 1960–85 period. Mankiw, Romer, and Weil (1992) also found a highly significant effect of education on growth among countries at all levels of development. Using data from the Summers and Heston (1984) Penn World Tables and UNESCO data on educational attainment, they found, first of all, that the standard Solow model accounted for about 60 percent of the cross-country variation in GDP per worker in a comprehensive sample of ninety-eight non-oil-producing countries over the 1960–85 period. Second, using their augmented Solow model (see Chapter 2 for a description of the model), it accounted for almost 80 percent of the cross-country variation in their sample.

Their education variable, SCHOOL, was computed as the fraction of the eligible population (aged twelve to seventeen) enrolled in secondary school multiplied by the fraction of the working-age population that was of school age (ages fifteen to nineteen). Two types of equations were estimated. In the first, the logarithm of GDP per working-age person in 1985 was the dependent variable. In the second, the rate of growth of GDP per working-age person over the 1960–85 period was the dependent variable. In both cases, the coefficient of the logarithm of SCHOOL was positive and significant at the 1 percent level. This held for the full sample of ninety-eight countries and a sample of seventy-five intermediate and less developed countries. For a sample of OECD countries, the coefficient was positive but significant at only the 5 percent level.

One interesting variant of this model was performed by Ram (2007). He added a measure of IQ to the same estimating equation used by Mankiw, Romer, and Weil (1992). His IQ measure was gleaned from IQ tests given in eighty-one countries and standardized by Lynn and Vannhanen (2002) for cross-country comparability. He found that his IQ measure had a positive and significant effect (at the 1 percent level) on the rate of growth of GDP per working-age person over the 1960 to 1985 period for the same sample of ninety-eight countries. Moreover, when the IQ variable was included in the regression equation, both the size and the significance level of the coefficient of SCHOOL decreased substantially, and, in fact, SCHOOL was no longer significant at the 5 percent level.

Hanushek and Kimko (2000) also found that direct measures of labor force quality were more strongly linked to productivity growth than raw measures of schooling. They used international mathematics and science test scores as a measure of labor quality. The tests were administered by the International Association for the Evaluation of Educational Achievement and by the International Assessment of Educational Progress. Test scores were available for eighty countries. They combined all of the information on international math and science tests available for each country through 1991. They looked at the effects of these test scores on the rate of growth of real GDP per capita from 1960 to 1990 obtained from the Penn World Tables on both test scores and various measures of schooling, including mean years of schooling and enrollment rates at different levels of schooling. Their main finding was that the coefficient of their test score variables was positive and highly significant (usually at the 1 percent level). Moreover, once the test score variable was included in the regression equation, the coefficient of their schooling variables became, in most cases, statistically insignificant.[5]

Mamuneas, Savvides, and Stengos (2001) argued that the relation between economic growth and education may be nonlinear in nature rather than the usual linear relation imposed in most cross-country regressions. They noted that the vast majority of these studies on the empirics of economic growth assumed that human capital exerts the same effect on economic growth both across countries (intratemporally) and across time (intertemporally) and assumed a linear or log linear relationship. The authors here used panel data over three decades – 1960–70, 1970–80, and 1980–90. They used educational data derived from Barro and Lee (1996). They used a variety of variables, including mean years of schooling, mean years of schooling at

[5] Two more recent papers on the subject, Jamison, Jamison, and Hanushek (2006) and Hanushek and Wößmann (2007), provided similar findings using more updated data and an expanded sample of countries.

the primary level, mean years at the postprimary level, educational enrollment rates at the primary and secondary levels, and educational attainment separately for males and females. Their sample covered ninety-three countries at various stages of development. They used a semiparametric estimation technique to allow for nonlinearities in the data. Their main finding was that education exerted a nonlinear effect on per capita income growth. There were also important differences in the growth effect of educational attainment by gender and by level of education.

Another approach to this issue is to look at the effects of the *change* in educational attainment on the growth in output per worker. As discussed in Chapter 5, this approach is more consistent with the growth accounting literature than relating the growth in productivity to the initial *level* of education in a country. The results reported in Chapter 5, as well as the earlier results of Wolff (2000), indicated that among OECD countries at least, there was generally no statistically significant effect of the change in education, as measured by mean schooling, various enrollment rates, and various measures of education attainment, on the growth of output per worker, though a couple of papers differed in this result.

Benhabib and Spiegel (1994) reported similar results for a sample of seventy-eight countries at all levels of development over the period from 1965 to 1985. Their per capita income data were taken from the Penn World Tables, and their measure of human capital was based on mean years of schooling provided by Kyriacou (1991).Using cross-country estimates of physical and human capital stocks, they estimated growth accounting regressions implied by a Cobb-Douglas aggregate production function. Their results indicated that the change in human capital did not enter significantly in explaining income per capita growth rates. However, they did find that in an alternative model in which TFP growth depended on a nation's human capital stock level the regression results indicated a positive role for human capital.

Krueger and Lindahl (2001) took issue with these and similar results on the relation between the growth in human capital and per capita income growth. They started out with the standard Mincerian wage equation:

$$\mathrm{Ln}\,W_i = a_0 + a_1 \ln S_i + u_i$$

where W_i is the earnings of individual i, a_0 is a constant term, a_1 is the rate of return to schooling, S_i is the schooling level of individual i, and u_i is a stochastic error term. They then showed how the Mincerian wage equation with the added assumption that the rate of return to schooling is constant over time led to a specification akin to equation (9.4)

$$\ln\left(RGDPW_1 \,/\, RGDPW_0\right) / \left(t_1 - t_0\right) = b_0 + b_1\Delta\left(EDUC\right) + \varepsilon$$

where $\ln(RGDP_1/RGDP_0)/(t_1 - t_0)$ is the annual rate of growth in real GDP per worker from time 0 to time 1, $\Delta(EDUC)$ is the change in the average education of the workforce, and ε is a stochastic error term. They argued that the finding of little or no correlation between the growth of output per worker and the change in average schooling appeared to be a spurious result of the extremely high rate of measurement error in first-differenced cross-country education data. After accounting for measurement error, Krueger and Lindahl (2001) showed that the effect of changes in educational attainment on income growth in cross-country data was at least as great as microeconometric estimates of the rate of return to years of schooling derived from the standard Mincerian wage equation. Moreover, they argued that another finding of the macrogrowth literature – that economic growth depends positively on the initial stock of human capital – resulted from imposing linearity and constant-coefficient assumptions on the estimates. These restrictions were often rejected by the data, and once either assumption was relaxed the initial level of education had little effect on economic growth for the average country.

Thus, what the statistical results suggest is that few if any nations can be totally excluded from the convergence process. For many of them it would appear to be a latent influence, waiting to emerge. Apparently, an important means to achieve this emergence is provision of education to its population to a degree commensurate with that of the most industrialized countries.

9.5 International Trade and Foreign Direct Investment

As noted previously, openness to trade should have a positive impact on the catch-up process of more backward economies, since trade is an important conduit of new technology and knowledge. However, unlike investment and education, trade openness appears to be a weak force for convergence.

The effect of trade openness on per capita GDP growth was tested for with the following specification:

$$\ln\left(RGDP_{91} \,/\, RGDP_{60}\right) = b_0 + b_1 RGDP_0 + b_2 INVRATE$$
$$+ b_3 EDUC + b_4 TRADE + \varepsilon \qquad (9.6)$$

Trade openness (TRADE) was measured in several ways: (i) exports of goods and nonfactor services as a proportion of GDP in 1984, (ii) merchandise exports as a proportion of GDP in 1984, (iii) merchandise imports as a proportion of GDP in 1984, and (iv) the average of merchandise exports and merchandise imports as a proportion of GDP in 1984.

Results shown in Table 9.2 confirmed the significance of all the trade measures on GDP per capita growth. All four variables had positive coefficients, as predicted; the first was significant at the 5 percent level, and the other three at the 1 percent level. Merchandise imports as a share of GDP had a stronger effect than that of either total exports or merchandise exports as a share of GDP, as indicated by their respective coefficients and t-ratios.

Several other studies have also documented the positive effects of openness on economic growth. Nishimizu and Robinson (1984) used data for Japan, Korea, Turkey, and Yugoslavia, mainly from the 1960s and 1970s. In general, they found that policies that promoted import substitution (reduced import openness) had a negative effect on output growth, whereas export promotion regimes had a positive effect on growth. Kormendi and Meguire (1985) used a sample of forty-seven countries drawn from the *International Financial Statistics* of the International Monetary Fund for the period 1950–77. Their regression specification included a catch-up term (initial per capita income) and the mean growth of exports as a proportion of a country's output as a measure of openness. They found some evidence of a positive effect of the export measure on country output growth, though its statistical significance depended on the particular specification used. Dollar (1992) used as his measure of trade openness an index of foreign exchange rate distortion (the greater the distortion, the less open was international trade in the country). His sample covered ninety-five less developed countries over the period 1976 to 1985. He reported a negative and significant relation between the growth in income per capita and his measure of foreign exchange distortion.

Hallak and Levinsohn (2004) criticized many of these "standard" studies on the effects of trade on productivity growth on methodological grounds. These studies used macroeconomic data on the growth of output per worker (or per capita) and a measure of trade openness such as the ratio of exports plus imports to GDP. In the standard growth regression, the former was regressed on the latter as well as a number of other control variables. However, such regressions were subject to two kinds of problems: endogeneity and omitted variable bias. The former arose because trade policy was endogenous to economic performance. The usual conclusion was that more openness induced greater growth. However, causality might run the other way. Countries with poor economic performance might have a greater propensity to restrict international trade through protective tariffs and the like. The latter problem arose if variables omitted from the regression were those that really determine the relationship between openness and productivity performance. One example was the role of institutional infrastructure. It is likely that "good" institutions may both foster growth and be correlated with trade openness policies. In this case, it may be the quality of institutions that really induces growth.

Several attempts have been made to get around the problem of endogeneity and omitted variable bias. Ben-David (1996) examined the relation between international trade and productivity growth by focusing on groups of countries comprising major trade partners. He used trade data for forty-three countries at different levels of development and matched countries on the basis of their principal trading partners in terms of both imports and exports for the year 1960. He then examined the degree of convergence in per capita income over the period 1960 to 1985 for each of the trading groups. His main finding was that the majority of these trade-based groups exhibited significant convergence in income per capita. Furthermore, a comparison of the trade-based groups with a group of randomly selected countries found that the former exhibited more convergence than the latter.

Frankel and Romer (1999) used geography as a way of avoiding the problem of endogeneity. The trade intensity of a country depends on both policy-related and geographical barriers to trade. A problem with policy-related trade barriers, as Hallak and Levinsohn (2004) argued, is that they are influenced by both income performance (the endogeneity problem) and other factors omitted from the usual growth regressions (the omitted variables problem). Geographical trade barriers, such as distance to other countries and proximity to oceans and major population centers, are affected neither by economic performance nor by any omitted variable that also affects economic performance. (Omitted variables may still be correlated with geographical trade barriers, even though they do not affect them.) Frankel and Romer (1999) based their estimation strategy on the exogenous character of geographical barriers to trade, which they used as an instrument for trade intensity in an instrumental variables regression. The instrumental variables approach then essentially used the relationship between geography and income or productivity growth to estimate the effect of policy-induced barriers to trade.

Frankel and Romer (1999) used bilateral trade data from the IFS Direction of Trade Statistics. They were obtained for sixty-three countries in 1985. The income and population data were from the Penn World Tables

Mark 5.6. They found that the geography-related trade component affected income growth. They estimated that an increase of 10 percentage points in the share of trade in GDP raised per capita income by about 10 to 20 percent. This result was consistent with the earlier results, which thus appear robust to the instrumentation of trade intensity with geographic (predetermined) variables.

In any case, as Hallak and Levinsohn (2004) noted, the result on the positive effect of trade was not robust to alternative empirical specifications that control for omitted variables. This was also true for variables related to the geographic location of a country. In this case, geography is thought of as a direct determinant of long-run growth, in contrast to the use Frankel and Romer (1999) made of geographical trade barriers. One example is the distance of a country from the equator. Easterly and Levine (2003) pointed to the fact that in comparison to temperate climates, tropical environments tended to have poor crop yields, more debilitating diseases, and endowments that could not effectively use production technologies developed in more temperate zones to motivate the inclusion of "distance from the equator" in the empirical specification.

Rodriguez and Rodrik (2001) included this variable as an additional control in the Frankel and Romer (1999) regression framework and found that the effect of trade on income per capita was substantially reduced and, indeed, was no longer statistically significant. Other geographic variables, such as the percentage of a country's land area that was in the Tropics or a set of other regional dummies, were also considered in alternation. The inclusion of these variables had similar dampening effects on the estimation results, with the positive and significant coefficient of trade on growth disappearing.

Chang, Kaltani, and Loayza (2005) investigated how the effect of trade openness on economic growth depended on complementary reforms that helped a country take advantage of international competition. Their sample consisted of an unbalanced panel comprising eighty-two countries. For each, the data set included at most eight observations consisting of nonoverlapping five-year averages over the period from 1960 to 2000. The countries covered both developed and less developed economies. They then presented panel evidence on how the growth effect of openness depended on a variety of structural characteristics. This was based on a nonlinear growth regression specification that interacted a proxy of trade openness with proxies of educational investment, financial depth, inflation stabilization, public infrastructure, governance, labor-market flexibility, ease of firm entry, and ease of firm exit. Their main finding was that the growth effects of openness were positive and economically significant if certain complementary reforms were also undertaken.

Galor and Mountford (2008) examined the effects of international trade on productivity for a wide cross section of countries. Their interest was to explain the role of trade in the "great divergence" in productivity performance between the advanced industrialized countries and the less developed economies. Their paper argued that the differential effects of international trade on the demand for human capital across countries had been a major determinant of the worldwide distribution of income and population. In the advanced countries the gains from trade were directed toward investment in education and growth in income per capita, whereas a significant portion of the gains in less developed economies were channeled toward population growth. They used data for 132 countries over the period 1985 to 1990. Their cross-country regression results showed that, as predicted, trade had positive effects on fertility and negative effects on education in non-OECD economies and, conversely, had a negative effect on fertility and a positive effect on human capital formation in OECD economies.

Vamvakidis (2002) took a historical perspective on the relation between trade and growth. He first verified previous results of a positive effect of trade openness on growth for the period 1970 to 1990 on the basis of Penn World Tables data for eighty-three countries. He used six indicators of openness, including tariff rates, tariff barriers, import duties as a share of total imports, and the average trade share. He also controlled for the investment rate, schooling, and a catch-up effect. However, for the period 1950 to 1970, he did not find a statistically significant relation between trade openness and the growth in per capita income. Moreover, for the 1920 to 1940 period, the correlation between the two variables was actually negative. He concluded that the positive effect of trade openness on growth was only of recent origin (since about 1970).

As discussed in Chapter 4, foreign direct investment (FDI) is a factor affecting income convergence highly related to trade. Several studies have looked at the impact of FDI. Aitken and Harrison (1999) looked at both productivity and FDI data on a sample of Venezuelan plants between 1976 and 1989. FDI penetration was measured by the share of employment of foreign-owned firms in total employment. Their main finding was of a *negative* relation between increased FDI presence and the TFP growth of domestic plants. This effect, as Aitken and Harrison noted, could be a short-term response. The relationship might change in the long run.

Akin and Kose (2007) investigated the changing nature of growth spillovers between advanced economies, "the North," and less developed countries, "the South," as affected by rising international trade and FDI. They used a database of macroeconomic and sectoral level variables for 106 countries spanning the period 1960 to 2005. They further divided the South into two groups, the "Emerging South" and the "Developing South," on the basis of the extent of their integration into the global economy. Using a panel regression framework, they found that the impact of the northern economic activity on the Emerging South as measured by output growth declined during the globalization period, 1986 to 2005. In contrast, the growth linkages between the North and Developing South were rather stable over time.

Das, Nath, and Yildiz (2008) used data for ninety-three countries at all levels of development over the period from 1970 to 2000 to examine the effects of FDI on cross-country differences in productivity. They constructed a spatial Gini coefficient of labor productivity across countries and weighted indices of FDI and gross domestic investment (GDI). They found little evidence that FDI decreased differences in productivity for the entire sample of countries. However, they did find that FDI, GDI, and labor productivity levels were cointegrated for developed and high and middle income developing countries. They concluded that FDI reduced disparities in productivity among high and middle income developing countries while it increased productivity gaps among advanced industrialized countries. In middle income developing countries, GDI had a significant effect in reducing productivity differences. Granger causality tests further indicated that FDI caused productivity differences among oil exporting countries.

In sum, the evidence on the effects of trade and FDI on productivity growth are decidedly mixed and nonrobust The results are sensitive to the sample of countries used, the period covered, the choice of ancillary explanatory variables, and the use of controls for endogeneity. As a result, trade openness and FDI would fall under my rubric of weak forces.

9.6 The Role of Science and Technology

9.6.1 The Role of R&D in Development

This section is based largely on Gittleman and Wolff (1995), who used cross-national data on real GDP per capita, obtained from the Penn World Table Mark V, and on expenditures for R&D taken from *UNESCO Statistical Yearbooks*, covering the period 1960–88. Gittleman and Wolff

(GW hereafter) found that R&D activity was significant in explaining cross-national differences in growth only among the more developed countries. Among middle income and less developed ones, the effects were statistically insignificant. Their analysis also suggested that R&D activity changed in importance over time, with returns to R&D diminishing sharply between the 1960s and 1970s, followed by a modest recovery in the 1980s. Though R&D is classified as a strong force among developed countries, among all countries of the world it would appear to fall into the category of a weak force.

Countries whose productive techniques are located away from the world technological frontier can benefit in their attempts to improve efficiency by the fact that such laggards can learn from the leaders. This "advantage of backwardness," which has been discussed by Gerschenkron (1952) and Kuznets (1973) among others, indicates that diffusion of technology from the leading economies to the more backward ones can potentially be a strong force in enabling productivity levels to converge among countries. Later work, such as Abramovitz (1986), argued that these potential advantages of backwardness are by no means automatically realized. Other preconditions must be met, among them high levels of investment, the social capability of the country, the presence of a skilled workforce, and appropriate macroeconomic and microeconomic policies.

A further prerequisite may be an adequate level of research and development (R&D) activity. With the requisite scientific and technical effort, nations will find it easier to imitate the technology that they encounter in international trade or through foreign direct investment. As an example, R&D activity might enable domestic firms to realize spillovers from the transfer of technology by multinational corporations.[6] In addition, a country's R&D activity will enhance its ability to make product and process innovations of its own.

Lall (1987) emphasized the former – the adaptation and imitation of technology – rather than the latter – new innovations – in developing what he referred to as technological capability. This was likely to be particularly relevant for developing countries, since it is improbable that movements of the international frontier of technology will occur outside the industrialized nations. As Lall argued, it requires costly technological efforts for firms to "change the technological point at which they operate, to gain the knowledge required to assimilate a given technology, to adapt it and to improve on

---

[6] For a discussion of the transfer of technology by multinational corporations and its connection to productivity convergence, see Blomström and Wolff (1994).

it." While R&D activity is not the only prerequisite for a country to develop its technological capabilities, clearly investment in R&D and the presence of manpower with sufficient training to engage in R&D are important components of this task.

A few studies looked at the role of R&D across both developed and less developed countries.[7] Lichtenberg (1992) addressed the role a nation's own R&D activity played in explaining cross-country differences in productivity growth among countries at varying levels of development. He found a positive and significant coefficient on R&D intensity (the ratio of R&D expenditures to GDP) in explaining growth in GDP per adult between 1960 and 1985.

Coe, Helpman, and Hoffmaister (1997), following up the work of Coe and Helpman (1995), examined the extent to which imports from developed countries (the "North") could boost the productivity performance of underdeveloped countries (the "South"). They first noted that almost the entire R&D activity in the world was concentrated in the industrialized countries of the world. In 1990, for example, according to UNESCO figures, the industrial nations accounted for 96 percent of world R&D expenditures. Moreover, within the OECD countries, the seven largest economies (the G-7 countries) accounted for 92 percent of total R&D spending. R&D leads to the development of new products, materials, and technologies, as well as to the improvement of existing production techniques, particularly within manufacturing. The main issue that they addressed was how much the benefits from the R&D activities of the industrialized countries of the world spilled over to the less developed countries. Using a sample of seventy-seven developing countries over the period from 1971 to 1990, they found evidence of substantial R&D spillovers from the industrial countries of the North to the developing countries in the rest of the world. The estimated elasticity of TFP with respect to foreign R&D capital stocks was positive and significant and of the order of 10 percent, and the marginal benefit from foreign R&D was found to be larger in countries that were more open to foreign trade.

Connolly (2003) used panel data consisting of three five-year periods, 1970–4, 1975–9, and 1980–4, for a cross section of up to forty countries. The country sample included both developed and underdeveloped countries. International patent data were used to create proxies for imitation and innovation. The author's main finding was that high technology imports positively affected both domestic imitation and innovation. Moreover,

---

[7] See Section 5.5 of Chapter 5 for a review of the cross-country literature on R&D and growth for the industrial (OECD) economies.

while both foreign and domestic innovation contributed positively to the growth in real per capita income, foreign technology from developed countries played a far greater role than did domestic technology.

The empirical work in this section considers the relationship between R&D and productivity growth over the period 1960 to 1988. It relies heavily on the Summers and Heston (1991) data set, which covers countries at all levels of development. This source is supplemented with UNESCO data on R&D intensity. The present section addresses two issues. First, it looks at the effects of R&D on productivity growth for different groups of countries, including industrial market economies (OECD countries), middle income countries, and lower income ones. Second, it investigates the effects for three different subperiods – the 1960s, the 1970s, and the 1980s. There are important reasons to believe that R&D activity may not be as effective in developing countries as in developed ones. There is also cause to speculate that the effectiveness of R&D varies over time as the types of technologies on the cutting edge change, along with the degree to which R&D activity can aid in the imitation and innovation of these technologies.

GW used a standard linear model in estimating the relationship between productivity growth and R&D. This was also true for most of the empirical studies on this issue. The main reason is that even though a more dynamic relationship exists between the two variables (for example, innovation leads to a growth in demand, which, in turn, induces more R&D, causing positive feedback effects), data limitations (particularly, the lack of annual time series data on R&D expenditures for most countries) prevent the estimation of more than a simple specification.

The results indicate, first, that R&D activity is significant in explaining cross-national differences in growth only among the more developed countries. Among middle income and less developed ones, the effects are insignificant. Second, the analysis suggests that R&D activity has changed in importance over time, in terms of its ability to explain international differences in productivity growth. The exact pattern of this change depends on the sample, but it appears that returns to R&D diminished sharply between the 1960s and 1970s, followed by a modest recovery in the 1980s.

9.6.2 Research and Development Activity by Level of Development

Expenditure for R&D as a percentage of GNP (or GDP) is used to measure R&D activity. The variable is derived from *UNESCO Statistical Yearbooks*. The earliest R&D data available were for 1960, and, for the vast majority

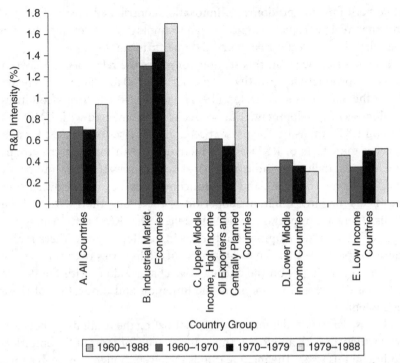

Figure 9.2 Mean ratio of R&D expenditures to GDP by country group and period, 1960–1988 (in percentage).

of countries, such measures were available only for a few scattered years between 1960 and 1988. For the purposes of regression analysis, the variable was averaged over all available years for the period of interest. If the measures are stable over time, little bias will be introduced by this procedure.[8]

Figure 9.2 shows averages for four different periods and for five different samples of countries (also see Appendix Table 9.2 for more details). The first grouping includes all countries for which the requisite data are available. In addition, the sample is divided into the following four groups,

---

[8] It is well known that, at least in industrialized nations, R&D investment tends to be stable over time, especially in comparison with spending on physical capital. Lichtenberg (1992), like Verspagen (1993), distinguished R&D investment by source of funds (private versus government) and by whether the expenditure was for basic or applied research. Such a distinction is not made here because to do so would severely limit the sample size when the regression analysis is conducted by level of development and period

on the basis of World Bank definitions: (1) industrial market economies; (2) upper middle income countries, including centrally planned and high income oil exporting economies; (3) lower middle income countries; and (4) low income countries.[9]

Discerning patterns, both across countries and over time, is made difficult by the fact that the components of the samples do not remain constant over time. This thorny problem – the trade-off between the desires to include as many countries as possible and to maintain a sample that is constant over time – is unfortunately a hindrance in interpreting trends throughout the work on this subject. Despite this, several are apparent. It is evident that the richer countries devoted a higher proportion of their resources to technological activity – about twice the level of other countries of the world that engaged in R&D activity. While this may be expected, since such countries are the centers of technological advance, it may be somewhat surprising that the relationship between per capita income and R&D expenditure was not so strong. That is, on average, there was little difference among the R&D levels of the other three country groupings, with the low income countries, in fact, allocating proportionately more of their resources to R&D than the lower middle income nations did.

Patterns over time for each of the country groupings, except the industrialized nations, tend to be obscured by changes in sample size. Among all nations, R&D intensity appeared to remain almost unchanged between the 1960s and 1970s and then showed a marked increase in the 1979–88 period. For the richest nations, there was a pronounced upward trend in R&D intensity between the 1960s and 1980s, while for the other country groups, the patterns were mixed or hard to interpret because of changing sample size.

Another interesting dimension is afforded by the variation in R&D activity among countries, as measured by the coefficient of variation (see Figure 9.3). The variation in R&D activity was lowest among the industrial market economies and highest among the upper middle income countries.[10] Among all countries, the coefficient of variation remained remarkably stable over time, while among low income, lower middle income, and upper middle income countries, no clear pattern emerged (partly because of changing country samples). However, among

---

[9] The World Bank country groupings change over time, depending on the levels of per capita income. The World Bank's 1986 definitions are used to standardize the analysis.

[10] The upper middle income countries were a diverse group, which includes the newly industrialized countries (NICs), centrally planned economies, and high income oil exporters. However, even when the latter two types of economies were excluded, there was still high variation in R&D activity for the group.

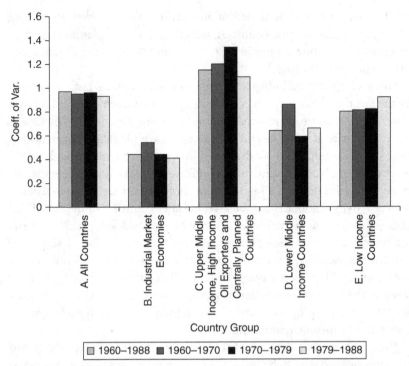

Figure 9.3 Coefficient of variation of the ratio of R&D expenditures to GDP by country group and period, 1960–1988.

the advanced countries, there was a noticeable downward trend in this dimension between the 1960s and the 1980s, suggesting some convergence in R&D intensity.[11]

9.6.3 R&D, the Convergence Process, and Growth

The proper specification for cross-country growth regressions is a matter of some controversy, particularly in light of the findings of Levine and Renelt (1992) that results of such regressions are very sensitive to the specification. The dependent variable here is the rate of growth of real GDP per capita (RGDP), and the main explanatory variable of interest is R&D intensity. GW used the standard specification (see Griliches, 1979, for example) by

[11] A similar finding was reported by Archibugi and Pianta (1994) for total R&D intensity among 20 OECD countries. However, interestingly, they found no evidence of convergence in R&D intensity on the industry level among OECD countries.

regressing the growth in RGDP on the ratio of R&D to GNP.[12] Following previous work (for example, Baumol, Blackman, and Wolff, 1989; Barro, 1991; Mankiw, Romer, and Weil, 1992; and Wolff and Gittleman, 1993), GW included initial per capita income as a catch-up term, the investment rate, and the educational level of the population. As discussed in Section 9.2 the catch-up term has been found to be highly significant in a wide range of specifications, when other variables such as investment or education have been included in the model to allow for conditional convergence.[13] The positive influence of investment as a share of GDP on RGDP growth has been found to be quite robust (see Section 9.3 and Levine and Renelt, 1992). Since Wolff and Gittleman (1993) raised questions about the proper measure of the stock of human capital resident in the labor force, alternative specifications are tried with a variety of enrollment and attainment rate variables.

An additional justification for including education in the specifications – besides its role as a prerequisite for conditional convergence – is that having a more educated workforce may make it easier for countries to adopt and implement new technologies (see Nelson and Phelps, 1966).[14] Since this is a role played by R&D activity as well, it is important to see whether measures of R&D remain influential even after controlling for the human capital stock of the workforce.

The basic estimating equation is:

$$\ln \left(RGDP_1 / RGDP_0 \right) / T = b_0 + b_1 RGDP_0 + b_2 INVRATE_{01} \\ + b_3 EDUC + b_4 RDGNP_{01} + \varepsilon \qquad (9.7)$$

---

[12] Modeling R&D activity at the firm level is rather complicated, as determinants include technological opportunity, appropriability, market structure, firm size, and other factors. The situation is even more complex at the national level, given that level of development will be a determinant and that national technology policy and R&D spending will interact. The regression specifications here are not meant to suggest, however, that consideration of the forces determining a natiodn's R&D activity is unimportant. In addition, they are not meant to imply that a country could profitably increase one of the variables without appropriate adjustments of other variables – for example, to speed growth by increasing R&D investment without raising spending on capital equipment that embodies new technology. Rather, the use of this type of specification is aimed at assessing whether – after controlling for other prerequisites for growth such as an educated workforce and high levels of capital investment – R&D acts as a spur to growth.

[13] As Mankiw, Romer, and Weil (1992) define the terms, "unconditional convergence" means that less productive countries will grow faster than more productive ones irrespective of any other characteristics of the countries. "Conditional convergence" implies that given other characteristics (such as the investment rate and the stock of human capital), poorer countries experience faster productivity growth than richer ones.

[14] See Benhabib and Spiegel (1992) for a discussion of the Nelson-Phelps model in a cross-country growth context.

where ln $(RGDP_1/RGDP_0)/T$ measures the annual average growth rate of real GDP per capita from time 0 to time 1 (T years), $RGDP_0$ is real GDP per capita at the beginning of the period and $RGDP_1$ at the end of the period, $INVRATE_{01}$ is the average ratio of investment to GDP over the period of analysis, and $RDGNP_{01}$ is a measure of average research and development activity during the appropriate time span. As noted, the catch-up hypothesis predicts that the coefficient b_1 will be negative (that is countries further behind at the beginning will show more rapid increases in GDP per capita), while b_2 and b_3 should be positive. The coefficient b_4 is also predicted to be positive, and its value is usually interpreted as the rate of return to R&D investment.

Six alternative measures are employed for the education variable, EDUC: gross enrollment rates for primary, secondary, and higher education and the three corresponding educational attainment rates. Enrollment rates are recorded as of the beginning of the period (or the closest year available), while attainment rates are recorded as of the midpoint of the period under consideration (or the closest year available) in order to measure the average educational input during the period more accurately.

The first stage of the analysis examines whether R&D is important in explaining cross-country differences in per capita income growth among countries at different levels of development. The period considered here is 1960–88, since this was the period for which pertinent R&D data were available. While the Summers and Heston (1991) data set contained data on RGDP for 138 countries for this period, R&D expenditure data were available for only 80 countries. Moreover, the inclusion of certain educational attainment variables further reduced the sample size to between 73 and 80 countries.

As shown in Table 9.3, clearly for the total sample of countries, R&D intensity was *not* a significant determinant of per capita income growth. The R&D variable was significant in no cases, and its coefficient was negative in several. The catch-up effect, as reflected in initial RGDP, was negative and significant at the 1 percent level in all cases. Investment in physical capital was positive and significant at the 1 percent level in all equations.

The coefficients of the education variables were all positive. They were significant at the 1 percent level only for primary enrollment and at the 5 percent level for secondary attainment when R&D intensity was used. They were not significant in the other cases. This finding raises the possibility that at least some portion of the impact of education on growth, which has been reported in many previous studies and in Section 9.4, may be attributable to the effects of a more specialized form of human capital, that engaged in R&D, on growth.[15]

GW were hard pressed to reconcile their results on R&D expenditures with those of Lichtenberg (1992), who found a positive and significant coefficient on R&D intensity in explaining growth in GDP per adult between 1960 and 1985. He also used the nominal ratio of R&D expenditures to GNP averaged over all years of available data between 1964 and 1989. His sample size was somewhat smaller – seventy-four countries (though it was smaller for some of his specifications). His model, derived from Mankiw, Romer, and Weil (1992) and based on a Cobb-Douglas production function with physical, human, and R&D capital, was different, as was his use of nonlinear estimation techniques. Despite the differences in data and specification, it is still surprising that the two sets of results were so much at odds with each other.

On the other hand, Goel and Ram (1994) reported results very similar to those of GW. They used a sample of fifty-two countries at all levels of development and a subsample of thirty-four LDCs. They performed several regressions with the rate of growth of GDP between 1980 and 1988 as their dependent variable. After controlling for the capital investment rate and the growth in employment, they found that the coefficient of R&D expenditure as a ratio to GDP was positive and significant at the 5 percent level for the full sample but positive and insignificant for the restricted LDC sample.

9.6.3.1 The Role of R&D by Level of Development and Period

The impact of R&D on growth is likely to vary by level of development for several reasons. First, R&D tends to be concentrated in manufacturing industries. As a result, those countries in the early stages of industrialization are likely to spend less on R&D than those with a well-developed manufacturing sector and to find such expenditures less effective as well.[16] Second, a significant portion of the return to a country's R&D expenditures is likely to be in the form of productivity improvements spilling over from the firm actually undertaking the R&D to other enterprises. The information

---

[15] GW also tested to see whether the impact of R&D varied by the educational level of the workforce by interacting the secondary school enrollment rate with the R&D measure. However, the interaction variable did not prove to be statistically significant.

[16] An alternative perspective was offered by Pack (1988). Citing evidence from Evenson (1981), he argued that the most important source of technology transfer to LDCs has not been industrial but rather agricultural technology from international agricultural research centers, which was then adapted by local institutes.

Table 9.3. *Regressions of RGDP Growth on Initial RGDP, the Investment Rate, Educational Enrollment and Attainment Rates, and R&D Intensity, 1960–1988*

Constant	Initial RGDP	INVRATE	Education Variable	RDGNP	R²	Adjusted R²	Standard Error	Sample Size	Education Variable
-0.001	-0.010**	0.130**			0.50	0.48	0.015	80	
(0.79)	(1.03)	(4.77)							
-0.002	-0.010**	0.126**		0.120	0.50	0.48	0.015	80	
(0.36)	(6.13)	(5.55)		(0.42)					
-0.014**	-0.011**	0.081**	0.026**	0.044	0.58	0.55	0.013	80	PRIME65
(2.72)	(7.38)	(3.36)	(3.72)	(0.17)					
0.000	-0.010**	0.093**	0.021	-0.179	0.52	0.49	0.014	80	SECE65
(0.13)	(6.48)	(3.24)	(1.84)	(0.55)					
0.000	-0.010**	0.114**	0.048	-0.171	0.51	0.49	0.014	80	HIGHE65
(0.11)	(6.22)	(4.78)	(1.45)	(0.49)					
-0.003	-0.010**	0.098**	0.015*	-0.139	0.51	0.49	0.015	73	PRIMA70
(0.64)	(6.22)	(3.48)	(2.10)	(0.42)					
0.000	-0.010**	0.113**	0.027	-0.250	0.52	0.49	0.015	76	SECA70
(0.20)	(6.29)	(4.49)	(1.72)	(0.67)					
-0.001	-0.010**	0.122**	0.043	0.028	0.50	0.47	0.015	77	HIGHA70
(0.20)	(1.20)	(4.54)	(1.12)	(0.08)					

Notes: t-ratios are shown in parentheses below the coefficient estimate

Key:

Dependent variable: $\ln(RGDP_{88}/RGDP_{60})/28$

Initial RGDP: RGDP per capita at beginning of period, as indicated, measured in units of $10,000s (1985 international dollars). *Source:* Summers and Heston (1991)

INVRATE: investment as a share of GDP (both in 1985 international prices) averaged over the appropriate period, *Source:* Summers and Heston (1991)

PRIME65: Gross enrollment rate in primary school in 1965

SECE65: Gross enrollment rate in secondary school in 1965

HIGH65: Gross enrollment rate in higher education in 1965

Source for enrollment rates: World Bank (1986), table 29

PRIMA70: Proportion of the population age 25 and older who have attended primary school or higher in 1970

SECA70: Proportion of the population age 25 and older who have attended secondary school or higher in 1970

HIGHA70: Proportion of the population age 25 and older who have attended an institution of higher education in 1970

Sources and methods for educational attainment: The basic data were obtained from UNESCO, Statistics of Educational Attainment and Literacy, 1945–74, Statistical Reports and Studies, No. 22, table 5, "Educational Attainment by Age and Sex, 1945 Onwards," and UNESCO Statistical Yearbook 1990, table 1.4, "Percentage Distribution of Population 25 Years of Age and Over, by Educational Attainment and by Sex." For many countries, no data were available, so missing values were imputed on the basis of a regression of available educational attainment rates for year t on educational enrollment ratios (collected from various UNESCO Statistical Yearbooks) for year t and for 15 years prior and on per capita income for year t. See Wolff and Gittleman (1993) for details

RDGNP: R&D expenditures as a percentage of GNP, averaged over all available years between 1960 and 1988. Source: UNESCO Statistical Yearbooks

* significant at the 5 percent level, 2-tail test

** significant at the 1 percent level, 2-tail test

networks needed for firms to take advantage of this public goods aspect of R&D are likely to be more developed in the higher income nations.

Third, technical progress is more important in enhancing labor productivity for more developed countries than for less developed ones. For example, Chenery, Robinson, and Syrquin (1986) found that, on average, increases in total factor productivity accounted for about a third of growth in value added in developing countries and nearly one-half for the developed economies. Since R&D activity is likely to be more important in improving labor productivity by raising technology levels rather than by increasing capital intensity, the lower rates of technical progress in LDCs also suggest reduced scope for R&D activity.

The issue of changes in the return to R&D over time is somewhat less clear. Perhaps the major technological development since the 1970s was the widespread introduction of computers and computer-based equipment. Some (for example, Piore and Sabel, 1984) argued that this represented a change in technological regime (the "fourth industrial revolution") from the previous mass production paradigm to one dominated by information technology (IT). GW suspected that traditional R&D activity might have less relevance to measured productivity change in an IT-dominated technology, while developments in computer software, factory downsizing, and office reorganization might be more important.

Two sets of results are presented in Table 9.4. The first includes all countries with the relevant R&D data in a given period, while the second includes only countries that have the pertinent data for all three periods.[17] For the whole 1960–88 period the R&D variable is significant only for the industrial market economies. The coefficient of the R&D expenditure variable is quite high for this group of countries – a rate of return of 55 percent. For the other two groups, the coefficients are insignificant (negative in some cases).[18]

Looking at changes over time for the same group of industrialized countries, GW found that R&D intensity was significant only for the 1960–70 period. Moreover, its estimated rate of return was 97 percent – twice the level estimated for the 1970s or 1980s. There was also a slight upward trend

---

[17] The regressions for which the results are shown contain initial RGDP, the investment rate, and the secondary education enrollment rate as regressors in addition to the R&D variable. The results for the R&D variables change little if other education variables are used or if none is included.

[18] The sample was divided into quartiles on the basis of per capita income in 1960 and the same set of regressions run. The only group for which the R&D variables are significant is the top quartile.

Table 9.4. *Regressions of RGDP Growth on Initial RGDP, the Investment Rate, Education, and R&D Intensity over Various Periods*

Country Group	Varying Country Samples				Constant Country Samples			
	1960–88	1960–70	1970–9	1979–88	1960–88	1960–70	1970–9	1979–88
A. All Countries								
R&D Coefficient	−0.18	0.28	−0.39	0.45	0.40	0.35	−0.58	0.97
t–ratio	(0.55)	(0.61)	(0.74)	(1.00)	(1.11)	(0.74)	(0.86)	(1.70)
R²	0.52	0.38	0.26	0.21	0.60	0.54	0.27	0.30
Adjusted–R²	0.49	0.33	0.22	0.15	0.55	0.49	0.19	0.23
Sample Size	80	56	77	57	41	41	41	41
B. Industrial Market Economies								
R&D Coefficient	0.55*	0.97*	0.41	0.46	0.55*	0.97*	0.41	0.46
t–ratio	(2.31)	(2.27)	(1.02)	(1.55)	(2.31)	(2.27)	(1.02)	(1.55)
R²	0.68	0.68	0.38	0.30	0.68	0.68	0.38	0.30
Adjusted–R²	0.59	0.59	0.20	0.11	0.59	0.59	0.20	0.11
Sample Size	19	19	19	19	19	19	19	19
C. Industrial Market and Upper Middle Income Economies								
R&D Coefficient	−0.03	0.89*	−0.25	0.63	0.69*	0.97*	−0.11	0.94
t–ratio	(0.07)	(2.13)	(0.67)	(1.40)	(2.23)	(2.58)	(0.23)	(1.84)
R²	0.71	0.62	0.68	0.32	0.63	0.69	0.42	0.41
Adj. R²	0.67	0.56	0.64	0.24	0.56	0.64	0.32	0.30
Sample Size	38	30	39	32	28	28	28	28
D. Lower Middle and Low Income Economies								
R&D Coefficient	−0.54	−0.97	−0.06	−1.36	−1.14	−1.79	0.34	−2.29
t–ratio	(0.66)	(0.86)	(0.03)	(0.91)	(0.56)	(1.35)	(0.12)	(0.50)
R²	0.12	0.12	0.08	0.21	0.54	0.49	0.40	0.28
Adj. R²	0.02	−0.04	0.04	0.05	0.30	0.23	0.11	−0.07
Sample Size	42	26	38	25	13	13	13	13

Notes: Regressions also include a constant term, initial RGDP, the investment rate, and an education variable. The education variable used for 1960–88 and 1960–70 is the secondary enrollment ratio in 1965. For 1970–9, it is the average of the secondary enrollment ratio in 1965 and that in 1983. For 1979–88, it is the secondary enrollment ratio in 1983. R&D variables are averaged over the corresponding period. The dependent variable is $\ln(\text{RGDPt}_1/\text{RGDPt}_0)/(t_1-t_0)$, with years t_1 and t_0 as indicated

 * significant at the 5 percent level, 2-tail test
** significant at the 1 percent level, 2-tail test

between the 1970–9 and 1979–88 periods. The only other case of a significant R&D variable was that for the combined sample of industrial market and upper middle income economies in 1960–70, though here the results appeared to be dominated by the OECD countries (the total sample size was only thirty).

In sum, the results indicated that the effectiveness of R&D varied by level of development. Only for the most industrialized countries were the two R&D measures significant. The poorer countries did not benefit as much from investments in R&D, presumably because there was less of a need to acquire the latest in technology, the composition of their economies tended to be away from R&D intensive sectors, and, relative to the richer countries, growth resulted more from increases in capital intensity and the reallocation of resources to more productive sectors than from technical progress. The regression results also suggested a decline in effectiveness between the 1960s and the 1970s, with a slight recovery during the 1980s.

9.6.4 Concluding Remarks on R&D and Growth

Perhaps the most surprising finding was the fall off in the return to R&D after 1970 among the advanced economies. GW suggested previously that this may have been the consequence of the shift in technological regime to IT based processes. As a result, the avenue to productivity growth was less likely to result from traditional R&D than from software related innovations and the type of industrial restructuring they might have spawned.

Two other possible explanations of why R&D effectiveness has fallen over time are (1) a decline in technological opportunities, leading to diminishing returns on R&D investment; and (2) a speed-up in the pace of international spillovers of knowledge, so that while R&D still makes important contributions to productivity growth at a world level, it does not have a measurable impact on relative national growth rates.

The slowdown in productivity growth in the United States during the 1970s spawned a vast literature seeking to determine its causes (see Chapter 8). Naturally, one important hypothesis warranting examination is that R&D was making less of a contribution to technical progress than previously. The results of Griliches (1980) and others led some to speculate that technological opportunities were being exhausted, reducing the contribution of R&D to growth.[19] Later work by Griliches and others has since come to an opposite conclusion.[20] As Nadiri (1993) observed, however, a survey of the literature left one with the impression that the contribution of R&D to growth may have diminished in the early 1970s and then strengthened in the late 1970s and 1980s. For example, Lichtenberg and Siegel (1991), who analyzed the period 1973–85 in the United States, found that while R&D

---

[19] For a more detailed discussion, see Baily and Chakrabarti (1988).
[20] See, for example, Griliches and Lichtenberg (1984a), Griliches (1986), and Lichtenberg and Siegel (1991).

was significant in boosting TFP growth throughout the period, its impact strengthened in the latter half of the period.[21]

Another strand of the technical change literature took note of the fact that the ratio of patents to real R&D investment and its ratio to scientists and engineers employed in R&D (S&E) declined in the United States and other developed economies. The patent/S&E ratio in 1990 was at 55 percent of its level in 1969–70 in the United States, 44 percent in the United Kingdom, 42 percent in Germany, and 40 percent in France (Evenson, 1993). Whether this implied diminishing returns to R&D is a matter of some dispute. Evenson (1993) argued that there was some evidence that invention potential was being exhausted. Griliches (1989), on the other hand, favored an explanation focusing on a declining tendency to patent.

Thus, while certainly not conclusive, the evidence from more developed countries seemed to suggest that changes over time in the returns to R&D formed part of the explanation for the patterns on returns to R&D found in these regressions. These findings could have reflected the shift in technological regime from one more amenable to R&D-type innovation (mass production) to one less susceptible (IT).

A second potential explanation is that the pace of spillovers of knowledge across borders quickened, so that R&D was still productive in terms of world growth, but the returns to each country's own R&D declined. While it was clear that it still took a major investment for a country to enhance its technological capability, common sense suggested that the increasing integration of the world economy would lead to greater spillovers via multinational corporations and other means. GW tested this hypothesis directly by including a measure of imported R&D in their regressions. They failed to find support for this hypothesis, but this may be due to limitations in the data.[22] This result also appeared at odds with Coe and Helpman (1995) and Coe, Helpman, and Hoffmaister (1995), who reported that foreign R&D capital stocks had a significant effect on domestic total factor productivity

---

[21] It should be kept in mind that as Scherer (1983) argued, continued strong returns to R&D investment do not necessarily mean that technological opportunities are not diminishing, since firms can cut back on R&D expenditures if they do not deem them to be profitable. Unfortunately, it is not easy to assess this hypothesis in a cross-national context, since a reasonably complete time series on R&D investment is not available for most countries.

[22] The variables for imported R&D were calculated as follows: Using UN trade data, for each country they calculated the share of its imports from each of its trading partners. These shares, in combination with the R&D measures, were used to compute an import-weighted index of the R&D of the country's trading partners. Given that they did not have measures of R&D for all countries, substantial measurement error was likely. In addition, determining the extent to which technology was being imported required information on the content of the trade, which the authors did not have as well.

growth in both developed and developing countries (see Chapter 5 for more discussion). Differences in data sources and methodology and specification may account for the disparity in results. Moreover, neither of the Coe *et al.* studies attempted to determine whether the pace of international R&D spillovers quickened over time. Time series data collected by the OECD on international payments for patents, licenses, and technical know-how seemed to suggest, however, that the pace of international technology transfer became more rapid.[23]

9.7 The Role of Other Factors

9.7.1 Population Growth

I next consider several other factors in the regression analysis that are often believed to influence the rate of productivity growth in a country. These almost without exception would be classified as weak forces in productivity growth. The first of these is population growth, which, as I argued earlier, is included in order to control for any country whose population growth is so rapid as to swamp any gains from the advantages of backwardness. In these cases, any gains in productivity from the introduction of new technology may be offset by rapid population growth and, as a result, do not show up as increases in per capita income. An opposing argument, often made, is that rapid population growth may stimulate production by providing a rapidly expanding domestic market. Thus, population growth may act as a positive stimulant to the growth in per capita income.

I first estimate the simple equation:

$$\ln\left(\text{RGDP}_{91} / \text{RGDP}_{60}\right) = b_0 + b_1 \text{RGDP}_0 + b_2 \text{POPGRT} + \varepsilon \qquad (9.8)$$

where POPGRT is the annual rate of population growth over the 1960–91 period. The coefficient of population growth is negative and statistically significant at the 1 percent level (results not shown), indicating that it has a strong depressing effect on the growth in RGDP. However, when I next include INVRATE in the equation, the coefficient of POPGRT remains negative but becomes statistically insignificant. This indicates that high population growth in a country lowers savings and hence investment, since more resources must be devoted to consumption. Independently of its effect on investment, it exerts no significant impact on the growth in per capita income.

---

[23] See Nadiri (1993) for further discussion of this point.

A similar result is obtained when the education variables are added to population growth in the regression equations. When primary school enrollment is added, the population growth variable remains negative but becomes marginally significant. When secondary school enrollment is added, population growth remains insignificant. Thus, rapid population growth, by increasing the number of children and diverting resources from investment in education, depresses per capita income growth indirectly by lowering educational enrollment rates, particularly for secondary school. Finally, when both investment and education are included in the equation:

$$\ln\left(RGDP_{91} / RGDP_{60}\right) = b_0 + b_1 RGDP_0 + b_2 INVRATE \\ + b_3 EDUC + b_4 POPGRT + \varepsilon \qquad (9.9)$$

population growth becomes statistically insignificant.

9.7.2 Military Expenditures

I then look at several sociopolitical variables to determine whether they exert any independent influence on the growth in per capita income. The general form of these equations is:

$$\ln\left(RGDP_{91} / RGDP_{60}\right) = b_0 + b_1 RGDP_0 + b_2 INVRATE + b_3 EDUC \\ + b_4 TRADE + b_5 OTHER + \varepsilon \qquad (9.10)$$

The OTHER variables take the form of "dummy variables"; that means that they take on the value of 1 if the characteristic is present and 0 otherwise.

The first of these is MIL82, military expenditure in 1982 as a percentage of GNP. This variable is generally positive but not statistically significant (see Table 9.5). This is true for the various forms with investment and education and in the regression equation with only $RGDP_{60}$ included. Thus, contrary to popular wisdom, the relative extent of military expenditures does not appear to be detrimental to growth in per capita income; nor does it appear to be especially helpful. The possible reason is that, while military spending diverts resources from productive investment, it might also stimulate the acquisition of advanced technology.

Other studies have produced mixed results. Faini, Annez, and Taylor (1984) found a negative relation between defense spending and the growth rate of national output for a sample of sixty-nine LDCs over the 1952–70 period. Biswas and Ram (1986), on the basis of a sample of fifty-eight LDCs over the 1960–77 and 1970–7 periods, concluded that there was not a consistently significant relation between the rate of output growth and defense

Table 9.5. *Regressions of Growth in RGDP on Initial Relative RGDP, the Investment Rate, Education, Population Growth, and Other Factors, 1960–91*

Constant	$RGDP_{60}$	INVRATE	Education		POPGRT	Other		Adj.-R^2	Std. Error	Sample Size	Other Factor
			PRIM	SCND		Factor	R^2				
-0.40*	-0.34**	0.028**	0.53**		-2.71	0.92	0.53	0.50	0.35	99	MIL82
(2.26)	(4.40)	(4.69)	(3.10)		(0.67)	(1.17)					
-0.36*	-0.47**	0.027**		0.78**	6.11	0.24	0.52	0.49	0.35	99	MIL82
(2.03)	(4.54)	(4.28)		(2.77)	(1.11)	(0.30)					
-0.47*	-0.32**	0.028**	0.60**		-4.88	0.13	0.52	0.49	0.35	100	VOTING
(2.49)	(3.91)	(4.78)	(3.50)		(1.01)	(1.22)					
-0.40*	-0.45**	0.028**		0.83**	3.32	0.14	0.50	0.47	0.36	100	VOTING
(2.11)	(4.29)	(4.29)		(2.88)	(0.58)	(1.24)					
-0.4**	-0.31**	0.027**	0.56**		-4.92	0.10	0.51	0.48	0.35	96	VIOLNCE
(2.01)	(3.68)	(4.30)	(3.17)		(1.01)	(0.82)					
-0.37	-0.43**	0.027**		0.80**	2.84	0.12	0.49	0.47	0.36	96	VIOLNCE
(1.82)	(4.10)	(3.94)		(2.81)	(0.49)	(1.02)					

Notes: t-ratios are shown in parentheses below the coefficient estimate

Key:

Dependent variable: ln(RGDP91/RGDP60)

See notes to Table 9.3 for the key. In addition, MIL82: Ratio of military expenditures to GNP in 1982. The data source is Savard (1985), table 11

VOTING: Dummy variable for limitations on the right to vote – equals0 if none; 1 if one-party control, other restrictions, or no voting. The data source is Savard (1985), p. 24

VIOLNCE: Dummy variable for official violence against citizens – equals zero if none; one if some or frequent. The data source is Savard (1985), p.24

* significant at the 5 percent level, 2-tail test

** significant at the 1 percent level, 2-tail test

spending. Grobar and Porter (1989), using a cross section of forty-four countries, reported a positive correlation between GDP growth and the share of GDP spent on defense. Adams, Behrman, and Boldin (1988), using the more representative Summer and Heston sample for the period 1974 to 1986, found a positive and significant relation between military spending and GDP growth for "nonwarring" countries. When "warring" nations were included in the sample, the effects of military spending on GDP growth became negative, suggesting that wars themselves are detrimental to output growth. However, it should be noted that none of these three analyses included a "catch-up" effect in its specifications, so that their results are not strictly comparable to those here.

The next two studies included a catch-up term in their statistical analysis. Hess (1989), using a sample of sixty-six LDCs over the 1970–85 period, found no relation between the share of national spending on defense and the rate of output growth. Barro (1991) found no significant negative effect of defense spending as a proportion of GDP on per capita GDP growth for the Summers-Heston sample (excluding the oil exporters) over the 1960–85 period but found that war had a negative and significant effect on both per capita GDP growth and the investment rate.

9.7.3 Political Factors

I then include a proxy variable for democracy, VOTING, which reflects the extent of voting rights in a country (see Table 9.5). When included with only $RGDP_{60}$, the variable is negative and statistically significant at the 1 percent level (restrictions on voting lower RGDP growth). However, when the investment rate is included in the equation, the variable becomes statistically insignificant. The results suggest that the absence of democracy slows productivity growth indirectly by inhibiting savings and investment. An almost identical result is obtained for VIOLNCE, a variable that reflects the presence or absence of official "violence" against citizens. When included with only $RGDP_{60}$, the variable is negative and significant at the 1 percent level, but once the investment rate is included, the variable becomes insignificant. Thus, domestic repression also appears to inhibit savings and investment and thereby indirectly lowers the growth in per capita income.

Earlier studies reported similar findings. Kormendi and Meguire (1985) used a sample of forty-seven countries drawn from the *International Financial Statistics* of the International Monetary Fund for the period 1950–77. Their regression specification included a catch-up term (initial per capita income) as well as a measure of "civil liberties," which reflected, among others, the degree of due process in criminal procedure, the extent of freedom of expression, the presence or absence of political prisoners, and the independence of the judiciary, in a country. As reported here, he found that the investment rate was positively related to the extent of civil liberties, but civil liberties had very little independent effect on a country's output growth rate. Barro (1991) used the same civil liberties index as Kormendi and Meguire and applied it, with a catch-up term, to the Summers-Heston sample (excluding the oil exporters) over the 1960–85 period. He found a significant positive effect of civil liberties on per capita income growth.

Later studies have produced somewhat mixed results. Barro (1996) reanalyzed the relation between democracy and growth using a panel of about one hundred countries over the period from 1960 to 1990. His measure of democracy was an index of political rights compiled by Gastil *et al.* (1982). He argued first that the favorable effects of democracy on growth include the maintenance of the rule of law, free markets, small government consumption, and high human capital formation. However, once these effects are controlled for, a well as the initial level of real GDP per capita, the effect of democracy on the growth of real GDP per capita was found to be weakly negative.

Rivera-Batiz (2002) examined how democracy affected long-run growth by influencing the quality of governance. The strength of democratic institutions was measured using the Freedom House (1997) index of political rights. The quality of governance was measured by the Hall and Jones (1999) index that evaluated countries on the basis of the institution and governmental policies that determined the economic environment for production and capital accumulation. He first reported that measures of governmental quality were substantially higher in more democratic countries than less democratic ones. His regression results showed that democracy was a significant determinant of TFP growth between 1960 and 1990 in a cross section of 115 countries, but this contribution occurred only insofar as stronger democratic institutions were associated with greater quality of governance.

Aghion, Alesina, and Trebbi (2007) showed that though empirical evidence of a positive effect of democracy on economic growth was weak, democracy influenced productivity growth in different sectors differently and that this differential effect may be one of the reasons for the ambiguity of the aggregate results. They used the Freedom House index of civil liberties and political rights. Sectoral data were obtained from the UNIDO database for twenty-eight manufacturing industries (see Chapter 6). The country sample size was 180. Their regressions were run over six five-year periods: 1970–5, 1975–80, 1980–5, 1985–90, 1990–5, and 1995–2000. They also included time and country-industry fixed effects in their regressions in order to account for unobserved heterogeneity across industries and countries. Their results indicated that political rights were conducive to growth in more advanced sectors of an economy, but they actually had a negative effect on growth in sectors far away from the technological frontier. They argued that the results could be explained by the beneficial effects of democracy and political rights on the freedom of entry into markets. Overall, democracies tend to have much lower entry barriers than autocracies, because political accountability reduces the protection of vested interests, and entry in turn is known to be generally more growth-enhancing in sectors that are closer to the technological frontier. They found empirical evidence to support the entry explanation.

Acemoglu *et al.* (2008) questioned the widely accepted modernization hypothesis that claims that per capita income causes the creation and the consolidation of democracy. They argued that previous studies found empirical support for this hypothesis because they failed to control for the presence of omitted variables. There are many underlying historical factors that affect both the level of income per capita and the likelihood of democracy in a country, and failing to control for these factors may introduce a spurious relationship between income and democracy. They used the Freedom House measure of democracy and GDP per capita data from the Penn World Tables over the period from 1970 to 1995 and from Maddison (2003) over the years 1900 to 2000. Using country samples ranking from 95 to 150 nations, they found that controlling for these historical factors by including fixed country effects and instrumental variable econometric techniques removed the correlation between income and democracy. In addition, the association between income and the likelihood of transitions to and from democratic regimes was also eliminated. They argued that critical historical junctures can lead to divergent political-economic development paths, some leading to prosperity and democracy and others to relative poverty and nondemocracy. They presented evidence of diverging development paths within the former colonial world, particularly between former Spanish and Portuguese colonies, on the one hand, and English colonies, on the other hand.

Doucouliagos and Ulubasoglu (2006) noted that despite a sizable empirical literature on the subject, no firm conclusions have yet been drawn regarding the impact of democracy on economic growth. The authors applied metaregression analysis to 483 previous estimates derived from eighty-four studies on democracy and growth (as of 2006). Using traditional metaanalysis estimators, the bootstrap, and fixed and random effects metaregression models, they derived several robust conclusions. Using all the available published evidence together, they concluded that democracy did not have a direct impact on economic growth. However, they did find that democracy had robust, significant, and positive indirect effects through higher human capital, lower inflation, lower political instability, and higher levels of economic freedom. There also appeared to be country- and region-specific effects of democracy on growth.

Several studies have also found negative effects of wars and violence on economic development. Yamarik, Johnson, and Compton (2007) investigated the long-run impact of interstate conflict on real GDP per capita for a cross section of 112 to 118 countries over the period 1960 to 2000. They constructed a casualty-weighted conflict variable that took into account both the severity and the endogeneity of individual confrontations. Their regression results indicated that interstate war had a decidedly negative impact on long-run growth in real GDP per capita. A one standard deviation increase in casualty-weighted conflict led to an 18 percent reduction in real GDP per capita in 2000.

Bodea and Elbadawi (2008) investigated the economic growth impact of organized political violence. The authors argued that under plausible assumptions regarding attitudes toward risk, the overall effects of organized political violence are likely to be much higher than its direct capital destruction impact. They distinguished among three levels of political violence – riots, coups, and civil war. They found using panel data (GMM) regressions on sixty-eight countries over six five-year nonoverlapping periods over the time span 1970 to 1999 that organized political violence, especially civil war, significantly lowered long-term economic growth. They also found that ethnic fractionalization had a negative and direct effect on growth, though its effect was substantially lessened by the institutions specific to a nonfactional partial democracy. The results also showed that Sub-Saharan Africa had been disproportionately impacted by civil war, which explained a substantial share of its economic decline, including the widening income gap relative to East Asia.

Chen, Loayza, and Reynal-Querol (2007) employed an "event-study" methodology to analyze the aftermath of civil war in a cross section of about forty-one countries over the period 1960 to 2003. It focused on those countries in which the end of conflict marked the beginning of a relatively lasting peace. The paper considered basic indicators of economic performance, health and education, political development, demographic trends, and conflict and security issues. For each of these indicators, the authors compared the post- and prewar situations and then examined their trend over the postconflict period. They found that, even though war had devastating effects and its aftermath could be immensely difficult, when the end of war marked the beginning of lasting peace, recovery and improvement were indeed achieved.

9.7.4 The Role of Central Planning

Another factor is central planning. Though it was abandoned in the early 1990s by almost all of the former Soviet republics and Eastern European countries, central planning might have accounted for slower productivity growth in these centrally planned economies (CPEs) than in market economies, after controlling for initial productivity, investment, education, trade openness, and other factors. Using the Summers-Heston sample for 111 countries over the 1960–85 period, Wolff (1992) found that CPEs grew as rapidly as other countries of the world. Moreover, when compared to a set of industrialized and middle income economies, CPEs generally fared as well as they, given the relevant attributes of the countries. However, CPEs grew significantly more slowly than OECD countries. Yet, even in the latter case, it may not be central planning per se that was at fault, but, instead, the lack of civil liberties.

Basic statistics for the countries for which the pertinent data are available are shown in Figure 9.4 (also see Appendix Table 9.3 for more details). Comparative figures are also shown for the average of industrialized and "upper middle income" countries in Appendix Table 9.3. It is first of interest to compare the relative standing of the CPEs in 1985. According to the Summers-Heston data, the German Democratic Republic (GDR) had by far the highest RGDP in 1985 (70 percent of the U.S. level), followed by Czechoslovakia (59 percent), the USSR (50 percent), and Hungary (46 percent). Bulgaria, Poland, and Yugoslavia followed at about 40 percent of the U.S. level, with Romania (34 percent) and China (20 percent) at the bottom.

It is next of interest to ascertain which CPE countries narrowed the per capita income gap with respect to the United States and which did not over the postwar period. All the CPEs were in the former group, with Bulgaria, China, GDR, Romania, and Yugoslavia more than doubling their per capita income level relative to the United States over the 1950–85 period. The other countries all advanced relative to the United States, but, since their 1950 RGDP was higher relative to the United States than these other countries, their relative advance was smaller. For example, the USSR increased from

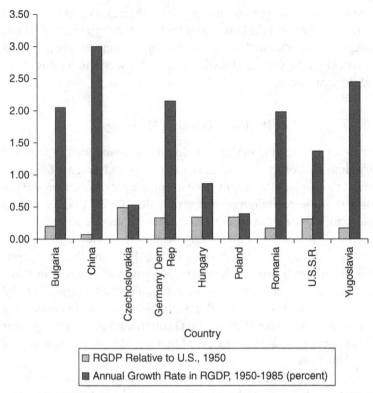

Figure 9.4 RGDP relative to the United States, 1950, and annual growth rate in RGDP, 1950–1985, for centrally planned economies.

31 percent to 50 percent of the U.S. level over the period, Czechoslovakia from 49 percent to 59 percent, and Hungary from 34 percent to 46 percent. Moreover, as a group, the CPEs grew from 52 percent of the average RGDP level of the industrial market economies in 1950 to 59 percent in 1985. Thus, on the surface at least, the performance of the CPEs over the postwar period was somewhat better than that of the industrialized economies. A comparison with the upper middle income countries also leads to a similar conclusion. In 1950, this group of countries was ahead of the CPEs (.30 compared to .27). However, by 1985, the CPEs had surpassed this group of countries (.44 compared to .37).

Figure 9.5 shows comparative enrollment rates by schooling level (also see Appendix Table 9.3). Primary school enrollment rates were all quite high in the CPEs, ranging from 88 to more than 100 percent, and comparable to those of industrial market economies and upper middle income countries. Secondary school enrollment rates, ranging from 35 to 99 percent in

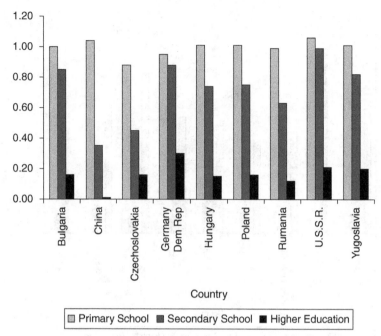

Figure 9.5 Gross enrollment rates by level of schooling, 1983, for centrally planned economies.

1983, were somewhat lower on average than those of the industrial market economies, though the differences were not great. However, interestingly, enrollment rates in higher education in the CPEs, which were comparable to those in the advanced market economies in 1965 (15 percent), had fallen to half their level in 1983. Indeed, enrollment in higher education remained almost constant between 1965 and 1983 in the CPEs.

Unfortunately, the early Summers and Heston data set did not contain information on investment for CPEs. The analysis here used investment data from Alton (1985) for Bulgaria, Czechoslovakia, GDR, Hungary, Poland, and Romania and from the Central Intelligence Agency (1988) for the USSR. Of the CPEs, only data on China and Yugoslavia were missing. Moreover, the investment data for the CPEs were available for only the 1965–81 period. Of course, investment data for the CPEs were subject to many caveats, particularly because they were based on the material product system (MPS) of accounting, which excluded most services from measures of the national product. Though both Alton and the CIA attempted to correct for these difficulties, it was not clear how successful they were. The average investment rate over the 1965–81 period in the CPEs was almost

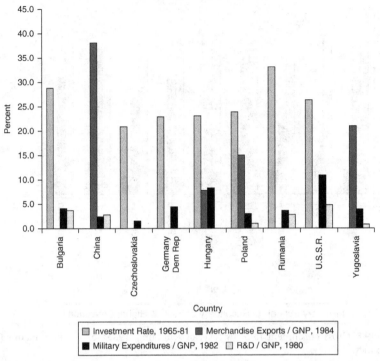

Figure 9.6 Investment rates and related statistics for centrally planned economies, 1960–1985.

identical to that of the advanced market economies (see Figure 9.6 and Appendix Table 9.3). Of course, as noted previously, there were method-ological difficulties with the investment data for the CPEs. However, on the surface, there did not appear to be a sizable gap in savings performance in the two groups of countries.

Population growth was also almost identical in the CPEs and the indus-trial market economies, but much greater in the middle income countries. Merchandise trade for the CPEs, based on incomplete data, appeared lower than in the advanced market economies, and considerably lower than in the upper middle income nations. Military expenditures as a proportion of GNP were considerably higher in the CPEs than in the advanced countries, with the USSR particularly high at 11 percent of GNP (and with some other esti-mates as high as 20 to 25 percent of GNP). On the basis of UNESCO data, it appeared that CPEs spent a much higher percentage of national product on R&D than the advanced economies. The upper middle income countries, on the other hand, ranked considerably lower on this technology dimension.

On the surface at least, neither the productivity performance nor the education, investment, and technology indicators appeared to be deficient in the CPEs relative to either the advanced industrial economies or the upper middle income countries. To analyze this further, Wolff (1992) performed the same set of regressions as shown in Table 9.5 except that a dummy variable (CENPLAN) was included for the CPEs. Three country samples were used. The first consisted of all the countries of the world with pertinent data (the 111 nations of the Summers-Heston sample). The second consisted of the CPEs and the industrial market economies. The third added to the second sample the upper middle income countries.

Results are shown in Table 9.6 for the coefficient of CENPLAN. For the sample of all countries, the coefficient of CENPLAN was negative but, in every case, statistically insignificant. For the sample of CPEs and industrial market economies, the coefficient was negative in every case and, in most cases, statistically significant at the 5 percent level. However, when controlling for the ratio of R&D to GNP, the significance level increased to the 1 percent level. This suggests that, given the large expenditures on R&D by the CPEs, they should have had significantly higher productivity growth than they actually did. On the other hand, when controlling for the presence or absence of civil liberties, there was no significant difference in RGDP growth between the CPEs and the advanced market economies. Indeed, the variable VOTING was perfectly collinear with CENPLAN – that is, the CPEs all lacked civil liberties, while the advanced market economies all enjoyed these rights.

When the upper middle income countries were added to the sample, the coefficient of CENPLAN remained negative but was generally insignificant. The coefficient of CENPLAN became significant when civil liberties and R&D intensity were included in the equation. It is also of interest that the coefficients of both VOTING and VIOLENCE were positive and statistically significant (results not shown) – suggesting that for countries at this level of development, authoritarian governments were conducive to growth.

In conclusion, there had been considerable debate about the relative advantages and disadvantages of centrally planned economies. Some argued that such a state apparatus introduced too much inflexibility into economic structure and may thus have acted as an impediment to economic growth. However, others suggested that central planning might increase the amount of capital available for expansion and improve its allocation over free market forms of economies.

Has central planning had a detrimental effect on productivity growth? In the context of all the countries of the world, the answer was no. When

Table 9.6. *Regressions of Growth in RGDP on Initial Relative RGDP, CENPLAN, and Other Factors: The Coefficient of CENPLAN*

Sample 1	Sample 2	Sample 3	Other Factor
−0.05	−0.18*	−0.20	none
(0.35)	(2.22)	(1.43)	
−0.15	−0.31*	−0.25	EXPMGDP
(0.63)	(2.34)	(1.18)	
−0.12	−0.33*	−0.23	IMPMGDP
(0.51)	(2.52)	(1.08)	
−0.06	−0.21*	−0.19	MIL82
(0.41)	(2.27)	(1.57)	
−0.12	−0.34**	−0.40*	RDGDP
(0.62)	(3.05)	(2.17)	
−0.12	−0.33*	−0.31	SCIPOP
(0.61)	(2.66)	(1.80)	
−0.18	a	−0.71**	VOTING
(1.03)		(3.98)	
−0.06	a	−0.18	WAR
(0.40)		(1.46)	
−0.13	−0.35	−0.52**	VIOLENCE
(0.78)	(2.04)	(3.28)	

Notes: Dependent variable: $\ln(RGDP_{85}/RGDP_{60})$. Independent variables: Constant, $RGDP_{60}$, INVRATE, PRIM, POPGRT, other factor, and CENPLAN: Dummy variable – 1 for centrally planned economy; 0 for market economy. classification based on Summers and Heston (1988). (See Table 2). t-ratios are shown in parentheses below the coefficient estimate of CENPLAN

Sample 1: all countries (maximum sample size: 109)

Sample 2: CPEs and industrial market economies (maximum sample size: 27)

Sample 3: CPEs, industrial market economies, and upper middle income countries (maximum sample size: 42)

[a] Multicollinear matrix

* significant at the 5 percent level, 2-tail test

** significant at the 1 percent level, 2-tail test

controlling for initial per capita income, investment performance, educational levels, and other relevant factors, CPEs grew as rapidly as other countries of the world. Moreover, when compared to a set of industrialized and middle income economies, CPEs generally fared as well as they, given the relevant attributes of the countries. However, vis-a-vis OECD countries themselves, the answer was yes. CPEs did grow significantly more slowly than this select group of countries. Yet, even in the context of the latter, it may not be central planning per se that was the culprit, but, instead, the lack of voting rights and other civil liberties, which appeared to stimulate these other economies.

Why, then, did Eastern Europe and the USSR abandon central planning? There were several possible reasons. First, their major reference point was their European neighbors, and, compared to them, the CPEs did not fare very well. Second, their relative position may have deteriorated quite substantially in the late 1980s (the data here extend only until 1985) relative to other countries of the world, and particularly to Western Europe. Third, some of the other requisite ingredients for growth – import openness, particularly with respect to OECD countries; joint ventures with Western transnational corporations; and civil liberties – may have been incompatible with the state apparatus associated with central planning.

9.8 The Role of Income Inequality

A large literature has now emerged on the effects of income inequality on economic growth. In this section, I will focus on this relationship. There is an equally large (and growing) literature on the effects of development on inequality and poverty. I will say a few words about this first but then focus on the effects of inequality on growth.

9.8.1 The Kuznets Curve

When we consider relative income inequality for countries at all levels of development, the pattern of inequality that ensues follows a well-known pattern referred to as the Kuznets curve (see, Kuznets, 1955). In this article, he speculated that in the course of economic development, the level of income inequality normally rises during the early phase, levels off during the intermediate phase, and then declines during the later stages. This speculation, now referred to as the Kuznets hypothesis, thus proposes an inverted U-shaped relation between income inequality and the level of development, where the latter is most often measured by the level of per capita income.

Kuznets based this speculation on an analysis of time series data for the United States, England, and Germany and of cross-sectional data involving these three countries as well as Ceylon, India, and Puerto Rico. For the United States, he found that share of income received by the bottom two quintiles of the income distribution rose from 13.5 percent in 1922 to 18 percent in about 1950, while the share of the top 5 percent declined from 31 to 20 percent and that of the top quintile from 55 to 44 percent during the same period. In the United Kingdom, the share of the top 5 percent declined from 46 percent of total income in 1880 to 43 percent in about 1910, to 33 percent in 1929, and to 24 percent in 1947. On the other side of the ledger, the share of the bottom 85 percent of the income distribution rose from about 41 percent in 1880 to 55 percent in 1947. In Prussia, income inequality increased slightly from 1875 to 1913; in Saxony there was almost no change from 1880 to 1913; while for Germany as a whole, income inequality fell sharply between 1913 and the 1920s but then returned to pre–World War I levels during the 1930s.

Various explanations or models have been put forward to try to account for the Kuznets relation. Kuznets himself in his 1955 article suggested a dualistic model (a "traditional" and a "modern" sector) to explain the movement of inequality with development, and most of the subsequent models have taken this form. The basic logic of this approach as originally suggested by Kuznets is as follows. Most underdeveloped countries are characterized by a very large share of the labor force employed in the low income, slow-growing "traditional" sector of the economy, which is primarily agrarian. In the early phase of development, income inequality tends to rise because both the population and the labor force shift into the faster growing, high income "modern" sector of the economy. It is the disparity in mean incomes between these two sectors that causes income inequality to rise. Income inequality is further heightened as the mean income in the modern sector increases more rapidly than the mean income in the traditional sector (which, by some accounts, actually falls in absolute terms). Moreover, the movement toward greater overall inequality is further intensified if the modern sector also has the property of greater within-sector inequality than the traditional sector.

In the later phase of development, several factors operate to moderate and eventually reverse the increase in income inequality. First, as the modern sector expands, it absorbs an increasingly higher proportion of the labor force and population, and this shift in proportions between the traditional and modern sectors will by itself reduce income inequality. Second, the absorption of an increasing share of the labor force and population in the modern sector will also reduce population pressure in the traditional sector and thereby cause income differences between the traditional and modern sectors to narrow. Third, there are also forces that serve to reduce

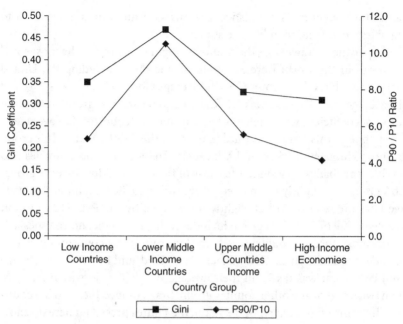

Figure 9.7 Income inequality by country group (averages), around the year 2000.

income inequality *within* the modern sector. These include the expansion of the educational system and the creation of a skilled labor force, which results in a more equal distribution of skills within the labor force and hence greater equality of labor earnings within the modern sector. The increased skill level of the labor force combined with the development of trade unions also cause the share of income going to labor to increase, further reducing income inequality within the modern sector.

Figure 9.7 presents relative income distribution figures for a selection of countries at various levels of development around the year 2000 (also see Appendix Table 9.4 for more details). These data were collected by the World Bank. The countries are organized into four groups by the World Bank, depending on the country's per capita income level. The World Bank provides both the Gini coefficient and the P90/P10 ratio.[24] However, no attempt was made to make the underlying income concepts consistent. Moreover, in some cases, the income shares correspond to per capita income, in other cases to family income, and for some countries, to consumption expenditure

---

[24] The P90/P10 ratio is the ratio of the income (expenditure) of the 90th percentile to that of the 10th percentile.

rather than income. For statistical reasons, consumption surveys tend to show less inequality than income surveys.

Despite these drawbacks, the results are highly suggestive. The most equal countries in the world were the high income ones, including the United States and other OECD countries. The average Gini coefficient was 0.31 and the average P90/P10 ratio was 4.1. The second most equal group in terms of the Gini coefficient were the upper middle income countries (an average of 0.33), though this group was third in terms of the P90/P10 ratio. This group includes Hungary, Turkey, and Venezuela. The low income countries had levels of inequality very similar to those of the upper middle income group. This group was slightly more unequal according to the Gini index (an average Gini index of 0.35) but slightly more equal by the P90/P10 ratio (an average value of 5.3). This group includes India, Pakistan, and Indonesia.

The most unequal countries were the lower middle income group, which includes the Philippines, Colombia, Peru, Poland, and Brazil. Their average Gini coefficient was 0.47 and their average P90/P10 ratio was 10.5, more than twice that of any other country group. Brazil topped the list of all countries in terms of inequality. In the main, the figures presented here do show an inverted U-shaped relation between per capita income and inequality and thus give support to the Kuznets hypothesis.

9.8.2 Effects of Inequality on Growth

According to Barro (2000), theories on the macroeconomic relationship between inequality and economic growth fall into four broad categories corresponding to the main feature stressed: credit-market imperfections, political economy, social unrest, and saving rates. (Also, see Benabou, 1996, and Aghion, Caroli, and Garcia-Penalosa, 1999, for other surveys of this literature.)

As Galor and Zeira (1993) and Piketty (1997) show, in models with imperfect credit markets, the limited ability to borrow implies that rates of return on investment are not necessarily equated at the margin. The credit-market imperfections can reflect asymmetric information or the limitations of legal institutions. For example, creditors may have difficulty in collecting on defaulted loans because of imperfect law enforcement or of bankruptcy laws that protect the assets of debtors. With limited access to credit, the exploitation of investment opportunities depends, to some extent, on the assets and income of individuals. As a result, poor people may forgo investments in education and other forms of human capital that offer relatively high rates of return. In this case, a redistribution of assets and incomes from rich people to poor people will raise the average productivity of investment. By this vehicle, a reduction in inequality will raise the rate of economic growth, at least during a transition to the steady state.

An offsetting effect comes about if investments require some kind of setup cost, so that the returns to investment are increasing over some range of the value of investments. One example is that formal education may benefit the individual only if it is pursued beyond some minimal level. Another example is that a business may be productive only if its scale of operation exceeds some minimal threshold level. If there are imperfections in the credit market, then larger inequality (particularly in assets) may lead to higher investment and growth.

If capital markets and legal institutions tend to improve as an economy develops, then the effects of capital-market imperfections on economic growth are more important in poor economies than in rich ones. As a result, the effects of inequality on economic growth would be larger in magnitude for poor economies than for rich ones, though, as discussed previously, it is still ambiguous whether the effect will be positive or negative.

Political economy explanations typically revolve around voting models of a society. If the mean income in an economy exceeds the median income, then majority voting will often lead to a redistribution of resources from rich to poor (see, for example, Perotti, 1993; Alesina and Rodrik, 1994; Persson and Tabellini, 1994; and Benabou, 1996). Such redistribution programs may involve explicit transfer payments but may also appear as public-expenditure programs such as education, health, and child care.

A greater degree of inequality will generally induce more redistribution through the political process. Typically, the transfer payments and associated taxes distort economic decisions. For example, welfare payments and taxes on labor earnings may discourage work effort. In such a case, more redistribution will lead to more distortions and will tend, in general, to reduce the level of investment. As a result, economic growth will decline, at least in the transition to the steady state. According to this theory, a greater amount of before-tax (and pretransfer) inequality leads to a greater amount of redistribution, and thus in this case greater inequality will lead to lesser growth.

Many of these political economy models assume that the distribution of political power is equal to – or, at least, more equal than – that of economic resources. However, the rich may prevent redistributive policies through campaign spending, lobbying, and buying the votes of legislators. In such a case, a higher degree of economic inequality would require more of these activities in order to prevent redistribution of income through the political process. Both the lobbying activities and campaign contributions would use up resources and potentially promote corruption of public officials. These effects would also have adverse consequences for economic performance. Here, too, inequality will have a negative effect on economic growth through the political process even if no redistribution of income occurs in the equilibrium.

Another set of models revolves around the possibility of social or political unrest (see, for example, Gupta, 1990; Alesina and Perotti, 1996; and Benhabib and Rustichini, 1996). The general argument is that economic inequality may induce poor people to engage in crime, riots, and other socially disruptive activities. Inequality may even lead to political revolution. The participation of the poor in crime and other socially disruptive activities wastes economic resources that could otherwise be devoted to productive activity. Moreover, defensive efforts taken by potential victims such as hiring bodyguards or investing in burglar alarm systems are a further loss of economic resources. In addition, the threat to property rights may reduce investment. Because of the threat of political unrest, more inequality will lead to lower productivity of an economy, and the rate of economic growth will decline as well.

However, as in many of the other models, there is an offsetting effect. In this case, economic resources may be required for the poor to be effective in generating disruption and social unrest that threaten the stability of an established regime. Hence, redistributive transfers may promote political stability only to the extent that the first force, the incentive of the poor to engage in crime and civil unrest, dominates the second factor, the need for resources to cause civil disruption.

Even in an autocratic government, leaders might favor some level of redistributive transfers if the net effect were to reduce the amount of civil unrest and political instability. These considerations would lead to a prediction of some form of a social safety net independently of the form of the government. Moreover, insofar as redistribution of income tends to decrease crime rates and civil unrest, this redistribution and the greater income equality that resulted should increase economic growth.

The fourth set of models focuses on the effects of inequality on the overall saving rate in a society. There is ample empirical evidence that personal saving rates increase with the level of income. If this relationship holds, then a redistribution of resources from the poor to the rich would lead to a higher aggregate saving rate in an economy. By this mechanism, a decline in inequality would actually lower overall investment and lower economic growth. This effect would be amplified if, as discussed earlier, imperfect credit markets coupled with relatively large setup costs for investment implied that greater inequality of asset ownership would be beneficial for the economy. These two arguments imply that aggregate saving rates would be enhanced, together with overall economic growth, if economic inequality were higher.[25]

In sum, the theory is decidedly ambiguous about how inequality affects economic growth. Some models predict a positive effect while others predict a negative effect, though even here ambiguity exists since some models have offsetting effects. It may be that inequality increases economic growth among high income countries (the savings effect dominates) while it retards growth among low income countries (political economy considerations dominate).

The empirical findings, perhaps not surprisingly, have also been ambiguous and, in any case, not very robust. Most of these studies use cross-country data sets (principally, the Penn World Tables) and regress overall growth of GDP or of GDP per capita on control variables plus a measure of income inequality. Some studies use straight cross-country regressions, others use panel data estimates, and still others use instrumental variable techniques.

Perotti (1993) found an overall tendency for inequality to lower economic growth in cross-country regressions. Benabou (1996) reported similar findings. On the other hand, Li and Zou (1998) and Forbes (2000) found that higher inequality was associated with higher economic growth. Forbes used the Deininger and Squire (1996) data set on inequality by country and panel estimation controlling for time-invariant country-specific effects, which eliminated one source of omitted-variable bias. Her estimation period was from 1965 to 1995. She found that her estimated relationship was highly robust across different samples, variable definitions, and model specifications.

Barro (2000) found that the overall effects of inequality on both economic growth and the investment rate were weak and generally statistically insignificant. He also used the Deininger and Squire (1996) data set, and his period of coverage was also 1965 to 1995. His sample size varied, depending on the subperiod of analysis, but was generally about eighty countries. However, he did find evidence of a negative effect of inequality on growth among poor countries (GDP per capita less than $2,000 in 1985 U.S. dollars)

---

[25] Other models emphasize somewhat different relationships. For example, higher inequality may be associated with greater lobbying activity and corruption, more rent-seeking activities of business leaders, or lower overall trust and social capital in a country. Each of these effects might lead to lower economic growth.

but of a positive relationship for richer countries (GDP per capita above $2,000). Barro (2008) updated some of his earlier work. He used the United Nations World Income Inequality Database in his more recent work and his period of coverage was from 1965 to 2004. His estimates from a cross-country growth equation showed that income inequality was negatively related to the growth in per capita income but that this effect diminished as per capita GDP increased and might, indeed, be positive for the high income countries.

Banerjee and Duflo (2003) also made use of the Deininger and Squire (1996) data set on inequality and their period of coverage was from 1970 to 1990, though it varied by country. Their main finding was that the relationship between inequality and growth was nonlinear. In particular, they found strong evidence that the growth rate in per capita income was an inverted U-shaped function of net changes in inequality. Changes of inequality *in any direction* were associated with reduced growth in per capita GDP in the next period.

Several papers looked at the relationship between economic inequality and the institutional structure of a country. Chong and Gradstein (2007) argued that inequality might affect the institutional quality of a country, and conversely. They used the Deininger and Squire (1996) data set on country level inequality, and their period of coverage was 1960 to 2000. They had data for 121 countries. Their measure of institutional quality was based on the International Country Risk Guide (2005). This risk-rating system assigns a numerical value on the basis of five dimensions of institutional quality: (i) government stability, (ii) degree of corruption, (iii) law and order, (iv) democratic accountability, and (v) bureaucracy quality. They found strong evidence of a double causality between institutional strength and a more equal distribution of income on the basis of a dynamic panel and linear feedback analysis.

Fielding and Torres (2005) also argued that a bidirectional relationship might exist between income inequality and other indicators of social and economic development. Their measure of institutional quality was similar to that of Chong and Gradstein (2007). It was computed as an unweighted average of five other indicators: corruption, rule of law, bureaucratic quality, government repudiation of contracts, and risk of expropriation. They found that overall lower inequality was associated with improvements in these other development indicators. A related paper by Bjørnskov (2008) argued that the association between income inequality and economic growth rates might be related to the political ideology of the incumbent government. Using a database compiled by Freedom House (2005), they classified governments as either left wing or right wing. Their estimates indicated that inequality was negatively related to growth under left wing governments but positively associated with inequality under right wing governments.

All in all, the results on inequality and growth are decidedly mixed, and it is safe to say that at best the level of income inequality is a weak force in economic growth.

9.9 The Role of Institutions

There is a large literature on how institutions affect economic development, beginning, perhaps, with North and Thomas (1973). They defined institutions as the formal and informal rules that govern human, social, economic, and political interactions. They argued that progress in the Western world occurred because of the development of economic institutions that fostered economic growth through granting and protecting property rights of individuals. North and Thomas (1973), as well as, more recently, North (2005) revealed that countries of fourteenth- to eighteenth-century Europe experienced divergent economic paths because England, through the success of its parliament, promoted institutions that supported economic growth, whereas Spain adopted a more centralized, protax approach to governing. These early differences eventually led to divergent growth paths in which England became the dominant economic power during the eighteenth century while Spain's wealth became dissipated.

Olson (1996) also emphasized the importance of institutions in explaining why some nations are rich and others poor. Putnam (1993) put the emphasis on what he called "social capital," which encompasses interpersonal trust, norms of civic cooperation, associational activity, cooperative norms, and the like.

Bockstette, Chanda, and Putterman (2002) looked at when different countries were first established, a variable they called "state antiquity." They were able to find information about ninety countries regarding the time when they were first established as independent states (the earliest being China and the most recent Mauritania in their sample). Using cross-country regression analysis, they found that state antiquity was significantly correlated with measures of political stability and institutional quality, with income per capita, and with the rate of growth of per capita income from 1960 to 1995. They also computed that about half of the difference in growth rates of per capita income between China and Mauritania could be explained by differences in state antiquity.

Easterly, Ritzan, and Woolcock (2006) looked at the effects of "social cohesion," which for them was reflected in such variables as income inequality and ethnic fractionalization. They argued that social cohesion endogenously determined institutional quality, which in turn causally determined growth. They defined social cohesion as the nature and extent of social and economic divisions within society. These divisions, whether by income, ethnicity, political leanings, caste, language, or the like, represent points around which societal cleavages can develop. They measured institutional quality by voice and accountability, the extent of civil liberties, government effectiveness, and freedom from corruption. Using data for eighty-two countries in the mid-1990s, they found in their econometric analysis that lower initial inequality (as measured by a larger class share for the middle class) and less ethnolinguistic fractionalization (as measured by more linguistic homogeneity) had a positive and significant effect on institutional quality. Moreover, using three-stage least squares regressions, they found that each of the institutional measures was positively related to the growth of per capita income.[26]

Babetskii and Campos (2007) performed a metastudy of the literature on how structural reform policy affects economic outcomes among countries at different levels of development. As the authors note, despite the fact that most economists believe that economic reforms contribute to economic growth, the empirical literature so far had failed to establish a positive and significant effect of such reforms on economic outcomes. The authors collected data from forty-three econometric studies, including three hundred coefficient estimates. They found that about one-third of these coefficients were positive and significant, one-third negative and significant, and the other third not statistically significant. They attributed the wide variance in results to different definitions of reform and to differences in econometric controls for institutions and initial conditions.

Several papers looked into the effects of "social capability" for economic growth. Three appeared in the *Quarterly Journal of Economics* in successive years. Temple and Johnson (1998) used indices of social development

---

[26] See Alesina and La Ferrara (2005) for an extended review of the literature on ethnic diversity and economic performance. As they concluded, they found overwhelming evidence that public good provision was lower in fragmented societies. However, the evidence was mixed on whether societal fragmentation led to lowered economic performance. They called attention to rich democratic countries like the United States that have both high economic growth and rich ethnic diversity. Moreover, even within the developing world, similar levels of ethnic diversity were associated with very different degrees of conflict and interethnic cooperation. They also called attention to the endogenous formation of political jurisdictions with respect to ethnic diversity.

constructed by Adelman and Morris (1967) in the early 1960s. Adelman and Morris began with data on social, political, and economic indicators for seventy-four less developed countries over the period from 1957 to 1962. Adelman and Morris performed factor analysis on the underlying data to construct an index of socioeconomic development. Temple and Johnson used the principal component of this technique, a variable they called SOCDEV, as a regressor in a cross-country regression of the change in GDP per capita over the 1960 to 1985 period. The sample size was sixty countries. Temple and Johnson found that SOCDEV was positive and significant, generally at the 1 percent level, in explaining GDP per capita growth. They interpreted their results as indicating the importance of social capital as an ingredient in growth in the developing world.

Similar results were obtained by Knack and Keefer (1997). They also developed a measure of social capital that reflected underlying indicators of trust and civic norms from the World Value Surveys for a sample of twenty-nine advanced economies. They developed a measure of "trust" that included such factors as confidence in government, bureaucratic efficiency, property rights, and contract enforceability. Using data on per capita income growth over the period 1980 to 1992 for the twenty-nine countries as the dependent variable, they found first of all that membership in formal groups, which Putnam (1993) emphasized in his measure of social capital, was not associated with greater "trust" or improved economic performance. However, they did find that their measure of "trust" had a positive and significant effect on the growth in per capita income.

Hall and Jones (1999) noted first that differences in physical and human capital could only partially explain the variation in output per worker among countries of the world. Instead, they found that the variations in capital accumulation, productivity, and hence output per worker were due to differences in institutions and government policies, which they called social infrastructure. They used data for 137 countries in 1988 from the Penn World Tables Mark 5.6. For their measure of social infrastructure, they used both the Knack and Keefer (1997) index and the Sachs and Warner (1995) index of trade openness. They argued that social infrastructure was an endogenous factor in growth, so that they used instrumental variable regressions. They used both spoken language and distance from the equator as instruments and found that social infrastructure had a positive and significant effect on output per worker.

Acemoglu, Johnson, and Robinson (2001, 2002) argued that colonial institutions made a large and long-lasting impact on the growth and development of the world's economies. Their econometric analysis relied on the use of mortality rates of settlers in the colonial period as an instrument. They argued that the feasibility of European settlement influenced the type of institutions created by the European colonizers. In places with low mortality rates, European colonists attempted to replicate European institutions by emphasizing private property and checks on government power. In contrast, where mortality rates were high, the colonists created extractive states, with institutions that did not safeguard against government expropriation. Using settler mortality rates as an instrument for institutions, they found that institutional difference between colonial powers (particular, English versus Spanish colonies) was a statistically significant factor in explaining differences in economic growth among former European colonies four hundred years later. They also found long-lived impacts of colonial origin on recent outcomes in terms of social, economic, and political well-being of societies.

In sum, it is clear that basic institutions like the rule of law, the existence of a stable state with a monopoly of force over a given territory, "good government" with some degree of accountability of the state to its citizens and checks and balances on power, social infrastructure, and related factors discussed by Douglas North are essential ingredients for sustained economic growth. These would fall under my category of strong forces. Though often "unseen," these institutions provide a necessary framework for economic development.

9.10 A Potpourri of Additional Factors

9.10.1 Financial Development

Another aspect of institutional capability is the degree of financial development of a country. Several researchers have found that a more developed financial system in a country is positively associated with a higher rate of economic growth.

King and Levine (1993) studied the relation between economic growth and financial development using a sample of seventy-seven countries at all levels of development over the years 1960 to 1989. They controlled for various factors associated with economic growth, including initial income, educational attainment, inflation, black market exchange rate premia, government spending, openness to trade, and political instability. Their measure of financial development was called DEPTH, which was defined as the liquid liabilities of the financial system (currency plus demand and interest-bearing liabilities of banks and nonbank financial intermediaries) divided by GDP.

As they noted, an important weakness with this measure of financial development is that while DEPTH measured the size of the financial intermediary sector it might not accurately represent the functioning of the financial system. It might not indicate how well bank research firms exert corporate control or provide risk management services to clients. Despite this drawback, their results were quite robust to alternative measures of financial development. They used three dependent variables to measure growth: (1) the average rate of real per capita GDP growth, (2) the average rate of growth in the capital stock per person, and (3) TFP growth. In their regression analysis, they found a statistically significant and economically large relationship between DEPTH and (a) long-run real per capita income growth, (b) capital accumulation, and (c) TFP growth. They estimated that a country that increased DEPTH from the mean of the slowest growing quartile of countries (0.2) to the mean of the fastest growing quartile of countries (0.6) would have increased its per capita income growth rate by almost 1 percent per year.

Levine and Zervos (1998) added measures of stock market and banking development to cross-country studies of growth, thereby examining two components of the financial system: banks and equity markets. Their measure of stock market development was the turnover ratio, defined as the total value of shares traded on a country's stock exchanges divided by the total stock market capitalization (the value of listed shares on the country's exchanges). The turnover ratio measured the volume of trading relative to the size of the market. To measure banking sector development, they used a variable "Bank Credit" that measured bank credit to the private sector as a share of GDP. This measure of banking development excluded credit issued by the government and the central bank and excluded credits issued to the government and public enterprises. In their regression analysis, they found that the initial level of stock market liquidity and the initial level of banking development (Bank Credit) were positively and significantly correlated with economic growth, capital accumulation, and TFP growth after controlling for initial income, schooling, inflation, government spending, the black market exchange rate premium, and political stability.

Later studies of Levine and associates also confirmed the positive impact of financial development on economic growth. To control for simultaneity bias, Beck, Levine, and Loayza (2000) used cross-country instrumental variables and found a very strong connection between the exogenous component of financial intermediary development and economic growth. They also found that the exogenous component of financial development was linked to both capital accumulation and TFP growth. Beck and Levine

(2004) employed data averaged over five-year periods to abstract from business-cycle fluctuations and extended the sample through 1998, which mitigated the potential effect of the Asian stock market boom in the 1990s on the results. Using panel data methods in their regressions, they found that the exogenous component of both stock market development and bank development was both positively and significantly related to economic growth.

In more recent work, Luintel, Khan, Arestis, and Theodoridis (2008) investigated the effects of financial structure on economic growth for a sample of fourteen low and middle income countries, including Venezuela, Mexico, Brazil, and India, over the period 1978 to 2005. They used two measures of financial structure. The first, which they called "Finance Size," was computed as the logarithm of the product of the private credit ratio and the level of stock market capitalization. The second, which they called "Finance Activity," was computed as the logarithm of the product of the private credit ratio and the stock market value traded ratio. Using a dynamic panel regression framework to prevent endogeneity problems, they found a positive and significant effect of financial development on output levels. The results were robust to various sensitivity tests.

9.10.2 Natural Resources and Geography

There are several avenues by which the abundance (or lack thereof) of natural resources may affect economic growth that have been discussed in the pertinent literature. An abundance of or heavy dependence on natural resources is usually taken to affect some intermediate factor that either helps or impedes growth. In particular, natural resource dependence is usually believed to "crowd out" other types of capital and thereby slow economic growth (the so-called natural resource curse).

Gylfason (2004) listed five reasons. The first avenue is through the so-called Dutch disease (associated with the discovery of natural gas deposits in the Netherlands in the North Sea in the late 1950s and early 1960s). Under this scenario, the export revenue generated by the exports of natural gas is expected to cause the nominal exchange rate to appreciate and to cause higher inflation. These factors drive up the real exchange rate and undercut the international competitiveness of the other export sectors of the economy. In this way, natural resources in a country tend to reduce the level of total exports and/or bias the composition of exports away from high tech or high value added manufacturing and service exports that may be more beneficial for growth over the long term.

A second avenue is that very large natural resource rents, particularly conjoined with limited property rights, imperfect markets, or lax legal systems, in many developing countries may lead to substantial rent-seeking behavior on the part of firms. This activity will, in turn, divert resources away from more fruitful economic activities that may promote growth in the long run. A third path is that resource abundance may inhibit private investment in human capital because of a high level of nonwage income (rents and dividends, for example). A fourth channel is that natural resource dependence may lower private incentives to save and invest and thereby lower economic growth. When the share of income that accrues to the owners of natural resources increases, the demand for capital will fall, and this will lead to less rapid growth. A fifth avenue is that in countries with poorly developed institutions, this last effect may be compounded if natural resource abundance also inhibits the development of financial institutions.

Gylfason (2004) provided evidence on each of these effects. He presented empirical cross-country results on the basis of eighty-five or so countries (the number varied, depending on the variable under consideration) and for the period 1965–98 (again, the period varied, depending on the variable under consideration) that countries that depended more heavily on their natural resources tended to have (a) less trade and foreign investment, (b) more corruption, (c) less political liberty, (d) less education, (e) less domestic investment, and (f) less financial development than others that were either less well endowed with, or less dependent on, natural resources.

Papyrakis and Gerlagh (2007) presented similar evidence on the basis of a cross section of states in the United States. They used state level data on the growth of income per capita over the period from 1986 to 2000, initial income per capita, and a measure of resource endowments defined as the share of the state's primary sector's production (agriculture, forestry, fishing, and mining) in the real gross state product. They found that the growth of per capita income was negatively related to the level of resource abundance after controlling for initial income per capita.

A related issue is the effect of natural climate on economic growth. Several studies have found that tropical countries (and states) grew more slowly than those in temperate climates. Gallup, Sachs, and Mellinger (1999) investigated how geography may matter directly for growth, controlling for economic policies and institutions, as well as the effects of geography on policy choices and institutions. Using data for seventy-five countries over the 1965 to 1990 period, they found that location and climate had large effects on income levels and income growth through their effects on transport costs, disease burdens, and agricultural productivity, among other channels. Moreover, geography appeared to play a role in the choice of economic policy itself. When they looked at geographical regions that were not conducive to modern economic growth, they identified areas that were located far from the coast, and thus that faced large transport costs for international trade, as well as tropical regions of high disease burden.

Sachs (2001) argued that one of the strongest links in explaining per capita income growth is the ecological zone or physical geography of a country. Almost all of the tropical countries, with the notable exceptions of Hong Kong and Singapore, were underdeveloped at the start of the twenty-first century. When temperate-zone economies are not rich, there is typically a straightforward explanation, such as decades under communism. Sea navigable regions are generally richer than landlocked nations. Those that are both tropical and landlocked – including Bolivia, Chad, Niger, Mali, Uganda, Rwanda, Burundi, Zimbabwe, Zambia, Lesotho, and Laos – were among the very poorest in the world in 2000.

He estimated that between 1820 and 1992, GNP per capita in the temperate region grew at an average annual rate of 1.4 percent, compared with 0.9 percent a year in the nontemperate region. Between 1960 and 1992, both regions grew at about 2.3 percent per year. This reflected fast growth in nontemperate zones of Asia of 2.9 percent per year and continued poor performance in Africa and Latin America. Production technology in the Tropics lagged behind temperate-zone technology in the two critical areas of agriculture and health. The difficulty of mobilizing energy resources in tropical economies also contributed to slow economic growth. The problems of applying temperate-zone technological advances to the tropical setting amplified these factors. Technologies that could diffuse within ecological zones could not diffuse across them. For major crops like rice, maize, and wheat, productivity was considerably higher in the temperate zone than in the tropical zone. The gap was due to differences in soil formation and erosion, pests and parasites, water availability, and the effects of tropical climates on plant respiration.

Ram (1999) also found that "tropicality" was a factor in explaining differences in economic growth across states in the United States. He performed a straightforward regression of personal income per capita for the states for the years 1920, 1950, 1970, and 1990 on each state's distance from the equator. He found that distance from the equator was positively related to state per capita income. However, he also found that the "tropicality" penalty declined substantially over time, from 1929 to 1990.

9.10.3 The Foreign Aid Debate

There are two sharply contrasting views on the effectiveness of foreign aid in promoting development among less developed countries. The first, represented by David Dollar, believes that foreign aid can be effective when coupled with appropriate institutional and political changes. The second, represented by the William Easterly camp, feels that foreign aid is ineffective in promoting growth.

The "pro side" is represented by Burnside and Dollar (2000). They investigated the relationship between foreign aid, economic policy, and the growth of GDP per capita using a database that contained information on foreign aid that was developed by the World Bank. They ran a set of regressions across developing countries in which the dependent variable was the growth rate of GDP per capita and the independent variables were initial GDP per capita, an index that measured institutional and policy distortions (a weighted average of budget deficits/GDP, inflation, and an index of openness to trade), foreign aid measured in dollars, and an interaction term between foreign aid and a set of policy measures. Their sample consisted of fifty-six less developed countries. To avoid the problem that foreign aid and growth in per capita income might be correlated over periods of a few years but not on a year-to-year basis, they subdivided their sample into six four-year periods covering the years from 1970–3 to 1990–3. In certain specifications, they also included variables for the degree of ethnic fractionalization, whether assassinations occurred, dummy variables for certain regions, and a measure of imports of armaments. In many of their specifications, they found the interaction term between foreign aid and "good policy" to be positive and statistically significant. They concluded, "We find that aid has a positive impact on growth in developing countries with good fiscal, monetary, and trade policies but has little effect in the presence of poor policies" (p. 847).

Since the Burnside and Dollar (2000) paper, many papers have reacted to their results, including Hansen and Tarp (2001), Dalgaard and Hansen (2001), Guillamont and Chauvet (2001), and Lensink and White (2001). These papers conducted variations on the Burnside and Dollar econometric specification, introducing variables such as the square of foreign aid, terms of trade shocks, variability of agricultural output and exports, and interaction terms between foreign aid and terms of trade shocks. Some of these papers confirmed the Burnside and Dollar finding that foreign aid was beneficial for growth only in conjunction with a good policy environment, while others found that when particular variables were added, the coefficient on the interaction between foreign aid and policy became close to zero and/or statistically insignificant.

Easterly (2003) argued that the Burnside and Dollar (2000) results were flawed. He cited Easterly, Levine, and Roodman (2003), who expanded the Burnside and Dollar data set to include newer data and then investigated how their results were affected even within the original data set by different definitions of "aid" and "good policy." Easterly, Levine, and Roodman first used the same specification as Burnside and Dollar (2000) but simply added more data that had become available since their study was performed. Using a sample covering the period 1970–97, they carried out the same regression with the same control variables including terms for foreign aid, their policy index, and the interaction between aid and the policy index. They reported that the coefficient on the crucial interaction term between aid and policy was insignificant in the expanded sample, which indicated no support for the conclusion that "aid works in a good policy environment."

They also showed that even in the original Burnside and Dollar (2000) sample and period, the significance of the interactive variable between aid and public policy was not robust to other, equally plausible definitions of "aid," "policies," and "growth." Their definition of aid was the grant element of aid, excluding the loan component of "concessional" loans, which were made at extremely low interest rates. When this component of aid was added in, they found that the interactive term between aid and policy was no longer statistically significant. With regard to "good policy," Burnside and Dollar (2000) constructed an index number that included the budget surplus, the inflation rate, and a measure of the openness of an economy. As an alternative, Easterly, Levine, and Roodman used the black market premium and a measure of financial depth (the ratio of M2 to GDP) as a variable in the policy index and found once again that the interactive term of aid and good policy was no longer statistically significant.

Rajan and Subramanian (2008) presented more recent evidence on this debate. They examined the effects of aid on growth, both in cross-sectional regressions and in panel data regressions, and after correcting for the bias that aid typically went to poorer countries or to countries after they registered poor growth performance. They used data for four periods – 1960–2000, 1970–2000, 1980–2000, and 1990–2000 – and for sixty-nine to seventy-seven less developed countries in their sample (depending on the period covered). Even after these statistical corrections for possible endogeneity, they reported little robust evidence of a positive (or even negative) relationship between aid inflows into a country and its economic growth. They also found no evidence that foreign aid worked better in better policy environments or in "better" geographical environments, or that certain forms of foreign aid worked better than others.

9.10.4 The Regulatory Framework

Several papers have looked at the effects of product market and labor market regulation on productivity growth across countries. Nicoletti and Scarpetta (2003) investigated the effect of regulation on TFP levels on the basis of cross-country data for several industrial sectors and including a regulatory variable directly in the productivity equation. TFP was calculated for seventeen manufacturing and six service industries in eighteen OECD countries. They found when using a time invariant country level measure of liberalization collected by the OECD in 1998 that the regulation variables were not significant on their own in regressions that did not include a country effect. However, the regulation variables were significant when interacted with the technology gap of the country. Time varying measures of privatization were also introduced on their own, and they generally had a positive and significant effect on productivity growth. When a time varying measure of liberalization based on information in seven service sectors was introduced, they found that the privatization index was insignificant while the time varying measure of regulation was significant and positive.

Loayza, Oviedo, and Serven (2005) considered the effect of regulation on the economic performance of a wide set of countries, including developing countries. Their work used time invariant indices on product market regulation, which was a composite of entry, trade, financial markets, bankruptcy, and contract enforcement indices. An index of labor market regulation was also constructed. These indices were used as regressors in standard cross-country growth regressions for output per capita over the 1990s, with interaction terms for the quality of governance. They found a negative and significant direct effect of product and labor market regulation on the growth of output per capita. However, results on the interaction terms suggested that better governance lessened the negative effect of regulation. The overall effect of regulation was sizable and negative for most developing countries, while it was zero or even mildly positive for countries with good quality of governance.

Delis, Molyneux, and Pasiouras (2008) investigated the relation between the regulatory and supervision framework and the productivity of banks in twenty-two Eastern European countries and former Soviet republics over the period 1999–2006. Their measure of regulation related to capital requirements, official supervisory power, market discipline, and restrictions on bank activities. After controlling for country-specific and bank-specific characteristics, they used a bootstrap procedure in their regression analysis. They found that regulations and incentives that promoted private monitoring had a positive impact on productivity in the banking sector. Restrictions on the activities of banks with regard to their involvement in securities, insurance, real estate, and ownership of nonfinancial firms likewise had a positive impact on the productivity performance of the banking sector. However, regulations relating to capital requirements and official supervisory power did not have a statistically significant impact on productivity in the sector.

9.11 Africa, East Asia, and the Former Communist Bloc

Both Sub-Saharan Africa and East Asia stand as outliers to the development paths of most other regions of the world. Arbache and Page (2007a, 2007b) documented the development of Sub-Saharan Africa between 1976 and 2005. As they noted, the path of GDP per capita followed a U-shaped pattern, first falling in absolute terms from the mid-1970s to the mid-1990s and then rising after that. By 2005, GDP per capita did not yet recover to the levels of the mid-1970s. The African growth story, moreover, contrasted strongly with that of other regions. Whereas all other regions of the world experienced significant improvements in GDP per capita between the 1970s and the 2000s, Africa's per capita income shrank.

They also found considerable volatility in growth rates of per capita income over time. Between 1975 and 2005, Africa had a considerable number of growth acceleration episodes but also nearly a comparable number of growth collapses, offsetting most of the gains of the growth periods. They estimated that GDP per capita in Africa would have been 30 percent higher in 2005 had Africa avoided its growth collapses.

Barro (1991) and Levine and Renelt (1992), among others, found a low growth effect in Africa that remained even after controlling for such conventional variables as the investment rate, education, and macroeconomic policies. The growth in physical capital per worker in Africa was less than 0.5 percent per year from 1960 to 2005, far slower than the world average of 1.0 percent. As reported by Bosworth and Collins (2003), capital deepening was actually negative between 1990 and 2003. Moreover, TFP growth was actually negative, -0.4 percent per year, from 1990 to 2003.

Explanations of the poor economic performance of Sub-Saharan Africa tend to focus on "poor institutions." Easterly and Levine (2003) and Acemoglu, Johnson, and Robinson (2003) found this to be the case in their

analyses. The latter also pointed to distortionary macroeconomic policies that allowed groups in power to reap rents and remain in power. This,
in turn, led the economies into further difficulties in dealing with political and economic shocks and made economic adjustments in the face of
such external shocks more difficult to handle. As discussed earlier, Bodea
and Elbadawi found that Sub-Saharan Africa had been disproportionately
impacted by civil war, which explained a substantial share of its economic
decline.

The East Asian story is exactly the opposite. The average annual growth
rate of GDP per capita of the "original" Asian Tigers was 4.66 percent from
1970 to 2003. A protracted debate ensued over what factors were behind
the success of the tigers. The two major (and opposing) views were that
(1) their success was driven by government industrial policy, particularly
export-oriented trade policies; and (2) high investment was the chief cause
of their economic success.

Amsden (1989, 1991) and Wade (1990) argued in favor of the first
view and the central role of export-led growth. Their basic argument was
that during the 1950s East Asian countries, principally South Korea and
Taiwan, engaged in traditional import-substitution policies, with multiple exchange rates, high levels of trade protection, and controlled financial markets. By the end of the decade, the countries had exhausted this
strategy. As a result, beginning in the 1960s, both countries changed their
economic strategy and pursued export-oriented policies. These included
the adoption of single exchange rates accompanied by devaluation, duty-
free access for exporters to imported inputs, and partial liberalization
of import restrictions. Moreover, the governments in the two countries
adopted specific industrial policies and, in fact, intervened in the market
through export subsidies, trade restrictions, administrative guidance, and
credit allocation in order to direct comparative advantage in the desired
direction. As a result, each country specialized its production in these
"favored" industries and exports boomed by the mid-1960s. Exports as a
share of GDP rose from virtually 0 in Korea in the early 1960s to 30 percent by the early 1980s and from about 10 percent in Taiwan to more than
40 percent over the same years.

Rodrik (1995), in contrast, favored the second view. His work focused
on South Korea and Taiwan. He argued that most explanations of their economic success since the early 1960s placed heavy emphasis on export orientation. However, it was difficult to see how export orientation could have
played a significant causal role in their economic development. One reason
was that the increase in the relative profitability of exports during the 1960s

was much too small to explain the explosion in exports that followed over the next two decades. A second reason was that exports as a share of GDP was initially too insignificant to have a major impact on overall economic performance. Instead, he argued that a more reasonable explanation centered on the investment boom that took place in both countries. In the early 1960s both economies had an extremely well-educated labor force relative to their physical capital stock, rendering the latent return to capital quite high. By subsidizing and coordinating investment decisions, the government policy of the two countries led to a substantial climb in the private return to capital. Moreover, a high degree of income equality helped by rendering government intervention effective and keeping it free of rent seeking. The outward orientation of the economy was the result of the increase in demand for imported capital goods, not the reverse.

Rodrik argued that the key reason for the investment boom that began in the early 1960s was that the two governments removed a number of impediments to investment and established a sound investment climate. They also engaged in a number of strategic interventions, including investment subsidies, administrative guidance, and the formation of public enterprises. His main evidence for this line of argument was the extraordinary increase in investment, which climbed from about 10 percent of GDP in the two countries in the late 1950s to about 30 percent in 1980. Moreover, on the basis of econometric analysis, he found that this rise in investment, in turn, led to the sharp rise in exports documented previously.

A similar argument was made by Dollar (2007) regarding the extraordinary growth achieved by China since the early 1980s. As documented by Dollar, between 1990 and 2005 China accounted for 28 percent of the world's economic growth, measured as purchasing power parity (PPP). In terms of the growth of per capita GDP, China achieved an annual rate of 8.7 percent over this period in comparison to an average of 2.7 percent for the rest of the developing world. Dollar argued that the main reason that China achieved this extraordinary growth was that it started its reform process with a better base of human capital, was more open to foreign trade and investment, and created good investment climates in coastal cities in comparison with other LDCs. In terms of exports, China achieved a spectacular 15.0 percent per year growth in exports over the years 1990 to 2005. In terms of human capital, the average years of schooling of the adult population in China was 5.2 years, compared to 3.5 years in the rest of developing Asia. In terms of investment, about half of the growth in output per worker could be attributed to the growth of physical capital per worker (the other half was due mainly to a very rapid rise in TFP).

The opposite story characterized the former Soviet republics and Eastern European countries since the early 1990s, with the breakup of the Soviet state and the end of central planning. Åslund and Genish (2006) first documented the extraordinary economic collapse of these countries after the fall of Communism in 1989 and then recovery in the late 1990s and early 2000s.

When the transition to a market economy started, recorded output plummeted in all countries. In 1990 only Poland and Hungary launched their transitions, and the very sharp declines in their registered production caused a shock. When other countries in Central Europe entered the transition in 1991, their output plummeted even more, but these falls were nothing in comparison with those of the CIS countries, several of which saw real collapse.

Not only were the declines in output huge, they lasted for years. Poland took an early lead by returning to growth in 1992. By 1994 the whole of Central Europe recorded growth, and three of the most vigorous reformers in the former Soviet Union had also seen some positive growth: Armenia, Lithuania, and Latvia. In 1995 other reformers followed, namely, Estonia, Georgia, and Kyrgyzstan. However, several former Soviet republics experienced a prolonged decline followed by stagnation. These included Russia, the Ukraine, Moldova, and Kazakhstan. Only at the end of the decade did they return to economic growth. The total fall in output was shocking. According to official statistics, the aggregate decline in GDP was 19 percent in Central Europe and 29 percent in Southeast Europe. In the former Soviet Union, the collapse was truly stunning, with 44 percent in the Baltics and 53 percent in the CIS.[27]

The early literature on the causes of the output collapses, as summarized by Åslund and Genish (2006), concluded that the more radical and comprehensive the market economic reform, the earlier a country returned to economic growth and the more vigorous its growth. The three major points of the transition were macroeconomic stabilization, deregulation, and privatization.

Almost all transition countries started out with high inflation, and output continued to fall until inflation had been brought under control. Deregulation was the basis for the formation of a market economy, and the earlier econometric results showed the rising importance of deregulation

---

[27] These declines are probably overstated because the Soviet system of national accounts exaggerated output during the era of central planning for the purpose of achieving plan targets.

for growth. The privatization policies were always more debatable, but the econometric analysis that included the share of GDP arising from the private sector showed that privatization had a clear positive impact on growth. However, the standard factors in explaining long-term economic growth, including the ratio of investment to GDP and education, appeared to be of little importance. With regard to the latter, human capital was already well developed in these countries before the transition and did not play a role in explaining the recovery.

Economic growth was also correlated with the expansion of exports. Imports took off slightly later. The countries that joined the European Union benefited from privileged access to the large EU market. A common finding was that the closer a country was to Brussels, the higher its economic growth. With regard to politics, the 1990s evidenced strong, positive correlation among democracy, comprehensive market reforms, and economic growth because in the early transition the threat against successful market reforms did not arise from the many losers but from the few winners who engaged in excessive rent seeking. Also, as a result, corruption was negatively correlated with economic growth. In sum, radical market reform, macroeconomic stabilization, privatization, EU accession, export expansion, democracy, and reasonable governance all went together. However, GDP growth rates remained very low, and only Poland had exceeded its economic level of 1989 by 2000.

9.12 Concluding Comments

The material presented in Section 9.2 provides very little evidence of *unconditional* productivity convergence among countries of the world at all levels of development over the postwar period. However, conditional convergence was strong among these countries, and once controls for investment and education were included in the regression models, the coefficient on initial productivity (or real GDP per capita) was negative and highly significant at the 1 percent level. Thus, the catch-up effect acts as a strong force among the whole range of countries of the world in fostering economic growth.

Three other strong forces were identified. The first of these was investment. My own work and other literature confirmed that the investment rate (the ratio of investment to GDP) and the rate of growth of the capital-labor ratio were both highly significant factors in explaining country-level productivity growth. The second was the *level* of education of a country's population. It is clear from my own work and that of others in the literature that regression analysis almost universally finds a positive and significant effect of the level of schooling (particularly, primary and secondary schooling) on the rate of productivity growth. However, it is not clear that there is a strong (or, indeed, any) relation between the change in educational attainment and productivity growth on the country level.

The third factor might be termed a good institutional framework. The latter includes such factors as the rule of law, the existence of a stable polity, "good government," and a developed social infrastructure. These factors almost invariably show up as positive and statistically significant effects in economic development.

Many other factors have been considered in the existing literature on economic development and growth. These produce mixed or weak results and, in some cases, even counterintuitive findings. This list would include the degree of trade openness, foreign direct investment, investment in R&D (at least, among countries at all levels of development), population growth, military expenditures, political factors such as voting rights and the degree of democracy in a society, the level of income inequality in a society, the degree of financial development in an economy, the abundance of natural resources, the level of foreign aid received, and the degree of product market and labor market regulation.

APPENDIX TO CHAPTER 9

Appendix Table 9.1. *Real GDP per Capita (RGDPL) by Country Group and for Selected Countries, 1970–2003*

Country	1970	1980	1990	2000	2003	Average Annual Growth Rate (AAGR) 1970–2003
1. Industrialized Market Economies						
Switzerland	21,081	24,043	27,447	28,831	28,792	0.94
United States	17,430	21,681	27,174	34,365	34,875	2.10
Luxembourg	16,820	20,382	32,033	48,217	49,261	3.26
Ireland	7,752	10,615	13,462	24,948	28,247	3.92
Average (23 countries)	13,222	16,952	20,810	25,950	26,697	2.13
2. High Income Oil Producers						
Saudi Arabia	14,964	30,968	17,420	15,827	16,010	0.20
Bahrain	11,834	18,494	17,191	18,652	19,561	1.52
United Arab Emirates	9,756	46,960	25,287	32,182	35,676	3.93
Average (5 countries)	12,155	24,330	17,358	18,658	19,416	1.42
3. The Original Asian "Tigers"						
Macao	7,005	14,291	21,867	24,224	30,420	4.45
Hong Kong	6,988	13,326	22,003	27,236	27,656	4.17
Singapore	6,844	13,001	19,472	29,434	27,004	4.16
Taiwan	2,872	5,945	11,284	19,184	19,886	5.86
Korea, Republic of	2,621	4,557	9,591	15,702	17,595	5.77
Average (5 countries)	5,266	10,224	16,844	23,156	24,512	4.66

4. The New Asian "Tigers"

Malaysia	2,572	5,010	6,924	11,406	12,131	4.70
Thailand	1,748	2,742	4,845	6,474	7,275	4.32
Indonesia	1,279	2,083	2,917	3,772	4,121	3.55
India	1,154	1,350	1,897	2,644	2,990	2.88
China	500	751	1,678	4,002	4,970	6.96
Average (5 countries)	1,451	2,387	3,652	5,659	6,297	4.45

5. Upper Middle Income Countries

Argentina	9,740	10,807	8,231	11,332	10,172	0.13
Venezuela	7,761	8,815	7,484	7,323	6,251	-0.66
South Africa	6,404	7,514	7,723	8,226	8,835	0.98
Chile	6,165	6,675	7,143	11,430	12,141	2.05
Hungary	5,725	8,503	10,087	11,383	13,016	2.49
Mexico	5,109	7,201	6,877	8,082	7,939	1.34
Average (20 countries)	8,460	10,359	11,011	13,243	13,709	1.46

6. Lower Middle Income Countries

Brazil	3,976	6,669	6,834	7,194	7,204	1.80
Poland	3,898	6,236	5,897	8,611	9,217	2.61
Colombia	3,469	4,823	5,442	6,080	6,095	1.71
Turkey	3,031	3,588	4,768	5,715	5,634	1.88
Average (21 countries)	3,679	4,932	5,738	7,244	7,552	2.18

(continued)

Appendix Table 9.1. (continued)

Country	1970	1980	1990	2000	2003	Average Annual Growth Rate (AAGR) 1970–2003
7. Low Income Countries						
Zimbabwe	2,880	3,227	3,448	3,256	2,438	-0.51
Cuba	2,675	3,749	6,726	5,699	6,288	2.59
Philippines	2,427	3,293	3,209	3,826	3,576	1.17
Romania	2,375	5,627	5,637	5,211	6,058	2.84
Iraq	2,003	3,386	2,538	2,445	1,230	-1.48
Egypt	1,892	2,572	3,384	4,536	4,759	2.80
Afghanistan	1,731	2,121	1,751	478	588	-3.27
Congo, Dem. Rep.	1,419	1,154	974	359	436	-3.58
Somalia	1,374	1,137	994	682	682	-2.12
Sierra Leone	1,326	1,343	1,178	684	713	-1.88
Congo, Republic of	1,235	2,089	2,646	1,286	1,421	0.43
Pakistan	1,235	1,591	2,197	2,477	2,592	2.25
Botswana	1,184	2,764	5,395	7,256	8,054	5.81
Zambia	1,147	1,289	1,117	866	946	-0.58
Kenya	1,134	1,261	1,351	1,268	1,218	0.22
Central African Republic	1,118	1,071	1,006	945	888	-0.70
Niger	1,106	1,224	997	807	835	-0.85
Cambodia	1,087	458	388	514	580	-1.90
Syria	1,066	1,900	1,519	2,001	2,016	1.93
Uganda	1,059	749	709	1,058	1,114	0.15

Rwanda	1,057	1,255	1,006	1,018	1,297	0.62
Ghana	1,041	1,140	1,153	1,392	1,440	0.98
Nigeria	1,031	987	1,060	1,074	1,223	0.52
Tanzania	576	571	498	817	912	1.39
Average (71 countries)	1,487	1,904	2,115	2,390	2,543	1.63
All countries (150 countries)						
Mean	5,003	6,803	7,725	9,473	9,906	
Standard deviation	4,980	7,370	7,865	9,888	10,273	
Coeff. Of Var.	1.00	1.08	1.02	1.04	1.04	
Correlation (AAGR, RGDP70)						0.068

Notes: All countries in Penn World Tables Version 6.2 with per capita income figures in 1970 and 2003 are included in the sample with the exception of Qatar, Kuwait, and Brunei. These three countries are excluded because their per capita income is more than three times the per capita income of any other country in the sample. Countries are classified according to their RGDP in 1970

Appendix Table 9.2. *Research and Development Expenditure by Country Group*
(Period Averages)

Country Group	Ratio of R&D Expenditure to GNP (percentage)			
	1960–88	1960–70	1970–9	1979–88
A. All Countries				
Mean	0.68	0.73	0.7	0.94
Standard Deviation	0.66	0.69	0.68	0.87
Coeff. of Variation	0.97	0.95	0.96	0.93
Number	84	58	77	59
B. Industrial Market Economies				
Mean	1.49	1.3	1.43	1.7
Standard Deviation	0.66	0.71	0.63	0.69
Coeff. of Variation	0.44	0.54	0.44	0.41
Number	19	19	19	19
C. Upper Middle Income, High Income Oil Exporters and Centrally Planned Countries				
Mean	0.58	0.61	0.54	0.9
Standard Deviation	0.66	0.73	0.73	0.99
Coeff. of Variation	1.15	1.2	1.34	1.09
Number	20	12	20	15
D. Lower Middle Income Countries				
Mean	0.34	0.41	0.35	0.3
Standard Deviation	0.22	0.35	0.21	0.2
Coeff. of Variation	0.64	0.86	0.59	0.66
Number	25	15	21	16
E. Low Income Countries				
Mean	0.45	0.34	0.49	0.51
Standard Deviation	0.36	0.28	0.4	0.46
Coeff. of Variation	0.8	0.81	0.82	0.92
Number	20	12	17	9

Note: The division of the countries into groups follows the World Bank convention
Source: UNESCO statistical yearbooks, various years.

Appendix Table 9.3. *Comparative Statistics for Centrally Planned Economies, Industrial Market Economies, and Upper Middle Income Countries, 1950–1985*

Country Group	Summers and Heston RGDP, International Prices, Relative to U.S.						Growth Rate 1950–85 (annual %)
	1950	1960	1970	1980	1985		
Centrally Planned Economies							
Bulgaria	0.20	0.32	0.41	0.43	0.41		2.05
China	0.07	0.10	0.11	0.14	0.20		3.00
Czechoslovakia	0.49	0.61	0.61	0.61	0.59		0.53
Germany Dem Rep	0.33	0.58	0.62	0.69	0.70		2.15
Hungary	0.34	0.44	0.46	0.48	0.46		0.86
Poland	0.34	0.38	0.41	0.44	0.39		0.39
Romania	0.17	0.23	0.27	0.35	0.34		1.98
USSR	0.31	0.40	0.47	0.49	0.50		1.37
Yugoslavia	0.17	0.24	0.31	0.42	0.40		2.44
Average	0.27	0.37	0.41	0.45	0.44		1.40
Memo							
Industrial Market Economies: Average[a]	0.52	0.61	0.70	0.76	0.74		1.01
Upper Middle Income Countries: Average[b]	0.30	0.29	0.33	0.38	0.37		0.60

(continued)

425

Appendix Table 9.3. (continued)

| Country Group | Gross Enrollment Rates | | | | | |
| | Primary School | | Secondary School | | Higher Education | |
	1965	1983	1965	1983	1965	1983
Centrally Planned Economies						
Bulgaria	1.03	1.00	0.54	0.85	0.17	0.16
China	0.89	1.04	0.24	0.35	0.00	0.01
Czechoslovakia	0.99	0.88	0.29	0.45	0.14	0.16
Germany Dem Rep	1.09	0.95	0.60	0.88	0.19	0.30
Hungary	1.01	1.01	0.63	0.74	0.13	0.15
Poland	1.04	1.01	0.58	0.75	0.18	0.16
Romania	1.01	0.99	0.39	0.63	0.10	0.12
USSR	1.03	1.06	0.72	0.99	0.30	0.21
Yugoslavia	1.06	1.01	0.65	0.82	0.13	0.20
Average	1.02	0.99	0.52	0.72	0.15	0.16
Memo						
Industrial Market Economies: Average[a]	1.04	1.01	0.62	0.89	0.15	0.30
Upper Middle Income Countries: Average[b]	0.99	1.06	0.33	0.61	0.07	0.17

Country Group	Investment Rate, 1965–81 (%)	Population Growth, 1960–85 (annual %)	Merchand. Exports / GNP, 1984 (%)	Merchand. Imports / 1984 (%)	Military Expend./ GNP, 1982 (%)	R&D/ GNP, 1980 (%)
Centrally Planned Economies						
Bulgaria	28.8	0.52			4.1	3.7
China		0.25	38.1	36.0	2.4	2.8
Czechoslovakia	20.9	0.84			1.5	
Germany Dem Rep	22.9	–0.08			4.4	
Hungary	23.1	1.84	7.8	8.2	8.3	1.0
Poland	23.9	0.91	15.0	13.6	3.0	2.8
Romania	33.1	0.55			3.6	2.8
USSR	26.3	1.05			10.9	4.8
Yugoslavia		0.91	21.0	24.6	3.9	0.8
Average	25.6	0.76	20.5	20.6	4.7	2.7
Memo						
Industrial Market Economies: Average[a]	26.8	0.76	26.4	26.7	2.9	1.5
Singapore	35.5	1.76	132.5	157.4	5.6	0.3
Upper Middle Income Countries: Average[b]	23.9	2.05	34.4	38.0	5.3	0.4

Notes: [a]Industrial market economies include Australia, Austria, Belgium, Canada, Denmark, Finland, France, Federal Republic of Germany, Ireland, Italy, Japan, the Netherlands, New Zealand, Norway, Spain, Sweden, Switzerland, United Kingdom, and the United States
[b] Upper middle income countries include Argentina, Brazil, Greece, Hong Kong, Israel, Republic of Korea, Malaysia, Mexico, Panama, Portugal, Singapore, South Africa, Uruguay, and Venezuela

Appendix Table 9.4. *Income Distribution Comparisons for Countries at Various Levels of Development, around 2000*

Country	Year	y/c	Income (y) or consumption (c) inequality	
			Gini index	P90/P10 ratio
A. Low Income Countries				
Bangladesh	2000	y	0.31	3.9
Ghana	1999	c	0.41	7.3
India	1999/2000	c	0.33	–
Indonesia	2000	c	0.34	–
Nigeria	2003	c	0.41	7.3
Pakistan	2001	c	0.27	3.1
Sri Lanka	2002	c	0.38	5.0
Average			0.35	5.3
B. Lower Middle Income Countries				
Philippines	2000	c	0.46	–
Cote d'Ivoire	2002	c	0.45	6.8
Morocco	1998	c	0.38	5.3
Guatemala	2000	y	0.58	16.8
Jamaica	2001	c	0.42	5.9
Colombia	1999	y	0.54	15.0
Peru	2000	c	0.48	14.6
Costa Rica	2000	y	0.46	9.7
Poland	2002	c	0.31	4.0
Malaysia	1997	y	0.49	–
Brazil	2001	y	0.59	16.3
Average			0.47	10.5
C. Upper Middle Income Countries				
Hungary	2002	c	0.24	3.0
Slovenia	1998	c	0.28	–
Turkey	2002	c	0.37	5.7
Venezuela	2000	y	0.42	7.9
Average			0.33	5.5
D. High Income Economies				
Spain	2000	y	0.35	4.7
Israel	2001	y	0.31	4.3
Singapore	1998	y	0.43	–
New Zealand	1997	y	0.37	–
Australia	1994	y	0.32	4.9
United Kingdom	1999	y	0.34	5.0
Italy	2000	c	0.31	4.3
Belgium	2000	y	0.26	3.2
Netherlands	1999	y	0.29	3.9

Country	Year	y/c	Income (y) or consumption (c) inequality	
			Gini index	P90/P10 ratio
France	1994	y	0.31	–
Canada	2000	y	0.33	4.5
Denmark	1997	y	0.27	–
Germany	2000	y	0.28	3.6
Finland	2000	y	0.25	3.1
Sweden	2000	y	0.25	3.2
United States	2000	y	0.38	6.3
Norway	2000	y	0.27	3.0
Japan	1993	y	0.25	–
Switzerland	1992	y	0.31	–
Average			0.31	4.1

Source: World Bank, World Development Report 2006 (New York: Oxford University Press, 2006), table A2, pp. 280–1.

10

Recapitulation and Future Prospects for Growth

10.1 Introduction

In this chapter I summarize the major findings of the book and speculate on "lessons to be learned" and future prospects for growth around the world. I first review the basic results on convergence around the world and among OECD countries in particular both over the long term and over the postwar period (Section 10.2). In the next two sections I summarize the evidence on the factors that have been found to play a role in the convergence process. I divide the myriad factors into two groups. The first of these, what I have called "strong forces," are discussed in Section 10.3. These include the catch-up effect (the initial productivity level), capital formation, education, R&D and technological spillovers, and basic social and political institutional factors. These factors explain the vast majority of the variation in the growth rates of GDP per capita or productivity (by some estimates as much as 90 percent).

The second set of factors, which I have termed "weak forces," is discussed in Section 10.4. These comprise almost all the other variables used in the analysis of convergence. These include international trade and FDI, the role of democracy and political institutions, inequality, financial development, geography and resource availability, regulation, structural change, and foreign aid. These factors collectively might account for another 5 percent of the variation in the growth rates of GDP per capita or productivity. One odd feature of the research in this area is that there seems to be an inverse relation between the amount of work done on a subject (inequality, for example) and its importance as a determinant of growth.

Section 10.5 provides a summary of the "lessons" about growth that can be inferred from the works surveyed in the book. It starts out with a brief summary of the major factors affecting growth and convergence. It then provides a short overview of the state of the world in terms of development and recent growth experiences. This is followed by a brief assessment of the prospects for future growth among (today's) advanced industrialized countries. Finally, it speculates on some of the lessons that are most relevant for today's middle income and less developed countries.

As a cautionary note, it should be emphasized again that many of the results reported in the works cited in the book were not robust. In particular, as Levine and Renelt (1992) discussed, coefficient estimates and significance levels often changed with the data used, the periods used, and the econometric specification. In addition, it is often hard to establish the direction of causation. Moreover, as discussed in Chapter 3, measures of labor productivity and, in particular, TFP are quite sensitive to the methodology used. As discussed in Chapter 3, work in this area is often plagued by severe econometric problems. Perhaps foremost among these is endogeneity, in which many of the explanatory variables used in the analysis are themselves codetermined with the dependent variable. This situation will produce biased coefficient estimators in the regression analysis. Another important problem is sample selection. Results are found to be quite sensitive to the countries included in the sample. A third is the omitted variable bias. This refers to a variable that is an important determinant of the dependent variable but is excluded from the list of explanatory variables used in the regression equation (perhaps because of lack of the appropriate data). This exclusion will also lead to biased coefficient estimates. A fourth is measurement error, which in most cases will cause the coefficient estimate to be biased downward toward zero.

10.2 Patterns of Convergence

I begin with a review of the evidence on patterns of convergence in both GDP per capita and productivity. The focus here is on unconditional convergence or σ-convergence (see Chapter 2 for an explanation of these terms). I start with convergence over the long term among the advanced industrial countries and then discuss convergence among the same group of countries in the postwar period. The third part will look into convergence and growth in the very long term. The final part will present the evidence on postwar convergence among all countries of the world.

10.2.1 Long-Term Results

The central argument on convergence is from Gerschenkron's notion of the advantage of relative backwardness. The argument is that countries and industries that are particularly far behind the technological frontier have the most potential to gain from technology transfer and should grow most rapidly.

Baumol (1986) was among the first to document this convergence in labor productivity levels over the long term. His data covered the period from 1870 to 1979 and was based on the so-called Maddison-16 sample, drawn from Maddison (1982). The results gave strong evidence of σ-convergence and catch-up. Indeed, between 1870 and 1938, the coefficient of variation in labor productivity levels among this sample fell almost by half, from 0.49 to 0.27. However, because of the destruction of capital stock in many European countries and in Japan during World War II, the coefficient of variation climbed back to a value of 0.42 in 1950. There followed a remarkable degree of convergence from 1950 to 1979, with the coefficient of variation falling by 61 percent, from 0.42 to 0.17.

He also found that the overall correlation coefficient between 1870 productivity levels and the annual rate of productivity growth from 1870 to 1979 was –0.93. The results were almost as strong for the postwar period alone. In this case, the correlation coefficient between initial labor productivity levels in 1950 and the rate of labor productivity growth over the 1950–79 period was –0.89.

The original Baumol results were challenged in two major directions. First, Abramovitz (1986) showed that the pattern of convergence was not very uniform even for this group of countries, and for the period 1870 to 1979, and, indeed, for some periods, there was actually divergence in productivity levels. He also found that labor productivity convergence was considerably slower between 1870 and 1938 than between 1950 and 1979. Moreover, between 1938 and 1950, productivity levels actually diverged, though this was partly attributable to the differential effects of World War II on the various economies of the world. Abramovitz also found that there were significant changes in leadership and the rank order of countries over time (for example, Australia was the early leader in productivity but ranked only ninth of sixteen in 1979). This result was at variance with a simple convergence hypothesis. Abramovitz argued that convergence depended on the appropriate social capabilities of a country and his conditional convergence argument won the day.

The second criticism was by De Long (1988). His basic argument was that Baumol's results suffered from sample selection bias. In particular, the countries chosen for the Maddison sample included only those countries that had proved successful – that is, the OECD countries. In fact, using data from a wider sample of countries, including Ireland, Chile, Portugal, and

Spain, de Long found that the correlation between initial productivity and productivity growth over this period was much weaker.

Baumol and Wolff (1988) in response showed that the de Long criticisms were not as cutting as they first appeared. Using the Summers and Heston data on GDP per capita (RGDP) for seventy-two countries between 1950 and 1980, they found that σ-convergence held up for top thirty-five to forty countries in the sample as ranked by RGDP in 1950. The simple convergence story then petered out for countries beyond (that is, lower than) this point. However, despite the rebuttal of Baumol and Wolff (1988), the original Baumol (1986) results were chipped away at seriously.

Wolff (1991a) was one of the first papers to look at the convergence of TFP over the long term. The basic data on output, employment, and capital stock were also drawn from Maddison (1982), and the sample consisted of the G-7 countries – Canada, France, Germany, Italy, Japan, the United Kingdom, and the United States. Using the coefficient of variation to measure σ-convergence, he found only moderate convergence between 1880 and 1938, followed by a sharp increase in dispersion between 1938 and 1950, and then dramatic convergence from 1950 to 1979. The correlation of TFP growth rates with initial TFP was –0.83 for the 1880–1979 period and –0.96 for the 1950–79 period.

10.2.2 Postwar OECD

Convergence in productivity levels was very strong from the beginning of the postwar period to about 1980 but dissipated after that. As shown in Chapter 5, the coefficient of variation in labor productivity (RGDPW) among twenty-four OECD countries declined by half between 1950 and 1980. Between 1980 and 1990, there was only a slight further reduction in the coefficient of variation. Moreover, from 1990 to 2002, the coefficient of variation actually increased from 0.24 to 0.34. The reason is the huge increase in RGDPW in Luxembourg over this period, more than doubling in value. If Luxembourg is excluded, then the coefficient of variation was actually only slightly higher in 2002 than in 1990 – 0.24 compared to 0.23. Catch-up was also evident, as indicated by the correlation coefficient between the 1950 RGDPW level and the rate of growth of RGDPW from 1950 to 2002. The correlation coefficient was -0.85 among all OECD countries (–0.90 excluding Luxembourg).

As discussed in Chapter 7, the U.S. aggregate labor productivity advantage in manufacturing in the early 1960s was rooted in superior labor productivity in virtually all industries. The United States had higher TFP than other OECD countries in each manufacturing industry and employed more capital per worker in each industry. It is interesting that the U.S. capital abundance at that time was reflected almost totally in the use of more capital per worker in industries. It was not the case that U.S. capital abundance led to employment of a larger share of its workforce in capital intensive industries. Indeed, there was no significant difference between the U.S. employment mix and those of other developed countries in relation to the capital or labor intensity of production.

Between the early 1960s and the mid-1970s labor productivity levels of other OECD countries converged on the United States in every manufacturing industry. Convergence of TFP was the primary source of this development, with convergence of capital-labor ratios playing a secondary role. In addition, there is evidence that countries and industries that lagged particularly far behind in terms of technological capability experienced the most rapid TFP convergence.

In the period 1963–72 there was also a positive correlation between TFP convergence and convergence of capital intensity. This result can be interpreted in two ways: Advanced technology was embodied in machines and hence rapid capital accumulation occasioned rapid TFP growth, or high TFP growth, through acquisition of disembodied technology, improved the profitability of an industry, hence attracting new investment. These issues of causality were difficult to sort out, but it was likely that the causality ran in both directions.

By the mid-1970s TFP levels of industrial countries were fairly similar, though the United States continued to hold a lead in most industries. There was no further convergence of TFP between the mid-1970s and the mid-1980s. Convergence of labor productivity within industries continued over this period, though at a slower rate than before, and in the late 1970s to the mid-1980s resulted almost entirely from capital accumulation. By the late 1980s differences in capital-labor ratios among OECD countries were minor.

The nature of the international economy changed significantly between the 1960s and the 1980s. In the former period, the United States had labor and total factor productivity advantages in all manufacturing industries. By the mid- to late 1980s different countries developed modest labor and total factor productivity leads in different industries. With this kind of international specialization, dispersion of productivity measures was greater within industries than in the aggregate. These results accord with the conclusion drawn by Abramovitz (1994) that industrial countries today had become nearly equal technological rivals by the late 1980s.

10.2.3 Very Long Term

Returning to data on the Maddison-16 sample for consistency with the earlier data, I reported time trends in GDP per capita from the year 1 to 2006 AD on the basis of newer data from Angus Maddison. It was found that over the very long term (and even the more recent long term) there was no clear pattern of convergence even among this select sample of countries. Indeed, the very long term was as much marked by divergence in per capita income levels as in convergence of per capita income. Divergence characterized the periods 1000–1700, 1820–90, and 1938–50; convergence occurred during the 1700–1820, 1890–1938, and 1950–80 periods; and no clear trend was apparent during the 1980–2006 period.

Going still further back in time, Galor and Weil (2000) developed a unified growth model to explain the long transition process from thousands of years of Malthusian stagnation through the demographic transition to the modern growth area (since about 1700). They identified three regimes that historically characterized economic development. The first was the Malthusian regime, which was characterized by slow technological progress and population growth that was high enough to prevent any sustained increase in income per capita. The second was what they called the post-Malthusian period, in which technological progress increased relative to the first period and population continued to increase but not enough to absorb the full increase of output growth. The third (and final) one is the modern growth regime. This was entered when a demographic transition that reversed the positive association between income growth and population growth occurred. The modern regime is characterized by sustained income growth and lowered population growth.

During the Malthusian regime, which characterized almost all of human history until the last few centuries, both technological progress and population growth were extremely slow, particularly by modern standards. Moreover, in contrast to the modern period, there was a positive relationship between population growth and income per capita. During the post-Malthusian regime, the positive association between population growth and income per capita was still in place, but output grew enough so that per capita income rose during this period. Finally, in the modern growth regime, the relationship between per capita income and population growth reversed and became negative. Today, for example, the highest rates of population growth are found in the poorest countries, and many advanced nations have population growth rates close to zero (or even negative). Galor and Weil (2000) argued that over the very long term, the Malthusian trap was escaped by improving the quality of children in exchange for smaller families.

10.2.4 Postwar Convergence among All Countries of the World

There are striking similarities between the state of the economies of today's advanced industrial countries 200 years ago and the state of the world's economies today. In many respects, the situation of today's poor countries is very similar to the state of the advanced countries 200 years ago in terms of per capita income, level of technology, and capital per worker.

As discussed in Chapter 9, on the basis of the variable RGDPL, real GDP per capita in 2000 constant prices (using the Laspeyre price index), from the Penn World Tables (PWT) database, there is no evidence of σ-convergence (or unconditional convergence) in per capita income among their sample of 150 countries (excluding three oil producers) over the period 1970 to 2003. The coefficient of variation of RGDPL was virtually the same in 2003 as in 1970 (actually, slightly higher). The correlation between the growth rate of RGDPL and initial RGDPL was slightly positive instead of negative.

10.3 Strong Forces

10.3.1 The Catch-Up Effect

Also known as β-convergence, the catch-up effect is the star variable in almost all growth regressions. Its coefficient is very robust and holds up through many samples and specifications. However, more advanced econometric techniques show that the size of coefficient is smaller than in the standard OLS specification.

The long-term data provide strong support of the catch-up effect. As noted previously, Baumol (1986) used the Maddison-16 sample, drawn from Maddison (1982), for the period from 1870 to 1979 and found that the overall correlation coefficient between 1870 productivity levels and the annual rate of productivity growth from 1870 to 1979 was negative, −0.93, and the correlation coefficient between initial labor productivity levels in 1950 and the rate of labor productivity growth over the 1950–79 period was −0.89. Wolff (1991a) also based his results on the Maddison (1982) data. The catch-up effect (the initial relative TFP level) had the expected negative sign, with a value of −0.04, and was significant at the 1 percent level in explaining labor productivity growth.

As reported in Chapter 5, the initial RGDPW level of the country relative to the U.S. level was by far the most powerful explanatory variable in accounting for differences in labor productivity growth among OECD countries. By itself, the catch-up variable explained 74 percent of the variation in RGDPW growth over the 1950–2000 period. In the Mankiw, Romer, and Weil (1992) (MRW) specification, the logarithm of the initial RGDPW of the country relative to the U.S. level explained 80 percent of the variation in RGDPW growth over the 1950–2000 period.

When we consider countries at all levels of development, the story is a bit different. As discussed in Chapter 9, for the 1960–91 PWT sample, I began with the top twenty countries, as ranked by 1960 RGDP, and then the sample was expanded by successively adding the next twenty countries. The coefficient of initial per capita income (RGDP) was negative for all samples, statistically significant at the 1 percent level for all samples except the full sample (101 countries), where the coefficient was significant at the 5 percent level. It appeared that convergence was a powerful force operating through all levels of development, though the force was much stronger among the industrialized and middle income countries than among the less developed ones. This was apparent by examining the coefficient estimate of initial RGDP and its t-ratio and the R^2 and adjusted-R^2 statistics, all of which declined as the sample was expanded to lower income countries. Among the top twenty countries, the R^2 statistic was 0.69, whereas among the full sample, the R^2 was only 0.05.

10.3.2 Capital Formation

There are two primary ingredients in the growth of labor productivity: technological innovation and the accumulation of capital through saving (and the subsequent investment of those savings). Most studies find that innovation and the international transfer of its products have played the major role in the converging productivity levels of a number of relatively successful industrialized economies. But many studies also find that substantial capital accumulation is also required to put the inventions into practice and to effect their widespread employment.

Though the association between capital and output of an economy is very close, the direction of causation may run two ways. On the one hand, a nation with a large amount of capital can be expected to produce a relatively high output level. On the other, a nation with a large output can be expected to have a correspondingly high investment rate. Statistical tests tend to show that both effects are present, but their relative strengths are difficult to ascertain (see Abramovitz, 1979, for further discussion of these points).

Capital investment appears to be the second most important variable in explaining growth. As reported in Chapter 5, the catch-up effect, measured by the initial RGDPW level of the country relative to the U.S. level, explained 74 percent of the variation in RGDPW growth among OECD countries over the 1950–2000 period. The coefficient of INVRATE was positive and generally significant at the 1 or 5 percent level. The average investment rate, together with the catch-up variable, explained 80 percent of the variation in RGDPW growth.

Among all countries of the world, as discussed in Chapter 9, the coefficient of the investment rate variable in a regression whose dependent variable was the growth rate of RGDP was positive and significant at the 1 percent level for a sample of 102 countries over the 1960–91 period. Initial RGDP and the average investment rate explained 44 percent of the variation of country RGDP growth rates over the 1960–91 period. The inclusion of the investment rate caused the R^2 to jump from 0.06 (with the catch-up term only) to 0.44

10.3.2.1 The Vintage Effect

There are a couple of ways in which capital investment and productivity growth may have positive interactions or complementarities. First, it is likely that capital accumulation is necessary to put new inventions into practice and to effect their widespread employment. This association is often referred to as the "embodiment effect," since it implies that at least some technological innovation is embodied in capital. It is also consistent with the "vintage effect," which states that new capital is more productive than old capital per (constant) dollar of expenditure. A second way is that the introduction of new capital may lead to better organization, management, and the like. This may be true even if no new technology is incorporated in the capital equipment. A third is through learning by doing, which would also imply a positive relation between technological advance and the accumulation of capital stock. A fourth is that potential technological advance may stimulate capital formation, because the opportunity to modernize equipment promises a high rate of return to investment.

As discussed in Chapter 4, Wolff (1991a) pointed to the extreme reduction in the average age of the capital stock among Germany, Italy, Japan, the United Kingdom, and the United States over the postwar period. The average age of the capital stock for the five countries declined from twenty-eight years in 1950 to fifteen years in 1979. Perhaps the most telling result is the extreme *rejuvenation* of the capital stock during the 1950s and 1960s, during which the average age fell by 6.1 and 5.6 years, respectively. In regression analysis on the basis of the Maddison (1982) data, Wolff found that the change in the average age of the capital stock had the expected negative sign and the variable was significant at the 5 percent level. The effect was surprisingly large: a one-year reduction in the average age of capital was associated with about a *1* percentage point increase in labor productivity growth.

Also, as shown in Chapter 5, regressions were run on three periods – 1960–73, 1974–9, and 1979–92 – on the basis of the ISDB database for fourteen OECD countries. The coefficient of DEL(KGRT) had the expected positive sign (an acceleration in capital growth is equivalent to a reduction in the average age of the capital stock) and was significant at the 1 percent level.

10.3.3 The Role of Education

As discussed in Chapter 6, there are three paradigms that appear to dominate models of the role of education in economic growth. The first stems from human capital theory, which views schooling as an investment in skills and hence as a way of augmenting worker productivity. This approach leads to growth accounting models in which productivity growth is related to the *change* in educational attainment.

The second views education in the context of a productivity catch-up model. In this approach, education is viewed as one index of the social capability of the labor force to borrow existing technology. In these models, education is treated as a *threshold effect* in that a certain level of schooling might be considered a necessary condition for the borrowing of advanced technology. Econometrically, the *rate* of productivity growth is related to the *level* of educational attainment. The endogenous growth models of Lucas (1988), Romer (1990), and Aghion and Howitt (1992) also predict that output and productivity growth should be directly related to the educational *level* of a country (see Chapter 2 for a discussion of these models). The MRW model, on the other hand, has both an educational growth and an educational level prediction.

The third approach, emanating from the work of Arrow (1962) and Nelson and Phelps (1966), emphasizes interactions between education and technological change. One implication of their models is that an educated labor force should learn faster than a less educated group and thus increase efficiency faster. The Arrow and Nelson-Phelps line of reasoning suggests that there may be interaction effects between the educational attainment of the labor force and measures of technological activity, such as the R&D intensity of a country.

As reported in Chapter 6, the evidence on education as a source of growth is a bit spotty at best, and even peculiar in some instances. Both cross-sectional and panel regressions of RGDPW growth over the 1950–2000 period among OECD countries were estimated on a catch-up term, the investment rate, R&D intensity, and various indicators of education. The educational enrollment rates had positive coefficients in all cases but were not significant. The coefficients of attainment rates were insignificant for secondary and university attainment but significant for primary school attainment levels (at the 5 percent level). The results for primary education make little sense because this is the level of schooling that would appear to have least relevance to the types of sophisticated technology in use among OECD countries in the post–World War II period. The coefficient of mean years of schooling was also insignificant. The coefficient of the change in schooling (over the 1960 to 2000 period) was positive in all cases but statistically significant in only one: the change in university enrollment rates at the 10 percent level. An interaction term was included between the various measures of schooling and R&D. However, the interaction term was insignificant in all cases, casting some doubt, at least, on this interpretation of the Arrow and Nelson-Phelps models.

In the MRW specifications, the logarithms of the educational enrollment rates had positive coefficients in all cases. The coefficients of the logarithms of both the primary and secondary school enrollment rates were significant at the 10 percent level, while that of the university enrollment rate was significant at the 1 percent level. The coefficients of the logarithm of the attainment rates were insignificant for secondary and university attainment but significant at the 1 percent level for the primary school attainment level. The coefficient of the change in schooling was positive in all cases but statistically significant in only one: the change in university enrollment rates, at the 5 percent level.

The coefficient of the interaction term between education and R&D was positive in all cases. The results for the enrollment rates seem to make sense since the coefficient of the interaction term was not significant for primary enrollment but was positive and significant at the 5 percent level for the secondary school enrollment rate and at the 1 percent level for the university enrollment rate. One would expect the interaction term to be stronger at higher levels of schooling. However, the results made little sense for the attainment rates since the coefficient was significant at the 1 percent level for primary school attainment but not significant at higher levels of education. The coefficient was also not significant for mean years of schooling. The results for the interaction effect between education and the investment rate were very similar. The coefficient of this term was positive in each case. As before, it was not significant for primary school enrollment rate, significant at the 5 percent level for the secondary school enrollment rate, and significant at the 1 percent level for the university enrollment rate. It was also significant at the 1 percent level for the primary school attainment rate, but it was not significant for attainment rates for higher levels or schooling or for mean schooling.

The findings of other researchers are also mixed. Frantzen (2000) used educational data from Barro and Lee (1993) to analyze the relation between human capital and TFP growth for twenty-one industrialized market economies in the OECD. He found that the coefficient of the *growth* in human capital was positive but not statistically significant. Fuente and Doménech (2006) found stronger results of the effect of education on growth for OECD countries by attempting to improve on the data quality of the Barro and Lee data set. They used the logarithm of the average number of years of schooling of the adult population as their measure of human capital. Using their corrected data on schooling, they obtained a positive coefficient significant at the 10 percent level for the logarithm of human capital in a regression in which TFP growth was used as the dependent variable and in which no country dummies or catch-up term was included. The coefficient did become significant at the 1 percent level when country dummies, period dummies, and a catch-up term were included.

Apergis (2007) used data from a panel of EU manufacturing industries over the 1980 to 2000 period and related the growth in industry-level TFP within a country to the growth in the country's level of human capital. Using a GMM estimator, he found a positive and significant (at the 1 percent level) coefficient on the growth in human capital based on the Fuente and Doménech (2006) corrected schooling variable. He also added a human capital "threshold effect" (that is, countries with mean years of schooling above a critical level) interacted with industry R&D intensity and found a positive and significant coefficient on this variable as well.

The evidence on the importance of education as a source of growth is much stronger among all countries of the world. In fact, it appears to be the third most important factor explaining growth after the catch-up effect and investment. In Chapter 9, I used two alternative statistics, one indicating the proportion of the relevant age group receiving formal primary education (PRIM), and the other being the corresponding figure for secondary education (SCND). In a regression of the growth of RGDP from 1960 to 1991 on a catch-up term, the investment rate, and education on a sample of 102 countries, the coefficients of the two education variables were positive and significant at the 1 percent level. Primary school enrollment seemed to have a slightly greater impact than secondary school enrolment, but the difference was not great. Moreover, the inclusion of the educational variable (in particular, PRIM) with initial RGDP and the investment rate caused the R^2 to increase from 0.44 to 0.50.

MRW (1992) reported similar results in a regression of the growth of RGDP on a similar set of variables. The coefficient of the logarithm of SCHOOL (their measure of education) was positive and significant at the 1 percent level for the full sample of ninety-eight countries and a sample of seventy-five intermediate and less developed countries. However, for a sample of OECD countries, the coefficient was positive but significant at only the 5 percent level.

With regard to the growth of human capital, Benhabib and Spiegel (1994) reported that the change in human capital did not enter significantly into an explanation of income per capita growth rates for a sample of seventy-eight countries at all levels of development over the period from 1965 to 1985. However, Krueger and Lindahl (2001) took issue with these and similar results on the relation between the growth in human capital and per capita income growth. They argued that the finding of little or no correlation between the growth of output per worker and the change in average schooling appeared to be a spurious result of the extremely high rate of measurement error in first-differenced cross-country education data.

In sum, the educational level (threshold) effect seems to be a powerful determinant of growth among samples that include all countries of the world (that is, the low and middle income ones) but not for high income ones alone. These results lend some credence to the endogenous growth models of Lucas (1988), Romer (1986 and 1990), and Aghion and Howitt (1992), which predict an educational *level* effect. Human capital theory and growth accounting, on the other hand, lead directly to a prediction that educational growth should be a factor in productivity growth, not educational *levels*. The results on this have been decidedly mixed.

10.3.4 R&D and Technological Spillovers

There is, of course, a voluminous literature that has demonstrated that R&D makes an important contribution to productivity growth at the firm, industry, and national levels. There is also recent empirical literature that has examined this issue in a cross-country context among OECD countries. This is included as a strong force since it almost always appears important in national and OECD regressions. However, it does not appear to prove significant as a determinant of growth among all countries of the world.

As reported in Chapter 6, in regressions of RGDPW growth among OECD countries over the 1950–2000 period, with a catch-up variable and the investment rate included, R&D intensity was significant in most regressions (and typically at the 10 percent level). In specifications without an interaction effect, R&D intensity was positive and significant at the 5 percent level in all cases. However, as discussed in Chapter 5, regressions were run on three periods – 1960–73, 1974–9, and 1979–92 – on the basis of the ISDB database for fourteen OECD countries. R&D intensity had the expected positive coefficient, a value of 0.31. However, the variable was not statistically significant.

Fagerberg (1988) reported a significant and positive effect of the average annual growth in civilian R&D on GDP growth for twenty-two countries over the 1973–88 period. Verspagen (1994) used a cross-country sample consisting of twenty-one OECD countries, South Korea, and Yugoslavia and covered the period 1970–85. He found that the growth in total R&D stock was a positive and significant determinant of GDP growth. A study, from Working Party No. 1 of the OECD Economic Policy Committee (1993), reported a positive but insignificant effect of the growth in R&D capital stock on labor productivity growth for a sample of nineteen OECD countries over four subperiods between 1960 and 1985.

Pyyhtiä (2007) used data from the OECD STAN database covering twelve EU countries and the United States over the period 1987 to 2003. He also included R&D data taken from the OECD ANBERD database. He found that in many ICT-producing and -using countries such as Denmark, Finland, Ireland, Sweden, and the United States the rate of technical progress accelerated during the decade of the 1990s. Using panel data estimation methods, he found that the acceleration in the rate of technological progress in ICT-intensive countries was associated with increased R&D investment.

Coe and Helpman (1995) used data for twenty-two OECD countries covering the period from 1971 to 1990. They found a positive and statistically significant effect of domestic R&D stock on TFP growth in their sample. They also included an estimate of foreign (imported) R&D capital stock and found this variable to have a positive and significant effect on TFP growth, particularly among the smaller OECD countries. This paper stimulated a lot of additional work on the importance of foreign spillovers from trade and

R&D. Park (1995), using aggregate data for ten OECD countries (including the G-7 countries), had similar results. However, Verspagen (1997) challenged the findings of Coe and Helpman. Verspagen constructed a technology flow matrix based on European patent data that indicated not only in which sector the patent originated but also in which sectors the patent was used. Using a panel data set of twenty-two sectors, fourteen OECD countries, and nineteen years (1974–92), Verspagen found very weak support for the Coe and Helpman results on foreign R&D spillovers. Keller (1998) replicated the set of regressions used by Coe and Helpman (1995) with what he termed "counterfactual import shares." On the basis of these results, he disputed the claim of Coe and Helpman that the import composition of a country was an important factor in explaining the country's productivity growth.

There are several studies that looked at the effects of R&D on growth for countries at different levels of development. Lichtenberg (1992) found a positive and significant coefficient on R&D intensity in explaining growth in GDP per adult between 1960 and 1985 in a sample of countries at all levels of development. Gittleman and Wolff (1995), on the other hand, failed to find a significant coefficient on R&D intensity as an explanatory variable for the growth of RGDP in a sample of eighty countries at different levels of development over the 1960–88 period. In contrast, the coefficient was positive and significant for a sample of nineteen industrialized market economies. Goel and Ram (1994) used a sample of fifty-two countries at all levels of development and a subsample of thirty-four LDCs. Their dependent variable was the rate of growth of GDP between 1980 and 1988. They found that the coefficient of R&D intensity was positive and significant at the 5 percent level for the full sample but positive and insignificant for the restricted LDC sample.

Coe, Helpman, and Hoffmaister (1997), using a sample of seventy-seven developing countries over the period from 1971 to 1990, found evidence of substantial R&D spillovers from the industrial countries of the North to the developing countries in the rest of the world. A similar finding was reported by Connolly (2003), who used five-year panels on international patent data from 1970 to 1984 for a cross section of up to forty countries. He found that high technology imports positively affected both domestic imitation and innovation. However, Gittleman and Wolff (1995), using data on R&D embodied in imports based on UN trade data for eighty countries over the 1960 to 1998 period, failed to replicate the Coe, Helpman, and Hoffmaister results.

In sum, R&D and technological spillovers appear to be consistently strong forces in explaining productivity growth among the advanced countries of the world. However, R&D and technological spillovers appear to be much weaker forces among countries at all levels of development,

10.3.5 Social Institutions

The last of the strong forces are basic social institutions. There is a large literature on how institutions affect economic development, beginning, perhaps, with North and Thomas (1973). They defined institutions as the formal and informal rules that govern human, social, economic, and political interactions. They argued that progress in the Western world occurred because of the development of basic economic institutions that fostered economic growth through establishing the rule of law and granting and protecting property rights of individuals.

Many papers have now looked into the effects of institutions or what Abramovitz called "social capability" on economic growth (see Chapter 9). Three, in particular, which appeared in the *Quarterly Journal of Economics* in successive years – Knack and Keefer (1997), Temple and Johnson (1998), and Hall and Jones (1999) – developed (or adapted) alternative measures of socioeconomic development. Knack and Keefer reported that their measure of social capital that reflected underlying indicators of trust and civic norms had a positive and significant performance on the growth in per capita income over the period 1980 to 1992 for a sample of twenty-nine advanced economies. Temple and Johnson found that their measure of socioeconomic development was positive and significant, generally at the 1 percent level, in explaining GDP per capita growth over the 1960 to 1985 period. Hall and Jones found that their measure of social infrastructure had a positive and significant effect on output per worker over the 1960 to 1985 period for their sample of 137 countries.

10.4 Weak Forces

10.4.1 International Trade and FDI

Another important economic factor in the catch-up process is the extent of openness of an economy, which reflects the degree to which a country is involved in international trade. Results of previous studies generally support the argument that openness is an important ingredient in economic growth. Countries with more open economies have been found to have higher rates of productivity catch-up than those that close their borders to trade. Generally, import openness was a stronger factor than the degree of export orientation of an economy. This result is consistent with the advantages of backwardness argument, since imports from advanced countries provide a more direct source of information on new technologies than the exports sent abroad by a country.

As shown in Chapter 5, regressions were run on three periods – 1960–73, 1974–9, and 1979–92 – on the basis of the ISDB database for fourteen OECD countries. Import intensity had the expected positive sign and was significant at the 5 percent level. A 1 percentage point increase in import openness (the ratio of imports to GNP) was associated with an increase of TFP growth of 0.023 percentage point – a relatively small effect.

For OECD countries, international trade (particularly, imports) has generally been found to be a significant determinant of the growth in GDP per capita. Helliwell and Chung (1991) used OECD national accounts data for nineteen industrialized countries over the 1960–85 period. They found that convergence was faster for countries whose degree of openness to international trade was increasing over time, with the coefficients of their trade openness variable typically significant at the 5 percent level. Ben-David (1993) used a sample of EEC countries over the 1950–85 period. He found a very strong relation between the degree of trade liberalization and the convergence in per capita income among this sample of countries. Rassekh (1992) used a sample of OECD countries for the 1950–85 period and a measure of trade openness defined as the ratio of the sum of exports and imports to GDP in each country. He found a positive relation between per capita GDP growth and the growth of this index of trade openness.

Many of the earlier studies of trade on growth have been criticized for relating the size of trade to the growth in income per capita (or per worker). This approach suffers from both problems of endogeneity and an omitted variable bias. One way around the endogeneity problem is to look at changes in (exogenous) trade policy. Ben-David (1993) chose a small number of advanced countries that decided formally to liberalize trade. He found support for the hypothesis that movements toward freer trade led to convergence rather than the converse. Another way around the endogeneity problem is to look at first differences. Ben-David and Kimhi (2004) examined the impact of changes in trade between countries on changes in the rate of reduction in the size of the income gap between these countries. Their major finding was that an increase in trade between trade partners was positively related to an increase in the rate of convergence in per capita income between the two countries.

An alternative vehicle for the transmission of technical know-how is through foreign direct investment (FDI). Lichtenberg and van Pottelsberghe de la Potterie (2001) analyzed the importance of FDI as a source of international technology diffusion in thirteen OECD countries over the period from 1971 to 1990. They did not find significant effects on country productivity from inward FDI. Baldwin, Braconier, and Forslid (2005) reported some positive inward FDI spillover effects on the industry level, but overall, the results were decidedly mixed.

When we consider countries at all levels of development, the results reported in Chapter 9 confirmed the significance of trade openness to GDP per capita (RGDP) growth among ninety to ninety-four countries over the period from 1960 to 1991. Import intensity had a positive coefficient, which was significant at the 1 percent level. Adding import intensity to initial RGDP, the investment rate, and education increased the R^2 from 0.50 to only 0.54.

Several other studies reported similar results. For example, Dollar (1992) used as his measure of trade openness an index of foreign exchange rate distortion (the greater the distortion, the less open was international trade in the country). Using a sample of ninety-five less developed countries over the period 1976 to 1985, he reported a negative and significant relation between the growth in income per capita and his measure of foreign exchange distortion.

Hallak and Levinsohn (2004) criticized many of these "standard" studies on the effects of trade on productivity growth on methodological grounds. Several attempts were made to get around the problem of endogeneity, including Ben-David (1996) and Frankel and Romer (1999). Their studies also found a positive and significant effect of trade openness on per capita income growth. However, the omitted variable bias seemed to be hard to get around. For example, Rodriguez and Rodrik (2001) included the distance of a country from the equator as a right-side variable in the regression equation and found that the effect of trade on income per capita was substantially reduced and, indeed, was no longer statistically significant.

The results on the effects of FDI on growth for middle income and LDCs were fairly negative. Aitken and Harrison (1999) looked at a sample of Venezuelan plants between 1976 and 1989. FDI penetration was measured by the share of employment of foreign-owned firms in total employment. Their main finding was of a *negative* relation between increased FDI presence and the TFP growth of domestic plants. Das, Nath, and Yildiz (2008) used data for ninety-three countries at all levels of development over the period from 1970 to 2000 and found little evidence that FDI decreased differences in productivity for the entire sample of countries.

Among advanced countries, the preponderance of the evidence is that trade openness (particularly on the import side) promotes growth. However, for middle income and LDCs, the results on trade are decidedly mixed. Moreover, FDI does not appear to be an important determinant of growth in per capita income either among advanced countries alone or among countries at all levels of development.

10.4.2 Democracy and Political Institutions

Many growth studies have considered the political structure and the degree of democracy of a country's government, measured in various ways, such as the extent of voting rights within a country or the presence or absence of "official violence" against citizens. Are democratic governments more conducive to economic growth? Some have argued that they are for several reasons. First, they may be more consonant with the freedom to invest and to make entrepreneurial decisions. Second, they may provide greater legal security to the owners of the enterprises within a country and reduce the fears of expropriation, thus increasing the incentive to invest. Third, such forms of government may create greater political stability, thus mitigating against capital flight out of the country. On the other hand, some have suggested that authoritarian regimes, particularly in the third world, may provide for greater political stability and legal security of ownership. These alternative views have also been subjected to empirical testing.

As reported in Chapter 9, in a regression of RGDP growth on initial RGDP and a proxy variable for democracy, VOTING, which reflected the extent of voting rights in a country over the 1960–91 period for a sample of 100 countries, the coefficient of VOTING was negative and statistically significant at the 1 percent level. However, when the investment rate was included in the equation, the variable became statistically insignificant. The results suggested that the absence of democracy slows productivity growth indirectly by inhibiting savings and investment. An almost identical result was obtained for VIOLENCE, a variable that reflected the presence or absence of official "violence" against citizens. When included with initial RGDP, the variable was negative and significant at the 1 percent level, but once the investment rate was included, the variable became insignificant. Thus, domestic repression also appears to inhibit savings and investment and thereby indirectly lowers the growth in per capita income.

Earlier studies reported similar findings. Kormendi and Meguire (1985) used a sample of forty-seven countries for the period 1950–77. Their regression specification included initial per capita income as well as a measure of "civil liberties," which reflected, among others, the degree of due process in criminal procedure, the extent of freedom of expression, the presence or absence of political prisoners, and the independence of the judiciary, in a country. He found that the investment rate was positively related to the extent of civil liberties, but civil liberties had very little independent effect on a country's per capita income growth rate. Barro (1991) used the same civil liberties index as Kormendi and Meguire and found a significant positive effect of civil liberties on per capita income growth over the 1960–85 period.

Later studies produced mixed results. Barro (1996) reanalyzed the relation between democracy and growth using a panel of about 100 countries over the period from 1960 to 1990. He argued first that the favorable effects of democracy on growth include the maintenance of the rule of law, free markets, small government consumption, and high human capital formation. However, once these effects were controlled for, as well as the initial level of real GDP per capita, the effect of democracy on the growth of real GDP per capita was found to be weakly negative. Rivera-Batiz (2002) found that that his measure of democracy was a significant determinant of TFP growth between 1960 and 1990 in a cross section of 115 countries, but this contribution occurred only insofar as stronger democratic institutions were associated with greater quality of governance.

A related factor is the extent of military expenditures and wars. There is some dispute about the import of the first factor. Some have argued that military expenditures may drain resources from productive investment and thus inhibit the process of technological catch-up. In contrast, others have argued that the production or import of advanced military equipment may be a source of new technology. As reported in Chapter 8, in a regression of RGDP growth on initial RGDP, the investment rate, education, and military expenditures as a share of GDP over the 1960–91 period for a sample of ninety-nine countries, the coefficient of the military expenditure variable was positive but not statistically significant. Other studies have produced mixed results, including Faini, Annez, and Taylor (1984), Biswas and Ram (1986), Grobar and Porter (1987), and Adams, Behrman, and Boldin (1988).

With regard to wars, several studies have found a negative impact of warfare on GDP growth. For example, Yamarik, Johnson, and Compton (2007), using a sample of 112 to 118 countries over the period 1960 to 2000, found that interstate war had a decidedly negative impact on long-run growth in real GDP per capita.

10.4.3 Inequality

According to Barro (2000), theories of the macroeconomic relationship between inequality and economic growth fall into four broad categories: credit-market imperfections, political economy, social unrest, and saving rates. Credit-market imperfections may force poor people to forgo investments in education and other forms of human capital, and a reduction in inequality will generally lead to higher economic growth. Political economy explanations typically revolve around voting models of a society. If the mean income in an economy exceeds the median income, then majority voting will often lead to a redistribution of resources from rich to poor. A greater degree of inequality will generally induce more redistribution through the political process and thereby lead to lesser growth.

With regard to the possibility of social or political unrest, the general argument is that economic inequality may induce poor people to engage in crime, riots, and other socially disruptive activities and thereby lower economic growth. With regard to the last set of models, there is ample empirical evidence that personal saving rates increase with the level of income. If this relationship holds, then a redistribution of resources from the poor to the rich would lead to a higher aggregate saving rate in an economy and greater output growth. Almost in concordance with the ambiguous predictions of these models, the empirical findings of the rather vast literature on this subject have also been ambiguous and, in any case, not very robust (see, for example, Barro, 2000 and 2008).

10.4.4 Financial Development

Another aspect of institutional capability is the degree of financial development of a country. Several researchers have found that a more developed financial system in a country is positively associated with a higher rate of economic growth.

King and Levine (1993) studied the relation between economic growth and financial development using a sample of seventy-seven countries at all levels of development over the years 1960 to 1989. Their measure of financial development was called DEPTH, which was defined as the liquid liabilities of the financial system (currency plus demand and interest-bearing liabilities of banks and nonbank financial intermediaries) divided by GDP. They found a statistically significant and economically large relationship between DEPTH and long-run real per capita income growth. Levine and Zervos (1998) added measures of stock market and banking development to cross-country studies of growth. Examining two components of the financial system, banks and equity markets, they found that the initial level of stock market liquidity and the initial level of banking development were positively and significantly correlated with economic growth. Later studies of Levine and associates also confirmed the positive impact of financial development on economic growth, including Beck, Levine, and Loayza (2000) and Beck and Levine (2004).

10.4.5 Economic Geography and Natural Resources

The effect of the abundance (or lack thereof) of natural resources on economic growth has also been extensively analyzed in the growth literature. For example, natural resource dependence is usually believed to "crowd out" other types of capital and thereby slow economic growth (the so-called natural resource curse).

Boulhol, de Serres, and Molnar (2008) examined how much of the disparities in productivity growth among OECD countries could be explained by economic geography factors. Their econometric analysis, based on a panel data set comprising twenty-one countries over the years 1970–2004, indicated that endowments in natural resources had a significant positive effect on GDP per capita.

Results that considered countries at all levels of development generally had contradictory results. Gylfason (2004) presented cross-country results on the basis of eighty-five or so countries over the period 1965–98 that countries that depended more heavily on their natural resources tended to have (a) less trade and foreign investment, (b) more corruption, (c) less political liberty, (d) less education, (e) less domestic investment, and (f) less financial development than others that were either less well endowed with, or less dependent on, natural resources.

A related issue is the effect of natural climate on economic growth. Several studies have found that tropical countries (and states) grew more slowly than those in temperate climates. Gallup, Sachs, and Mellinger (1999), using data for seventy-five countries over the 1965 to 1990 period, found that climate had large effects on income levels and income growth. Sachs (2001) estimated that between 1820 and 1992, GNP per capita in the temperate region grew at an average annual rate of 1.4 percent, compared with 0.9 percent a year in the nontemperate region.

10.4.6 The Role of IT

The role of information technology (IT) on productivity growth has also been extensively analyzed. Gust and Marquez (2004) looked into the growing gap in productivity growth between the United States and other industrialized countries during the 1990s. They used panel data from 1992 to 1999 for thirteen OECD countries. They used two variables to measure the extent of IT. The first was IT production as a share of GDP. The second was the ratio of expenditures on IT to GDP. They found that both these variables were positive and significant (at the 5 percent level). They concluded that both the production and adoption of IT played an important role in the divergence of productivity growth between the United States and European countries.

Van Ark, O'Mahony, and Timmer (2008) also examined the growing productivity gap between Europe and the United States. They first of all reported that the average annual rate of labor productivity growth in the United States accelerated from 1.2 percent in the 1973–95 period to 1.5 percent in the 1995–2006 period. In contrast, among the fifteen EU countries, annual labor productivity growth declined from 2.4 percent in the first period to 1.5 percent during the second. The authors found that the slower emergence of IT in Europe compared to the United States was responsible for the growing divergence in productivity performance. The paper also emphasized the key role played by market services in accounting for the widening of the productivity gap. In particular, while productivity growth stagnated or fell in European market services, it increased on the American scene. This difference was attributable to the greater investment made by American service providers in IT.

10.4.7 Regulation

Several papers have looked at the effects of product market and labor market regulation on productivity growth across countries. With regard to OECD countries, many of the service industries in the industrialized countries have been until recently tightly regulated by the state. Many economists have argued that this has created a serious restriction on their potential for future productivity advance.

Gust and Marquez (2004), using panel data from 1992 to 1999 for thirteen OECD countries, developed three variables to measure the extent of regulation in a country reflecting employment protection legislation, overall administrative regulatory burdens, and regulatory burdens on start-up companies. They found that the extent of regulation in a country had a negative effect on IT spending. Barone and Cingano (2008) used data for seventeen OECD countries and fifteen manufacturing industries to look at the effect of regulation in service industries on the productivity performance of manufacturing industries that used these services. They considered three types of regulations: (i) entry barriers, (ii) vertical integration restrictions, and (iii) conduct regulation. They found that countries with lower levels of regulation of their service industries exhibited faster rates of productivity growth among manufacturing industries using these services.

Results for countries at all levels of development were more mixed. Loayza, Oviedo, and Serven (2005) considered indices of product and labor market regulation for a wide set of countries in the 1990s. They found a negative and significant direct effect of product and labor market regulation on the growth of output per capita. However, results on the interaction terms suggested that better governance lessened the negative effect of regulation. The overall effect of regulation was sizable and negative for most developing countries, while it was zero or even mildly positive for countries with good quality of governance.

10.4.8 Structural Change

Another factor affecting overall growth is shifts in the shares of employment among the various sectors of an economy. As shown in Chapter 5, regressions were run on three periods – 1960–73, 1974–9, and 1979–92 – on the basis of the ISDB database for fourteen OECD countries. The change in the share of employment in agriculture had the expected negative sign and was significant at the 1 percent level. The coefficient was also quite large – a 1 percentage point decline in the agricultural share was associated with a 1.0 percentage point overall increase in TFP growth. The change in the share of employment in services had the expected negative sign but was insignificant. However, the coefficient was also quite large – a 1 percentage point decline in the services share was associated with a 0.5 percentage point increase in TFP growth.

10.4.9 Infrastructure

Another factor that has steadily gained attention in recent years involves the quantity and quality of infrastructure and its effects on economic growth. At the basis of this interest is the belief that infrastructure capital is an important ingredient in economic growth. Aschauer (1989a), using time series data for the United States, included public sector capital in an aggregate production function for the U.S. economy and found that it exerted a very large effect on private sector productivity growth. Munnell (1990) and Eberts (1990) also reported qualitatively similar though smaller effects. However, Holtz-Eakin and Schwartz (1995) developed an augmented neoclassical growth model and found little support for claims of a dramatic productivity boost from increased infrastructure outlays.

10.4.10 Foreign Aid

There are two opposing views with regard to the effectiveness of foreign aid in promoting economic growth. The first, represented by David Dollar, believes that foreign aid can be effective when coupled with appropriate institutional and political changes. The second, represented by the William Easterly camp, feels that foreign aid is ineffective in promoting growth. Here, the evidence is decidedly mixed. Whereas Burnside and Dollar (2000) found positive and significant effects of foreign aid on income growth when conjoined with "good" institutions, Easterly (2003) argued that the Burnside and Dollar (2000) results were flawed.

10.5 Lessons We Have Learned and Prospects for Future Growth

10.5.1 A Brief Recap

The results reported in this book provide strong support to the argument that the advantage of backwardness is a strong effect operating at all levels of development. The importance of the convergence phenomenon becomes particularly clear when controlling for other factors, such as investment, educational attainment, degree of openness of an economy, and political attributes. Thus, even the least developed economies have a latent tendency to catch up in terms of overall output per capita on those ahead of them with similar levels of education, investment, involvement in the international economy, and political characteristics.

This book also highlights the importance of the international transfer of technology. As I argued in Chapter 1 of the book concerning the logic of productivity convergence, the main mechanism is the constant diffusion of technology from the leading countries to those behind. In this regard, the main player is not the entrepreneur associated with the original invention and innovation process but rather the one who recognizes previously unexploited opportunities for profitable transfer of productive knowledge that is already in use elsewhere. In a sense, it is imitative rather than innovative entrepreneurship that occupies central stage in this explanation of the convergence process.

The reason is that, while an initial innovation within a country may confer some transitory advantage to that economy, the *transfer* of technology tends rapidly to wipe out further differential gains. The technology transfer process has become particularly rapid in recent years. In high tech industries, product designs and production techniques have an amazing degree of similarity across countries (compare computers made in the United States, Japan, and Korea). This is also true in core manufacturing industries. For example, a U.S. automobile plant of 2010 bears more resemblance to corresponding 2010 plants in Germany or Japan than to a U.S. plant twenty years earlier. It is likely that over long periods, priority in invention may matter less to the relative productivity performance of an economy than do the activities of its imitative entrepreneurs.

There are some other general inferences that can be drawn from our own results and those of studies surveyed in this book. Not surprisingly, education and investment are both crucial ingredients in the growth of productivity over time. The establishment of basic social institutions such as the rule of law is another essential ingredient for sustained productivity growth. Moreover, involvement in international trade generally appears as an important ingredient in the catch-up process (though there is some dispute about this). This is particularly true for import openness, even more so than for export orientation. A low rate of population growth tends to raise both the investment rate and educational attainment level of the population. Democracy and citizens' rights both tend to stimulate investment (or, conversely, authoritarian rule and repression tend to discourage domestic investment), though it is not unanimously agreed that democracy by itself has a positive impact on growth. Finally, both external wars and internal strife also retard investment and lower productivity growth, and they also appear to have directly deleterious effects on economic growth.

It should be noted that the explained variation (the R^2 statistic) of regressions reported here, which include a full range of countries at all levels of development, generally never exceeded about 0.60. Thus, these variables explain at most about 60 percent of the differences in per capita income growth rates among the countries of the world. The remaining 40 percent or so is due to factors that have not been specifically addressed. These may include specific cultural and historical influences pertinent to particular cultures and national histories.

Indeed, even among OECD countries alone, the R^2 statistic is typically around 80 to 85 percent, including a catch-up term, the investment rate, education, and R&D intensity. The remaining variables explain a trivial amount of the variation in per capita growth rates or productivity growth rates.

10.5.2 Where We Stand Today

Today's industrialized (OECD) countries give spectacular evidence of the power of the catch-up effect. Between 1950 and 1980 the coefficient of variation in average labor productivity levels fell by half among this group of twenty-four countries. This process was aided by a healthy rate of capital investment and its attendant embodiment effect of new technology. Some countries saw spectacular growth rates in productivity over this period, including Greece, Ireland, Japan, Portugal, and Spain.

However, by 1980 the catch-up effect had generally petered out in this group of countries at least as growth cooled. Indeed, the United States began to pull ahead of these other countries in the 1990s and early 2000s. This, as several researchers argued, was due to substantial IT investment. Other success stories connected with the IT revolution during this period were Ireland, Sweden, and Finland.

Outside the (original) OECD, only a few other countries participated in the so-called takeoff as described by Rostow (1960), which refers to a productivity spurt that leads to a relatively long period of *sustained* growth. These include what are now referred to as "original" Asian Tigers, including Hong Kong, Singapore, Taiwan, and South Korea, whose average annual growth rate of GDP per capita of the was 4.7 percent from 1970 to 2003. Taiwan and South Korea had annual growth rates of 5.9 and 5.8 percent, respectively. More recently, since 1980 or so, a similar story has been unfolding for the "new" Asian Tigers, including Malaysia, Thailand, Indonesia, India, and, most notably, China. Their average annual growth rate of RGDPL was 4.5 percent over the period. China registered a figure of 7.0 percent (even higher after 1980). India appears to be on the move recently, with an annual per capita GDP growth rate of 3.5 percent from 1990 to 2003. The most likely reason for the success of these countries was high capital investment, which was likely combined with a strong technology embodiment effect (see Rodrik, 1995, and Dollar, 2007). Chile also has recently shown some impressive gains in per capita income, an annual rate of 4.1 percent from 1990 to 2003. Brazil, on the other hand, showed remarkable growth in the 1970s, an annual growth of per capita income of 5.2 percent, but then sputtered out.[1]

Sub-Saharan Africa calls for special attention. The path of GDP per capita of Sub-Saharan Africa between 1976 and 2005 followed a U-shaped pattern, first falling in absolute terms from the mid-1970s to the mid-1990s and then rising after that. By 2005, GDP per capita did not yet recover to the levels of the mid-1970s. Explanations of the poor economic performance of Sub-Saharan Africa tend to focus on "poor institutions" (see Easterly and Levine, 2003, and Acemoglu, Johnson, and Robinson, 2003.) In fact, in the earlier growth regressions, a dummy variable ("a measure of our ignorance") was often inserted for Sub-Saharan Africa because of its very poor growth performance. In recent analyses, the dummy variable could be removed when variables reflecting institutional quality were included.

A similar story characterized the former Soviet republics and Eastern European countries since the early 1990s, with the breakup of the Soviet state and the end of central planning. Their per capita income also experience a U-shaped pattern with the extraordinary economic collapse of these countries after the fall of Communism in 1989 and then recovery in the late 1990s and early 2000s. However, GDP growth rates remained very low, and only Poland had exceeded its economic level of 1989 by 2000.

10.5.3 Prospects for Future Growth among the Advanced Industrialized Countries

What are the prospects for future growth in the world? Here I include some speculations on the factors that might prove important in the future. I begin with the (currently) advanced industrialized countries of the world.

As noted previously, by 2005, there was relatively little remaining gap in TFP levels between the United States and the other advanced countries (between 16 and 18 percent). As a result, the rate of further diminution of the TFP gap is rather limited. Thus, it is already the case that the catch-up effect has dissipated and it is unlikely that the catch-up effect will contribute much more to future productivity growth among this group of countries.

Both the ISDB data and the Maddison data show a slowdown in the rate of growth of capital between the 1960s and the 2000s for the advanced countries (see Chapter 5). There is not likely to be much of a surge in capital investment in the future. Moreover, the average age of the capital stock is

---

[1] Also see Rodrik (2004) for additional descriptions of episodes of rapid growth among countries of the world.

likely to remain fairly constant, so that it is unlikely that the vintage effect will be a major source of (or hindrance to) future productivity growth.

The growth in mean education has slowed dramatically between the 1970s and 2000s. Further growth in mean education is limited both by constraints on public spending and by a saturation effect as students reach ability limitations in the amount of education that they can absorb. However, since part of the growth of average schooling of the labor force is a cohort effect – younger people with more education replace older people with less education in the labor force – there will still be continued growth in average years of schooling among workers in the future, though not as dramatically as in the past. I do not see rising education as a major source of productivity growth in the future.

The rate of increase in trade openness slowed considerably in the 1990s and 1980s, relative to the 1960s and especially to the 1970s. There are natural limits to the degree of openness, particularly as the advanced countries move more toward service economies. As a result, I do not foresee much further gain in the degree of openness. On the other hand, import intensity rose faster than total trade openness during the 1980s and 1990s. Still, a further increase in the ratio of imports to GNP is not likely to be great, and its impact on productivity growth (its coefficient) is relatively small in any case.

R&D intensity, after growing very rapidly during the 1960s, has grown much more slowly in the 1970s, 1980s, 1990s, and early 2000s. Here, again, there are natural limits to this variable – particularly, as the marginal rate of return to R&D falls off very quickly as expenditures on R&D increase. R&D intensity among the industrialized countries is not likely to increase much more in the future.

Shifts in employment shares are limited by both 0 percent and 100 percent. After a rapid decline in the share of employment in agriculture during the 1950s and 1960s, its rate of decline has slowed considerably during the 1970s and 1980s and approached 0 in the 1990s and early 2000s. Further gains in productivity from the shift of employment out of agriculture are therefore fairly limited.

Conversely, the share of employment in services increased very rapidly during the 1960s and 1970s but slowed considerably during the 1980s and 1990s. Here again, the rate of further increase is likely to be much slower than in the past. In this case, the negative effect of a rising share of employment in services on productivity growth is also likely to be relatively small in the future.

In sum, there are likely to be three main sources of future productivity growth over the next couple of decades or so from traditional factors:

(1) The productivity drag of the vintage effect (deceleration in the growth of the capital stock) will moderate substantially; (2) R&D intensity and trade openness will continue to undergo a modest increase; and (3) the productivity drag effect of the shift into services will continue to diminish. Offsetting these factors will be (1) a reduction in the gains from the catch-up effect and (2) diminished growth in mean years of schooling. All in all, the overall average rate of labor productivity growth for the industrialized countries is likely to subside to its long-term historical average of about 2 percent per year.

There are, of course, many other factors that may influence future productivity growth among the advanced industrialized countries. In the remainder of this section, I will try to assess the importance of three such factors that may have an impact on future productivity performance. The three are particularly relevant to service sector performance: (1) the deregulation of service industries, (2) the influence of computerization and information technology on service sector productivity, and (3) the outsourcing of service activities from manufacturing.

As discussed in Chapter 5, the prevailing wisdom is that deregulation is generally beneficial for TFP growth, though Gordon (1992), in particular, disputed this conclusion. Generally, the estimates show that deregulation increased TFP growth by about 1 percentage point per year. Since the main locus of future deregulation in OECD countries is likely to be the communications and transportation industries, the likely effect of complete deregulation of this sector on future TFP growth for the whole economy will probably be on the order of a 0.07 percentage point per year improvement (calculated by multiplying 1 percentage point by the share of total employment in the communications and transportation industries). Additional mileage from future deregulation of these sectors is therefore rather limited. Moreover, increasing environmental regulation may more than offset even this modest improvement. In addition, the financial deregulation of the 1990s and 2000s seems to have had some deleterious effects on growth, as evidenced by the 2008 meltdown in world financial markets and world growth. This suggests that most advanced countries will impose additional regulations on their financial industries in the future.

Computerization and IT may provide another vehicle for future productivity growth. Fantastic increases in productivity were found for both computers and software in the early literature on this subject. Berndt and Griliches (1993) estimated a real price decline of microcomputers of 28 percent per year between 1982 and 1988. Gandal (1994) estimated a real price reduction in computer spreadsheets of *15* percent per year over the 1986–91 period.

Many economists feel that the growing use of IT throughout the sectors of the economy should result in an acceleration of TFP growth in the near future. Lichtenberg (1995), using production data on the firm level throughout the U.S. business sector over the years 1988–91; Brynjolfsson and Hitt (1993), on the basis of a sample of 367 large firms in the United States over the period 1987–91; and Hendel (1994), using a sample of 7,895 establishments covering all major sectors of the economy in the United States in 1984 and 1988 all estimated that the return to investment in computer capital was much higher than the return to other types of capital.

Later studies showed even larger effects of IT on productivity growth. For example, Stiroh (1998) and Jorgenson and Stiroh (1999, 2000) used a growth accounting framework to assess the impact of computers on output growth. Jorgenson and Stiroh (2000) found relatively higher growth in total factor productivity (TFP) and average labor productivity between 1958 and 1996 in manufacturing. Within manufacturing, the annual growth rates of average labor productivity for computer-producing industries were far higher than for other industries: 4.1 percent for Industrial Machinery and Equipment and 3.1 percent for Electronic and Electric Equipment, compared to 2.6 percent for the next highest industry, Instruments. Jorgenson and Stiroh (1999) calculated that one-sixth of the 2.4 percent annual growth in output could be attributed to computer outputs, compared to about 0 percent over the 1948–73 period. The effect resulted from capital deepening rather than from enhanced productivity growth.

A study by Oliner and Sichel (2000) provided strong evidence for a substantial role of IT in the recent spurt of productivity growth during the second half of the 1990s. Using aggregate time series data for the United States, they found that both the use of IT in sectors purchasing computers and other forms of IT, as well as the production of computers, appeared to have made an important contribution to the speedup of productivity growth in the latter part of the 1990s. Also, as mentioned, Van Ark, O'Mahony, and Timmer (2008) attributed most of the growing productivity gap between Europe and the United States to the greater investment made by American service providers in IT.

In sum, the results from this set of studies taken as a whole suggest that the return to investment in IT was much higher than that to other types of capital by the early 1990s at least. Suppose this trend remains unchanged in the future, the return to IT is about twice as great as the return to other investment, and about 10 percent of new investment is in the form of IT equipment. Then if TFP growth averaged about 1 percentage point per year, a doubling of IT investment to 20 percent should add another 0.1 percentage point (1 percentage point multiplied by 0.1) to overall TFP growth.

"Outsourcing" refers to the process of replacing in-house services, such as legal, advertising, accounting, and related business services, with services purchased from outside the firm (see, for example, Postner, 1990, for a discussion of this issue from an accounting point of view). This process has two effects of interest for us. First, it may speed up the shift of employment out of goods industries to services. Second, by sloughing off the more stagnant service activities, manufacturing should experience more rapid TFP growth.

With regard to the first, a study by Siegel and Griliches (1991) calculated that the share of purchased intermediate services in manufacturing increased by 8 percent between 1977 and 1982. A similar figure was reported by ten Raa and Wolff (2001). With regard to the second issue, ten Raa and Wolff (1993, 2001), using input-output data for the United States, calculated that outsourcing may have increased TFP growth within manufacturing by 0.2 percentage point over the 1947–82 period. The effects of outsourcing were weaker for all goods industries, about 0.1 percentage point. If we use the ten Raa and Wolff (2001) figure that outsourcing added 0.1 percentage point to TFP growth in goods industries, then continued outsourcing may add 0.03 percentage point (0.1 percentage point multiplied by the share of employment in goods industries) to aggregate TFP growth.

On the basis of the preceding rather crude analysis, I predict at most an additional 0.2 percentage point in TFP growth from these three factors. These are, of course, over and above the contributions of the more traditional factors to overall productivity growth. In any case, there is not likely to be much of a productivity resurgence from continued deregulation, increased IT investment, and outsourcing

In sum, future projections suggest that average annual labor productivity growth will remain in the order of 2 percent per year. The concurrence of factors very favorable to growth that happened in the early postwar period largely dissipated by 1980 or so. In particular, the strong catch-up effect, rapid rates of capital growth, with the concomitant strong vintage effect, rapid gains in educational attainment, large increases in trade openness, rapid acceleration in R&D intensity, and rapid structural shifts in employment will likely be absent over the next couple of decades or so.

10.5.4 Prospects for Middle Income and Less Developed Countries of the World

It is not possible to conduct a quantitative analysis of the future prospects of growth among the other countries of the world because of their extensive heterogeneity and varied growth performances over the last half-century. However, there are several "lessons" that can be drawn for this group of countries, particularly the LDCs.

(1) The first lesson is that it is necessary to develop basic social institutions in order to achieve sustained growth. There is almost unanimous agreement on the importance of socioeconomic development as a prerequisite for economic development. A solid set of social and economic institutions, such as the rule of law and little corruption, seems a must for economic growth. The development of financial institutions seems to be another principal ingredient for successful economic development.

(2) The second is to establish a solid and sustainable set of political institutions. A stable political environment is another necessary condition for successful economic development. Fagerberg and Srholec (2008) also stress the importance of good governance as a prerequisite for growth. However, this does not necessarily require democracy, as long as the government is stable over time. Indeed, as Fagerberg and Srholec noted, there are several examples of countries during the 1990s and 2000s that have successfully industrialized and that have not adapted Western political institutions (such as China and Vietnam). Also, it is important to avoid wars, both interstate and civil encounters. These appear to be very bad for a country's economic health.

(3) Low income and middle income countries cannot rely on the catch-up effect per se to promote growth. The catch-up effect (or unconditional convergence effect) is too weak at lower levels of development. However, conditional on other factors such as investment and education, the catch-up effect can become a powerful force.

(4) Capital investment is crucial for development. It may be the major force promoting economic growth. However, FDI by itself does not appear to be an important ingredient in economic development. Nor does foreign aid help very much (nor hurt very much either).

(5) It appears to be crucial for the population to reach a minimal level of education. The educational threshold effect seems to be another powerful force in development. However, advanced education (at the university level or even the upper secondary school level) does not seem to matter as much.

(6) Trade openness seems to have positive effects on economic growth, though the early results concerning the positive effect of trade on productivity

growth have been gradually whittled away as researchers employed more econometrically sophisticated techniques that adequately control for endogeneity and the omitted variable bias.

(7) Inequality does not seem to be much of a problem for economic development (though it may be bad for other reasons such as leading to a high rate of impoverishment of the population and unstable political conditions).

(8) R&D investment does not appear to be very important for growth during the catch-up phase of development but may become important once a country reaches a more advanced level of development.

(9) Product and labor market deregulation does not appear to have strong positive effects on output growth. However, in conjunction with "good" social, political, and economic institutions, regulation of these markets can help to promote growth.

(10) Natural resources abundance can be a "curse" for economic development among LDCs. However, the negative effects can be avoided with the right institutions and good government.

(11) Tropical countries seem to be subject to particular disadvantages because of their climate. However, there is not much that can be done about that (unless the country can move to a colder climate).

(12) An additional factor is the development of a so-called national innovation system. A "national innovation system" refers to the set of institutions in a country that promote the development of new technology and innovation. This may consist of some combination of privately financed and sponsored R&D, government owned or sponsored research laboratories, university-based research, the patenting system of a country, and other institutions. Different countries are characterized by different combinations of these institutions. The effectiveness of different countries in generating new technology and innovations may therefore differ considerably.

Fagerberg and Srholec (2008), for example, called attention to the importance of national innovation systems as a factor in explaining growth differences among 115 countries over the period from 1992 to 2004. They used a factor analytical technique to identify the components of national innovation systems, as well as the weightings of the different components. They found that this variable was strong, positive, and statistically significant in explaining the growth in GDP per capita among these countries over this period. They concluded that countries that have succeeded in catch-up gave high priority to this dimension of development. In fact, a well-functioning innovation system appears to be an essential (though not sufficient) prerequisite for development.

Bibliography

Abramovitz, Moses (1979), "Rapid Growth Potential and Its Realization: The Experience of Capitalist Economies in the Post-War Period," in Edmond Malinvaud, editor, *Economic Growth and Resources*, Vol. 1 (London: Macmillan).

(1986), "Catching Up, Forging Ahead, and Falling Behind," *Journal of Economic History*, Vol. 46, No. 2, June, pp. 385–406.

(1994), "Catch-Up and Convergence in the Postwar Growth Boom and After," in William J. Baumol, Richard R. Nelson, and Edward N. Wolff, editors, *Convergence of Productivity: Cross-National Studies and Historical Evidence* (New York: Oxford University Press), pp. 86–125.

Abramovitz, Moses, and Paul A. David (1973), "Reinterpreting Economic Growth: Parables and Realities," *American Economic Review*, Vol. 63, No. 2, May, pp. 428–39.

Acemoglu, Daron, Simon Johnson, and James A. Robinson (2001), "The Colonial Origins of Comparative Development: An Empirical Investigation," *American Economic Review*, Vol. 91, No. 5, pp. 1369–1401.

(2002), "Reversal of Fortune: Geography and Institutions in the Making of the Modern World Income Distribution," *Quarterly Journal of Economics*, Vol. 117, No. 4, pp. 1231–94.

(2003), "Institutional Causes, Macroeconomic Symptoms: Volatility, Crises and Growth," *Journal of Monetary Economics*, Vol. 50, pp. 49–123.

Acemoglu, Daron, Simon Johnson, James A. Robinson, and Pierre Yared (2008), "Income and Democracy," *American Economic Review*, Vol. 98, No. 3, pp. 808–42.

Acemoglu, Daron, and Fabrizio Zilibotti (2001), "Productivity Differences," *Quarterly Journal of Economics*, Vol. 116, No. 2, May, pp. 563–606.

Acharta, Ram C., and Wolfgang Keller (2008), "Estimating the Productivity Selection and Technology Spillover Effects of Imports," NBER Working Paper No. 14079, October.

Adams, F. Gerard, J. R. Behrman, and Michael Boldin (1988), "Defense Expenditures and Economic Growth in LDCs: An Application of the Feder Approach to Military and Non-Military Government Spending," paper presented to the Peace Science Society (International), December 29, New York.

Adelman, Irma, and Cynthia Taft Morris (1967), *Society, Politics, and Economic Development* (Baltimore, MD: Johns Hopkins University Press).

Aghion, Philippe, Alberto Alesina, and Francesco Trebbi (2007), "Democracy, Technology, and Growth," NBER Working Paper No. 13180, June.

Aghion, P., E. Caroli, and C. Garcia-Penalosa (1999), "Inequality and Economic Growth: The Perspective of the New Growth Theories," *Journal of Economic Literature*, Vol. 37, No. 4, pp. 1615–60.

Aghion, Philippe, and Peter Howitt (1992), "A Model of Growth through Creative Destruction," *Econometrica*, Vol. 60, No. 2, March, pp. 323–51.

Aitken, B., and A. Harrison (1999), "Do Domestic Firms Benefit from Foreign Direct Investment? Evidence from Venezuela," *American Economic Review*, Vol. 89, pp. 605–18.

Akin, Ciğdem, and M. Ayhan Kose (2007), "*Changing North-South Linkages: Stylized Facts and Explanations,*" mimeo, George Washington University.

Alam, M. Shahid (1992), "Convergence in Developed Countries: An Empirical Investigation," *Weltwirtschaftliches Archiv*, Vol. 128, pp. 189–201.

Alesina Alberto, and Eliana La Ferrara (2005), "Ethnic Diversity and Economic Performance," *Journal of Economic Literature*, Vol. 43, September, pp. 762–800.

Alesina Alberto, and Roberto Perotti (1996), "Income Distribution, Political Instability and Investment," *European Economic Review*, Vol. 81, No. 5, pp. 1170–89.

Alesina, Alberto, and Dani Rodrik. (1994), "Distribution Politics and Economic Growth," *Quarterly Journal of Economics*, Vol. 109, pp. 465–90.

Alton, T. P. (1985), "East European GNPs: Origins of Product, Final Uses, Rates of Growth, and International Comparisons," in Joint Economic Committee of the U.S. Congress, Selected Papers, *East European Economies: Slow Growth in the 1980s*, Volume 1, Economic Performance and Policy (Washington, DC: Government Printing Office).

Amable, Bruno (1993), "Catch-Up and Convergence: A Model of Cumulative Growth," *International Review of Applied Economics*, Vol. 7, No. 1, January, pp. 1–25.

Amsden, Alice H. (1989), *Asia's Next Giant: South Korea and Late Industrialization* (Baltimore, MD: Johns Hopkins Press).

(1991), "Diffusion of Development: The Late-Industrializing Model and Greater East Asia," *American Economic Review*, Vol. 81, No. 2, May, pp. 282–86.

An, Galina, and Murat F. Iyigun (2004), "The Export Technology Content, Learning by Doing and Specialization in Foreign Trade," *Journal of International Economics*, Vol. 64, No. 2, December, pp. 465–83.

Apergis, Nicholas (2007), "Technology, Human Capital and Productivity Growth: Should We Care about Threshold Effects? Evidence from a Panel of EU Industries," University of Piraeus, February.

Arbache, Jorge Saba, and John Page (2007a), "Patterns of Long Term Growth in Sub-Saharan Africa," World Bank Policy Research Working Paper No. 4398, November.

(2007b), "More Growth of Fewer Collapses? A New Look at Long Run Growth in Sub-Saharan Africa," World Bank Policy Research Working Paper No. 4384, November.

Archibugi, Daniele, and Mario Pianta (1992), "Specialization and Size of Technological Activities in Industrial Countries: The Analysis of Patent Data," *Research Policy*, Vol. 21, pp. 79–93.

(1994), "Aggregate Convergence and Sectoral Specialization of Innovation," *Journal of Evolutionary Economics*, Vol. 4, pp. 17–33.

Arrow, Kenneth (1962), "The Economic Implications of Learning by Doing," *Review of Economic Studies*, Vol. 29, No. 2, June, pp. 155–73.

(1973), "Higher Education as a Filter," *Journal of Public Economics*, Vol. 2, No. 3, pp. 193–216.

Arthur, W. Brian (1989), "Competing Technologies, Increasing Returns, and Lock-in by Historical Events," *Economic Journal*, Vol. 99, pp. 116–31.

Aschauer, David A. (1989a), "Is Public Expenditure Productive?" *Journal of Monetary Economics*, Vol. 23, pp. 177–200.

(1989b), "Public Investment and Productivity Growth in the Group of Seven," *Economic Perspectives*, Vol. 13, pp. 17–25.

Åslund, Anders, and Nazgul Genish (2006), "The Eurasian Growth Paradox," Institute for International Economics Working Paper No. 06–5, June.

Atrostic, B. K., J. Gates, and R. Jarmin (2000), "Measuring the Electronic Economy: Current Status and Next Steps," Center for Economic Studies, U.S. Bureau of the Census, Working Paper CES-01-11.

Babetskii, Ian, and Nauro F. Campos (2007), "Does Reform Work? An Econometric Examination of the Reform-Growth Puzzle," IZA Discussion paper No. 2638, February, Bonn, Germany.

Baily, M. N. and A. K. Chakrabarti (1988), *Innovation and the Productivity Crisis* (Washington, DC, The Brookings Institution).

Baily, Martin, and Robert Gordon (1988), "The Productivity Slowdown, Measurement Issues, and the Explosion in Computer Power," *Brookings Papers on Economic Activity*, Vol. 2, pp. 347–432.

Baily, Martin Neil, and Robert Z. Lawrence (2001), "Do We Have a New E-Economy," *American Economic Review*, Vol. 91, No. 2, May, pp. 308–12.

Bairoch, Paul (1976), "Europe's Gross National Product, 1800–1973," *Journal of European Economic History*, Vol. 5, pp 213–340.

(1993), *Economics and World History: Myths and Paradoxes* (Chicago: University of Chicago Press).

Baldwin, R. (1971), "Determinants of the Commodity Structure of U.S. Trade," *American Economic Review*, Vol. 61, pp. 126–46.

Baldwin, R., H. Braconier, and R. Forslid (2005), "Multinationals, Endogenous Growth and Technological Spillovers: Theory and Evidence," *Review of International Economics*, Vol. 13, pp. 945–63.

Banerjee, Abhijit V., and Esther Duflo (2003), "Inequality and Growth: What Can the Data Say?" *Journal of Economic Growth*, Vol. 8, pp. 267–99.

Barker, Terry (1990), "Sources of Structural Change for the UK Service Industries 1979–84," *Economic Systems Research*, Vol. 2, No. 2, pp. 173–83.

Barker, Terry, and Osmo Forssell (1992), "Manufacturing, Services and Structural Change, 1979–1984," in C. Driver and P. Dunne editors, *Structural Change in the UK Economy* (Cambridge: Cambridge University Press).

Barone, Guglielmo, and Federico Cingano (2008), "Service regulation and growth: Evidence from OECD countries," Banca D'Italia Working Paper No. 675, June.

Barro, Robert J. (1991), "Economic Growth in a Cross Section of Countries," *Quarterly Journal of Economics*, Vol. 106, pp. 407–43.

(1996), "Democracy and Growth," *Journal of Economic Growth*, Vol. 1, March, pp. 1–27.

(2000), "Inequality and Growth in a Panel of Countries," *Journal of Economic Growth*, Vol. 5, March, pp. 5–32.

(2008), "Inequality and Growth Revisited," Asian Development Bank Working Paper Series, January.

Barro, Robert J., and Jong-Wha Lee (1993), "International Comparisons of Educational Attainment," *Journal of Monetary Economics*, Vol. 32, pp. 363–94.

(1996), "International Measures of Schooling Years and Schooling Quality," *American Economics Review*, Vol. 86, No. 2, pp. 218–23.

(2000), "International Data on Educational Attainment: Updates and Implications," manuscript, Harvard University, February, http://www.cid.harvard.edu/ciddata/ciddata.html.

Barro, Robert J., and Xavier Sala-i-Martin (1992), "Convergence," *Journal of Political Economy*, Vol. 199, No. 2, pp. 97–108.

(1995), *Economic Growth* (New York: McGraw-Hill).

Bartel, Ann P., and Frank R. Lichtenberg (1987), "The Comparative Advantage of Educated Workers in Implementing New Technology," *Review of Economics and Statistics*, Vol. 69, pp. 1–11.

Bartelsman, Eric J. and Doms, Mark (2000), "Understanding Productivity: Lessons from Longitudinal Microdata," *Journal of Economic Literature*, Vol. 38, September, pp. 569–94.

Baumol, William J. (1967), "Macroeconomics of Unbalanced Growth: The Anatomy of Urban Crisis," *American Economic Review*, Vol. 57, June, pp. 415–26.

(1986), "Productivity Growth, Convergence, and Welfare: What the Long-Run Data Show?" *American Economic Review*, Vol. 76, No. 5, December, pp. 1072–85.

Baumol, William J., Sue Anne Batey Blackman, and Edward N. Wolff (1985), "Unbalanced Growth Revisited: Asymptotic Stagnancy and New Evidence," *American Economic Review* Vol. 75, No. 4, September, pp. 806–17.

(1989), *Productivity and American Leadership: The Long View* (Cambridge, MA.: MIT Press).

Baumol, William J., and Edward N. Wolff (1984), "On Interindustry Differences in Absolute Productivity," *Journal of Political Economy*, Vol. 92, No. 6, December.

(1988), "Productivity Growth, Convergence, and Welfare: Reply," *American Economic Review*, Vol. 78, No. 5, December, pp. 1155–59.

Beaudry, Paul, Fabrice Collard, and David A. Green (2002), "Decomposing the Twin-Peaks in the World Distribution of Output per Worker," NBER Working paper No. 9240, October.

Beck, T. and R. Levine (2004), "Stock Markets, Banks and Growth: Panel Evidence," *Journal of Banking and Finance*, Vol. 28, No. 3, March, pp. 423–42.

Beck, T., Levine, R., and Loayza, N. (2000), "Finance and the Sources of Growth, *Journal of Financial Economics*, Vol. 58, pp. 261–300.

Becker, Gary S. (1975), *Human Capital: A Theoretical and Empirical Analysis*, 2nd edition (New York: Columbia University Press and National Bureau of Economic Research).

Behrman, Jere, and Mark Rosenzweig (1994), "Caveat Emptor: Cross-Country Data on Education and the Labor Force," *Journal of Development Economics*, Vol. 44, No. 1, pp. 147–71.

Benabou, Roland (1996), "Inequality and Growth," *NBER Macroeconomics Annual, 1996*, pp. 11–73.

Ben-David, Dan (1993), "Equalizing Exchange: Trade Liberalization and Income Convergence, *Quarterly Journal of Economics*, Vol. 108, pp. 653–79.

(1996), "Trade and Convergence among Countries," *Journal of International Economics*, Vol. 40, pp. 279–98.

Ben-David, Dan, and Ayal Kimhi (2004), "Trade and the Rate of Income Convergence," *Journal of International Trade & Economic Development*, Vol. 13, No. 4, December, pp. 419–41.

Benhabib, Jess and Aldo Rustichini (1996), "Social Conflict and Growth," *Journal of Economic Growth*, Vol. 1, No. 1, pp. 129–46.

Benhabib, Jess, and Mark Spiegel (1992), "The Role of Human Capital and Political Instability in Economic Development," *Rivista de Politica Economica*, Vol. 11, pp. 55–93.

Benhabib, Jess, and Mark A. Spiegel (1994), "The Role of Human Capital in Economic Development: Evidence from Aggregate Cross-Country Data," *Journal of Monetary Economics*, Vol. 34, No. 2, October, pp. 143–74.

Bennet, Paul (1979), "American Productivity Growth: Perspective on the Slowdown," *Federal Reserve Bank of New York Quarterly Review*, Autumn, pp. 25–31.

Berg, Andy, Jonathan D. Ostry, and Jeromin Zettelmeyer (2008), "What Makes Growth Sustained?" IMF Working Paper No. 08/59, March.

Bernard, Andrew A., and Steven Durlauf (1996), "Interpreting Tests of the Convergence Hypothesis," *Journal of Econometrics*, Vol. 71, No. 1&2, March/April, pp. 161–73.

Bernard, Andrew A., and J. Bradford Jensen (2004), "Exporting and Productivity in the USA," *Oxford Review of Economic Policy*, Vol. 20, No. 3, pp. 343–57.

Bernard, Andrew B., and Charles I. Jones (1996a), "Productivity across Industries and Countries: Time Series Theory and Evidence," *Review of Economics and Statistics*, Vol. 78, No. 1, February, pp. 135–46.

(1996b), "Comparing Apples to Oranges: Productivity Convergence and Measurement across Industries and Countries," *American Economic Review*, Vol. 86, No. 5, December, pp. 1216–38.

(2001), "Comparing Apples to Oranges: Productivity Convergence and Measurement across Industries and Countries: Reply," *American Economic Review*, Vol. 91, No. 4, September, pp. 1168–69.

Berndt, Ernst R. (1980), "Energy Price Increases and the Productivity Slowdown in United States Manufacturing," in *The Decline in Productivity Growth* (Boston: Federal Reserve Bank of Boston).

Berndt, E., and Fuss, M. (1986), "Productivity Measurement with Variations in Capacity Utilization and Other Forms of Temporary Equilibrium, *Journal of Econometrics*, Vol. 33, pp. 7–29.

Berndt, Ernst R., and Catherine J. Morrison (1995), "High-Tech Capital Formation and Economic Performance in U.S. Manufacturing Industries," *Journal of Econometrics*, Vol. 69, pp. 9–43.

Berndt, Ernst R., Ann F. Friedlaender, Judy Shaw-Er Wang Chiang, and Christopher A. Vellturo (1993), "Cost Effect of Mergers and Deregulation in the U.S. Railroad Industry," *Journal of Productivity Analysis*, Vol. 4, No.2, pp. 127–44

Berndt, Ernst R., and Zvi Griliches (1993), "Price Indices for Microcomputers: An Exploratory Study," in Murray F. Foss, Marilyn E. Manser, and Alwyn H. Young, editors, *Price Measurements and Their Uses*, Studies in Income and Wealth, Vol. 57 (Chicago: University of Chicago Press), pp. 63–93.

Berndt, Ernst R., and Catherine J. Morrison (1997), "Assessing the Productivity of Information Technology Equipment in U.S. Manufacturing Industries," *Review of Economics and Statistics*, Vol. 79, No. 3, pp. 471–81

Bishop, John H. (1989), "Is the Test Score Decline Responsible for the Productivity Growth Decline? *American Economic Review*, Vol. 79, No. 2, March, pp. 178–97.

Biswas, Basudeb, and Rati Ram (1986), " Military Expenditure and Economic Growth in Less Developed Countries: An Augmented Model and Further Evidence," *Economic Development and Cultural Change*, Vol. 34, pp. 361–72.

Bjørnskov, Christian (2008), "The Growth-Inequality Association: Government Ideology Matters," *Journal of Development Economics*, Vol. 87, pp. 300–308.

Blitzer, Jürgen, Ingo Geishecker, and Holger Görg (2007), "Productivity Spillovers through Vertical Linkages: Evidence from 17 OECD Countries," University of Nottingham Research Paper 2007/26.

Blomström, Magnus, and Ari Kokko (1998), "Multinational Corporations and Spillovers," *Journal of Economic Surveys*, Vol. 2, pp. 247–77.

Blomström, Magnus, and Edward N. Wolff (1994), "Multinational Corporations and Productivity Convergence in Mexico," in William J. Baumol, Richard R. Nelson, and Edward N. Wolff, editors, *Convergence of Productivity: Cross-National Studies and Historical Evidence* (New York: Oxford University Press), pp. 263–84.

Blundell, R. W. and Bond, S. R. (1998), "Initial Conditions and Moment Restrictions in Dynamic Panel Data Models," *Journal of Econometrics*, Vol. 87, No. 1, pp. 115–43.

Bockstette, Valerie, Areendam Chanda, and Louis Putterman (2002), "States and Markets: The Advantage of an Early Start," *Journal of Economic Growth*, Vol. 7, pp. 347–69.

Bodea, Cristina, and Ibrahim A. Bodea, and Elbadawi (2008), "Political Violence and Economic Growth," World Bank Policy Research Paper 4692, August.

Bosworth, B. P., and S. M. Collins (2003), "The Empirics of Growth: An Update," *Brookings Papers on Economic Activity*, Vol. 2, pp. 113–206.

Boulhol, Hervé, Alain de Serres, and Margit Molnar (2008), "The Contribution of Economic Geography to GDP per Capita," OECD Working Paper No. 602, Paris.

Boussemart, Jean-Philippe, Walter Briec, Isabelle Cadoret, and Christophe Tavera (2006), "A Re-Examination of the Technological Catching-Up Hypothesis across OECD Industries," *Economic Modeling*, Vol. 23, Issue 6, December 2006, pp. 967–77.

Bowen, Harry P. (1983), "Changes in the International Distribution of Resources and Their Impact on U.S. Comparative Advantage, *Review of Economics and Statistics*, Vol. 65, August, pp. 402–15.

Braconier, Henrik, and Fredrik Sjöholm (1998), "National and International Spillovers from R&D: Comparing a Neoclassical and an Endogenous Growth Approach," *Weltwirtschaftliches Archiv*, Vol. 134, pp. 638–63.

Bresnahan, Timothy F., and Manuel Trajtenberg (1995), "General Purpose Technologies: Engines of Growth?" *Journal of Econometrics*, Vol. 65, No. 1, pp. 83–108.

Broadberry, Stephen N. (1994a), "Technological Leadership and Productivity Leadership in Manufacturing since the Industrial Revolution: Implications for the Convergence Debate," *Economic Journal*, Vol. 104, March, pp. 291–302.

(1994b), "Comparative Productivity in British and American Manufacturing during the Nineteenth Century," *Explorations in Economic History*, Vol. 31, October, pp. 521–48.

(1997), *The Productivity Race: British Manufacturing in International Perspective, 1850–1990* (Cambridge: Cambridge University Press).

Bronfenbrenner, Martin (1985), "Japanese Productivity Experience," in William J. Baumol and Kenneth McLennan, editors, *Productivity Growth and U.S. Competitiveness* (New York: Oxford University Press).

Brynjolfsson, Erik, and Lorin Hitt (1993), "*New Evidence on the Returns to Information Systems*," mimeo, MIT Sloan School, Cambridge, MA, October.

Buchele, Robert, and Jens Christiansen (1999), "Labor Relations and Productivity Growth in Advanced Capitalist Economies, *Review of Radical Political Economics*, Vol. 31, No. 1, pp. 87–110.

Burnside, Craig, and David Dollar (2000). "Aid, Policies, and Growth," *American Economic Review*, Vol. 90, No. 4, September, pp. 847–68.

Carter, Anne P. (1970), *Structural Change in the American Economy* (Cambridge, MA: Harvard University Press).

Castellacci, Fulvio (2008), "Technology Clubs, Technology Gaps, and Growth Trajectories," Norwegian Institute of International Affairs (NUPI) Working Paper 731, Oslo, Norway.

Castellacci, Fulvio, and Daniele Archibugi (2008), "The Technology Clubs: The Distribution of Knowledge across Nations," *Research Policy*, Vol. 37, pp. 1659–73

Caves, Douglas, Laurits Christensen, and Erwin Diewert (1982a), "The Economic Theory of Index Numbers and the Measurement of Input, Output, and Productivity," *Econometrica*, 50(6), pp. 1393–1414.

(1982b), "Multilateral Comparisons of Output, Input and Productivity Using Superlative Index Numbers," *Economic Journal*, 92 (365), pp. 73–86.

Central Intelligence Agency (1988), *Handbook of Economic Statistics, 1988* (Washington, D.C.: Government Printing Office).

Chakraborty, Atreya, and Mark Kazarosian (2001), "Marketing Strategy and the Use of Information Technology: New Evidence from the Trucking Industry," *Research in Transport Economics*, Vol. 6, pp. 71–96.

Chang, W. (1979), "Some Theorems of Trade and General Equilibrium with Many Goods and Factors," *Econometrica*, Vol. 47, pp. 709–26.

Chang, Roberto, Linda Kaltani, and Norman Loayza (2005), "Openness Can be Good for Growth: The Role of Policy Complementarities," NBER Working Paper No. 11787, November.

Chen, Siyan, Norman V. Loayza, and Marta Reynal-Querol (2007), "The Aftermath of Civil War," World Bank Working Paper 4190, April.

Chenery, H., Robinson, S., and Syrquin, M. (1986), *Industrialization and Growth: A Comparative Study* (New York: Oxford University Press).

Christensen, Laurits R., Dianne Cummings, and Dale W. Jorgenson (1980), "Economic Growth, 1947–73: An International Comparison," in *New Developments in Productivity Measurement*, Studies in Income and Wealth 40, John W. Kendrick and Beatrice Vaccara, editors (Chicago: National Bureau of Economic Research and Chicago University Press), pp. 595–691.

Christensen, Laurits R. and Dale W. Jorgenson (1969), "The Measurement of U.S. Real Capital Input, 1929–1967, *Review of Income and Wealth*, Vol. 15, pp. 293–320.

Christensen, Laurits R., and Dale W. Jorgenson (1970), "U.S. Real Product and Real Factor Input, 1929–1967, *Review of Income and Wealth*, Vol. 16, pp. 19–50.

Christensen, Laurits R., Dale W. Jorgenson and L. J. Lau (1971), "Conjugate Duality and the Transcendental Logarithmic Production Function," *Econometrica*, Vol. 39, pp. 255–56.

Chong, Alberto, and Mark Gradstein (2007), "Inequality and Institutions," *Review of Economics and Statistics*, Vol. 89, No. 3, pp. 454–65.

Clark, Gregory, Kevin H. O'Rourke, and Alan M. Taylor (2008), "Made in America? The New World, the Old, and the Industrial Revolution," NBER Working Paper No. 14077.

Clark, Peter K. (1979), "Issues in the Analysis of Capital Formation and Productivity Growth," *Brookings Papers on Economic Activity*, 2, pp. 423–31.

Cobb, C. W., and Paul H. Douglas (1928), "A Theory of Production," *American Economic Review*, Vol. 18, No. 1, Supplement, pp. 139–72.

Coe, David T., and Elhanan Helpman (1995), "International R&D Spillovers," *European Economic Review*, Vol. 39, pp. 859–87.

Coe, Davit T., Elhanan Helpman, and Alexander W. Hoffmaister (1997), "North-South R&D Spillovers," *The Economic Journal*, Vol. 107, No. 440, January, pp. 134–49.

Coe, David, and Gerald Holtham (1983), "Output Responsiveness and Inflation: An Aggregate Study," *OECD Economic Studies*, No. 1, Autumn.

Cohen, W. M. and D. A. Levinthal (1989), "Innovation and Learning: The Two Faces of R&D," *Economic Journal*, 99, pp. 569–96.

Comin, Diego, William Easterly, and Erick Gong (2006), "Was the Wealth of Nations Determined in 1000 B.C.?" NBER Working Paper No. 12657, October.

Comin, Diego, Bart Hobijn, and Emilie Rovito (2006), "World Technology Usage Lags," NBER Working Paper No. 12677, November.

Connolly, Michele P. (2003), "The Dual Nature of Trade: Measuring Its Impact on Imitation and Growth," *Journal of Development Economics*, Vol. 72, Issue 1, pp. 31–55.

Cook, David (2002), "World War II and Convergence," *Review of Economics and Statistics*, Vol. 84, No. 1, pp. 131–38.

Council of Economic Advisers (various years), *Economic Report of the President* (Washington, D.C.: U.S. Government Printing Office).

Crafts, Nicholas (1998), "Forging Ahead and Falling Behind: The Rise and Relative Decline of the First Industrial Nation," *Journal of Economic Perspectives*, Vol. 12, No. 2, Spring, pp. 193–210.

Crandall, Robert W. (1980), "Regulations and Productivity Growth," in *The Decline in Productivity Growth* (Boston: Federal Reserve Bank of Boston).

Dalgaard, Carl-Johan, and Henrik Hansen (2001), "On Aid, Growth and Good Policies," *Journal of Development Studies*, Vol. 37, No. 6, August, pp. 17–41.

Dalum, Bent, Keld Laursen, and Bart Verspagen (1999), "Does Specialization Matter?" *Industrial and Corporate Change*, Vol. 8, No. 2, pp. 267–88.

Das, Gouranga G., Hiranya K. Nath, and Halis Murat Yildiz (2008), "Foreign Direct Investment and Inequality in Productivity across Countries," mimeo.

David, Paul A. (1991), "Computer and Dynamo: The Modern Productivity Paradox in a Not-Too-Distant Mirror," in *Technology and Productivity: The Challenge for Economic Policy* (Paris: OECD), pp. 315–48.

Deane, Phyllis, and W. A. Cole (1964), *British Economic Growth, 1688–1959: Trends and Structure* (Cambridge: Cambridge University Press).

Deininger, Klaus, and Lyn Squire (1996), "A New Data Set Measuring Income Inequality, *World Bank Economic Review*, Vol. 10, No. 3, September, pp. 565–91.

Delis, Manthos D., Philip Molyneux, and Fotios Pasiouras (2008), "Regulations and Productivity Growth in Banking," Working Paper No. 2008.06, University of Bath, School of Management.

De Long, J. Bradford (1988), "Productivity Growth, Convergence, and Welfare: Comment," *American Economic Review*, Vol. 78, No. 5, December, pp. 1138–54.

Denison, Edward F. (1962), *Sources of Economic Growth and the Alternatives before Us* (New York: Committee for Economic Development).

(1967), *Why Growth Rates Differ* (Washington, DC: The Brookings Institution).

(1973), "The Shift to Services and the Rate of Productivity Change," *Survey of Current Business*, 53, Vol. 10, October, 20–35.

(1974), *Accounting for United States Economic Growth* (Washington, DC: The Brookings Institution).

(1979a), "Explanations of Declining Productivity Growth," *Survey of Current Business*, Vol. 59, No. 8, Part 2, August, pp. 1–24.

(1979b), *Accounting for Slower Economic Growth* (Washington, D.C.: Brookings Institution).

(1980), "Discussion," in *The Decline in Productivity Growth* (Boston: Federal Reserve Bank of Boston).

(1983), "The Interruption of Productivity Growth in the United States," *Economic Journal*, Vol. 93, pp. 56–77.

Denny, Michael, Fuss, Melvyn, and Waverman, Leonard (1981), "The Measurement and Interpretation of Total Factor Productivity in Regulated Industries, with an Application to Canadian Telecommunications," in Cowing, Thomas E., and Stevenson, Rodney E., editors, *Productivity Measurement in Regulated Industries*, Academic Press, pp. 179–247.

Diewert, W. Erwin (1976), "Exact and Superlative Index Numbers," *Journal of Econometrics*, 4, pp. 115–45.

Diewert, W. Erwin and Alice Nakamura (2007), "The Measurement of Productivity of Nations," *The Handbook of Econometrics*, Volume 6A, edited by James J. Heckman and Edward E. Leamer, Amsterdam: North-Holland, pp. 4501–86.

Dollar, David (1991), "Convergence of South Korean Productivity on West German Levels, 1966–78," *World Development*, Vol. 19, 1991, 263–73.

(1992), "Outward-Oriented Developing Economies Really Do Grow More Rapidly: Evidence from 95 LDCs, 1976–85," *Economic Development and Cultural Change*, Vol. 40, No. 3, pp. 523–44.

(2007), "Asian Century or Multi-Polar Century?" World Bank Policy Research Working Paper No. WPS4174, March.

Dollar, David, and Edward N. Wolff (1988), "Convergence of Industry Labor Productivity among Advanced Economies, 1963–1982" *Review of Economics and Statistics*, Vol. 40, No. 4, November, 549–58.

(1993), *Competitiveness, Convergence, and International Specialization* (Cambridge, MA: MIT Press).

Dosi, Giovanni, Keith Pavitt, and Luc Soete (1990), *The Economics of Technical Change and International Trade* (London: Harvester Wheatsheaf).

Doucouliagos, Hristos, and Mehmet Ulubasoglu (2006), "Democracy and Economic Growth: A Meta-Analysis," SWP 2006/04, Melbourne, Australia: Deakin University Faculty of Business and Law.

Dowrick, Steve, and Duc-Tho Nguyen (1989), "OECD Comparative Economic Growth 1950–85: Catch-Up and Convergence," *American Economic Review*, Vol. 79, No. 5, December, pp. 1010–31.

Dowrick, Steve, and John Quiggin (1997), "True Measures of GDP and Convergence," *American Economic Review*, Vol. 87, No. 1, March, pp. 41–64.

Easterlin, Richard A. (1996), *Growth Triumphant: the Twenty-First Century in Historical Perspective* (Ann Arbor: University of Michigan Press).

Easterly, William (2001), *The Elusive Quest for Growth: Economists' Adventures and Misadventures in the Tropics* (Cambridge, MA: MIT Press).

(2003), "Can Foreign Aid Buy Growth?" *Journal of Economic Perspectives*, Vol. 17, No. 3, Summer, pp. 23–48.

Easterly, William and Ross Levine (2003), "Tropics, Germs, and Crops: How Endowments Influence Economic Development," *Journal of Monetary Economics*, Vol. 50, pp. 3–39.

Easterly, William, Ross Levine, and David Roodman (2003), "New Data, New Doubts: A Comment on Burnside and Dollar's 'Aid, Policies, and Growth' (2000)," *American Economic Review*, Vol. 91, No. 4, September, pp. 795–813.

Easterly, William, Jozef Ritzan, and Michael Woolcock (2006), "Social Cohesion, Institutions, and Growth," Center for Global Development Working Paper No. 94, August.

Eaton, Jonathan, and Samuel Kortum (1996), "Trade in Ideas: Patenting and Productivity in the OECD," *Journal of International Economics*, Vol. 40, pp. 251–78.

(1999), "International Patenting and Technology Diffusion: Theory and Measurement," *International Economic Review*, Vol. 40, pp. 537–70.

Eberts, Randall W. (1990), "Public Infrastructure and Regional Economic Development," *Economic Review*, Federal Reserve Bank of Cleveland, Quarter 1, 1990, pp. 15–27.

Eckstein, Otto (1980), "Core Inflation, Productivity, Capital Supply, and Demand Management," in Walter E. Hoadley, editor, *The Economy and the President: 1980 and Beyond* (Englewood Cliffs, NJ: Prentice-Hall).

Engerman, Stanley L., and Robert E. Gallman, editors (1986), *Long-Term Factors in American Economic Growth*, Studies in Income and Wealth, series 51 (Chicago: University of Chicago Press).

Ehrlich, Isaac (2008), "The Mystery of Human Capital as Engine of Growth, or Why the US Became the Economic Superpower in the Twentieth Century," in Barry Smith, David Mark, and Isaac Ehrlich, editors, *The Mystery of Capital and the Construction of Social Reality* (Chicago: Open Court).

Evenson, Robert E. (1981), "Benefits and Obstacles to Appropriate Agricultural Technology," *The Annals of the American Academy of Political and Social Science*, No. 458, pp. 54–67.

(1993), "Patents, R&D and Invention Potential: International Evidence," *American Economic Review*, Vol. 83, May, pp. 463–68.

Fagerberg, Jan (1987), "A Technology Gap Approach to Why Growth Rates Differ," *Research Policy*, Vol. 16, pp. 87–99.

(1988), "Why Growth Rates Differ," in Giovanni Dosi, Christopher Freeman, Richard Nelson, Gerald Silverberg, G., and Luc Soete, editors, *Technical Change and Economic Theory* (London: Pinter).

(1994), "Technology and International Differences in Growth Rates," *Journal of Economic Literature*, Vol. 32, September, pp. 1147–75.

Fagerberg, Jan, and Martin Srholec (2008), "National Innovation Systems, Capabilities and Economic Development," *Research Policy*, Vol. 37, pp. 1417–35.

Faini, R., Annez, P., and Taylor, L. (1984), "Defense Spending, Economic Structure, and Growth: Evidence among Countries and over Time," *Economic Development and Cultural Change*, Vol. 32, pp. 487–498.

Fecher, F. and Perelman, S. 1989. "Productivity Growth, Technological Progress and R&D in OECD Industrial Activities," in *Public Finance and Steady Economic Growth* (The Hague, the Netherlands: International Institute of Public Finance).

Fellner, William (1979), "The Declining Growth of American productivity: An Introductory Note," in William Fellner, editor, *Contemporary Economic Problems, 1979* (Washington, DC: American Enterprise Institute).

Fielding, David, and Sebastian Torres (2005), "A Simultaneous Equation Model of Economic Development and Income Inequality," *Journal of Economic Inequality*, Vol. 4, pp. 279–301.

Filer, Randall K. (1980), "The Downturn in Productivity Growth: A New Look at Its Nature and Causes," in Shlomo Maital and Noah M. Melz, editors, *Lagging Productivity Growth* (Cambridge, MA: Ballinger).

Fogel, Robert W. (1999), "Caching Up with the Economy," *American Economic Review*, Vol. 89, No. 1, March, pp. 1–21.

Forbes, Kristin J. (2000). "A Reassessment of the Relationship between Inequality and Growth," *American Economic Review*, Vol. 90, No. 4, September, pp. 869–87.

Foster, Andrew D., and Mark R. Rosenzweig (1996), "Technical Change and Human-Capital Returns and Investments: Evidence from the Green Revolution, *American Economic Review*, Vol. 86, No. 6, pp. 931–53.

Franke, R. H. (1989), "Technological Revolutions and Productivity Decline: The Case of U.S. Banks," in T. Forester, editor, *Computers in the Human Context: Information Technology, Productivity, and People* (Cambridge, MA: MIT Press).

Frankel, Jeffrey A., and David Romer (1999), "Does Trade Cause Growth?" *American Economic Review*, Vol. 89, No. 3, June, pp. 379–99.

Frantzen, Dirk (2000), "R&D, Human Capital and International Technology Spillovers: A Cross-Country Analysis," *Scandinavian Journal of Economics*, Vol. 102, No. 1, pp. 57–75.

Fraumeni, Barbara, and Dale W. Jorgenson (1981), "Capital Formation and U.S. Productivity Growth, 1948–1976," in Ali Dogramaci, editor, *Productivity Analysis: A Range of Perspectives* (Boston/The Hague/London: Martinus Nijhoff).

Freedom House (1997), *Freedom in the World: The Annual Survey of Political Rights and Civil Liberties, 1996–97* (New Brunswick, NJ: Transaction).

Freeman, Christopher (1987), "Information Technology and the Change in Techno-Economic Paradigm," in Christopher Freeman and Luc Soete, editors, *Technical Change and Full Employment* (Oxford: Basil Blackwell).

Friedman, Milton (1992), "Communication: Do Old Fallacies Ever Die?" *Journal of Economic Literature*, Vol. 30, pp. 2129–32.

Fuente, Angel de la, and Rafael Doménech (2001), "Schooling Data, Technological Diffusion, and the Neoclassical Model," *American Economic Review*, Vol. 91, No. 2, May, pp. 323–27

(2006), "Human Capital Growth Regressions: How Much Difference Does Data Quality Make?" *Journal of the European Economics Association*, Vol. 4, No. 1, pp. 1–36.

Gallup, John Luke, Jeffrey D. Sachs, and Andrew D. Mellinger (1999), "Geography and Economic Development," *International Science Review*, Vol. 22, No. 2, August, pp. 179–232.

Galor, Oded, and Andrew Mountford (2008), "Trading Population for Productivity: Theory and Evidence," CEPR Discussion paper No. 6678.

Galor, Oded, and Daniel Tsiddon (1997), "Technological Progress, Mobility, and Economic Growth," *American Economic Review*, Vol. 87, No. 3, June, pp. 363–99.

Galor, Oded, and David N. Weil (2000), "Population, Technology, and Growth: From Malthusian Stagnation to the Demographic Transition and Beyond," *American Economic Review*, Vol. 90, No. 4, March, pp. 806–28.

Galor, O. and J. Zeira (1993), "Income Distribution and Macroeconomics," *Review of Economic Studies*, Vol. 60, No. 1, pp. 35–52.

Gandal, Neil (1994), "Hedonic Price Indexes for Spreadsheets and an Empirical Test of the Network Externalities Hypothesis," *Rand Journal of Economics*, Vol. 25, No. 1, Spring, pp. 160–70.

Gastil, Raymond D., et. al. (1982), *Freedom in the World* (Westport, CT: Greenwood Press).

Geary, R. C. (1958), "A Note on the Comparison of Exchange Rates and Purchasing Power Between Countries," *Journal of the Royal Statistical Society*, Series A. Vol. 121, Part I, pp. 97–99.

Gerschenkron, Alexander (1952), "Economic Backwardness in Historical Perspective," in B. F. Hoselitz, editor, *The Progress of Underdeveloped Areas* (Chicago: University of Chicago Press).

Gilbert, M., and I. B. Kravis (1954), *An International Comparison of National Products and Purchasing Power* (Paris: OECD).

Gill, Indermit S., 1989. "Technological Change, Education, and Obsolescence of Human Capital: Some Evidence for the U.S." Mimeo, November.

Girma, S., and K. Wakelin (2001), "Regional Underdevelopment: Is FDI the Solution? A Semi-Parametric Analysis," GEP Research Paper 2001/11, University of Nottingham, U.K.

Gittleman, Maury, Thijs ten Raa, and Edward N. Wolff (2006), "The Vintage Effect in TFP-Growth: An Analysis of the Age Structure of Capital," *Structural Change and Economic Dynamics*, Volume 17, Issue 3, September, pp. 306–28.

Gittleman, Maury, and Edward N. Wolff (1995), "R&D Activity and Cross-Country Growth Comparisons." *Cambridge Journal of Economics*, Vol. 19, No. 1, pp. 189–207.

Globerman, S., A. Kokko, and F. Sjöholm (2000), "International Technology Diffusion: Evidence from Swedish Patent Data," *Kyklos*, Vol. 53, pp. 17–38.

Goel, Rajeev K., and Rati Ram (1994), "Research and Development Expenditures and Economic Growth: A Cross-Country Study," *Economic Development and Cultural Change*, Vol. 42, No. 2, pp. 403–11.

Gollop, Frank M., and Dale W. Jorgenson (1980), "U.S. Productivity Growth by Industry," in John W. Kendrick and Beatrice N. Vaccara, editors, *New Developments in Productivity Measurement and Analysis* (Chicago: University of Chicago Press).

Goodfriend, Marvin, and John McDermott (1995), "Early Development," *American Economic Review*, Vol. 85, No. 1, March, pp. 116–33.

Gordon, Robert J. (1979), "The End of Expansion Phenomenon in Short-Run Productivity Behavior," *Brookings Papers on Economic Activity*, Vol. 2, pp. 447–61.

(1990), *The Measurement of Durable Goods Prices* (Chicago: University of Chicago Press).

(1992), "Productivity in the Transportation Sector," in Zvi Griliches, editor, *Output Measurement in the Service Sector*, Studies in Income and Wealth, Vol. 56 (Chicago: Chicago University Press).

Gouyette, Claudine, and Sergio Perelman (1997), "Productivity Convergence in OECD Service Industries," *Structural Change and Economic Dynamics*, Vol. 8, pp. 279–95.

Gray, Wayne B., and Ronald J. Shadbegian (1993), "Environmental Regulation and Manufacturing Productivity at the Plant Level," NBER Working Paper No. 4321, April.

(1994), "Pollution Abatement Costs, Regulation, and Plant-Level Productivity," mimeo.

Greenwood, Jeremy, and Boyan Jovanovic (2001), "Accounting for Growth," in Charles R. Hulten, Edwin R. Dean, and Michael J. Harper, editors, *New Developments in Productivity Analysis* (Chicago: University of Chicago Press).

Griffith, Rachel, Stephen Redding, and John van Reenen (2004), "Mapping the Two Faces of R&D: Productivity Growth in a Panel of OECD Industries," *Review of Economics and Statistics*, Vol. 86, No. 4, pp. 883–95.

Griliches, Zvi (1970), "Notes on the Role of Education in Production Functions and Growth Accounting," in W. Lee Hansen, editor, *Education, Income, and Human Capital*, Studies in Income and Wealth 35 (New York: National Bureau of Economic Research and Columbia University Press), pp. 71–115.

(1979), "Issues in Assessing the Contribution of Research and Development to Productivity Growth," *Bell Journal of Economics*, Vol. 10, No. 1, Spring, pp. 92–116.

(1980), "R&D and the Productivity Slowdown," *American Economic Review*, Vol. 70, No. 2, May, pp. 343–47.

Griliches, Z. (1986). "Productivity, R&D and Basic Research at the Firm Level in the 1970's," *American Economic Review*, Vol. 76, March, pp. 141–54.

(1989), "Patents: Recent Trends and Puzzles," *Brookings Papers on Economic Activity*, Microeconomics, pp. 291–330.

Griliches, Zvi (1979) (1992), "The Search for R&D Spillovers," *Scandinavian Journal of Economics*, Vol. 94, pp. 29–47.

(1996), "Education, Human Capital, and Growth: A Personal Perspective," NBER Working Paper No. 5426, January.

Griliches, Zvi, and Frank Lichtenberg (1984a), "R&D and Productivity Growth at the Firm Level: Is There Still a Relationship?" in Zvi Griliches, editor, *R&D, Patents, and Productivity* (Chicago: University of Chicago Press), pp. 465–96.

(1984b), "Interindustry Technology Flows and Productivity Growth: A Reexamination," *Review of Economics and Statistics*, Vol. 61, pp. 324–29.

Grobar, L. M., and R. C. Porter (1989), "Benoit revisited: defense spending and economic growth in LDCs," *Journal of Conflict Resolution*, Vol. 33, pp. 318–45.

Grossman, G. M., and E. Helpman (1991), "Quality Ladders in the Theory of Economic Growth," *Review of Economic Studies*, Vol. 58, pp. 43–61.

Grossman, Michael, and Victor R. Fuchs (1973), "Intersectoral Shifts and Aggregate Productivity Change," *Annals of Economic and Social Measurement*, Vol. 2, No. 3, pp. 227–43.

Guillamont, Patrick and Lisa Chauvet (2001), "Aid and Performance: A Reassessment," *Journal of Development Studies*, Vol. 37, No. 6, August, pp. 66–92.

Gupta, D. (1990), *The Economics of Political Violence* (New York: Praeger).

Gust, Christopher, and Jaime Marquez (2004), "International Comparisons of Productivity Growth: the Role of Information Technology and Regulatory Practices," *Labour Economics*, Vol. 11, No. 1, February, pp. 33–58.

Gylfason, Thorvaldur (2004), "Natural Resources and Economic Growth: From Dependence to Diversification" CEPR Discussion Paper No. 4804, London, December.

Hall, Robert E., and Charles I. Jones (1999), "Why Do Some Countries Produce So Much More Output per Worker than Others?" *Quarterly Journal of Economics*, Vol. 114, pp. 83–116.

Hallak, Juan Carols, and James Levinsohn (2004), "Fooling Ourselves: Evaluating the Globalization and Growth Debate," NBER Working Paper No. 10244, January.

Hansen, Henrik and Finn Tarp (2001), "Aid and Growth Regressions," *Journal of Development Economics*, Vol. 64, No. 2, pp. 547–70.

Hanushek, Eric A., and Dennis D. Kimko (2000), "Schooling, Labor-Force Quality, and the Growth of Nations," *American Economic Review*, Vol. 90, No. 5, December, pp. 1184–1208.

Hanushek, Eric A., and Ludger Wößmann (2007), "The Role of Education Quality in Economic Growth," World Bank Policy Research Working paper No. 4122, February.

Hanushek, Eric A., and Ludger Woessman (2009a), "Do Better Schools Lead to More Growth? Cognitive Skills, Economic Outcomes, and Causation," NBER Working Paper No. 14633, January.

(2009b), "Schooling, Cognitive Skills, and the Latin American Growth Puzzle," NBER Working Paper No. 15066, June.

(2010a), "Sample Selectivity and the Validity of International Student Achievement Tests in Economic Research," NBER Working Paper No. 15867, April.

(2010b), "The Economics of International Differences in Educational Achievement, NBER Working Paper No. 15949, April.

(2010c), "How Much Do Educational Outcomes Matter in OECD Countries?, NBER Working Paper No. 16515, November.

Haskel, J., S. Pereira, and M. Slaughter (2002), "Does Inward Foreign Direct Investment Boost the Productivity of Domestic Firms?" NBER Working Paper No. 8724.

Hecksher, E. (1919), "The Effect of Foreign Trade on the Distribution of Income," *Ekonomisk Tidskriff*, pp. 497–512 (Translated as chapter 13 in American Economic Association, *Readings in the Theory of International Trade* [Philadelphia: Blakiston, 1949], pp. 272–300).

Helliwell, John F., and Alan Chung (1991), "Macroeconomic Convergence: International Transmission of Growth and Technical Progress," NBER Working Paper No. 3264.

Helpman, Elhanan, and Manuel Trajtenberg (1998), "A Time to Sow and a Time to Reap: Growth Based on General Purpose Technologies," in E. Helpman, editor, *General Purpose Technologies and Economic Growth* (Cambridge: MIT Press).

Hendel, Igal (1994), "Estimating Multiple-Discrete Choice Models: An Application to Computerization Returns," NBER Technical Working Paper No. 168, October.

Hess, Peter (1989), "The Military Burden, Economic Growth, and the Human Suffering Index: Evidence from the LDCs, *Cambridge Journal of Economics*, Vol. 13, pp. 497–515.

Heston, Alan, Robert Summers, and Bettina Aten (2006), "Penn World Tables Version 6.2," Center for International Comparisons of Production, Income and Prices at the University of Pennsylvania, September.

Hobijn, B. and P. H. Franses (2001), "Are Living Standards Converging?" *Structural Change and Economic Dynamics*, Vol. 12, pp. 171–200.

Hobsbawm, Eric J. (1969), *Industry and Empire* (Harmondsworth: Penguin Books).

Holtz-Eakin, Douglas, and Amy Ellen Schwartz (1995), "Infrastructure in a Structural Model of Economic Growth," *Regional Science and Urban Economics*, Vol. 25, No. 2, April, pp. 131–51.

Howell, David R., and Edward N. Wolff (1991), "Trends in the Growth and Distribution of Skills in the U.S. Workplace, 1960–85," *Industrial and Labor Relations Review*, Vol. 44, No. 3, April, pp. 486–502.

(1992), "Technical Change and the Demand for Skills by US Industries," *Cambridge Journal of Economics*, Vol. 16, pp. 127–46.

Hubbard, Thomas N. (2001), "Information, Decisions, and Productivity: On-Board Computers and Capacity Utilization in Trucking," mimeo, March 26.

Hudson, E. A., and Dale W. Jorgenson (1978), "Energy Prices and the U.S. Economy, 1972–76," *Natural Resources Journal*, Vol. 18, No. 4, October, pp. 877–97.

Hulten, Charles R. (1978), "Growth Accounting with Intermediate Inputs," *Review of Economic Studies*, Vol. 45, No. 3, October, pp. 511–18.

(1992), "Growth Accounting When Technical Change Is Embodied in Capital," *American Economic Review*, Vol. 82, No. 4, September, pp. 964–80.

Hulten, Charles R., and Anders Isaksson (2007), "Why Development Levels Differ: The Sources of Differential Economic Growth in a Panel of High and Low Income Countries," NBER Working Paper No. 13469, October.

Hungerford, Thomas L. (2012), "Taxes and the Economy: An Economic Analysis of the Top Tax Rates Since 1945," Congressional Research Service Report 7-5700, September 14, www.crs.gov/R42729

International Country Risk Guide (2005), http:/www.icrg.net.

Inwood, Kris (2002), "Economic Growth and Global Inequality in Long Run Perspective," *Review of Income and Wealth*, Vol. 48, No. 4, December, pp. 581–93.

Islam, Nazrul (2003), "What Have We Learnt from the Convergence Debate?" *Journal of Economic Surveys*, Vol. 17, No. 3, pp. 309–60.

Jaffe, Adam (1986), "Technological Opportunity and Spillovers of R&D: Evidence from Firms' Patents, Profits, and Market Value," *American Economic Review*, 76, December, pp. 984–1001.

Jaffe, A., M. Trajtenberg, and R. Henderson (1993), "Geographic Localization of Knowledge Spillovers as Evidenced by Patent Citations," *Quarterly Journal of Economics*, Vol. 108, pp. 577–98.

Jamison, Eliot A., Dean T. Jamison, and Eric A. Hanushek (2006), "The Effects of Education Quality on Income Growth and Mortality Decline," NBER Working Paper No. 12652, October.

Japan Economic Planning Agency, Department of National Accounts, Economic Research Institute (1988), "Gross Capital Stock of Private Enterprises, 1965–1986," February.

Johnson, D. Gale (1954), "The functional distribution of income in the United States, 1850-1952," *Review of Economics and Statistics*, Vol. 36, No. 2, pp. 175–82.

Jorgenson, Dale W., and Barbara M. Fraumeni (1993), "Education and Productivity Growth in a Market Economy," *Atlantic Economic Journal*, Vol. 21, No. 2, pp. 1–25.

Jorgenson, Dale W., Frank M. Gollop, and Barbara M. Fraumeni (1987), *Productivity and U.S. Economic Growth* (Cambridge, MA: Harvard University Press).

Jorgenson, Dale W., and Z. Griliches (1967), "The Explanation of Productivity Change," *Review of Economic Studies*, 34(2), No. 99, July, pp. 249–80.

Jorgenson, Dale W., Masahiro Kuroda, and Mieko Nishimizu (1987), "Japan-U.S. Industry-Level Productivity Comparison, 1960–1979," *Journal of the Japanese and International Economies*, Vol. 1, Issue 1, pp. 1–30.

Jorgenson, Dale W., and Mieko Nishimizu (1978), "US and Japanese Economic Growth, 1952–1974: An International Comparison," *Economic Journal*, Vol. 88, pp. 707–26.

Jorgenson, Dale W., and Kevin J. Stiroh (1999), "Information Technology and Growth," *American Economic Review*, Vol. 89, No. 2, May, pp. 109–15.

(2000), "Raising the Speed Limit: U.S. Economic Growth in the Information Age," *Brooking Papers on Economic Activity*, No. 1, pp. 125–211.

Kaldor, N. (1956), "Alternative Theroies of Distribution," *Review of Economic Studies*, Vol. 23, No. 2, pp. 83–100.

(1967), *Strategic Factors in Economic Development* (Ithaca, NY: Cornell University Press).

Keller, Wolfgang (1998), "Are International R&D Spillovers Trade Related? Analyzing Spillovers among Randomly Matched Trade Partners," *European Economic Review*, Vol. 42, pp. 1469–81.

(2002), "Geographic Localization of International Technology Diffusion," *American Economic Review*, Vol. 92, No. 1, pp. 120–42.

(2004), "International Technology Diffusion," *Journal of Economic Literature*, Vol. 42, No. 3, September, pp. 752–82.

Kendrick, John (1980a), "Productivity Trends in the United States," in Shlomo Maital and Noah M. Meltz, editors, *Lagging Productivity Growth* (Cambridge, MA: Ballinger).

(1980b), "Remedies for the Productivity Slowdown in the United States," in Shlomo Maital and Noah M. Meltz, editors, *Lagging Productivity Growth* (Cambridge, MA: Ballinger).

Kendrick, John W. (1984), editor, *International Comparisons of Productivity and Causes of the Slowdown* (Cambridge, MA: Ballinger).

Khamis, S. H. (1970), "Properties and Conditions for the Existence of a New Type of Index Numbers," *Sankhya*, Series B, Vol. 32, pp. 81–98.

King, R. G., and Levine, R. (1993), "Finance and Growth: Schumpeter Might Be Right," *Quarterly Journal of Economics*, Vol. 108, pp. 717–38.

Kinoshita, Y. (2001), "R&D and Technology Spillover Via FDI: Innovation and Absorptive Capacity," CEPR Discussion paper No. 2775.

Klette, Tor Jakob (1999), "Market Power, Scale Economies and Productivity: Estimates from a Panel of Establishment Data," *The Journal of Industrial Economics*, Vol. 47, No. 4 (December), pp. 451–76.

Knack, Stephen, and Philip Keefer (1997), "Does Social Capital Have an Economic Payoff? A Cross-Country Investigation," *Quarterly Journal of Economics*, Vol. 112, pp. 1251–88.

Kopcke, Richard W. (1980), "Capital Accumulation and Potential Growth," in *The Decline in Productivity Growth* (Boston: Federal Reserve Bank of Boston).

Kormendi, R. C., and Meguire, P. G. (1985), "Macroeconomic Determinants of Growth: Cross-Country Evidence," *Journal of Monetary Economics*, Vol. 16, pp. 141–63.

Kremer, Michael (1993), "Population Growth and Technological Change: One Million B.C. to 1990," *Quarterly Journal of Economics*, Vol. 108, No. 3, August, pp. 681–716.

Krueger, Alan B., and Mikael Lindahl (2001), "Education for Growth: Why and for Whom?" *Journal of Economic Literature*, Vol. 39, No. 4, December, pp. 1101–36.

Krueger, Dirk, and Krishna Kumar (2003), "US-Europe Differences in Technology-Driven Growth: Quantifying the Role of Education," NBER Working Paper No. 10001, September.

Krugman, Paul (1979), "Increasing Returns, Monopolistic Competition, and International Trade," *Journal of International Economics*, Vol. 9, pp. 469–79.

(1980), "Scale Economies, Product Differentiation, and the Patterns of Trade," *American Economic Review*, Vol. 70, No. 5, December, pp. 950–59.

Krugman, Paul R. (1991), "Increasing Returns and Economic Geography," *Journal of Political Economy*, Vol. 99, pp. 483–99.

Kumar, Subodh, and Robert Russell (2002), "Technological Change, Technological Catch-up, and Capital Deepening: Relative Contributions to Growth and Convergence," *American Economic Review*, Vol. 92, No. 3, June, pp. 527–48.

Kutscher, R. E., J. A. Mark, and J. R. Norsworthy (1977), "The Productivity Slowdown and Outlook to 1985," *Monthly Labor Review*, Vol. 100, May, pp. 3–8.

Kuznets, Simon (1955), "Economic Growth and Income Inequality," *American Economic Review*, Vol. 45, No. 1, March, pp. 1–28.

(1973), *Population, Capital, and Growth: Selected Essays* (New York: W. W. Norton).

Kyriacou, Georges Andreas (1991), "Growth, Human Capital, and the Convergence Hypothesis: A Cross-Country Study." New York University Ph.D. Dissertation, January.

Lall, S. 1987. *Learning to Industrialize: The Acquisition of Technological Capability by India* (London, Macmillan Press).

Leamer, E. (1984), *Sources of International Comparative Advantage: Theory and Evidence*, (Cambridge, MA: MIT Press).

Lehr, William, and Frank Lichtenberg (1998), "Computer Use and Productivity Growth in US Federal Government Agencies, 1987–92," *Journal of Industrial Economics*, Vol. 44, No. 2, June, pp. 257–79.

—— (1999), "Information Technology and Its Impact on Productivity: Firm-Level Evidence from Government and Private Data Sources, 1977–1993," *Canadian Journal of Economics*, Vol. 32, No. 2, April, pp. 335–62.

Lensink, Robert and Howard White (2001), "Are There Negative Returns to Aid?" *Journal of Development Studies*, Vol. 37, No. 6, August, pp. 42–65.

Levine, R. and D. Renelt (1992), "A Sensitivity Analysis of Cross-Country Growth Regressions," *American Economic Review*, Vol. 82, No. 4, pp. 942–63.

Levine, R., and Zervos, S. (1998), "Stock Markets, Banks, and Economic Growth," *American Economic Review*, Vol. 88, pp. 537–58.

Li, H. and H. Zou (1998), "Income Inequality Is Not Harmful for Growth: Theory and Evidence," *Review of Development Economics*, Vol. 2, pp. 318–34.

Lichtenberg, Frank R. (1992), "R&D Investment and International Productivity Differences," in Horst Siebert, editor, *Economic Growth in the World Economy* (Tubingen: J. C. B. Mohr).

—— (1995), "The Output Contribution of Computer equipment and Personnel: A Firm Level Analysis," *Economics of Innovation and New Technology*, Vol. 3, No. 4, pp. 201–17.

Lichtenberg, Frank R., and Moshe Kim (1989), "The Effects of Mergers on Prices, Costs, and Capacity Utilization in the U.S. Air Transportation Industry, 1970–84," NBER Working Paper No. 3197, December.

Lichtenberg, F. R. and D. Siegel (1991), "The Impact of R&D Investment on Productivity: New Evidence Using Linked R&D-LRD Data," *Economic Inquiry*, Vol. 29, April, pp. 203–28.

Lichtenberg, Frank, and Bruno van Pottelsberghe de la Potterie (2001), "Does Foreign Direct Investment Transfer Technology across Borders?" *Review of Economics and Statistics*, Vol. 83, No. 3, pp. 490–97.

Lipsey, R. E. and Kravis, I. B. (1987), *Saving and Economic Growth: Is the United States Really Falling Behind?*(New York: The Conference Board).

Loayza N. V., A. M. Oviedo, and L. Serven (2005), "Regulation and Macroeconomic Performance," World Bank, September, *mimeo*.

Loveman, G. W. (1988), "An Assessment of the Productivity Impact of Information Technologies," in *Management in the 1990s* (Cambridge, MA: MIT Press).

Lucas Jr., Robert E. (1988), "On the Mechanics of Development Planning," *Journal of Monetary Economics*, Vol. 22, No. 1, July, pp. 3–42.

Luintel, Kul B., Mosahid Khan, Philip Arestis, and Konstantinos Theodoridis (2008), "Financial Structure and Economic Growth," *Journal of Development Economics*, Vol. 86, pp. 181–200.

Lynn, R., and T. Vannhanen (2002), *IQ and the Wealth of Nations* (Westport, CT: Praeger).

Maddison, Angus (1982), *Phases of Capitalist Development* (Oxford: Oxford University Press).

(1987), Growth and Slowdown in Advanced Capitalist Economies: Techniques of Quantitative Assessment," *Journal of Economic Literature*, Vol. 25, June, pp. 649–706.

(1989), *The World Economy in the 20th Century* (Paris: OECD).

(1991), *Dynamic Forces in Capitalist Development* (Oxford: Oxford University Press).

(1993a), "Standardized Estimates of Fixed Capital Stock: A Six Country Comparison," *Innovazione e Materie Prime*, April, pp. 1–29.

(1993b), "Average Age Gross Stock of Non Residential Structures and of Machinery and Equipment," Worksheet data supplied to the author by Angus Maddison, November 16.

(1995), *Monitoring the World Economy, 1820–1992* (Paris: OECD).

(2001), *The World Economy: A Millennial Perspective* (Paris: OECD).

(2003), *The World Economy: Historical Statistics* (Paris: OECD).

(2005), "Measuring and Interpreting World Economic Performance 1500–2001," *Review of Income and Wealth*, Vol. 51, No. 1, March, pp. 1–35.

(2007), *Contours of the World Economy: 1–2030 AD: Essays in Macroeconomic History* (Paris: OECD).

(2008), "Shares of the Rich and the Rest in the World Economy: Income Divergence between Nations, 1820–2030," *Asian Economic Policy Review*, Vol. 3, pp. 67–82.

Madsen, Jakob B. (2007), "Technology Spillover through Trade and TFP Convergence: 135 Years of Evidence for the OECD Countries," *Journal of International Economics*, Vol. 72, pp. 464–80.

Malmquist, S. (1953), "Index Numbers and Indifference Surfaces," *Trabajos de Estadistica*, Vol. 4, pp. 209–42.

Mamuneas, Theofanis P., Andreas Savvides, and Thanasis Stengos (2001), "Measures of Human Capital and Nonlinearities in Economic Growth," *Journal of Economic Growth*, Vol. 6, pp. 229–54.

Mankiw, N. Gregory, David Romer and David N. Weil (1992), "A Contribution to the Empirics of Economic Growth," *Quarterly Journal of Economics*, Vol. 107, pp. 407–38.

Mansfield, Edwin (1965), "Rates of Return from Industrial Research and Development," *American Economic Review*, Vol. 55, No. 2, May, pp. 310–22.

(1980), "Basic Research and Productivity Increase in Manufacturing," *American Economic Review*, Vol. 70, No. 5, December, pp. 863–73.

Mansfield, Edwin, Anthony Romeo, Mark Schwartz, David Teece, Samuel Wagner, and Peter Brach (1982), *Technology Transfer, Productivity, and Economic Policy* (New York: W. W. Norton).

Matthews, R. C. O., C. H. Feinstein, and J. C. Odling-Smee, J. C. (1982), *British Economic Growth, 1856–1973* (Stanford, CA: Stanford University Press).

Meyer-zu-Schlochtern, F. J. M. (1988), "An International Sectoral Data Base for Thirteen OECD Countries," Working Paper, OECD Department of Economics and Statistics.

Middendorf, Torge (2005), "Human Capital and Economic Growth in OECD Countries, RWI Discussion Paper No. 30, Essen, Germany, June.

Mincer, Jacob (1974), *Schooling, Experience, and Earnings*, (New York: National Bureau of Economic Research).

Mincer, Jacob, and Yoshio Higuchi (1988), "Wage Structures and Labor Turnover in the United States and Japan," *Journal of the Japanese and International Economies*, Vol. 2, pp. 97–113.

Mohnen, Pierre (1992), *The Relationship between R&D and Productivity Growth in Canada and Other Major Industrialized Countries* (Ottawa: Canada Communications Group).

Morrison, Catherine, and Amy Ellen Schwartz (1996), "State Infrastructure and Productive Performance," *American Economic Review*, Vol. 86, No. 5, December, pp. 1095–1111.

Mowery, David C., and Richard R. Nelson, Editors (1999), *Sources of Industrial Leadership: Studies of Seven Industries* (Cambridge: Cambridge University Press).

Munnell, Alicia (1990), "How Does Public Infrastructure Affect Regional Economic Performance?" in Alicia Munnell, editor, *Is There a Shortfall in Public Capital Investment?* (Boston: Federal Reserve Bank of Boston).

Murphy, Kevin, Andre Schleifer, and Robert W. Vishny (1991), "Allocation of Talent: Implications for Growth," *Quarterly Journal of Economics*, Vol. 106, pp. 503–30.

Musgrave, John C. (1986a), "Fixed Reproducible Tangible Wealth in the United States: Revised Estimates," *Survey of Current Business* Vol. 66, No. 1, January, pp. 51–75.

(1986b), "Fixed Reproducible Tangible Wealth in the United States, 1982–1985," *Survey of Current Business*, Vol. 66, No. 8, August, pp. 36–39.

Nadiri, Mohammed I. (1970), "Some Approaches to the Theory and Measurement of Total Factor Productivity," *Journal of Economics Literature*, Vol. 8, No. 4, December, 1137–78.

Nadiri, M. Ishaq (1980), "Sectoral Productivity Slowdown," *American Economic Review*, Vol. 70, No. 2, May, pp. 349–52.

Nadiri, M. I. (1993), "Innovation and Technological Spillovers," NBER Working Paper No. 4423, August.

Nadiri, M. Ishaq, and Mark A. Shankerman (1981), "Technical Change, Returns to Scale, and the Productivity Slowdown," *American Economic Review*, Vol. 71, No. 2, May, pp. 314–19.

Nakamura, Shinichiro (1989), "Productivity and Factor Prices as Sources of Differences in Production Costs between Germany, Japan, and the U.S.," *The Economic Studies Quarterly*, Vol. 40, March, pp. 701–15.

Nelson, Richard R. (1964), "Aggregate Production Functions and Medium-Range Growth Projections," *American Economic Review*, Vol. 54, No. 5, September, pp. 575–605.

(1991), "Diffusion of Development: Post-World War II Convergence among Advanced Industrial Nations," *American Economic Review*, Vol. 81, No. 2, May, pp. 271–75.

Nelson, Richard R. and Edmund S. Phelps (1966), "Investment in Humans, Technological Diffusion and Economic Growth," *American Economic Review*, Vol. 61, No. 2, pp. 69–75.

Nelson, Richard, and Sydney Winters (1982), *An Evolutionary Theory of Economic Change* (Cambridge, MA: Harvard University Press).

Nelson, Richard R., Sydney Winter, and H. L. Schuette (1976), "Technical Change in an Evolutionary Model," *Quarterly Journal of Economics*, Vol. 90, 90–118.

Nelson, Richard R., and Gavin Wright (1992), "The Rise and Fall of American Technological Leadership: The Postwar Era in Historical Perspective," *Journal of Economic Literature*, Vol. 30, No. 4, December, pp. 1931–64.

Neumayer, Eric (2003), "Beyond Income: Convergence in Living Standards Big Time," *Structural Change and Economic Dynamics*, Vol. 14, pp. 275–96.

Nicoletti, G., and S. Scarpetta (2003), "Regulation, Productivity and Growth: OECD Evidence," *Economic Policy*, Vol. 18, No. 36, pp. 11–72.

Nishimizu, M. and S Robinson (1984), "Trade Policies and Productivity Change in Semi-Industrialized Countries", *Journal of Development Economics*, Vol. 16, pp. 177–210.

Nordhaus, William D. (1972), "The Recent Productivity Slowdown," *Brookings Papers on Economic Activity*, No. 3, pp. 493–536.

(2004), "Retrospective on the 1970s Productivity Slowdown," NBER Working Paper No. 10950, December.

Norsworthy, J. R. and Michael Harper (1979), "*The Role of Capital Formation in the Recent Slowdown in Productivity Growth*," Bureau of Labor Statistics Working Paper no. 87 (Washington, D.C.: U.S. Government Printing Office).

Norsworthy, J. R., M. J. Harper, and K. Kunze (1979), "The Slowdown in Productivity Growth: Analysis of Some Contributing Factors," *Brookings Papers on Economic Activity*, No. 2, pp. 387–421.

Norsworthy, J. R., and David H. Malmquist (1983), "Input Measurement and Productivity Growth in Japanese and US Manufacturing," *American Economic Review*, Vol. 73, 1983, pp. 947–67.

(1985), "Recent Productivity Growth in Japanese and U.S. Manufacturing," in William J. Baumol and Kenneth McLennan, editors., *Productivity Growth and U.S. Competitiveness* (New York: Oxford University Press), pp. 58–69.

North, Douglass C. (2005), *Understanding the Process of Economic Change* (Princeton, NJ: Princeton University Press).

North, Douglass C., and Robert Paul Thomas (1973), *The Rise of the Western World: A New Economic History* (New York: Cambridge University Press).

Ochoa, Rolando A. (1996), *Growth, Trade, and Endogenous Technology* (New York: St. Martin's Press).

OECD (1980), *Main Economic Indicators, 1960–1979* (Paris: Organization for Economic Cooperation and Development).

(1998), *Education at a Glance: OECD Indicators*, Paris: OECD.

Ohlin, B. (1933), *Interregional and International Trade*, (Cambridge, MA: Harvard Univeristy Press).

Oliner, Stephen, and Daniel Sichel (1994), "Computers and Output Growth Revisited: How Big Is the Puzzle?" *Brookings Papers on Economic Activity*, Vol. 2, pp. 273–334.

(2000), "The Resurgence of Growth in the Late 1990s: Is Information Technology the Story?" mimeo, Federal Reserve Board of Washington, May.

Olley, G. Steven, and Ariel Pakes (1994), "The Dynamics of Productivity in the Telecommunications Equipment Industry," Mimeo, New York University, October.

Olley, G. Steven and Ariel Pakes (1996), "The Dynamics of Productivity in the Telecommunications Equipment Industry," *Econometrica*, Vol. 64 No. 6, pp. 1263–97.

Olson, Jr., Mancur (1996), "Big Bills on the Sidewalk: Why Some Nations Are Rich, and Others Poor," *Journal of Economic Perspectives*, Vol. 10, No. 2, Spring, pp. 3–24.

Oniki, Hajime, Tae Hoon Oum, Rodney Stevenson, and Yimin Zhang (1994), "The Productivity Effects of the Liberalization of Japanese Communication Policy," *Journal of Productivity Analysis*, Vol. 5, pp. 63–79.

O'Rourke, Kevin H., Ahmed S. Rahman, and Alan M. Taylor (2007), "Trade, Knowledge, and the Industrial Revolution," Institute for International Integration Studies Discussion Paper, No. 219, April.

Pack, H. 1988. "Industrialization and Trade," in H. Chenery, and T. N. Srinivasan, editors, *Handbook of Development Economics*, Volume I (Amsterdam: Elsevier Science Publishers B.V.).

Papyrakis, Elissaios, and Reyer Gerlagh (2007), "Resource Abundance and Economic Growth in the United States," *European Economic Review*, Vol. 51, pp. 1011–39.

Park, W. (1995), "International R&D Spillovers and OECD Economic Growth," *Economic Inquiry*, Vol. 23, pp. 571–91.

Parsons, Daniel J., Calvin C. Gotlieb, and Michael Denny (1993), "Productivity and Computers in Canadian Banking," *Journal of Productivity Analysis*, Vol. 4, June, pp. 91–110.

Pavitt, Keith, and Luc G. Soete (1982), "International Differences in Economic Growth and the International Location of Industry," in Herbert Giersch, editor, *Emerging Technologies: Consequences for Economic Growth, Structural Change, and Employment* (Tubningen: J. C. B. Mohr (Paul Siebeck)), pp. 105–33.

Perloff, Jeffrey M., and Michael L. Wachter (1980), "The Productivity Slowdown: A Labor Problem," in *The Decline in Productivity Growth* (Boston: Federal Reserve Bank of Boston).

Perotti, R. (1993), "Political Equilibrium, Income Distribution and Growth," *Review of Economic Studies*, Vol. 60, pp. 755–76.

Perry, G. L. (1977), "Potential Output and Productivity," *Brookings Papers on Economic Activity*, No. 1, pp. 11–47.

Persson, T., and G. Tabellini (1994), "Is Inequality Harmful for Growth? Theory and Evidence," *American Economic Review*, Vol. 84, pp. 600–21.

Petit, P. (1993), "Technology and Employment: Main Issues in a Context of High Unemployment," September, mimeo, Paris, CEPREMAP.

Piketty, Thomas (1997), "The Dynamics of the Wealth Distribution and Interest Rates with Credit Rationing," *Review of Economic Studies*, Vol. 64, pp. 173–89.

Piore, M. J., and C. F. Sabel (1984), *The Second Industrial Divide* (New York: Basic Books).

Postner, Harry H. (1990), "The Contracting-Out Problem in Service Sector Analysis: Choice of Statistical Unit," *Review of Income and Wealth*, Series 36, No. 2, June, 177–86.

Pritchett, Lant (1997), "Divergence, Big Time," *Journal of Economic Perspectives*, Vol. 11, No. 3, Summer, pp. 3–17.

Psacharopoulos, George, and Ana Maria Arriagada (1986), "The Educational Attainment of the Labor Force: An International Comparison," *International Labor Review*, Vol. 125, No. 5, pp. 561–74.

Putnam, Robert (with Robert Leonardi and Raffaella Y. Nanetti) (1993), *Making Democracy Work* (Princeton, NJ: Princeton University Press).

Pyyhtiä, Limo (2007), "Why Is Europe Lagging behind?" Bank of Finland Research Discussion Paper 3.

Rajan, Raghuram G., and Arvind Subramanian (2008), "Aid and Growth: What Does the Cross-Country Evidence Really Show?" *Review of Economics and Statistics,* Vol. 90, No. 4, pp. 643–65.

Ram, Rati (1999), "Tropics and Income: A Longitudinal Study of the U.S. States," *Review of Income and Wealth,* Vol. 45, No. 3, September, pp. 373–78.

(2007), "IQ and Economic Growth: Further Augmentation of Mankiw-Romer-Weil Model," *Economic Letters,* Vol. 94, No. 1, January, pp. 7–11.

Rama, Simon (1980), "The U.S. Technology Slip: A New Political Issue," in Walter E. Hoadley, Editor, *The Economy and the President: 1980 and Beyond* (Englewood Cliffs, N.J.: Prentice-Hall).

Rasche, R. H., and J. A. Tatom (1977a), "The Effects of the New Energy Regime on Economic Capacity, Production and Prices," *Federal Reserve Bank of St. Louis Monthly Review,* May, pp. 2–12.

(1977b), "Energy Resources and Potential GNP," *Federal Reserve Bank of St. Louis Monthly Review,* June, pp. 10–24.

Rassekh, Farhad (1992), "The Role of International Trade in the Convergence of Per Capita GDP in the OECD 1950–1985," *International Economic Review,* Vol. 6, No. 4, Winter, pp. 1–16.

Rees, Albert (1979), "Improving the Concepts and Techniques of Productivity Measurement," *Monthly Labor Review,* September, pp. 23–27.

Rivera-Batiz, Francisco L. (2002), "Democracy, Governance, and Economic Growth: Theory and Evidence," *Review of Development Economics,* Vol. 6, No. 2, pp. 225–47.

Robson, M., J. Townsend, and K. Pavitt (1988), "Sectoral Patterns of Production and Use of Innovations in the UK: 1945–1983," *Research Policy,* Vol. 17, pp. 1–14.

Rodriguez, Francisco, and Dani Rodrik (2001), "Trade Policy and Economic Growth: A Skeptic's Guide to Cross-National Evidence," in Benjamin Bernanke and Kenneth Rogoff, editors, *NBER Macroeconomics Annual 2000,* Cambridge, MA: MIT Press.

Rodrik, Dani (1995), "Getting Interventions Right: How South Korea and Taiwan Grew Rich," *Economic Policy,* Vol. 10, No. 2, April, pp. 53–107.

(2004), "Rethinking Growth Strategies," WIDER Annual Lecture 8, United Nations University, Helsinki, November.

Romer, Paul M. (1986), "Increasing Returns and Long-Run Growth," *Journal of Political Economy,* Vol. 94, October, pp. 1002–37.

(1990), "Endogenous Technological Change," *Journal of Political Economy,* Vol. 98, No. 5, Part 2, pp. S71–S102.

Rostow, Walt W. (1960), *The Stages of Economic Growth: A Non-Communist Manifesto* (Cambridge: Cambridge University Press).

Rowthorn, Robert E. (1992), "Productivity and American Leadership," *Review of Income and Wealth,* Series 38, No. 4, December 1992, pp. 475–96.

Sachs, Jeffrey D. (2001), "Tropical Underdevelopment," NBER Working Paper No. 8119, February.

Sachs, Jeffrey D., and Andrew M. Warner (1995), "Economic Reform and the Process of Global Integration," *Brookings Papers on Economic Activity,* Vol. 1, pp. 1–95.

(1997), "Fundamental Sources of Long-Run Growth," *American Economic Review*, Vol. 87, No. 2, May, pp. 184–88.

Samaniego, Roberto M. (2006), "Organizational Capital, Technology Adoption and the Productivity Slowdown," *Journal of Monetary Economics*, Vol. 53, No. 7, October, pp. 1555–69.

Samuelson, P. (1953), "Prices of Factors and Goods in General Equilibrium," *Review of Economic Studies*, Vol. 21, pp. 1–20.

Savard, R. L. (1985), *World Military and Social Expenditures 1985* (Washington, D.C.: World Priorities).

Sato, Ryuzo, and Martin J. Beckmann (1970), "Shares and Growth under Factor-Augmenting Technical Change," *International Economic Review*, Vol. 11, No. 3, October, pp. 387–98.

Scherer, Frederic M. (1983), "R&D and Declining Productivity Growth," *American Economic Review*, Vol. 73, May, pp. 215–18.

Schultz, Theodore W. (1960), "Capital Formation by Education," *Journal of Political Economy* Vol. 68, No. 6, pp. 571–83.

(1961), "Investment in Human Capital," *American Economic Review* Vol. 51, No. 1, pp. 1–17.

(1964), *Transforming Traditional Agriculture* (New Haven, CT: Yale University Press).

(1971), *Investment in Human Capital: The Role of Education and of Research* (New York: Free Press).

Schumpeter, Joseph (1936), *The Theory of Economic Development* [1911] (Cambridge, MA.: Harvard University Press), English translation, 1936.

Schumpeter, Joseph A. (1950), *Capitalism, Socialism, and Democracy*, 3rd edition (New York: Harper & Row).

Siegel, Donald (1997), "The Impact of Computers on Manufacturing Productivity Growth: A Multiple-Indicators, Multiple-Causes Approach," *Review of Economics and Statistics*, Vol. 79, pp. 68–78.

Siegel, Donald, and Zvi Griliches (1991), "Purchased Services, Outsourcing, Computers, and Productivity in Manufacturing," NBER Working Paper No. 3678, April.

(1992), "Purchased Services, Outsourcing, Computers, and Productivity in Manufacturing," in Zvi Griliches, editor, *Output Measurement in the Service Sector* (Chicago: University of Chicago Press).

Sjöholm, F. (1996), "International Transfer of Knowledge: The Role of International Trade and Geographic Proximity," *Weltwirtschaftliches Archiv*, Vol. 132, pp. 97–115.

Skoczylas, Les, and Bruno Tissot (2005), "Revisiting Recent Productivity Developments across OECD Countries," BIS Working Paper No. 182, Bank for International Settlements, Basel, Switzerland.

Smith, Adam (1776), *The Wealth of Nations* (London: Nuthuen University Paperbacks, edition 1961).

Soete, Luc (1987), "The Impact of Technological Innovation on International Trade Patterns: the Evidence Reconsidered," *Research Policy*, Vol. 16, pp. 101–30.

Soete, Luc, and Bart Verspagen (1993), "Technology and Growth: The Complex Dynamics of Catching Up, Falling Behind, and Taking Over," in A. Szirmai, B. Van Ark, and D. Pilat, editors, *Explaining Economic Growth* (Amsterdam: Elsevier Science Publishers B.V.), pp. 101–27.

Solow, Robert M. (1956), "Contribution to the Theory of Economic Growth," *Quarterly Journal of Economics*, Vol. 70, February, pp. 65–94.

(1957), "Technical Change and the Aggregate Production Function," *Review of Economics and Statistics*, Vol. 39, August, pp. 312–20.

(1988), "Growth Theory and After," *American Economic Review*, Vol. 78, No. 3, June, pp. 307–17.

Sørenson, Anders (2001), "Comparing Apples to Oranges: Productivity Convergence and Measurement across Industries and Countries: Comment," *American Economic Review*, Vol. 91, No. 4, September, pp. 1160–67.

Spence, Michael (1973), "Job Market Signalling," *Quarterly Journal of Economics*, Vol. 87, No. 3, pp. 355–74.

Statistics Canada (1987), *Fixed Capital Flows and Stocks*, Science, Technology and Capital Stock Division, Ottawa, Canada, September.

Steindel, Charles (1992), "Manufacturing Productivity and High-Tech Investment," *Federal Reserve Bank of New York Quarterly Review*, Vol. 17, December, pp. 39–47.

Stiroh, Keven J. (1998), "Computers, Productivity, and Input Substitution," *Economic Inquiry*, Vol. 36, No. 2, April, pp. 175–91.

(2002), "Are ICT Spillovers Driving the New Economy?" *Review of Income and Wealth*, Vol. 48, No. 1, March, pp. 33–57.

Summers, Robert, and Alan Heston (1984), "Improved International Comparisons of Real Product and Its Composition, 1950–1980," *Review of Income and Wealth*, Vol. 30, pp. 207–62.

(1988), "A New Set of International Comparisons of Real Product and Prices: Estimates for 130 Countries, 1950–1985," *Review of Income and Wealth*, Vol. 34, pp. 1–26.

(1991), "The Penn World Table (Mark V): An Expanded Set of International Comparisons," *Quarterly Journal of Economics*, Vol. 106, pp. 327–36.

Tatom, John A. (1979), "The Productivity Problem," *Federal Reserve Bank of St. Louis Monthly Review*, September, pp. 3–16.

Temple, Jonathan (1999), "The New Growth Evidence," *Journal of Economic Literature*, Vol. 37, March, pp. 112–56.

Temple, Jonathan, and Paul A. Johnson (1998), "Social Capability and Economic Growth," *Quarterly Journal of Economics*, Vol. 113, pp. 965–90.

ten Raa, Thijs, and Edward N. Wolff (2000), "Engines of Growth in the U.S. Economy," *Structural Change and Economic Dynamics*, Vol. 11, No. 4, December, pp. 473–89.

(2001), "Outsourcing of Services and the Productivity Recovery in U.S. Manufacturing in the 1980s and 1990s" *Journal of Productivity Analysis*, Vol. 16, No. 2, 2001, pp. 149–65.

Terleckyj, Nestor W. (1980), "Direct and Indirect Effects of Industrial Research and Development on the Productivity Growth of Industries," in John W. Kendrick and Beatrice Vaccara, editors, *New Developments in Productivity Measurement* (New York: National Bureau of Economic Research), 359–77.

Theil, H. (1968), "On the Geometry and the Numerical Approximation of Cost of Living and Real Income Indices," *De Economist*, Vol. 116, pp. 677–89.

Thurow, Lester (1979), "The U.S. Productivity Problem," *Data Resource Review*, Vol. 69, August, pp. 14–19.

(1980), "Comment," in *The Decline in Productivity Growth* (Boston: Federal Reserve Bank of Boston).

Tilton, John E. (1971), *International Diffusion of Technology: The Case of Semiconductors* (Washington, D.C.: Brookings Institution).

Triplett, Jack E., and Barry Bosworth (2004), *Productivity in the U.S. Services Sector* (Washington, D.C.: Brookings Institution).

UNESCO (1963–1990), *Statistical Yearbooks* (Paris: UNESCO).

Vamvakidis, Athanasios (2002), "How Robust Is the Growth-Openness Connection? Historical Evidence," *Journal of Economic Growth*, Vol. 7, No. 1, March, pp. 57–80.

Van Ark, Bart, Mary O'Mahony, and Marcel Timmer (2008), "The Productivity Gap between Europe and the United States: Trends and Causes," *Journal of Economic Perspectives*, Vol. 22, No. 1, Winter, pp. 25–44.

Van Biesebroeck, Johannes (2006), "The Sensitivity of Productivity Estimates: Revisiting Three Important Productivity Debates," *Journal of Business and Economic Statistics*, October.

(2007), "Robustness of Productivity Estimates," *Journal of Industrial Economics*, Vol. 55, No. 3,(July), pp. 529–69.

Vanek, J. (1968), "The Factor Proportions Theory: The N-Factor Case," *Kyklos*, Vol. 21, pp. 749–756.

Verdoorn, P. J. (1949), "Fattori che regolano lo sviluppo della produttivita del lavoro," *L'industria*, Vol. 1, pp. 3–10.

Vernon, R. (1966), "International Investment and International Trade in the Product Cycle," *Quarterly Journal of Economics*, Vol. 80, pp. 190–207.

(1979), "The Product-Cycle Hypothesis in a New International Environment," *Oxford Bulletin of Economics and Statistics*, Vol. 41, No. 4, pp. 255–67.

Verspagen, Bart (1991), "A New Empirical Approach to Catching Up or Falling Behind," *Structural Change and Economic Dynamics*, Vol. 2, No. 2, December, pp. 359–80.

(1993), "R&D and Productivity: A Broad Cross-Section Cross-Country Look," Maastricht, the Netherlands, MERIT Working Paper 93–007.

(1994), "Technology and Growth: The Complex Dynamics of Convergence and Divergence," in Gerald Silverberg and Luc Soete, editors, *The Economics of Growth and Technical Change: Technologies, Nations, Agents* (Aldershot, UK: Edward Elgar), pp. 154–81.

(1997), "Estimating International Technology Spillovers Using Technology Flow Matrices," *Weltwirtschaftliches Arhiv*, Band 133, Heft 2, pp. 226–48.

Wade, Robert (1990), *Governing the Market: Economic Theory and the Role of Government in East Asian Industrialization* (Princeton, NJ: Princeton University Press).

Ward, Michael (1985), *Purchasing Power Parities and Real Expenditures in the OECD* (Paris: Organization for Economic Cooperation and Development).

Wasmer, Etienne (2003), "Interpreting European and US Labour Market Differences: The Specificity of Human Capital Investments," CEPR Discussion paper No. 3780, January.

Welch, Finis R. (1970), "Education in Production," *Journal of Political Economy*, Vol. 78, pp. 35–59.

Williamson, Jeffrey G. (1984), "Why Was British Growth So Slow during the Industrial Revolution?" *Journal of Economic History*, Vol. 44, September, pp. 687–712.

Winter, Sydney (1984), "Schumpeterian Competition under Alternative Technological Regimes," *Journal of Economic Behavior and Organization*, Vol. 5, No. 3-4, September/December, pp. 287-320.

Wolff, Edward N. (1985), "Industrial Composition, Interindustry Effects, and the U.S. Productivity Slowdown," *Review of Economics and Statistics*, Vol. 67, No. 2, May, pp. 268-77.

    (1991a), "Capital Formation and Productivity Convergence over the Long-Term," *American Economic Review*, Vol. 81, No. 3, June, pp. 565-79.

    (1991b), "Productivity Growth, Capital Intensity, and Skill Levels In the U.S. Insurance Industry, 1948-86," *Geneva Papers on Risk and Insurance*, Vol. 16, No. 59, April, pp. 173-90.

    (1992), "International Convergence in Productivity Levels: Has Central Planning Mattered?" in Pierre Pestieau, editor, *Public Finance in a World of Transition*, Vol. 47, (Munich: International Institute of Public Finance), pp. 122-37.

    (1994), "The Emergence of New Technology and Development: What Asia Can Learn from Its Recent History," in M. Blomstrom, editor, *Transnational Technology towards the Year 2000 in the ESCAP Region* (New York: United Nations), pp. 27-50.

    (1994), "Technology, Capital Accumulation, and Long Run Growth," in Jan Fagerberg, Nick von Tunzelmann, and Bart Verspage, editors, *The Dynamics of Technology, Trade, and Growth* (London: Edward Elgar), pp. 53-74.

    (1996a), "The Productivity Slowdown: The Culprit at Last?" *American Economic Review*, Vol. 86, No. 5, December, pp. 1239-52.

    (1996b), "Technology and the Demand for Skills," *OECD Science, Technology and Industry Review*, 18, pp. 96-123.

    (2000), "Human Capital Investment and Economic Growth: Exploring the Cross-Country Evidence," *Structural Change and Economic Dynamics*, Vol. 11, No. 4, December, pp. 433-72.

    (2009), *Poverty and Income Distribution*, 2nd edition, (Chichester, U.K.: Wiley-Blackwell).

Wolff, Edward N., and Maury Gittleman (1993), "The Role of Education in Productivity Convergence: Does Higher Education Matter?" in Eddy Szirmai, Bart van Ark, and Dirk Pilat, editors, *Explaining Economic Growth* (Amsterdam: Elsevier Science Publishers B.V.), pp. 147-67.

Wolff, Edward N., and M. I. Nadiri (1993), "Spillover Effects, Linkage Structure, and Research and Development," *Structural Change and Economic Dynamics*, Vol. 4, No. 2, December, pp. 315-31.

Working Party No. 1 of the OECD Economic Policy Committee (1993), "*Medium-Term Productivity Performance in the Business Sector: Trends, Underlying Determinants and Policies*," Paris, OECD, September.

World Bank (various years), *World Development Report* (New York: Oxford University Press).

    (1991). *World Tables, 1991* (Washington, DC: World Bank).

Wright, Gavin (1990), "The Origins of American Industrial Success, 1879-1940," *American Economic Review*, Vol. 80, No. 4, September 1990, pp. 651-68.

Xu, B. (2000), "Multinational Enterprises, Technology Diffusion, and Host Country Productivity Growth," *Journal of Development Economics*, Vol. 62, pp. 477-93.

Xu, B., and J. Wang (1999), "Capital Goods Trade and R&D Spillovers in the OECD," *Canadian Journal of Economics*, Vol. 32, pp. 1258–74.

Yamarik, Steven, Noel D. Johnson, and Ryan A. Compton (2007), "War! What Is It Good For?" http://ssrn.com/abstract=1080947.

Young, Alwyn (1992), "A Tale of Two Cities: Factor Accumulation and Technical Change in Hong Kong and Singapore," in Olivier Jean Blanchard and Stanley Fischer, editors, *NBER Macroeconomic Annual* (Cambridge, MA: MIT Press), pp. 13–54.

Index